Praise for the second edition

From basic to complex, this book gives you the tools to create beautiful data visualizations.
—Claudio Rodriguez, Cox Media Group

The best reference for one of the most useful DataViz tools.
—Jonathan Rioux, TD Insurance

From toy examples to techniques for real projects. Shows how all the pieces fit together.
—Scott McKissock, USAID

A clever way to immerse yourself in the D3.js world.
—Felipe Vildoso Casti, University of Chile

T0293294

D3.js in Action
THIRD EDITION

ELIJAH MEEKS
ANNE-MARIE DUFOUR
FOREWORD BY ANDY KIRK

MANNING
SHELTER ISLAND

For online information and ordering of this and other Manning books, please visit
www.manning.com. The publisher offers discounts on this book when ordered in quantity.
For more information, please contact

> Special Sales Department
> Manning Publications Co.
> 20 Baldwin Road
> PO Box 761
> Shelter Island, NY 11964
> Email: orders@manning.com

Manning Publications Co.
20 Baldwin Road
PO Box 761
Shelter Island, NY 11964

Development editor:	Elesha Hyde
Technical editor:	Jon Borgman
Review editor:	Aleksandar Dragosavljević
Production editor:	Keri Hales
Copy editor:	Julie McNamee
Proofreader:	Melody Dolab
Technical proofreader:	Alain Lompo, Elena Ghisalberti
Typesetter and cover designer:	Marija Tudor

ISBN 9781633439177
Printed in the United States of America

To my three As

brief contents

contents

foreword

In my capacity as a freelance data visualization educator, consultant, and designer, I've been deeply immersed in most corners of the data visualization world since the late 2000s and been fortunate to have a front-row seat to a huge amount of change. The technological landscape is always shifting. From the evolution of the tools of our trade to the platforms on which our work reaches its audience, there are always new forces pushing and pulling.

Where once this was a small, niche community of specialists, the elevated mainstream exposure of visualization led to substantial growth, both in the volume of enthusiastic participants and through the improved widening in their diversity. A field is only as rich as the breadth of its sensibilities and cultures, and the trajectory is hopeful.

This expanding pool of talent continues to inject fresh thinking. Traditional discourse and so-called established convictions are being challenged. A heightened appetite for experimentation has led to innovative methods impacting audiences in novel ways. The boundaries of creative possibility are being stretched beyond *just* the chart and *just* the visual.

What remains unchanged is a desire among data visualization designers and developers to attain maximum technical *expressiveness* and *fluency*. This is the ultimate capability. *Expressiveness* is having access to the broadest set of representation and presentation options. It's being able to create more than—or at least as much as—you're able to imagine. For many years, D3.js has been *the* JavaScript library that offers this.

Fluency is about accomplishing tasks that are too hard to do well by hand or too laborious to repeat by hand. Fluency minimizes the friction from not knowing how to perform certain technical tasks or from not knowing whether they're even possible. Fluency is about having the discipline to know when and why you should and shouldn't make certain choices.

This is where the third edition of *D3.js in Action* comes in. The previous editions skillfully presented readers with an understanding of *what* D3.js can do and *how* to do it. The third edition transcends these technical contents, addressing the *when, why,* and for *whom,* in the context of contemporary data visualization practices.

The most valuable books in any discipline tackle topics that have steep and, perhaps for some, overwhelming learning curves. They make those curves gentler and more surmountable. They work simultaneously as introductory texts for beginners and as sophisticated references for more advanced practitioners. They weave together the apparent objectivity of technology with the inherently subjective craft of visual communication. *D3.js in Action* delivers against these demands.

This is a book that is to be *used*. "In Action" reflects the applied nature of the teaching it delivers with relevant examples, valuable exercises, and inspiring case studies helping learners to take their learning from the page and put it into practice.

This is a book that promotes being *useful*. The essence of doing things because you *should*, not because you *could*, is a persistent theme. You want to make functionally cool things? Of course. You wish to make aesthetically beautiful things? Who doesn't? This book will satisfy those cravings but through the lens of what is right and what is relevant. Your results will be useful to the people they're designed for.

The book is also about visualization that is *usable*. To design visualizations effectively is to create work that is responsive to the myriad platforms through which it may be consumed, elegantly adapting to different shapes, sizes, and feature compatibilities. To be usable, visualizations must also be equally accessible for all characteristics and abilities of the people using them. This text gives due importance to this often-neglected topic.

The foundations of this book, through its early editions, come from the vital work of Elijah Meeks, who has been a champion developer, a prominent promoter of community and better practices, and a thoughtful critic of data visualization practice from his real-world perspective developing data visualizations in industry.

Anne-Marie Dufour is the perfect candidate to have taken on this new edition for the latest cohort of learners. She possesses that rare combination of being a highly accomplished data visualization developer and having a keen eye for design and instinct for creativity. Her substantial technical and communicative talents are perfectly supplemented by a natural flair for breaking down complex subjects into digestible and understandable parts. Anne-Marie's own learning journey informs how she helps others, and there is no better person to take the wheel and drive you through this exciting subject.

ANDY KIRK
INDEPENDENT DATA VISUALIZATION EXPERT

preface

Back in 2017, I was working as a frontend developer and found myself yearning for my next professional step. Although I enjoyed developing websites, something was missing. I was looking to bridge my background in engineering and my love for teaching with my new coding skills. That's when my partner suggested I have a look at data visualization. For some reason, he thought I'd enjoy exploring this booming field. When I googled "data visualization," I stumbled upon the project Data Sketches (www .datasketch.es) by Nadieh Bremer and Shirley Wu. Like so many others, I was deeply inspired and knew I had to learn how to build such projects. That's when I discovered a library called D3.js that they used to create their work.

I started to learn D3 here and there, subscribing to courses and reading blog posts. But my frustration kept growing as I discovered that many of the code snippets I was learning were outdated. I was confused by the lack of a straightforward step-by-step approach to learning and building D3 projects. When the first wave of the COVID-19 pandemic hit and the world went into shutdown, I finally had time to sit down and start building my first projects. Slowly, the philosophy behind D3 began to make sense and became more and more intuitive.

A while later, thanks to a kind nudge from Andy Kirk, I was contacted by Nicole Butterfield at Manning. She told me they were looking to build a course about D3 and asked if I'd be interested. With all the enthusiasm from my first dataviz projects, I jumped headfirst into that challenge and started to put together a strategy for learning D3. After a few months, *Interactive Visualization with D3.js* (http://mng.bz/jXrz) came to life.

While building this course with the second edition of *D3.js in Action* as a reference, my early frustrations came back. Much had changed with D3 since the book's release, keeping us from using it to its full potential. In all my naiveté, I suggested to Nicole that I'd be willing to update the book and was lucky that Elijah and Manning allowed me to add my touch to this manuscript and bring my vision to life.

With this new edition, I wish to provide you, the reader, with a road map toward creating unique and insightful data visualizations. This book and the projects it contains will help you learn the basics and the more advanced concepts, and I hope it will serve you as a reference for years to come.

acknowledgments

Before working on this manuscript, I had a vague idea that writing a book would be a ton of work, and it is. But little did I know how many people are crucial to bringing such a project to life. First, I'd like to thank Nicole Butterfield and Brian Sawyer at Manning, who believed in my ability to produce this new edition and gave me the green light to get started. I'm also grateful to Elijah Meeks for allowing me to mess with his work. I can only imagine the weird feeling of having somebody you barely know making your baby their own. Thanks a ton for your trust!

A huge shoutout goes to Elesha Hyde, my content editor at Manning, and Jon Borgman, my technical editor and a senior software engineer with 20+ years of full-stack engineering and architect experience. I've worked closely with both of them for the past year and a half. They have been my cheerleaders along the way, and this book wouldn't be half as good without their thoughtful reviews.

A massive team of people worked behind the scenes at Manning to make this book possible—some of whom I've been briefly in contact with, some I didn't have the chance to meet. Thank you so much for your dedicated work! To all the reviewers: Alain Couniot, Alain Lompo, Amogh Raghunath, Art Bergquist, Ashley Eatly, Chris Thomas, Deborah Mesquita, Elena Ghisalberti, Eli Rabinovitz, Esref Durna, Gregorio Piccoli, Hans Donner, James J Byleckie, Jereme Allen, Jonathan Boiser, Juan M. Carrillo de Gea, Leonard Grey, Mario Ruiz, Michael Bright, Patrice Maldague, Pierfrancesco D'Orsogna, Prasanth Rasam, Rodney Weis, Simon Verhoeven, Sriram Macharla, Thamizh Arasu S., and Yves Dorfsman—your suggestions helped make this a better book.

Another thank-you goes to my small but mighty network of friends in the field of data visualization. Inbal Rief, Cédric Scherer, and Georgios Karamanis, you have witnessed all the big moments. From the "I got the gig!" to the numerous "I'm almost to the end . . . not quite yet, but almost." Your early reviews, design feedback, and constant enthusiasm encouraged me along the way. In addition, thanks to Andy Kirk, who, in his continued kindness, agreed to write the foreword to this piece. We are many who consider you as one of the leading mentors of data visualization. Thank you for all that you do for our craft!

Finally, it proved impossible to have a healthy work-life balance while working on this project, and I couldn't have done it without my team at home. Ádám, you are my rock. Thank you for supporting me in all my wild endeavors! Albert and Arnó, thank you for all the hugs and kisses during those long hours at my desk. I hope you'll enjoy taking a peek at this book, knowing you were right by my side while I created it.

about this book

Who should read this book

This book is for all those who want total creative freedom with their data visualization work, from customized classical charts to creating unique data visualization layouts. You might come from a data analysis background, be a journalist, a designer, or even a dataviz enthusiast. Congrats for considering learning D3.js! You'll quickly realize that this is a wise investment of your time. By mastering D3, you'll unlock a level of freedom and potential for creativity that is unmatched by the gazillion data visualization tools available today.

How this book is organized: A road map

As you may know, D3 lives within an ecosystem of frontend development tools: HTML, CSS, and JavaScript. Before you dive into chapter 2, you'll want to ensure that you understand the basics of those tools and how we combine them to create beautiful and interactive web pages. By no means do you need to be an expert, but a little prior knowledge will make your D3 learning experience way more manageable. If you're looking to brush up your frontend development skills, we recommend the following resources:

- *2023 Web Development Bootcamp* by Maximilian Schwarzmüller (http://mng .bz/WEe4)
- *Complete Intro to Web Development* by Frontend Masters (http://mng.bz/8wyZ)

This book is organized in a progressive fashion. Part 1 covers the fundamentals such as working with data and creating simple charts, while part 2 focuses on meeting the new digital expectations by making our projects interactive and responsive, improving their accessibility, and combining D3 with a JavaScript framework such as React or Svelte. Each chapter in part 3 covers more advanced data visualizations: hierarchies, networks, and maps. Finally, in part 4, we invite you behind the scenes of the creation of a fully customized visualization layout, and we discuss performance and how to combine D3 with Canvas.

If you're new to D3, we recommend you go through chapters 1 to 7 in order. Those early chapters will help you build your mental model of D3 and ensure you have all the building blocks in your toolbox before approaching more advanced topics. D3 has a bad reputation for having a steep learning curve, but by following the steps from those early chapters, it can become very intuitive.

If you have prior D3 knowledge and are comfortable with the basics, you might want to pick your own adventure. Chapters 8 to 15 focus on specific concepts or chart types, and it might be worth reading them when your current projects call for this knowledge.

But to all of you, we highly recommend that you not only READ the book but that you DO the book. Each chapter contains its own data visualization project(s), which were crafted to help you integrate the concepts explained in the text. Putting those notions into practice will make all the difference in the world, making your learning journey smoother and swifter.

For each project and exercise, you can access the starting code files and solutions on the book's GitHub repository (http://mng.bz/Xqjv). You'll also find the solutions to the exercises in appendix D. All the code files and code snippets in this book use D3 Version 7, which is the latest at the time of writing. To run and edit the code, you'll need only a code editor and a browser. We recommend VS Code and Chrome or Firefox.

About the code

This book contains many examples of source code both in numbered listings and in line with normal text. In both cases, source code is formatted in a `fixed-width font like this` to separate it from ordinary text. Sometimes code is also **in bold** to highlight what has changed from previous steps in the chapter, such as when a new feature adds to an existing line of code.

In many cases, the original source code has been reformatted; we've added line breaks and reworked indentation to accommodate the available page space in the book. In rare cases, even this was not enough, and listings include line-continuation markers (➥). Additionally, comments in the source code have often been removed from the listings when the code is described in the text. Code annotations accompany many of the listings, highlighting important concepts.

You can get executable snippets of code from the liveBook (online) version of this book at https://livebook.manning.com/book/d3js-in-action-third-edition. The complete code for the examples in the book is available for download from the Manning website at www.manning.com/books/d3js-in-action-third-edition, and from GitHub at http://mng.bz/Xqjv.

liveBook discussion forum

The purchase of *D3.js in Action, Third Edition,* includes free access to liveBook, Manning's online reading platform. Using liveBook's exclusive discussion features, you can attach comments to the book globally or to specific sections or paragraphs. It's a snap to make notes for yourself, ask and answer technical questions, and receive help from the author and other users. To access the forum, go to https://livebook.manning .com/book/d3js-in-action-third-edition/discussion. You can also learn more about Manning's forums and the rules of conduct at https://livebook.manning.com/ discussion.

Manning's commitment to our readers is to provide a venue where a meaningful dialogue between individual readers and between readers and the author can take place. It isn't a commitment to any specific amount of participation on the part of the author, whose contribution to the forum remains voluntary (and unpaid). We suggest you try asking the author some challenging questions lest their interest stray! The forum and the archives of previous discussions will be accessible from the publisher's website as long as the book is in print.

about the authors

ELIJAH MEEKS has spent the past two decades working with data visualization at some of the most dynamic organizations in the world, including Stanford, Netflix, and Apple. He cofounded Noteable, a start-up focused on the intersection of computational notebooks, business intelligence, and AI. He was also the cofounder and is the current publications director of the Data Visualization Society, a professional society dedicated to advancing the field of data visualization. At present, he is a principal engineer at Confluent.

Elijah is a prolific writer and speaker on the topic of data visualization, including authoring *D3.js in Action* from Manning and creating the Pearson video series *Designing for the Data Visualization Lifecycle*. He is the author of libraries such as Semiotic, as well as interactive works such as *ORBIS: The Transportation Network Model of the Roman Empire*.

ANNE-MARIE DUFOUR has an original background in mechanical engineering, computational fluid dynamics, and frontend development. She specialized in data visualization to combine her love for science, coding, design, and teaching. This unique skill set has helped her develop a solid understanding of how data visualization can help us grasp complex phenomena and realities and how to translate them into modern web applications. She currently works as a data visualization engineer at PingThings.

While teaching diverse engineering subjects such as fluid dynamics, heat transfer, and the environmental and social impacts of engineering projects, she developed a strong sense for how to structure information and present it in a digestible yet challenging way to keep students motivated and eager to learn. Recently she has created the liveProject series *Interactive Visualization with D3.js* for Manning Publications.

about the cover illustration

The figure on the cover of *D3.js in Action, Third Edition,* "Habit of a Moorish Pilgrim Returning from Mecca in 1586," is taken from a book by Thomas Jefferys, published between 1757 and 1772.

In those days, it was easy to identify where people lived and what their trade or station in life was just by their dress. Manning celebrates the inventiveness and initiative of the computer business with book covers based on the rich diversity of regional culture centuries ago, brought back to life by pictures from collections such as this one.

Part 1

D3.js fundamentals

Welcome to the world of D3.js! We know you are impatient to build mind-blowing data visualizations. You're going to get there soon, we promise! But first, let's make sure that you get the basics right. The notions you'll encounter in this section are the ones you'll meet repeatedly in your D3 journey, and understanding them in depth will give you a definite advantage once you approach more complex visualizations.

In chapter 1, we'll discuss why and when someone might want to use D3 and its ecosystem. We'll also introduce concepts that will support your learning: drawing Scalable Vector Graphics (SVG) shapes, manipulating data with JavaScript, and method chaining.

Then, in chapters 2 and 3, we'll use D3 to build our first data visualization: a bar chart. For that, we'll discuss how to manipulate the document object model (DOM) and work with data. In chapters 4 and 5, we'll already build more complex visualizations with the help of D3's shape and layout generators. We'll finish this part in chapter 6 by discussing distributions, a subject that all data visualization practitioners meet from time to time.

An introduction to D3.js

This chapter covers

- Understanding the role of D3.js and the philosophy behind it
- Recognizing the tools used in combination with D3.js to create data visualizations
- Creating and styling Scalable Vector Graphics (SVG) with code
- Learning how data visualization best practices support your journey as a D3.js developer

Given the plethora of data visualization tools that emerged in the past decade, you might wonder if learning D3 is worth the trouble. Let us be clear: learning D3 is a wise investment. Although the learning curve can be steep and require dedication, you'll not only be rewarded with the ability to create all the traditional charts that other libraries offer and customize them at will but also gain the freedom to get off the beaten track and create visualizations that are truly tailored to your data and audience.

D3.js is the library behind most of the exciting data visualizations on the web. It's the tool of choice when you want total creative and technical freedom over your data visualizations, whether you make interactive prototypes for research, responsive data dashboards, or scrollytelling data stories such as "Why Budapest, Warsaw, and Lithuania split themselves in two" by Maarten Lambrechts, as shown in figure 1.1.

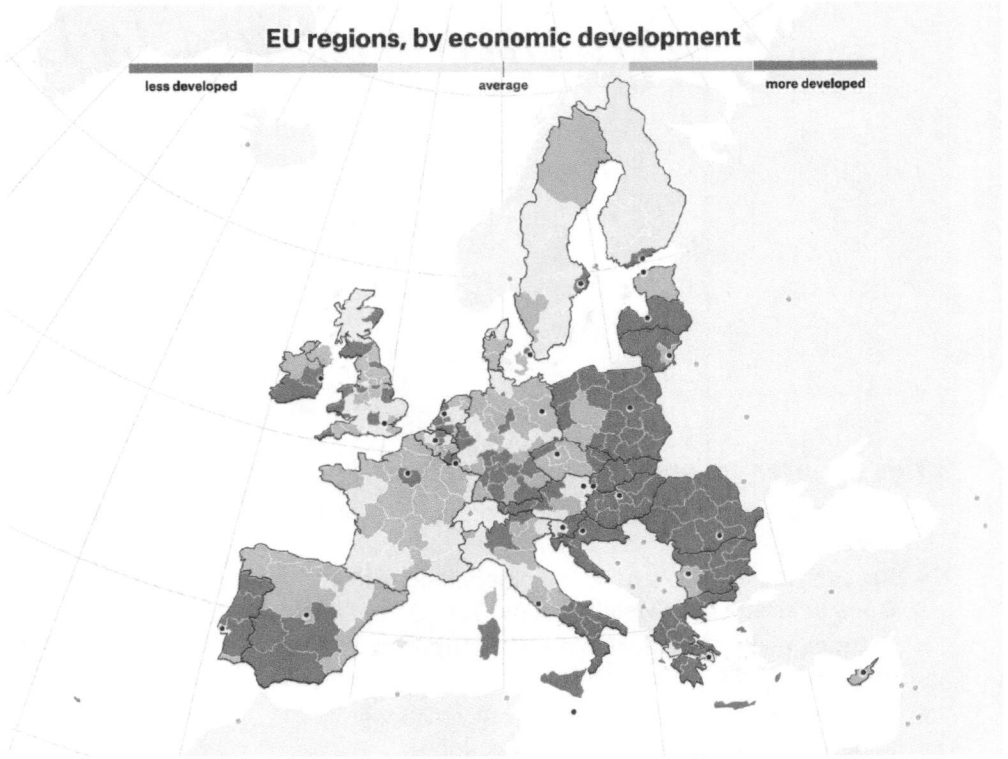

Figure 1.1   D3 developers have access to a wide range of data representations, such as maps. Here's an example by Maarten Lambrechts (https://pudding.cool/2019/04/eu-regions/).

In this first chapter, we'll introduce D3's ecosystem and a few concepts, such as SVG graphics and JavaScript object manipulation methods, which are crucial to comprehend before diving into digital data visualizations.

NOTE   Throughout the book, we'll use the names D3.js and D3 interchangeably.

1.1   *What is D3.js?*

D3.js stands for *Data-Driven Documents*. It's an open source JavaScript library created in 2011 by Mike Bostock to generate dynamic and interactive data visualizations for the web. Many new data visualization libraries have been introduced since, but they generally use D3 under the hood, thanks to its power and flexibility.

1.1.1   *A need for web-accessible data visualizations*

D3 was created to fill a pressing need for web-accessible, sophisticated data visualizations. Let's say your company is using a business intelligence tool, but it doesn't show the kind of patterns in the data that your team needs. They ask you to build a custom dashboard that shows exactly how your customers are behaving, tailored for your specific domain. That dashboard needs to be fast, interactive, and shareable around the organization. D3 is a natural choice for such a task.

Or imagine that you're hired to create a scrollytelling piece that visualizes how the rights of the LGBTQ+ community evolved in the past decades and across the world. This page should contain many creative visualizations that transform as the user scrolls, reveal more information with mouse events, and adapt to the size of the screen. D3 is the tool of choice to build such a project.

Mike Bostock originally created D3 to take advantage of emerging web standards, which, as he puts it, "avoids proprietary representation and affords extraordinary flexibility, exposing the full capabilities of web standards such as CSS3, HTML5, and SVG" (http://d3js.org). D3.js version 7, the latest iteration of this popular library at the time of writing, continues this trend by modularizing the various pieces of D3 to make it fully compatible with ECMAScript modules to package JavaScript code for reuse and modern web development.

D3.js affords developers the capacity to make richly interactive projects that are styled and served like traditional web content, such as "The Inside Scoop of Ben & Jerry's" shown in figure 1.2. This makes them more portable, more amenable to

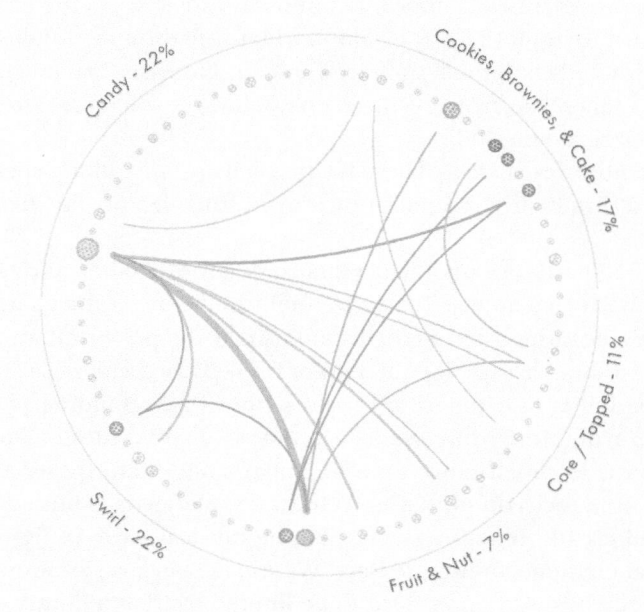

Figure 1.2   D3 is a low-level library, giving us complete technical and creative freedom. This chord diagram is part of the project "The Inside Scoop of Ben & Jerry's," by Hesham Eissa and Lindsey Poulter (https://benjerry .heshlindsdataviz.com/).

growth, and more easily maintained by large groups where other team members might not know the specific syntax of D3.

The decision on Bostock's part to deal broadly with data and to create a library capable of presenting maps as easily as line charts and networks also means that a developer doesn't need to understand the abstractions and syntax of one library for maps, another for dynamic SVG path creation, and yet another for networks. Instead, the code for running an interactive D3 network visualization is close to pure Java-Script and also similar to the code representing dynamic points on a D3 map. The methods are the same, but the data also could be the same, formulated in one way for the nodes and links of a network, while formulated in another way for geospatial representations on a map. Although the learning curve is steeper than with other tools, learning D3 is a wise investment.

Not only can D3 create complex and varied graphics, it can embed the high level of interactivity that users expect, which is crucial to modern web development. With D3, every element of every chart, from a spinning globe to a slice of a pie chart, is made interactive in the same way. And because D3 was written by someone well-versed in data visualization practice, it includes interactive components and behaviors such as selecting nodes in a network, as shown in figure 1.3, that are standard in both data visualization and web development.

1.1.2   When do we use D3.js?

The field of data visualization is enjoying a boom in popularity, and the number of tools available to generate data-bound graphics has exploded in the past decade. We have business intelligence tools such as Microsoft Excel, a common entryway to data visualization, and Power BI, the Microsoft solution to build dashboards. On the other hand, data scientists often turn to ggplot2 for R or Matplotlib for Python to visualize data.

Browser-based point-and-click tools such as Tableau, Flourish, Datawrapper, and RAWGraphs have also taken the front of the scene, allowing you to create stunning work with minimal technical knowledge.

Finally, JavaScript libraries such as Highcharts, Chart.js, and Plotly specialize in developing web-based interactive visualizations. And this list is far from being exhaustive.

So where does D3 fall in this ocean of data visualization tools? When and how do we use it? We can probably say that although D3 can totally build any of the charts offered by the data visualization libraries listed here, it's not usually the preferred option when building simple traditional charts or for the exploration phase, where we investigate which type of visualization is best suited to represent our data. Building D3 projects requires time, and D3 truly shines in complex, interactive, and custom-tailored projects. Data visualization is so much more than line charts and scatterplots! While the tools just mentioned often focus on predefined charts, D3 allows us to bind data to any graphical element and create something new, like the musical score in figure 1.4, by combining these visual elements in unique ways. We use D3 because we want the freedom to think outside the box and don't want to be limited by what a library offers.

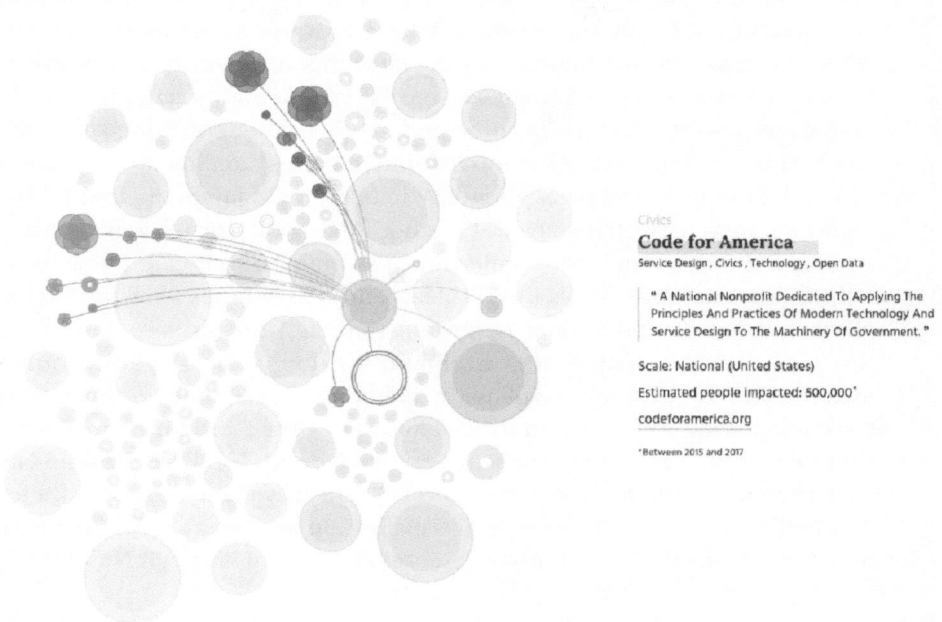

Civics

Code for America

Service Design , Civics , Technology , Open Data

" A National Nonprofit Dedicated To Applying The
Principles And Practices Of Modern Technology And
Service Design To The Machinery Of Government. "

Scale: National (United States)

Estimated people impacted: 500,000*

codeforamerica.org

*Between 2015 and 2017

Figure 1.3   Interactivity is at the heart of D3. On this network visualization, mouse interactions reveal the relationships between different organizations as well as information specific to the selected node (http://mng.bz/QROG).

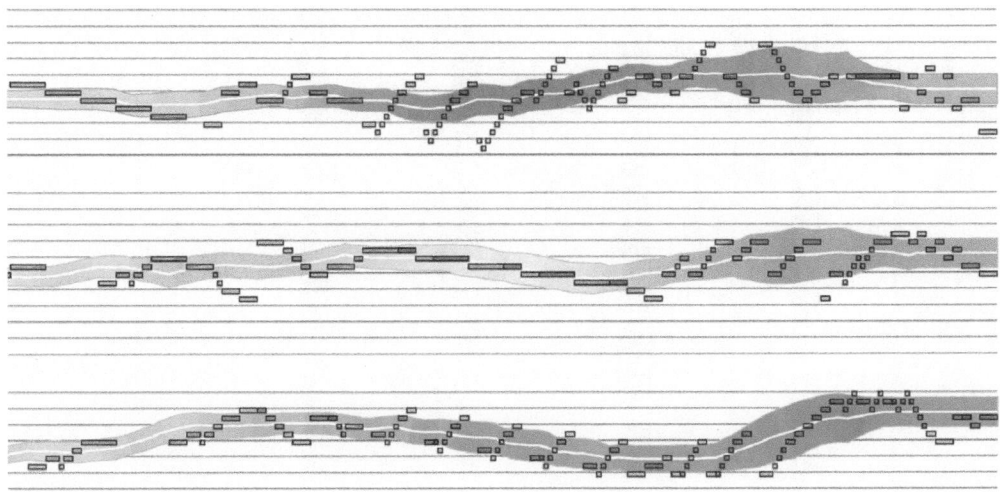

Figure 1.4   D3 has SVG and Canvas drawing functions, allowing developers to build custom visualizations such as this representation of musical scores by Elijah Meeks.

Here's an example of how we can use D3 within the scope of a data visualization project. First, we start with a preexisting dataset or with data gathered manually. We usually spend a significant amount of time cleaning, formatting, and preparing the data before beginning the data analysis process. Programming languages such as Python and R are powerful for this purpose and can help us identify the story hidden within the data. Excel can also do the job for simple data wrangling and data analysis, and it requires a less technical background. We can even use JavaScript and D3 for basic data exploration, as they offer statistical methods that we'll discuss later in this book.

Once the data analysis is underway, it's common to create a few prototypes that help refine our story. Tools like Tableau and RAWGraphs allow us to generate such charts quickly. That's a super important step, and the visualizations created during this phase aren't usually fancy or refined. We don't want to get too attached to our ideas during this prototyping phase by spending a lot of time on them. We might find ourselves having to "kill our darlings" and start over a few times until we identify the best-suited visualization for the story we want to tell. Network diagrams might be an exception here, and jumping right into D3 generally makes sense for these projects.

Finally, once we know the type of visualization we'll create, like the Sankey diagram in figure 1.5, it's time to roll up our sleeves and code it with D3! Nowadays, the coding

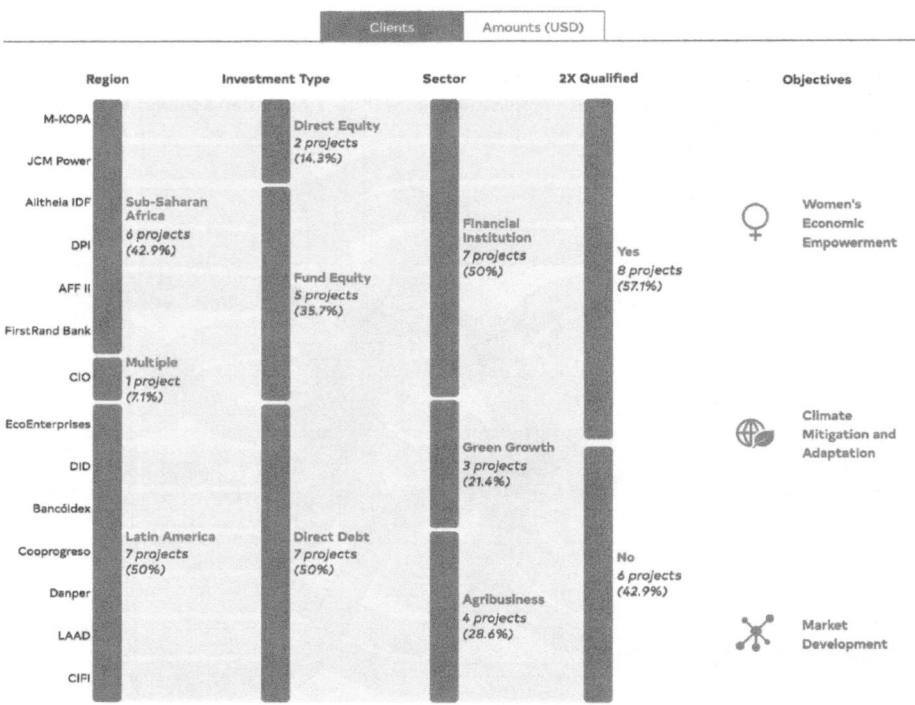

Figure 1.5   "A portfolio of inclusive businesses for a sustainable future" is an award-winning project created by Voilà: (https://chezvoila.com/project/findevportfolio/).

step often occurs within single-page applications (SPAs), using frameworks such as React or Svelte.

1.1.3 How D3.js works

You might have already experimented with D3 and found that it isn't easy to get into. Maybe that's because you expected it to work like a charting library. A case in point is creating a bar chart, which we'll do in chapters 2 and 3. D3 doesn't have one single function to create a bar chart. Instead, it has a function that appends an `<svg>` container into the document object model (DOM) and another set of functions that appends one `<rect>` element for each data point. We then use scales to calculate the length of the rectangles that compose our histogram and set their `height` attributes. Finally, we call another set of functions that adds an x- and a y-axis to the bar chart.

As you can see in figure 1.6, it's a much longer process than using a dedicated charting library such as Highcharts. But the explicit manner in which D3 deals with data and graphics is also its strength. Although other charting libraries conveniently allow you to make line charts and pie charts quickly, they often break down when you want to create a visualization that falls outside of the traditional charts spectrum or when it comes to implementing custom interactions. Not D3—it allows you to build whatever data-driven graphics and interactivity you can imagine.

In figure 1.7, you see a mind map of how we generally approach the coding of a data visualization with D3. We start with a dataset, often a CSV or a JSON file, and we use the d3-fetch module to load this dataset into our project. We then usually need to perform a few manipulations to format the data. For example, we ensure that our numbers and dates are correctly formatted. If we didn't do it previously, we might also want to interrogate our dataset to find its main characteristics. For instance, knowing its maximum and minimum values in advance is often helpful. We're then ready to start building our visualization, for which we'll combine the different D3 functions that you'll learn in this book. Finally, we add interactivity by listening to mouse events, allowing users to filter the data or zoom in on the visualization.

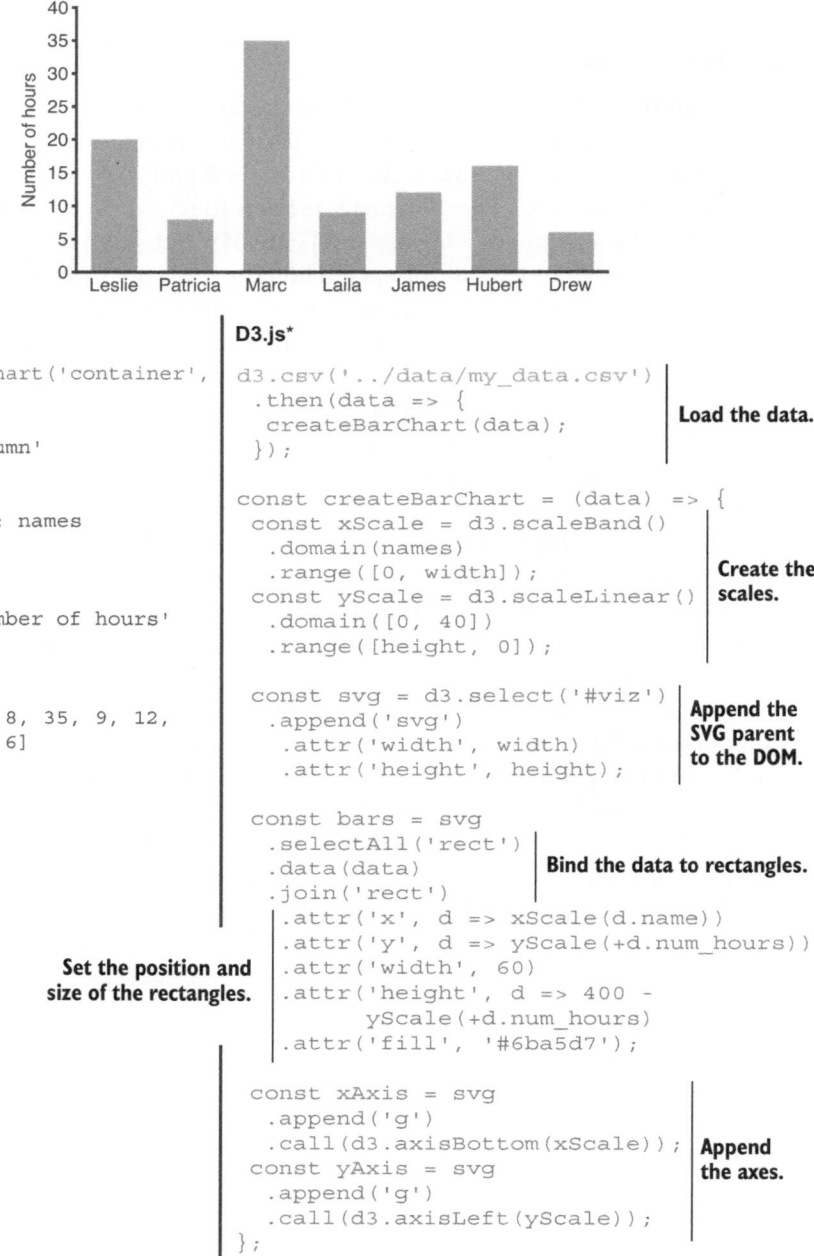

Average time spent working with D3.js each week

Highcharts

```
Highcharts.chart('container',
{
 chart: {
  type: 'column'
 },
 xAxis: {
  categories: names
 },
 yAxis: {
  title: {
   text: 'Number of hours'
  }
 },
 series: [{
  data: [20, 8, 35, 9, 12,
         16, 6]
 }]
}
);
```

Set the position and
size of the rectangles.

D3.js*

```
d3.csv('../data/my_data.csv')
 .then(data => {
  createBarChart(data);
 });
```
Load the data.

```
const createBarChart = (data) => {
 const xScale = d3.scaleBand()
  .domain(names)
  .range([0, width]);
 const yScale = d3.scaleLinear()
  .domain([0, 40])
  .range([height, 0]);
```
Create the
scales.

```
 const svg = d3.select('#viz')
  .append('svg')
  .attr('width', width)
  .attr('height', height);
```
Append the
SVG parent
to the DOM.

```
 const bars = svg
  .selectAll('rect')
  .data(data)
  .join('rect')
```
Bind the data to rectangles.

```
  .attr('x', d => xScale(d.name))
  .attr('y', d => yScale(+d.num_hours))
  .attr('width', 60)
  .attr('height', d => 400 -
        yScale(+d.num_hours))
  .attr('fill', '#6ba5d7');
```

```
 const xAxis = svg
  .append('g')
  .call(d3.axisBottom(xScale));
 const yAxis = svg
  .append('g')
  .call(d3.axisLeft(yScale));
};
```
Append
the axes.

* We have simplified this D3.js code for conciseness.

Figure 1.6   A bar chart generated with Highcharts vs. with D3.js. The Highcharts' code is simpler and shorter, but D3.js is more versatile.

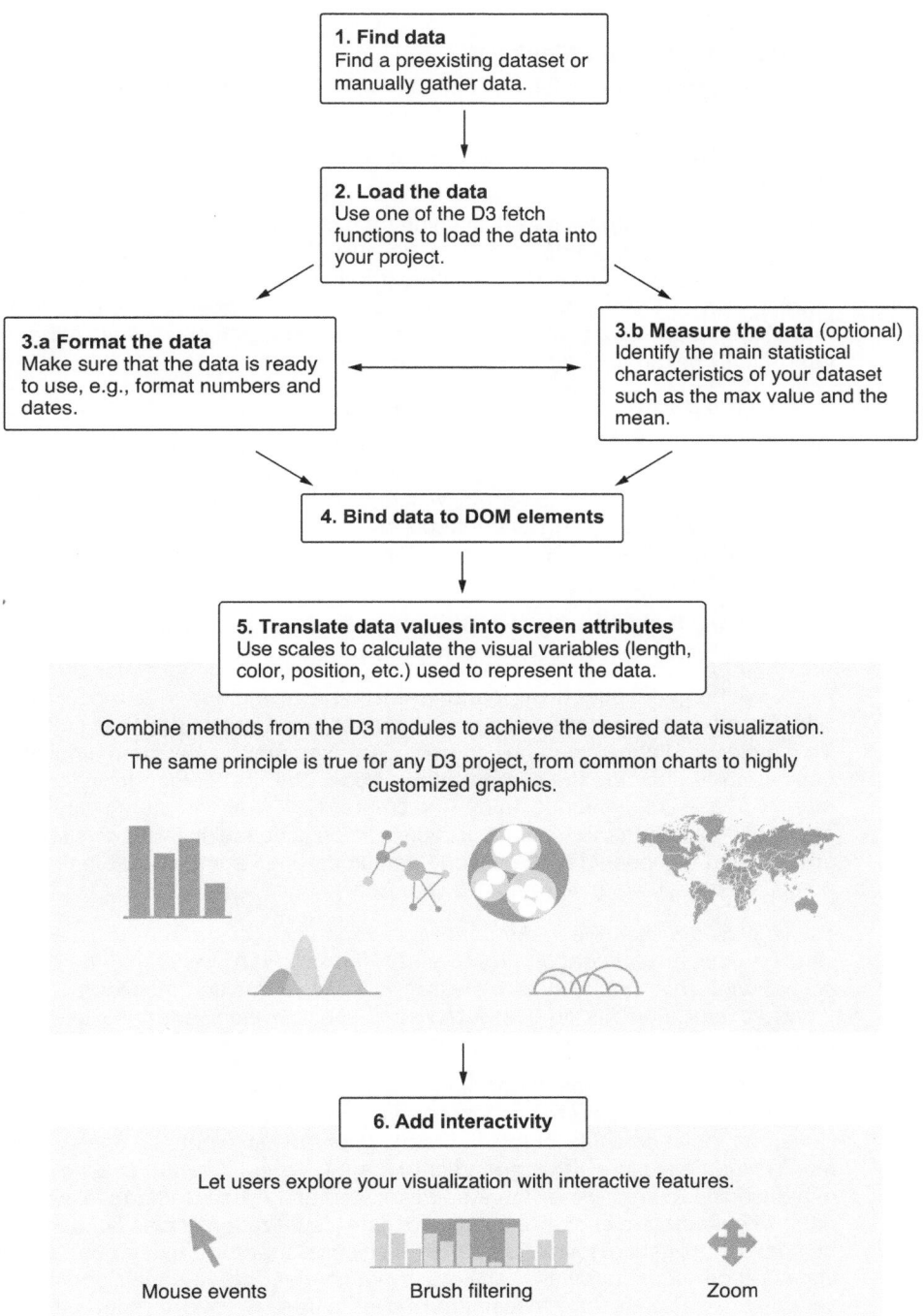

Figure 1.7   How to approach data visualization with D3.js

Interview with Elijah Meeks

Meeks is a data visualization engineer and the author of the first two editions of *D3.js in Action*.

Can you tell us a little bit about your background and how you entered the field of data visualization?

I've done data visualization work in some form or another for almost 15 years at organizations like Apple, Netflix, the Data Visualization Society, Stanford, and at Noteable, a startup I cofounded. I got into data visualization in an unconventional way, starting with GIS (Geographic Information System) to support my PhD work on state formation in early China. From there, I started to work with network visualization and, later, finally began to make bar charts and line charts.

How did you discover D3, and what inspired you to learn more about this library?

Early on in my career, I used Flash with ActionScript3 to create interactive apps that used data visualization. When it became clear that Flash was dying, I started to explore Protovis as an alternative, which was quickly replaced by D3. The more I understood D3, the more I understood data visualization. More than that, I found using D3 to visualize data helped me learn more about data structures, analytics, and machine learning.

You wrote the first two editions of D3.js in Action at a time when there weren't a lot of D3-related resources available. How did this project come to life?

I'll always be grateful for the opportunity Manning gave me to write those books. That work forced me to understand D3 more fully and comprehensively than I did just using it for projects. Writing about how to use D3 caused me to grow more ambitious in my usage and in planning the content of the book. The first edition included examples for how to use D3 almost as an MVC to create HTML content, creating custom touch events on your charts for phones or tablets, alongside making your own layouts, generators, and components. The second edition dropped some of that in favor of more practical content like integrating D3 with React.

You've played a vital role in the data visualization field over the past decade, starting as the first data visualization engineer at Netflix and later becoming the CIO of Noteable. During this time, you've witnessed significant transformations in the industry. What are your thoughts on how data visualization development has evolved over the years, and where do you believe it's headed?

I'm a firm believer in eras in any culture, and data visualization practice is no different. We started with computers providing us with simple charting options in order to visualize tabular data (like charts in Excel). When D3 came out, the energy of the community was on exploring that grammar of graphics and understanding how you could use encoding to create ever more sophisticated and dynamic charts. Now we're at a point when there are enough examples of data visualization across domains (whether business intelligence, journalism, or data science) that the expectations for the data visualization products being made cross boundaries that in earlier periods seemed very distinct. Rather than focusing on novel charts, we see a focus on more integrated data visualization approaches that allow different roles with different skills and expectations to work on the same data-driven products.

1.2 The D3 ecosystem: What you need to know to get started

D3.js is never used alone but rather is part of an ecosystem of technologies and tools that we combine to create rich web interfaces. Like any web page, D3 projects are built within the DOM and use the power of HTML5. Although D3 can create and manipulate traditional HTML elements such as divisions (<div>) and lists (<ul>, <ol>), we mainly generate our visualizations with SVG graphics or within Canvas, an HTML element that renders bitmap images from scripts. Then we might also use good old CSS stylesheets, which can enhance D3 projects and make their design easier to maintain, especially across broad teams.

Given that D3 is a JavaScript library, we naturally tend to combine D3 methods with native JavaScript functions to access and manipulate the data. D3 now fully supports the ECMAScript 2015 or ES6 revision of JavaScript and most of the latest updates. D3 also comes as modules that can be integrated into the recent frameworks and libraries we build web projects with (React, Svelte, etc.). Using these modules is often the preferred approach because it doesn't pollute the global scope of our applications.

In this section, we'll briefly discuss these technologies and their role in the D3 ecosystem. Because SVG knowledge is foundational to understanding D3, we'll spend time explaining in greater detail the basics that you'll need to comprehend to start building visualizations. If you're already familiar with HTML, SVG elements, CSS, JavaScript, and JavaScript modules, feel free to skim or skip ahead to section 1.3.

1.2.1 HTML and the DOM

When you land on a web page, the first file to be loaded is an HTML file, like the following example. The browser parses the HTML file to build the DOM, the programming interface used for web documents. We often refer to it as the DOM tree because it consists of a set of nested elements, also called nodes or tags. In our example, the <head> and the <body> elements are children of the <html> parent. Similarly, the <body> tag is the parent of the <h1>, the <div>, and the <p> tags. The <h1> title is also a sibling of the <div> element. When you load a web page, what you see on the screen are the elements contained within the <body> tag:

```
<!DOCTYPE html>
<html>
  <head>
    <meta charset="UTF-8">
    <title>A simple HTML file | D3.js in Action</title>
  </head>
  <body>
    <h1>I am a title</h1>
    <div>
      <p>I am a paragraph.</p>
      <p>I am another paragraph.</p>
    </div>
  </body>
</html>
```

In the DOM, three categories of information about each element define its behavior and appearance: styles, attributes, and properties. *Styles* determine color, size, borders, opacity, and so on. *Attributes* include classes and IDs, though some attributes can also determine appearance, depending on which type of element you're dealing with. For SVG elements, attributes are used to set the position, size, and proportions of the different shapes. *Properties* typically refer to states, such as the "checked" property of a check box, which is true if the box is checked and false if the box is unchecked. Although the terms "attribute" and "property" are often used interchangeably, they're two separate things. An attribute appears as the initial state when the DOM is rendered. A property is the current state of an element and can change as the user interacts with the interface. In chapter 2, we'll discuss the D3 methods used to generate or modify the styles and attributes of HTML and SVG elements.

The DOM also determines the onscreen drawing order of elements, with child elements drawn after and inside parent elements. Although the CSS property z-index gives us partial control over the order in which traditional HTML elements are drawn onto the screen, SVG elements strictly follow the order in which they appear in the DOM. Per the painter's model, what is drawn after appears on top of what was drawn before.

1.2.2 *Scalable Vector Graphics*

The introduction of Scalable Vector Graphics (SVG) changed the face of the web—literally. Within a few years, SVG became a major web development tool. While raster graphics (PNG and JPG) are composed of tiny pixels that become visible when we zoom in too close, vector graphics are built with math and geometry. They maintain a crisp look at any size and any screen resolution. Another considerable advantage of SVG graphics is that they can be injected directly into the DOM, allowing developers to manipulate and animate their elements and making them accessible to screen readers. If built properly, SVG graphics are also performant, as their file size is only a fraction of their equivalent raster images.

When creating data visualizations with D3, we usually inject SVG shapes into the DOM and modify their attributes to generate the visual elements that compose the visualization. Understanding how SVG works, the main SVG shapes, and their presentational attributes is essential to most D3 projects. In this section, we'll cover the SVG shapes that you'll keep reusing over and over throughout your D3 project. If you're not familiar with SVG, take the time to code along with us. We promise it will make working with D3 way easier down the road.

How to access the code files

Every chapter in this book includes code-along exercises designed to support your learning experience. We highly recommend that you "do" the book rather than just "read" the book, which means completing the exercises as you read the chapters. You'll retain much more information this way and will soon be on your way to building your own D3 projects!

For every exercise and project, you have access to ready-to-use code files. You can find them on the book's GitHub repository (http://mng.bz/Xqjv). If you're familiar with Git, you can clone the repository on your computer. You can also download the zipped files.

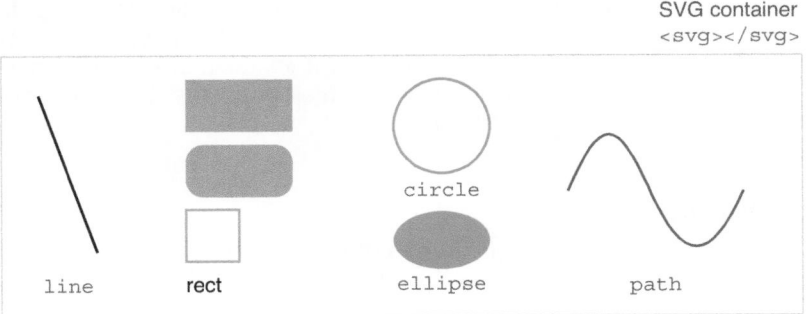

Download the code files from the GitHub repository.

Each chapter has its own folder that contains one or multiple exercises numbered per the sections in each chapter. The exercises include a `start` folder containing all the files you need to get started. You'll find the complete solution to the exercise in the `end` folder. As you progress through a chapter's sections, you can keep coding in the file you used for the previous section or start anew with the folder dedicated to that section. Both options will lead to the same result.

Let's start exploring vector graphics. Go to the code files provided with this book. Find the `end` folder in `chapter_01/SVG_Shapes_Gallery`, and right-click on the `index.html` file. In the menu, go to Open With, and select a browser. We recommend working with Chrome or Firefox for their great inspector tools. The file will open in a new browser tab, and the vector graphic that you see in figure 1.8 will appear. You can also view these SVG shapes on the GitHub-hosted project (http://mng.bz/yZmB).

Figure 1.8 Gallery of fundamental SVG shapes that we'll build in this section

The SVG graphic you're looking at contains the shapes you'll use most often as you create D3 visualizations: lines, rectangles, circles, ellipses, paths, and text.

When working with D3, you usually tell the library which shapes it should append to the DOM. You're also responsible for knowing which presentational attributes need to be included for the shapes to have the dimensions, color, and position that you're looking for. In the following exercise, you'll write the code that creates each of the SVG elements from figure 1.8. We'll refer to this exercise as our *Gallery of SVG Shapes*. Afterwards, you'll know all the SVG basics you need to get started.

Open the `index.html` file from the `start` folder of exercise `SVG_Shapes_Gallery` in your code editor of choice. We recommend *Visual Studio Code (VS Code)*, a code editor that is free, easy to use, and has multiple functionalities that you'll find helpful for frontend development.

As you can see in listing 1.1, `index.html` is a simple HTML file. If you open this file in your browser (right-click on the file and choose a browser in the Open With menu), you'll only see a blank page because the `<body>` element is empty. In the next subsections, we'll add SVG shapes into this `<body>` element.

Listing 1.1   Starting HTML for the Gallery of SVG Shapes exercise

```
<!DOCTYPE html>
<html>
<head>
  <meta charset="UTF-8">
  <meta name="viewport" content="width=device-width, initial-scale=1.0">
  <title>SVG Shapes Gallery | D3.js in Action</title>
</head>
<body>

</body>
</html>
```

Where to find more information

The following sections will introduce multiple SVG elements and their attributes. As frontend developers, we heavily rely on online resources when building our projects, using SVG elements that we're not familiar with, or looking for a JavaScript function to perform a specific action. MDN Web Docs (https://developer.mozilla.org/) is always a reliable and comprehensive resource. It contains easy-to-understand and often editable examples of SVG elements and their attributes, CSS properties, and JavaScript functions.

RESPONSIVE SVG CONTAINER

In the world of SVG graphics, the `<svg>` container is the whiteboard on which we draw. Every single SVG shape is nested inside a `<svg>` parent. To see it in action, edit index.html, and add an SVG container inside the <body> element. Reload your page in the browser. Nothing is visible yet:

```
<body>
  <svg></svg>
</body>
```

Open the inspector tool of your browser (right-click in your browser window, and choose Inspect). Within the inspector window, you'll see the DOM that composes the page. Find the <svg></svg> container, also called the SVG node. When you pass your mouse over it in the inspector, the SVG element gets highlighted on the page. You can see this effect in figure 1.9.

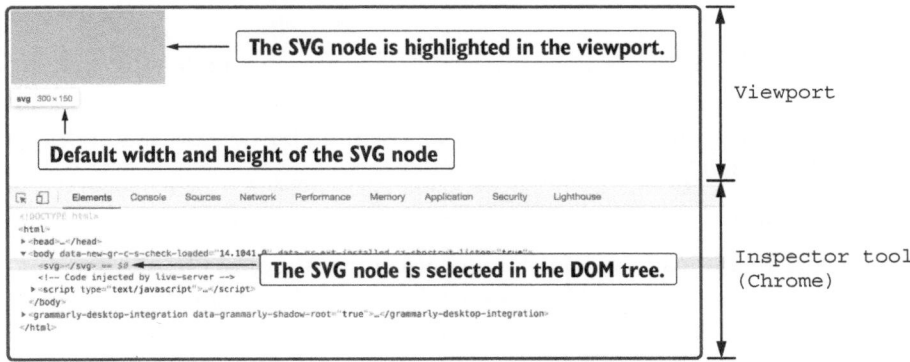

Figure 1.9   SVG node selected in the DOM tree and highlighted in the viewport

By default, the browser gives a width of 300 px and a height of 150 px to the SVG container. But we can also use attributes to assign these values. Attributes are there to provide additional information about HTML elements. With inline SVG, we mainly use attributes to set the size and positions of the shapes that compose an SVG graphic.

For example, we can set the width and height attributes of an SVG element. Go back to your text editor, and add a width and a height attribute to the SVG container. Set their values to 900 and 300, respectively, and save the file:

```
<svg width="900" height="300"></svg>
```

Reload your project in the browser, and find the SVG node in the inspector tool. Note that the width and height attributes now appear on the SVG element. If you pass your mouse over the SVG node in the DOM tree of the inspector tool, you'll also see that the SVG container in the viewport now has a size of 900 px by 300 px, as shown in figure 1.10.

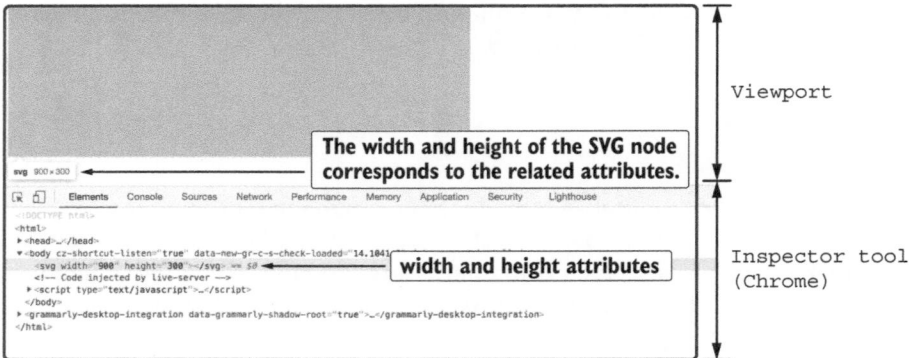

Figure 1.10   SVG node taking the size specified by its attributes

To help us see the SVG container without having to highlight it from the inspector, let's give it a border. Add a style attribute to the SVG element, and insert the CSS `border` property. In the next snippet, we used the border shorthand property to create a black, solid border of 1 px width:

```
<svg width="900" height="300" style="border:1px solid black;"></svg>
```

Save your file, reload the page, and confirm that there is a border around your SVG container. Now resize your browser window until it's smaller than the SVG container. You'll observe that the SVG container keeps a fixed width and height and doesn't adapt to the browser window's size. Let's try to make our SVG container responsive (adapting automatically to the window size).

Previously, we've set the SVG attributes as absolute values (900 and 300), and the browser interpreted them as measurements in pixels (900 px and 300 px). But we can also use percentages. In your text editor, change the width attribute to a relative value of `"100%"`, save the file, and reload the page:

```
<svg width="100%" height="300" style="border:1px solid black;"></svg>
```

Resize your browser again, and notice how the SVG takes the full width available and keeps a fixed height of 300 px. That's better, but we've lost our original aspect ratio.

To make responsive SVG elements, we can use the `viewBox` attribute. In your code editor, remove the `width` and the `height` attributes from the SVG container, and replace them with a `viewBox` attribute. Give it a value of `"0 0 900 300"`:

```
<svg viewBox="0 0 900 300" style="border:1px solid black;"></svg>
```

Play again with resizing your browser window. What do you notice? The SVG container now adapts to any screen size while maintaining its aspect ratio of 900:300. We have a responsive SVG!

As you've seen, the `viewBox` attribute consists of a list of four values. The first two numbers specify the origin of the coordinate system of the `viewBox` (x and y). In this book, we'll always use 0 0, but it's good to know that these values can change which portion of the SVG container is visible on the screen. The last two numbers of the viewBox attribute are its width and height. They define the aspect ratio of the SVG and ensure that it scales perfectly to fit within any container without distortion.

Fitting within a container is the key here. So far, the container of our inline SVG is the <body> element, which generally extends to fit the browser's viewport. If the viewport gets very large, the SVG gets very large too. Usually, we want our SVG to have a maximum width so that it doesn't get larger than the rest of the content on the page. To do so, wrap the SVG container inside a div with a width of 100% and a max-width of 1200px. For simplicity, we've set these properties as inline styles. Note that we've also added a margin of value 0 auto to center the SVG horizontally on the page:

```
<div style="width:100%; max-width:1200px; margin:0 auto;">
  <svg viewBox="0 0 900 300" style="border:1px solid black;"> ... </svg>
</div>
```

Try resizing your browser one more time and see how our SVG adapts gracefully to any screen size while respecting the maximum width of its container. This strategy is helpful to inject D3 visualizations into responsive web pages, and we'll use it throughout the book.

SVG COORDINATE SYSTEM

Now that you know how to make inline SVG responsive, it's important to address how the SVG shapes are positioned within the SVG container. The SVG container is like a blank sheet on which we draw vectorial shapes. Vectorial shapes are defined with basic geometric principles and positioned in reference to the coordinate system of the SVG container.

The SVG coordinate system is similar to the Cartesian coordinate system. Its 2D plane uses two perpendicular axes to determine the position of elements, referred to as x and y. These two axes originate from the *top-left corner* of the SVG container, as you can see in figure 1.11. It means that the positive direction of the y-axis goes *from top to bottom.* Remembering this will save you from a few headaches!

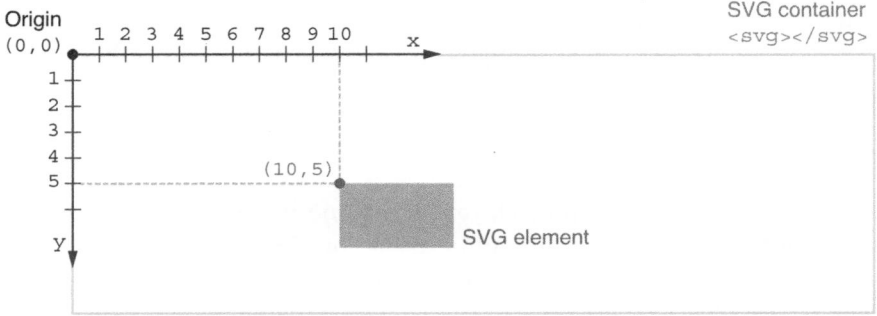

Figure 1.11   Coordinate system of the SVG container and position of an element

To position an element inside the SVG container, we start from the origin at the top-left corner and move toward the right. This will give us the horizontal position (x) of the element. For the vertical position (y), we start at the top and move down. These positions are defined by the presentational attributes of each SVG shape.

We'll now look at the SVG shapes that you'll often meet while building D3 projects. We'll also discuss their main presentational attributes. The goal here is by no means to write a comprehensive guide to all the shapes and features SVG has to offer, but rather to cover the basic knowledge that will support your D3 journey.

Data visualization tip: Geometric primitives

Accomplished artists can draw anything with vector graphics, but you're probably looking at D3 with more pragmatic goals in mind. From that perspective, it's essential to understand the concept of geometric primitives (also known as graphical primitives). *Geometric primitives* are simple shapes such as points, lines, circles, and rectangles. These shapes, which can be combined to make more complex graphics, are particularly convenient for displaying information visually.

Primitives are also useful for understanding complex information visualizations that you see in the real world. Tree layouts, like the ones we'll build in chapter 11, are far less intimidating when you realize they're only circles and lines. Interactive timelines are easier to understand and create when you think of them as collections of rectangles and points. Even geographic data, which primarily comes in the form of polygons, points, and lines, is less confusing when you break it down into its most basic graphical structures.

LINE

The line element is probably the simplest of all SVG shapes. It takes the position of two points, set as attributes, and draws a straight line between them. Go back to the `index.html` file, and add a `<line />` element inside the SVG container. Declare its attributes x1 and y1, and give them a value of 50 and 45, respectively. This means that the starting point of our line is positioned at (50, 45) in the coordinate system of the SVG container. If you start at the top-left corner of the SVG container and move 50 px to the right and 45 px down, you'll meet the line's starting point. Similarly, set the line's endpoint to (140, 225) using the attributes x2 and y2, as in figure 1.12:

```
<svg>
  <line x1="50" y1="45" x2="140" y2="225" />
</svg>
```

If you save and reload your project, your line won't be visible, and you might wonder what's going on. For an SVG line to be visible on the screen, we also need to set its `stroke` attribute, which controls the line's color. The value of the `stroke` attribute is similar to the CSS color property. It can be a color name (black, blue, etc.), an RGB color (rgb(255,0,0)), or a hexadecimal value (#808080). Add a `stroke` attribute to

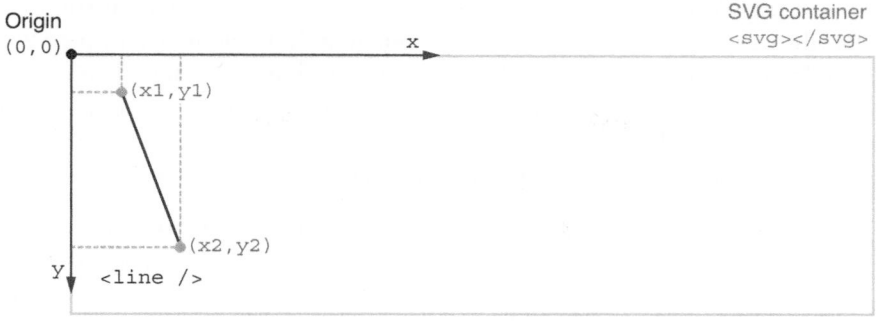

Figure 1.12   Positioning a line element in the coordinate system of an SVG container

your line, and give it the color of your choice (we used black). It should now be visible on the screen:

```
<line x1="50" y1="45" x2="140" y2="225" stroke="black" />
```

If we want to set the width of the line, we use the `stroke-width` attribute. This attribute accepts an absolute number, which translates into pixels, or a relative value (%). For example, the following line will have a `stroke-width` of 3 px. If the `stroke-width` attribute isn't declared, the browser applies a default value of 1 px:

```
<line x1="50" y1="45" x2="140" y2="225" stroke="black" stroke-width="3" />
```

Open the inspector tool of your browser, and find the SVG node and the line it contains. Double-click on one of the attributes, change its value, and observe how the new value modifies the line's starting or endpoint. Take the time to play with different values to confirm that you understand how the attributes x1, y1, x2, and y2 affect the position and length of the line.

Now give a value of -20 to the x1 attribute. Do you see how the starting point of the line disappeared, as shown in figure 1.13? Any shape or portion of a shape that falls

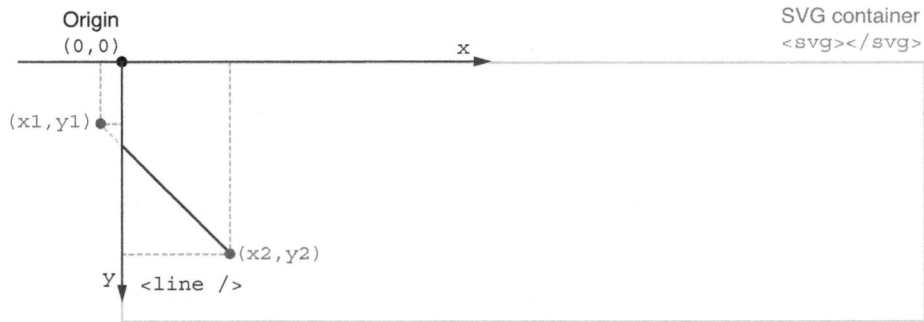

Figure 1.13   SVG line partially hidden when outside of the SVG container

outside of the SVG `viewBox` *is not* visible on the screen. The element still exists in the DOM, though, so we can access and manipulate it. If an element in your SVG isn't visible and you don't know why, the first thing to check is if it's outside of the SVG `view-Box`! Remember that you can always find it by using the developer tools to inspect the DOM. As we did earlier, if you pass your mouse over the element in the inspector tool, it will be highlighted in the viewport, even if it's outside of the SVG `viewBox`.

> **NOTE** Most SVG elements need only a self-closing tag (we use `<line />` rather than `<line></line>`). Like some of the other HTML tags, the inherent structure of SVG elements provide all the required information within the self-closing tag. This will be different for SVG text elements, where the text is placed between an opening and a closing tag.

RECTANGLE

As its name suggests, the rectangle element `<rect />` draws a rectangular shape on the screen. The `<rect />` element requires four attributes to be visible. The attributes `x` and `y` declare the position of the rectangle's top-left corner, while the attributes `width` and `height` respectively control its width and height, as shown in figure 1.14. Add the following `<rect />` element and its attributes in your SVG container:

```
<rect x="260" y="25" width="120" height="60" fill="#6ba5d7" />
```

In our example, the top-left corner of the rectangle is positioned 260 px to the right and 25 px below the origin of the SVG container. It has a width of 120 px and a height of 60 px. As with other positional attributes, we can set these values using percentages instead of absolute numbers. For instance, if we set the `width` attribute to 50%, the rectangle will spread on half of the width of the SVG container.

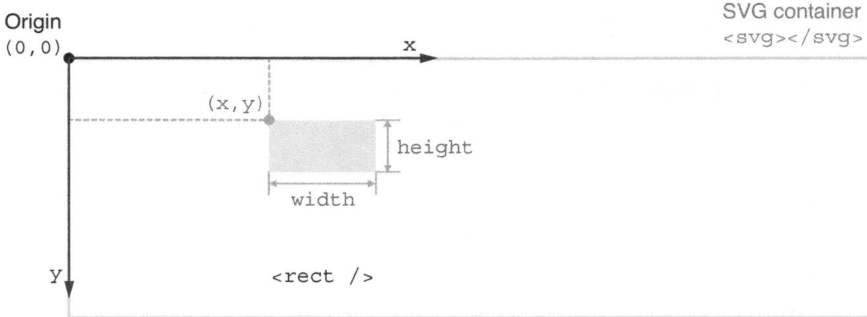

Figure 1.14   Positioning and sizing a rectangle in the coordinate system of an SVG container

You might have noticed that our rectangle is black at first. By default, browsers apply a black fill to most SVG shapes. We can change that color by setting the fill attribute and giving it any CSS color property. If we want to add a border to the rectangle, we add a stroke attribute. Figure 1.15 shows a few examples. Note how no border is drawn around the rectangle if you don't declare a `stroke` attribute. In addition, in the last rectangle, the attributes fill-opacity and stroke-opacity are used to make both the `fill` and the `stroke` semitransparent. Like in CSS, the opacity can be set as an absolute value (between `0` and `1`) or a percentage (`30%`). All the attributes related to the fill and the stroke can also be set or modified from a CSS file.

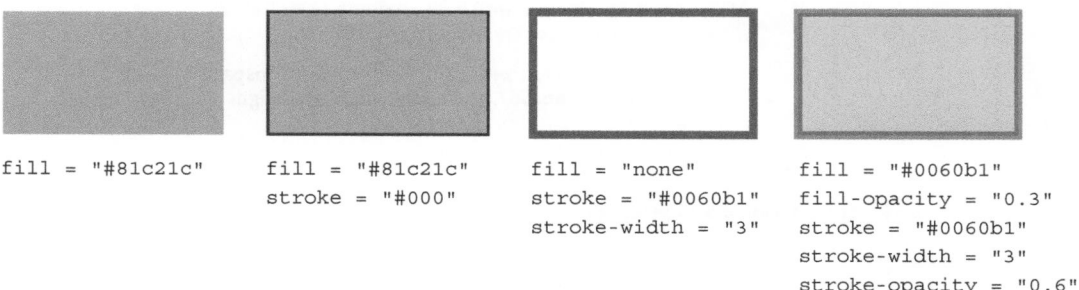

```
fill = "#81c21c"        fill = "#81c21c"       fill = "none"          fill = "#0060b1"
                        stroke = "#000"        stroke = "#0060b1"     fill-opacity = "0.3"
                                               stroke-width = "3"     stroke = "#0060b1"
                                                                      stroke-width = "3"
                                                                      stroke-opacity = "0.6"
```

Figure 1.15 Different styling attributes applied to rectangle SVG shapes

If you want your rectangle to have rounded corners, you simply need to add the `rx` and `ry` attributes, which, respectively, represent the horizontal and vertical corner radius. These attributes accept absolute (in pixels) and relative values (percentages). For example, each corner of the rectangle in the following code has a radius of 20 px. Add this rectangle to your gallery of shapes:

```
<rect x="260" y="100" width="120" height="60" rx="20" ry="20"
fill="#6ba5d7" />
```

At this point, you might wonder if there is an element to draw square shapes in SVG. We don't need one! In SVG, we draw squares with `<rect />` elements by giving them equal `width` and `height` attributes. For example, the following `<rect />` element will draw a square of 60 px × 60 px. Add it to your gallery of shapes as well:

```
<rect x="260" y="175" width="60" height="60"  fill="transparent"
stroke="#6ba5d7" />
```

As a reference, we now have three types of SVG rectangles in our gallery of shapes: a classic rectangle, a rectangle with rounded corners, and a square. For fun, we gave them a color of #6ba5d7 and played with their `stroke` and `fill` attributes. Note that only the stroke is visible on the square because its `fill` attribute has a value of `transparent` (`none` would be the same). Your rectangles should look similar to the ones in figure 1.16, unless you used different attributes, which we encourage you to do:

```
<rect x="260" y="25" width="120" height="60" fill="#6ba5d7" />
<rect x="260" y="100" width="120" height="60" rx="20" ry="20"
    fill="#6ba5d7" />
```

```
<rect x="260" y="175" width="60" height="60" fill="transparent"
  stroke="#6ba5d7" />
```

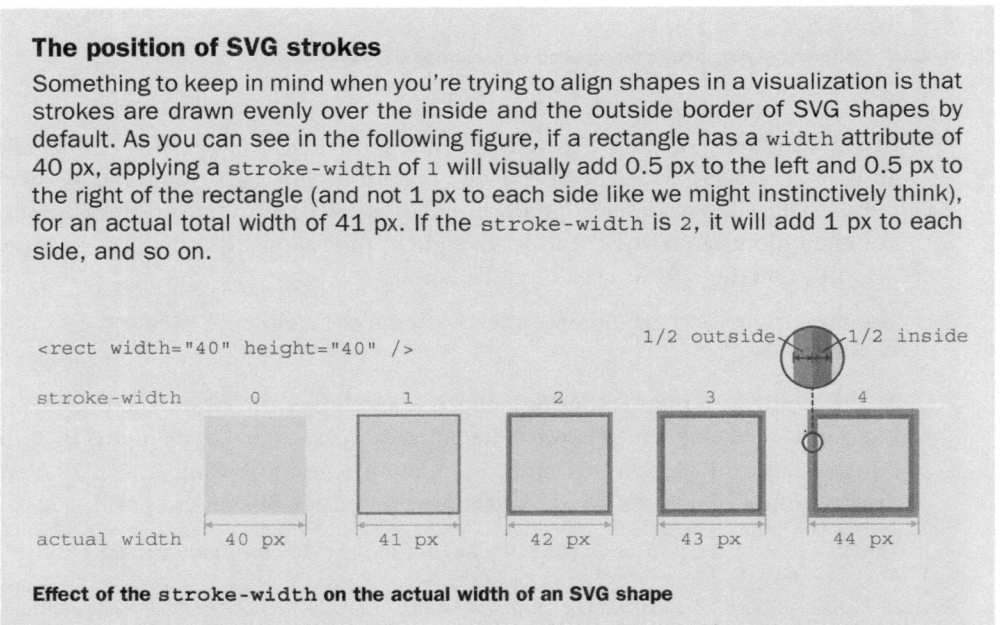

Figure 1.16   Three types of SVG rectangles

The position of SVG strokes

Something to keep in mind when you're trying to align shapes in a visualization is that strokes are drawn evenly over the inside and the outside border of SVG shapes by default. As you can see in the following figure, if a rectangle has a `width` attribute of 40 px, applying a `stroke-width` of 1 will visually add 0.5 px to the left and 0.5 px to the right of the rectangle (and not 1 px to each side like we might instinctively think), for an actual total width of 41 px. If the `stroke-width` is 2, it will add 1 px to each side, and so on.

Effect of the `stroke-width` on the actual width of an SVG shape

CIRCLE AND ELLIPSE

Circular shapes are used regularly in data visualization. They naturally attract the eye and make the visualization feel more friendly and playful. We draw SVG circles with the `<circle />` element. Its required attributes are the position of the center of the circle (cx, cy) and its radius (r), as shown in figure 1.17. A circle's radius is the length of a line drawn from its center to any point on its circumference. Add the following circle to your gallery of shapes. Position its center at (530, 80), and give it a radius of 50 px:

```
<circle cx="530" cy="80" r="50" />
```

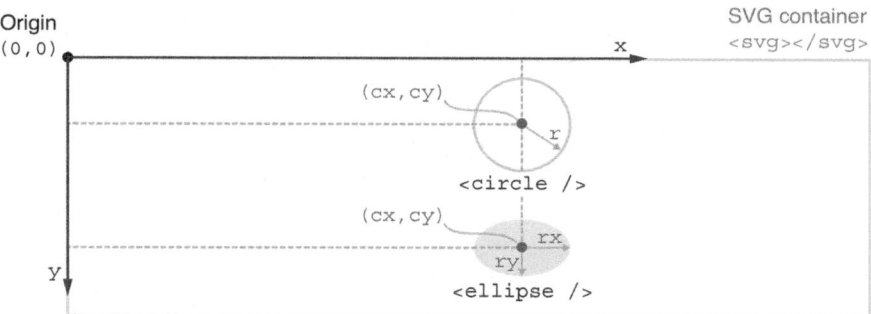

Figure 1.17   Positioning and sizing a circle and an ellipse in the coordinate system of an SVG container

You can also play with the fill and the stroke attributes of the circle. To generate the one from our Gallery of shapes, we used a transparent fill and a stroke of 3 px with the color #81c21c.

Similarly, the <ellipse /> element requires attributes for the position of the center of the shape (cx, cy). While circles have a constant radius, the radius of ellipses varies, giving them a flattened shape. We create this flattened effect by declaring a horizontal radius (rx) and a vertical radius (ry). Add the next snippet to your gallery. It will draw an ellipse below the circle, with a horizontal radius of 50 px and a vertical radius of 30 px:

```
<ellipse cx="530" cy="205" rx="50" ry="30" />
```

PATH

SVG paths are by far the most flexible of all the SVG elements. They are extensively used in D3 to draw pretty much all the complex shapes and curves that can't be represented by one of the shape primitives discussed so far (line, rectangle, circle, and ellipse).

We instruct the browser on how to draw a path by declaring its d attribute, which stands for "draw." The d attribute contains a list of commands, from where to start drawing the path to the types of curves to use, up to specifying if we want the path to be a closed shape or not. As an example, add the following path element to your gallery of shapes:

```
<path d="M680 150 C 710 80, 725 80, 755 150 S 810 220, 840 150" fill="none"
stroke="#773b9a" stroke-width="3" />
```

In this example, illustrated in figure 1.18, the d attribute starts with M680 150, which means "move (M) to the coordinate (680, 150)." Then we draw a cubic Bézier curve from the starting point (680 150) to the endpoint specified by the last coordinate (840 150) in the d attribute. A cubic Bézier curve also needs control points to define how steep the curve is and the directions in which it bends. Those control points start right after the letter C ("cubic curve") and stop right after the letter S ("stop").

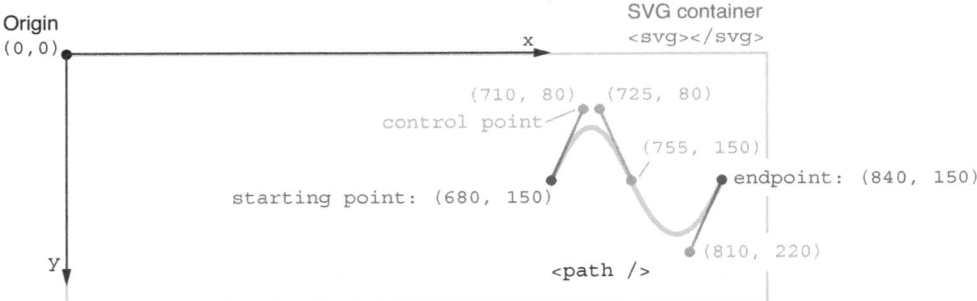

Figure 1.18   A simple SVG path and its control points

> **NOTE** For a deep dive into SVG paths, refer to MDN's tutorial at http:// mng.bz/amn7.

Manually writing the d attribute is feasible for simple shapes but gets tedious as the shapes increase in complexity. Fortunately, D3 has powerful shape generators that calculate the d attribute for us. We'll introduce them in chapter 4.

Another important thing to remember about paths is that browsers will fill them with black color, unless we set their fill attribute to none or transparent. This is true even if the path isn't closed, as in our example.

TEXT

One of the most significant advantages of inline SVG graphics is that the text they contain is available to screen readers. This is a big plus for accessibility. Because data visualizations often contain multiple labels, it's necessary to understand how to manipulate SVG text using the <text> element. Let's add labels to our gallery of shapes to understand the basic principles of SVG text.

The SVG shapes discussed so far use a self-closing tag (<line />, <rect />, <path />, etc.). When working with SVG <text> elements, we need to use both an opening and a closing tag. We position the text to display in between these two tags. For example, let's add a <text> element into our SVG that says "line":

```
<text>line</text>
```

Save your file and reload the page. You might expect the text to appear at the top-left corner of the SVG container, but it's nowhere to be seen. Why is that? By default, the position of SVG text is calculated in reference to its baseline, controlled by the `dominant-baseline` attribute. If the coordinate of the text's baseline is `(0, 0)`, you can see in figure 1.19 how the actual text ends up outside of the SVG container. Because any element positioned outside of the SVG container is invisible, we don't see our text.

Figure 1.19   Text positioned outside of the SVG container

Another point to consider when working with SVG text is how the content will flow. Regular HTML elements are positioned on the page following specific rules that control the flow of content. If you insert a bunch of `<div>` elements into your page, they will naturally stack one over another, and their text will break lines so that it never goes outside of their container. SVG text doesn't flow at all, and we must set the x and y attributes of each text element individually. If we use these attributes to place our text at `(60, 260)`, the label "line" will appear below the SVG line in our gallery of shapes:

```
<text x="60" y="260">line</text>
```

To practice, create a new text element that positions a label "rect" below the rectangle and square shapes.

So far, we've used the x and y attributes to declare the position of the bottom-left corner of our text elements. But what if we want to set the position of the middle point of our text instead? We can do so by using the attribute `text-anchor` with a value of `middle`, as illustrated in figure 1.20. For example, we can center a text label for our circle shape using this attribute:

```
<text x="530" y="155" text-anchor="middle">circle</text>
```

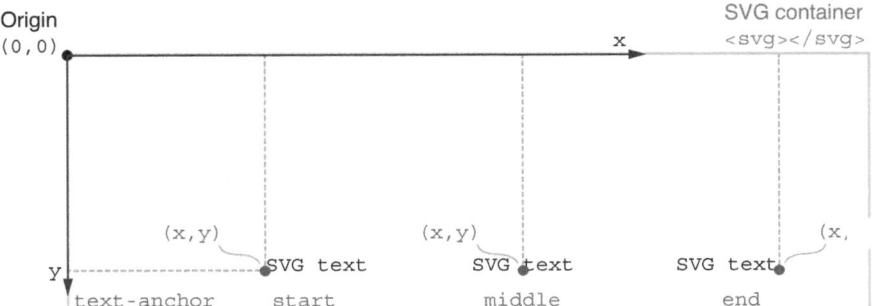

Figure 1.20   The `text-anchor` attribute affects the alignment of SVG text. Its default value is `start`. To align a text element based on its middle, we apply a `text-anchor` attribute of `middle`. Similarly, to align a text based on its end, we apply a `text-anchor` attribute of `end`.

Finish by adding a label for the ellipse and another one for the path element. By default, SVG text is black. You can change its color with the `fill` attribute.

GROUPING ELEMENTS

The final SVG element that we'll discuss in this section is the group element. The group or `<g>` element is distinct from the SVG elements we've discussed so far in that it has no graphical representation and doesn't exist as a bounded space. Instead, it's a logical grouping of elements. You'll want to use groups extensively when creating visualizations made of several shapes and labels.

If we want the square and the "rect" label to be displayed together and move as one within the SVG container, we can place them inside a `<g>` element, as in the following example. Note how the top-left corner of the `<rect>` element has been changed to (0, 0). The `<text>` is positioned at (0, 85) to maintain it below the `<rect>`:

```
<g>
  <rect x="0" y="0" width="60" height="60" />
  <text x="0" y="85">rect</text>
</g>
```

The group containing the square and its label now appear at the top-left corner of the SVG container. We can move this group and all the elements it contains wherever we want them within the SVG container while maintaining the alignment between the square and its label.

Moving a group around the SVG container is done with the `transform` attribute. The `transform` attribute is a little more intimidating than the attributes discussed so far but is identical to the CSS `transform` property. It takes a transformation (translate, rotate, scale, etc.) or a stack of transformations as values. To move a group, we use the `translate(x, y)` transformation. If we want to move our `<rect>` and `<text>` elements back to their original position, we need to apply a translation of 260 pixels to the right and 175 pixels down. To do so, we set the `transform` attribute of the `<g>` element to `transform="translate(260,175)"`:

```
<g transform="translate(260,175)">
  <rect x="0" y="0" width="60" height="60" />
  <text x="0" y="85">rect</text>
</g>
```

Another helpful aspect of the `<g>` element is that its children inherit its styling attributes. To illustrate this, let's group all remaining text elements within a `<g>` element, except the label "rect", which we've already grouped with the square:

```
<g>
  <text x="60" y="260">line</text>
  <text x="530" y="155" style="text-anchor:middle">circle</text>
  <text x="530" y="260" style="text-anchor:middle">ellipse</text>
  <text x="730" y="260">path</text>
</g>
```

If we apply a fill attribute of `#636466` to the group, each `<text>` element inside that group will inherit the same color. Similarly, if we add a style attribute to the group, for instance, with the `font-family` and the `font-size` properties, the text inside the group will inherit these properties:

```
<g fill="#636466" style="font-size:16px; font-family:monospace">
  <text x="60" y="260">line</text>
  <text x="530" y="155" style="text-anchor:middle">circle</text>
  <text x="530" y="260" style="text-anchor:middle">ellipse</text>
  <text x="730" y="260">path</text>
</g>
```

Reload your page one last time, and observe how the labels inside the group inherit the group's color and font, while the label that remained outside of that group kept its original look. This technique of applying shared attributes to a group element is quite handy and can help you apply the Don't Repeat Yourself (DRY) coding principle to your work. It will also make your life easier when you need to update these attributes.

Congrats on completing the first exercise of this book! You can find the complete code of the *Gallery of SVG Shapes* in the next listing and in the end folder of the coding files. Use this exercise as a reference when you build your first D3 projects.

Listing 1.2   Completed HTML for the Gallery of SVG Shapes exercise

```
<!DOCTYPE html>
<html>
<head> [...] </head>
<body>
  <div style="width:100%; max-width:1200px; margin:0 auto;">
    <svg viewBox="0 0 900 300" style="border:1px solid black;">

      <line x1="50" y1="45" x2="140" y2="225" stroke="black" />

      <rect x="260" y="25" width="120" height="60" fill="#6ba5d7" />
      <rect x="260" y="100" width="120" height="60" rx="20" ry="20"
fill="#6ba5d7" />
      <g transform="translate(260, 175)">
        <rect x="0" y="0" width=60" height="60" fill="transparent"
stroke="#6ba5d7" />
        <text x="0" y="85">rect</text>
      </g>

      <circle cx="530" cy="80" r="50" fill="none" stroke="#81c21c" stroke-
width="3" />
      <ellipse cx="530" cy="205" rx="50" ry="30" fill="#81c21c" />

      <path d="M680 150 C 710 80, 725 80, 755 150 S 810 220, 840 150"
fill="none" stroke="#773b9a" stroke-width="3" />

      <g fill="#636466" style="font-size:16px; font-family:monospace">
        <text x="60" y="260">line</text>
        <text x="530" y="155" style="text-anchor:middle">circle</text>
        <text x="530" y="260" style="text-anchor:middle">ellipse</text>
```

```
            <text x="730" y="260">path</text>
          </g>

      </svg>
    </div>
  </body>
</html>
```

Exercise: Create an SVG graphic

Now it's your turn! Create the SVG graphic shown in the following figure. You can work in the `start` folder inside `02_SVG_exercise` of this chapter's code files. Here are a few guidelines:

- Create a responsive SVG container with a width and a height of 400 px (when there's enough room on the screen).
- Draw a square shape with a width and a height of 200 px. Center it within the SVG container, and give it a transparent fill and a 5 px black stroke.
- Add a circle with a radius of 100 px to the center of the SVG container. Set its fill attribute to the CSS color name "plum."
- Draw two diagonal black lines with a stroke of 5 px. One goes from the top-left corner of the square to its bottom-right corner. The other one goes from the top-right corner of the square to its bottom-left corner.
- Add the text "SVG is awesome!" above the square, and center it within the SVG container. Give the text the following style properties: a `font-size` of `18` px and a `font-family` of `sans-serif`.

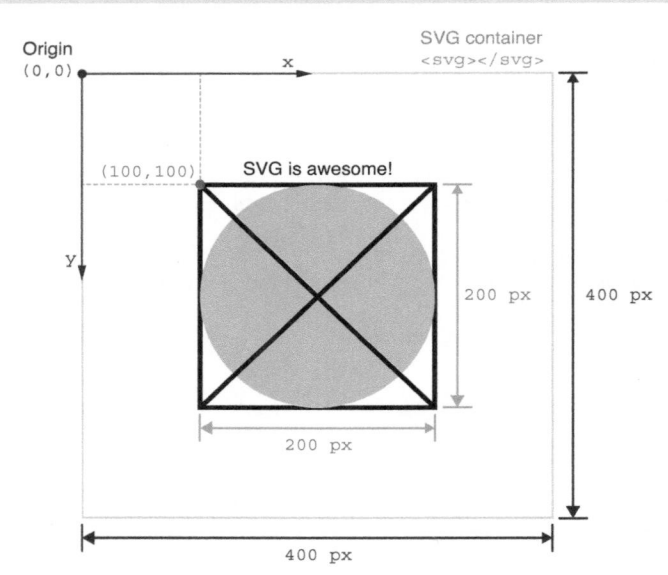

We encourage you to build this SVG graphic to reinforce the concepts discussed in this section.

You'll find the solution in section D.1.1 of appendix D and folder `02_SVG_exercise/end` of this chapter's code files. We encourage you to try to complete it on your own.

1.2.3   Canvas and WebGL

Although we usually build D3 projects with SVG elements, we might occasionally need to create complex visualizations from large datasets, for which the traditional SVG approach can generate performance problems. It's important to remember that D3 appends one or many SVG elements to the DOM for each graphical detail in a data visualization. A typical example is a large network visualization made of thousands of nodes and links. These may leave your browser huffing and puffing. Although the number of objects that browsers can comfortably handle is constantly increasing as they get more performant, a generally accepted rule of thumb is that we should consider using Canvas rather than SVG if a visualization contains more than 1,000 elements.

Canvas is a client-side drawing API that uses a script, often JavaScript, to create visuals and animations. It doesn't add XML elements to the DOM, which dramatically improves performance when building visualizations from large datasets. Canvas doesn't provide the same crisp rendering as SVG and makes interactions more complex to handle, so we generally stick with SVG. It's all a question of compromise.

Canvas also allows you to use the Web Graphics Library (WebGL) API to create 3D objects. Although learning WebGL is outside this book's scope, creating 3D data visualizations for the web is possible. At the moment, it's mainly used in experimental projects. In chapter 15, we'll cover how to build visualization with Canvas and discuss its pros and cons.

1.2.4   CSS

CSS (which stands for *Cascading Style Sheets*) is the language that describes how DOM elements are displayed on the screen and what they look like. From the overall grid layout of a page to the family of fonts used for the text, up to the color of the circles in a scatterplot, CSS can turn a plain HTML file into an awe-inspiring web page. In D3 projects, we generally apply CSS styles using inline styles or via an external stylesheet.

Inline styles are applied to elements with the `style` attribute. The `style` attribute can be used both on traditional HTML and SVG elements, and D3 has a handy method to set or modify this attribute that we'll discuss in chapter 2. The following example shows the `style` attribute with inline styles:

```
<div style="padding:10px; background:#00ced1;"> ... </div>
<text style="font-size:16px; font-family:serif;"> ... </text>
```

Inline styles affect only the element to which they are applied. If we want to propagate the same design to multiple elements, we need to apply the same `style` attribute to every one of them (or to an SVG group that wraps all the elements together). It certainly works, but it's not the most efficient way to go.

On the other hand, external CSS stylesheets are perfect for applying styles globally. A strategy is to ask D3 to add the same class name to multiple elements. We then use this class name as a selector in an external stylesheet and apply the same styling properties to the targeted group of elements, as in the following examples in the stylesheet

```
.my-class {
  font-size: 16px;
  font-family: serif;
}
```

and in the DOM:

```
<text class="my-class"> ... </text>
```

This approach is much more efficient, especially when maintaining large projects. It also follows the separation of concerns principle, where we separate behaviors, controlled with JavaScript, from styles, regulated with CSS. Note that CSS preprocessors such as Syntactically Awesome Stylesheets (SASS) and Leaner Stylesheets (LESS) are part of the external stylesheet approach described here.

> **TIP**   Remember that inline styles take precedence over the ones applied from an external stylesheet. In any frontend development project, it's important to plan the architecture of your CSS styles with the cascading order in mind.

1.2.5 *JavaScript*

D3 is a JavaScript library that adds new methods on top of the existing core features of JavaScript. This means that a little bit of prior experience with JavaScript is helpful when working with D3. In addition, when building D3 projects, you have access to all the existing JavaScript features.

A real introduction to JavaScript deserves its own book. In this section, we'll only discuss two JavaScript topics that are used extensively in D3 projects: *method chaining* and *object manipulation*.

METHOD CHAINING

If you search for examples of D3 projects on the web, you'll notice that methods are called one after another on the same selection. This technique is what we call method chaining and helps to keep the code concise and readable.

We can think of method chaining as we would of a car assembly line. Let's say we write the script that runs such an assembly line. As you can see in the following example, we would first declare a `car` variable that creates a new `Car()` object. We then call the function `putOnHood()`, which puts a hood on top of the car, and we continue by calling the functions that handle wheels, tires, and lights. Each successive call adds an element to the `Car()` object, and, once all the methods have been executed, the car has a hood, wheels, tires, and lights. Each method passes the updated car object to the next, thus the "chaining." Note that each call is separated by a dot and that the methods are executed in the order in which they are chained. In our car assembly line example, we need the wheels to be installed before we can put tires on them. The example looks like this:

```
let car = new Car().putOnHood().putOnWheels().putOnTires().putOnLights();
```

Let's now look at how we would use method chaining in D3. Imagine that we want to grab all the <div>s from the DOM and add a paragraph element into each of them. The paragraph elements should have a class attribute of my-class and contain the text "Wow". We then want to insert a <span> element into each paragraph, with the text "Even More Wow" in bold. Without method chaining, we would need to store each action into a constant, and then call this constant when performing the next action, as shown here (it's exhausting just to look at it):

```
const mySelection = d3.selectAll("div");
const myParagraphs = mySelection.append("p");
const myParagraphsWithAClass = myParagraphs.attr("class", "my-class");
const myParagraphsWithText = myParagraphsWithAClass.text("Wow");
const mySpans = myParagraphsWithText.append("span");
const mySpansWithText = mySpans.text("Even More Wow")
const myBoldSpans = mySpansWithText.style("font-weight", "900");
```

Thanks to method chaining, the same example becomes much more concise:

```
d3.selectAll("div").append("p").attr("class", "my-class").text("Wow")
    .append("span").text("Even More Wow").style("font-weight", "900");
```

In D3, it's very common to break lines, which JavaScript ignores, and to indent the chained methods. This makes the code easier to read, and the indentation helps us see which element we're working on:

```
d3.selectAll("div")
  .append("p")
    .attr("class", "my-class")
    .text("Wow")
  .append("span")
    .text("Even More Wow")
    .style("font-weight", "900");
```

Don't worry if you don't fully understand yet how the previous code works. For now, we only want you to get familiar with how methods can be chained in JavaScript. We'll cover the D3-specific jargon in chapter 2.

ARRAYS AND OBJECTS MANIPULATION

D3 is all about data, and data is often structured as JavaScript objects. Understanding the construction of these objects and how to access and manipulate the data they contain will be a tremendous help as you build visualizations.

Let's first talk about simple arrays, which are a list of elements. In data-related projects, arrays are usually an ordered list of numbers or strings:

```
const arrayOfNumbers = [17, 82, 9, 500, 40];
const arrayOfStrings = ["blue", "red", "yellow", "orange"];
```

Each element in an array has a numeric position, called the *index*, and the first element has an index of 0 (we say that JavaScript arrays are *zero-indexed*):

```
arrayOfNumbers[0]    // => 17
arrayOfStrings[2]    // => "yellow"
```

Arrays have a `length` property that, for nonsparse arrays, specifies the number of elements they contain. Because arrays are zero-indexed, the last element in an array has an index corresponding to the array's length minus 1:

```
arrayOfNumbers.length;                          // => 5
arrayOfStrings[arrayOfStrings.length - 1]   // => "orange"
```

We can also determine if an array contains a specific value with the method `includes()`. This method returns `true` if one of the elements from the array corresponds exactly to the value passed as an argument; otherwise, it returns `false`:

```
arrayOfNumbers.includes(9)        // => true
arrayOfStrings.includes("pink")   // => false
arrayOfStrings.includes("ellow")  // => false
```

However, most datasets aren't simple lists of numbers or strings, and each of their data points is usually composed of multiple properties. Let's imagine a database of employees from a fictional agency, represented in table 1.1. The table contains four columns: the ID, name, and position of each employee, and whether the employee works with D3 or not.

Table 1.1 A small dataset with employees and their position

ID	Name	Position	Works_with_d3
1	Zoe	Data analyst	False
2	James	Frontend developer	True
3	Alice	Fullstack developer	True
4	Hubert	Designer	False

Each row in the dataset, or data point, can be represented by a JavaScript object such as `row1`:

```
const row1 = {
          id:"1",
          name:"Zoe",
          position:"Data analyst",
          works_with_d3:false
        };
```

We can easily access the value of each property in the object with dot notation:

```
row1.name            // => "Zoe"
row1.works_with_d3   // => false
```

We can also access these values with bracket notation. Bracket notation is handy if the property name contains special characters, such as empty spaces, or if we previously saved the property name in a constant or a variable:

```
row1["position"]                              // => "Data analyst"

const myProperty = "works_with_d3";
row1[myProperty]                              // => false
```

In real life, datasets are generally formatted as arrays of objects. For example, if we load the dataset contained in table 1.1 with D3, as you'll learn to do in chapter 3, we obtain the following array of objects that we can save in a constant named `data`:

```
const data = [
  {id:"1", name:"Zoe", position:"Data analyst", works_with_d3:false},
  {id:"2", name:"James", position:"Frontend developer", works_with_d3:true},
  {id:"3", name:"Alice", position:"Fullstack developer",works_with_d3:true},
  {id:"4", name:"Hubert", position:"Designer", works_with_d3:false}
];
```

We can iterate through each element, or datum, in the `data` array with a loop. More specifically, the JavaScript `forEach` loop is convenient and easy to write and read. A common use case for iterating through a dataset is data wrangling. When we load an external CSV file, the numbers are often formatted as strings. Let's take our `data` array as an example and convert the values of the property `id` from strings into numbers.

In the following example, the array iterator `d` gives us access to each datum. Using dot notation, we convert each `id` into a number using the + operator:

```
data.forEach(d => {
  d.id = +d.id;
});
```

JavaScript provides many array iterator methods that help us interact with data and even reshape it when needed. Let's say we want to position each employee from our dataset onto a visualization. Creating a simple array that only contains the names of the employees might come in handy, and we'd use the `map()` method for that:

```
data.map(d => d.name);    // => ["Zoe", "James", "Alice", "Hubert"]
```

Similarly, if we want to isolate only the employees that work with D3, we could use the `filter()` method:

```
data.filter(d => d.works_with_d3);

// => [
    {id:2, name:"James", position:"Frontend developer", works_with_d3:true},
    {id:4, name:"Hubert", position:"Designer", works_with_d3:true}
  ];
```

Finally, we could find the employee with an ID of 3 with the `find()` method. Note that the `find()` method stops iterating after finding the value it's looking for. We can only use this method when searching for one unique data point:

```
data.find(d => d.id === 3);

// => {id:"3", name:"Alice", position:"Fullstack developer",
works_with_d3:true}
```

The methods discussed in this section are far from covering all the array and object manipulation techniques that JavaScript offers, but they are probably the ones you'll keep coming back to when working with data. Whenever you need to find another way to access or manipulate your data, MDN Web Docs (https://developer.mozilla.org/) is always a solid reference with plenty of examples.

1.2.6   *Node and JavaScript frameworks*

JavaScript has seen major changes in the past decade. The two most significant trends in modern JavaScript are the rise of node.js and the establishment of JavaScript frameworks as the standard for most projects.

The major node technology we want to know for D3 projects is Node Package Manager (NPM). NPM allows you to install "modules," or small libraries of JavaScript code, to use in your projects. You don't have to include a bunch of `<script>` tag references to individual files, and if the module has been built so that it's not one monolithic structure, modules can reduce the amount of code shipped by your application.

D3.js Version 7, which came out in mid-2021, takes advantage of module importing. Throughout this book, you'll see examples of using D3 in one of two ways. Either we'll load the entire D3 library, as we'll do in chapter 2, or we'll include only the individual parts of D3 that we need, as you'll see in later examples. We can do so with script tags, but starting in section 2, we'll import D3 modules using NPM because this is considered standard practice today. You'll likely need to get familiar with it if you ship professional D3 projects.

If you already participate in professional web projects, there's also a good chance that you're working with JavaScript frameworks, such as React, Angular, Vue, or Svelte. Frameworks provide developers with the foundation to build web projects with modular, reusable, and testable code. These frameworks are in charge of building and updating the DOM, which is what the D3 library does as well. In chapter 8, we'll discuss strategies to avoid conflicts when building D3 visualization within JavaScript frameworks.

Finally, in a professional working environment, you might use D3 in combination with TypeScript. TypeScript is a syntactical superset of JavaScript that enhances project scalability and code maintainability. Although we won't discuss it in detail in this book, D3 methods' types can be installed with the NPM package @types/d3 (www.npmjs .com/package/@types/d3). In chapter 8, we'll use such types in an Angular project.

1.2.7   *Observable notebooks*

If you search for examples of D3 projects on the web, you'll undoubtedly come across Observable notebooks (https://observablehq.com). Observable is a collaborative playground for data science and visualization, similar to Jupyter Notebook for Python. The Observable platform was created by Mike Bostock and replaced *blocks*, the previous online D3 sandbox. All the official D3 examples now live on Observable, and the D3 community is quite active over there.

It's important to know that Observable requires you to learn a way to handle D3 projects that is specific to this platform. In addition, you can't directly copy and paste an Observable notebook into a frontend development environment (although Observable 2.0 is making it easier). Because the focus of this book is to build D3 visualizations in an environment that resembles how we ship D3 projects for production, we won't cover Observable notebooks. If you're interested in learning Observable, there is an excellent series of tutorials at https://observablehq.com/tutorials. Most of the techniques and concepts that you'll learn in this book can be translated into Observable notebooks.

1.3   *Data visualization best practices*

Data visualization has never been as popular as it is today. The wealth of maps, charts, and complex representations of systems and datasets is present not only in the workplace but also in our entertainment and our everyday lives. With this popularity comes a growing library of data visualizations, as well as aesthetic rules to promote legibility and comprehension. Your audience, whether the general public, academics, or decision-makers, has grown accustomed to what we once considered incredibly abstract and complicated representations of trends in data. This makes libraries such as D3 popular not only among data scientists but also with journalists, artists, scholars, IT professionals, and even data visualization enthusiasts.

Such a wealth of options can seem overwhelming, and the relative ease of modifying a dataset to appear in a streamgraph, treemap, or histogram tends to promote the idea that information visualization is more about style than substance. Fortunately, well-established rules dictate which charts and methods to use for different data types. This book doesn't aim to cover every best practice in data visualization, but we'll touch on a few. Although developers use D3 to revolutionize the use of color and layout, most want to create visual representations of data that support practical concerns.

As you build your first visualization projects—and when in doubt, simplify—it's often better to present a histogram than a violin plot, or a hierarchical network layout (e.g., a dendrogram) than a force-directed one. The more visually complex methods of displaying data tend to inspire more excitement, but they can also lead an audience to focus on the aesthetics of the graphics rather than the data. There's nothing wrong with creating cool and jaw-dropping visualizations, but we should never forget that the primary goal of any data visualization is to tell a story. Asking around to see if people understand your visualization and how they interpret it is a crucial step. Do they need explanation? Which conclusions can they draw from interacting with your project? Does the story get told?

Still, to properly deploy information visualization, you should know what to do and what not to do. You need to have a firm understanding of your data and your audience. D3 grants us immense flexibility, but remember, "With great power comes great responsibility." While it's good to know that certain charts are better suited to represent a specific type of data, it's even more important to remember that data visualizations can carry misinformation when not architected with care and from an informed perspective. If you plan to design your own visualizations, educating yourself on data visualization best practices is essential.

The best way to learn this is to review the work of established designers and information visualization practitioners. Although an entire library of works deals with these best practices, here are a few resources that we've found useful and that can get you oriented on the basics. These are by no means the only texts for learning data visualization, but they are a great place to start:

- *Better Data Visualizations* (Columbia University Press, 2021), Jonathan Schwabish
- *The Functional Art* (New Riders, 2013), *The Truthful Art* (New Riders, 2016), and *How Charts Lie* (W.W. Norton, 2020), Alberto Cairo
- *Data Visualisation: A Handbook for Data Driven Design* (SAGE, 2019), Andy Kirk
- *The Visual Display of Quantitative Information Envisioning Information* (Graphics Press, 2001), Edward Tufte
- *Design for Information* (Rockport, 2013), Isabel Meirelles
- "Pattern Recognition" (published thesis, 2008, Rhode Island School of Design), Christian Swinehart
- *Visualization Analysis and Design* (A K Peters, 2014), Tamara Munzner

One thing to keep in mind while reading about data visualization is that the literature is often focused on static charts. With D3, you'll be making interactive and dynamic visualizations. A few interactions can make a visualization not only more readable but also significantly more engaging. Users who feel like they're exploring rather than reading, even if only with a few mouse events, might find the content of the visualization more compelling and memorable than if they read the static equivalent. But this added complexity requires learning about user experience. We'll get into this in more detail in chapter 7.

This concludes our first chapter! Although we haven't used D3 yet, you now have all the knowledge you need to get started. Keep coming back to this chapter when you're unsure about which SVG element you should use in your visualizations or if you need a reminder on how to manipulate data with JavaScript. From the next chapter, we'll roll up our sleeves and create D3 visualizations.

Interview with Hesham Eissa and Lindsey Poulter

Eissa and Poulter are data visualization designers and developers.

In one of your blog posts, you wrote that before the Ben & Jerry's project, you both had experience designing data visualizations in Tableau. What made you want to learn D3 instead of other data visualization tools? (https://heshameissa.com/blog/learn-d3/)

We both enjoyed the work we saw from *The Pudding*, Nadieh Bremer, the Information is Beautiful Awards, and various news outlets producing data journalism pieces. We had taken note that D3 was the common thread behind all the work we enjoyed.

Additionally, we both had a passion for finding creative ways to display data and didn't want to be tied to the visualizations that a particular software allowed for. With D3, and web-based visualizations in general, we felt that we could create anything we wanted. The only barrier was our own ability to make it!

About the same blog post, I love how you have structured your learning process, given that you had no prior experience with frontend development and that you had the patience to do it step by step. What did you find the hardest in this learning journey? What did you enjoy the most?

The hardest part in the learning journey was that there were so many different parts to learn and understand. On top of that, the world of frontend development is changing so quickly that we also had to learn how to keep up and get used to adapting examples from different versions. We sometimes found ourselves jumping ahead, so having patience to fully understand a concept before moving on was also difficult in its own way.

The most enjoyable part was when we finally reached the stage where we could directly apply our learnings to data visualization. Seeing our first SVG render on the page was a big moment of joy. As we dug into the different D3 modules, we thoroughly enjoyed understanding all the powerful ways each one could be used in the future. Modules like d3-force had so much flexibility and applicability and really expanded the way we thought about approaching data visualization.

Where did you find help when you got stuck?

The best part about learning alongside someone else is having a built-in partner to ask questions. If we didn't understand a concept, we would ask each other. This either reaffirmed we both were confused and needed to spend more time on it, or it allowed one person the opportunity to explain it in a completely different way.

Outside of each other, we spent a lot of time trying to understand the code of other people in the field or how they executed a specific concept. One of the best parts about the data visualization community is the willingness to share. Mike Bostock's examples on Observable and the greater Observable community were lifesavers. Usually, the first place we looked when creating a new chart was his examples—99% of the time he had what we were looking for. *The Pudding* and Nadieh Bremer had a lot of code on their respective GitHubs, so oftentimes we would say "How are they doing transitions?" and find real working examples. Funnily enough, we also bought the first edition of this book one weekend when we were confused about a concept and couldn't find the answers online.

However, we will say there were definitely times where we really got stuck. Part of it was that our vocabulary wasn't expansive enough yet to properly Google what we needed, and part of it was that we were trying to find very niche things. We weren't afraid to spend several days (or weeks) in a row just trying out whatever we could and experimenting. Ultimately, not having easy access to everything about web-based data visualization really forced us to learn and understand (and not just copy and paste).

Is there something you particularly like and/or dislike about D3.js, maybe compared to other data visualization tools?

D3 takes more time up front to learn how to use. Instead of taking a few clicks to create a bar chart, it can sometimes take 50+ lines of code. However, ultimately that is what we love the most about D3—we can control *everything*!

Featured project: "The Inside Scoop of Ben & Jerry's" (https://benjerry.heshlindsdata viz.com/)

(continued)

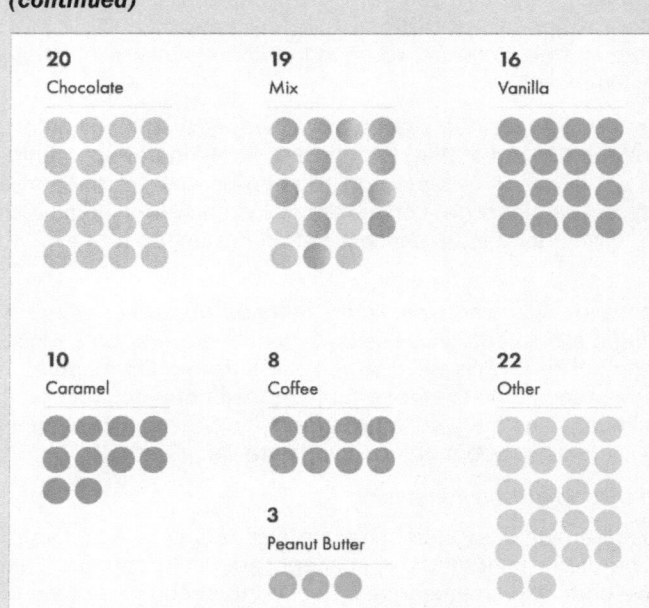

"The 98 flavors of Ben & Jerry's" project

You worked on the Ben & Jerry's project together. How did you split the work? Did one of you focus more on design and the other one on development, or did you both work on these two aspects?

We probably approached this unconventionally, and given that we were in the middle of peak lockdown in a global pandemic, we had a lot of time to kill. Our approach to this was not to split the work but to both learn and both focus on the entire process from start to finish. We would storyboard and explore the data together and then set out on a goal. We would say "Let's build a chord diagram that shows the combination of ice cream add-ins," and then both separately try to figure out how to build it. Once we were both done, we would compare our code to see if one person had found a better method, merge it together, and set out on the next task. Once we started to feel confident in our abilities, probably about half of the way through, we did begin to divide and conquer. We didn't necessarily divide it up so that one person did XYZ and the other did ABC—we both just did whatever needed to be done!

This project uses both graphics made of SVG elements and Canvas. Some visualizations are SVG-based, such as "The Complete Ben & Jerry's Flavor Guide," whereas others are mainly Canvas-based, such as "The 98 Flavors of Ben & Jerry's." The chord diagram of "The 79 Additions of Ben & Jerry's" even uses a combination of both. How did you decide when to use SVG versus Canvas graphics? Did you have this structure in mind from the start, or did you opt for canvas during the implementation, maybe for performance purposes?

We did not have the structure in mind from the start! Honestly, we probably didn't even know what Canvas was when we started. Once we had determined what visualizations we wanted to do, we began working on adding the transitions and quickly realized that the performance was really bad. This led us to research different performance options, which led us to Canvas.

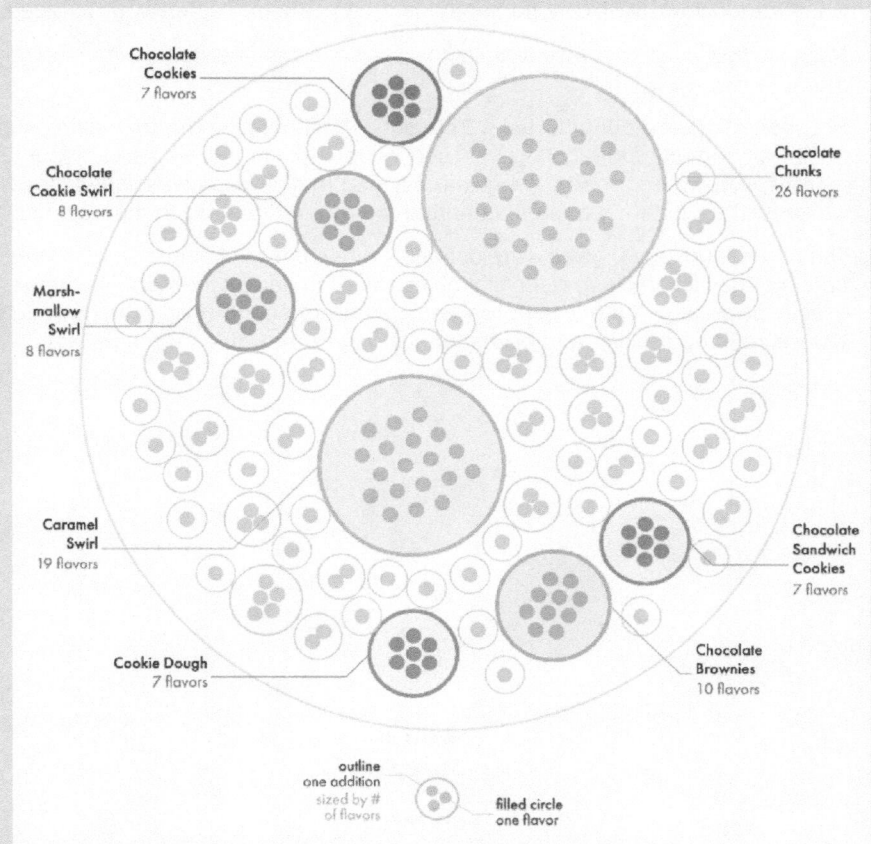

"The 79 Additions of Ben & Jerry's" project chord diagram

You have managed to make your whole project work well on mobile, including your rich radial visualizations. Do you remember if you had to make hard decisions like tweaks to your original ideas to accommodate smaller touch screens? Do you have a preference between the mobile-first or desktop-first approaches when it comes to web-based visualizations?

Once we got to the divide and conquer phase, mobile was one of the last things we did. We definitely learned the hard way that saving it for last wasn't the best approach, as there were compromises we had to make. We had to deal not just with what we need to change—but how do we actually do that? Utilizing scrollytelling (http://mng.bz/g7MV) helped us on mobile, both because we could have the text scroll on top of the visuals and because it allowed us to replace interactions with highlighting important data points.

(continued)

A desktop-first approach gives you a lot more real estate to play with, which can allow for more intricate interactions and designs. However, mobile forces you to distill each visualization down to its core purpose, which can be helpful when trying to create clarity.

Roughly, how long did it take to build this project? Was one step much longer or harder than the others?

Between this being our first real D3 project and learning on the fly, making sure everything was perfect, and redoing every section multiple times, we spent about four solid months working on it daily. We eventually had to give ourselves a deadline because we knew if we didn't, we would continue to redo, refine, and find problems.

The harder and longer parts were definitely those things that are more frontend development specific and less visualization related. We had all the visualizations and story exactly as we wanted but then realized we had to spend even more time to make it work across all devices and browsers—and perform well on them as well.

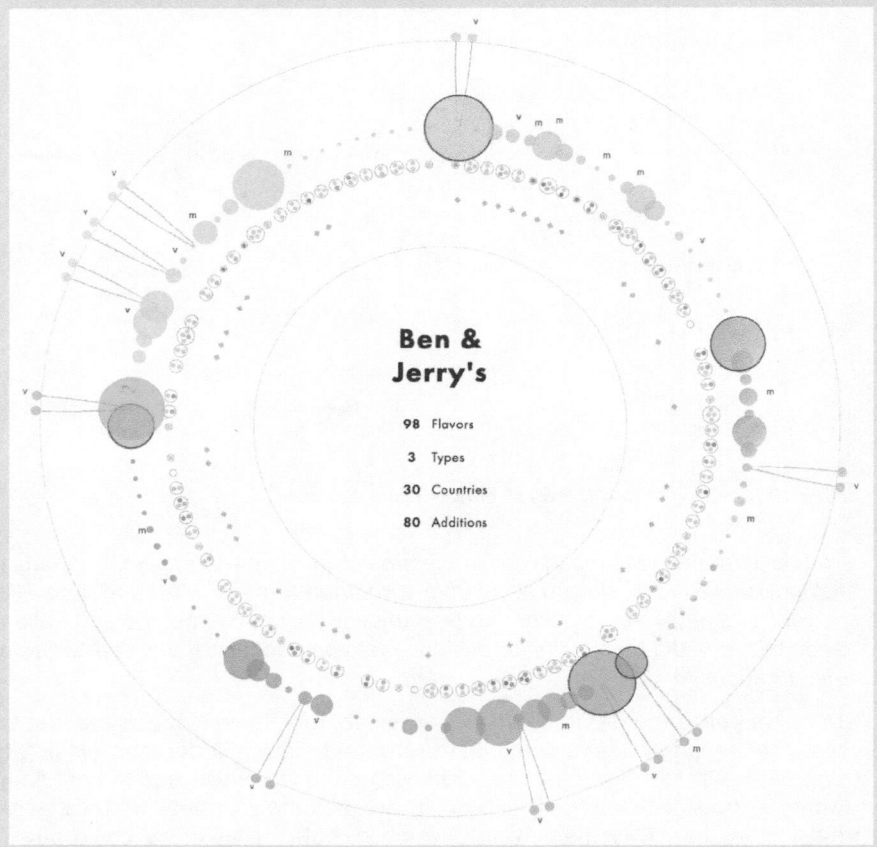

"The Complete Ben & Jerry's Flavor Guide" project

Is there a specific D3 feature or module that you wish to explore and/or master better in the near future?

There are definitely a few things where we are more in the "copy and paste" phase instead of fully understanding how it works. Chords, Sankeys, and geography modules are all on that list! Additionally, mastering more mathematical functions in general can help us better make use of what D3 has to offer.

Summary

- D3 is the tool of choice when you want to have total creative and technical freedom with your data visualizations.
- D3 applications are styled and served like traditional web content.
- D3 is never used alone but is rather part of an ecosystem of technologies and tools that we combine to create rich web interfaces: HTML, CSS, JavaScript, SVG, Canvas, and frameworks such as React or Svelte.
- The SVG shapes that we use most often as we build data visualizations are lines, rectangles, circles, ellipses, paths, and text.
- You need a basic understanding of these shapes and their main attributes to work with D3.
- Before working with D3, you should familiarize yourself with two JavaScript subjects—method chaining and object manipulation:
  - Method chaining is a pattern where multiple methods are called one after the other on the same object.
  - In D3, datasets are often structured as arrays of objects. JavaScript offers multiple methods to access and manipulate the data within these structures.
- As a D3 developer, it's important to develop a solid understanding of data visualization best practices. Multiple resources can help you start your learning journey.

Manipulating the DOM

This chapter covers

- Setting up a local development environment for D3 projects
- Selecting elements from the DOM
- Adding HTML or SVG elements to a selection
- Setting and modifying the attributes and styles of DOM elements

Now that we've discussed D3's ecosystem, it's time to get to work! In this chapter, we'll set the foundations of our first visualization while learning how to manipulate the document object model (DOM) with D3.

DOM manipulation is a foundational feature of D3, and the techniques that you'll learn in this chapter are probably the ones you'll use most often as a D3 developer (as long as you're not working with a JavaScript framework like React or Svelte, which we'll discuss in chapter 8). First, we'll cover selections, which allow us to grab a single element or multiple elements from the DOM. You'll see that D3 makes selections very easy and intuitive. Then, once we have a selection, we'll want to do something with it. An action that we regularly perform in D3 projects is adding HTML or

Scalable Vector Graphics (SVG) elements to a selection. For example, to create a visualization, we often append SVG shapes inside an SVG container. Finally, we adjust the positions, sizes, and colors of these SVG shapes by setting their attributes and styles.

Because this book focuses on building projects in a local development environment, you'll need to have one before we dive into D3 techniques. In section 2.2, we'll explain how to use Visual Studio Code (VS Code) and its Live Server extension to have a local environment ready to go within a few minutes.

2.1 *Your first D3 visualization*

In this chapter and the next, you'll develop your first D3 visualization: the bar chart shown in figure 2.1. Although we've mentioned in chapter 1 that D3 isn't necessarily

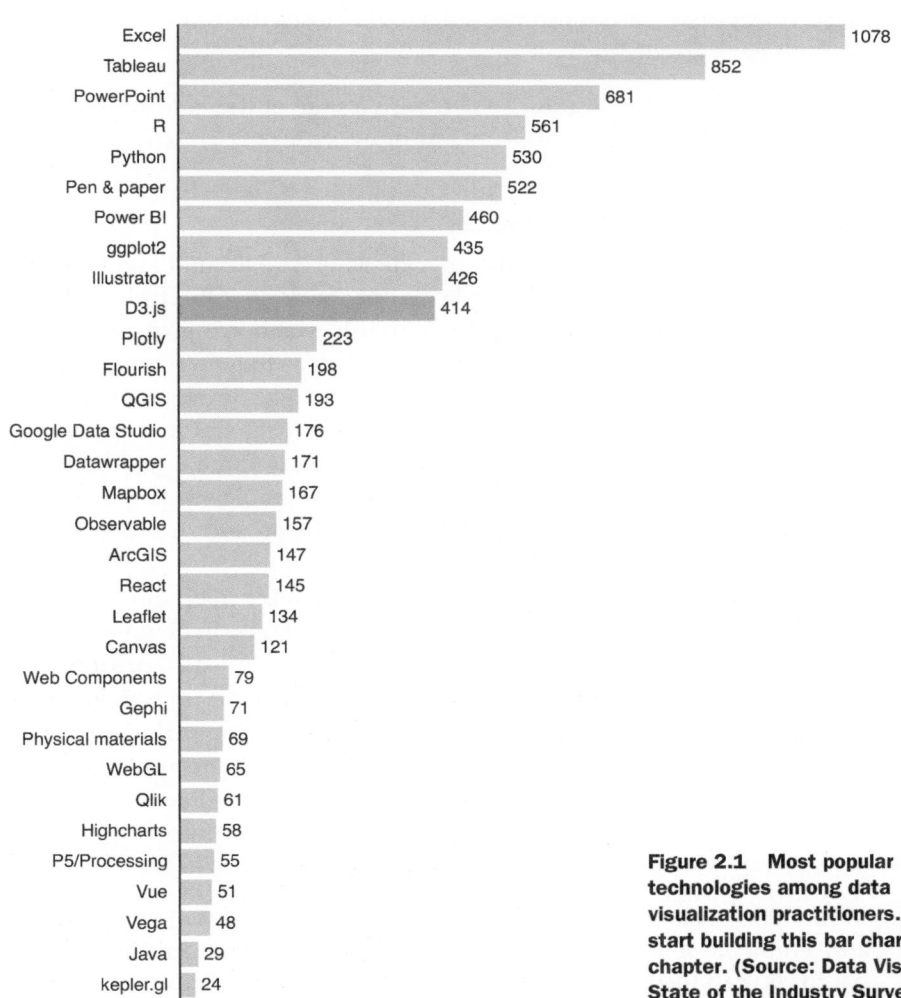

Figure 2.1   Most popular technologies among data visualization practitioners. We'll start building this bar chart in this chapter. (Source: Data Visualization State of the Industry Survey 2021, Data Visualization Society)

the most efficient tool for making simple, classical charts, a bar chart is perfect for introducing D3's fundamental concepts. Stick with us, and soon you'll have a solid foundation that will allow you to build complex visualizations with ease.

The data behind our bar chart comes from the 2021 Data Visualization State of the Industry Survey, hosted by the Data Visualization Society (www.datavisualizationsociety .org).

The 2021 State of the Industry Survey was answered by 2,181 data visualization practitioners, from professionals to students to hobbyists. We'll visualize the answers to one question from the survey—"What technologies do you use often to visualize data?"—for which the respondents could select all the tools that apply from a predefined list. In figure 2.1, you can see the resulting bar chart, where the tools are listed vertically, and the length of each bar represents the number of respondents that selected this tool. According to this survey, D3 closes the top 10 of data visualization tools. Let's get started!

> **NOTE**   The Data Visualization Society runs a state of the industry survey every year. To get the latest insights from our industry, access fresh data at www.data visualizationsociety.org/survey.

2.2   *Preparing your environment*

Before we start using D3, we need to decide where we'll build and run our projects. We could work with an online code editor, such as Observable (https://observ ablehq.com) or CodePen (https://codepen.io), which are great for quickly testing and sharing code. But because the goal of this book is to help you get ready to ship D3 projects into websites and web apps, we'll opt for a local development environment.

Now, if the idea of setting up a development environment makes you cringe, don't worry. Far gone are the days where you had to spend half a day sweating and crying through this process. Thanks to modern tools, your whole setup shouldn't take more than a few minutes the first time, and then you'll be up and running with the click of a button.

At this point, you might wonder why we can't simply open our HTML files with a browser like we did for the Gallery of SVG Shapes exercise in chapter 1. Although this approach could sometimes work just fine, it will eventually lead to the browser refusing to perform specific tasks and throwing errors. Some browsers prevent loading local files with JavaScript for security reasons and require loading them via a web server instead. In D3 projects, we usually have to load a data file, so we do need a web server.

Throughout this book, we'll be using VS Code as our code editor, often combined with its Live Server extension, which provides a local web server. But if you already have a preferred setup, feel free to use it and skip to section 2.2.1.

> **NOTE**   The project structure we'll use in the first part of this book is trivial and a little old school. Our goal is to keep the environment as simple as possible so you can focus on learning D3. But if you're a more advanced developer and want to work with module-based projects, you can totally do so. Refer to

chapter 8, section 8.2, for instructions on installing D3 via Node Package Manager (NPM) and importing the library into files.

VS Code is wildly popular among developers. It's free, open source, and easy to use—yet powerful. It has built-in Git commands (no need to have a terminal window open on the side!) and is highly customizable. If you don't have VS Code already installed on your computer, you can download it from the VS Code website at https://code .visualstudio.com/Download. Once you have VS Code, you'll want to install its Live Server extension. Refer to appendix A if you need help with the installation. This appendix also contains explanations on how to start and stop your local web server using the Live Server extension.

> **NOTE** If you haven't already, download the code files from the book's GitHub repository (http://mng.bz/Xqjv). In this chapter, we'll work with the `start` folder of this chapter's code files. If you get stuck and need to look at the solution, you'll find it in the `end` folder. When working with the chapter's code files, open only one `start` or one `end` folder in your code editor. If you open them all at once and use the Live Server extension to serve the project, some paths won't work as expected, especially when loading a dataset into the project. The code files are broken down into sections, so when we move to a new section in the book, you can keep working in your initial code files or start anew with the folder dedicated to that section. Both options will lead to the same result.

2.2.1 *The structure of our first D3 project*

The D3 projects that we'll work on in the next chapters will all have a similar structure, represented in figure 2.2.

Figure 2.2 Folder structure of our first D3 project

At the root of the project, we have an `index.html` file, where the initial markup of our project lives. This is also where, in the first section of this book, we'll load the D3 library, our JavaScript file(s), and our CSS file(s) into the project. We then have three folders:

- The `/css` folder contains any CSS file relevant to the project. Although this book doesn't focus on CSS, we'll use it occasionally. For simplicity, we'll also group our styles in a minimal number of files. But keep in mind that in professional projects, the structure of the CSS folder can be much more sophisticated and often involves a CSS preprocessor such as Syntactically Awesome Stylesheets (SASS) or Leaner Stylesheets (LESS).
- The `/data` folder contains our dataset(s). For the bar chart, our dataset is a CSV file, where values are separated with a comma. Each line of the dataset contains

a technology, followed by the count, that is, how many times the survey respondents have selected this technology.

- Finally, the /js folder contains our JavaScript file(s). To keep things simple, we'll write our D3 code in one single file, main.js. But later, we'll discuss how you can split the code into multiple files, or components, for better maintainability and testability.

2.2.2 Loading D3 into a project

Before we start, check that your web server is running by looking at the lower-right corner of the VS Code window. You should see Port 5500 (or another port number) indicating that the server is running. If you see Go Live instead, click it to start the live server. Your project can now be accessed in a browser at http://localhost:5500/ or whichever port the server is using.

Now that we have a web server up and running, there's one more thing we need to do before we can start coding with D3: load the D3 library into our project. In this book, there are two main approaches that we'll use. The first one is to add a script tag to index.html that links to the latest version of D3. We can use this approach to load the entire D3 library or only specific modules. The second approach is to load D3 as NPM modules; this approach is mainly suited to sites built with React or another JavaScript framework.

In this chapter, we'll opt for the first approach because it's the simplest. As the book progresses, we'll start using the second approach, which is more representative of how professional D3 projects are built today.

In VS Code or in your code editor of choice, open the index.html file, located at the root of the folder. Just before the closing body tag (</body>), load version 7 of the D3 library, the latest version at the time of writing this book, using a script tag. Add another script tag to load the main.js file located in the /js folder, and save your project. You can see how to proceed in listing 2.1:

```
<script src="https://d3js.org/d3.v7.min.js"></script>
<script src="js/main.js"></script>
```

The browser reads the JavaScript files in the same order as the script tags are listed in index.html. We must load the D3 library before main.js. Otherwise, the browser won't have access to the D3 methods used in main.js. It will throw errors, and the code won't execute.

We also want the scripts to be the last thing to load on a web page, so we position the script tags just before the closing body tag (</body>). With this approach, we reduce the loading time of our page, not having to wait for the scripts to execute before the DOM is displayed. It also ensures that the DOM is available before we try to manipulate it from the script files.

NOTE During local development, you might want to consider loading the non-minified library instead (https://d3js.org/d3.v7.js) to give you access to a readable version of the source code. For performance purposes, you'll want to swap it for the minified version when you ship your code to production.

> **Listing 2.1 Loading the entire D3 library in a `script` tag: `index.html`**

```
<!DOCTYPE html>
<html>
<head> ... </head>
<body>
  <div class="container">
    <h1>You are about to start working with D3!</h1>
  </div>

  <script src="https://d3js.org/d3.v7.min.js"></script>    <———  Script tag loading the
                                                                 minified D3 library

  <script src="js/main.js"></script>    <———  Script tag loading
                                               the file main.js
</body>    <———  Closing
</html>          body tag
```

Now let's test that the D3 library and the `main.js` file are properly loaded into our project. In your code editor, go to the `/js` folder, and open `main.js`. Copy the following code snippet into `main.js`, and save the file:

```
d3.select("h1").style("color", "plum");
```

In the next section, we'll explain in detail what the D3 methods from this code snippet are for, but for now, we've selected the title `h1` and changed its color to the CSS color name `"plum"`. If you look at your project in the browser, the color of the title should have changed, like in figure 2.3.

> You are about to start working with D3!

Figure 2.3 Title color modified with D3

Now that we've confirmed that D3 is loaded into our project, you can delete the snippet from `main.js` and the `h1` title from `index.html`. In the next section, we'll introduce D3 selections.

> **NOTE** Selecting and manipulating the DOM with D3 is a little old-fashioned. Nowadays, we generally build frontend projects with a framework such as React or Svelte and let the framework handle changes to the DOM. We're teaching you these methods because they will help you understand how D3 works and because you'll likely use them in smaller, sandbox-like projects. From chapter 8 onward, we'll use a more modern approach.

2.3   *Selecting elements*

When building D3 projects, we constantly manipulate the DOM, and any DOM manipulation starts with a selection. Selections are like grabbing an element from the DOM and holding it ready for further manipulations. D3 has two methods for selections: `d3.select()` and `d3.selectAll()`.

The `d3.select()` method takes a selector as a parameter and returns the first element that matches that selector. This method is chained to the `d3` object and used to select one single element. As you can see in figure 2.4, the selector parameter can be a class attribute, an ID, a tag name, or any combination of these—exactly like the selectors we use in CSS.

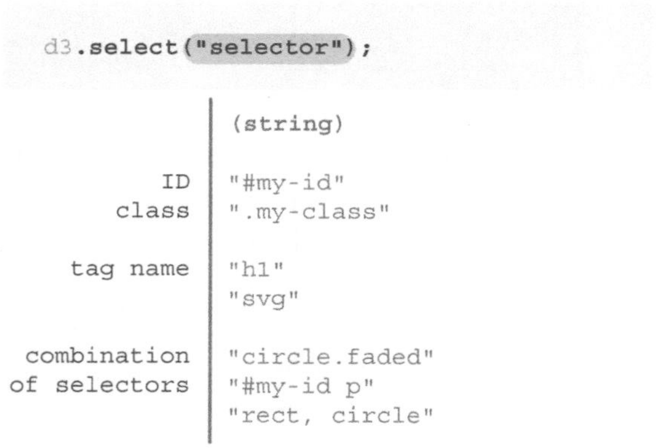

```
d3.select("selector");
```

	(string)
ID	`"#my-id"`
class	`".my-class"`
tag name	`"h1"`
	`"svg"`
combination of selectors	`"circle.faded"`
	`"#my-id p"`
	`"rect, circle"`

Figure 2.4   The `select()` method

Let's take the fictional DOM sample illustrated in figure 2.5 as an example. It consists of a `div` element that contains an `h1` title, a paragraph element with the class `intro`, and another `div` with the ID `viz-container`. This `div` wraps together another paragraph and an SVG container. Finally, the SVG container encompasses three `circle` elements. The first and the last of these circles have the class `faded`.

If we want to select the `h1` title, we can use its tag name as a selector passed to the `d3.select()` method, as follows:

```
d3.select("h1");
```

Similarly, if we want to select the paragraph with the class `intro` or the `div` with the id `viz-container`, we can use their respective class or

```
<div>

  <h1>A title</h1>

  <p class="intro"> ... </p>

  <div id="viz-container">

    <p> ... </p>

    <svg>

      <circle class="faded" />

      <circle />

      <circle class="faded" />

    </svg>

  </div>

</div>
```

Figure 2.5   A fictional DOM sample

ID attributes as selectors. Like in CSS selectors, class names are preceded by a dot (.) and IDs by a hashtag (#):

```
d3.select(".intro");
d3.select("#viz-container");
```

We can also use a combination of selectors. For instance, if we want to select the paragraph element inside the div with an ID of viz-container, we leave a space between the two selectors:

```
d3.select("#viz-container p");
```

Such a combined selector will have the same effect as chaining two select() methods:

```
d3.select("#viz-container").select("p");
```

One important thing to keep in mind is that the method d3.select() returns only the first element from the DOM that matches its selector. For example, there are three circle elements in our DOM sample illustrated in figure 2.6. But the selection d3.select("circle") only returns the first one and ignores the others.

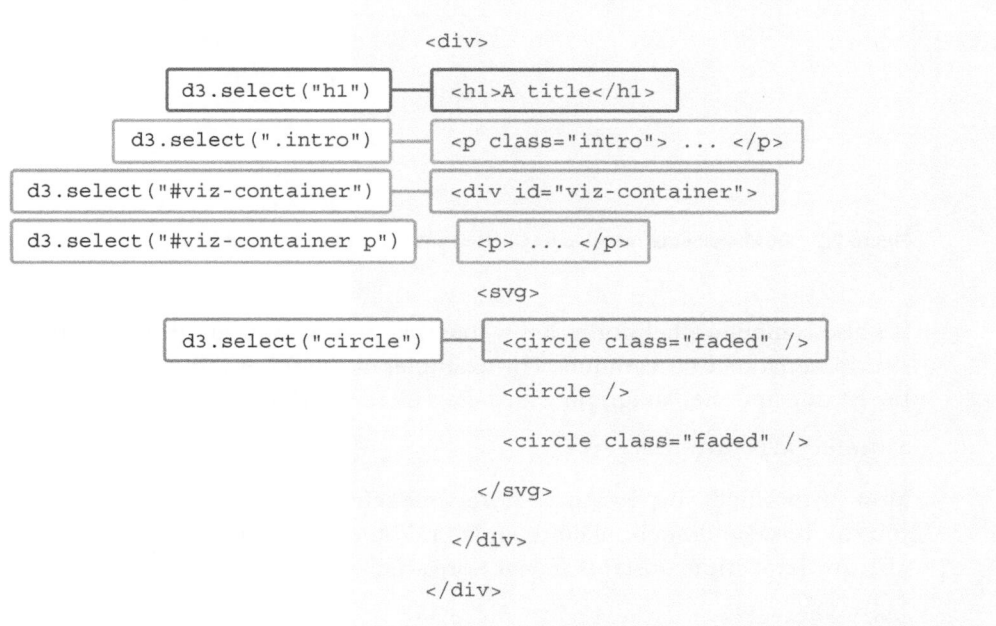

Figure 2.6 DOM elements returned by the d3.select() **method**

So what can we do if we need to include more than one element in a selection? This is when we use the `d3.selectAll()` method. `d3.selectAll()` works similarly to `d3.select()`, except that it returns all the DOM elements matching its selector. For example, if we go back to our fictional DOM sample, `d3.selectAll("circle")` returns all the circle elements contained in the DOM, as illustrated by figure 2.7.

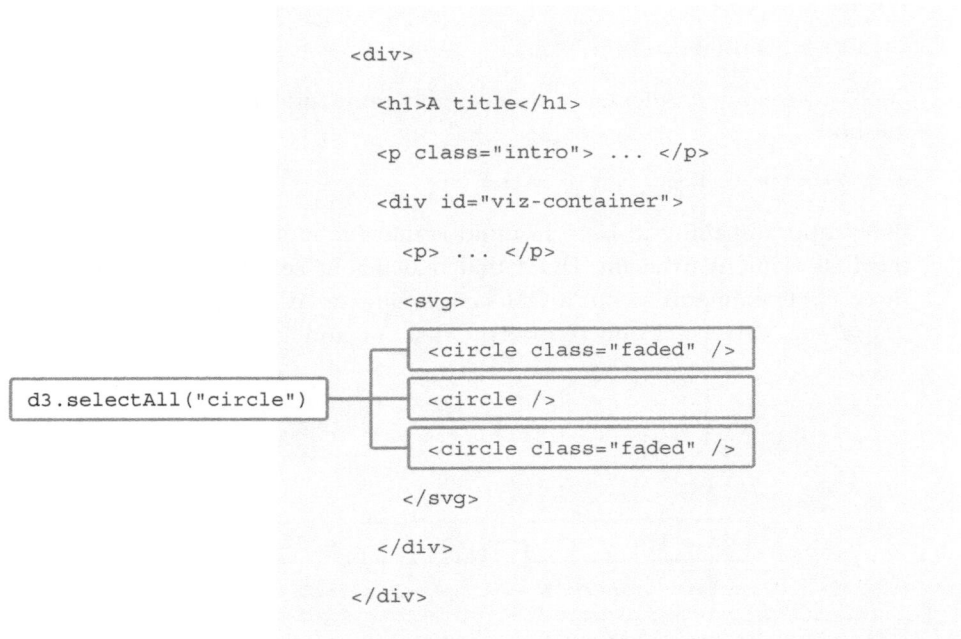

Figure 2.7   DOM elements returned by the `d3.selectAll()` method

It's also sometimes helpful to know that, like in CSS, we can group multiple selector strings, separated by a comma. For example, in the following snippet, we select both the `h1` title and the paragraph with a class of `intro`, as shown in figure 2.8:

```
d3.selectAll("h1, .intro");
```

Most of the time, you'll want to store your selections in JavaScript constants so that you can reuse and manipulate them later. You can store D3 selections like you would with any JavaScript constants (`const`) or variables (`let`):

```
const myCircles = d3.selectAll("circle");
```

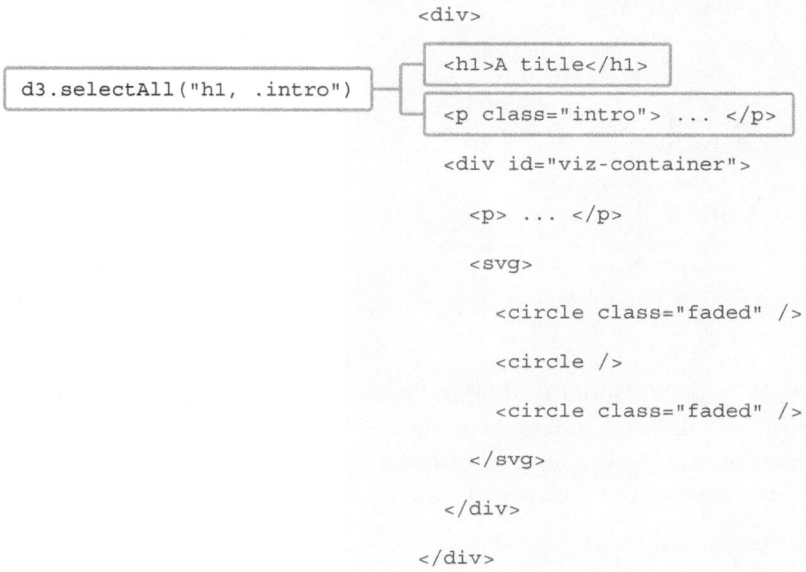

Figure 2.8   Grouping selectors with a comma

Accessing documentation for the D3 modules

D3 consists of a collection of modules that we can use independently and combine based on our needs. Each module contains multiple methods that perform related tasks.

All the methods that we discuss in this chapter are part of the module d3-selection This module is covered on the official D3 documentation website (https://d3js .org/), a trustworthy and always up-to-date resource.

If you're new to web development, such API documentation might be intimidating at first, but the more you refer to it, the better you'll start to understand its technical language.

2.4   Adding elements to a selection

Selections are nice, but they aren't much use if we don't do anything with them. A typical pattern in D3 is to perform a selection in order to append another element into it. Although vanilla JavaScript already allows us to append elements, D3 makes it much easier.

The main D3 method used to add an element to a selection is `selection.append()`. The `append()` method adds a new element as the *last child* of the selection and takes the type of the element, or the name of the tag, as a parameter (see figure 2.9).

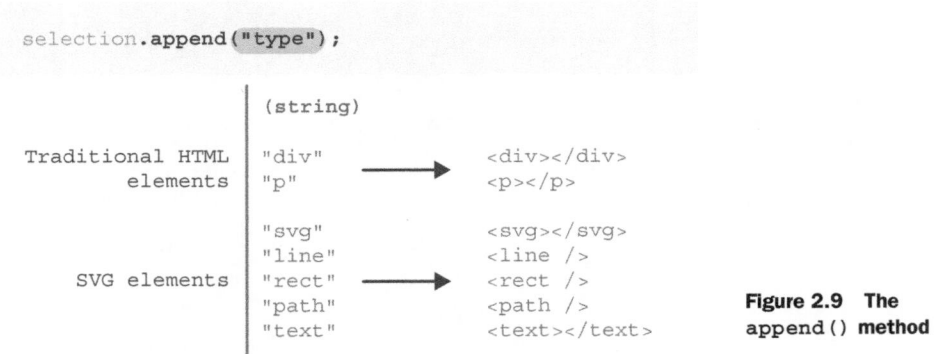

Figure 2.9 The append() method

Let's go back to our fictional DOM sample. If we want to add a rectangle element as the last child of the SVG container, we first select the SVG container and then chain the `append()` method to the selection (see figure 2.10). The type of node to append, a `rect` element, is passed to the `append()` method as a parameter:

```
d3.select("svg").append("rect");
```

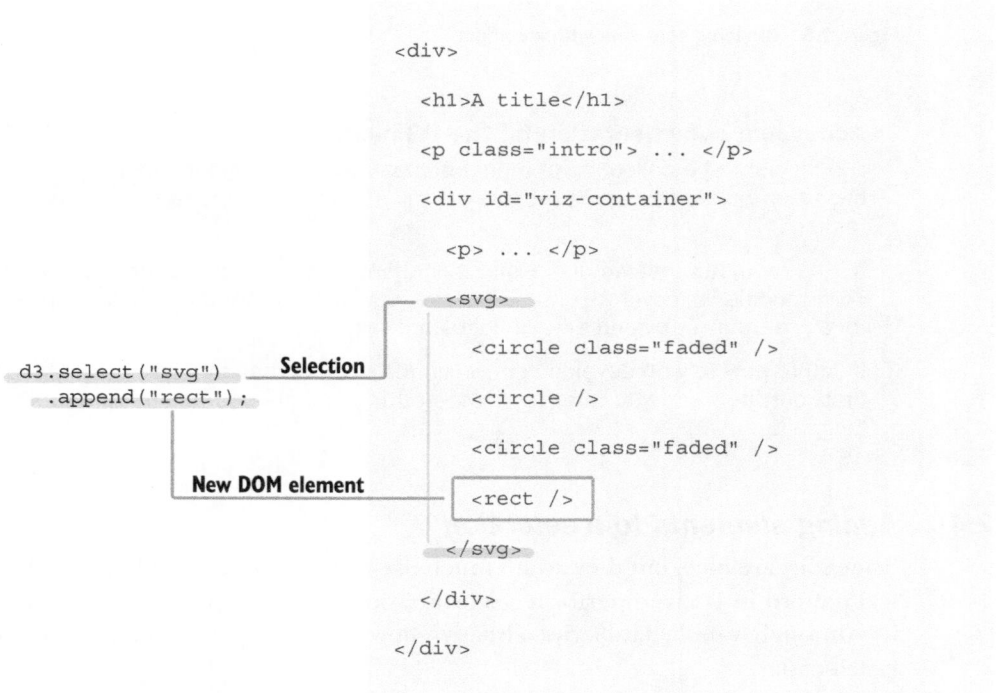

Figure 2.10 Using the `selection.append()` method to add an element as the last child of a selection

We could also use `d3.selectAll("div")` to select every `div` node in the DOM and append a paragraph element into each of them, as you can see in figure 2.11:

```
d3.selectAll("div").append("p");
```

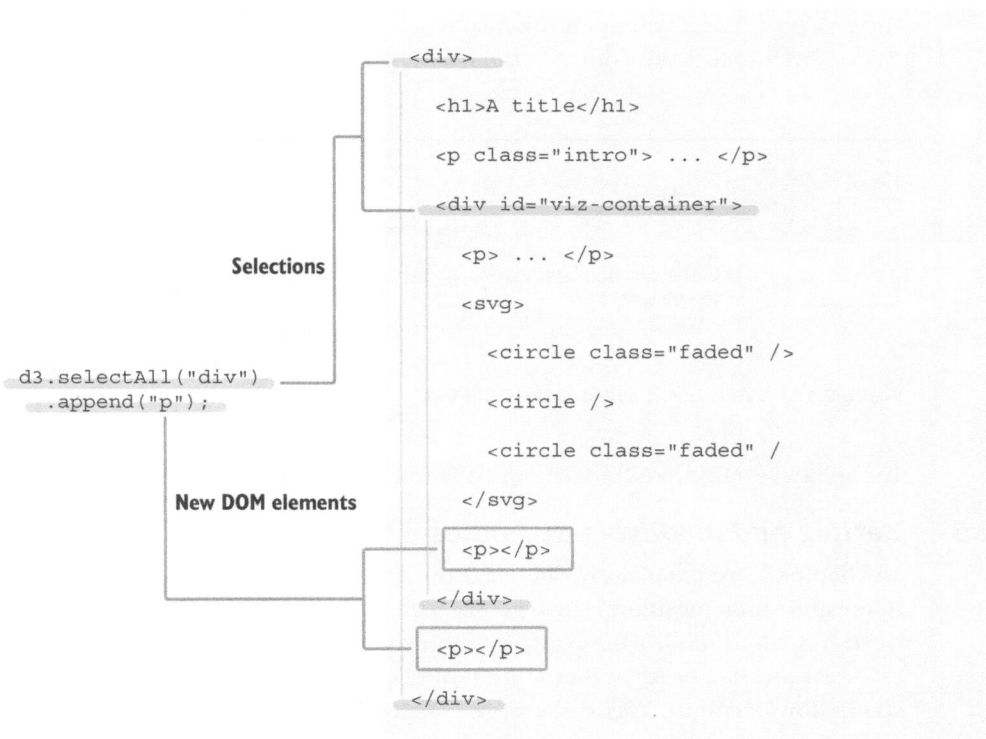

Figure 2.11 When combined with `d3.selectAll()`, the append method adds nodes into each element of the selection.

To put what you've learned into practice, let's start building the bar chart described in the introduction of this chapter.

Make sure that the `start` folder of chapter's 2 code files is still open in your code editor and that your local web server is running. Refer to appendix A if you need a refresher on how to start a web server with VS Code's Live Server extension. Open the `index.html` file; note that it contains a `div` element with the class `responsive-svg-container`.

As discussed in chapter 1, most D3 visualizations are built with SVG elements, and our bar chart is no exception. To do so, we need an SVG container into which the SVG shapes will go. We'll now add this SVG element.

Open the `main.js` file contained in the `/js` folder. Using method `d3.select()`, select the `div` with a class of `responsive-svg-container`, and add an SVG element inside this `div`. The following snippet shows how the `append()` method is chained to the selection:

```
d3.select(".responsive-svg-container")
  .append("svg");
```

Save the `main.js` file, and look at the project in the browser. No change is visible in the viewport, but if you open the inspector as shown in figure 2.12, you'll see that the SVG element has been added to the DOM, precisely as we wanted!

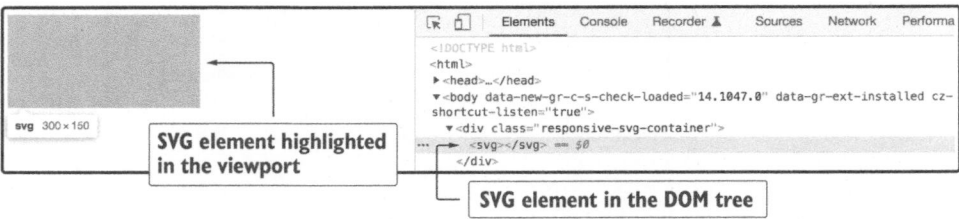

Figure 2.12   SVG element added to the DOM tree

In the next section, we'll make our SVG responsive by giving it a `viewBox` attribute.

2.5 *Setting and modifying attributes*

In chapter 1, we extensively discussed the main SVG elements and the attributes that determine their position and size. We also explained that as a D3 developer, you'll need to set and modify these attributes in your code. Now's the time to learn how!

Attributes can be set and modified with D3 method `selection.attr()`, where "attr" stands for "attribute." As you can see in figure 2.13, the `attr()` method takes two

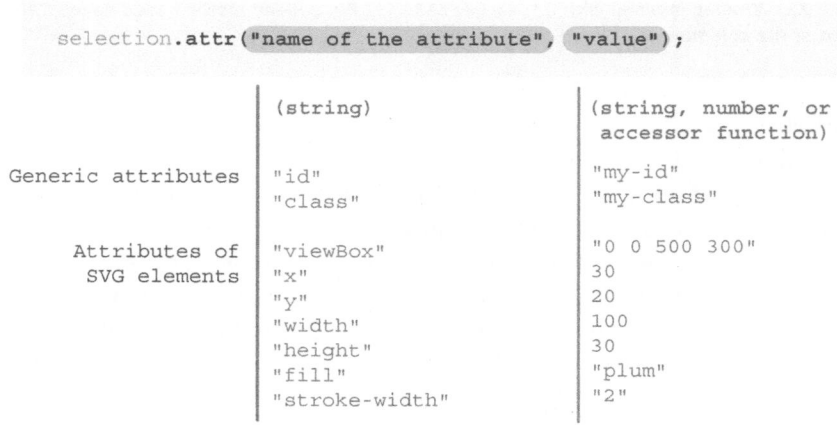

Figure 2.13   The `attr()` method

parameters: the first one is the name of the attribute, and the second one is its value. The value can be set directly or via an accessor function, as we'll discuss in chapter 3.

In our bar chart exercise, the `div` element that surrounds our SVG container has the class `responsive-svg-container`. If you open the `main.css` file in the `/css` folder, you'll see that this class applies all the styles needed for the container of a responsive SVG element, as discussed in chapter 1, section 1.2.2. Here the container has a `max-width` property of 1,200 px, which will also be the maximum width of our bar chart.

For our SVG container to maintain its aspect ratio while adapting to its container, we only need to set its `viewBox` attribute. We'll use the `attr()` method for that. As you can see in the following code snippet, the first parameter passed to the `attr()` method is the name of the attribute, which is `viewBox` in this case. Note how the "B" letter of this attribute's name is a capital letter. The presentation attributes are case sensitive, and it's essential to respect the CamelCase notation of the `viewBox` attribute for the browser to recognize it.

The second parameter is the value of the `viewBox` attribute, which is a list of four numbers. The first two numbers are the origin of the coordinate system of the `view-Box`, located at (0,0); the last two numbers are the width and height of the `viewBox`. The width corresponds to the `max-width` property of the container `div`, hence 1,200 px, and let's estimate the height at 1,600 px. We can adjust it later if we need to. Our `viewBox` attribute then has a value of `"0 0 1200 1600"`:

```
d3.select(".responsive-svg-container")
  .append("svg")
    .attr("viewBox", "0 0 1200 1600");
```

Set the `viewBox` attribute of the SVG element, save `main.js`, and take a look at your project in the inspector. You'll see that the `viewBox` attribute has been added to the SVG element, as shown in figure 2.14. In addition, if you make your browser's viewport smaller, the SVG element will adapt while keeping its aspect ratio of 1200:1600.

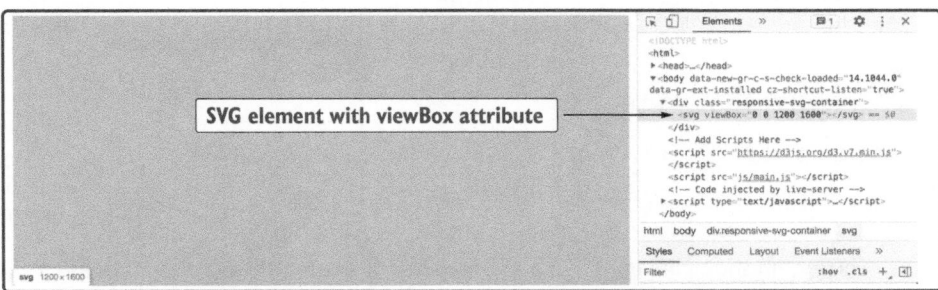

Figure 2.14 SVG **element with a** `viewBox` **attribute**

Let's take our latest bit of code and save it into a JavaScript constant named `svg` that we'll soon reuse:

```
const svg = d3.select(".responsive-svg-container")
  .append("svg")
    .attr("viewBox", "0 0 1200 1600");
```

Every time we add a new element to a selection with the `.append()` method, we change the element returned by the selection. For instance, when we reuse the constant `svg`, it won't return the `div` with a class of `responsive-svg-container` but rather the SVG container that we've added into it.

The D3 indentation convention

Before we go further, let's discuss the D3 indentation convention. In our last snippets of code, you might have noticed that each chained method is written on a new line. Doing so helps with readability, especially when more than two or three methods are chained together. You might also have noticed that the `append()` method is indented with two spaces, while the `attr()` method uses four spaces of indent. Per D3's indentation convention, each level of nesting gets an additional two-space indent.

In D3, every time we append a new element to a selection, we update the DOM element(s) targeted by the selection. As we set the attributes and styles of the newly added element(s), a proper indentation helps us know to which selection the attributes and styles are applied.

The D3 indentation convention

The indentation convention is especially handy when multiple elements are appended one after the other. Imagine that after adding our SVG element and setting the `viewBox` attribute, we append a group element into the SVG container, with a class of `my-group`. Then we append a rectangle element to the group and set its required attributes. As you can see in the previous figure, we need to chain multiple methods to make that happen. But thanks to the indentation convention, the chain is easy to read, and we see at a glance to which selection, or element, each attribute is applied.

Bar charts like the one we're building are composed of SVG rectangles, which are created with the `rect` element. Just to practice selections and the `attr()` method, we'll add one rectangle to our bar chart, which will represent the number of data visualization practitioners that selected the tool D3.js in the survey. If you open the `data.csv` file in the `/data` folder, you'll find that 414 practitioners said they use D3 regularly.

In `main.js`, start by calling the constant `svg`, which returns the SVG container. Add a `rect` element inside the SVG container. Save your project, and confirm that the `rect` element has been added inside the SVG:

```
const svg = d3.select(".responsive-svg-container")
  .append("svg")
    .attr("viewBox", "0 0 1200 1600");

svg
  .append("rect");
```

The `rect` element exists in the DOM but isn't yet visible on the screen because its required attributes haven't been set. We know that SVG rectangles need four attributes in order to appear on the screen. You can refer to chapter 1, section 1.2.2, to review these notions. The `x` and the `y` attributes control the position of the top-left corner of the rectangle. Let's place it at (`10, 10`) for now. The width of the rectangle corresponds to how many practitioners selected D3 as a tool, which is 414, and its height can be any number—we'll use 16. By giving the `width` and the `height` attributes values of 414 and 16, respectively, our rectangle will have a width of 414 px and a height of 16 px. The values of these four attributes are passed as numbers:

```
svg
  .append("rect")
    .attr("x", 10)
    .attr("y", 10)
    .attr("width", 414)
    .attr("height", 16);
```

Finally, the `fill` attribute of the rectangle is set to the CSS color name `"turquoise"` and is passed as a string:

```
svg
  .append("rect")
    .attr("x", 10)
    .attr("y", 10)
    .attr("width", 414)
    .attr("height", 16)
    .attr("fill", "turquoise");
```

Note how we use the indentation convention here: the new selection created when we append the rectangle uses two spaces of indent while the `attr()` methods use four spaces. This way, we make it obvious that the attributes are applied to the `rect` element. Once your project is saved, the rectangle will be visible in the viewport of your browser, as in figure 2.15.

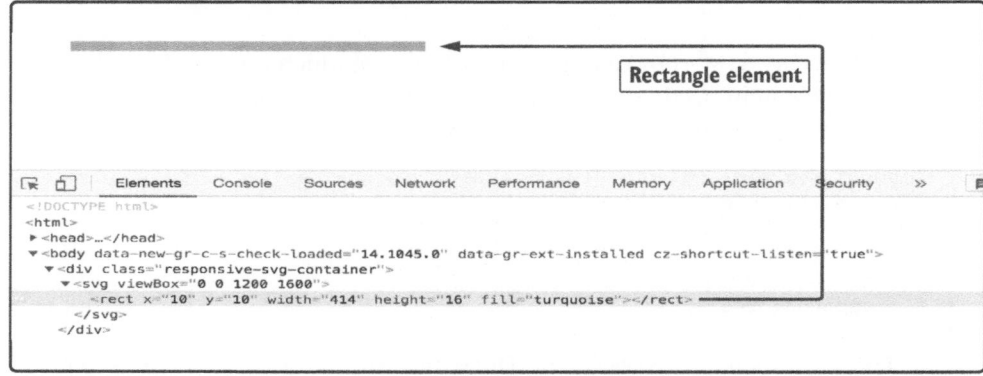

Figure 2.15   Rectangle element appended into the SVG container

2.6   *Setting and modifying styles*

For our visualization elements to have the look and feel that we want, we need to apply styles to them. The traditional CSS stylesheet approach is a good one and often a better option for maintainability purposes. But sometimes, setting and modifying the style attribute directly with D3 is handy, especially when the styles dynamically change with data.

D3 allows us to set and modify the style attribute of elements with method `selection.style()`. This method takes two parameters: the name of the style property and its value, as demonstrated in figure 2.16.

```
selection.style("name of style property", "value");
```

(string)	(string, number or accessor function)
"fill"	"cyan"
"fill-opacity"	0.6
"stroke"	"plum"
"stroke-width"	2
"font-size"	"14px"

Figure 2.16   The `style()` method

Go back to our bar chart exercise, and in `main.js`, chain a `style()` method to the SVG container selection, the one stored in the constant named `svg`. Like in the following snippet, use the `style()` method to apply a border to the SVG container. You can give it any value you'd like. Here we use the shorthand property to apply a black border with a width of 1 px:

```
const svg = d3.select(".responsive-svg-container")
  .append("svg")
    .attr("viewBox", "0 0 1200 1600")
    .style("border", "1px solid black");
```

The border around the SVG container will help us visualize the space we're working in and understand how the `style()` method works.

Save your project, and look at it in your browser. Locate the SVG container in the DOM inspector. You should see the `border` property added within a `style` attribute, as shown in figure 2.17. This means that the `style()` method injects what we call inline styles.

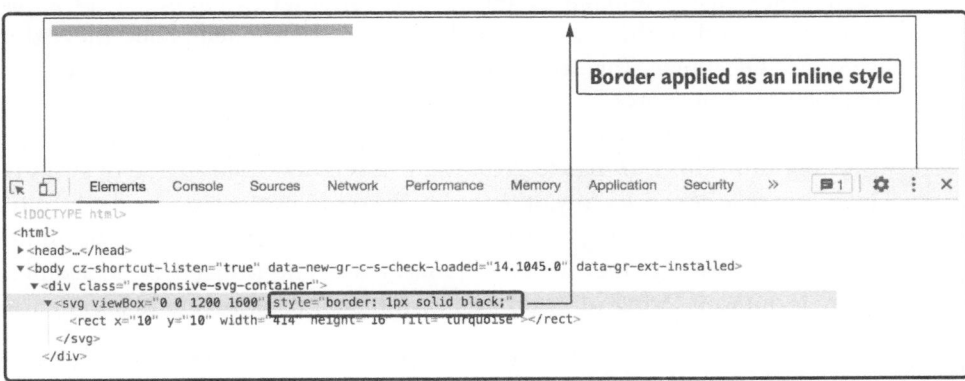

Figure 2.17 Border applied with the `style()` method

When working with SVG elements, some styles can be applied as an attribute or using inline styles, such as the `fill` and the `stroke` properties. There is no strict rule that we should use the `attr()` or the `style()` method to apply such properties, but some developers prefer to be consistent and always apply presentational attributes as CSS or inline styles rather than using attributes. This can be a good idea, especially when we want to keep our cascade of styles easy to manage by separating the code that makes shapes from the code that dictates how they look. In this book, we'll use both the `attr()` and the `style()` methods, as well as external CSS files to set the presentational attributes of SVG elements.

Let's illustrate this with an example. In `main.js`, chain a `style()` method to the rectangle selection, and use this method to apply a second fill of a different color to the rectangle. In the following snippet, we use the CSS color `"plum"`:

```
svg
  .append("rect")
    .attr("x", 10)
    .attr("y", 10)
    .attr("width", 414)
    .attr("height", 16)
    .attr("fill", "turquoise")
    .style("fill", "plum");
```

Now open the `main.css` file, and add a third `fill` property to the rectangle. Here we used the CSS color `"orange"`:

```
rect {
  fill: orange;
}
```

Our rectangle now has three fill properties, applied differently. It has a fill of color `"turquoise"` that is applied as an attribute, another of color `"plum"` applied as an inline style, and a third one of color `"orange"` applied from the external CSS stylesheet. Of course, this isn't something we would do in real life and is only for demonstration purposes.

Save your project, and notice how the fill applied with the `style` property overwrites the two others. In figure 2.18, you can see how the cascade of styles is applied. The inline style overrides any other styles, followed by the style applied from an external CSS stylesheet. The `fill` attribute comes last. Keeping this rule in mind will help you develop a strategy that fits your habits, team, and projects while avoiding pulling your hair out wondering why one style is visible on the screen and another one isn't.

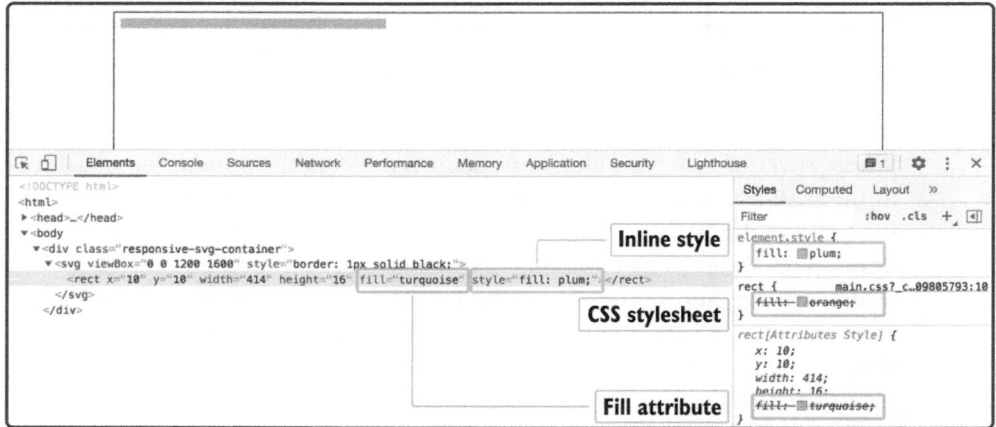

Figure 2.18   Fill applied as an attribute, from an external stylesheet, and as an inline style

We now know how to perform selections, add elements to the DOM, and position and style those elements. But adding the rectangles one by one to our bar chart like we did here isn't efficient at all. In the next chapter, we'll learn how data binding can help us add all the rectangles at once. Before we get there, remove the bit of code related to the rectangle from main.js and main.css. The main.js file now only contains the code from the next listing. In chapter 3, we'll start from there to build our bar chart.

Listing 2.2 Content of `main.js` at the end of chapter 2

```
const svg = d3.select(".responsive-svg-container")
  .append("svg")
    .attr("viewBox", "0 0 1200 1600")
    .style("border", "1px solid black");
```

Interview with Nadieh Bremer

Nadieh Bremer is a data visualization artist.

Can you tell us a little bit about your background and how you entered the field of data visualization?

I graduated as an astronomer, after which I started working as a data scientist. However, after a few years, I realized that I was missing the creative side of my work. When I saw someone else call themselves a "Data Visualization Specialist," I knew instantly that that's where I could get both: being creative while still investigating data, finding stories, and playing with math.

What brought you to learn D3, even if you didn't have a web development background? What were your main challenges, and how did you overcome them?

I attended a D3.js workshop at a conference (in 2013) where they showed the possibilities of D3, such as the interactions. Especially at that time, I had never seen something like it before, and I knew that I wanted to be able to create such interactive dataviz as well. I got the book *Interactive Data Visualization for the Web* (O'Reilly, 2017) by Scott Murray and started from there. My main challenge was that HTML/CSS/JavaScript were all new to me (although I knew how to program in R), so I had to learn those besides D3. And, in my ignorance, I didn't know what was unique to D3 or what was vanilla JavaScript, so I could get stuck on the smallest of things, not really knowing how to search for it online. Usually, extreme perseverance and making sure that I was working on projects that I was passionate about kept me going. And without consciously realizing it, I started to understand more and more. It took me a full year to wrap my head around the enter-update-exit flow of D3, ha ha.

Do you use visualization tools other than D3? What's the place of D3 in your current data visualization workflow? For example, I see that you often use R in your projects.

D3 really is my main tool. I load it in 90% of my dataviz projects when I start on the final visual. Other than that, I use vanilla JavaScript with some other libraries, such as Chroma.js for colors or SimplexNoise for noise functions. I do always start with a data analysis and data preparation phase in R, creating lots of simple charts so I can

(continued)

personally get an understanding of the data. However, I never use these as the final visuals.

Featured project: "Space Wars" (www.visualcinnamon.com/portfolio/space-wars/)

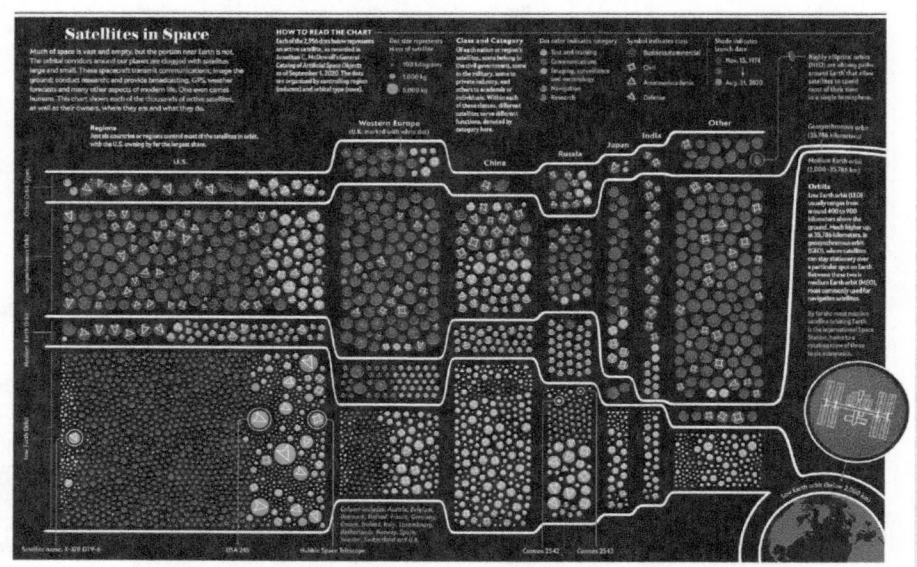

Visualization of satellites in space by Nadieh Bremer, as published in *Scientific American*

Please describe your project, "Space Wars," which you created for the November 2020 edition of Scientific American.

The "Space Wars" visual shows all the satellites that are still active in space (at that point in time). The main point was to show who owned the satellites and in what orbits they could be found. However, by keeping each satellite as a separate circle but grouping them by country and orbit, the visualization reveals a very detailed look into the satellites themselves, such as their weight, age, classification, and more.

Can you explain the process of creating this project?

The data was thankfully gathered by an expert in satellites, so I didn't have to do any data wrangling, only some analysis to get an understanding of what I had. I drew a few ideas in a little notebook. I knew that I wanted to play with the countries and orbits. However, I had so much metadata about each satellite that I just wanted to show each separately. I don't know how the thought came to me, but at some point,

I drew the approach of a treemap filled with circles for the satellites. After that idea was clear to me, the rest was split between the technical part of figuring out how to use circles within a treemap and how to make the design look good. It looked awful at the start, but then I took some time to look for inspiration in terms of colors from some of my favorite sci-fi movies, and it was exactly what the visual needed.

As an outsider, it looks like you combined D3's treemap method with the force layout to generate this visualization. Is that the case? Combining methods from different modules to create unseen-before layouts is one of the things I love the most about D3. Actually, in your Skillshare course "Data Visualization: Customizing Charts for Beauty & Impact," you suggest combining different types of charts.

Yes, that's it exactly. I use a treemap method to get the region (in x, y and width, height) where I should place each group of satellites. Within each rectangle, I then run a force layout simulation to position all the circles, making sure none overlap. Knowing how big each square for the treemap should be comes from adding the surface area of each circle (which scales with the satellite's weight) with a conversion factor, and sometimes some manually defined "magic" number for some minor tweaking here and there.

Yes, being able to get really creative with how you use D3 is definitely one of my favorite things about it!

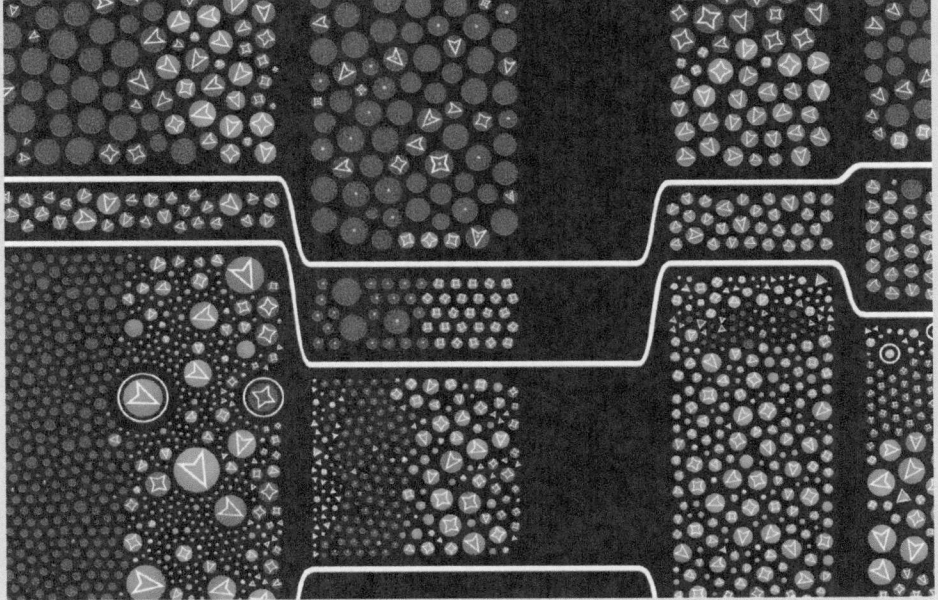

The circles representing satellites are grouped by controlling region and orbital type in a treemap chart. Their exact position is then calculated with D3's force layout.

(continued)

Can you tell us a little more about using D3 to generate static visualization for a print medium? I think we don't speak nearly enough about this possibility!

I love creating static visuals, and I almost always use D3.js while doing this. One thing that is important for creating a visual for print is that you should probably create it as an SVG (instead of using an HTML5 canvas) so the editors at the magazine can have a vector file that can still be scaled. Furthermore, aspects such as fonts and titles can still be adjusted (e.g., fonts) and tweaked (e.g., the wording). Most of the styles you apply are copied over if you take the visual from the browser into a vector editor (Illustrator has been the best in copying most CSS styles/settings I've found).

With your project and book Data Sketches *(A K Peters, 2021) cocreated with Shirley Wu, you inspired so many of us to get more inventive in the way we approach data. What advice would you give to someone who's getting started in the field?*

I'm so, so happy to hear that *Data Sketches* has been an inspiration. It's strange to think back to when Shirley and I started on *Data Sketches*, expecting that it was just a silly project that only we and some close friends would appreciate.

My main point of advice is two-fold. One is to create. Create as many visuals as you can. With each new visual, you'll learn new things (sometimes even without realizing it), come across new pitfalls, and think of new creative ways to overcome them. When I look back on my own journey and visuals along that path, it's so clear to see how I got more confident in coding, in being creative, and how that affected what I could make.

The second part is to try and work on data and topics that truly interest you, even if the data isn't readily available but needs (manual) work to gather. Working on a data-viz about a topic that you're really into makes it much easier to keep going even when you're stuck (technically or design-wise). You can see this all through the *Data Sketches* book. We never took the "easy" route in terms of data but always tried to let our interests guide us, and somehow the data was out there somewhere in nearly all cases.

Summary

- D3 projects require a web server in order to run properly. A quick and easy way to have access to a web server in a local development environment is to use the Live Server extension of VS Code.
- There are two ways to load the D3 library into a project: by adding a `script` tag to `index.html` that links to the library or as an NPM module. In the first chapters of this book, we use the `script` tag approach for simplicity.
- The D3 library can be loaded in its entirety, or we can load only the D3 modules that we need, which can improve the performance of our projects.
- When loading files and libraries via `script` tags, the order in which the `script` tags are listed is the same as the order in which the browser will read the scripts.

This means that the `script` tag that links to the D3 library must appear before the `script` tags that are loading the JavaScript file(s) where we use D3. Otherwise, the browser won't have access to the D3 methods used in the JavaScript file(s) and will throw errors.

- In D3, we can select elements from the DOM with methods `d3.select()` and `d3.selectAll()`. The first method returns only the first element, while the second returns all the DOM elements that match its selector.

- The selector strings passed as an argument to the `select()` and `selectAll()` methods are identical to the selectors used in CSS stylesheets. They use tag names, class names, IDs, or a combination of those to identify DOM elements.

- The `append()` method allows you to add an element as the last child of a selection.

- The `attr()` method is used to add or modify attributes to an element. It requires two arguments: the name of the attribute and its value.

- The `style()` method allows you to set and modify the style attribute of DOM elements. It also requires two arguments: the name of the style property and its value.

- With the `style()` method, we apply inline styles, overwriting styles applied from external CSS stylesheets and via presentation attributes.

Working with data

This chapter covers

- Recognizing data types and dataset formats
- Loading, formatting, and measuring data
- Binding data to DOM elements
- Using scales to translate data into visual attributes
- Adding labels to a chart

The common denominator of any data visualization is, obviously, the underlying presence of data. As data visualization developers, we meet different types of data and datasets that we need to understand and manipulate to generate visualizations. In this chapter, we'll discuss a data workflow that applies to most D3 projects. This strategy, illustrated in figure 3.1, starts with finding data for our project. This data can contain different data types, such as nominal or ordinal data, and can come in different dataset formats, such as CSV or JSON files. There's usually a lot of work implied at this stage to prepare and clean the data, but we won't cover that in this book.

Once a dataset is assembled, we can use D3 to load, format, and measure the data. Then we're ready to generate visual elements, usually SVG shapes, based on the data. This powerful process is called data binding, and we'll use it to generate all the rectangles for the bar chart we've started building in chapter 2.

The values contained in a dataset aren't always directly applicable on the screen. The numbers might be too big to be used directly as the size of visual elements in pixels, or we might want to represent specific values with colors. This is where D3 scales come into play. In this chapter, we'll discuss the different types of scales and how to use them. We'll then use linear and band scales to position and size the rectangles on our bar chart (http://mng.bz/mjor).

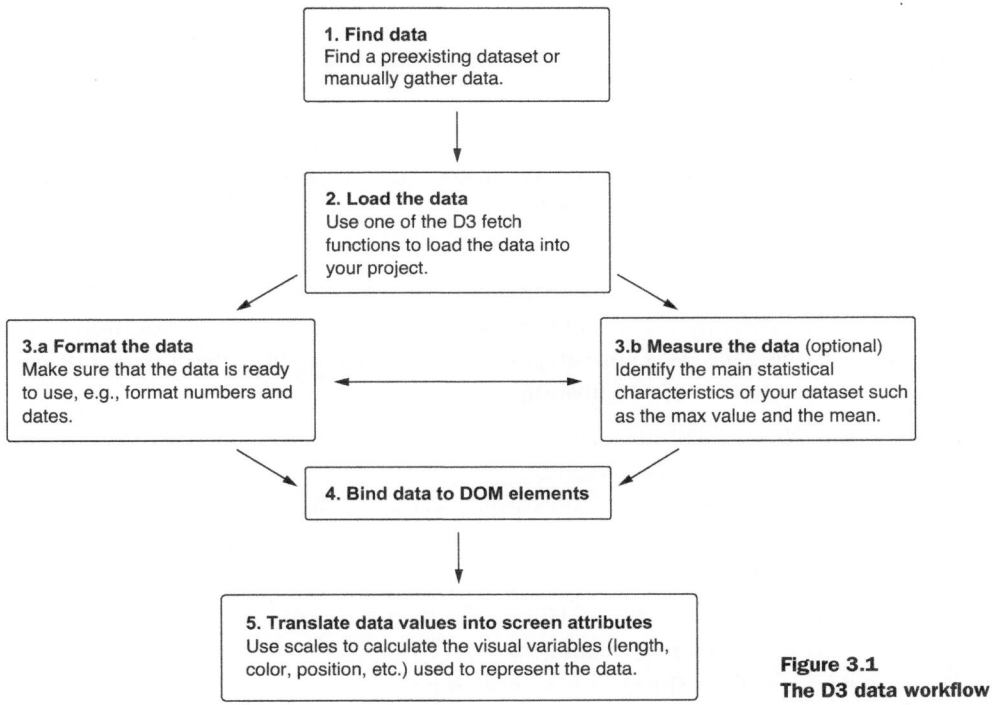

Figure 3.1
The D3 data workflow

Figure 3.2 shows a simplified version of the data workflow that we'll use as we progress through this chapter.

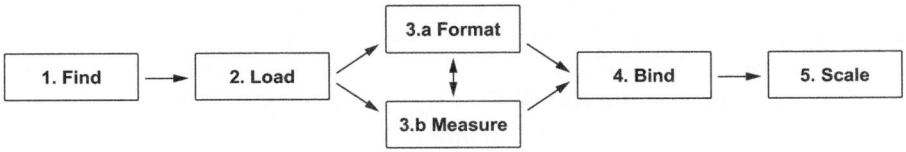

Figure 3.2 Simplified diagram of the D3 data workflow

3.1   *Understanding data*

The first step of the D3 data workflow is finding or gathering data, as illustrated in figure 3.3. Before we dive into D3 data techniques, we'll briefly discuss the different data types and dataset formats you'll encounter as a D3 developer. This little bit of theory will help you read and understand the data you work with, which is essential to proper data visualization architecture. It will also help you later to select the appropriate scales for your projects.

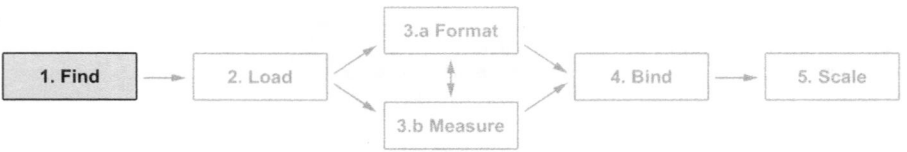

Figure 3.3   The first step of the D3 data workflow is finding or gathering data. Data comes in different types and dataset formats.

3.1.1   *Finding data*

Although you might gather your own data from time to time, you'll mostly work with preexisting datasets. There are a lot of resources on the web for data, but here's a non-exhaustive list of website-hosting public datasets:

- Data.world (https://data.world/)
- Kaggle (www.kaggle.com/)
- World Bank Open Data (https://data.worldbank.org/)
- Our World in Data (https://ourworldindata.org/)
- EarthData (www.earthdata.nasa.gov/)
- EU Open Data Portal (https://data.europa.eu/)
- Data.gov (https://data.gov/)
- openAfrica (https://africaopendata.org/)
- Dataportal.asia (https://dataportal.asia/)

3.1.2   *Data types*

When building data visualizations, we work with two main data types: quantitative and qualitative. Quantitative data is numerical information such as time, weight, or countries' gross domestic product (GDP). As you can see in figure 3.4, quantitative data can be discrete or continuous. Discrete data consists of whole numbers, also called integers, that can't be subdivided. For example, a company can have 16 employees but not 16.3 employees. On the other hand, continuous data can be divided into smaller units and still make sense. A typical example of continuous data is temperature. We can say that it's 17°C today, but we can also measure it with even more precision and realize that it's actually 16.8°C. As a rule of thumb, continuous data can be measured with an instrument, while discrete data can be counted but not measured.

Qualitative data, on the other hand, is made up of nonnumerical information such as text. It can be nominal or ordinal. Nominal values don't have a specific order, for instance, gender identity labels or city names. Ordinal values, on the other hand, can be classified by order of magnitude. If we take T-shirt sizes as an example, we usually list them in ascending size order (XS, S, M, L, XL).

Data types will affect the sort of visualization that we can choose to communicate the data. Line charts work great for continuous data but aren't an option for discrete values. Nominal values can be represented by a set of categorical colors, while we might opt for a sequential or diverging color palette for ordinal values.

We also keep the data types in mind when selecting a D3 scale. Linear scales are used with quantitative data, while D3 has specific scales for qualitative data. We'll discuss scales in greater detail in section 3.4.

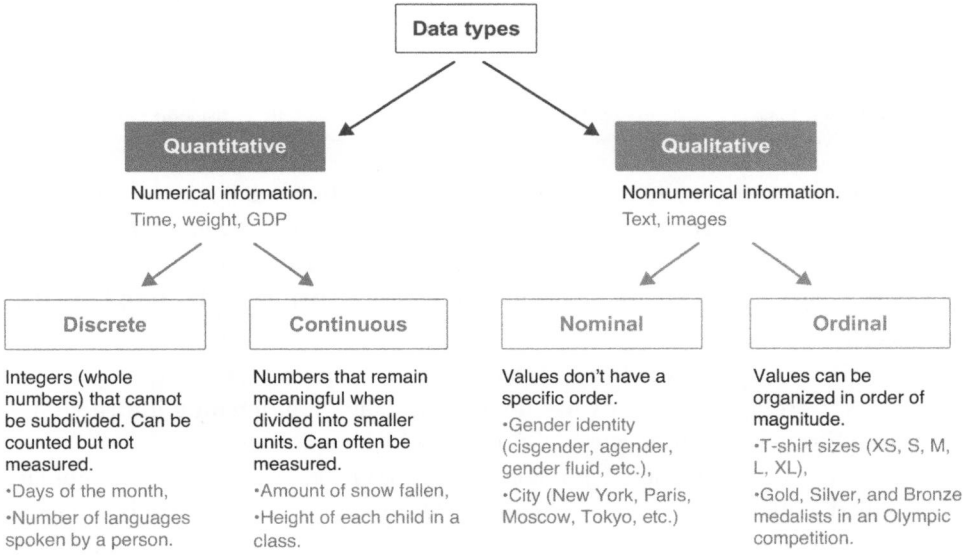

Figure 3.4 A classification of data types

3.1.3 *Data formats and structures*

Data can be formatted in a variety of manners for various purposes. Still, it tends to fall into a few recognizable structures: tabular data, JavaScript objects (JSON), nested data, networks, geographic data, or raw data. Those structures aren't mutually exclusive.

TABULAR

Tabular data appears in columns and rows and is typically found in a spreadsheet or a table in a database. Tabular data is separated with a particular character, called a delimiter, which defines its format. The most common tabular data format is Comma-Separated Values (CSV) files, where the delimiter is a comma. We can also meet

Tab-Delimited Values (TSV) files or any other Delimiter-Separated Values (DSV) files that use specific delimiters such as pipes or semicolons.

As an example, let's take a sample from our fictional employees' dataset, discussed in chapter 1. If we saved this data as a CSV, TSV, or DSV file, values would be respectively separated by a comma, a tab, or another delimiter, as listed in table 3.1. In tabular datasets, the first line usually lists the column headers, and each row of data is listed on a new line.

Table 3.1   Delimited data expressed in CSV, TSV, and DSV formats

CSV: Comma-Separated Values	TSV: Tab-Separated Values	DSV: Delimiter-Separated Values (with a pipe delimiter)
`id,name,works_with_d3`	`id name works_with_d3`	`id|name|works_with_d3`
1,Zoe,false	1 Zoe false	1|Zoe|false
2,James,true	2 James true	2|James|true
3,Alice,true	3 Alice true	3|Alice|true
4,Hubert,false	4 Hubert false	4|Hubert|false

D3 provides three different functions to load tabular data: `d3.csv()`, `d3.tsv()`, and `d3.dsv()`. The only difference between them is that `d3.csv()` is built for comma-delimited files, `d3.tsv()` is for tab-delimited files, and `d3.dsv()` allows you to declare a delimiter. You'll see `d3.csv()` in action in this chapter and throughout the book.

JSON

JavaScript Object Notation (JSON) files are a common way to store simple data structures. Developers regularly use them, especially when fetching information from API endpoints, which often provide data in JSON format only.

If we stored the data from table 3.1 in a JSON format rather than tabular, it would look like the following array of objects. Although it's not the most compact, the object notation has the significant advantage of making the data key-value pairs easy to access with the JavaScript dot notation discussed in chapter 1:

```
[
  {
    id": 1,
    "name": "Zoe",
    "position": "Data analyst",
    "works_with_d3": false
  },
  {
    "id": 2,
    "name": "James",
    "position": "Frontend developer",
    "works_with_d3": true
  },
```

```
  {
    "id": 3,
    "name": "Alice",
    "position": "Fullstack developer",
    "works_with_d3": true
  },
  {
    "id": 4,
    "name": "Hubert",
    "position": "Designer",
    "works_with_d3": false
  }
]
```

In D3, we use the function `d3.json()` to load JSON files. But even when you load another type of tabular data, such as a CSV file, D3 will transform the data into an array of objects, hence ending up with a JSON-like structure.

NESTED

Nested data, with objects exist-ing as children of objects recur-sively, is common. Many of the most intuitive layouts in D3 are based on nested data, which can be represented as trees, such as the one in figure 3.5, or packed in circles or boxes. Pulling out nested datasets requires a bit of additional scripting, but the flexibility of this representation is worth the effort. You'll see hierarchical data in detail in chapter 11.

NETWORK

Networks are everywhere. Whether they're the raw output of social networking streams, transportation networks, or a flowchart, networks are a power-ful method of delivering an understanding of complex sys-tems. Networks are often repre-sented as node-link diagrams, as shown in figure 3.6. Like geo-graphic data, network data has many standards, but this text

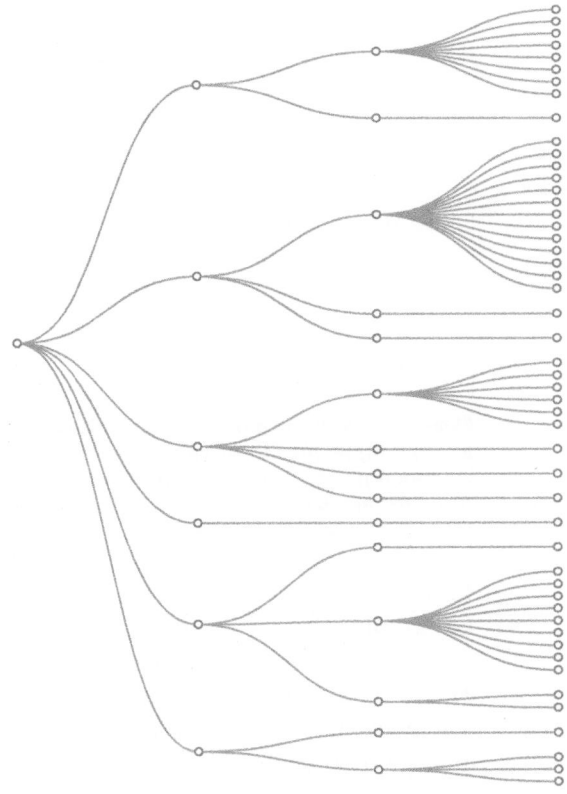

Figure 3.5 Nested data represents parent/child relationships of objects, typically with each object having an array of child objects, and is represented in a number of forms, such as this dendrogram. Notice that each object can have only one parent.

focuses on node/edge lists. Network data can also be easily explored by using a freely available network analysis tool such as Gephi (available at https://gephi.org). We'll examine network data and network data standards when we deal with network visualizations in chapter 12.

Figure 3.6   Network data consists of objects and the connections between them. The objects are typically referred to as nodes or vertices, and the connections are referred to as edges or links. Networks are often represented using force-directed algorithms, such as the example here, that arrange the network in such a way as to pull connected nodes toward each other.

GEOGRAPHIC

Geographic data refers to locations either as points or shapes, and it's used to create the variety of online maps seen on the web today, such as the world map in figure 3.7 or the ones in Observable's gallery (https://observablehq.com/@d3/gallery#maps). The incredible popularity of web mapping means that you can get access to a massive amount of publicly accessible geodata for any project. Geographic data has a few standards, but the focus in this book is on two: the GeoJSON and TopoJSON standards. Although geodata may come in many forms, readily available geographic information systems (GIS) tools such as PostGIS (https://postgis.net) allow developers to transform the data into GIS format for ready delivery to the web. We'll look at geographic data closely in chapter 13.

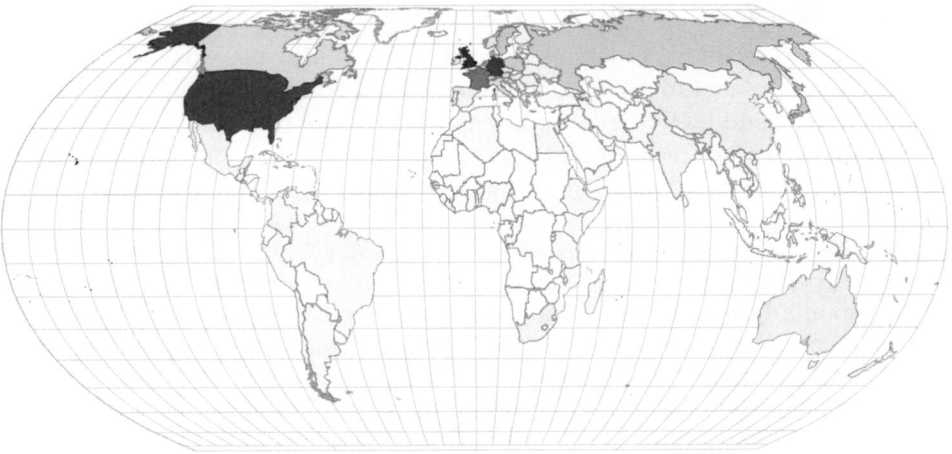

Figure 3.7 Geographic data stores the spatial geometry of objects. Each country in this image is represented as a separate feature with an array of values indicating its shape. Geographic data can also consist of points (e.g., for cities) or lines (e.g., for roads).

RAW

As you explore the field of data visualization, you'll discover that everything is data, including images, blocks of text, and a website's markup. Although information visualization typically uses shapes encoded by color and size to represent data, sometimes the best way to visualize it in D3 is with linear narrative text, an image, or a video. If you develop applications for an audience that needs to understand complex systems, but you consider the manipulation of text or images to be somehow separate from the representation of numerical or categorical data as shapes, then you arbitrarily reduce your capability to communicate. The layouts and formatting used when dealing with text and images, typically tied to older modes of web publication, are possible in D3.

3.2 Preparing data

Once we have a dataset ready, we use D3 to load the data into our project, per step 2 in figure 3.8. We then ensure that the data values are correctly formatted, and we might want to measure different aspects of the data. In this section, we discuss the D3 methods used to perform these tasks and prepare the data for our bar chart.

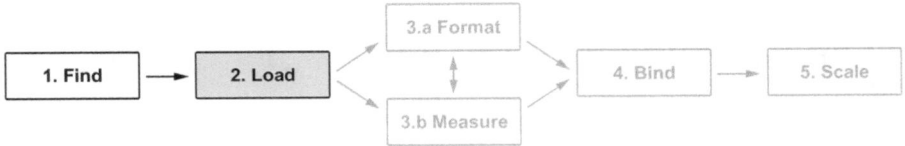

Figure 3.8 The second step of the D3 data workflow is to load a dataset into our project using one of the D3 fetch functions.

3.2.1   *Loading a dataset into a D3 project*

D3 has convenient functions to load datasets into projects. The function that we choose is related to the format of the dataset. For instance, CSV files are loaded with `d3.csv()`, and JSON files are loaded with `d3.json()`. We pass the path to the data file as the function's first argument. D3 also has functions to load text or even XML files. They are all part of the d3-fetch module (https://d3js.org/d3-fetch).

> **NOTE**   You can find the code files for chapter 3 in the book's GitHub repository (http://mng.bz/Y7Po). The code for each section is found in corresponding folders under the repository. You can expect to find the code for section 3.2 in a folder starting with `3.2` and then a subject such as `3.2 -Preparing_data`. Each folder has a `start` and `end` folder. Use the `start` folder if you want to start fresh with the bare minimum code. If you get stuck, the `end` folder will show you the section's final code. When working with the chapter's code files, open only one `start` *or* one `end` folder in your code editor. If you open all the chapter's files at once and use the Live Server extension to serve the project, some paths won't work as expected, especially when you load a dataset into the project.

Let's go back to the bar chart exercise started in chapter 2 and load our sample dataset from the 2021 Data Visualization State of the Industry Survey (www.datavisualizationsociety.org/survey). The dataset is in CSV format and is located in the `/data` folder. You can see the content of the `data.csv` file in listing 3.1. The first line of the file lists the column headers, `technology` and `count`, which respectively represent the data visualization tools available in the survey, from `ArcGIS` to `P5`, and how many data visualization practitioners selected each tool, which was 414 for `D3.js` and 530 for `Python`.

Listing 3.1   Tools most used by data practitioners (`data.csv`)

```
technology,count
ArcGIS,147
D3.js,414
Angular,20
Datawrapper,171
Excel,1078
Flourish,198
ggplot2,435
Gephi,71
Google Data Studio,176
Highcharts,58
Illustrator,426
Java,29
Leaflet,134
Mapbox,167
kepler.gl,24
Observable,157
```

```
Plotly,223
Power BI,460
PowerPoint,681
Python,530
QGIS,193
Qlik,61
R,561
React,145
Tableau,852
Vega,48
Vue,51
Web Components,79
WebGL,65
Pen & paper,522
Physical materials,69
Canvas,121
P5/Processing,55
```

Because our dataset is a CSV file, we can load it into our project using function `d3.csv()`, passing the path to the data file as the first parameter. Knowing that our data file is located in the `/data` folder, the relative path from `main.js` is `"../data/data.csv"`. With the two dots (`".."`), we go back one level, which brings us outside the `/js` folder, at the project's root. We then go inside the `/data` folder and arrive at the file `data.csv`:

```
d3.csv("../data/data.csv");
```

This completes step 2 of our data workflow, but now we need to understand how to access the data to perform the formatting and measuring steps. It's important to know that loading data is an *asynchronous process*. Asynchronous operations are requests for which the result isn't available immediately. We need to wait for D3 to fetch the data before we can read or manipulate it. We can safely know that the data is done loading and is ready for manipulation by accessing it through the callback function of `d3.csv()` and/or by using a JavaScript Promise.

3.2.2 Formatting a dataset

In this section, we'll discuss how we can handle data formatting with D3. This is the third step in figure 3.9.

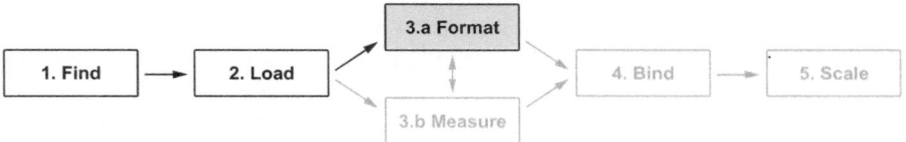

Figure 3.9 The third step of the D3 data workflow consists initially of formatting the data so that it's ready to use when you start building your visualization.

The callback function of d3.csv(), also called the row conversion function, gives access to the data row by row. In the following snippet, the first argument of d3.csv() is the path to the data, and the second one is the callback function, where we log the data into the console. Copy this snippet into main.js, and save your project:

```
const svg = d3.select(".responsive-svg-container")
  .append("svg")
    .attr("viewBox", "0 0 1200 1600")
    .style("border", "1px solid black");

d3.csv("../data/data.csv", d => {
  console.log(d);
});
```

Open the inspector of your browser, and go to the Console tab. You'll see that as shown in figure 3.10, the data is logged one row at a time, each row being a JavaScript object containing a technology and a count.

```
▸ {technology: 'ArcGIS', count: '147'}
▸ {technology: 'D3.js', count: '414'}
▸ {technology: 'Angular', count: '20'}
▸ {technology: 'Datawrapper', count: '171'}
▸ {technology: 'Excel', count: '1078'}
▸ {technology: 'Flourish', count: '198'}
▸ {technology: 'ggplot2', count: '435'}
▸ {technology: 'Gephi', count: '71'}
▸ {technology: 'Google Data Studio', count: '176'}
▸ {technology: 'Highcharts', count: '58'}

    . . .

▸ {technology: 'Physical materials', count: '69'}
▸ {technology: 'Canvas', count: '121'}
▸ {technology: 'P5/Processing', count: '55'}
```

Figure 3.10 Fetched data (partial) logged into the console from the callback function of d3.csv()

Note how the values from the count column have been fetched as strings instead of numbers. This is a common problem when importing data and is due to the type conversion of the dataset from CSV to JSON. Because the callback function of d3.csv() gives us access to the data one row at a time, it's a great place to convert the counts back into numbers. Doing so will ensure that the count values are ready to be used to generate our visualization later.

In the next snippet, instead of logging each data row into the console, we return an object containing the technology and the count key-value pairs. The values are made available with the d parameter via the dot notation. With the d parameter, we're looping through the objects previously logged in to the console (refer to figure 3.10). We can then access the technology with d.technology and count d.count. Finally, we convert the count into a number using the + operator:

```
d3.csv("../data/data.csv", d => {
  return {
    technology: d.technology,
    count: +d.count
  };
});
```

It's important to know that the key-value pairs returned in the callback function are the only ones you'll have access to once the dataset is fully loaded. This strategy can be an efficient way to get rid of columns from the original dataset that you don't need. But if the dataset contains a lot of columns that all need to be kept, returning the keys and values one by one can be redundant. In this case, you might want to skip working in the callback function and perform the formatting once D3 has returned the complete dataset. We discuss how to access the entire dataset at once in the next section.

3.2.3 Measuring a dataset

The third step of D3's data workflow optionally includes data measurements, as suggested in figure 3.11. While retrieving the data row by row can be useful, we also need to access the dataset as a whole. This is where JavaScript Promises come into play. A Promise is the result of an asynchronous operation, stored as an object, such as the one returned by d3.csv(). A simple way to retrieve a Promise is with the then() method.

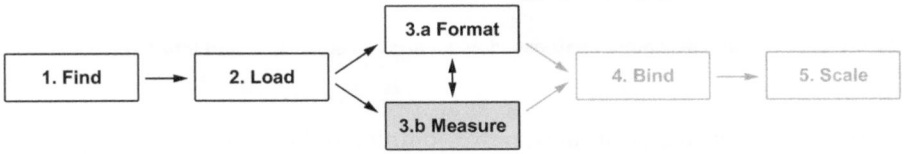

Figure 3.11 In the second part of the third step, we can measure and explore the data.

In the following snippet, we chain the then() method to d3.csv(). Once the data is fully loaded, the Promise is fulfilled, and the complete dataset is available in the callback function of the then() method. Log the complete dataset into the console, and save your project:

```
d3.csv("../data/data.csv", d => {
  return {
    technology: d.technology,
    count: +d.count
```

```
  };
}).then(data => {
  console.log(data);
});
```

In the console, you'll see that the dataset has been converted into an array of objects, each object being a line from the original CSV dataset. This way, D3 makes the data iterable, which is useful for developing visualizations. In figure 3.12, we can also confirm that the count values have been properly converted into numbers. If you look at the last item in our data array, you'll see that D3 exposed the column headers from the CSV dataset. Although we won't need it to build our bar chart, this array can sometimes come in handy.

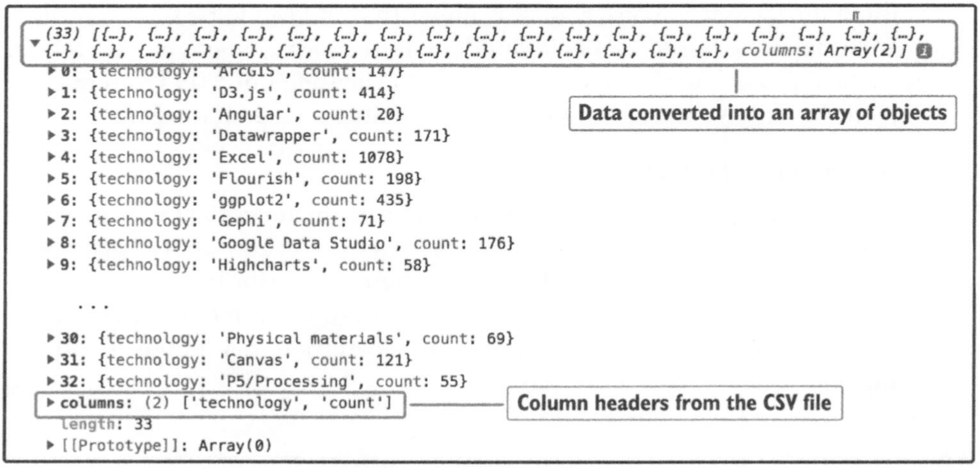

```
  (33) [{…}, {…}, {…}, {…}, {…}, {…}, {…}, {…}, {…}, {…}, {…}, {…}, {…}, {…}, {…}, {…}, {…},
  {…}, {…}, {…}, {…}, {…}, {…}, {…}, {…}, {…}, {…}, {…}, {…}, {…}, columns: Array(2)]
  ▶0: {technology: 'ArcGIS', count: 147}
  ▶1: {technology: 'D3.js', count: 414}
  ▶2: {technology: 'Angular', count: 20}        ┌─────────────────────────────────────────┐
  ▶3: {technology: 'Datawrapper', count: 171}   │ Data converted into an array of objects │
  ▶4: {technology: 'Excel', count: 1078}        └─────────────────────────────────────────┘
  ▶5: {technology: 'Flourish', count: 198}
  ▶6: {technology: 'ggplot2', count: 435}
  ▶7: {technology: 'Gephi', count: 71}
  ▶8: {technology: 'Google Data Studio', count: 176}
  ▶9: {technology: 'Highcharts', count: 58}

     . . .

  ▶30: {technology: 'Physical materials', count: 69}
  ▶31: {technology: 'Canvas', count: 121}
  ▶32: {technology: 'P5/Processing', count: 55}
  ▶columns: (2) ['technology', 'count'] ──────── ┌──────────────────────────────────┐
  length: 33                                      │ Column headers from the CSV file │
  ▶[[Prototype]]: Array(0)                        └──────────────────────────────────┘
```

Figure 3.12   Complete dataset expressed as an array of objects logged into the console

In step 3.a of our data workflow, we've completed the data formatting part, but we can still explore and measure our data using D3. Measuring specific aspects of the data can help you to get situated before diving into the actual crafting of a data visualization.

Although there's no strict rule about where to proceed, the then() method of our data Promise is a great place to perform an initial exploration of the dataset. The first thing we might want to know is how many technologies it contains. For that, we can directly look at the length property of our data array. If we log the length property in the console, we get 33, which means that our bar chart will have 33 rectangles:

```
d3.csv("../data/data.csv", d => {
  . . .

}).then(data => {
```

```
console.log(data.length);    // => 33
});
```
◄─┐ **How many rows
   │ the dataset contains**

We might also want to know which technology is the most popular in our survey data and how many data practitioners said that they use it regularly. And how about the least popular? You can get these values with methods d3.max() and d3.min(). As you can see in the following snippet, these methods take two parameters. The first one is the iterable from which we want to know the maximum or minimum value, hence the data returned by the Promise. The second parameter is an accessor function, where we specify on which key from our data objects we want to compare values—here, the count.

If we log the maximum and the minimum values into the console, still inside the then() method of the Promise, we obtain 1078 and 20:

```
d3.max(data, d => d.count)      // => 1078
d3.min(data, d => d.count)      // => 20
d3.extent(data, d => d.count)   // => [20, 1078]
```

> **NOTE** We could also use method d3.extent(), which takes the same parameters and returns an array containing both the minimum and the maximum values.

Knowing the maximum and minimum values in our data helps us make a rough mental image of how long our bars will need to be in the chart and if the difference between the highest and the lowest value will be easy to represent on the screen or not.

It's common practice for bar charts to sort the data in descending order. It makes the charts easier to read and allows viewers to know at a glimpse which technologies are used more or less than others. The JavaScript sort() method allows us to sort the data easily. It takes a compare function as an argument, as you can see in the next snippet, in which it compares the count value of two technologies, represented as the a and the b parameters. If the count of b is greater than the count of a, b should appear before a in the sorted array, and so on:

```
data.sort((a, b) => b.count - a.count);
```

You can sort your data in the then() method. If you log it into the console, you'll see that Excel is at the top of the technologies' list, with a count of 1078, followed by Tableau, with 852. The last technology in the bar chart will be Angular, with a count of 20, as shown in figure 3.13.

The d3-array module (https://d3js.org/d3-array) contains many other methods to measure and transform data, some of which we'll explore throughout this book. But d3.max(), d3.min(), and d3.extent() are probably the ones that you'll use most often.

```
sorted data                                                          main.js:22
 ▾ (33) [{…}, {…}, {…}, {…}, {…}, {…}, {…}, {…}, {…}, {…}, {…}, {…}, {…}, {…}, {…}, {…}, {…},
    {…}, {…}, {…}, {…}, {…}, {…}, {…}, {…}, {…}, {…}, {…}, {…}, {…}, columns: Array(2)] ▣
     ▸ 0: {technology: 'Excel', count: 1078}
     ▸ 1: {technology: 'Tableau', count: 852}
     ▸ 2: {technology: 'PowerPoint', count: 681}
     ▸ 3: {technology: 'R', count: 561}
     ▸ 4: {technology: 'Python', count: 530}
     ▸ 5: {technology: 'Pen & paper', count: 522}
     ▸ 6: {technology: 'Power BI', count: 460}
     ▸ 7: {technology: 'ggplot2', count: 435}
     ▸ 8: {technology: 'Illustrator', count: 426}
     ▸ 9: {technology: 'D3.js', count: 414}

       . . .

     ▸ 30: {technology: 'Java', count: 29}
     ▸ 31: {technology: 'kepler.gl', count: 24}
     ▸ 32: {technology: 'Angular', count: 20}
     ▸ columns: (2) ['technology', 'count']
       length: 33
     ▸ [[Prototype]]: Array(0)
```

Figure 3.13   Technologies dataset sorted in descending order

Once we're done loading, transforming, and measuring our data, it's common practice to pass the dataset to another function that will take care of building the visualization. In the next listing, you can see the state of main.js at this stage and how, at the end of the then() method, we call and pass the data to function createViz(). We'll start working in this function from the next section.

Listing 3.2   Loading, transforming, and measuring the data (main.js)

```
const svg = d3.select(".responsive-svg-container")
  .append("svg")
    .attr("viewBox", "0 0 1200 1600")        Append an
    .style("border", "1px solid black");      SVG container.

d3.csv("../data/data.csv", d => {            Load the
                                              dataset.
  return {
    technology: d.technology,                Format the data.
    count: +d.count
  };

}).then(data => {

  console.log(data.length); // => 33
  console.log(d3.max(data, d => d.count)); // => 1078    Measure the
  console.log(d3.min(data, d => d.count)); // => 20      dataset.
  console.log(d3.extent(data, d => d.count));
    // => [20, 1078]
                                                         Sort the data in
  data.sort((a, b) => b.count - a.count);                descending order.
```

```
    createViz(data);
});

const createViz = (data) => {};
```

Pass the data to
another function.

Function where we'll
build the bar chart

Before we wrap up this section, you can find an overview of the data loading, row conversion, and Promise concepts discussed so far in figure 3.14. Here's a recap:

1 Load the data using a fetch function, such as d3.csv().
2 Format the data in the row conversion function.
3 Chain a then() method to access the entire dataset once the data loading is complete. This last method is a great place to measure the data and perform any operation that requires the whole dataset.
4 Pass the data to another function that will handle the building of the visualization.

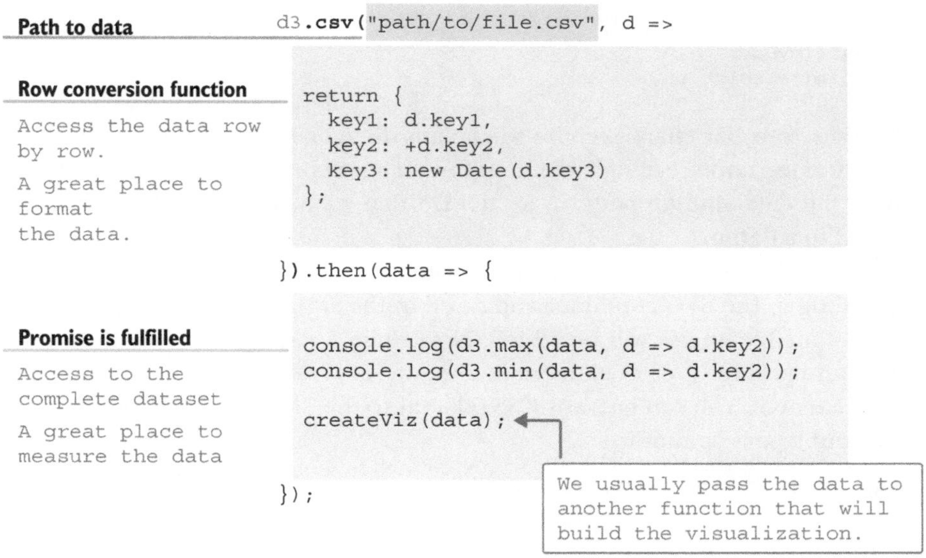

Path to data

```
d3.csv("path/to/file.csv", d =>
```

Row conversion function

Access the data row
by row.

A great place to
format
the data.

```
return {
  key1: d.key1,
  key2: +d.key2,
  key3: new Date(d.key3)
};

}).then(data => {
```

Promise is fulfilled

Access to the
complete dataset

A great place to
measure the data

```
console.log(d3.max(data, d => d.key2));
console.log(d3.min(data, d => d.key2));

    createViz(data);

});
```

We usually pass the data to
another function that will
build the visualization.

Figure 3.14   How and where to load, transform, and measure data in D3

3.3   Binding data to DOM elements

We're now ready to introduce one of the most exciting features of D3: data binding. With data binding, we can couple datum (a single piece of data) to DOM elements. For instance, each SVG rect element composing our bar chart will be coupled with a technology and its corresponding count value. At the data-binding step of the data workflow (the fourth step in figure 3.15), the visualization really starts to come to life—and that's always a joyful moment for a visualization developer!

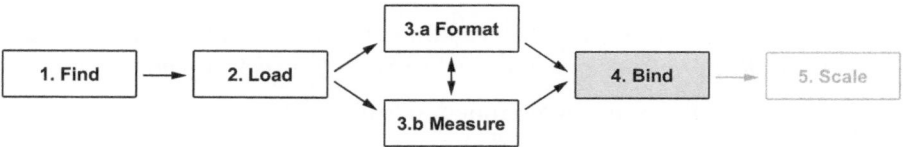

Figure 3.15   The fourth step of the D3 data workflow consists of creating and binding data to DOM elements that will be the core of the visualization.

To bind data, you only need to use the pattern shown in the next snippet, which is composed of three methods (`selectAll()`, `data()`, and `join()`) chained to a selection:

```
selection
  .selectAll("selector")
  .data(myData)
  .join("element to add");
```

We'll use our bar chart exercise to explain the data-binding pattern. In this visualization, we need one rectangle element for each row in our dataset, also called a datum. With the data-binding pattern, we tell D3 that each rectangle element should correspond to a datum.

Go back to `main.js`, and inside the function `createViz()`, call the selection corresponding to the SVG container and saved in the constant named `svg`. The selection is where our rectangles will be added. Now chain a `selectAll()` method to the selection, and pass the type of element that we want to add as a parameter, which is an SVG `rect` element. You can pass any CSS selector to the `selectAll()` method, but using an element type is common:

```
const createViz = (data) => {

  svg
    .selectAll("rect")

};
```

You might wonder why we're selecting elements that don't even exist yet! This is what we call an *empty selection*. But D3 doesn't know yet how many rectangles it needs to add. This is why we chain the `data()` method and pass our dataset as a parameter. Now D3 knows that it needs to create one `rect` element for each row in the data:

```
svg
  .selectAll("rect")
  .data(data)
```

Finally, the rectangles enter the DOM with the join() method:

```
svg
  .selectAll("rect")
  .data(data)
  .join("rect")
```

Save your file, and take a look at the DOM in the inspector. In figure 3.16, you can see that the SVG container now contains 33 rectangles, one for each technology in the dataset.

```
▼<div class="responsive-svg-container">
  ▼<svg viewBox="0 0 1200 1600" style="border: 1px solid black;">
      <rect></rect>
      <rect></rect>
      <rect></rect>
      <rect></rect>
      <rect></rect>
      <rect></rect>

        . . .

      <rect></rect>
      <rect></rect>
      <rect></rect>
   </svg>
 </div>
```

Figure 3.16 Data-bound rectangles added to the DOM

Figure 3.17 illustrates the data-binding process. We start with a selection, here the SVG container. Then we create an empty selection with the selectAll() method and pass a selector. We pass the dataset to the data() method. Finally, D3 appends one rectangle for each datum via the join() method. Once the data binding is complete, the selection becomes the *combination* of the elements and the data together. Whenever we reuse or manipulate elements from this selection, we have access to their corresponding data!

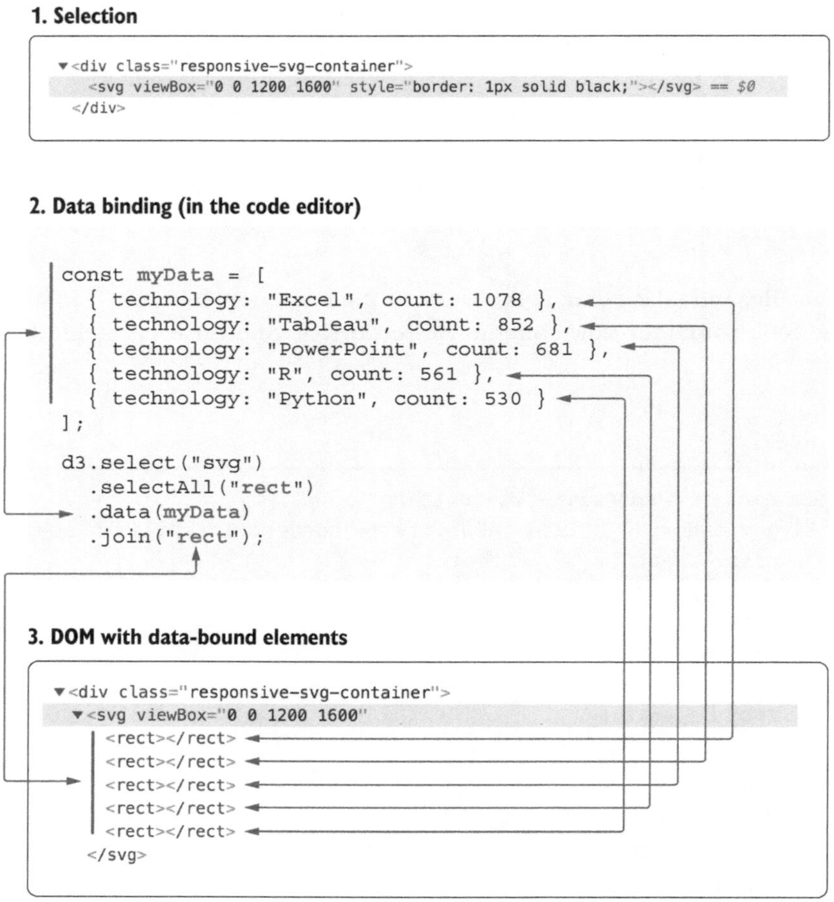

1. Selection

```
▼<div class="responsive-svg-container">
    <svg viewBox="0 0 1200 1600" style="border: 1px solid black;"></svg> == $0
  </div>
```

2. Data binding (in the code editor)

```
const myData = [
  { technology: "Excel", count: 1078 },
  { technology: "Tableau", count: 852 },
  { technology: "PowerPoint", count: 681 },
  { technology: "R", count: 561 },
  { technology: "Python", count: 530 }
];

d3.select("svg")
  .selectAll("rect")
  .data(myData)
  .join("rect");
```

3. DOM with data-bound elements

```
▼<div class="responsive-svg-container">
  ▼<svg viewBox="0 0 1200 1600"
      <rect></rect>
      <rect></rect>
      <rect></rect>
      <rect></rect>
      <rect></rect>
    </svg>
```

Figure 3.17   The data-binding process

Another data-binding pattern

If you search for D3 code examples on the web, you'll undoubtedly come across a slightly different data-binding pattern where the `.enter().append()` methods are used instead of `.join()`:

```
selection
  .selectAll("selector")
  .data(myData)
  .enter().append("element type");
```

Although the `.enter().append()` approach is still valid, it has mainly been replaced by `.join()` since Version 6 of D3.

Under the hood, the `join()` method not only handles the elements to add to the selection based on data but also considers how many new elements are entering the DOM, how many are exiting, and how many are being updated. This more complex pattern is particularly powerful in interactive visualizations, where the data displayed in the visualization is evolving. By taking care of all of these aspects of data binding, `join()` is simpler to use than the previous `.enter().append()` approach.

We'll discuss this more complex approach in chapter 7. For now, it's only important for you to know that prior versions of D3 used a slightly different data-binding pattern and that you're likely to meet code that is still using it.

3.3.1 Setting DOM attributes dynamically with data

We mentioned earlier that after loading the CSV file into our project, D3 converted it into an iterable data structure, hence an array of objects. Then we bound each object from the iterable data structure to a rectangle element. This bound data not only adds the correct number of rectangle elements to the DOM but also can be accessed when we manipulate the rectangles with inline or accessor functions.

Let's see it in action for our bar chart. After the data-binding pattern, chain an `attr()` method to the rectangles selection. We'll use it to add a `class` attribute to each rectangle, but instead of simply passing the value as the second parameter, we'll enter the accessor function.

As you can see in the following snippet, the accessor function is structured as any JavaScript function and returns the value of the class, which is `"bar"` or any class name that you want to give to the rectangles:

```
svg
  .selectAll("rect")
  .data(data)
  .join("rect")
    .attr("class", d => {
      console.log(d);
      return `bar bar-${d.technology}`;
    })
```

The accessor function exposes the parameter d, for *datum*, which is the data bound to each rectangle. If you log d into the console, you'll see that each datum object, containing a technology and a count, is logged one after the other, precisely as if we were *looping* through the rectangles and their data.

Template literals vs. concatenated strings

In the previous snippet, we used template literals, also known as template strings, delimited with backticks (` `` `). They are used to combine traditional JavaScript strings with expressions, and the expressions are preceded by a dollar sign and wrapped in curly braces (`${expression}`).

(continued)

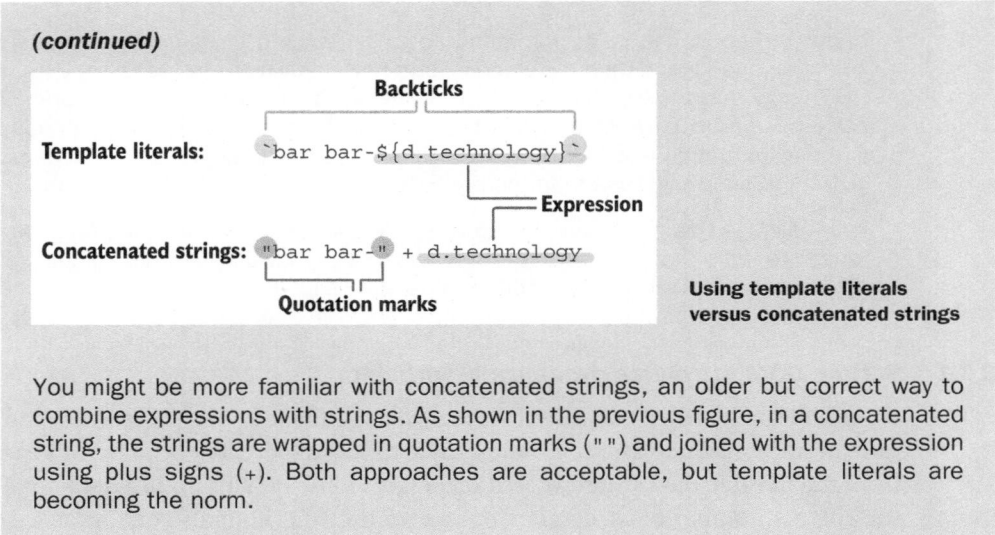

Using template literals versus concatenated strings

You might be more familiar with concatenated strings, an older but correct way to combine expressions with strings. As shown in the previous figure, in a concatenated string, the strings are wrapped in quotation marks (`" "`) and joined with the expression using plus signs (`+`). Both approaches are acceptable, but template literals are becoming the norm.

This way of accessing the bound data is advantageous for setting the position and size of each rectangle. We know that we want to stack the rectangles vertically in our bar chart, as shown in figure 3.18. The `width` attribute of each rectangle represents the number of practitioners that use a tool, stored in the `count` key of the bound data. The longer the rectangle, the more the technology is used, and vice versa. On the other hand, their `height` attribute is constant, and there's a little bit of vertical space between each rectangle.

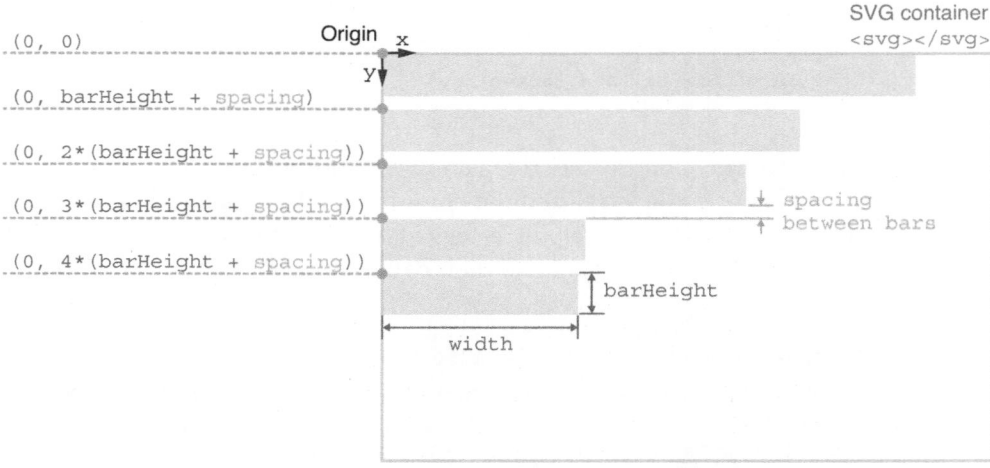

Figure 3.18   Finding a formula for the position of the top-left corner of each rectangle

If we store the height of the bars in a constant named `barHeight`, we can set the `width` and the `height` attributes of the rectangles selection as follows. Note how we access the `count` value bound to each rectangle with a callback function when setting the `width` attribute:

```
const barHeight = 20;
svg
  .selectAll("rect")
  .data(data)
  .join("rect")
    .attr("class", d => {
      console.log(d);
      return "bar";
    })
    .attr("width", d => d.count)
    .attr("height", barHeight)
```

Then we need to set the position of the rectangles by calculating their x and y attributes, which represent the position of their top-left corners within the coordinate system of the SVG container. If you refer to figure 3.18, you'll see that the rectangles are aligned with the left border of the SVG parent, meaning that their x attribute is always 0.

For the y attribute, we need to perform a small calculation. The top-left corner of the first rectangle is positioned at the top of the SVG container, where y is equal to 0. The second rectangle is positioned below the first one, with a distance corresponding to the height of the bars plus a little spacing (remember that the y coordinate of SVG elements goes from top to bottom). The third rectangle is again lower, at a y position corresponding to the height of two rectangles plus two times the vertical spacing between those rectangles. In figure 3.18, we can see a pattern taking shape. The y position of each rectangle corresponds to the number of rectangles before it, multiplied by the bars' combined height and vertical spacing.

To make this calculation in the callback function of the y attribute, we have access to a second parameter, often named i, for *index*. We've already stated that in the accessor function, it's as if we were looping through the data of the bound elements. In JavaScript loops, we generally have access to the index of each item, corresponding to their position in the looped array minus 1 (arrays are zero-indexed in JavaScript). In the following snippet, we use the index to calculate the vertical position of each rectangle and leave 5 px of empty space between each rectangle:

```
const barHeight = 20;
svg
  .selectAll("rect")
  .data(data)
  .join("rect")
    .attr("class", d => {
      console.log(d);
      return "bar";
    })
    .attr("width", d => d.count)
    .attr("height", barHeight)
```

```
    .attr("x", 0)
    .attr("y", (d, i) => (barHeight + 5) * i)
```

In the accessor functions, we use JavaScript arrow functions (ECMAScript 6 [ES6] syntax). When only one parameter is used, such as for the class and the width attribute, it doesn't require parentheses. When multiple parameters are used, they need to be wrapped in parentheses, such as (d, i) for the y attribute. In addition, accessor functions that spread over multiple lines require body braces ({}) and a return statement (e.g., for the class attribute), while simple, single-line functions don't need them (e.g., for the width attribute). These rules are summarized in figure 3.19.

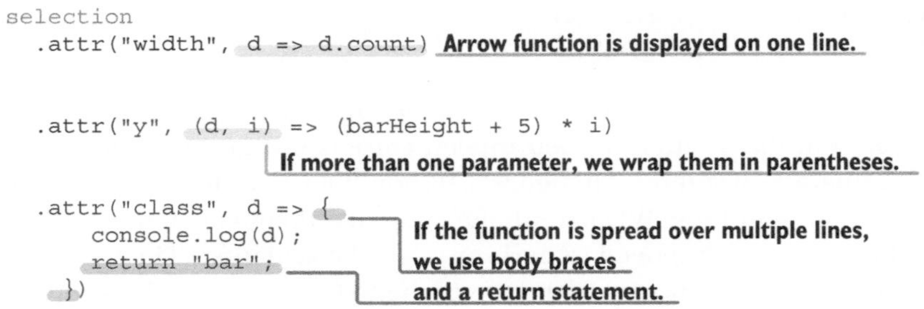

```
selection
    .attr("width", d => d.count)  Arrow function is displayed on one line.

    .attr("y", (d, i) => (barHeight + 5) * i)
                      If more than one parameter, we wrap them in parentheses.

    .attr("class", d => {
        console.log(d);           If the function is spread over multiple lines,
        return "bar";             we use body braces
    })                            and a return statement.
```

Figure 3.19   Formatting arrow functions

Save your project, and you'll see your rectangles take their place, as in figure 3.20. This is starting to look like a bar chart!

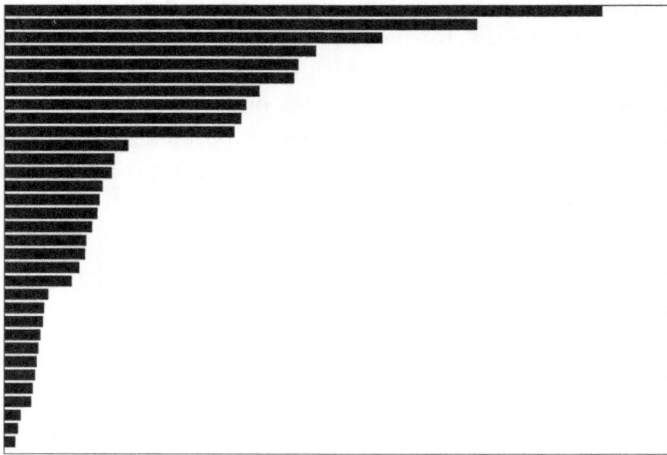

Figure 3.20   Rectangles positioned and sized with data

TIP In the next section, you'll learn how band scales can calculate the vertical position of each bar for you. But knowing how to determine the bars' position on your own is a valuable exercise. When we build D3 projects, we regularly have to make such small calculations of the position of elements on the screen, so it's important to get comfortable with the task. It might not be easy at first, but with practice, you'll get the hang of it! One of the best ways to approach such calculations is to draw a few elements from your visualization on a piece of paper and find their position within the coordinate system of the SVG parent, as we did earlier in figure 3.18. This exercise will help you better understand how your visualizations are built, which will be especially handy when you work on complex projects.

Now we'll make our graph a little more joyful by giving a blue color to the bars using their `fill` attribute. In the following snippet, we provide them with the CSS color name `"skyblue"`. Feel free to use another color if you prefer:

```
svg
  .selectAll("rect")
  .data(data)
  .join("rect")
    ...
    .attr("fill", "skyblue");
```

As a last step, let's interrogate the data bound to the rectangles to identify the one corresponding to D3.js. To do so, we use a JavaScript ternary operator that checks if the technology bound to the current rectangle is `"D3.js"`. If this is the case, the CSS color `"yellowgreen"` is given to the `fill` attribute; otherwise, `"skyblue"` is used, as in figure 3.21:

```
    ...
    .attr("fill", d => d.technology === "D3.js" ? "yellowgreen" : "skyblue");
```

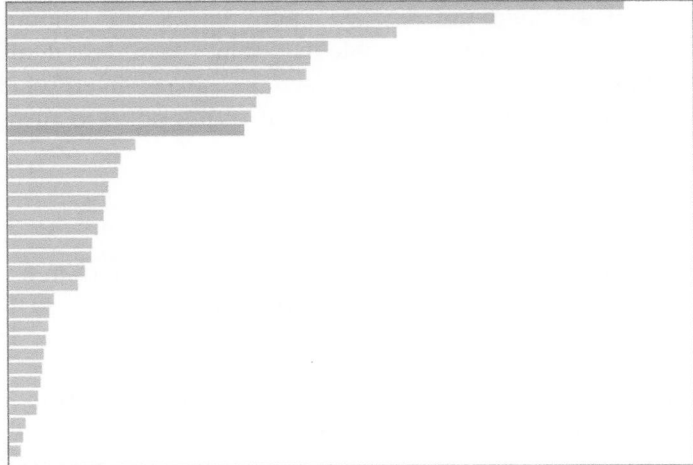

Figure 3.21 The bar corresponding to D3.js is colored in green, while the other ones are blue.

Our bar chart is really taking shape. Currently, we're directly using data to set the width of each rectangle, but this approach isn't always practical. Imagine if the numbers in the data were in the order of millions—we wouldn't be able to use these values directly. In the next section, we'll introduce scales, which are how we map data values into visual attributes in D3 projects.

3.4   *Adapting data for the screen*

When we create data visualizations, we translate the data into visual variables, such as the size of an element, its color, or its position on the screen. In D3 projects, this translation is handled with scales, the last step in figure 3.22.

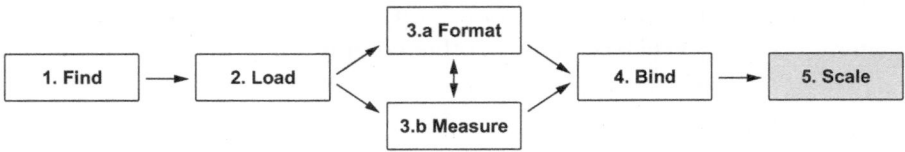

Figure 3.22   In the last step of the D3 data workflow, we use scales to translate data values into screen attributes such as length, position, and color.

3.4.1   *Scales*

Scales are functions that take a value from the data as an input and return an output value that can directly be used to set the size, position, or color of a data visualization element. More specifically, the input data is part of a *domain*, which is the spectrum of possible data values. On the screen, that domain is mapped onto a *range*, which is the spectrum of possible output values.

D3 has multiple scale functions that accept different types of domain and range. Let's take the linear scale function d3.scaleLinear() as an example. To initialize the scale function, we need to chain the domain() and the range() methods. The domain() method takes the spectrum of possible data values as an argument, from a minimum to a maximum value specified in an array. The range() method also takes an array of the corresponding minimum and maximum output values as an argument:

```
const myScale = d3.scaleLinear()
  .domain([0, 200])
  .range([0, 20]);
```

The scale can then be called like any JavaScript function. We pass a value from the domain as an argument, and the scale returns the corresponding value from the range:

```
myScale(100) => 10
```

The input and output values of a scale can be *continuous* or *discrete*. Continuous values can exist anywhere within a predetermined spectrum, for example, a floating-point number between 0 and 100 or a date between June 2020 and January 2021. You can think of continuous quantitative data like a sliding scale of values. On the other hand, discrete inputs and outputs have a predetermined set of values, for instance, a collection of T-shirts available in the sizes XS, S, M, L, and XL or a set of colors that includes blue, green, yellow, and red. Working with qualitative data is like throwing items into different boxes. Each item can only go in one box.

In D3, quantitative data generally couples to a scale with a continuous domain. Conversely, qualitative data implies a discrete domain, usually an array of the possible values. Hence, a scale with a continuous output allows any value within the specified range, while a discrete output will return values from a predefined list.

Based on this concept of continuous versus discrete inputs and outputs, we can group D3 scales into four families:

- Scales with a continuous input and a continuous output
- Scales with a discrete input and a discrete output
- Scales with a continuous input and a discrete output
- Scales with a discrete input and a continuous output

Let's say we make a Google search for TV series released in 2021 and group the first 10 results in a dataset (an exercise we did as we were writing this chapter). We then retrieve information about the genre of each series, its popular score on Rotten Tomatoes, the average score given by professional critics, and the platform on which it is available. This dataset, shown in table 3.2, contains both continuous values (the audience's and critics' scores) and discrete values (the genres and platforms). To create the bar chart in figure 3.23, we need to use a D3 scale from each family listed previously. Note that you don't need to build this bar chart; its purpose is only to illustrate the different types of scales and when to use them.

Table 3.2   TV series released in 2021 suggested by Google

Title	Genre	Audience Score (%)	Critics Score (%)	Platform
Nine Perfect Strangers	Drama	59	62	Prime
Maid	Drama	88	94	Netflix
Katla	Drama	78	100	Netflix
Jupiter's Legacy	Action	73	40	Netflix
Hit & Run	Action	72	82	Netflix
The Irregulars	Crime	54	80	Netflix
Shadow and Bone	Action	89	88	Netflix
Clickbait	Crime	64	56	Netflix
Sex/Life	Comedy	34	23	Netflix
The Wheel of Time	Action	64	82	Prime

Source: www.rottentomatoes.com

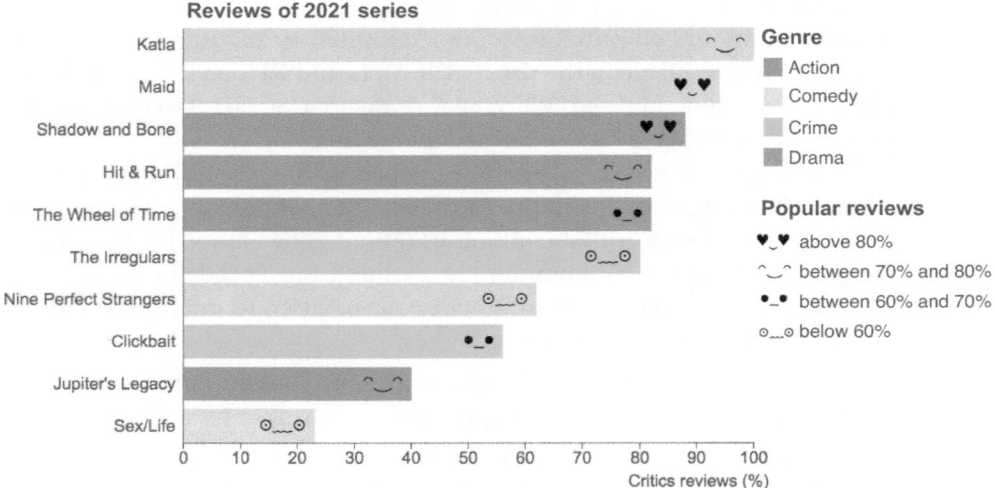

Figure 3.23   Critics and popular reviews of 2021 TV series: a visualization with a scale from each family

On the bar chart, each rectangle corresponds to a series, and its length is proportional to the average score given by critics. To calculate the length of the bars, we use a D3 scale from the first family that takes a continuous value as an input, a critic's score, and returns a continuous value as an output, the length of the corresponding bar.

This scale would have a domain between 0% and 100% (the spectrum of potential values from the critics' scores) and a range of the corresponding bar lengths in pixels:

```
domain => [0, 100] possible min and max values of the input, in %
range  => [0, 500] related min and max values of the output, in pixels
```

The color of the bars represents the genre of each series. To give the appropriate color to the bars, we need a scale from the second family that takes a discrete value as an input, the genre, and returns a discrete value as an output, the corresponding color. The domain of this scale is an array of genres, and the range is an array of related colors:

```
domain => ["Drama", "Action", "Crime", "Comedy"] possible inputs
range  => ["purple", "blue", "green", "yellow"]  corresponding outputs
```

At the tip of each bar, an emoji represents the score from the popular reviews. Series that received a score above 80% get a heart-eyed emoji, series that received between 70% and 80% get a smiley face, the ones that received a score between 60% and 70% get a neutral face, and the ones with a score below 60% get a grimacing face. Here we have a continuous input, the popular reviews, and a discrete output, the related emoji:

```
domain => [60, 70, 80] thresholds of the input values
range  => ["o͟o", "•_•", "-‿-", "♥‿♥"] corresponding output
```

Finally, the bars are distributed along the vertical axis of the graph. To calculate the position of each bar, we need a scale from the fourth family that takes a discrete input, the series' titles, and returns a continuous output, a position along the vertical axis:

```
domain => ["Nine Perfect Strangers", "Maid", "Katla", ...] list of inputs
range  => [0, 500] related min and max values of the output, in pixels
```

Each family of scales contains multiple scale functions. At the time of writing this book, there were more than 20 scale functions available in the d3-scale module (https://d3js.org/d3-scale). In this chapter, we'll introduce the functions `d3.scaleLinear()` and `d3.scaleBand()` because they are commonly used in D3 projects and because we'll need them to finalize our bar chart. Throughout the book, we'll cover many other scales. For an overview of all the scale functions available and a decision tree to help you select the right one for your project, see appendix B.

3.4.2 Linear scale

The type of scale that we use most often when developing D3 projects is, without a doubt, the linear scale (`d3.scaleLinear()`). This scale takes a continuous domain as an input and returns a continuous range of outputs:

```
const myLinearScale = d3.scaleLinear()
  .domain([0, 250])
  .range([0, 25]);
```

The output of a linear scale is directly proportional to its input, as depicted in figure 3.24. In the previous snippet, the domain covers any value between 0 and 250, while the corresponding range of outputs contains values between 0 and 25. If we call this scale function with an argument of 100, it returns 10. Similarly, if we pass a value of 150, it returns 15:

```
myLinearScale(100) => 10
myLinearScale(150) => 15
```

Let's get back to our bar chart exercise. In the previous section, we've used the count values from the data to set the `width` attribute of each rectangle. It worked fine because the counts were relatively small numbers, but using a scale to translate values from the data into SVG attributes is generally more practical.

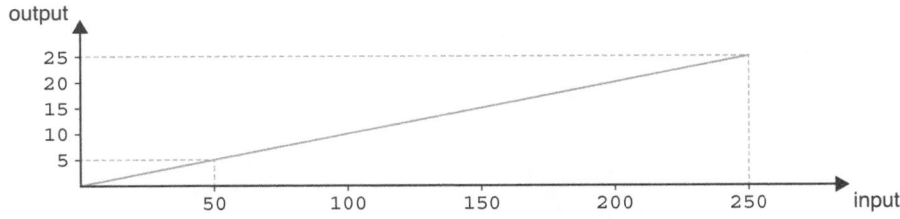

Figure 3.24 The output of a linear scale is linearly proportional to the input.

To illustrate this, let's say that the SVG container of our visualization has a size of 600 × 700 pixels instead of 1,200 × 1,600 pixels. Change the `viewbox` attribute of the SVG container in `main.js` to reflect this new width-height ratio:

```
const svg = d3.select(".responsive-svg-container")
  .append("svg")
  .attr("viewBox", "0 0 600 700")
  ...
```

In addition, modify the value of the `max-width` property of the `div` with a class of `responsive-svg-container` in `main.css`:

```
.responsive-svg-container {
  ...
  max-width: 600px;
  ...
}
```

If you save your project and go to your browser, you'll see that the first three bars of the chart are larger than the SVG container and that their tips are hidden. We'll fix that with a linear scale that will map the count values onto the space available in the SVG container, while leaving free space for labels.

We first declare a constant named `xScale` because this scale will be responsible for sizing and positioning elements along the x-axis. We then call function `d3.scale-Linear()` and chain the `domain()` and `range()` methods.

The possible `count` values from our dataset extend from 0, the theoretical minimum, to 1,078, the highest count corresponding to Excel as a data visualization technology. Note that we use 0 instead of the actual minimum count from the dataset. Like in most charts, we want our x-axis to start at 0. We pass the minimum and maximum values from our domain to the `domain()` method as an array (`[0, 1078]`).

Now we need to assess the horizontal space available, hence the range of the scale. Figure 3.25 shows the first five bars of the graph. You should not see the labels on the

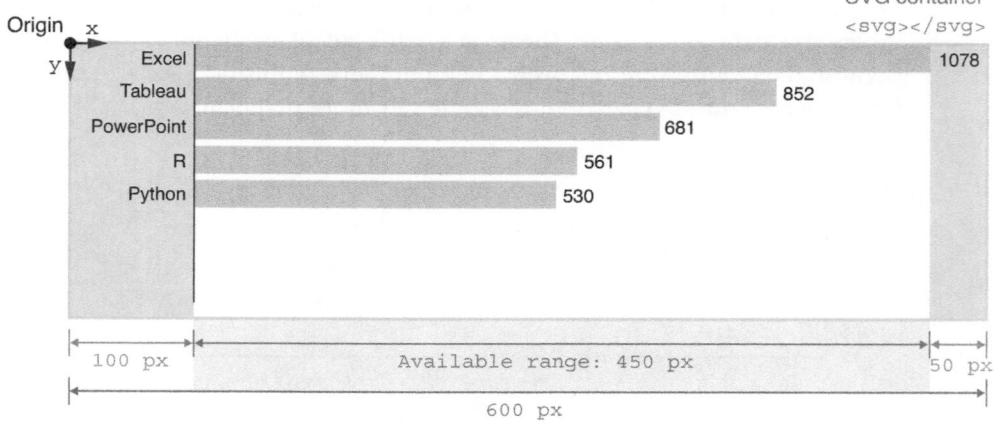

Figure 3.25 Assessing the horizontal space available for the bars

left and the right side of the chart on your project yet. We've added them to this illustration only to show why we need additional space.

We already know that the SVG container has a total width of 600 px. We want to leave 100 px of free space to the left for the technology labels and 50 px to the right for the count labels. This means that the length of the bars can range between 0 px and 450 px.

We can now declare xScale, with a domain varying between 0 and 1078 and a range between 0 and 450. Add the linear scale inside function createViz() before the data binding's code:

```
const createViz = (data) => {

  const xScale = d3.scaleLinear()
    .domain([0, 1078])
    .range([0, 450]);

  // Data-binding
  ...
}
```

We've mentioned that we can call D3 scales like any other JavaScript function. We pass a value from the domain as an argument, and the function returns the corresponding value from the range. For example, if we pass the value 1078 to xScale, corresponding to Excel's count value, the scale will return 450. If we pass 414, the number of practitioners that use D3, the scale returns 172.82, the width in pixels of the bar corresponding to D3.js:

```
xScale(1078)    // => 450
xScale(414)     // => 172.82
```

Try it for yourself by logging in to the console the output returned by the scale for a few values from the dataset and see if they correspond to the values in figure 3.26.

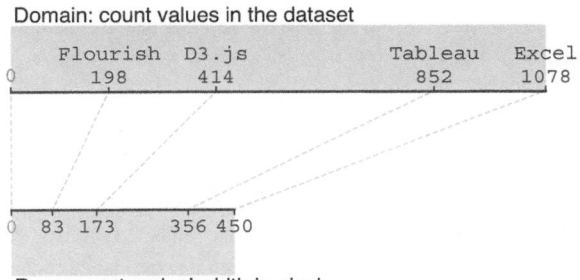

Figure 3.26 Count values from the data mapped by the linear scale into the bars' width

Now that our scale is declared, we can start using it to calculate the width of each rectangle in our bar chart. Find the line of code where the width attribute of the rectangles is set. Like in the next snippet, instead of using the count value directly, call xScale(), and pass the count value as an argument. Change the value of the x attribute to 100 to translate the rectangles to the right, and leave space for the technology labels shown in figure 3.25:

```
svg
  .selectAll("rect")
  .data(data)
  .join("rect")
    ...
    .attr("width", d => xScale(d.count))
    ...
    .attr("x", 100)
    ...
```

Save your project, and note how the bars fit within the SVG container and how whitespace is preserved for the labels on each side of the bars.

You now know how to use D3 scales! Although there are a lot of different types of scales available in D3, the principles of how to declare and use them remain similar. Switching from one scale to another only requires you to know the type of data accepted by the domain and the expected range.

3.4.3   *Band scale*

The second type of scale we'll need for our bar chart is a band scale. Band scales are from the fourth family: they accept a discrete input and return a continuous output. D3's band scale is especially useful for distributing the rectangles of a bar chart within the available space.

To declare a band scale, we call function d3.scaleBand(). In the following code snippet, we save the scale into a constant named yScale because this scale is responsible for distributing elements along the y-axis. The domain of our band scale is an array containing all the technologies from our dataset. We generate this array with the JavaScript map() function. (Go back to section 1.2.5 if you need a refresher on when and how we use the map() function.) Then our range covers all the vertical space available, from 0 px at the top of the SVG container, to 700 px at the bottom of the SVG container:

```
const yScale = d3.scaleBand()
  .domain(data.map(d => d.technology))
  .range([0, 700]);
```

Add the band scale inside createViz(), before the code related to data binding. When called with a technology from the dataset, the band scale returns the vertical position of the corresponding rectangle. For example, if we pass the string "Excel" to yScale, it returns 0. This makes sense because the bar that corresponds to Excel is the first one at the top of the graph. Similarly, if we call yScale passing the value "D3.js", it returns 272.72, which is the vertical position of the top-left corner of the bar corresponding to D3:

```
yScale("Excel")   // => 0
yScale("D3.js")   // => 272.72
```

Do you remember the calculations we had to perform earlier to set the y attributes of the rectangles? Thanks to the band scale, we can now set this attribute extremely easily by passing the name of the technology that is bound to each rectangle to yScale:

```
svg
  .selectAll("rect")
  .data(data)
  .join("rect")
    ...
    .attr("y", d => yScale(d.technology))
    ...
```

Band scales also have a very handy method, bandwidth(), that returns the thickness of the bars, which is proportional to the number of bars and the space available. In our bar chart, this thickness corresponds to the height attribute of the rectangles. You can see in the next snippet how calling the bandwidth() method on the band scale returns the height attribute:

```
svg
  .selectAll("rect")
  .data(data)
  .join("rect")
    ...
    .attr("height", yScale.bandwidth())
    ...
```

Save your project, and take a look at it in the browser. As you can see in figure 3.27, the bars cover all the vertical space available in the SVG container, but the absence of padding between them makes the graph look cramped and difficult to read.

We can fix it by setting the paddingInner() property of the band scale, which specifies the amount of padding between each band and accepts values between 0 and 1. Here we give it a value of 0.2, for 20% of the height of the bands:

```
const yScale = d3.scaleBand()
  .domain(data.map(d => d.technology))
  .range([0, 700])
  .paddingInner(0.2);
```

Once we're done, our bar chart layout breathes a little more, as you can see in figure 3.28. That's much better!

Figure 3.29 gives a recap of how the band scale works. First, it takes a domain, the list of technologies from our dataset, and distributes it within the range, the vertical space available in the SVG container. The vertical position of the top-left corner of each rectangle can be retrieved by calling the scale function and passing the technology as an argument (yScale("PowerPoint")). Similarly, we can obtain the height of the bars by calling the bandwidth() method on the scale (yScale.bandwidth()). Finally, by default, the padding between the bars is 0. We can tell D3 the amount of padding that we want between each band by setting the paddingInner() property of the band scale and giving it a value between 0 and 1.

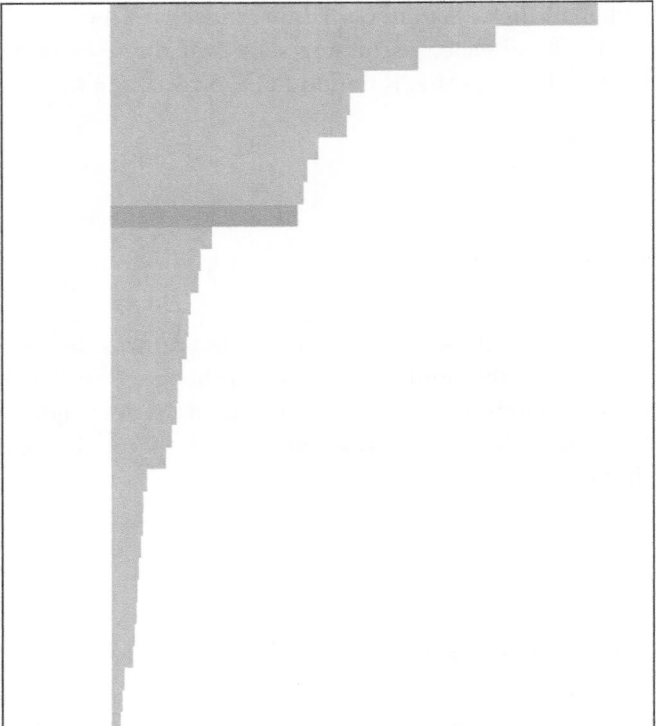

Figure 3.27 Bars distributed with a band scale and without padding

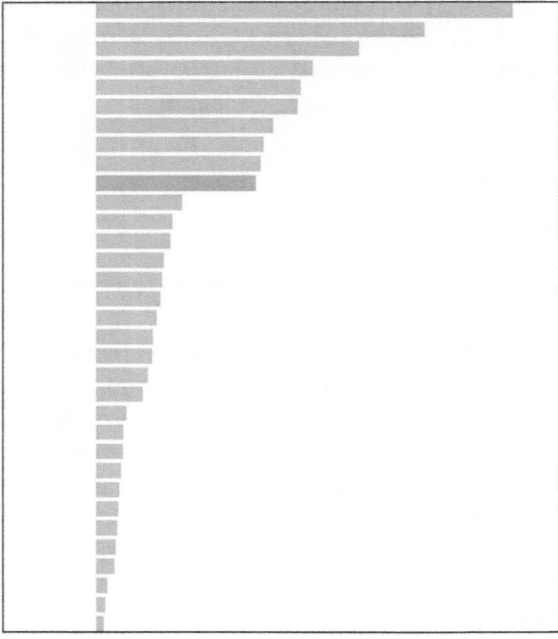

Figure 3.28 Bars distributed with a band scale and with padding

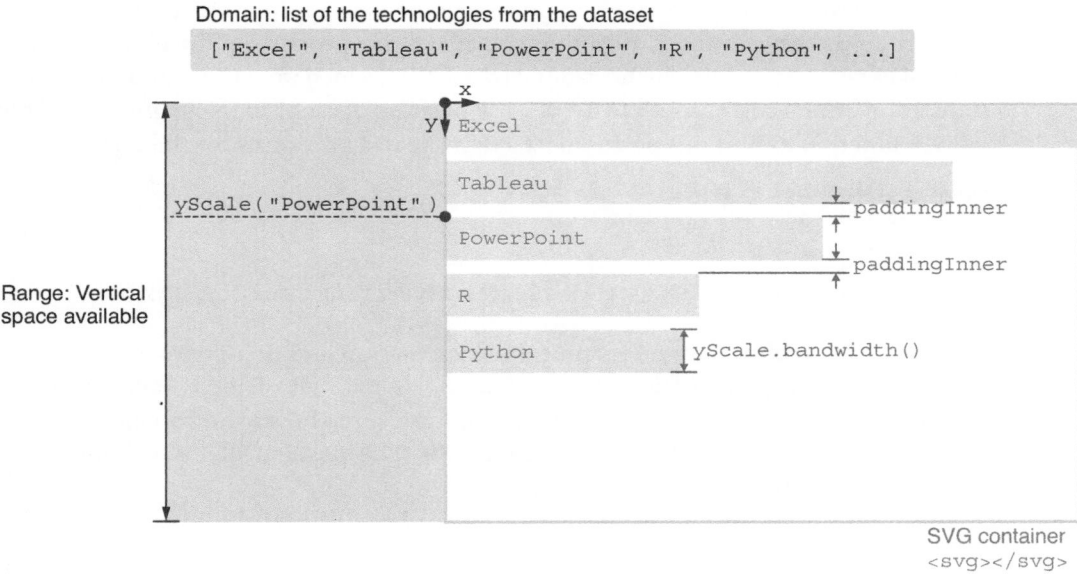

Figure 3.29 How the band scale distributes the list of technologies within the available vertical space

3.5 Adding labels to a chart

Our bar chart is almost complete, but it's currently impossible to know which rectangle corresponds to which technology and which values the lengths of the bars represent. We'll rectify this by adding two sets of labels to the chart. The first set of labels will be the name of the technologies listed on the left side. The second one will be the count associated with each bar and positioned at the tip of the rectangles.

In SVG-based visualizations, we make labels with SVG text elements. We'll have two text elements combined with each rectangle and will nest each rectangle and its related labels into an SVG group. If you remember our discussion about SVG groups from chapter 1, section 1.2.2, we use groups to move multiple elements as one. They are also handy for passing bound data to their descendants, as you'll see here.

Let's start by refactoring our code a little bit. First, comment out all the lines related to the attributes of the rectangle elements. We'll reuse them in a few minutes. In JavaScript, single-line comments start with two forward slashes (//), while multiline comments start with /* and end with */.

Now go back to the data-binding piece of code. Instead of binding data onto rectangles, use SVG groups (g). We also save the selection in a constant named barAndLabel:

```
const barAndLabel = svg
  .selectAll("g")
  .data(data)
  .join("g");
```

For the rectangles and their labels to move together, we apply a vertical translation to each group via the transform attribute. The translate property of the transform attribute takes two parameters: the horizontal translation, which we set to 0, and the vertical translation, which corresponds to the vertical position of each bar. Note how we call the yScale function to find this position, exactly as we did previously for the rectangles:

```
const barAndLabel = svg
  .selectAll("g")
  .data(data)
  .join("g")
    .attr("transform", d => `translate(0, ${yScale(d.technology)})`);
```

Although SVG groups have no graphical representation and don't exist as a bounded space, we can imagine them as boxes that encapsulate all of their child elements. Thanks to the transform attribute, the groups are spread over the vertical height of the SVG container, as illustrated in figure 3.30. The position of the rectangle and labels will be relative to their parent group.

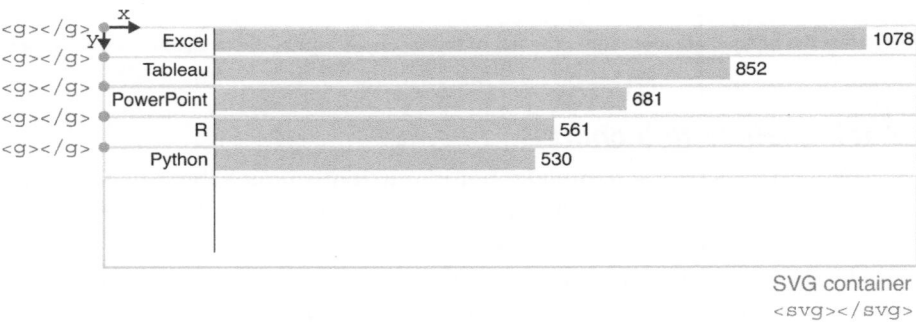

Figure 3.30   Groups positioned within the SVG container and encapsulating their descendent rectangle and labels

Now that our groups are ready, let's add back the rectangles. Call the barAndLabel selection, and append rectangle elements into it:

```
const barAndLabel = svg
  .selectAll("g")
  .data(data)
  .join("g")
    .attr("transform", d => `translate(0, ${yScale(d.technology)})`);

barAndLabel
  .append("rect");
```

Because the bar selection contains multiple group elements, one for each datum, D3 understands that it needs to add one rectangle element into each group. Save your project and look at the markup with the inspector tool. Confirm that the groups and rectangles have been added to the DOM, as in figure 3.31.

```
▼<div class="responsive-svg-container">
  ▼<svg viewBox="0 0 600 700" style="border: 1px solid black;">
    ▼<g transform="translate(0, 0)">
      ┌─────────────┐
      │<rect></rect>│ ◄──── Rectangle element
      └─────────────┘
    </g>
    ▶<g transform="translate(0, 21.34146341463415)">…</g>
    ▶<g transform="translate(0, 42.6829268292683)">…</g>
    ▶<g transform="translate(0, 64.02439024390245)">…</g>
    ▶<g transform="translate(0, 85.3658536585366)">…</g>
        . . .
    ▶<g transform="translate(0, 618.9024390243903)">…</g>
    ▶<g transform="translate(0, 640.2439024390244)">…</g>
    ▶<g transform="translate(0, 661.5853658536586)">…</g>
    ▶<g transform="translate(0, 682.9268292682927)">…</g>
  </svg>
</div>
```

Figure 3.31 Rectangle elements appended into groups

You can now uncomment the rectangles' attribute methods and apply them to the newly added `rect` elements. What is neat about data binding is that the bound data is passed to the descendent elements of the groups. We still have access to the data, exactly as we did before. The only difference is that because the vertical translation has already been applied to the groups, the y attribute of the rectangles can be set to 0:

```
barAndLabel
  .append("rect")
    .attr("width", d => xScale(d.count))
    .attr("height", yScale.bandwidth())
    .attr("x", 100)
    .attr("y", 0)          ◄────
    .attr("fill", d => d.technology === "D3.js" ? "yellowgreen":"skyblue");
```

The rectangles don't need a vertical translation anymore. Their position is relative to the one of their group parent.

Your rectangles should now be visible on your bar chart and look exactly as they did previously (refer to figure 3.28).

We're ready to add the labels! Call the `barAndLabel` selection again, and append a text element into it. This will add a text element to each group. We want the labels to display the name of the technology related to each rectangle. To do so, chain the `text()` method to the selection. This method accepts one parameter: the text to add to the SVG text element. Here we set the text dynamically based on the data bound to each element:

```
barAndLabel
  .append("text")
    .text(d => d.technology);
```

Then we position each label using the x and y attributes of the text elements. Horizontally, we want the end of the labels to align with the start of each rectangle.

Because the rectangles start at 100 px, we can say that the labels should end at around 96 px, leaving 4 px between the end of the labels and the start of the related rectangle. We also use the `text-anchor` attribute with a value of `end` to make the labels right-aligned. This means that the `x` attribute represents the position of the end of each label, as you can see in figure 3.32.

Figure 3.32   Calculating the position of the technology labels

Vertically, the position of each label is relative to its parent group. We need to move them down slightly until they are centered with the bars, keeping in mind that text elements are vertically positioned in reference to their baseline. Here we apply a translation of 12 px. Note that the values of the `x` and `y` attributes don't come out of thin air. We found these numbers by having a rough idea of where we wanted to display the labels and testing a few values until we found the right ones. The browser's inspector is a great place to make such quick assessments:

```
barAndLabel
  .append("text")
    .text(d => d.technology)
    .attr("x", 96)
    .attr("y", 12)
    .attr("text-anchor", "end");
```

Finally, we can set the `font-family` and `font-size` properties of the labels based on our preference and using the `style()` method. Here we use a sans-serif font with a size of 11 px. You can see the result in figure 3.33:

```
barAndLabel
  .append("text")
    .text(d => d.technology)
    .attr("x", 96)
    .attr("y", 12)
    .attr("text-anchor", "end")
    .style("font-family", "sans-serif")
    .style("font-size", "11px");
```

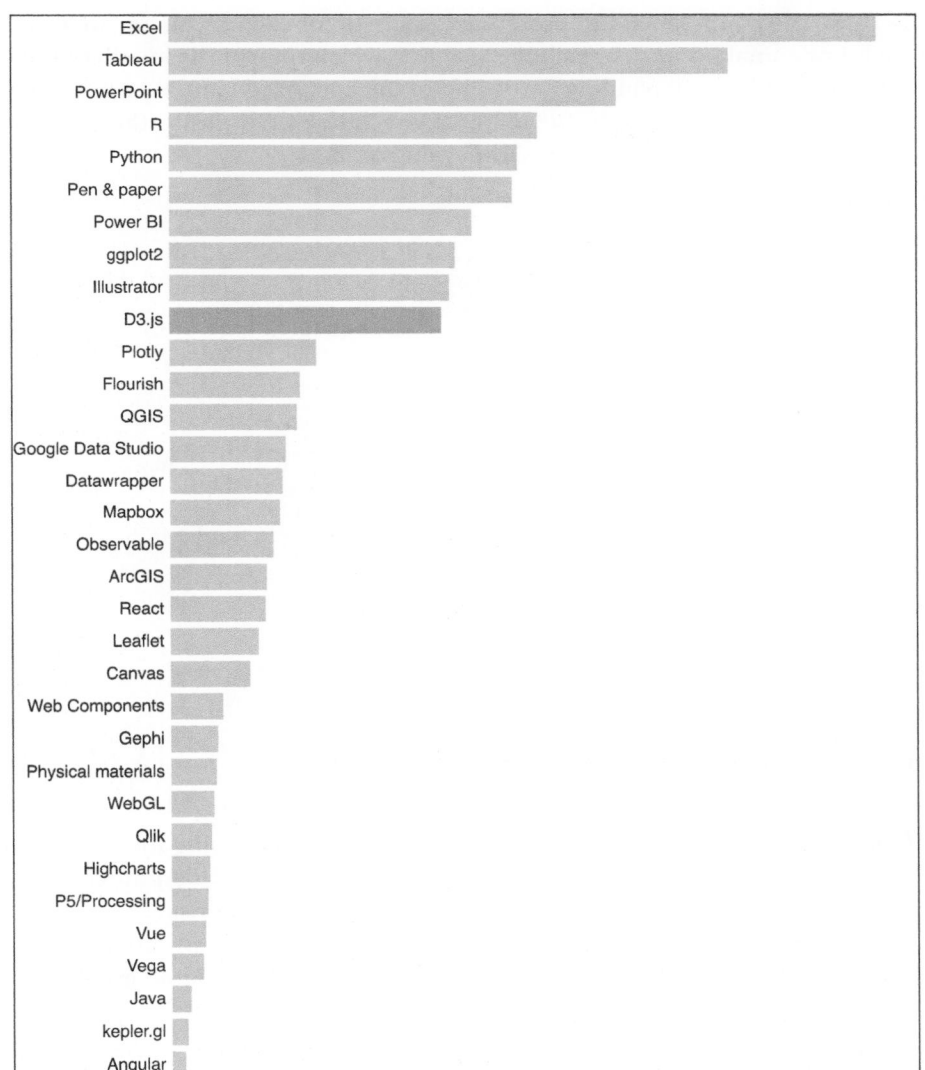

Figure 3.33   Bar chart with technology labels

We can now add a label at the rectangles' tip, representing how many times a technology was selected in the survey. The procedure is very similar to the one used for the technology labels. First, we call the `barAndLabel` constant, which contains the groups' selections, and append another text element into each group. The text of each label is set to the `count` value of each technology via the `text()` method:

```
barAndLabel
  .append("text")
    .text(d => d.count)
```

Because the count labels are positioned at the tip of each rectangle, we can calculate their horizontal position by calling xScale(), which returns the length of the bars. We also add a little bit of padding at the end of the bars (4 px) and take into account that there is a space of 100 px at the left of the rectangles. Vertically, the count labels are also pushed down with 12 px, as shown in figure 3.34:

```
barAndLabel
  .append("text")
    .text(d => d.count)
    .attr("x", d => 100 + xScale(d.count) + 4)
    .attr("y", 12)
```

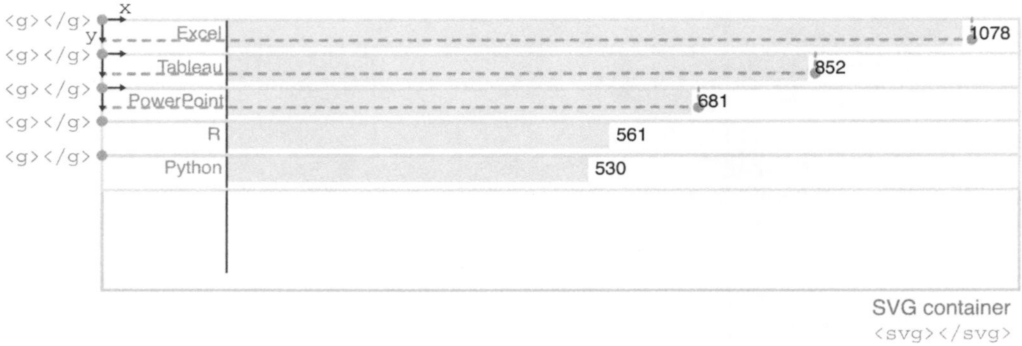

Figure 3.34   Calculating the position of the count labels

Finally, we set the font-family and font-size properties using the style() method. Notice how the font size of the count labels (9 px) is smaller than the one of the technology labels (11 px). We proceed this way to maintain the visual hierarchy between the two types of labels. The larger labels will catch the attention first, and the viewers will understand that the count labels are secondary to the technology labels:

```
barAndLabel
  .append("text")
    .text(d => d.count)
    .attr("x", d => 100 + xScale(d.count) + 4)
    .attr("y", 12)
    .style("font-family", "sans-serif")
    .style("font-size", "9px");
```

As a final step, let's add a vertical line to the left of the bars to act as a vertical axis. In the following code snippet, we append the line into the SVG container. The starting position of the line (x1, y1) is at (100, 0), the top of the SVG container, and its ending position (x2, y2) is at (100, 700), the bottom of the container. We also need to specify the stroke's color for the line to be visible:

```
svg
  .append("line")
```

```
.attr("x1", 100)
.attr("y1", 0)
.attr("x2", 100)
.attr("y2", 700)
.attr("stroke", "black");
```

If you remove the border from the SVG container, your bar chart should look like the one in figure 3.35 and on the GitHub hosted project (http://mng.bz/mjor). Note

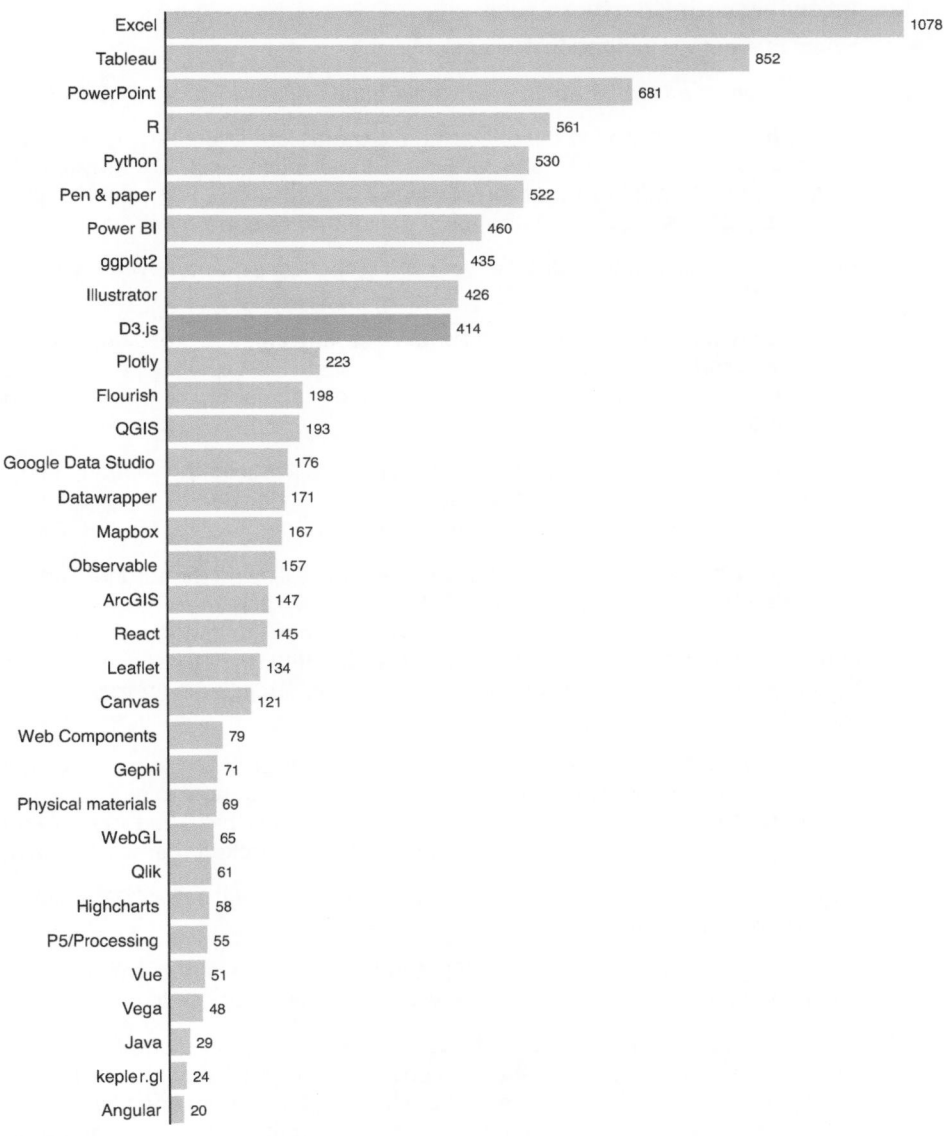

Figure 3.35 Completed bar chart (http://mng.bz/mjor)

that the approach we used in this chapter to preserve whitespace for labels is not conventional. We normally use the D3 margin convention, a concept we'll introduce in the next chapter and use throughout the rest of the book.

Congrats on making it to the end of this chapter—it was a dense one! Don't worry too much if you haven't yet mastered all the concepts we've discussed. We'll keep using these concepts in different contexts, and they will soon become second nature.

Interview with Krisztina Szűcs

Szűcs is a data visualization designer.

Can you tell us a little bit about your background and how you discovered D3.js?

I don't have a background in coding; I have a masters in graphic design but used a bit of ActionScript in the Flash era. First, I used processing for dataviz, but when I found out online in 2012 that everyone was using this new thing called d3.js and that it was very good for data visualization, I decided to give it a try and learn it.

How did you learn D3? What were your main challenges, and how did you overcome them?

I'm not very keen on learning new libraries or languages. I prefer to learn just one, then use it forever (ha ha). I'm usually very upset when a shiny new thing appears, and it seems to become standard, and I cannot deny anymore that I need to invest the time to learn it.

So when d3.js appeared, everyone started to talk about it. I already knew that I wanted to create interactive data visualizations, so I decided this was going to be the one (and only one) thing that I was going to learn.

I remember it was more difficult than I expected. I followed the tutorials from *Interactive Data Visualization for the Web* by Scott Murray and then tried to apply what I learned in my own projects. The tutorials worked when I followed every step, but when I finally tried to use those examples with my own data, they failed—because most of the time my real datasets were too complex, and I struggled a lot making them work with d3.js.

Also, I wanted to create big, unusual visuals from day one, and there were no specific tutorials for those, so it was difficult for me to figure out how to get from the simple bar charts to the unconventional, complicated designs that I had in my mind. I just practiced until I could get the result where every part looked the way I imagined.

Do you use visualization tools other than D3? What's the place of D3 in your current data visualization workflow?

I use design tools like Figma to design the look of my visualizations. And I also use Excel and Python, mostly when I work with my datasets or I collect my data.

When I use design tools, I have a designer mindset, and I do not think about the limitations I have to face or all the challenges I'll need to solve when I will actually develop the visualization. This helps me not to limit my ideas, and I can create better visuals this way. When the visual look is ready as a static picture, then I switch to "developer mindset," and I just try to re-create everything as I saw in my designs. Sometimes I make adjustments, but when I design something that is challenging to develop, I force myself to solve the coding problem and not go back and change the design to something simple just to make coding easier for myself. I've also found that for me this is the best way to learn D3.js.

Featured project: Animated Sport Results (https://krisztinaszucs.com/)

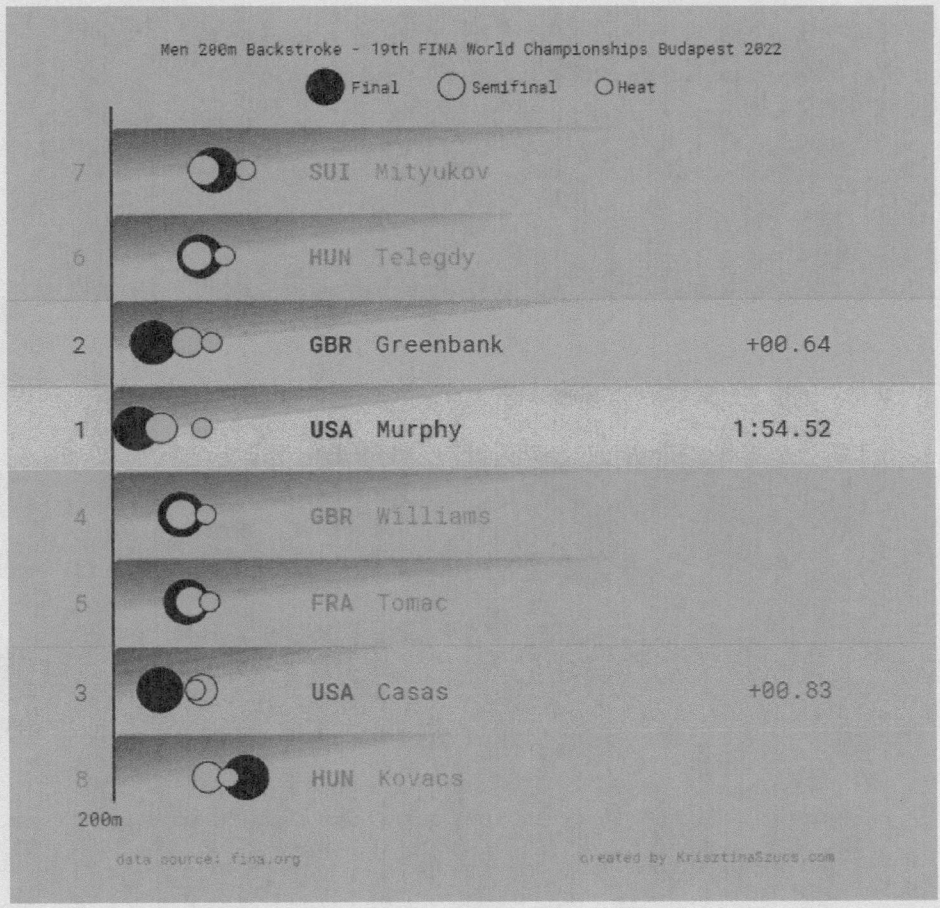

Animated visualization of the Men's 200 m Backstroke competition at the 2022 FINA World Championship

Please describe your project "Animated Sport Results."

I was planning to create a project for the 2020 Olympic Games. This is a big world event that many people are interested in, and sport result data is an available resource.

(continued)

I thought that if I created one match visualization, then I would be able to reuse it again many times for other sport events like world championships or even for other sport disciplines that use similar scoring rules.

I also wanted the viewers to relive the excitement of a match by not disclosing the final result at the start; I wanted to slowly show the progress.

I love similar visualizations from Chartball.com and the *New York Times*, and those were my inspirations for this project.

Can you explain the process of creating this project?

When I started to work on this project, I knew that I was going to create an animation, and the style would be minimalist with a hint of red, which I connected to Japan in my head (the Olympics were held in Tokyo in 2020).

Multiple data visualizations created by Krisztina Szűcs for the "Animated Sport Results" project

But I didn't know which sport event I was going to visualize, so I created a bunch of sketches for different sport disciplines like high jump, long jump, javelin or hammer throw, running, indoor cycling, etc. . . . also something for water polo, which was a score progress visualization (bottom-right image in figure 2.19). I quickly realized that the score progress visualization would be the one that I could reuse the most, and once I was happy with the look, I moved on to coding it.

Of course, this was months before the Olympics, and I didn't have any data yet, so I used previous Olympic results as sample data. I also created a UI for myself around the main visualization that made it easy for me to quickly switch between color palettes or datasets.

I was ready weeks before the Olympics, and the UEFA European Football Championship happened around that time, so even though I created my visualization for 10+ goal matches, I tried to test it with soccer results. I loaded soccer data files, and the visualization worked even with 1-3 goals. I also extended visualization with the penalty scores around this time.

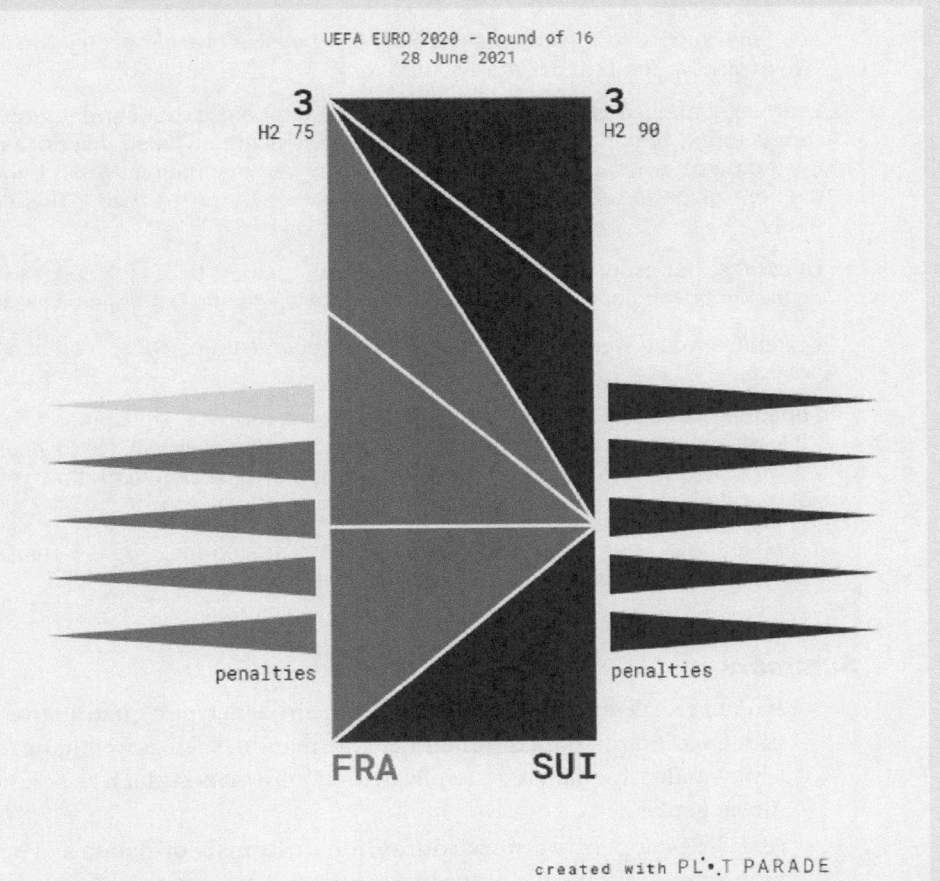

Score progress visualization exploring the results from the 2021 European Football Championship

But when the Olympics started, I could not get the data for the matches because they were published in a PDF format on the official website. I was able to create and publish only two to three animations because getting the data from the PDF was a tedious manual process which I didn't plan for.

(continued)

This taught me that I should have looked for better data sources, and luckily other events like world championships or sport associations' websites had better and more accessible data. I created a lot more of these animations after the Olympics when I had better data sources.

Did you create the animations with D3, or do you use another library or tool?

I only used D3.js, but for exporting the images I recorded my screen with a screen recording software—ScreenToGif.

You have such a recognizable style! How did it evolve over time? Any trick on finding "your voice" in the field of data visualization?

Learning graphic design in university gave me the basics, but current graphic design trends (print, brand design, packaging design, typography) also influence my style a lot. I browse graphic design sites daily looking for inspiration. When I find a visual element or pattern that I really like, I immediately start to think "This could be a dataviz."

Of course, not every visual trend can work with a chart, but I learn a lot while I try to figure out how it could be possible to re-create a specific but unusual look in D3.js.

Which tips would you share with our readers about learning D3 and creating personal projects?

Separate the design and the coding phase in your process. Design the final look first while deliberately avoiding thinking about how difficult it will be to develop what you've created. This way, you'll always encounter new problems that you need to solve and you'll learn lots of new tricks.

If design is not your strong suit, you can always search for a great visualization and then just try to re-create it from scratch as practice.

Summary

- In data visualization, we work with two main data types: quantitative and qualitative. Quantitative data is numerical information, such as weight or temperature, while qualitative data is generally textual information, such as country names or movie genres.
- As D3 developers, we work with different formats of datasets. The most common ones are tabular, such as CSV files and JavaScript objects found in JSON files. But data can also be organized in ways specific to hierarchical, network, or geographic visualizations.
- D3 offers functions to load specific dataset formats into a project. For example, the functions d3.csv() and d3.json() can respectively load a CSV or a JSON file. As it loads the data, D3 transforms it into an array of objects.
- When loading external datasets, we generally need to ensure that the data, especially numbers, is correctly formatted. The callback function of d3.csv()

and `d3.json()` gives access to the dataset row by row and can be a great place to perform type conversion and other data manipulation.

- Loading data into a project is an asynchronous process, which means that the browser continues to read and execute the script while the data is loading:
  - It's crucial to wait for the data to be fully available before manipulating it. To do so, we can use JavaScript Promises with the `then()` method.
  - The callback function of the `then()` method gives us access to the entire dataset once it's loaded. We can then measure and reorganize the data before building a visualization.
- The data-binding pattern generates as many SVG elements as there are datum (individual data points or rows in a tabular dataset):
  - The data-binding pattern is made of three methods chained to a selection: `selectAll()`, `data()`, and `join()`.
  - Once SVG elements are generated with the data-binding pattern, we have access to the data bound to each of them via inline functions.
  - Data bound to an element is also passed to its children.
- D3 scales allow translating values from a dataset into attributes applied to SVG elements, such as their size, position, or color:
  - We can group scales into four families depending on whether their input and output values are discrete or continuous.
  - Linear scales take an input from a continuous domain and return a value from a continuous range of outputs. The output is linearly proportional to the input value. Linear scales are widely used in D3 projects, for example, to calculate the length of the rectangles in a bar chart.
  - Band scales take an input from a discrete domain and return a value from a continuous range of outputs. They are especially useful for spreading rectangles over the available space in a bar chart.
- A translation applied to an SVG group affects all of its descendent elements.
- Labels are built with SVG text elements. Each text element must be positioned individually, using its `x` and `y` attributes. We can also make the text right-aligned with the `text-anchor` attribute.

Drawing lines, curves, and arcs

This chapter covers

- Adding axes to a chart and applying the margin convention
- Drawing a line chart with the line generator function
- Interpolating data points to turn lines into curves
- Drawing an area with the area generator
- Using the arc generator to create arcs

You're already familiar with the common SVG shapes that we use and combine to make data visualizations: lines, rectangles, and circles. You've even created a bar chart from scratch using rectangles. But there's only so much we can draw with primitive shapes. To create more complex visualizations, we generally turn to SVG paths. As we've discussed in chapter 1, SVG paths are the most flexible of all SVG elements and can take pretty much any form. We use them extensively in D3 projects; the simplest examples are drawing the lines and curves in line charts or creating the arcs in donut charts.

The shape of an SVG path is determined by its d attribute. This attribute is composed of commands dictating the starting point and endpoint of the path, the type of curves it uses to change direction, and whether the path is open or closed. The d attribute of a path can quickly become long and complex. Most times, we don't want to have to write it ourselves. This is when D3's shape generators come in handy!

In this chapter, we'll build the project shown in figure 4.1: a line chart of the evolution of temperature and a set of arcs visualizing the percentage of days with precipitation in New York City in 2021. You can find this project online at http://mng.bz/5orB. The underlying data comes from Weather Underground (www.wunderground.com).

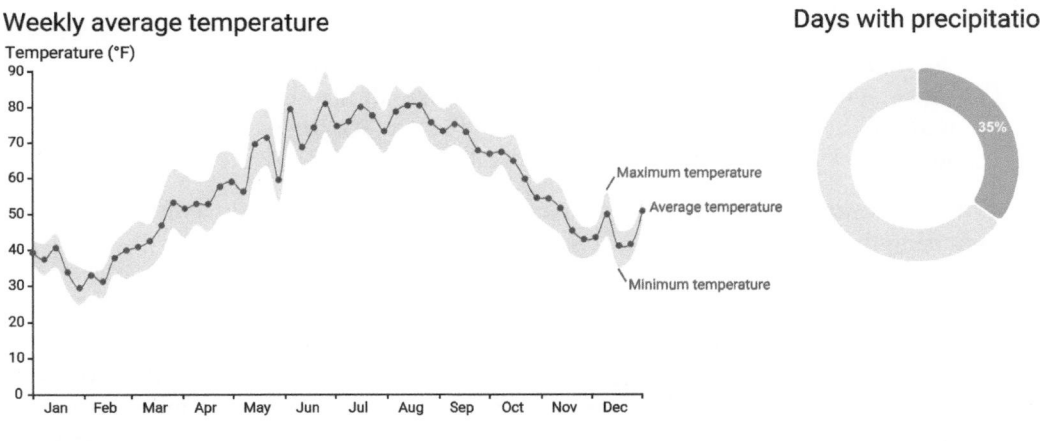

Figure 4.1   Project that we'll build in this chapter: a line chart of the temperature evolution in New York City in 2021 and a set of arcs showing the percentage of days with precipitation

We'll create both visualizations using D3's shape generator functions. But before we get started, we'll discuss D3's margin convention and how to add axes to a chart.

4.1   Creating axes

Developing data visualizations often requires planning how we'll use the space available in the SVG container. It's very tempting to start playing with the cool stuff first—aka the core of the visualization—but trust us, a little bit of preparation can save you a lot of execution time. It's true for all programming tasks and, well, life in general! During this planning phase, we not only think about the chart itself but also about the complementary elements that make a chart readable, such as axes, labels, and legends.

In this section, we'll introduce the margin convention, which is a way to facilitate allocating space for these different elements. We'll then discuss how to add axes to a visualization and the multiple SVG elements that comprise a D3 axis. We'll apply these concepts to the line chart shown in figure 4.1.

Before we get started, go to the code files of chapter 4. You can download them from the book's GitHub repository if you haven't already (http://mng.bz/Xqjv). In the `chapter_04` folder, the code files are organized by section. To get started with this chapter's exercise, open the `4.1-Margin_convention_and_axes/start` folder in your code editor, and start your local web server. Refer to appendix A if you need help setting up your local development environment. You can find more details about the project folder structure in the README file located at the root of this chapter's code files.

> **WARNING** When working with the chapter's code files, open only one `start` *or* one `end` folder in your code editor. If you open all the chapter's files at once and use the Live Server extension to serve the project, the path to the data file won't work as expected.

We'll start working in the file `line-chart.js` and load the weekly temperatures dataset using the `d3.csv()` method:

```
d3.csv("../data/weekly_temperature.csv");
```

In chapter 3, we explained that the type conversion performed by D3 when loading a tabular dataset can affect the type of the values. For example, the numbers from the original dataset become strings, and we need to turn them back into numbers to facilitate their manipulation. We've seen that the callback function of `d3.csv()`, where we have access to the data row by row, is a great place to perform such conversion. Here we'll introduce a little trick: instead of converting the numbers manually, we can call method `d3.autoType`. This function detects common data types, such as dates and numbers, and converts them into the corresponding JavaScript type:

```
d3.csv("../data/weekly_temperature.csv", d3.autoType);
```

Be aware that data types can be ambiguous and that `d3.autoType` sometimes picks the wrong type. For example, four-digit numbers, such as `2023`, can be both a number or a date. `d3.autoType` will opt for a number, but maybe that's not always what you want. For this reason, it's important to always double-check your data array once it's fully loaded. Observable has a great article on the topic if you want to learn more (https://observablehq.com/@d3/d3-autotype).

In the following snippet, we access the loaded dataset with a JavaScript Promise and log it into the console to confirm that the dates are formatted as JavaScript dates and the temperatures as numbers. You can see the result in figure 4.2:

```
d3.csv("../data/weekly_temperature.csv", d3.autoType).then(data => {
  console.log("temperature data", data);
});
```

```
▼ Array(53) ⊞
  ▼ 0:
      avg_temp_F: 39.3428571428571
    ▶ date: Fri Jan 01 2021 01:00:00 GMT+0100 (Central European Standard Time) {}
      max_temp_F: 43.2857142857143
      min_temp_F: 36.4285714285714
    ▶ [[Prototype]]: Object
  ▶ 1: {date: Fri Jan 08 2021 01:00:00 GMT+0100 (Central European Standard Time), max_temp_F: 42.2857142857143, avg_temp_F: 37.45714285714
  ▶ 2: {date: Fri Jan 15 2021 01:00:00 GMT+0100 (Central European Standard Time), max_temp_F: 45.1428571428571, avg_temp_F: 40.68571428571
  ▶ 3: {date: Fri Jan 22 2021 01:00:00 GMT+0100 (Central European Standard Time), max_temp_F: 37.8571428571429, avg_temp_F: 33.87142857142
  ▶ 4: {date: Fri Jan 29 2021 01:00:00 GMT+0100 (Central European Standard Time), max_temp_F: 35.8571428571429, avg_temp_F: 29.57142857142
  ▶ 5: {date: Fri Feb 05 2021 01:00:00 GMT+0100 (Central European Standard Time), max_temp_F: 34.7142857142857, avg_temp_F: 33.04285714285
  ▶ 6: {date: Fri Feb 12 2021 01:00:00 GMT+0100 (Central European Standard Time), max_temp_F: 35.4285714285714, avg_temp_F: 31.3, min_temp
  ▶ 7: {date: Fri Feb 19 2021 01:00:00 GMT+0100 (Central European Standard Time), max_temp_F: 42.7142857142857, avg_temp_F: 37.88571428571
  ▶ 8: {date: Fri Feb 26 2021 01:00:00 GMT+0100 (Central European Standard Time), max_temp_F: 45.8571428571429, avg_temp_F: 40.02857142857
  ▶ 9: {date: Fri Mar 05 2021 01:00:00 GMT+0100 (Central European Standard Time), max_temp_F: 48.5714285714286, avg_temp_F: 41, min_temp_F
  ▶ 10: {date: Fri Mar 12 2021 01:00:00 GMT+0100 (Central European Standard Time), max_temp_F: 48, avg_temp_F: 42.6142857142857, min_temp_
  ▶ 11: {date: Fri Mar 19 2021 01:00:00 GMT+0100 (Central European Standard Time), max_temp_F: 56, avg_temp_F: 47.0142857142857, min_temp_
  ▶ 12: {date: Fri Mar 26 2021 01:00:00 GMT+0100 (Central European Standard Time), max_temp_F: 63, avg_temp_F: 53.2714285714286, min_temp_
  • • •
```

Figure 4.2   Thanks to method `d3.autoType`, dates are formatted as JavaScript dates, and temperatures are formatted as numbers.

We used a JavaScript Promise to access the dataset because loading data is an asynchronous process (refer to chapter 3 if you need a refresher about loading and accessing data with D3). But now that we know our dataset is fully loaded and formatted correctly, we can start building our chart.

The `line-chart.js` file already contains a function named `drawLineChart()`, in which we'll create the line chart. Within the callback function of the JavaScript Promise, call function `drawLineChart()`, and pass the dataset as an argument:

```
d3.csv("../data/weekly_temperature.csv", d3.autoType).then(data => {
  console.log("temperature data", data);
  drawLineChart(data);
});
```

We're now ready to discuss the margin convention and apply it to our chart!

4.1.1   *The margin convention*

The D3 margin convention aims at reserving space around a chart for axes, labels, and the legends in a systematic and reusable way. This convention uses four margins: above, to the right side, below, and to the left side of the chart, as shown in figure 4.3. By stating these margins, we can know the position and the size of the area remaining for the core of the chart, which we'll call the *inner chart*.

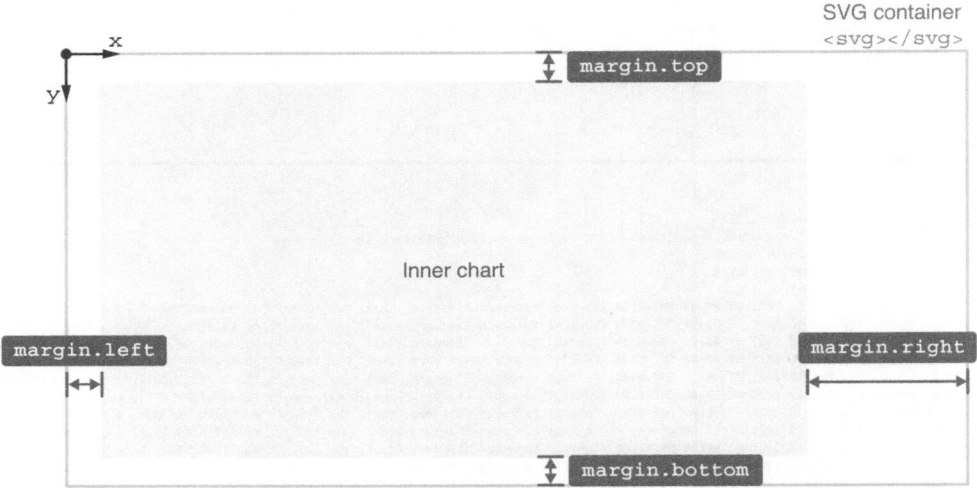

Figure 4.3   The D3 margin convention sets the value of the margins at the top, right, bottom, and left of a chart.

The margin values are declared in a margin object, composed of a top, right, bottom, and left margin. Let's create the margin object for our line chart. Inside function `drawLineChart()`, declare a constant named `margin`. As in the following snippet, give the top, right, bottom, and left margins the respective values of 40, 170, 25, and 40 px:

```
const drawLineChart = (data) => {
  const margin = {top: 40, right: 170, bottom: 25, left: 40};
};
```

Knowing in advance exactly how much space we'll need for the axes and labels usually isn't possible. We start with an educated guess and adjust them later if we need to. For example, look at the line chart in figure 4.1 or on the hosted project (http://mng.bz/ 5orB). You'll see that the labels displayed on the right side of the visualization are relatively long, hence the 170 px right margin. On the other hand, the axes' labels don't take much space, so the remaining margins can be much smaller.

Once our margin object is declared, we can start thinking about the size of the SVG container. Knowing the size of the SVG container and the margins, we can finally calculate two new constants named `innerWidth` and `innerHeight`, which represent the width and the height of the inner chart. These dimensions are shown in figure 4.4.

The inner chart's width corresponds to the width of the SVG container minus the margins on the left and the right. If the SVG container has a width of 1,000 px and margins of 170 px and 40 px on each side, 790 px remains for the inner chart. Similarly, if the SVG container's height is 500 px, we calculate the inner chart's height by

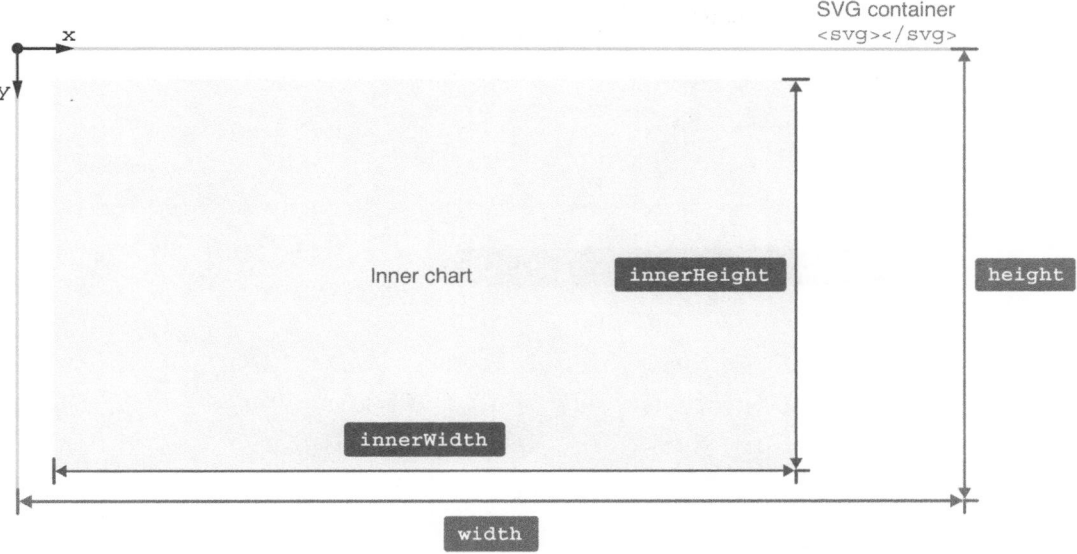

Figure 4.4 Knowing the dimensions of the SVG container and the margins, we can calculate the inner chart's width and height.

subtracting the top and the bottom margins from the total height, hence 435 px. By making the constants `innerWidth` and `innerHeight` proportional to the margins, we ensure that they will automatically adjust if we need to change the margins later:

```
const margin = {top: 40, right: 170, bottom: 25, left: 40};
const width = 1000;
const height = 500;
const innerWidth = width - margin.left - margin.right;
const innerHeight = height - margin.top - margin.bottom;
```

Let's now append the SVG container of our line chart. Still working inside function `drawLineChart()`, append an SVG element to the div with an id of `line-chart`, which already exists in the `index.html` file, and set its `viewBox` attribute using the `width` and `height` constants. You can also temporarily apply a border to the SVG element to help you see the area in which you're working (if you need a refresher on appending elements to the DOM or setting their attributes and styles, refer to chapter 2):

```
const svg = d3.select("#line-chart")
  .append("svg")
  .attr("viewBox", `0, 0, ${width}, ${height}`);
```

We've previously declared the margins that will dictate the area reserved for the inner chart. Knowing that the coordinate system of the SVG container starts at its top-left corner, every element of the inner chart will have to be moved toward its reserved area. Instead of applying this displacement to every element, we can wrap the inner chart within an SVG group and apply a translation only to that group. As you can see in figure 4.5, this strategy creates a new coordinate system for the inner chart.

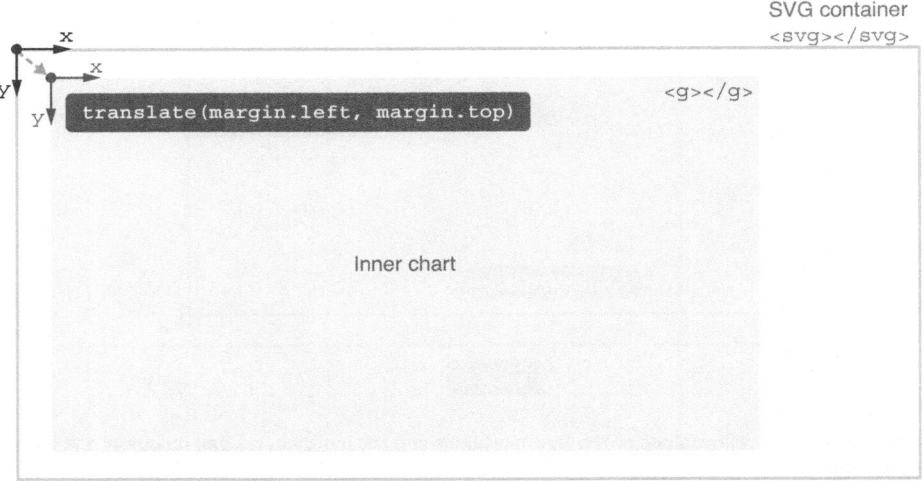

Figure 4.5   Translation applied to the SVG group that will contain the inner chart, creating a new coordinate system for the elements contained in the inner chart

To put this strategy into action, we append a group to the SVG container. We then apply a translation to the group based on the left and top margins. Finally, we save the SVG group into a constant named `innerChart` that we'll use to build the line chart later:

```
const innerChart = svg
  .append("g")
  .attr("transform", `translate(${margin.left}, ${margin.top})`);
```

The main advantage of the margin convention and the strategy presented here is that once implemented, we don't need to think about it anymore. We can go on to create our axes and chart while knowing that an area is preserved for the labels, legends, and other complementary information.

4.1.2   *Generating axes*

With our margin convention established, we're ready to add axes to the chart. Axes are an essential part of data visualizations. They serve as a reference for the viewer to understand the numbers and categories represented.

If you look at the line chart in figure 4.1 or on the hosted project (http://mng.bz/ 5orB), you'll see two axes. The horizontal axis, also called the x-axis, shows the position of each month. The vertical axis, or y-axis, serves as a reference for the temperature in Fahrenheit.

In D3, we create axes with the `axis()` component generator. This generator takes a scale as an input and returns the SVG elements that compose an axis as an output. If you remember the discussion we had about scales in chapter 3, you know they translate values from the domain into values from the range that we can then use to draw on the screen. For our line chart, scales will calculate for us the horizontal position of each date from the dataset or the vertical position of their related temperatures.

DECLARING THE SCALES

The first step to creating axes is actually to declare their scales. First, we need a scale that will position the dates horizontally. That's precisely the role of D3's time scale `d3.scaleTime()` (see appendix B for help selecting a D3 scale). The time scale is part of the first family of scales discussed in chapter 3. It takes a continuous input and returns a continuous output. The time scale behaves very similarly to the linear scale used in chapter 3 with the only difference being that it manipulates time-related data.

Let's declare our time scale and name it `xScale` because it will be responsible for positioning elements along the x-axis. The domain of our scale extends from the first to the last date in our dataset. In the following snippet, we use `d3.min()` and `d3.max()`, two methods from the d3-array module, to find these values.

The range covered by the scale extends along the horizontal space available within the inner chart (see figure 4.5). In the coordinate system of the inner chart, it means that the range extends from 0 to the `innerWidth` calculated earlier (refer to chapter 3 if you need a refresher on declaring the domain and range of D3 scales):

```
const firstDate = d3.min(data, d => d.date);
const lastDate = d3.max(data, d => d.date);
const xScale = d3.scaleTime()
  .domain([firstDate, lastDate])
  .range([0, innerWidth]);
```

The temperature, distributed along the y-axis, also requires a scale with a continuous input and output. A linear scale will be perfect here because we want the temperature and the vertical position on the line chart to be linearly proportional.

In the following snippet, we declare our temperature scale and name it `yScale` because it will be responsible for positioning elements along the y-axis. Here we want our y-axis to start at 0, so we pass `0` as the first value of the domain. Although the minimum temperature in the dataset is somewhere around 26°F, starting the y-axis at 0 is often a good idea and, in our case, will allow us to see the evolution of temperature correctly. But like most things in life, this isn't a hard rule, and there's no right or wrong answer for this chart, especially because the 0 in Fahrenheit isn't an absolute 0.

We pass the maximum temperature from the dataset as the second value of the domain. We find this value by interrogating column `max_temp_F` from the dataset with function `d3.max()`.

The range of our scale extends along the height of the inner chart. Because vertical values are calculated from top to bottom in the SVG coordinate system, the range starts at `innerHeight`, the position of the bottom-left corner of the inner chart, and ends at `0`, the position corresponding to its top-left corner:

```
const maxTemp = d3.max(data, d => d.max_temp_F);
const yScale = d3.scaleLinear()
  .domain([0, maxTemp])
  .range([innerHeight, 0]);
```

APPENDING THE AXES

With our scales initialized, we're ready to append the axes. D3 has four axis generators—`axisTop()`, `axisRight()`, `axisBottom()`, and `axisLeft()`—that respectively create the components of the top, right, bottom, and left axes. They are all part of the d3-axis module.

We mentioned that axis generator functions take a scale as input. For example, to create the bottom axis of our line chart, we call generator `axisBottom()` and pass `xScale` as an argument because this scale is responsible for distributing data along the bottom axis. We save the generator in a constant named `bottomAxis`:

```
const bottomAxis = d3.axisBottom(xScale);
```

The axis generator is a function that constructs the elements composing an axis. For these elements to appear on the screen, we need to call the axis generator from within a D3 selection using the `call()` method. In the following snippet, note how we've used the `innerChart` selection and appended a group element into it before calling the axis generator. The group has a class name of `axis-x`, which will help us position and style the axis later:

```
const bottomAxis = d3.axisBottom(xScale);

innerChart
  .append("g")
    .attr("class", "axis-x")
    .call(bottomAxis);
```

Take a look at the generated axis in your browser. By default, D3 axes are displayed at the origin of the selection—in this case, the top-left corner of the inner chart region, as shown in figure 4.6. We can move the axis to the bottom of the chart by applying a translation to the SVG group that contains the axis. Remember that transformations applied to a group are inherited by all of the group's children. In the following snippet, we translate the group containing the axis elements down with a value corresponding to the height of the inner chart:

```
const bottomAxis = d3.axisBottom(xScale);
innerChart
  .append("g")
    .attr("class", "axis-x")
    .attr("transform", `translate(0, ${innerHeight})`)
    .call(bottomAxis);
```

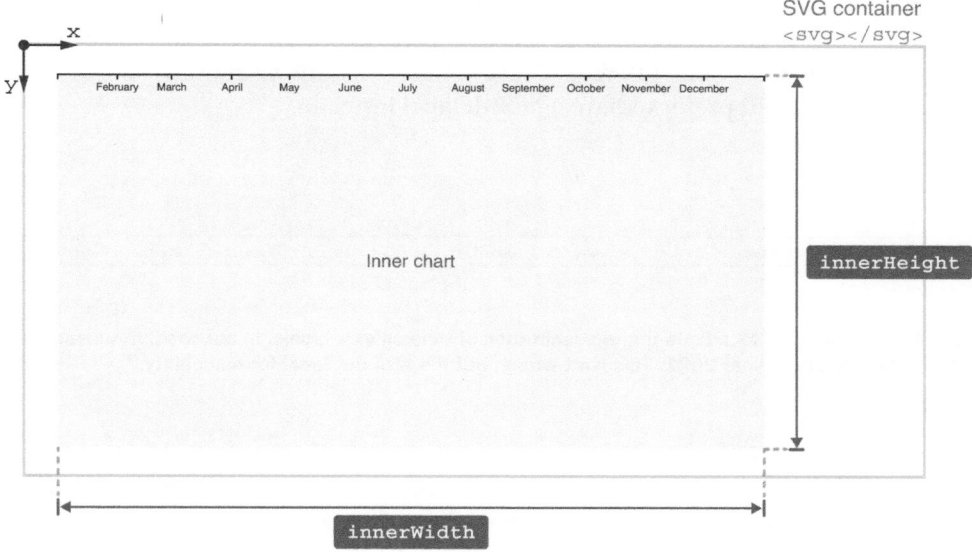

Figure 4.6 By default, D3 axes are generated at the origin of the selection, which is the top-left corner of the inner chart in this example. We need to apply a translation to move them to the desired location.

Another thing that we'll want to change is the formatting of the axis labels. By default, D3 adapts the representation of time on axes, displaying hours, days, months, or years labels based on the domain. But this default formatting doesn't always provide the labels we're looking for. Fortunately, D3 offers multiple methods to change the format of labels.

First, we note that the x-axis has labels for the months of February to December, which is great, except it doesn't have one for January. Depending on the time zone in which you live, the first date might not be exactly the first of January at midnight, which prevents D3 from recognizing it as the start of our first month. Because our dataset isn't dynamic, hardcoding the `firstDate` variable is a reasonable solution. To do so, we'll use the JavaScript `Date()` constructor.

In the following code snippet, `firstDate` becomes a new `Date()` object. Between the parentheses, we first declare the year (`2021`), the month (`00` because the month index is zero-indexed), and the day (`01`), and then optionally follow it with hours, minutes, and seconds (`0, 0, 0`):

```
const firstDate = new Date(2021, 00, 01, 0, 0, 0);
const lastDate = d3.max(data, d => d.date);
const xScale = d3.scaleTime()
  .domain([firstDate, lastDate])
  .range([0, innerWidth]);
```

If you save your project, you'll see that we now have a label at the location of January 1. But the label only gives us the year 2021, as shown in figure 4.7. This isn't wrong, given that `Fri Jan 01 2021 00:00:00` corresponds to the very start of the year 2021, but we would prefer to have a month label instead.

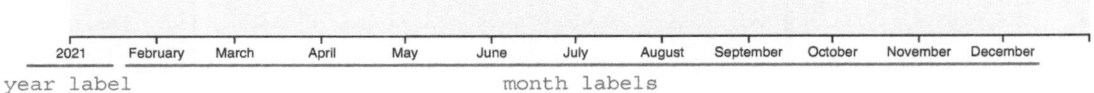

Figure 4.7   By default, D3 adapts the representation of time on axis labels. In our case, it represents January 1st as the beginning of the year 2021. This isn't wrong, but it's also not ideal for readability.

We can also change the format of the axis labels with method `axis.tickFormat()`, available in the d3-axis module. *Ticks* are the short vertical lines that you see on the axis. They are often, but not necessarily, accompanied by a tick label.

Let's say that we want our tick labels to be the abbreviated month names. In D3, we can format time-related values with method `d3.timeFormat()` from the d3-time-format module. This method accepts a format as an argument, for example, `%b` for the abbreviation of a month name. You can see the full list of available formats in the module.

In the following snippet, we chain the `tickFormat()` method to the bottom axis declared earlier and pass the time format as an argument:

```
const bottomAxis = d3.axisBottom(xScale)
  .tickFormat(d3.timeFormat("%b"));
```

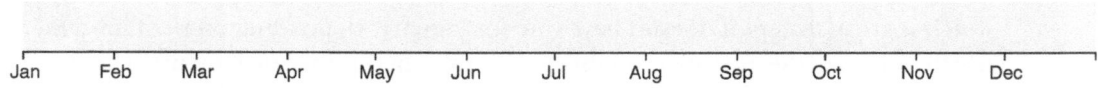

Figure 4.8   Bottom axis labels formatted with the abbreviated name of each month

Our labels are now formatted properly! They mark the beginning of each month, which isn't bad, but we could improve readability by centering the month labels between their respective ticks to suggest that each month extends from one tick to the next one.

To change the position of the tick labels, we first need to select them. Open your browser's inspector, and take a closer look at the SVG elements generated by D3 for the axis. First, we have a `path` element with the class `domain` that draws a horizontal line across the range (or the domain's representation). This path includes two outer ticks, that is, the short vertical lines at each end of the shape, as you can see in figure

4.9. The ticks and labels of the axis are composed of a line and a text element, organized into SVG groups with a class of `tick`. These SVG groups are translated along the axis to set the positions of their lines and text elements. The type and class of the elements created by the axis generator are part of D3's public API. You can use them to customize the axis appearance.

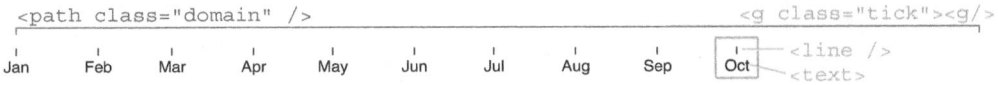

Figure 4.9 SVG elements composing an axis

With that structure in mind, we can select all the labels of the x-axis with the selector `".axis-x text"`, meaning that we grab every text element in the group that has the `axis-x` class. We then perform a few adjustments. First, we move the text elements down by 10 px using their `y` attribute. This increased vertical whitespace will improve readability. We also set their `font-family` to "Roboto", the font we already used in the project. By default, D3 sets the `font-family` of axis to "sans-serif", preventing the labels from inheriting the `font-family` property of the project's root. Finally, we increase their font-size to 14 px.

For separation of concerns purposes, these last two style adjustments should preferably be handled from a CSS file. But here we do it with D3 to simplify the instructions:

```
d3.selectAll(".axis-x text")
  .attr("y", "10px")
  .style("font-family", "Roboto, sans-serif")
  .style("font-size", "14px");
```

To center the month labels between their corresponding ticks, we'll use the `x` attribute. Because each month has a different length (between 28 and 31 days), we need to find the median position between the first day of the month and the first day of the following month for each label. Note that D3 already set the `text-anchor` property to "middle" on `g.axis-x`.

We know that the data attached by D3 to each label corresponds to the first day of the month. In the following snippet, we find the next month by applying the JavaScript method `getMonth()` to the current month or the value attached to the label. This method returns a number between 0 and 11, that is, 0 for January and 11 for December. We can then create a new JavaScript date by passing the year, next month, and the first day of the month to the `Date()` object. As mentioned in chapter 3, the first parameter provided by the callback function, often named `d`, corresponds to each row from the bound dataset. It's as if we were looping through the data array with a `forEach()` method.

Finally, we calculate the median distance between the start of the month and the start of the following month using xScale. Once completed, your axis should look like the one in figure 4.10:

```
d3.selectAll(".axis-x text")
  .attr("x", d => {
    const currentMonth = d;
    const nextMonth = new Date(2021, currentMonth.getMonth() + 1, 1);
    return (xScale(nextMonth) - xScale(currentMonth)) / 2;
  })
  .attr("y", "10px")
  .style("font-family", "Roboto, sans-serif")
  .style("font-size", "14px");
```

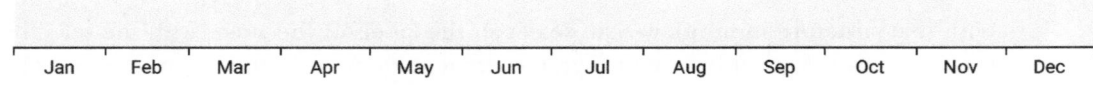

Figure 4.10   Formatted x-axis with the month labels centered between their respective ticks

That was a lot of manipulation, but it should give you an overview of the different ways you can customize D3 axes.

We'll now add the y-axis, for which the steps will be much more straightforward. We use the axis generator d3.axisLeft() because we want to position the y-axis on the left side of the chart. We pass yScale as an argument and save the axis in a constant named leftAxis:

```
const leftAxis = d3.axisLeft(yScale);
```

Once again, we want to add the axis to the inner chart. We append a group to the inner chart selection, give it a class of axis-y, and call leftAxis:

```
const leftAxis = d3.axisLeft(yScale);
innerChart
  .append("g")
  .attr("class", "axis-y")
  .call(leftAxis);
```

If you save your project and look at it in the browser, you'll see that the y-axis is already positioned correctly, as in figure 4.11. All we have to do is change the labels' font and increase their size. In the following snippet, we select all the text elements inside the group with the class axis-y. We move them slightly to the left for better readability using their x attribute and set their font-family and font-size properties:

```
d3.selectAll(".axis-y text")
  .attr("x", "-5px")
  .style("font-family", "Roboto, sans-serif")
  .style("font-size", "14px");
```

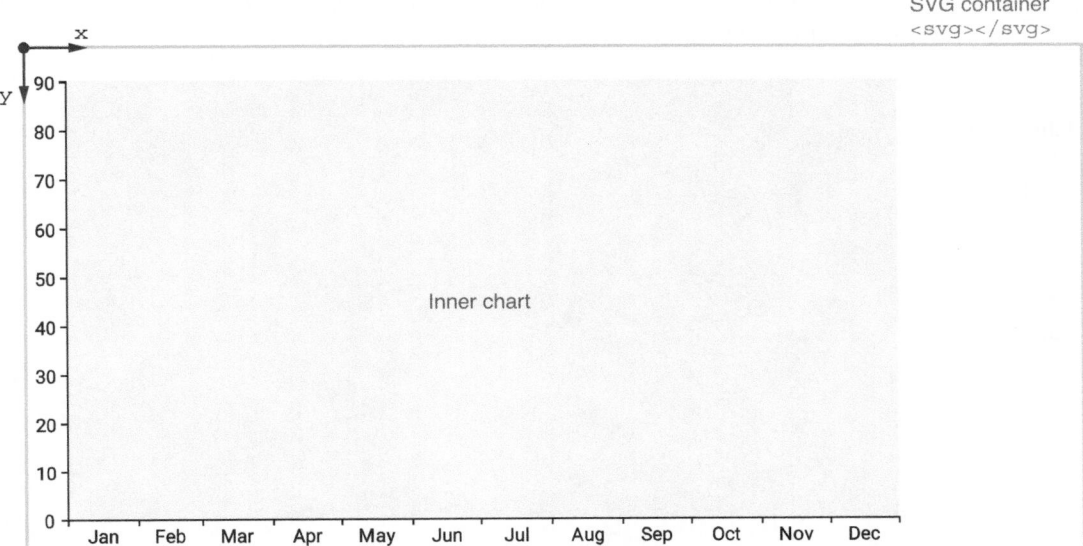

Figure 4.11 Completed x-axis and y-axis

You might have noticed the code repetition we had to do to set both axis labels' `font-family` and `font-size` properties. In a learning context, that's not a big deal, but we usually try to avoid such repetition in professional projects. A better solution, mentioned earlier, is to control these styles from a CSS file. Another solution is to apply them using a combined selector, as shown here:

```
d3.selectAll(".axis-x text, .axis-y text")
  .style("font-family", "Roboto, sans-serif")
  .style("font-size", "14px");
```

ADDING AXIS LABELS

We've completed our axes, but there's still one thing we should do to help readers understand our chart. The tick labels on the x-axis are self-explanatory, but the ones on the y-axis aren't. We know that they vary between 0 and 90, but we have no idea what they represent.

We can fix that by adding a label to the axis. In D3 projects, labels are simply text elements, so all we have to do is append a text element to the SVG container. We set its content to `"Temperature (°F)"` and its vertical position to 20 px below the origin of the SVG container:

```
svg
  .append("text")
  .text("Temperature (°F)")
  .attr("y", 20);
```

That's it! Your project should now look like the one in figure 4.12. In the next section, we'll draw the line chart.

Figure 4.12   **Completed axes and labels**

4.2   *Drawing a line chart*

We're now ready to build one of the most common data visualizations: a line chart. Line charts are composed of lines connecting data points or curves interpolating these data points. They are often used to show the evolution of a phenomenon over time. In D3, these lines and curves are built with SVG path elements whose shapes are determined by their d attributes. In chapter 1, we discussed how the d attribute is made of a series of commands that dictate how to draw a shape. We also said that it can quickly become complex. Thankfully, the d3-shape module provides line and curve generator functions that calculate the d attribute for us, easing the creation of line charts.

In this section, we'll draw a line/curve showing the evolution of the average temperature in New York City during the year 2021, like the one you can see on the hosted project (http://mng.bz/5orB) or in figure 4.1 shown earlier. But first, let's display each data point on the screen. Although this step isn't necessary for drawing a line chart, it will help us understand how D3's line generator works.

Working inside function drawLineChart(), we use the data-binding pattern to create one circle for each row in the weekly_temperature.csv dataset. We append these circles to the innerChart selection and give them a radius of 4 px. We then calculate their position attributes (cx and cy) using the x and y scales.

If you remember our discussion on data binding from chapter 3, you know that we can access the data bound to each circle with an accessor function. In the following snippet, d exposes the datum attached to each circle. Because data is a JavaScript object, we can access the date or the average temperature with dot notation. Refer to chapter 3, section 3.3.1, if you need to review this concept.

Note that we've declared a separate color constant named "aubergine" and used it to set the fill attribute of the circles. We'll reuse the same color a few times during this project, so having it in a constant will be handy. Feel free to use any color of your preference:

```
const aubergine = "#75485E";
innerChart
  .selectAll("circle")          Data-binding pattern to append one
  .data(data)                   circle for each row in the dataset
  .join("circle")
    .attr("r", 4)
    .attr("cx", d => xScale(d.date))        Use the scales to position the data
    .attr("cy", d => yScale(d.avg_temp_F))  points based on their related data.
    .attr("fill", aubergine);
```

Save your project, and take a look at the circles in your browser. They should be positioned between 29°F and 80°F and form a dome-like shape, as in figure 4.13.

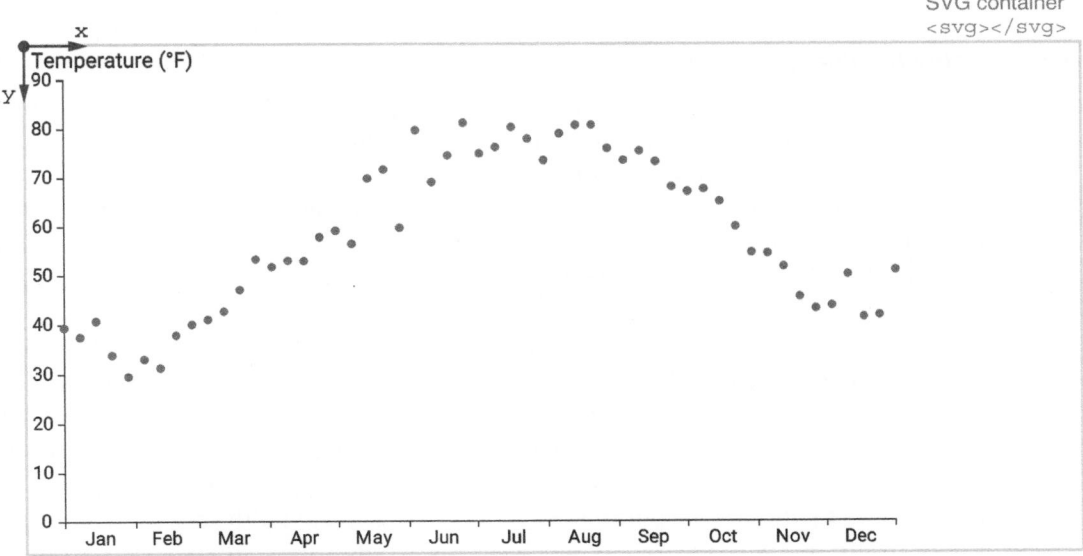

Figure 4.13   Data points of the evolution of average temperature over time

You can now draw scatterplots

A cool thing to point out at this stage is that even without noticing it, you now know how to draw scatterplots! A scatterplot is simply a chart showing a collection of data points positioned along the x-axis and y-axis and visualizing the relationship between two or more variables.

You know how to draw axes and how to position data points on the screen based on their bound data, so you can totally build a scatterplot! That's what's so cool about D3. You don't have to learn how to create specific charts. Instead, you build visualizations by generating and assembling building blocks. For a scatterplot, those building blocks can be as simple as two axes and a set of circles. In chapter 7, we'll build a scatterplot where the area of the circles changes based on a variable.

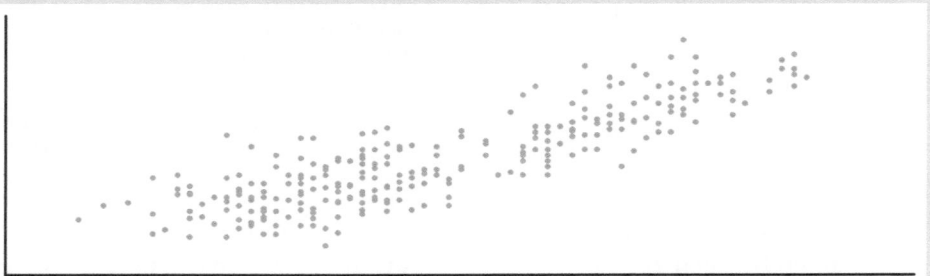

Example of a scatterplot

4.2.1   *Using the line generator*

Now that we clearly see the position of each data point, it will be easier to introduce D3's line generator. Line generator `d3.line()` is a function that takes the horizontal and vertical position of each data point as an input and returns the d attribute of an SVG path, or polyline, passing through these data points as an output. We usually chain the line generator with two accessor functions, `x()` and `y()`, respectively taking the data point's horizontal and vertical position as an argument, as shown in figure 4.14.

Let's declare a line generator function for our line chart. We first call method `d3.line()` and chain in with the `x()` and `y()` accessor functions. The `x()` accessor function takes the horizontal position of each data point as an argument. If we loop through our data as we've been doing so far, we can use the parameter d that gives us access to each datum or each individual data point. The horizontal position of the data points corresponds to the date the points represent and is calculated with `xScale()`. Similarly, the vertical position of the data points is proportional to the average temperature on

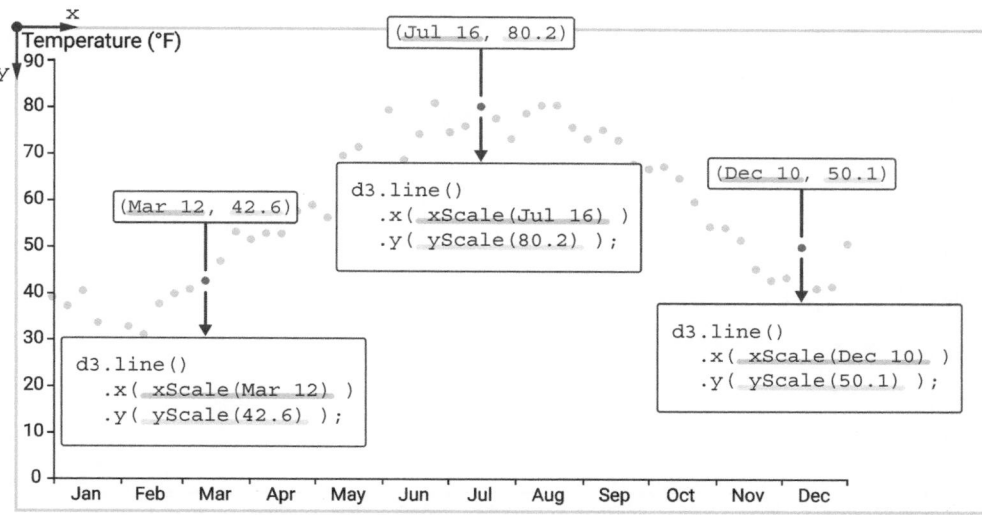

Figure 4.14 Line generator `d3.line()` is used in combination with two accessor functions, `x()` and `y()`, that respectively take the horizontal and vertical position of each data point as arguments.

that day and is returned by `yScale()`. We store the line generator function in a constant named `lineGenerator` so that we can call it later:

```
const lineGenerator = d3.line()
  .x(d => xScale(d.date))
  .y(d => yScale(d.avg_temp_F));
```

**Horizontal position
of each data point**

**Vertical position of
each data point**

Then we append a path element to the inner chart and set its `d` attribute by calling the line generator and passing the dataset as an argument.

By default, SVG paths have a black fill. If we want to see only a line, we need to set the `fill` attribute to `none` or `transparent` and set the `stroke` attribute to the color of our choice; here, the color stored in the `aubergine` constant. This stroke will become our line chart, as you can see in figure 4.15:

```
innerChart
  .append("path")
    .attr("d", lineGenerator(data))
```

**Call the line generator, and pass
the dataset as an argument.**

```
.attr("fill", "none")
.attr("stroke", aubergine);
```

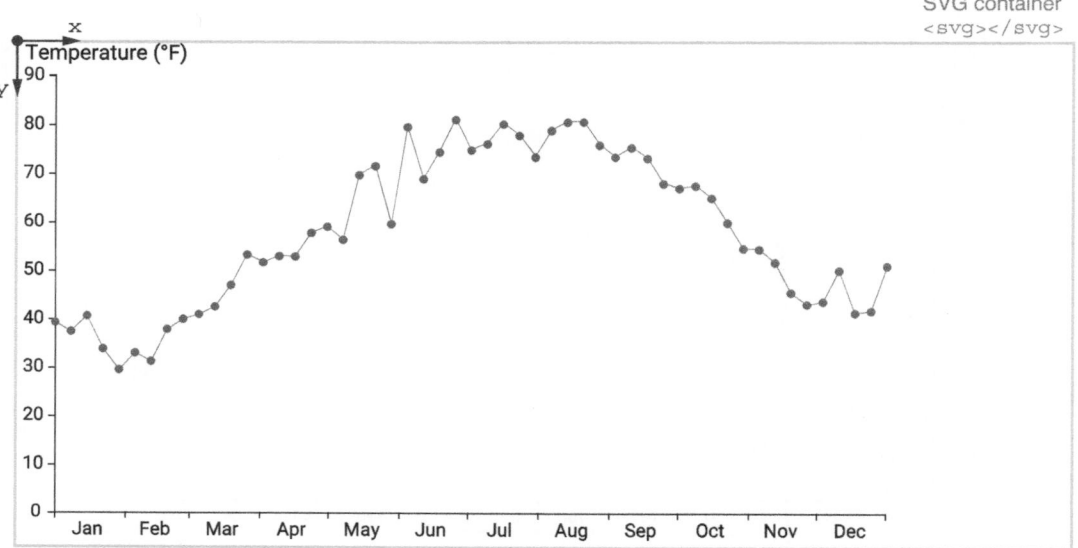

Figure 4.15   SVG path created with the line generator and passing through each data point, resulting in a line chart

4.2.2   *Interpolating data points into a curve*

In cases like our line chart, where the discrete data points cover the whole spectrum of data, representing the data points with a simple line is a good solution. But sometimes, we need to interpolate the data between points, for which D3 provides a variety of interpolation functions that generate curves.

Curve generators are used as an accessor function of d3.line(). To transform the line generator declared in the previous section into a curve generator, we simply chain the curve() accessor function and pass one of D3's interpolators. In the following snippet, we use interpolator d3.curveCatmullRom, which produces a cubic spline (a smooth and flexible shape passing through each data point and calculated with a third order polynomial function). The result of the following is shown in figure 4.16:

```
const curveGenerator = d3.line()
  .x(d => xScale(d.date))
  .y(d => yScale(d.avg_temp_F)
  .curve(d3.curveCatmullRom);
```

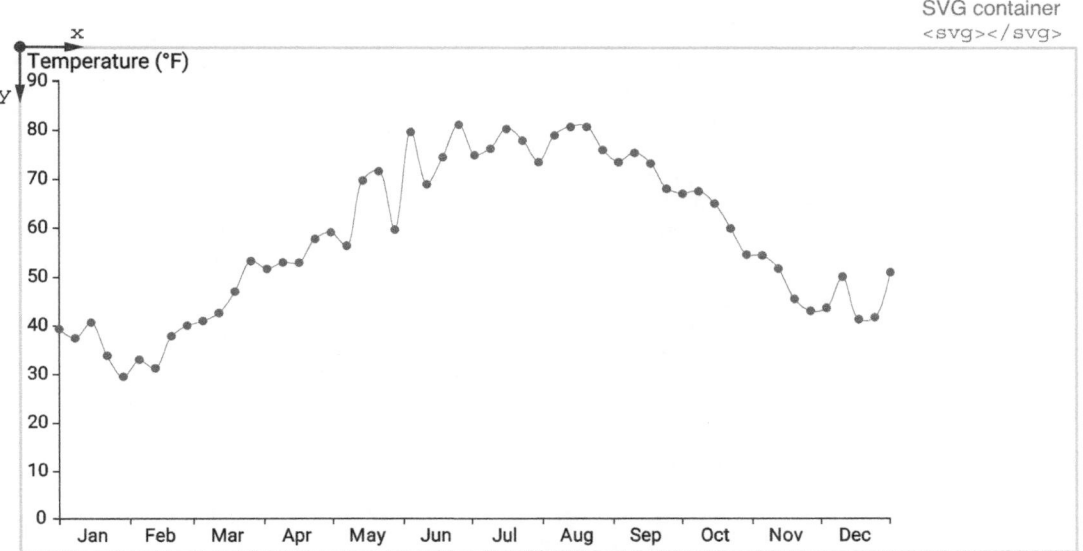

Figure 4.16   Line chart with a curve interpolation using a Catmull-Rom spline

What's the best interpolation?

Interpolations modify the data representation, and different interpolation functions create different visualizations. Data can be visualized in various ways, which are all correct from a programming perspective. But it's up to us to make sure the information we're visualizing reflects the actual phenomena.

Because data visualization deals with the visual representation of statistical princi- ples, it's subject to all the dangers of misusing statistics. The interpolation of lines is particularly vulnerable to misuse because it changes a clunky-looking line into a smooth, "natural" line.

In figure 4.17, you can see the same line chart traced with different curve interpola- tions and appreciate how they affect the visual representation. Choosing an adequate interpolation function depends greatly on the data you're working with. In our case, `d3.curveBasis` underestimates the sudden variations of temperature, while `d3.curveBundle` is meant to straighten a curve and reduce its variation, which isn't adequate for our data. If we didn't draw the data points on the chart, we'd have no idea that the curve doesn't represent them accurately. That's why it's important to select and test your curve interpolation function carefully.

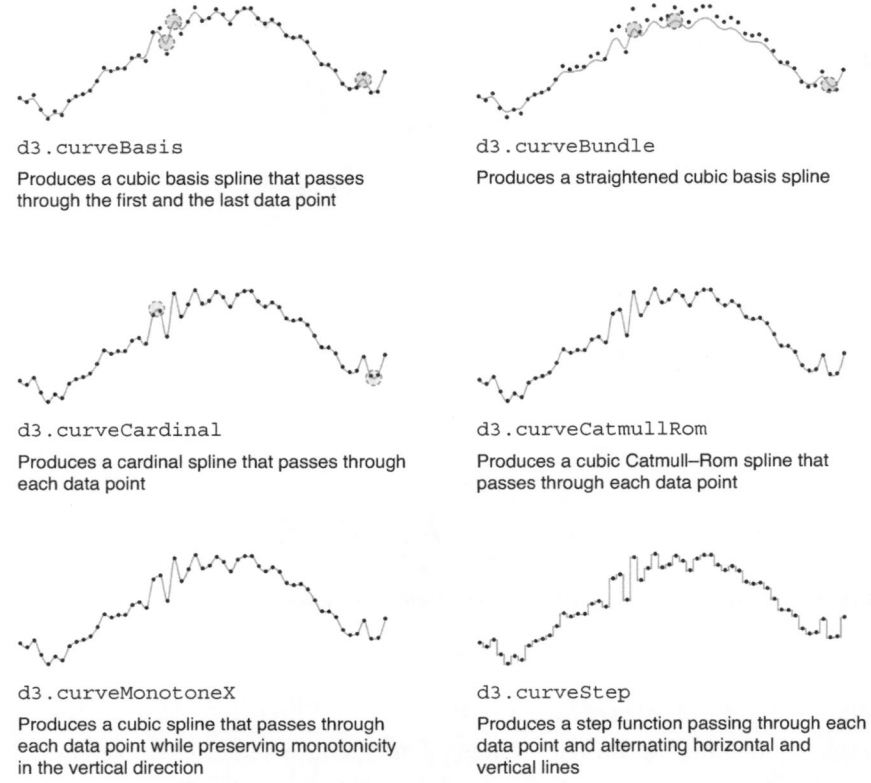

d3.curveBasis

Produces a cubic basis spline that passes
through the first and the last data point

d3.curveBundle

Produces a straightened cubic basis spline

d3.curveCardinal

Produces a cardinal spline that passes through
each data point

d3.curveCatmullRom

Produces a cubic Catmull–Rom spline that
passes through each data point

d3.curveMonotoneX

Produces a cubic spline that passes through
each data point while preserving monotonicity
in the vertical direction

d3.curveStep

Produces a step function passing through each
data point and alternating horizontal and
vertical lines

Figure 4.17   Different curve interpolations and how they modify the representation of data

On the other hand, functions d3.curveMonotoneX and d3.curveCatmullRom create curves that closely follow the data points and are similar to the original line chart. d3.curveStep can also provide an interesting interpretation of the data when the context is appropriate. The list of curve interpolations illustrated in figure 4.17 isn't exhaustive, and some of these interpolators also accept parameters that affect the shape of the final curve. Refer to the d3-shape module for all the available options.

You now know how to draw line charts with D3! To recap, we first need to initialize a line generator function and set its x() and y() accessor functions, as stated in figure 4.18. These will be responsible for calculating each data point's horizontal and vertical position. Then we can choose to turn the line into a curve by chaining the curve() accessor function and selecting an interpolation. Finally, we append an SVG path element to our chart and set its d attribute by calling the line generator and passing the data as an argument. In chapter 7, we'll make this line chart interactive with a tooltip. Feel free to go directly to that chapter if that's something you'd like to learn right away!

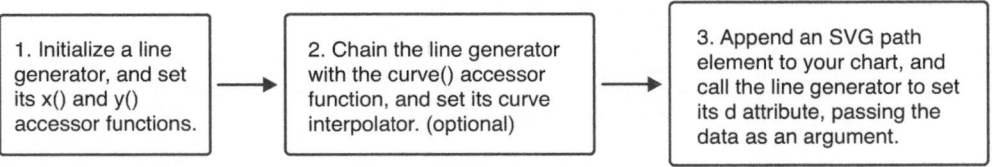

Figure 4.18 Steps to create a line chart

4.3   Drawing an area

In this section, we'll add an area behind our line chart that shows the range between the minimum and maximum temperatures for each date. The process of drawing an area in D3 is very similar to the one used to draw a line. Like lines, areas are created with SVG path elements, and D3 provides us with a handy area generator function, d3.area(), to calculate the d attribute of that path.

One thing to note before we get started is that we want to display the area *behind* the line chart. Because elements are drawn on the screen in the same order they are appended inside the SVG parent, the code to draw the area should be added to the JavaScript file *before* the code that creates the line chart.

4.3.1   Using the area generator

Let's first declare an area generator function and store it in a constant named area-Generator. As you can observe in the following snippet, the area generator requires at least three accessor functions. The first one, x(), is responsible for calculating the horizontal position of the data points, exactly like with the line generator. But now we don't just have one set of data points, but two: one along the lower edge of the area and another one on its upper edge, hence the accessor functions y0() and y1(). Note that in our case, the data points on the lower and upper edges of the area share the same horizontal positions:

```
const areaGenerator = d3.area()
  .x(d => xScale(d.date))
  .y0(d => yScale(d.min_temp_F))
  .y1(d => yScale(d.max_temp_F));
```

Figure 4.19 might help you visualize the lower and upper boundaries of the area and how the area generator computes the data related to the area.

As we did for the line chart, we interpolate the area's boundaries into curves by chaining the curve() accessor function to the area generator. Here we also use the same curve interpolator function, d3.curveCatmullRom:

```
const areaGenerator = d3.area()
  .x(d => xScale(d.date))
  .y0(d => yScale(d.min_temp_F))
  .y1(d => yScale(d.max_temp_F))
  .curve(d3.curveCatmullRom);
```

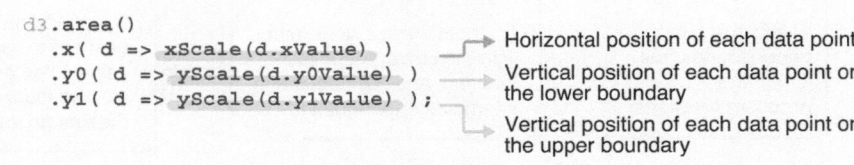

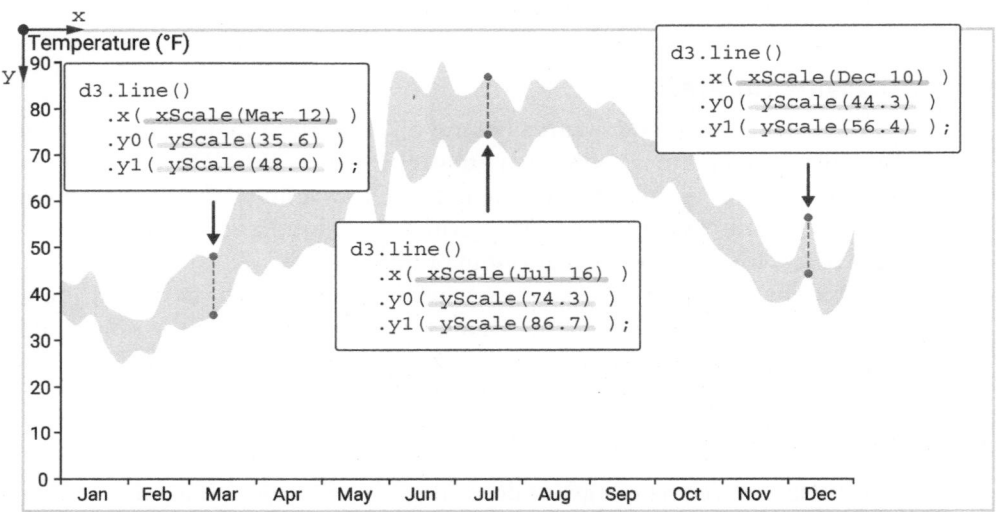

Figure 4.19   Area generator `d3.area()` **is used in combination with three or more accessor functions. To draw the area between the minimum and the maximum temperatures, we use** `x()`**,** `y0()`**, and** `y1()`**. The first one calculates the horizontal position of each data point, the second the vertical position of the data points on the lower boundary (here, the minimum temperature), and the third one the vertical position of the data points on the upper edge (here, the maximum temperature).**

Once the area generator is ready, all we need to do is append an SVG `path` element to the inner chart. To set its `d` attribute, we call the area generator and pass the dataset as an argument. The rest is related to aesthetics. We set the `fill` attribute to the aubergine color constant declared earlier and the `fill-opacity` to 20% to ensure that the contrast is sufficient between the area and the line chart, as you can see in figure 4.20. Note that the declaration of the aubergine constant needs to happen before we use it to set the fill of the area:

```
innerChart
  .append("path")
    .attr("d", areaGenerator(data))
    .attr("fill", aubergine)
    .attr("fill-opacity", 0.2);
```

As you can see, the process of drawing an area is very similar to the one of drawing a line. The main difference is that a line has only one set of data points between which

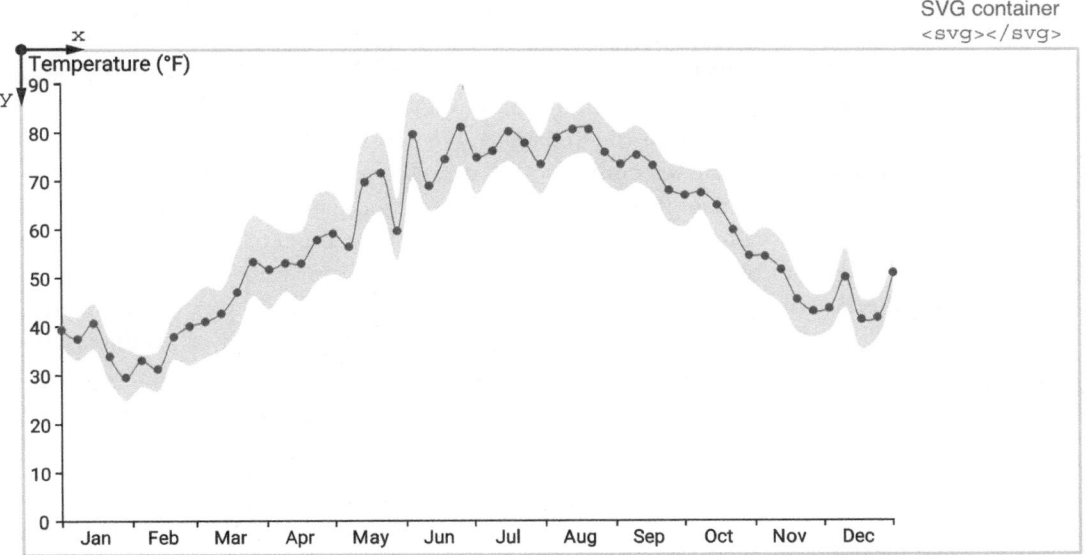

Figure 4.20   Line chart of the average temperature combined with an area showing the variation between the minimum and the maximum temperatures

the line is drawn, while an area is a region between two edges, with one set of data points for each edge. This is why the line generator requires only two accessor functions, x() and y(), while the area generator needs at least three, in our case, x(), y0(), and y1(), as explained in figure 4.21.

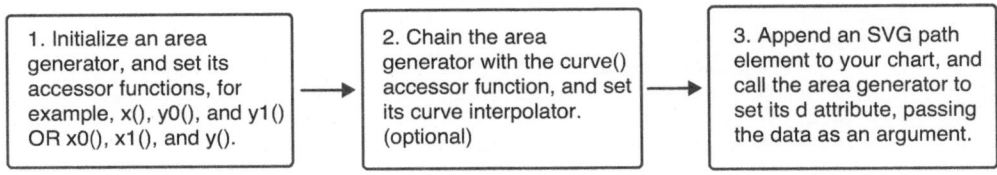

Figure 4.21   Steps to create an area

4.3.2   *Enhancing readability with labels*

We now have a line chart of the average temperature in New York City for the year 2021, combined with an area showing the variation between the minimum and the maximum temperatures. It looks pretty good already, but we need to ensure that the people who will see this chart will easily understand what the line and the area mean. Labels are an excellent tool for that!

We know that labels are simply SVG text elements that we position over our visualizations. Here we'll create three labels, one for the average temperature that we'll place at the end of the line chart, one for the minimum temperature positioned below the area, and one for the maximum temperature placed above the area.

Let's start with the label for the line chart. We first append an SVG `text` element to the inner chart and set its content to "Average temperature" using the `text()` method. We then calculate its position, controlled by the attributes x and y.

We want the label to be positioned at the end of the line chart or just after its last data point. We can obtain that position by passing the `lastDate` constant, calculated earlier when we declared our scales, to `xScale()`. We also add 10 px of extra padding.

For the vertical position, we don't already have a constant that gives us the last temperature value. Still, we can find the last row in the dataset with `data[data.length - 1]`, and use the dot notation to access the average temperature. We pass this value to the `yScale()` and obtain the vertical position of the label. We finally reuse the color constant aubergine for the color of the text, controlled by its `fill` attribute:

```
innerChart
  .append("text")
    .text("Average temperature")
    .attr("x", xScale(lastDate) + 10)
    .attr("y", yScale(data[data.length - 1].avg_temp_F))
    .attr("fill", aubergine);
```

If you save your project and look at it in the browser, you'll observe that the bottom of the label is vertically aligned with the center of the last data point on the line chart. By default, the baseline of SVG text is positioned at the bottom of the text, as shown in figure 4.22. We can change this with the dominant-baseline attribute. In the following snippet, we give this attribute a value of `middle` to shift the baseline to the vertical center of the text:

```
innerChart
  .append("text")
    .text("Average temperature")
    .attr("x", xScale(lastDate) + 10)
    .attr("y", yScale(data[data.length - 1].avg_temp_F))
    .attr("dominant-baseline", "middle")
    .attr("fill", aubergine);
```

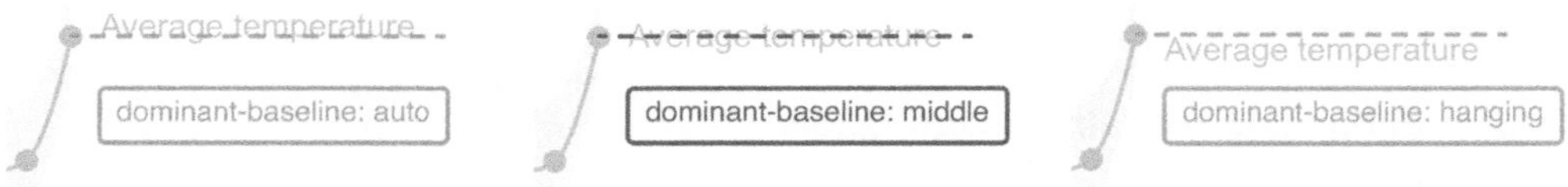

Figure 4.22   The y **attribute of SVG text sets the vertical position of its baseline, which by default is positioned at the bottom of the text. We can change that with the** dominant-baseline **attribute. If we give this attribute the value** "middle"**, the baseline of the text is shifted to its vertical middle, while the value** "hanging" **shifts the baseline to the top of the text.**

We'll then add a label for the lower boundary of the area, which represents the evolution of the minimum temperature. The strategy is very similar. We first append an SVG text element and give it a content of "Minimum temperature".

For its position, we opt for the last downward protuberance, which corresponds to the third to last data point. We pass the values of this data point to our scales to find its position and move the label down by 20 px and right by 13 px. These numbers were found simply by moving the label around until we found a position that looked right. The inspector tool of the browser is a great place to test such minor adjustments. Note that we've set the `dominant-baseline` of the label to `hanging`. As you've seen in figure 4.22, this means that the `y` attribute controls the position of the top of the text.

Finally, in the following snippet, you'll see that we've added a line to the label and traced between the downward protuberance of the area and the label to clarify what the label represents. You can see how it looks in figure 4.23. Again, we've used the scales to calculate the `x1`, `y1`, `x2`, and `y2` attributes of the line, which control the position of its starting and ending points:

```
innerChart
  .append("text")
    .text("Minimum temperature")
    .attr("x", xScale(data[data.length - 3].date) + 13)
    .attr("y", yScale(data[data.length - 3].min_temp_F) + 20)
    .attr("alignment-baseline", "hanging")
    .attr("fill", aubergine);
innerChart
  .append("line")
    .attr("x1", xScale(data[data.length - 3].date))
    .attr("y1", yScale(data[data.length - 3].min_temp_F) + 3)
    .attr("x2", xScale(data[data.length - 3].date) + 10)
    .attr("y2", yScale(data[data.length - 3].min_temp_F) + 20)
    .attr("stroke", aubergine)
    .attr("stroke-width", 2);
```

We use a very similar process to append a label for the upper boundary of the area, which represents the evolution of the maximum temperature. We position this label close to the upward protuberance corresponding to the fourth to last data point. Again, we draw a line between the label and the protuberance. Once you're done, the line chart is complete:

```
  innerChart
  .append("text")
    .text("Maximum temperature")
    .attr("x", xScale(data[data.length - 4].date) + 13)
    .attr("y", yScale(data[data.length - 4].max_temp_F) - 20)
    .attr("fill", aubergine);
innerChart
  .append("line")
    .attr("x1", xScale(data[data.length - 4].date))
    .attr("y1", yScale(data[data.length - 4].max_temp_F) - 3)
    .attr("x2", xScale(data[data.length - 4].date) + 10)
    .attr("y2", yScale(data[data.length - 4].max_temp_F) - 20)
```

```
.attr("stroke", aubergine)
.attr("stroke-width", 2);
```

Weekly average temperature

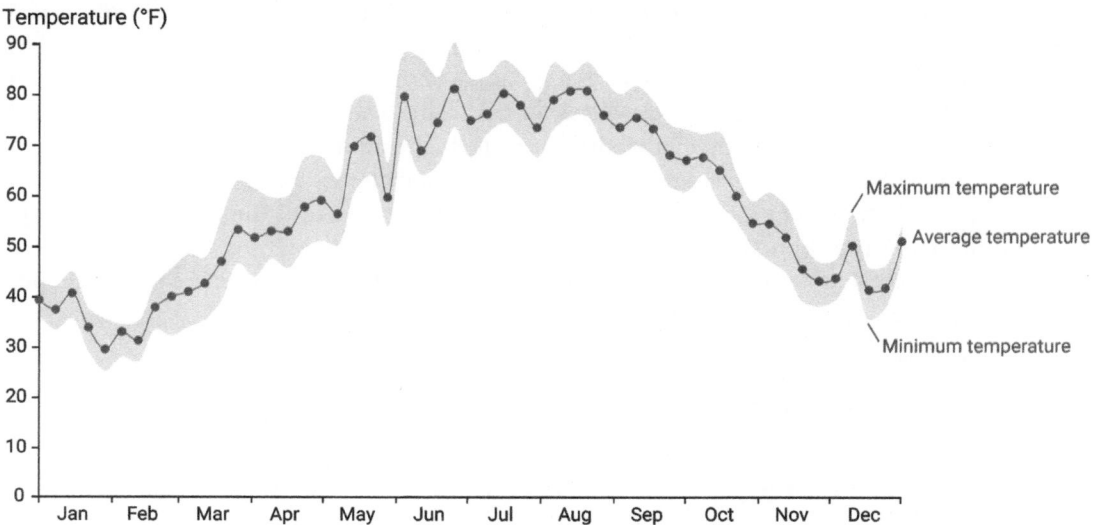

Figure 4.23   Completed line chart of the evolution of temperature in New York City for the year 2021

4.4   Drawing arcs

In this last section, we'll discuss how to draw arcs with D3. Arcs are a common shape in data visualization. They are used in pie charts, sunburst diagrams, and Nightingale rose charts to visualize how an amount relates to the total, and we regularly use them in custom radial visualizations.

Like lines and areas, arcs are drawn with SVG paths, and, as you've probably guessed by now, D3 provides a handy arc generator function that computes the d attribute of arc paths for us. Before discussing the arc generator in detail, let's prepare our project. Here we'll draw the arcs that compose the radial chart you can see under "Days with precipitation" in figure 4.1, shown earlier, or on the hosted project (http://mng.bz/5orB). The blue arc portrays the percentage of days with precipitation in New York City during 2021 (35%), while the gray arc represents the rest of the days.

First, open the arcs.js file. This is where we'll work for the rest of the chapter. As usual, we need to load a dataset—in this case, daily_precipitation.csv—which is included in the data folder. If you take a look at the CSV file, you'll see that it only contains two columns: the date column lists every day of 2021, while the total_ precip_in column provides the total precipitation, in inches, for each day.

In the following snippet, we fetch the dataset with `d3.csv()`, use `d3.autoType` to format the dates and numbers correctly, and chain it with a Promise, inside of which we log the data into the console:

```
d3.csv("./data/daily_precipitation.csv", d3.autoType).then(data => {
  console.log("precipitation data", data);
});
```

> **NOTE** We won't discuss the details of how to use `d3.csv()` here, but you can refer to chapter 3 for more explanations or to section 4.1 of this chapter for a discussion about `d3.autoType`.

If you look at the data in the console, you'll see that both the dates and numbers are correctly formatted. Great! We can take our formatted dataset and pass it to function `drawArc()`, which already exists in `arcs.js`:

```
d3.csv("./data/daily_precipitation.csv", d3.autoType).then(data => {
  console.log("precipitation data", data);
  drawArc(data);
});
```

Inside `drawArc()`, we can now append a new SVG container. As you can see in the following snippet, we give a width and height of 300 px to the SVG container and append it inside the `div` with an ID of `arc` that already exists in `index.html`. We use the strategy explained in chapter 1 to make the SVG responsive: setting the last two values of the `viewBox` attribute to its width and height and omitting the `width` and `height` attributes altogether. This way, the SVG container will adapt to the size of its parent while preserving its aspect ratio. Note that we save the SVG container selection in a constant named `svg`:

```
const pieChartWidth = 300;
const pieChartHeight = 300;
const svg = d3.select("#arc")
  .append("svg")
  .attr("viewBox", [0, 0, pieChartWidth, pieChartHeight]);
```

4.4.1   *The polar coordinate system*

As discussed in section 4.1, we'll wrap our chart inside an SVG group and translate this group to the desired position. The strategy is a little bit different this time, though. We don't need to reserve space for axis or labels, so we can omit the margin convention. But contrary to all the visualizations built so far, arcs live in a polar coordinate system rather than a Cartesian coordinate system.

As shown in figure 4.24, the coordinate system of an SVG container is Cartesian. It uses two perpendicular dimensions, x and y, to describe positions in the 2D space. A 2D polar coordinate system also uses two dimensions: a radius and an angle. The radius is the distance between the origin and a point in space, while the angle is calculated from 12 o'clock in the clockwise direction. This way of describing positions in space is particularly useful when working with arcs.

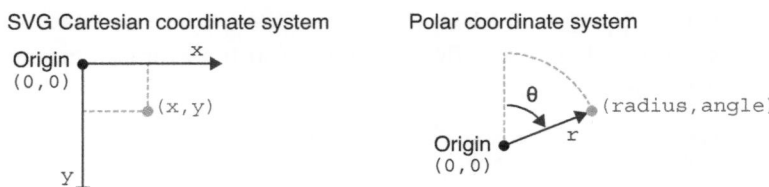

Figure 4.24   The dimensions of a Cartesian coordinate system are perpendicular to one another, while the polar coordinate system uses the radius and angle dimensions to describe a position in space.

Because elements are positioned around the origin in the polar coordinate system, we can say that the origin of the arcs visualization we're about to build is positioned at the center of the SVG container, as shown in figure 4.25.

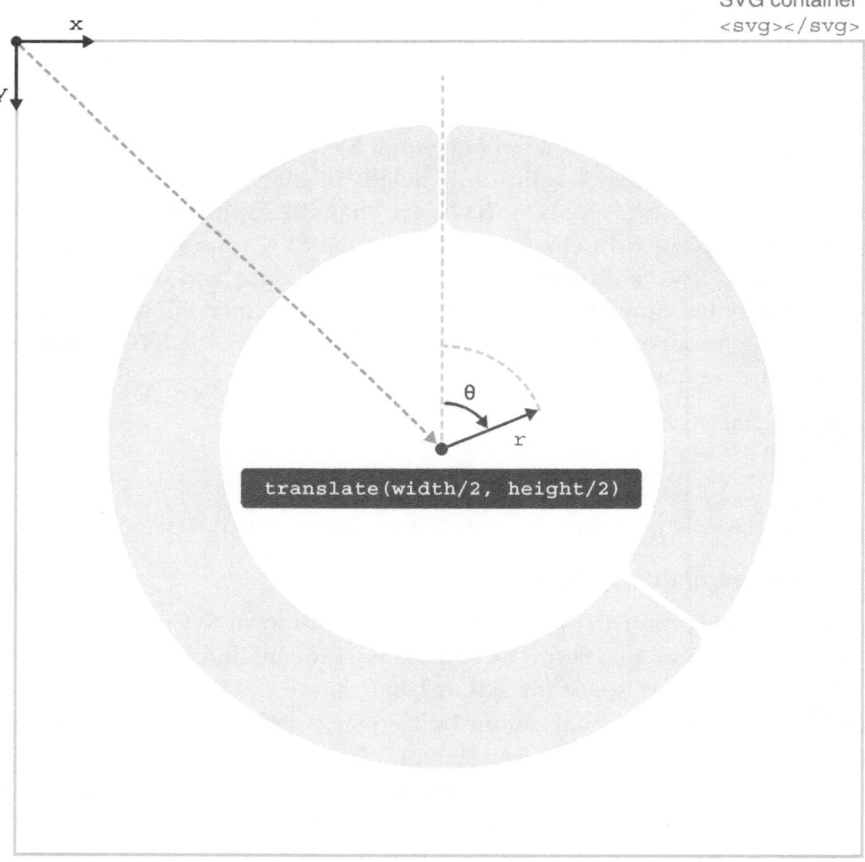

Figure 4.25   We facilitate the creation of a set of arcs by wrapping them into an SVG group and translating this group to the center of the SVG container. When we append arcs to the group, their position will be automatically relative to the center of the chart, which corresponds to the origin of their polar coordinate system.

In the next snippet, we take our SVG container selection and append a group inside of it. We translate the group to the center of the SVG container and save it in constant `innerChart`:

```
const innerChart = svg
  .append("g")
    .attr("transform", `translate(${pieChartWidth/2},
    ➥ ${pieChartHeight/2})`);
```

Before creating our arcs, we need to do one last thing: calculate the angle taken by the days with precipitation on our chart. When creating pie or donut charts with D3, we usually handle such calculations with the pie layout generator, which we'll introduce in the next chapter. But because we'll draw only two arcs here, the math is easy.

First, we can know the total number of days in 2021, which is 365, with the `length` property of our dataset. Then we find the number of days with precipitation by filtering the dataset to keep only the days for which precipitation is greater than 0, which is 126 days. Finally, we turn the number of days with precipitation into a percentage by dividing it by the total number of days, which gives 35%:

```
const numberOfDays = data.length;
const numberOfDaysWithPrecipitation = data.filter(d =>
➥ d.total_precip_in > 0).length;
const percentageDaysWithPrecipitation =
➥ Math.round(numberOfDaysWithPrecipitation / numberOfDays * 100);
```

We can then calculate the angle corresponding to the number of days with precipitation by multiplying this number by 360 degrees, the number of degrees in a full circle, to obtain 126 degrees. We start with degrees because it's more intuitive, but we also need to convert this value to radians. To do so, we multiply the angle covered by the percentage of days with precipitation, in degrees, by the number pi (3.1416) and divide it by 180 for an angle of about 2.2 radians that we save in constant `angleDays-WithPrecipitation_rad`.

We perform this conversion because the arc generator we'll use in a moment expects angles to be in radians rather than degrees. As a rule of thumb, when working with angles, JavaScript usually expects them to be in radians, while CSS uses degrees:

```
const angleDaysWithPrecipitation_deg = percentageDaysWithPrecipitation *
➥ 360 / 100;
const angleDaysWithPrecipitation_rad = angleDaysWithPrecipitation_deg *
➥ Math.PI / 180;
```

4.4.2 Using the arc generator

We're finally getting to the fun part: generating the arcs! First, we need to declare an arc generator as we did for lines and areas. Arc generator `d3.arc()` is part of the d3-shape module and, in our case, requires two main accessor functions: the inner radius and the outer radius of the arcs, respectively handled by the accessor functions `innerRadius()` and `outerRadius()` and given values of 80 px and 120 px. Note that if the inner radius is 0, we get a pie chart:

```
const arcGenerator = d3.arc()
  .innerRadius(80)
  .outerRadius(120);
```

We can personalize our arcs by adding padding between them with accessor function
`padAngle()` illustrated in figure 4.26, which accepts an angle in radians. Here we use
0.02 radians, which corresponds to a little more than 1 degree. We can also round the
corner of the arcs with `cornerRadius()`, which accepts a value in pixels. This accessor
function has a similar effect as the CSS `border-radius` property:

```
const arcGenerator = d3.arc()
  .innerRadius(80)
  .outerRadius(120)
  .padAngle(0.02)
  .cornerRadius(6);
```

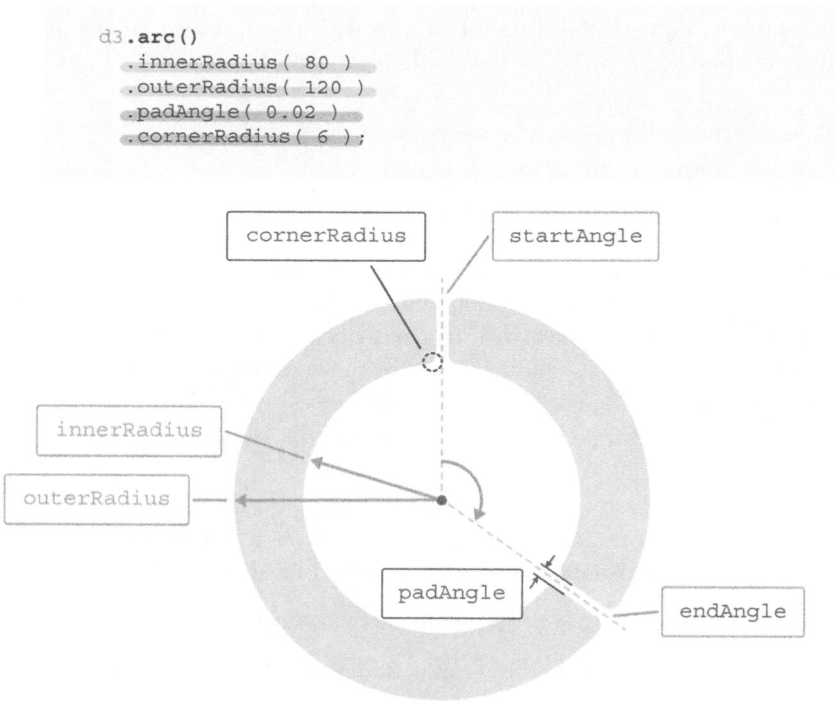

Figure 4.26   The arc generator uses multiple accessor functions to compute the d
**attribute of an arc. Here we set its inner radius, outer radius, padding angle, and
corner radius during the generator declaration. We'll pass each arc's start and end
angles when we append the path element to the chart.**

At this point, you might wonder why we didn't use accessor functions that handle the
angles covered by the arcs. In our case, because we've manually calculated our angle,

it's simpler to pass these values to the arc generator ourselves when we append the paths. But we'll see in the next chapter that this isn't always the case.

So let's append our first arc, the one showing the number of days with precipitation. In the following snippet, we first append a path element to the inner chart selection. Then we set its d attribute by calling the arc generator declared in the preceding snippet.

Observe how we pass the start and end angles to the generator as an object. The value of startAngle is 0, which corresponds to 12 o'clock, while the value of endAngle is the angle covered by the days with precipitation calculated earlier. Finally, we set the fill of the arc to the color #6EB7C2, a cyan blue:

```
innerChart
  .append("path")
    .attr("d", () => {
      return arcGenerator({
        startAngle: 0,
        endAngle: angleDaysWithPrecipitation_rad
      });
    })
    .attr("fill", "#6EB7C2");
```

We append the second arc in a similar fashion. This time, the arc starts where the previous one ended and ends at the circle's completion, corresponding to the angle 2*Pi in radians. We give a fill of #DCE2E2 to the arc, a color closer to gray, to suggest that these are the days without precipitation:

```
innerChart
  .append("path")
    .attr("d", () => {
      return arcGenerator({
        startAngle: angleDaysWithPrecipitation_rad,
        endAngle: 2 * Math.PI
      });
    })
    .attr("fill", "#DCE2E2");
```

After saving your project, your arcs should look like the ones in figure 4.27. We encourage you to play with the values passed to the generator's accessor functions, like the radii or corner radius, to get a feel for how they modify the appearance of arcs.

As you can see in figure 4.28, the process of drawing arcs is similar to the one of drawing lines and areas. The main difference is that the position of arcs in space is handled with polar coordinates rather than Cartesian, which is reflected in the accessor functions of the arc generator.

Days with precipitation

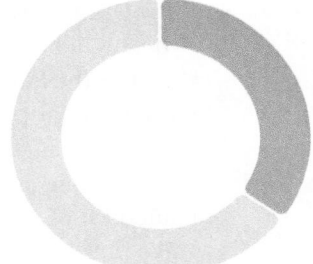

Figure 4.27 Arcs showing the ratio between days with precipitation and days without

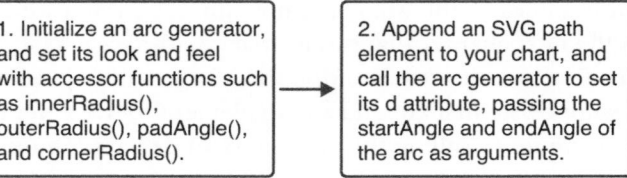

1. Initialize an arc generator, and set its look and feel with accessor functions such as innerRadius(), outerRadius(), padAngle(), and cornerRadius().

→

2. Append an SVG path element to your chart, and call the arc generator to set its d attribute, passing the startAngle and endAngle of the arc as arguments.

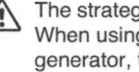 The strategy may vary. When using the pie layout generator, the startAngle and endAngle can be declared directly with the arc generator. We discuss this case in chapter 5.

Figure 4.28   Steps to draw an arc

4.4.3   *Calculating the centroid of an arc*

Pie charts and donut charts have recently got a lot of bad press in the data visualization community, mainly because we learned that the human eye isn't very good at estimating the ratio represented by an angle. These charts aren't always a poor choice, though, especially when they contain a small number of categories. But we can definitely help their readability with labels, and this is what we'll do here.

On the arc representing the number of days with precipitation, we'll add the label "35%", the percentage of days with precipitation calculated earlier. A great place to position this label is on the centroid of the arc, also known as its center of mass. This value can be provided by the arc generator.

In the following snippet, we call methods on the arc generator function initialized earlier. This time, we chain it with the startAngle() and endAngle() accessor functions, passing them the respective values of the start and end angles of the arc representing the days with precipitation. Finally, we chain method centroid(), which will calculate the midpoint of the arc:

```
const centroid = arcGenerator
  .startAngle(0)
  .endAngle(angleDaysWithPrecipitation_rad)
  .centroid();
```

Log the centroid into the console. You'll see that it consists of an array of two values: the horizontal and vertical position of the centroid, which in our case is [89, -45], relative to the origin of the inner chart.

In the next snippet, we create the label by appending a text element to the inner chart. For the label to include a "%" sign, we use method d3.format(".0%"), followed by the value in parentheses. This method is convenient for formatting numbers in a specific way, such as currencies, percentages, and exponents, or adding a particular suffix to these numbers, such as "M" for millions or "µ" for micro. You can find a detailed list of all the formats available in the d3-format module.

We then set the x and y attributes, using the first and second values returned in the centroid array. Note that we set the text-anchor and dominant-baseline attributes to ensure that the label is centered around the x and y attributes, both horizontally and vertically.

Finally, we give the label a white color and a font-weight of 500 to improve its legibility. Once saved, your arc with a label should look like the one in figure 4.29:

```
innerChart
  .append("text")
    .text(d => d3.format(".0%")(percentageDaysWith
    ➥ Precipitation/100))
    .attr("x", centroid[0])
    .attr("y", centroid[1])
    .attr("text-anchor", "middle")
    .attr("dominant-baseline", "middle")
    .attr("fill", "white")
    .style("font-weight", 500);
```

Days with precipitation

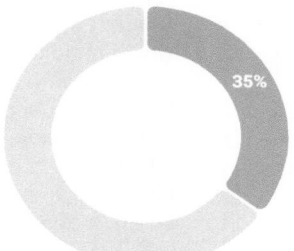

Figure 4.29   Completed arcs with a label

You now know how to draw lines, areas, and arcs with D3! In the next chapter, we'll use layout generators to bring these shapes to another level.

Interview with Francis Gagnon, Patricia Angkiriwang, and Olivia Gélinas from the Voilà:, Information Design Agency

- Gagnon is the founder of Voilà: and an information designer.
- Angkiriwang is a data visualization designer and developer.
- Gélinas is a full-stack developer and former programmer at Voilà:.

Can you tell us a little bit about your mission as an information design agency?

Francis: We're focused on sustainable development projects, meaning anything related to environmental protection, social development, and good governance. We also see ourselves as advocates for information design. The proposals to make the world better can appear complex at first, and they compete for attention with strong marketing campaigns. We want to help our clients get their important ideas across and have an effect for the best.

Which role does D3.js play in the spectrum of data visualization tools your team uses on a regular basis? Which place does it play in your workflow (from brainstorming to production-ready projects)?

Patricia: Our team regularly uses Microsoft Excel and Adobe Illustrator, along with other tools like RAWGraphs for our static data visualizations. D3.js complements Svelte in our interactive visualization workflow, which we use for prototyping and building more bespoke visualizations as well as anything interactive on the web. We like it for its handy utility functions (for example, d3-array, d3-format, d3-dsv), and its scales (d3-scale) and interpolators (d3-interpolate), which are essential for our data visualizations. If we end up coding anything radial or stacked, we inevitably turn to the d3-shape module.

In your experience, what are the main advantages and disadvantages of using D3, especially as a team where many people are involved in the same project?

Patricia: I would say that the main advantages are that D3 can serve as a common language and that you can find great documentation and examples online. A disadvantage is that even then, it's not readily accessible to the non-coders on a project.

(continued)

Olivia: I'd add that D3 gives full flexibility compared to other data visualization tools, which is quite powerful. It facilitates the creation of almost any visualization you can come up with, and has handy functions for many more complex visualizations (think Sankey or chord diagrams). Because of its flexibility, non-coders on a team quickly realize that we can implement "anything," which can quickly turn to implementing "everything"; it's hard to reliably express to a non-coder which types of tasks take longer to implement. So the challenge can sometimes involve requirements and scope management more so than technical problems.

Patricia: D3's imperative style can also make the code a little tricky to read, especially when passing code between team members. At the time when we first built this particular project, our code used D3.js for everything, including controlling SVG elements and handling the interactivity. When I adapted the project to use our new workflow, keeping track of all the event handlers that used d3-select to control each piece individually felt like piecing together a tangled riddle!

Featured project: "A Portfolio of Inclusive Business for a Sustainable Future" (https://chezvoila.com/project/findevportfolio/)

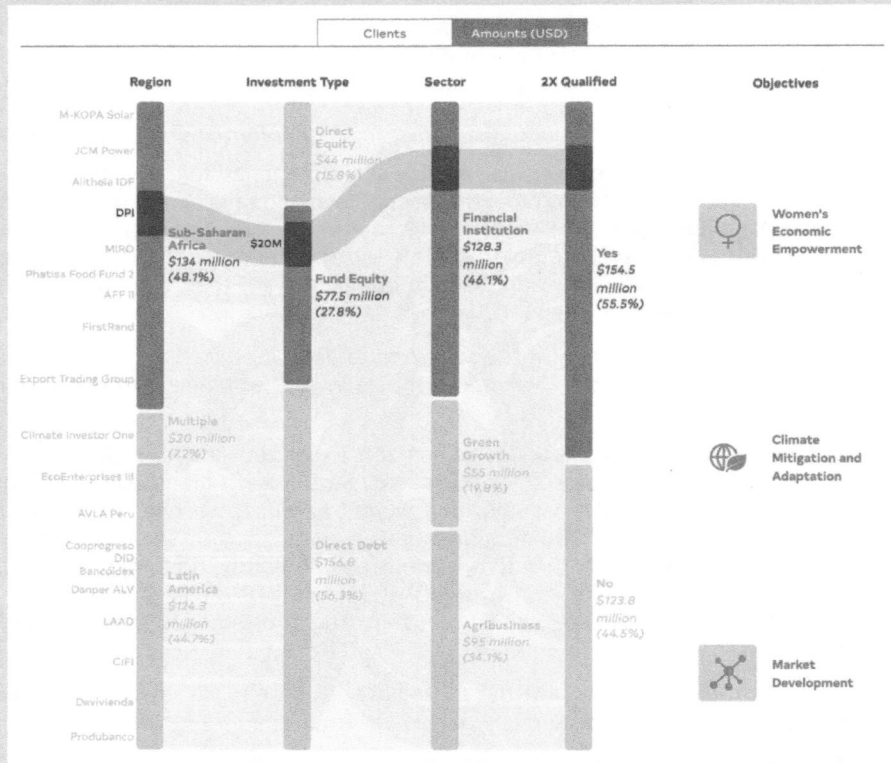

An interactive portfolio of international development projects visualized by an alluvial diagram. Created for FinDev Canada.

Please describe your project created for FinDev Canada.

Francis: It's an interactive portfolio of international development projects. FinDev Canada is an organization that supports the growth and sustainability of businesses in emerging markets. They asked us to build something that both informs the public of the nature of the projects in progress and serves as a dashboard for their employees. At the center of this project is an alluvial graph, a visualization that allows us to present different distributions of the same variable. In this case, that variable is the financial value (or number) of projects, as distributed across regions, investment types, sectors, and 2X eligibility. Each project is made visible by hovering the cursor over the graph, revealing that each column of the alluvial contains a proportional distribution of projects across categories.

Can you describe the process of creating this project?

Francis: Our starting point, provided by the client, was a PowerPoint slide with data and graphs that, at first glance, seemed unrelated. Then we realized that many of these categories were actually reorganizations of the same data. So we wanted to create a design that clarified this continuity and thus communicated the nature of the data. With an online whiteboard exercise, our team explored many ideas for visualizations before settling on the alluvial graph. We then mocked up a design, doing everything from the visual design to the animations, in PowerPoint. The first design we showed the client was more polished than what we now do, which was a big risk, but it paid off.

Olivia: Once the detailed mockups were approved, it was simply a question of implementing the graphic. I planned (on paper!) the main files, classes, and functions that would be used. I then implemented the code in a top-down approach starting by defining the classes, then the functions, and then filling everything in. I worked iteratively, checking with the team every so often and making any needed adjustments as I went. Since then, the iterations have continued, since the code is updated every so often with new data and other improvements.

Was this alluvial flowchart created with the d3-sankey module, or did you develop your own custom solution?

Patricia: Yes, we did use the d3-sankey module. We used it to calculate the positions of the nodes and links, as well as the shape of the link paths (we used `sankeyLink-Horizontal()` there). To customize it, we built custom sorters to determine the order of the nodes and the links. All we had to do then was to style the alluvial, manage the responsive sizing, and handle the interactivity!

Your solution for adapting the visualization to mobile screens is simple but very efficient and elegant. Knowing how making responsive data visualizations can be challenging, was this one the result of trial and error, or was it obvious?

Francis: It was a stroke of luck. We remembered late in the process that the client expected a mobile version—again, this was our first experience! We stared at it for a minute, and the solution was staring back at us: just rotate it 90 degrees. Our tests were immediately conclusive, and we told the client it was the idea all along. There was a bit more tweaking involved in making it work on multitouch without the hover action.

(continued)

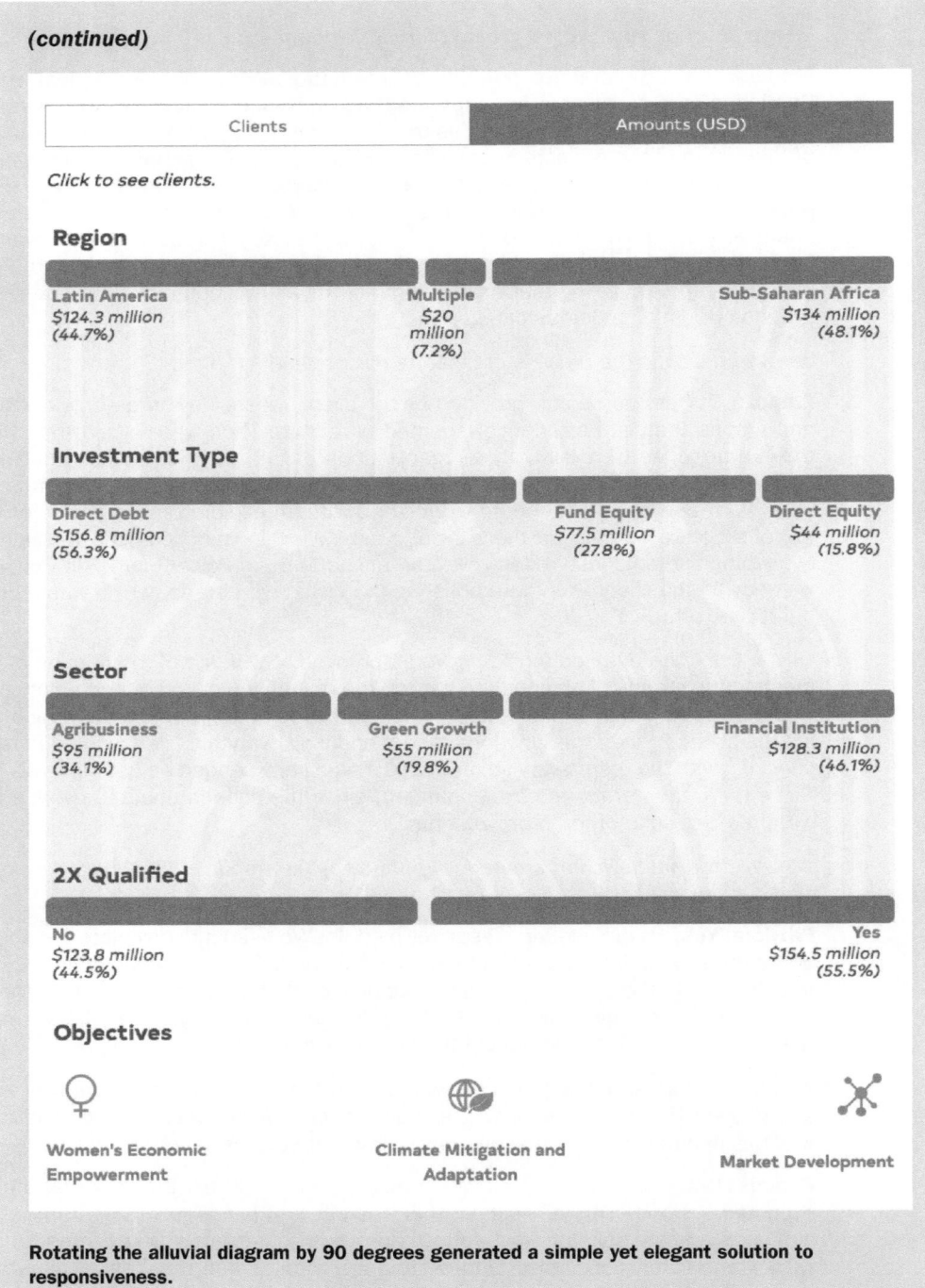

| Clients | Amounts (USD) |

Click to see clients.

Region

Latin America	Multiple	Sub-Saharan Africa
$124.3 million	$20 million	$134 million
(44.7%)	(7.2%)	(48.1%)

Investment Type

Direct Debt	Fund Equity	Direct Equity
$156.8 million	$77.5 million	$44 million
(56.3%)	(27.8%)	(15.8%)

Sector

Agribusiness	Green Growth	Financial Institution
$95 million	$55 million	$128.3 million
(34.1%)	(19.8%)	(46.1%)

2X Qualified

No	Yes
$123.8 million	$154.5 million
(44.5%)	(55.5%)

Objectives

| Women's Economic Empowerment | Climate Mitigation and Adaptation | Market Development |

Rotating the alluvial diagram by 90 degrees generated a simple yet elegant solution to responsiveness.

Which tips would you share with our readers about learning D3 and becoming a professional D3 developer?

Patricia: My tip would be to relieve yourself of the pressure of "mastering" D3. Even as I use D3 professionally, I've barely scratched the surface of what this library has to offer! I think it's useful to think of D3 as a set of tools you can pick and choose from. As you are learning, pick some relevant modules, and use those in the projects you are working on. Personally, the d3-scale module has transformed the way I think about and approach visualizations.

Summary

- The role of the D3 margin convention is to reserve space around a chart for axes, labels, and legends in a systematic and reusable way.
- We do so by declaring a `margin` object containing a value for the top, right, bottom, and left margin.
- A useful strategy is to wrap the elements constituting the chart itself into an SVG group and position this group inside the SVG container based on the margins. This creates a new origin for the chart elements and facilitates their implementation.
- D3 has four axis generators: `axisTop()`, `axisRight()`, `axisBottom()`, and `axisLeft()`, which create the respective components of top, right, bottom, and left axes.
- These axis generators take a scale as an input and return the SVG elements comprising an axis as an output (a line along the axis and multiple sets of ticks and labels).
- We append an axis to a chart by chaining the `call()` method to a selection and passing the axis as an argument.
- Line charts are one of the most common charts and are useful to show the evolution of a phenomenon over time. We draw line charts with lines or curves connecting data points:
  - To draw a line chart, we first initialize a line generator with method `d3.line()`. The line generator has two accessor functions, `x()` and `y()`, which calculate each data point's horizontal and vertical position.
  - We can turn a line chart into a curve with the `curve()` accessor function. D3 offers multiple curve interpolation functions, which affect data representation and must be selected carefully.
  - To make a line chart appear on the screen, we append a path element to a selection and set its `d` attribute by calling the line generator and passing the dataset as an attribute.
- An area is a region between two boundaries, and drawing an area with D3 is similar to drawing a line:

- – To draw an area, we first declare an area generator with method `d3.area()`. This method requires at least three accessor functions to calculate the position of each data point along the edges of the area, for example, `x()`, `y0()`, and `y1()` or `x0()`, `x1()`, and `y()`.
- – Like for lines, D3 provides interpolation functions that can be applied with the `curve()` accessor function.
- – To make an area appear on the screen, we append a path element to a selection and set its `d` attribute by calling the area generator and passing the dataset as an attribute.

- Labels are particularly useful to help readers understand our data visualizations. In D3, labels are simply text elements that we need to position within the SVG container:
  - – The position of SVG text is controlled by their `x` and `y` attributes.
  - – The `y` attribute sets the position of the text's baseline, which by default is positioned at its bottom. We shift the baseline of an SVG text with attribute `dominant-baseline`. The `middle` value moves the baseline to the vertical middle of the text, while the `hanging` value shifts the baseline to the top.

- Visualizations that use arcs are usually described with a polar coordinate system. This coordinate system uses a radius, the distance between the origin and a point, and an angle to describe a position in space.

- Arcs are created with SVG path elements, for which the `d` attribute is calculated with an arc generator:
  - – D3's arc generator (`d3.arc()`) has an accessor function that defines the starting and ending angle of an arc (`startAngle()` and `endAngle()`), as well as its inner and outer radius (`innerRadius()` and `outerRadius()`).
  - – We can also use accessor functions to round the corners of an arc (`cornerRadius()`) or to add padding between arcs (`padAngle()`).
  - – The arc generator expects angles to be expressed in radians.

- The center of mass of an arc can be calculated with the `centroid()` method. Chained to an arc generator, this accessor function returns an array containing the horizontal and vertical position of the center of mass.

Pie and stack layouts 5

This chapter covers
- Understanding D3 layout functions
- Drawing donut charts using the pie layout
- Stacking shapes to generate a stacked bar chart and a streamgraph
- Creating a simple legend

In the previous chapter, we discussed how D3 can calculate the d attribute of complex shapes such as curves, areas, and arcs with its shape generator functions. In this chapter, we'll take such shapes to another level with layouts. In D3, layouts are functions that take a dataset as an input and produce a new, annotated dataset as an output. This new dataset contains the attributes necessary to draw a specific visualization. For example, the pie layout calculates the angles of each slice of a pie chart and annotates the dataset with these angles. Similarly, the stack layout calculates the position of the piled shapes in a stacked bar chart or a streamgraph.

Layouts don't draw the visualizations, nor are they referred to in the drawing code like shape generators. Instead, they comprise a preprocessing step that formats your data so that it's ready to be displayed in the form you've chosen, as explained in figure 5.1.

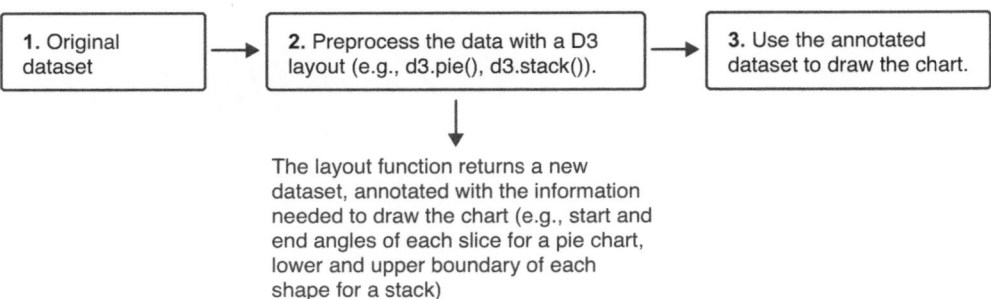

Figure 5.1   The layout function is a data preprocessing step used to calculate the information required to draw a specific chart.

In this chapter, we'll combine D3's pie and stack layouts with the arc and area shape generators discussed in chapter 4 to create the project shown in figure 5.2. You can also find it online at http://mng.bz/6nVo. This project visualizes sales per format in the music industry between 1973 and 2019. It's inspired by a challenge hosted by MakeoverMonday in 2020 (www.makeovermonday.co.uk).

Although this chapter discusses only the pie and the stack layouts, other layouts, such as the chord layout and more exotic ones, follow the same principles and should be easy to understand after looking at these.

Before we get started, go to the code files of chapter 5. You can download them from the book's GitHub repository if you haven't already (http://mng.bz/Xqjv). In the folder named `chapter_05`, the code files are organized by section. To get started with this chapter's exercise, open the `5.1-Pie_layout/start` folder in your code editor, and start your local web server. Refer to appendix A if you need help setting up your local development environment. You can find more details about the project's folder structure in the `README` file located at the root of this chapter's code files.

The three visualizations we'll build in this chapter are donut charts, a stacked bar chart, and a streamgraph. They will share the same data, dimensions, and scales. To avoid repetition, the project is broken into multiple JavaScript files, including one for the constants shared by the visualizations and one specifically for the scales. This approach will make our code easier to read and modify. In production code, we would likely use JavaScript imports and exports to access the different functions, in combination with Node and a bundler. We'll get there when discussing frontend frameworks in chapter 8, but for now, we'll stick to a legacy-like project structure to keep the focus on D3. Note that the D3 library and all the JavaScript files are already loaded in `index.html`.

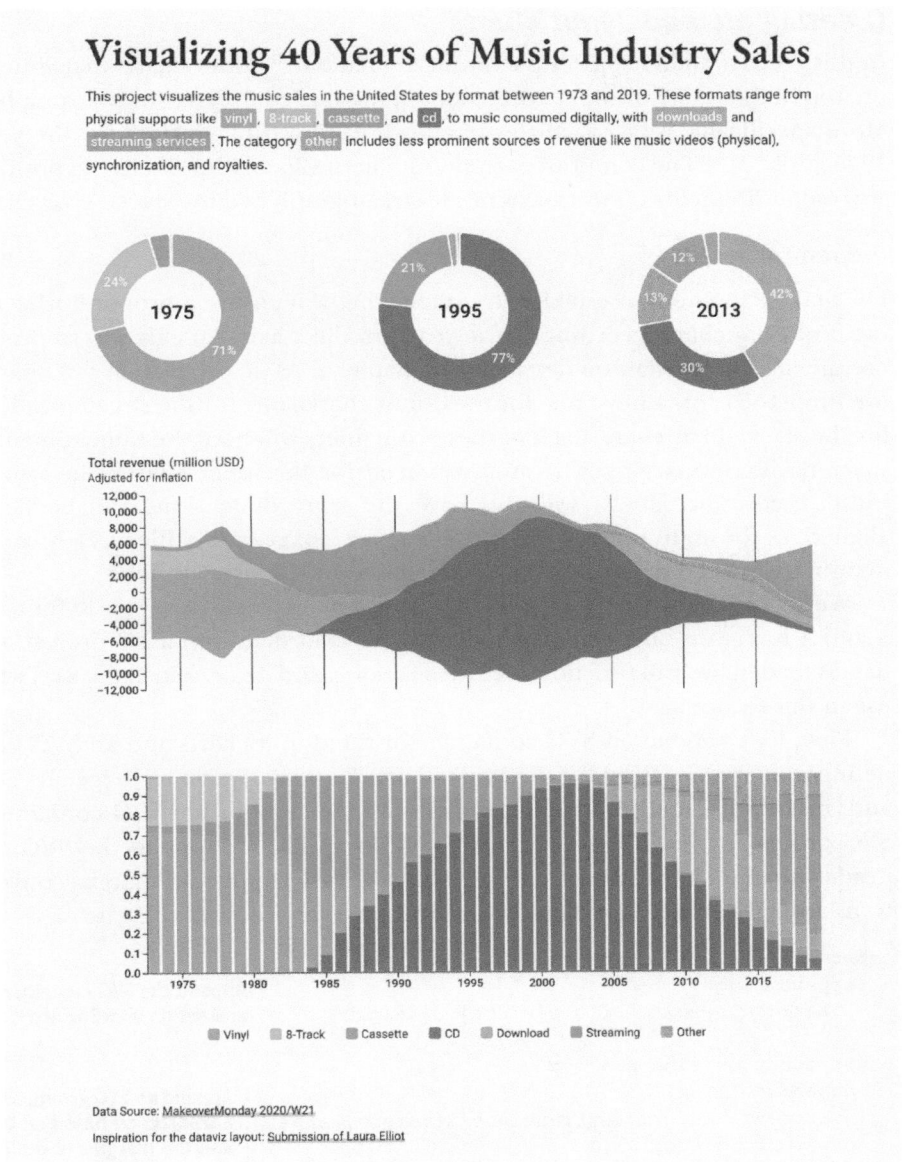

Figure 5.2 Visualization of the sales in the music industry between 1973 and 2019. This is the project that we'll build in this chapter.

WARNING When working with the chapter's code files, open only one `start` *or* one `end` folder in your code editor. If you open all the chapter's files at once and use the Live Server extension to serve the project, the path to the data file won't work as expected.

5.1   *Creating pie and donut charts*

In this section, we'll use D3's pie layout to create the donut charts that you can see at the top of figure 5.2, shown earlier, and on the hosted project (http://mng.bz/6nVo). More specifically, we'll visualize the sales breakdown per format for the years 1975, 1995, and 2013. The center of each donut chart will correspond to the position of the corresponding years on the x-axis of the streamgraph and the stacked bar chart below.

5.1.1   *Preparatory steps*

Let's take a moment to establish a strategy that will ensure a proper horizontal alignment of each chart according to the years on the x-axis. An easy way to proceed is to use the margin convention described in chapter 4. As we progress in this chapter, we'll use three SVG containers: one for the donut charts, one for the streamgraph, and one for the stacked bar chart. Each of these containers will have the same dimensions and share the same margins. The areas reserved for the inner charts (the visualizations without axes and labels) will also have the same dimensions and be horizontally aligned, as shown in figure 5.3. The `js/shared-constant.js` file already contains the margin object and dimension constants shared by the visualizations.

We've also loaded the CSV data file for you in `js/load-data.js`. Refer to chapters 3 and 4 for more information about how we load data into a D3 project. Once the data is loaded, we call functions `defineScales()` and `drawDonutCharts()`, which we'll use in this section.

First, let's append an SVG container for the donut charts and an SVG group that defines the area reserved for the inner chart. To do so, we go to `js/donut-charts.js` and, inside function `drawDonutCharts()`, we create both the SVG container and an SVG group. In the following snippet, you'll see that we append the SVG container inside the `div` with an ID of `"donut"`. Note that we apply the margin convention by translating the group based on the left and top margins of the charts:

```
const svg = d3.select("#donut")
  .append("svg")
    .attr("viewBox", `0 0 ${width} ${height}`);
```
Append the SVG container, and set its viewBox attribute.

```
const donutContainers = svg
  .append("g")
    .attr("transform", `translate(${margin.left},
    ${margin.top})`);
```
Append an SVG group, and apply a translation based on the left and top margins of the charts.

You might wonder why we need to apply the margin convention to the donut charts when there's no axis and labels to account space for. This is because each donut chart will be aligned with the corresponding year on the x-axis. Because we want the horizontal position of these years to be the same as in the streamgraph and the stacked bar chart below, we need to account for the margin convention that those charts will use later.

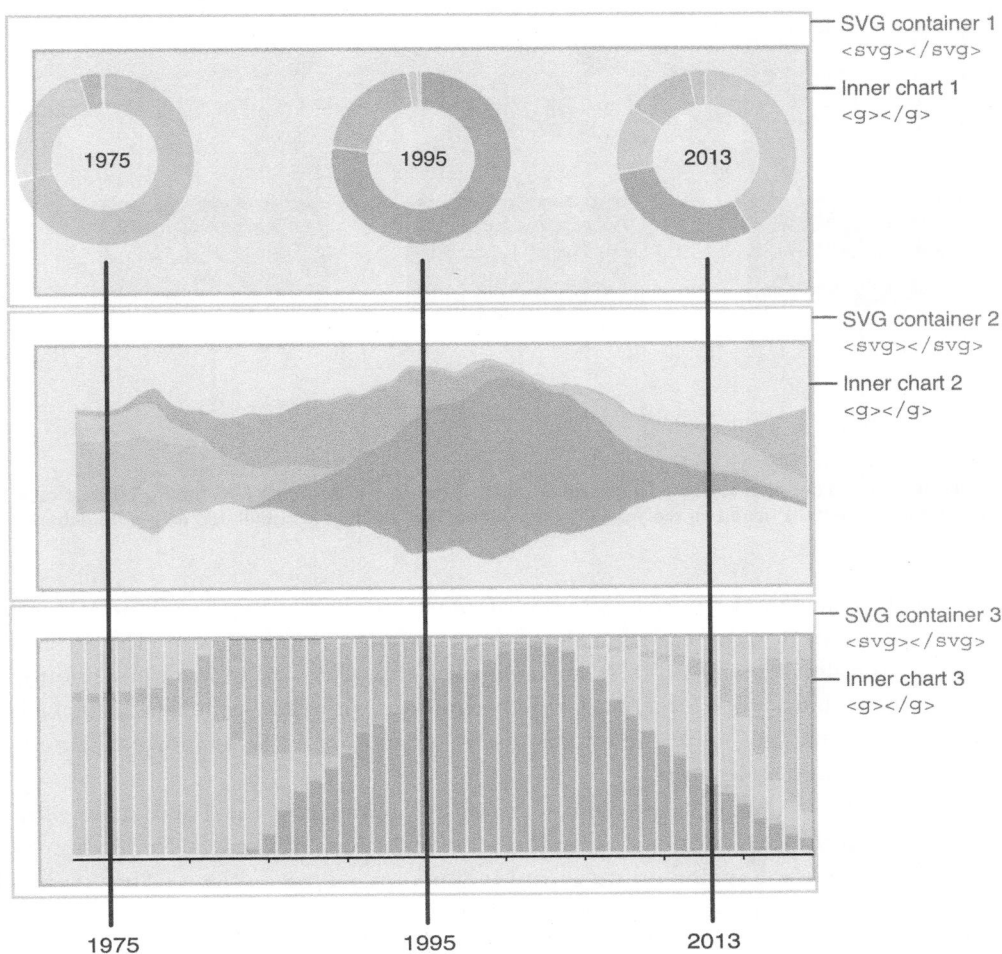

Figure 5.3   To create this chapter's project, we'll use three SVG containers: one for the donut charts, one for the streamgraph, and one for the stacked bar chart. This strategy will allow us to have a consistent area reserved for the inner chart and to align each chart on top of the other properly.

In chapter 4, we discussed polar coordinates and how we can facilitate the creation of a pie or donut chart by containing the arcs inside an SVG group and translating this group to the center of the chart. By proceeding this way, the arcs are automatically drawn around this center.

We'll apply the same strategy here with the only differences being that we have three donut charts to account for and the horizontal position of their center corresponds to the years they represent, as illustrated by figure 5.4.

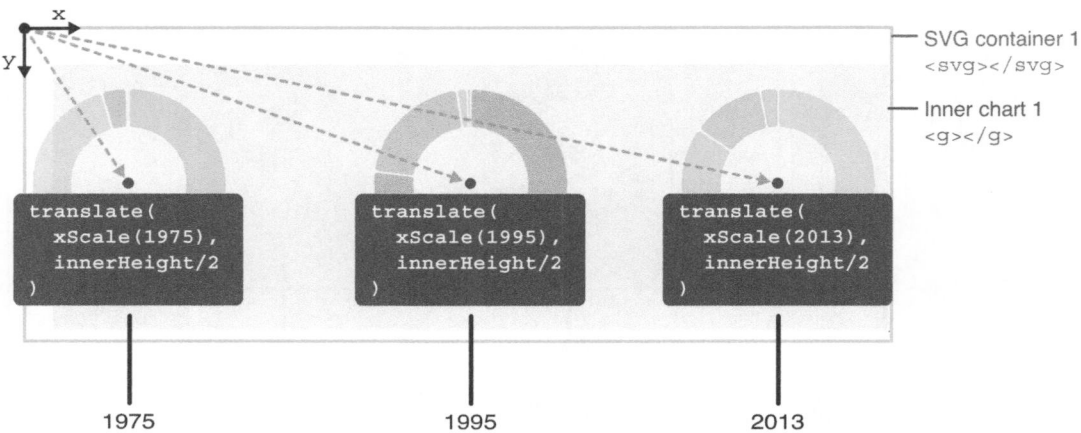

Figure 5.4   Each set of arcs composing a donut chart is contained inside an SVG group. These groups are translated horizontally based on the year they represent. This position is calculated with a D3 scale.

To calculate the horizontal position of each donut's center, we'll need a scale. As you know by now, we use D3 scales to translate data (the years) onto the screen attributes (the horizontal positions). A linear or a time scale would work just fine for our purpose, but we opt for a band scale because we know that we'll draw a stacked bar chart later that will share the same scale. Refer to chapter 3 for more explanations about how band scales work.

In the `js/scale.js` file, we start by initializing the band scale with function `d3.scaleBand()` and storing it in a constant named `xScale`. Notice how we declare the scale's domain and range inside function `defineScales()`. This approach lets us wait until the data is done loading before attempting to set the domain. `define-Scales()` is called from `load-data.js` once the data is ready. We declare constant `xScale` outside the function to make it accessible from the other JavaScript files.

Listing 5.1   Declaring the band scale (`scales.js`)

```
const xScale = d3.scaleBand();          ⟵┐  Declare the
                                         │  band scale.
const defineScales = (data) => {
  xScale
    .domain(data.map(d => d.year))      │  Set the scale's
    .range([0, innerWidth]);            │  domain and range.
};
```

Band scales accept a discrete input as a domain and return a continuous output from the range. In listing 5.1, we set the domain by creating an array with each year from the dataset using the JavaScript `map()` method. For the range, we pass an array containing the minimum value of the horizontal space available, which is `0`, and the maximum value, corresponding to the `innerWidth` of the chart.

We go back to function `drawDonutCharts()`, and as you can see in listing 5.2, we first declare an array, named `years`, that lists our years of interest: 1975, 1995, and 2013. Then, using a `forEach()` loop, we append an SVG group for each year and save it in a constant named `donutContainer`. We finally translate the groups by setting their `transform` attributes. The horizontal translation is calculated by calling `xScale`, to which we pass the current year, while the vertical translation corresponds to the half-height of the inner chart.

Listing 5.2 Appending a group for each donut (`donut-charts.js`)

```
const years = [1975, 1995, 2013];
years.forEach(year => {

  const donutContainer = donutContainers
    .append("g")
      .attr("transform", `translate(${xScale(year)}, ${innerHeight/2})`);

});
```

5.1.2 *The pie layout generator*

With the preparation steps completed, we can now focus on the donut charts. Pie and donut charts visualize part-to-whole relationships or the amount represented by each slice in regard to the total. The D3 pie layout generator helps us by calculating each slice's start and end angle based on the percentage it represents.

FORMATTING THE DATA

D3's pie generator expects the input data to be formatted as an array of numbers. For example, for the year 1975, we could have an array with the sales corresponding to each music format:

```
const sales1975 = [8061.8, 2770.4, 469.5, 0, 0, 0, 48.5];
```

Although such a simple array is enough to generate a pie chart, it prevents us from knowing the music format associated with each slice. To carry this information with us, we can use an array of objects that contains both the ID of the music format and the related sales for the year of interest.

In listing 5.3, we start by extracting the formats from the `columns` attribute of the dataset. When fetching data with method `d3.csv()`, for example, D3 attaches an array to the dataset containing each column's title from the original CSV dataset and accessible with the `data.columns` key. If you log the fetched data into the console, you'll see it at the end of the data array, as shown in figure 5.5. Because we're only interested in the music formats, we can filter the columns array to remove the "year" label.

```
data
▼Array(47) ℹ
  ▶ 0: {year: 1973, vinyl: 8268.55, eight_track: 2815.68, cassette: 437.611081081, cd: 0, …}
  ▶ 1: {year: 1974, vinyl: 8037.9, eight_track: 2848.01, cassette: 452.196559838, cd: 0, …}
  ▶ 2: {year: 1975, vinyl: 8061.75, eight_track: 2770.41, cassette: 469.496498141, cd: 0, …}
  ▶ 3: {year: 1976, vinyl: 8573.27, eight_track: 3047.22, cassette: 654.643671353, cd: 0, …}

    . . .

  ▶ 44: {year: 2017, vinyl: 411.551754832, eight_track: 0, cassette: 0, cd: 1107.92, …}
  ▶ 45: {year: 2018, vinyl: 432.206383393, eight_track: 0, cassette: 0, cd: 715.45199218, …}
  ▶ 46: {year: 2019, vinyl: 504.384866529, eight_track: 0, cassette: 0, cd: 616.192064248, …}
  ▶ columns: (8) ['year', 'vinyl', 'eight_track', 'cassette', 'cd', 'download', 'streaming', 'other']
    length: 47
```

columns attribute of the fetched data

Figure 5.5   When fetching data from a CSV file, for example, D3 attaches an array to the dataset that contains the titles of the columns from the original dataset. This array is accessible with the `data.columns` key.

To prepare the data for the pie generator, we also need to extract the data for the year of interest. We isolate this data with the JavaScript `find()` method and store it in a constant named `yearData`.

We loop through the music format's array and create an object for each format that contains the format ID and its related sales for the year of interest. Finally, we push this object into the `formattedData` array, declared previously.

Listing 5.3   Formatting the data (`donut-charts.js`)

```
const years = [1975, 1995, 2013];
const formats = data.columns.filter(format =>      Extract the formats from the columns attribute
  format !== "year");                              of the data, and filter out the "year" item.

years.forEach(year => {
  . . .
                                                   Retrieve the data related
  const yearData = data.find(d => d.year === year);  ◄── to the year of interest.

  const formattedData = [];      ◄──  Initialize an empty array for the
                                      formatted data.

  formats.forEach(format => {           For each format, create an object containing both
    formattedData.push({ format: format,  the format ID and its sales for the year of interest.
      sales: yearData[format] });       Push this object to the formatted data array.
  });

});
```

Once ready, the formatted data is an array of objects, and each object contains the format ID and its related sales for the year of interest:

```
// => formattedData = [
       { format: "vinyl", sales: 8061.8 },
       { format: "eight_track", sales: 2770.4 },
```

```
    { format: "cassette", sales: 469.5 },
    { format: "cd", sales: 0 },
    { format: "download", sales: 0 },
    { format: "streaming", sales: 0 },
    { format: "other", sales: 48.5 }
];
```

INITIALIZING AND CALLING THE PIE LAYOUT GENERATOR

Now that the data is formatted properly, we can initialize the pie layout generator. We construct a new pie generator with method d3.pie(), which is part of the d3-shape module. Because our formatted data is an array of objects, we need to tell the pie generator which key contains the value that will determine the size of the slice. We do so by setting the value() accessor function, as in the following snippet. We also store the pie generator in a constant named pieGenerator so that we can call it like any other function:

```
const pieGenerator = d3.pie()
  .value(d => d.sales);
```

To produce the annotated data for the pie layout, we simply call the pie generator function, pass the formatted data as an argument, and store the result in a constant named annotatedData:

```
const pieGenerator = d3.pie()
  .value(d => d.sales);
const annotatedData = pieGenerator(formattedData);
```

The pie generator returns a new, annotated dataset that contains a reference to the original dataset but also includes new attributes—the value of each slice, its index, and its start and end angles (in radians):

```
// => annotatedData = [
      {
        data: { format: "vinyl", sales: 8061.8 },
        value: 8061.8,
        index: 0,
        startAngle: 0,
        endAngle: 4.5,
        padAngle: 0,
      },
      ...
    ];
```

Note how padAngle, the padding between each slice, is also included and currently set to 0. We'll change that in a moment. It's important to understand that the pie layout generator isn't directly involved in drawing a pie chart. It's a preprocessing step that calculates the angles of a pie chart's slices. As described in figures 5.1 and 5.6, this process usually involves three steps:

1 Format the data.
2 Initialize the pie layout function.

3   Call the pie layout and pass the formatted data as an argument. Later, we'll use the annotated dataset returned by the pie layout to draw the arcs.

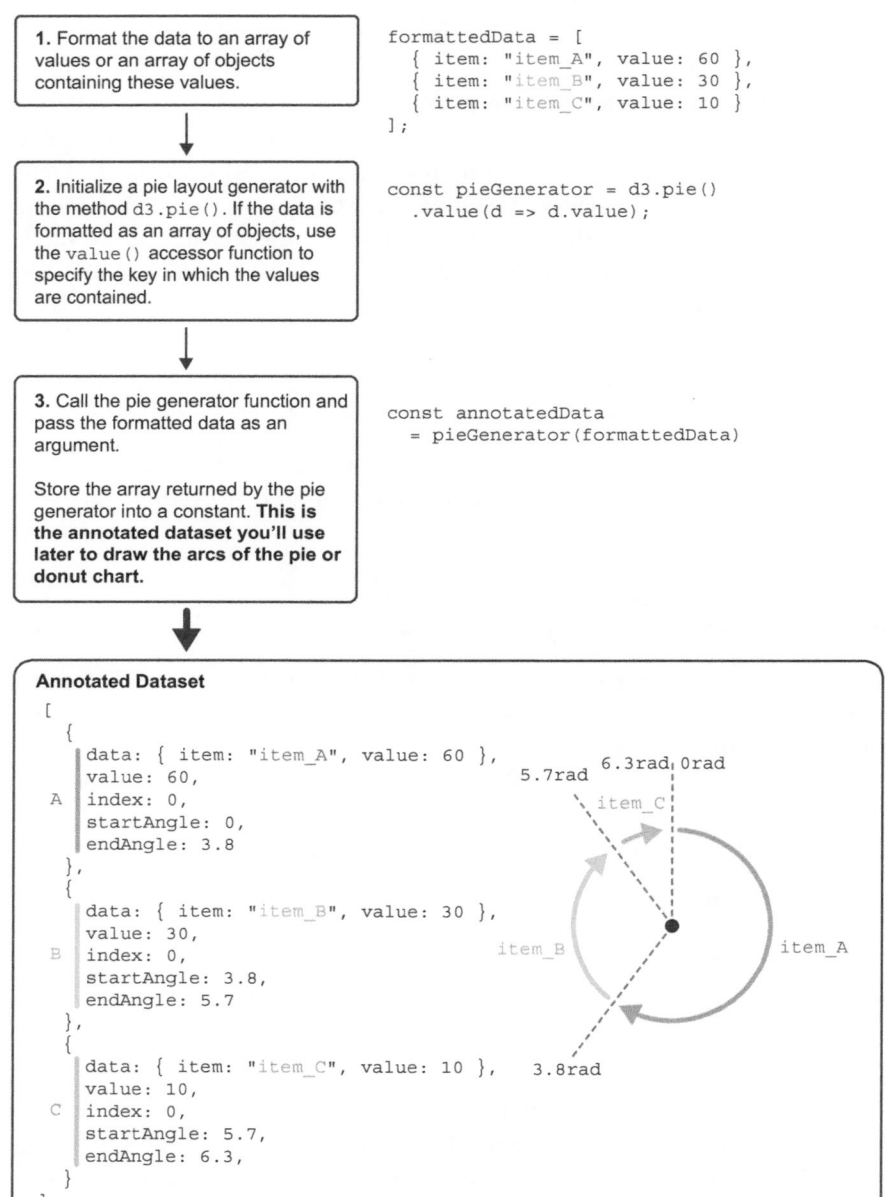

1. Format the data to an array of values or an array of objects containing these values.

```
formattedData = [
  { item: "item_A", value: 60 },
  { item: "item_B", value: 30 },
  { item: "item_C", value: 10 }
];
```

2. Initialize a pie layout generator with the method d3.pie(). If the data is formatted as an array of objects, use the value() accessor function to specify the key in which the values are contained.

```
const pieGenerator = d3.pie()
  .value(d => d.value);
```

3. Call the pie generator function and pass the formatted data as an argument.

Store the array returned by the pie generator into a constant. **This is the annotated dataset you'll use later to draw the arcs of the pie or donut chart.**

```
const annotatedData
  = pieGenerator(formattedData)
```

Annotated Dataset

```
[
  {
    data: { item: "item_A", value: 60 },
    value: 60,
A   index: 0,
    startAngle: 0,
    endAngle: 3.8
  },
  {
    data: { item: "item_B", value: 30 },
    value: 30,
B   index: 0,
    startAngle: 3.8,
    endAngle: 5.7
  },
  {
    data: { item: "item_C", value: 10 },
    value: 10,
C   index: 0,
    startAngle: 5.7,
    endAngle: 6.3,
  }
];
```

Figure 5.6   The pie layout generator is a preprocessing step that generates an annotated dataset containing the start and end angles of each slice of a pie chart. The process usually involves formatting our data, initializing the pie generator function, and calling that function to obtain the annotated data.

5.1.3   Drawing the arcs

With our annotated dataset ready, it's time to draw the arcs of the pie charts! You'll see that the following steps are very similar to how we drew arcs in the previous chapter. For this reason, we won't explain every detail. Refer to chapter 4 if you need a more in-depth discussion.

In listing 5.4, we start by initializing the arc generator by calling the `d3.arc()` method and its various accessor functions responsible for setting the inner and outer radius of the chart, the padding between the slices, and the radius of the slices' corners. If the inner radius is set to 0, we'll get a pie chart, whereas if it's greater than 0, we'll get a donut chart.

The only difference compared to the strategy used in chapter 4 is that this time, we can set the `startAngle()` and `endAngle()` accessor functions while declaring the arc generator. This is because these values are now included in the annotated dataset, and we can tell these accessor functions how to access them via `d.startAngle` and `d.endAngle`.

The last thing we need to do for the arcs to appear on the screen is to use the data-binding pattern to generate one path element for each object in the annotated dataset (there is one object for each arc or slice). Note that in listing 5.4, we give a specific class name to the arcs of each donut (`` `arc-${year}` ``) and use this class name as a selector in the data-binding pattern. Because we're creating the donuts in a loop, this will prevent D3 from overwriting each donut as it generates a new one. Finally, we call the arc generator function to calculate the d attribute of each path.

Listing 5.4   Generating and drawing the arcs (`donut-charts.js`)

```
const arcGenerator = d3.arc()
  .startAngle(d => d.startAngle)
  .endAngle(d => d.endAngle)
  .innerRadius(60)
  .outerRadius(100)
  .padAngle(0.02)
  .cornerRadius(3);
```

> Set the startAngle() and the endAngle() accessor functions, and provide the key from which these values are accessible in the annotated dataset.

```
const arcs = donutContainer
  .selectAll(`.arc-${year}`)
  .data(annotatedData)
  .join("path")
    .attr("class", `arc-${year}`)
    .attr("d", arcGenerator);
```

> Use the data-binding pattern to generate one path element for each object in the annotated dataset.

> Call the arcGenerator() function to obtain the d attribute of each path.

USING A COLOR SCALE

If you save your project and look at the donut charts in your browser, you'll see that their shape is correct, but the arcs are pitch black. This is normal because black is the default fill color in SVG. To improve readability, we'll apply a different color to each arc based on the music format it represents.

An easy and reusable way to apply the right color to each arc is to declare a color scale. In D3, color scales are often created with `d3.scaleOrdinal()`. Ordinal scales map a discrete domain onto a discrete range. In our case, the domain is an array of music formats, and the range is an array containing the color associated with each format.

In the `scales.js` file, we start by declaring an ordinal scale and saving it in the `colorScale` constant. We then set its domain by mapping each format ID from the `formatsInfo` array (available in `shared-constants.js`) into an array. We do the same with the colors, which you can personalize to your liking. Throughout the chapter, we'll reuse this color scale to create all the charts that compose our project:

```
const colorScale = d3.scaleOrdinal();

const defineScales = (data) => {

  colorScale
    .domain(formatsInfo.map(f => f.id))
    .range(formatsInfo.map(f => f.color));

};
```

Back to `donut-charts.js`, where we can set the `fill` attribute of the arcs by passing the music format ID bound to each arc to the color scale:

```
const arcs = donutContainer
  .selectAll(`.arc-${year}`)
  .data(annotatedData)
  .join("path")
    .attr("class", `arc-${year}`)
    .attr("d", arcGenerator)
    .attr("fill", d => colorScale(d.data.format));
```

Save your project, and take a look in your browser—it doesn't look bad! As you can see in figure 5.7, the arcs already appear in descending order, from the largest to the smallest, which can help with readability. We can already see how the face of music changed between 1975, 1995, and 2013, as evidenced by the dominant formats being completely different.

Figure 5.7   Donut charts for the years 1975, 1995, and 2013

5.1.4   Adding labels

In chapter 4, we mentioned that pie charts are sometimes hard to interpret, given that the human brain isn't very good at translating angles into ratios. We can improve the readability of our donut charts by adding a label with the value of each arc, in percentages, onto their centroid, as we did in the previous chapter.

In listing 5.5, we modify slightly the code used to create the arcs (from listing 5.4). First, we use the data-binding pattern to append SVG groups rather than path elements. We then append path elements (for the arcs) and SVG text elements (for the label) into these groups. Because parents pass bound data to children, we'll have access to the data as we shape the arcs and the labels.

We draw the arcs by calling the arc generator, precisely as we did previously. To set the label's text, we need to calculate the ratio, or percentage, represented by each arc. We perform this calculation by subtracting the arc's start angle from its end angle and dividing the result by 2π, the angle covered by a full circle in radians. Note how we store the percentage value into the bound data using bracket notation (`d["percentage"]`). This trick is useful when we need the same calculation for different attributes. It keeps you from repeating the computation multiple times. To return the label's text, we pass the calculated percentage to method `d3.format(".0%")`, which produces a rounded number and adds a percentage symbol at the end of the label.

We apply the same strategy to calculate the centroid of each arc, which is where we want to position the labels. When setting the x attribute of the labels, we calculate the centroid of the related arc (with the technique discussed in chapter 4) and store it in the bound data (`d["centroid"]`). Then, when setting the y attribute, the centroid array is already accessible via `d.centroid`.

For the labels to be horizontally and vertically centered with the centroid, we need to set their `text-anchor` and `dominant-baseline` attributes to `middle`. We also set their color to white with the `fill` attribute and increase their font size to 16 px and their font weight to 500 to improve readability.

If you save your project and look at the donut charts in the browser, you'll see that the labels are working well on large arcs but are almost impossible to read on smaller ones. In a professional project, we could solve this problem by moving the small arcs' labels outside the donut chart. For this project, we simply won't show these labels by setting their `fill-opacity` attribute to 0 when the percentage is smaller than 5%. You can see the final result in figure 5.8.

Listing 5.5 Adding labels on the centroids (`donut-charts.js`)

```
const arcs = donutContainer
  .selectAll(`.arc-${year}`)
  .data(annotatedData)           Use the data-binding pattern to append
  .join("g")              ◁──    SVG groups rather than path elements.
    .attr("class", `arc-${year}`);

arcs                                       Append a path element inside each
  .append("path")                          group, and draw the arcs by calling
    .attr("d", arcGenerator)               the arc generator. Set the fill
    .attr("fill", d => colorScale(d.data.format));   attribute with the color scale.

arcs                      Append a text element
  .append("text")   ◁──   inside each group.
```

```
.text(d => {
  d["percentage"] = (d.endAngle - d.startAngle)
    / (2 * Math.PI);
  return d3.format(".0%")(d.percentage);
})
.attr("x", d => {
  d["centroid"] = arcGenerator
    .startAngle(d.startAngle)
    .endAngle(d.endAngle)
    .centroid();
  return d.centroid[0];
})
.attr("y", d => d.centroid[1])
.attr("text-anchor", "middle")
.attr("dominant-baseline", "middle")
.attr("fill", "#f6fafc")
.attr("fill-opacity", d => d.percentage
  < 0.05 ? 0 : 1)
.style("font-size", "16px")
.style("font-weight", 500);
```

Set the text by calculating the percentage occupied by each arc. Store this value in the bound data (d["percentage"]).

Get the position of the centroid of each arc, and store it in the bound data (d["centroid"]). Then use it to set the x and y attributes of the labels.

Hide the labels positioned over arcs that represent a value smaller than 5%.

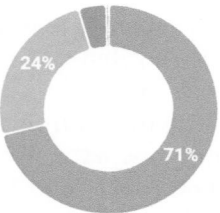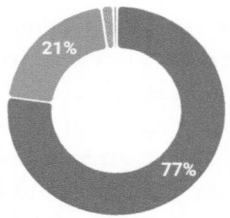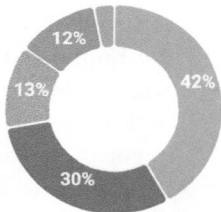

Figure 5.8   Donut charts with percentage labels

As a last step, we'll indicate the year represented by the donut charts with labels positioned in their center. We do so by appending a text element to each donut container. Because we're still looping through the years, we can directly apply the current year as the label's text. In addition, because the donut containers are positioned at the center of the charts, the text element is automatically positioned correctly. All we have to do is set its text-anchor and dominant-baseline properties to center it horizontally and vertically to get the result shown in figure 5.9:

```
donutContainer
  .append("text")
    .text(year)
    .attr("text-anchor", "middle")
    .attr("dominant-baseline", "middle")
    .style("font-size", "24px")
    .style("font-weight", 500);
```

And voilà—our donut charts are complete!

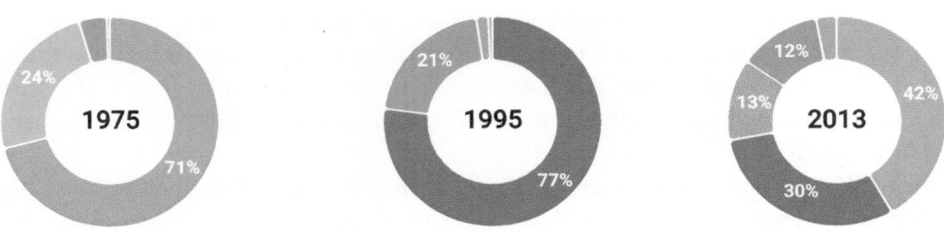

Figure 5.9   Completed donut charts with year labels

The steps to create a pie or donut chart are reviewed in figure 5.10. During the first step, we preprocess the data with layout function `d3.pie()` to obtain an annotated dataset with the angles for each slice. We then draw the arcs with the arc generator function that takes the angles from the annotated dataset and returns each path's `d` attribute. Finally, we add labels to improve the readability of the chart, using SVG text elements.

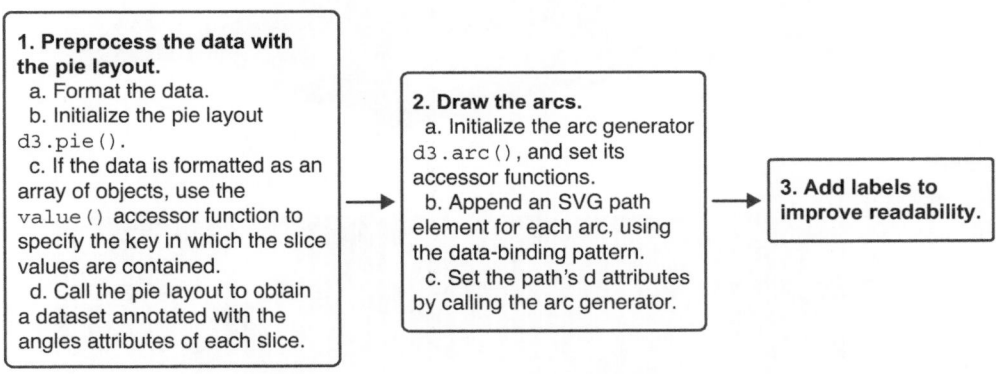

Figure 5.10   The main steps involved in the creation of a pie or donut chart

5.2   *Stacking shapes*

So far, we've dealt with simple examples of information visualization that we might easily create in any spreadsheet software. But you didn't get into this business to make Excel-like charts. You might want to wow your audience with beautiful data, win awards for your aesthetic je ne sais quoi, and evoke deep emotional responses with your representation of change over time.

The streamgraph is a sublime piece of information visualization that represents variation and change. It may seem challenging to create until you start to put the pieces together. Ultimately, a streamgraph is a variant of what's known as a stacked area chart. The layers accrete upon each other and adjust the area of the elements above and below, based on the space taken up by the components closer to the center. It appears organic because that accretive nature mimics the way many organisms grow and seems to imply the kinds of emergent properties that govern the growth and decay of organisms. We'll interpret its appearance later, but first, let's figure out how to build it.

We're looking at a streamgraph in the first section of this book because it's actually not that exotic. A streamgraph is a stacked chart, which means it's fundamentally similar to stacked bar charts, as shown in figure 5.11. Streamgraphs are also similar to the area behind the line chart we created in chapter 4, except that these areas are stacked over one another. In this section, we'll use D3's stack and area generators to create a stacked bar chart followed by a streamgraph.

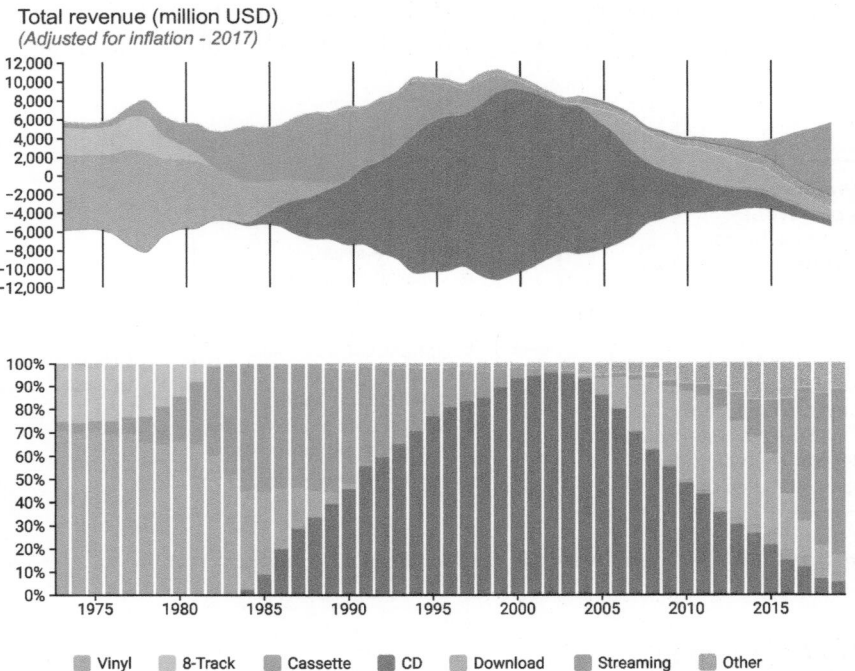

Figure 5.11   Streamgraphs are fundamentally similar to stacked bar charts. In D3, both are created with the stack layout generator.

In D3, the steps for creating a stacked bar chart or a streamgraph are similar, as explained in figure 5.12. First, we initialize a stack layout generator and set the parameters of the stack. Then we pass the original dataset to the stack generator, which will return a new annotated dataset indicating each data point's lower and upper boundary. If we make a streamgraph, we'll also have to initialize an area generator, similar to the line and curve generators discussed in the previous chapter. Finally, we bind the annotated dataset to the SVG shapes required to make our chart, that is, rectangles for a stacked bar chart or paths for a streamgraph. In the case of a streamgraph, the area generator is called to calculate the d attribute of the paths. We'll look at these steps in greater detail in the following subsections.

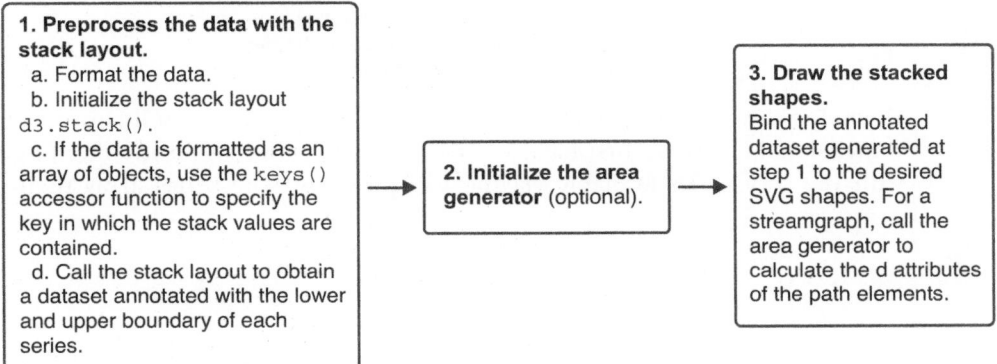

Figure 5.12   The steps to creating a stacked chart with D3

5.2.1   *The stack layout generator*

The stack layout generator is a D3 function that takes a dataset with multiple categories as an input. The dataset used in this chapter's example contains the total sales for different music formats for each year between 1973 and 2019. Each music format will become a series in the stacked chart.

Like the pie layout generator discussed earlier, the stack layout function returns a new, annotated dataset that contains the position of the different series when "stacked" one over the other. The stack generator is part of the d3-shape module.

Let's put the stack layout into action and start working in function drawStacked-Bars(), located in stacked-bars.js. Note that this function already contains the code that appends an SVG container to the div with an ID of "bars", as well as a group container for the inner chart. This is the same strategy that we used in chapter 4, in parallel with the margin convention.

In the following snippet, we start by declaring a stack generator with method d3.stack() and store it in a constant named stackGenerator. We then need to tell the generator which keys from the dataset contain the values we want to stack (what will become the series). We do that with the keys() accessor function, to which we pass an array of the category IDs—here, the identifier of each music format. We create this array by mapping the IDs from the formatsInfo constant. We could also have used the data.columns key attached to the dataset and filtered out the years, as we did in section 5.1.2.

Finally, we call the stack generator and pass the data as an argument to obtain the annotated dataset. We store the new dataset in a constant named `annotatedData`:

```
const stackGenerator = d3.stack()    ◄───┘ Initialize the stack
    .keys(formatsInfo.map(f => f.id));            layout generator.
                                          ◄───────
                                                   Tell the layout function which
const annotatedData = stackGenerator(data);  ◄─── keys from the dataset should
                                                   be used to create the series.
          Call the layout generator, passing the data as an
          argument, to obtain the annotated dataset.
          Store the annotated dataset in a constant.
```

If you log the annotated dataset into the console, you'll see that it consists of a multidimensional array. We first have an array for each series, as illustrated in figure 5.13, with the series' IDs available via the `key` property. The series array then contains

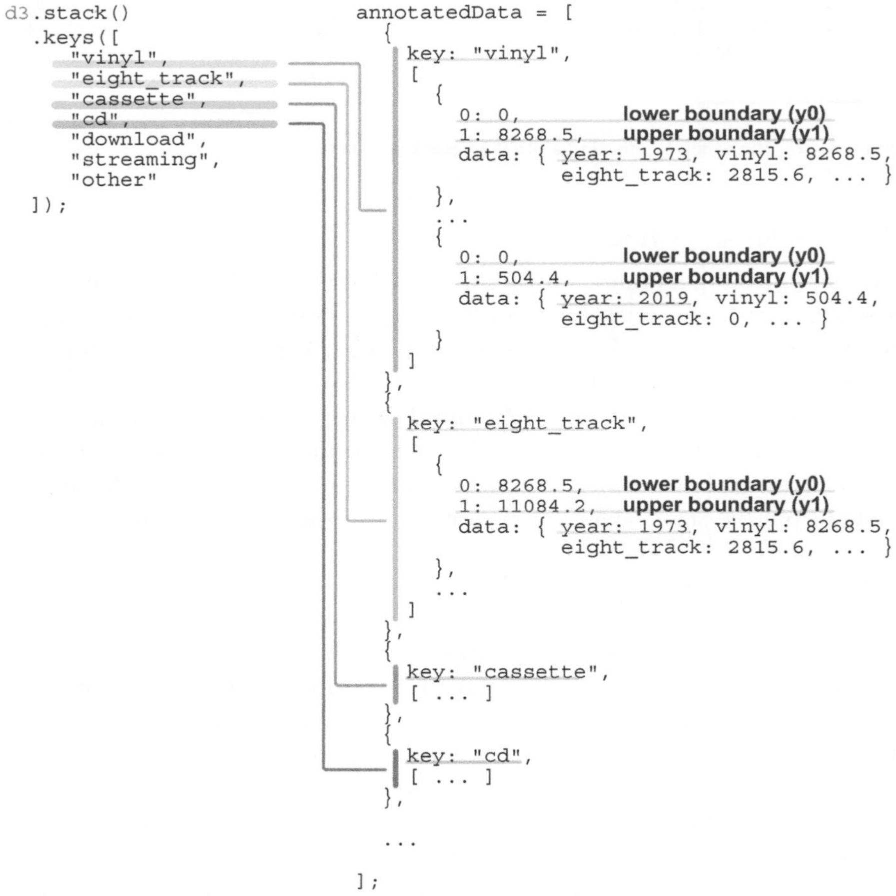

```
d3.stack()                      annotatedData = [
  .keys([                         {
     "vinyl",                       key:  "vinyl",
     "eight_track",                 [
     "cassette",                      {
     "cd",                              0:  0,          lower boundary (y0)
     "download",                        1:  8268.5,     upper boundary (y1)
     "streaming",                       data: { year: 1973, vinyl: 8268.5,
     "other"                                          eight_track: 2815.6, ... }
  ]);                               },
                                    {...
                                      {
                                        0:  0,          lower boundary (y0)
                                        1:  504.4,      upper boundary (y1)
                                        data: { year: 2019, vinyl: 504.4,
                                                        eight_track: 0, ... }
                                      }
                                    ]
                                  },
                                  {
                                    key:  "eight_track",
                                    [
                                      {
                                        0:  8268.5,     lower boundary (y0)
                                        1:  11084.2,    upper boundary (y1)
                                        data: { year: 1973, vinyl: 8268.5,
                                                        eight_track: 2815.6, ... }
                                      },
                                      ...
                                    ]
                                  },
                                  {
                                    key:  "cassette",
                                    [ ... ]
                                  },
                                  {
                                    key:  "cd",
                                    [ ... ]
                                  },

                                    ...

                                ];
```

Figure 5.13   Annotated dataset returned by the stack layout generator

another set of arrays, one for each year from the dataset. These last arrays include the lower and upper boundaries of the category for the related year and the original data for that year. The lower and upper boundaries are accessed by index `d[0]` and `d[1]`, respectively, if `d` corresponds to the array.

The format `"vinyl"` is the first key to be treated by the stack layout. Note how its lower boundary is always `0`, while its upper boundary corresponds to the sales of that format for the year. Then the following category is `"8-track"`. The lower boundary for 8-tracks corresponds to the upper boundary for vinyl, to which we add the sales of 8-tracks to get its upper boundary, which creates a stack.

If the notion of "stack" isn't clear yet, figure 5.14 might help. If we take a closer look at the year 1986 from the original dataset, we'll see that music was available primarily via three formats: vinyl with sales of \$2,825M, cassettes with \$5,830M, and CDs with \$2,170M. We show these data points, drawn independently, on the left side of figure 5.14.

When we use the stack layout, we create what we'll call "data columns" rather than "data points," with each column having a lower and an upper boundary. If our stack

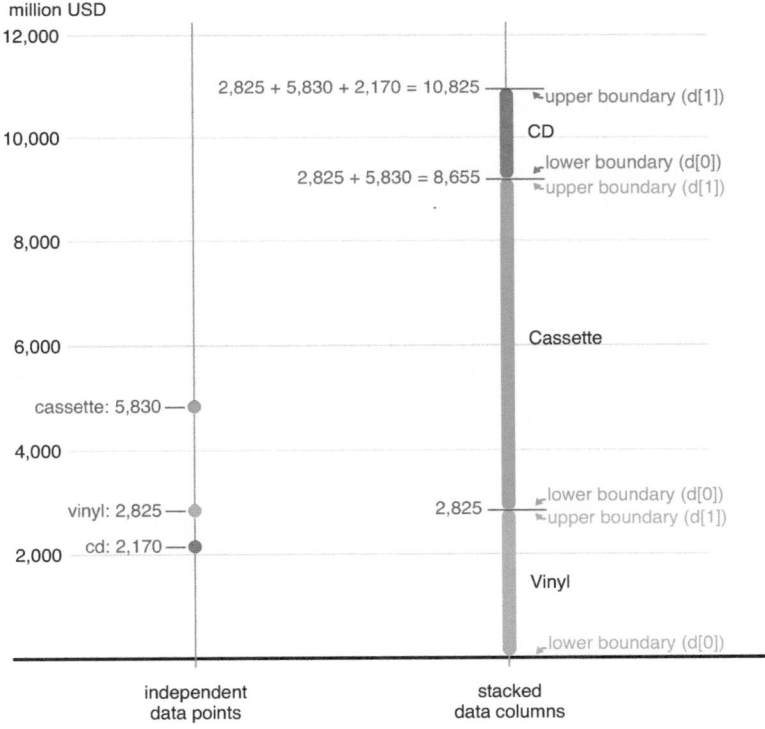

Figure 5.14 **The stack layout generator transforms data points into stacked data columns and returns an annotated dataset containing each data column's lower and upper boundaries. Here we see an example for the year 1986.**

starts with vinyl, the lower boundary is 0, and the upper boundary corresponds to the sales of vinyl for the year 1986: $2,825M. We then stack the cassette sales over it: the lower boundary corresponding to the upper boundary for vinyl ($2,825M), and the upper boundary being the addition of the sales for vinyl and cassette ($8,655M). This upper boundary becomes the lower boundary for CD sales, whose upper boundary corresponds to the addition of the sales from the three formats ($10,825M). These boundaries are accessed in the annotated dataset by index (`d[0]` and `d[1]`).

5.2.2   *Drawing a stacked bar chart*

In this section, we'll create the stacked bar chart that you've seen earlier at the bottom of figure 5.11. Stacked bar charts are similar to the bar charts we've already made in chapters 2 and 3, except that the bars are divided into multiple categories, or series. Stacked bar charts and stacked visualizations in general are often used to show the evolution of trends over time.

Like we did for the donut chart, we'll use the annotated dataset returned by the stack layout to draw the bars corresponding to each category. But first, we'll need a scale for the vertical axis to translate each rectangle's lower and upper boundary into a vertical position. We want the height of the bars to be linearly proportional to the sales, so in listing 5.6, we use a linear scale. Because this scale will need to access the annotated data, we'll declare it inside function `drawStackedBars()`.

The scale domain goes from 0 to the maximum upper boundary available in the annotated data. We know that this maximum value must live inside the last series of the annotated data, which will be positioned at the top of the chart. We can access this series with the length property (`annotatedData[annotatedData.length - 1]`). Then we use method `d3.max()` to retrieve the maximum value under property `d[1]`, which corresponds to the upper boundary.

The range of the vertical scale varies from `innerHeight`, the bottom of the inner chart, to 0, the top of the inner chart (remember that the SVG vertical axis is positive in the downward direction). Finally, we chain the scale declaration with method `.nice()`, which will ensure that the domain ends on "nice" round values rather than the actual maximum value in the annotated dataset.

Listing 5.6   Declaring the vertical scale (`stacked-bars.js`)

```
const maxUpperBoundary = d3.max(annotatedData[annotatedData.length - 1], d
⇢ => d[1]);

const yScale = d3.scaleLinear()
  .domain([0, maxUpperBoundary])
  .range([innerHeight, 0])
  .nice();
```

We're now ready to append the bars. To do so, we loop through the annotated data and append the series one after the other, as detailed in listing 5.7. We start with the data-binding pattern to append one rectangle for each year in the series array (there's one series for each music format). Note how we apply a class name related to the current series to the rectangles and use it as a selector. If we simply use `"rect"` elements as a selector, every time the loop executes, the rectangles previously created will be removed and replaced by the new ones.

We then set the rectangles' x attributes by passing the current year to xScale and their `width` attributes by calling the `bandwidth` property of the band scale. The y attribute, corresponding to the vertical position of the rectangle's top-left corner, is returned by the vertical scale declared previously, to which we pass the upper boundary of the rectangle (`d[1]`).

Similarly, the height of the rectangles is the difference between the position of their upper and lower boundaries. Here there's a bit of a catch. Because the SVG vertical axis is positive in the downward direction, `yScale(d[0])` returns a higher value than `yScale(d[1])`. We need to subtract the latter from the former to avoid giving a negative value to the y attribute, which would throw an error.

Finally, we set the `fill` attribute by passing the current music format to the color scale, which is accessible under the `key` property for each series, as shown previously in figure 5.13.

Listing 5.7 Appending the stacked bars (`stacked-bars.js`)

```
annotatedData.forEach(series => {        ◁──  Loop through each series
                                              from the annotated dataset.
  innerChart
    .selectAll(`.bar-${series.key}`)
    .data(series)
    .join("rect")
      .attr("class", d => `bar-${series.key}`)      Use the data-binding pattern to
                                                    append a rectangle for each year.
                                                    Apply a different class name to
                                                    each series, and use it as a selector
      .attr("x", d => xScale(d.data.year))          to avoid removing the previous
      .attr("y", d => yScale(d[1]))                 rectangles as the loop progresses.
      .attr("width", xScale.bandwidth())
      .attr("height", d => yScale(d[0]) - yScale(d[1]))
      .attr("fill", colorScale(series.key));

});
```

Use the scales to position the rectangles and set their fill attributes.

If you save your project, you'll see that there is no horizontal space between the bars. We fix that in the next listing by going back to the declaration of our band scale (xScale), and setting its `paddingInner()` accessor function to a value of 20%, as we did in chapter 3.

Listing 5.8 Adding padding between the bars (`scales.js`)

```
xScale
  .domain(data.map(d => d.year))
  .range([0, innerWidth])
  .paddingInner(0.2);
```

To complete our stacked bar chart, we need to add axes. In listing 5.9, we start by declaring a bottom axis with method `d3.axisBottom()` and passing `xScale` as a reference.

We chain the axis declaration with method `.tickValues()`, which allows us to state the exact ticks and labels that we want to see on the chart. Otherwise, D3 will provide a tick and label pair for each year, which will look cramped and hard to read. Method `.tickValues()` takes an array of values as an argument. We generate this array with method `d3.range()` and state that we want every integer from 1975 to 2020, with a step of 5.

We also hide the ticks at each end of the bottom axis with method `.tickSize-Outer()`, to which we pass a value of `0`. Methods `tickValues()` and `tickSizeOuter()` can both be found in the d3-axis module, while `d3.range()` is part of the d3-array module. Finally, we append the bottom axis to the chart with the `call()` method inside a group translated to the bottom and do the same for the left axis.

Listing 5.9   Appending the axes (`stacked-bars.js`)

```
const bottomAxis = d3.axisBottom(xScale)
  .tickValues(d3.range(1975, 2020, 5))
  .tickSizeOuter(0);

innerChart
  .append("g")
    .attr("transform", `translate(0, ${innerHeight})`)
    .call(bottomAxis);

const leftAxis = d3.axisLeft(yScale);
innerChart
  .append("g")
    .call(leftAxis);
```

Declare the bottom axis generator. Set the ticks and labels that we want on the chart with method .tickValues(), and hide the outer ticks with .tickSizeOuter(0).

Append the bottom axis inside an SVG group, and translate it to the bottom of the inner chart.

Declare and append the left axis.

If you save your project and take a look in your browser, you might find that the axis labels are a little too small. In addition, as mentioned in chapter 4, D3 applies the font family `sans-serif` to the SVG group that contains the axis elements, which means that the font family of the project isn't inherited by the axis labels. From CSS file `visualization.css`, we can target the axis labels with the `.tick text` selector and modify their style properties. In the following snippet, we change their `font-family`, `font-size`, and `font-weight` properties:

```
.tick text {
  font-family: 'Roboto', sans-serif;
  font-size: 14px;
  font-weight: 500;
}
```

Once completed, your stacked bar chart will look like the one in figure 5.15 but not like the one in figure 5.2 or from the hosted project (http://mng.bz/6nVo) yet. We'll get there in a moment.

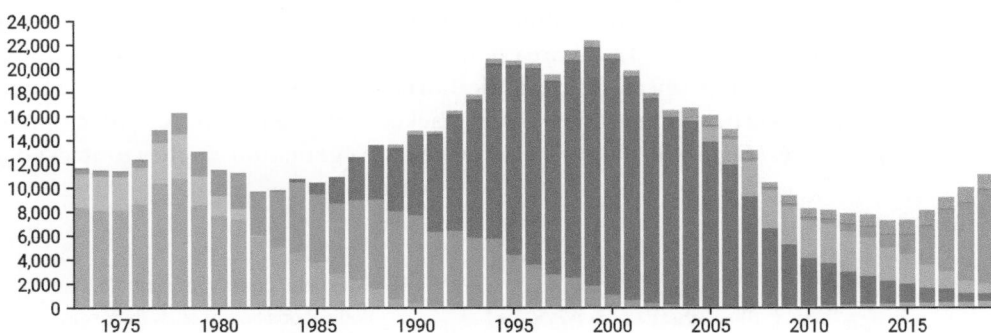

Figure 5.15   First version of the stacked bar chart

5.2.3   *Drawing a streamgraph*

In the previous subsection, we used the stack layout function to generate an annotated dataset from which we drew the rectangles of a stacked bar chart. Now we'll apply a similar strategy to draw a streamgraph. Although streamgraphs look more complex than stacked bar charts, they are simple to create with D3. The main difference is that for streamgraphs, we use the annotated dataset to append areas while we append rectangles for stacked bar charts.

In this subsection, we'll work in function drawStreamGraph(), which you can find in the streamgraph.js file. This function already contains code that appends an SVG container to the div with an ID of "streamgraph", as well as a group container for the inner chart. This is the same strategy that we used in chapter 4 in parallel with the margin convention.

In listing 5.10, we initialize the stack generator and call it to obtain the annotated data. We also declare a linear scale to calculate the position of the vertical boundaries. This is the exact same code we've used for the stacked bar chart. For now, don't worry about the fact that we're duplicating code. We'll come back to it in the next subsection.

Listing 5.10   **Declaring the stack generator (**streamgraph.js**)**

```
const stackGenerator = d3.stack()                      Initialize and call the stack generator
  .keys(formatsInfo.map(f => f.id));                   to obtain the annotated data.
const annotatedData = stackGenerator(data);

const maxUpperBoundary = d3.max(annotatedData[annotatedData.length - 1], d
  => d[1]);
```

```
const yScale = d3.scaleLinear()
  .domain([0, maxUpperBoundary])
  .range([innerHeight, 0])
  .nice();
```

Declare a linear scale for the vertical axis.

To draw the stacked areas, we'll need an area generator function that will be responsible for calculating the d attribute of each path element used to draw the series. As explained in chapter 4, the area generator uses at least three accessor functions; in our case, there is one to retrieve the horizontal position of each data point, one for the lower vertical boundaries of the stacked areas, and one for their upper vertical boundaries. Figure 5.16 illustrates how the area generator applies to stacked areas.

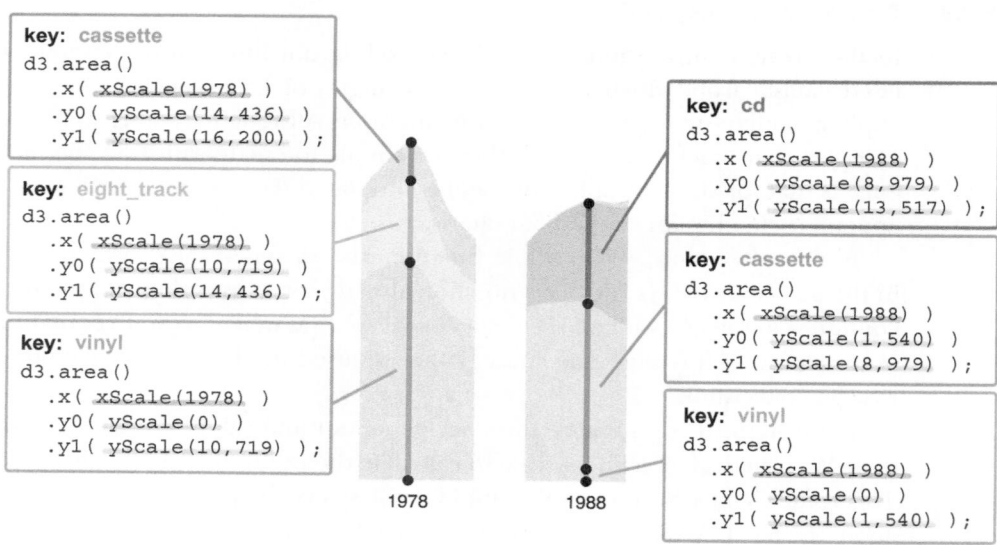

Figure 5.16 The area generator d3.area() is combined with three or more accessor functions. When employed in combination with the stack layout for a streamgraph, it uses the lower and upper boundaries (y0 and y1) of each data point to calculate the d attribute of the areas.

In the following snippet, we initialize area generator d3.area(). First, we use its x() accessor function to calculate the horizontal position of each data point. Because xScale is a band scale, it returns the position of the beginning of each band for the related year, which is accessible in the annotated dataset in the data object of each data point (d.data.year). If we want the data columns to align horizontally with the center of the bars of the stacked bar chart, we need to translate the data points toward the right by half the width of the bars, which we can calculate with the bandwidth() property of the band scale.

Then we use the y0() and y(1) accessor functions to determine the vertical position of the columns along the lower and upper boundary of each series. This position is calculated with yScale, declared earlier, to which we pass the values of the boundaries, accessible by their array index in the bound data: d[0] for the lower boundary and d[1] for the upper boundary.

Finally, if we want to interpolate the data points along each boundary to obtain curves rather than lines, we use the curve() accessor function. Here we chose curve interpolation function d3.curveCatmullRom:

```
const areaGenerator = d3.area()
  .x(d => xScale(d.data.year) + xScale.bandwidth()/2)
  .y0(d => yScale(d[0]))
  .y1(d => yScale(d[1]))
  .curve(d3.curveCatmullRom);
```

> **NOTE** As emphasized previously, curve interpolations modify the representation of data and must be chosen with care. Refer to chapter 4, section 4.2.2, for a discussion and demonstration.

We're now ready to draw the stacked areas! First, we use the data-binding pattern to generate an SVG path element for each series in the annotated dataset. We call the area generator function to obtain the d attribute of each path, and we call the color scale for their fill attribute.

Note how we've appended the paths inside an SVG group to keep the markup organized and easy to inspect. This will also help maintain a proper juxtaposition of the areas and vertical grid later:

```
innerChart
  .append("g")
    .attr("class", "areas-container")
  .selectAll("path")
  .data(annotatedData)
  .join("path")
    .attr("d", areaGenerator)
    .attr("fill", d => colorScale(d.key));
```

The last thing we'll do in this section is add axes and labels to the streamgraph. We start by declaring axis generator d3.axisLeft() and passing yScale as a reference. We then append the axis elements inside an SVG group, using the .call() method:

```
const leftAxis = d3.axisLeft(yScale);
innerChart
  .append("g")
  .call(leftAxis);
```

EXPANDING AXIS TICKS INTO A GRID

We could potentially omit the x-axis, given that the streamgraph is horizontally aligned with the stacked bar chart below and that this chart has the same x-axis. But we'll use this opportunity to discuss how the ticks on an axis can be expanded to create a grid behind a chart.

First, we need to remember that SVG elements are drawn in their order of appearance within the SVG container. So if we want the grid to appear behind the streamgraph, we need to draw it before. That's why the following code snippet should be positioned *before* the one that appends the streamgraph's paths.

So far, the code to generate the bottom axis is identical to the one used for the stacked bar chart, including the usage of the `tickValues()` and `tickSizeOuter()` methods:

```
const bottomAxis = d3.axisBottom(xScale)
  .tickValues(d3.range(1975, 2020, 5))
  .tickSizeOuter(0);

innerChart
  .append("g")
    .attr("class", "x-axis-streamgraph")
    .attr("transform", `translate(0, ${innerHeight})`)
    .call(bottomAxis);
```

To transform the ticks into a grid, all we have to do is extend their length using the `tickSize()` method. Via this method, we give the ticks a length corresponding to the height of the inner chart, multiplied by -1 to make them grow in the upward direction:

```
const bottomAxis = d3.axisBottom(xScale)
  .tickValues(d3.range(1975, 2020, 5))
  .tickSizeOuter(0)
  .tickSize(innerHeight * -1);
```

> **NOTE** We could also avoid translating the axis in the first place and set this length to a positive value to make the ticks grow in the top-to-bottom direction. This approach can also be applied to a left or a right axis whenever you need a horizontal grid.

Finally, we can choose to hide the horizontal line at the bottom of the axis and the years labels by giving them an opacity of 0. To do so, we use the class name given to the x-axis container used previously (x-axis-streamgraph) and use it as a selector in the CSS `visualization.css` file. As you can see in the following snippet, the opacity of the horizontal line accessed via `.x-axis-streamgraph path` is managed with the `stroke-opacity` property, while we need to use `fill-opacity` to hide the year labels (`.x-axis-streamgraph text`). We could also have used the D3 `style()` method to handle the opacity from within `streamgraph.js`:

```
.x-axis-streamgraph path {
  stroke-opacity: 0;
```

```
}
.x-axis-streamgraph text {
  fill-opacity: 0;
}
```

HANDLING COMPLEX SVG TEXT LAYOUTS

As a final touch, we'll add a label above the left axis to indicate what this axis represents. As you can see in figure 5.2, shown earlier, or on the hosted project (http://mng.bz/6nVo), the streamgraph's label is broken over two lines: the first text of "Total revenue (million USD)" and the second text of "Adjusted for inflation."

We'll build this label using SVG text. One thing that is important to know about SVG text is that it doesn't behave like HTML text. For example, if we add text inside HTML elements, the text will automatically break lines or reflow based on the space available horizontally. SVG text doesn't do that, and the position of each text element needs to be handled separately.

To manipulate subtext inside SVG text, we can use the `tspan` element. Breaking down text into multiple `tspan`s allows us to adjust their style and position separately by using their `x`, `y`, `dx`, and `dy` attributes—the first two being applied in reference to the coordinate system of the SVG container, and the last two in reference to the previous text or `tspan` element:

- `x`—Horizontal position of the text baseline, in reference to the coordinate system of the SVG container
- `y`—Vertical position of the text baseline, in reference to the coordinate system of the SVG container
- `dx`—Shifts the horizontal position of the text baseline, in reference to the previous text element
- `dy`—Shifts the vertical position of the text baseline, in reference to the previous text element

In all of these definitions, it's important to remember that the text baseline is controlled horizontally by its `text-anchor` attribute and vertically by its `dominant-baseline` attribute.

To create our label, we can use three `tspan` elements positioned inside an SVG text, as illustrated in figure 5.17. If the `dominant-baseline` attribute of the text element is set to `hanging`, the text will appear directly below and to the right of the origin of the SVG container. Using `dx` and `dy`, we can move the second and third span, respectively, to their proper positions based on figure 5.17.

```
<text>
  <tspan>Total revenue</tspan>
  <tspan>(million USD)</tspan>
  <tspan>Adjusted for inflation</tspan>
</text>
```

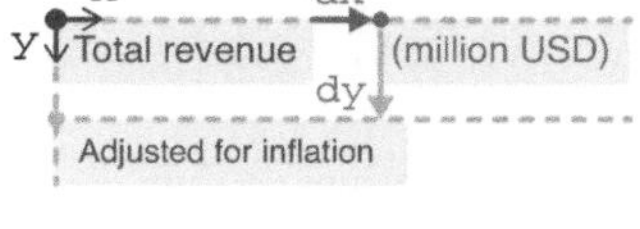

Figure 5.17 `tspan` elements allow for manipulating the style and position of subtext items separately. We use the attributes `dx` and `dy` to set a position relative to the previous text element.

In the following snippet, we put that strategy into action. First, we append a text element into our SVG container and set its `dominant-baseline` attribute to the value `hanging`, which means that the baseline of the text and its children will be positioned right above them.

We save the text selection into constant `leftAxisLabel` and reuse it to append three `tspan` elements into the text container. We set the text of the first `tspan` to `"Total revenue"`, the second one to `"(million USD)"`, and the third to `"Adjusted for inflation"`:

```
const leftAxisLabel = svg
  .append("text")
    .attr("dominant-baseline", "hanging");

leftAxisLabel
  .append("tspan")
    .text("Total revenue");

leftAxisLabel
  .append("tspan")
    .text("(million USD)");

leftAxisLabel
  .append("tspan")
    .text("Adjusted for inflation");
```

By default, the `tspan` elements appear one after another on the same horizontal line. Save your project, and take a look at the labels to confirm.

To move the second `tspan` slightly toward the right, we can set its `dx` attribute and give it a value of `5`. To move the third `tspan` below the first and the second, we can use the `y` or the `dy` attributes and give it a value of `20`. Both attributes will have the same effect in this particular case. Finally, if we want the left side of the third `tspan` to align with the left border of the SVG container, it's best to use the `x` attribute and set it to zero:

```
const leftAxisLabel = svg
  .append("text")
    .attr("dominant-baseline", "hanging");

leftAxisLabel
  .append("tspan")
    .text("Total revenue");

leftAxisLabel
  .append("tspan")
    .text("(million USD)")
    .attr("dx", 5);

leftAxisLabel
  .append("tspan")
    .text("Adjusted for inflation")
    .attr("x", 0)
    .attr("dy", 20);
```

Often, `tspan` elements are used to apply different styles to a portion of the text. As an example, we can reduce the opacity of the second and third `tspan` elements to give them a gray color and reduce the `font-size` of the third `tspan` because it conveys secondary information in comparison to the rest of the label:

```
const leftAxisLabel = svg
  .append("text")
    .attr("dominant-baseline", "hanging");

leftAxisLabel
  .append("tspan")
    .text("Total revenue");

leftAxisLabel
  .append("tspan")
    .text(" (million USD)")
    .attr("dx", 5)
    .attr("fill-opacity", 0.7);

leftAxisLabel
  .append("tspan")
    .text("Adjusted for inflation")
    .attr("x", 0)
    .attr("dy", 20)
    .attr("fill-opacity", 0.7)
    .style("font-size", "14px");
```

The first iteration of our streamgraph is now complete and is shown in figure 5.18. When the vertical baseline of such a chart is located at 0, we often name it a stacked area chart, while streamgraphs tend to have their areas positioned around a central baseline. In the next subsection, we'll discuss how we can change the baseline of the chart. But before we get there, it's interesting to observe how similar the stacked bar chart and the stacked area chart look at this point. The latter looks like a smoothed version of the first one.

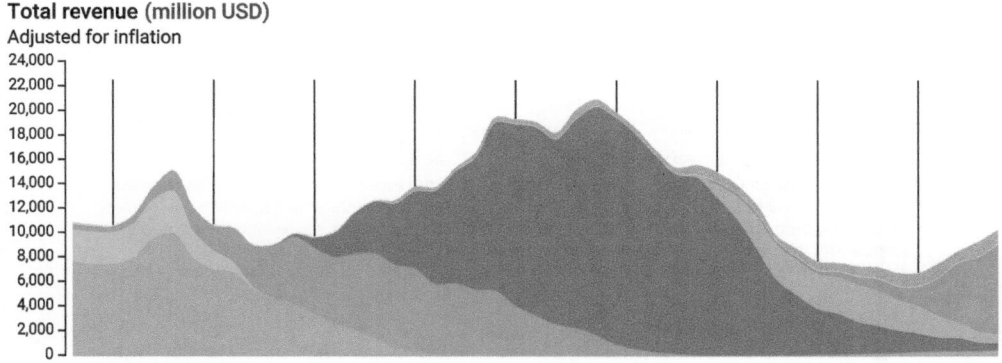

Figure 5.18 First iteration of our streamgraph, which is also referred to as a stacked area chart

5.2.4   *The stack order and stack offset properties*

We can bring our stacked bar and stacked area charts a step further by controlling the order in which the series are stacked and how they are vertically positioned around a zero baseline. This level of control is achieved with the `order()` and `offset()` accessor functions, both applied to the stack layout generator.

Let's first take a look at the `order()` accessor function, which controls the order in which the shapes are vertically stacked. D3 has six built-in orders that can be passed as an argument, as illustrated in figure 5.19.

`d3.stackOrderNone` is the default order, which means that it's the one that is applied if the `order()` accessor function isn't set. It stacks the shapes corresponding to each series in the same order as they are listed in the `keys` array, from bottom to

`d3.stackOrderNone`

The series are stacked in the same order as in the `key()` accessor function. If the order accessor function is not set, `d3.stackOrderNone` is used by default.

`d3.stackOrderReverse`

The series are stacked in the reversed order as in the `key()` accessor function.

`d3.stackOrderAscending`

The series are organized in ascending order of total sum, starting with the series with the smallest total sum at the bottom.

`d3.stackOrderDescending`

The series are organized in descending order of total sum, starting with the series with the highest total sum at the bottom.

`d3.stackOrderAppearance`

Finds the index at which each series reaches its maximum value and stacks the series in ascending order of that index, starting with the series with the earliest index at the bottom.

`d3.stackOrderInsideOut`

Finds the index at which each series reaches its maximum value. The series with the earliest index is positioned inside, and the ones with later indexes outside. This order is recommended for streamgraphs along with `d3.stackOffsetWiggle`.

Figure 5.19   D3 allows controlling the order in which the shapes are stacked with the `order()` accessor function. Here we see examples with stacked areas, but the same principles apply to stacked bar charts.

top. `d3.stackOrderReverse` reverses that order, starting with the last key at the bottom and ending with the first key at the top.

`d3.stackOrderAscending` calculates the total sum of each series. The series with the smallest total sum is positioned at the bottom, and the other ones are stacked following an ascending order. Similarly, `d3.stackOrderDescending` positions the series with the largest total sum at the bottom and stacks the series in descending order.

The last two orders calculate the index at which each series reaches its maximum value. `d3.stackOrderAppearance` stacks the series in the order in which they reach their peak values, which is great for readability, especially for stacks with a zero baseline. `d3.stackOrderInsideOut`, on the other hand, positions the series with the earliest peak value at the middle of the chart and the series with the latest peaks outside. This order works great for streamgraphs where the shapes are distributed around a central baseline.

The other accessor function of the stack layout, called `offset()`, controls the position of the zero baseline of the chart and how the shapes are distributed around it. D3 has five built-in offsets, as shown in figure 5.20.

`d3.stackOffsetNone`

Applies a zero baseline and position the shapes above it. If the offset accessor function is not set, `d3.stackOffsetNone` is used by default.

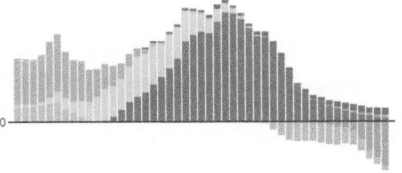

`d3.stackOffsetDiverging`

Moves positive values above the baseline and negative values below it. Best used with stacked bar charts rather than stacked areas.

`d3.stackOffsetSilhouette`

Shifts the baseline to the center of the chart by distributing the shapes above and below.

`d3.stackOffsetWiggle`

Shifts the baseline to minimize the wiggle in each series. This offset is recommended for streamgraphs along with `d3.stackOrderInsideOut`.

`d3.stackOffsetExpand`

Applies a zero baseline and normalizes the values between 0 and 1.

Figure 5.20   D3 allows controlling how the shapes are positioned in regard to the baseline with the `offset()` accessor function. Here we see examples with stacked areas and stacked bars.

d3.stackOffsetNone positions all the shapes above the zero baseline. It's the default offset. The following three offsets distribute the shapes above and below the baseline: d3.stackOffsetDiverging positions the positive values above the baseline and the negative ones below. This offset is best suited for stacked bar charts. d3.stack-OffsetSilhouette shifts the baseline to the center of the chart. d3.stackOffset-Wiggle acts similarly but optimizes the position of the baseline to minimize the wiggle, or the alternate up and down movement, of the series. These three offsets require adapting the domain of the vertical scale to accommodate the position of the baseline.

Finally, d3.stackOffsetExpand normalizes the data values between 0 and 1 so that the sum at each index is 100%. When normalizing values, the domain of the vertical scale also varies between 0 and 1.

When creating stacked layouts, we usually combine an order and an offset to achieve the desired result. Although there's no strict rule regarding when we should use one order or an offset over another, the goal should always be to improve readability and/or direct the reader's attention on the story we are trying to emphasize.

For this chapter's project, we'll use the order() and offset() accessor functions to transform the stacked area chart into a streamgraph with a central baseline and the stacked bar chart to represent relative values (between 0% and 100%).

One thing to note before we get started is that the order() and offset() accessor functions can significantly change the annotated dataset returned by the layout generator. For example, by turning the stacked area chart into a streamgraph, the sales value represented will no longer vary between 0 and 24,000, but rather between −12,000 and 12,000. Similarly, if we use d3.stackOffsetExpand to normalize the sales displayed by the stacked bar chart, the annotated data will be contained between 0 and 1. These different values must be taken into consideration when setting the domain of the vertical scale.

A simple way to consider the domain variation brought by different offset() accessor functions is to ensure that we always calculate the minimum and the maximum values in the annotated dataset and set the domain accordingly.

In listing 5.11, we start by declaring two empty arrays, one in which we'll store the minimum value of each series, and another one in which we'll store the maximum values. Then we loop trough the annotated dataset, find the minimum and maximum values for each series using d3.min() and d3.max(), and push them into their corresponding array. Finally, we extract the minimum and maximum values from each array and use them to set the domain.

This strategy can be applied to both the streamgraph and the stacked bar chart. For the stacked bar chart, you might want to remove the nice() method from the scale declaration to only show values between 0 and 1.

Listing 5.11   Updating yScale (stacked-bar.js + streamgraph.js)

```
const minLowerBoundaries = [];
const maxUpperBoundaries = [];
```
Declare two empty arrays, one to store the minimum value of each series, and another to store the maximum values.

```
annotatedData.forEach(series => {
  minLowerBoundaries.push(d3.min(series, d => d[0]));
  maxUpperBoundaries.push(d3.max(series, d => d[1]));
});
```
Loop through the annotated dataset, and find the minimum and the maximum value in each series. Push these values into the corresponding arrays.

```
const minDomain = d3.min(minLowerBoundaries);
const maxDomain = d3.max(maxUpperBoundaries);
```
Extract the minimum and maximum values from each array.

```
const yScale = d3.scaleLinear()
  .domain([minDomain, maxDomain])
  .range([innerHeight, 0])
  .nice();
```
Use the minimum and maximum values to set the domain.

With this modification in place, you'll be free to test any order of offset value, and the domain of `yScale` will adjust automatically.

Now, to turn the stacked area chart into a streamgraph, all we have to do is chain the `order()` and `offset()` accessor functions to its stack generator declared earlier. Here we use order `d3.stackOrderInsideOut` in combination with offset `d3.stackOffsetSilhouette`. We encourage you to test a few combinations to see how they affect the data representation:

```
const stackGenerator = d3.stack()
  .keys(formatsInfo.map(f => f.id))
  .order(d3.stackOrderInsideOut)
  .offset(d3.stackOffsetSilhouette);
```

> **TIP** Streamgraphs are aesthetically pleasing, and they certainly grab attention. But they can also be hard to read. They are a great option when you want to give an overview of the evolution of a phenomenon over time. But if you want your reader to be able to read and compare values precisely, stacked bar charts or paired bar charts are better options. Tooltips can also help with the readability of streamgraphs. We'll build one in chapter 7.

Similarly, we modify the stacked bar chart by setting its offset to `d3.stackOffset-Expand`, which will normalize the sales values between 0 and 1. We also set the order to `d3.stackOrderDescending` to emphasize how the CD format had dominated the market around the year 2000. Again, try a few combinations, and see how thay can change the focus of the story conveyed by the chart:

```
const stackGenerator = d3.stack()
  .keys(formatsInfo.map(f => f.id))
  .order(d3.stackOrderDescending)
  .offset(d3.stackOffsetExpand);
```

5.3 Adding a legend to a project

In this last section, we'll discuss how legends can be easily built with traditional HTML elements, and we'll put that into practice by placing a color legend below the stacked bar chart. Legends are an essential part of data visualization and help readers interpret what they see. They usually contain text, and we know that SVG text isn't always convenient to manipulate. If you look at the color legend we're about to build in figure 5.21, you'll see that it consists of a series of colored squares and labels. Building this legend with SVG elements would involve calculating the exact position of each rectangle and text element. That's possible, but there's an easier way.

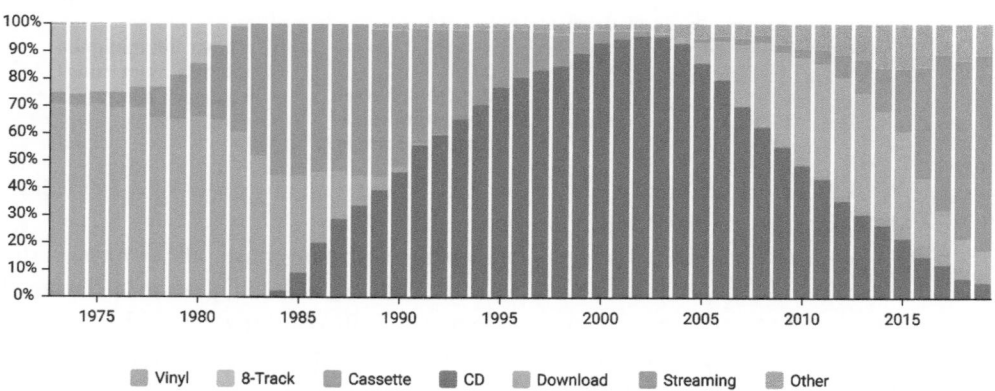

Figure 5.21   Color legend that we'll build in this section, positioned below the stacked bar chart

D3 isn't just used to control SVG elements; it can create and manipulate any element from the DOM. This means that we can build the legend with traditional HTML elements and use CSS to position them. There are many ways to proceed, but such a legend calls to be structured as an HTML unordered list (`<ul></ul>`). Each combination of color with a label can be stored in an `<li></li>` element, with one `<span></span>` element holding the color and another one containing the label, as shown in the following example:

```
<ul>
  <li>
    <span> color 1 </span>
    <span> label 1 </span>
  </li>
  <li>
    <span> color 2 </span>
    <span> label 2 </span>
  </li>

  ...

</ul>
```

To build this HTML structure with D3, we go to the `legend.js` file and start working inside function `addLegend()`. In the following snippet, we select the `div` with a class of `legend-container` that already exists in `index.html`. We append a `ul` element into this `div` and give it a class of `color-legend`.

Then we use the data-binding pattern to append an `li` element for each format included in the `formatsInfo` array, available in `shared-constants.js`. We save this selection into a constant named `legendItems`.

We call the `legendItems` selection, append a `span` element into it, and set the span's `background-color` attribute based on the related music format. To do so, we can directly access the color key from `formatsInfo` or call the color scale. Finally, we append another `span` element and set its text to the label key of the current format:

```
const legendItems = d3.select(".legend-container")
  .append("ul")
    .attr("class", "color-legend")
  .selectAll(".color-legend-item")
  .data(formatsInfo)
  .join("li")
    .attr("class", "color-legend-item");
```

Create an HTML unordered list (`<ul></ul>`), and use the data-binding pattern to append a list element (`<li></li>`) for each music format.

```
legendItems
  .append("span")
    .attr("class", "color-legend-item-color")
    .style("background-color", d => d.color);
```

Append a span element into each list item, and set its background-color property according to the music format.

```
legendItems
  .append("span")
    .attr("class", "color-legend-item-label")
    .text(d => d.label);
```

Append another span element into each list item, and set its text to correspond to the label of the music format.

If you applied the same class names as the ones used in the previous snippet, your legend should automatically look like the one from figure 5.21. This is because the following styles are already set in `base.css`:

```
.color-legend {
  display: flex;
  justify-content: center;
  flex-wrap: wrap;
  margin: 0;
  padding-left: 0;
}
.color-legend-item {
  margin: 5px 12px;
  font-size: 1.4rem;
}
.color-legend span {
  display: inline-block;
}
.color-legend-item-color {
  position: relative;
  top: 2px;
  width: 14px;
  height: 14px;
  margin-right: 5px;
  border-radius: 3px;
}
```

NOTE   We use the CSS `flexbox` property (http://mng.bz/qOMz) to handle the legend's layout. We won't spend time explaining this style snippet because you're likely familiar with CSS, and this isn't the focus of this book. The main takeaways here are that sometimes traditional HTML elements are the easiest way forward, and we can use D3 to bind data and manipulate any DOM element.

You now know how to work with D3 layouts like the pie layout and the stack layout! In chapter 7, we'll turn this project into an interactive visualization. Feel free to go there directly if that's something you'd like to do next.

Interview with Sarina Chen

Chen is a data scientist.

Can you tell us a little bit about your background and how you discovered D3.js?

I studied industrial engineering and operations research as an undergrad and then jumped into the analytics field. First, I worked as a project manager at a consulting firm where I led teams to build reporting for clients. I wanted to get more hands-on, so I switched to analytics at a startup. I wrote lots of SQL, built Tableau dashboards, and gradually worked up my Python chops to do more data engineering and modeling.

I also had a huge interest in visual design at work. Whenever I had to make presentations, I laid out everything as if it were an infographic to make data more interesting and easier to understand. My coworker saw several of my designs and recommended I check out D3 and Nadieh Bremer's website (www.visualcinnamon.com). I was awestruck, and the DIY side of me was inspired to try D3.

How did you learn D3? What were your main challenges, and how did you overcome them?

I started with the book *Interactive Data Visualization for the Web* by Scott Murray. While following the book examples, I also referenced Nadieh's open source JavaScript code from her early projects to reinforce my understanding.

When I dived into my first personal project, I often found that my visual sense always wanted to bite off more than my technical skills could chew. I have no background in JavaScript whatsoever, so I had to learn along the way. Besides objects like Promise, JavaScript is just really weird (for someone more used to Python).

Furthermore, the D3 functions were not intuitive either. When I coded up anything more complicated than a bar/line chart, it just wouldn't work. Nothing would render, and I would have no idea why. The JavaScript console wasn't helpful for debugging, so I did tons of googling. I would copy other people's examples word for word, hoping it would work. As I did it more, I got used to it and developed an intuition for D3.

Do you use visualization tools other than D3? What's the place of D3 in your current data visualization workflow?

From my work experience, I am fluent in a variety of tools, including Excel, Tableau, and Matplotlib (Python). Those tools are great for delivering quick insights and analyses but lack creativity. Enter D3!

In my usual workflow, D3 is close to the last step—most of the work done before D3 is planning what to draw.

Featured project: "Holst: The Planets" (https://planets.ifcolorful.com/)

Visualization of the movement Mercury, from the orchestral suite *The Planets* by Gustav Holst

Please describe briefly your project "Holst: The Planets."

My project is a data visualization of the seven movements from the symphony *The Planets* by Gustav Holst. Each movement represents a planet, which evokes a particular persona and emotion. For example, Venus is about beauty, and Jupiter is about jollity.

I started this project because one of my favorite YouTubers, TwoSet Violin, designed creative merchandise around this symphony. Having used Spotify data before, I wanted to take another chance at visualizing the data. I wanted my graphic to show a lot of information about the music, similar to the motion of a conductor looking at the full orchestra score and knowing all the individual parts that play at once.

Can you describe the process of creating this project?

My typical process is like this:

(continued)

Gather data: I knew I wanted to use Spotify audio analysis data, which I have used before. So I reused my code for calling the Spotify API.

Explore: I used pandas and Matplotlib (Python libraries) to do exploratory analysis. I wanted to look for interesting dimensions (backed by my musical knowledge) and had a good variety between the seven movements. I also figured out what not to use based on incompleteness or inaccuracy.

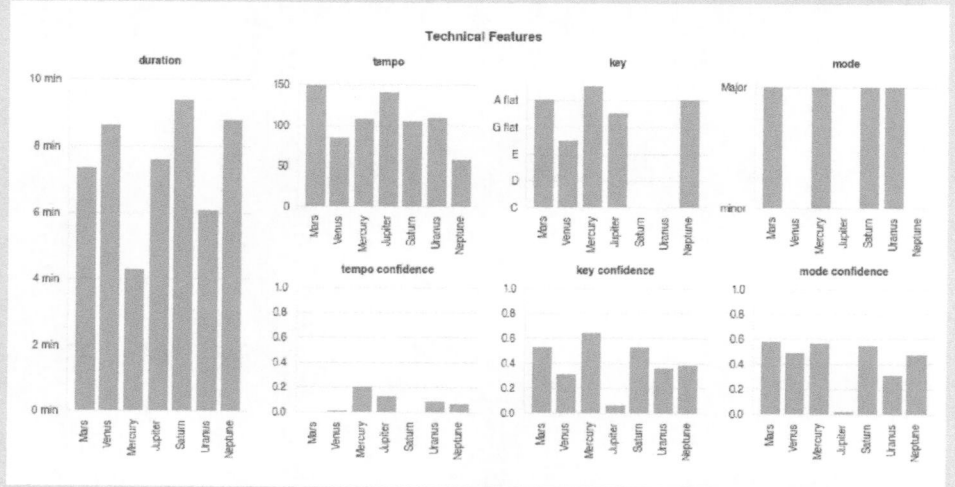

Exploration of the movements' technical features, by Sarina Chen

Decide on the story: Out of all the angles I explored in step 2, I came up with the main points I wanted to show in the visual. My approach for "The Planets" was to describe the emotion and context coming from each movement, so I mainly wanted to show how different elements of the music (e.g., loudness, rhythm, etc.) changed.

Mock up the design: I used pen and paper or Illustrator to brainstorm my charts' structure. I also had a lot of fun using Illustrator to come up with seven color palettes, one for each planet.

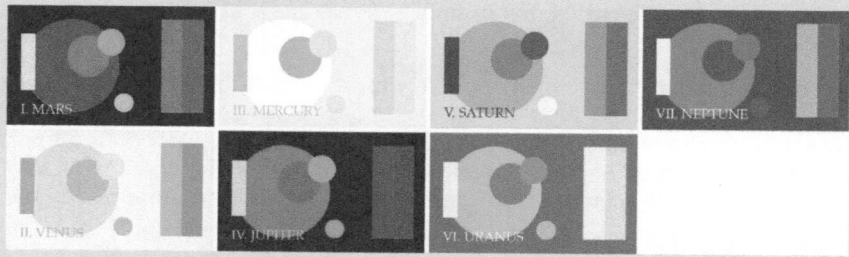

Color palettes created by Sarina Chen for each movement

Prepare the data: After knowing what data mapped to each visual coding I needed, I manipulated my data in Python and exported it as CSV or JSON for D3. I left detailed comments in my code so it would be easy to alter or revisit after a break.

Draw: At this point, I had everything I needed to create the visual, with a bit of rework in case I hit a road bump (such as realizing that a visual looks great in the mockup but terrible in practice).

Can you tell us a little more about combining D3 with Canvas? Which problem did it help you solve in this project?

I prefer sticking to SVG whenever possible, but it fails when there are too many elements to render. The rule of thumb is that if you're drawing more than 1,000 elements and introducing movement, you should switch to Canvas to prevent performance from deteriorating. Canvas is a single HTML element, so it will make those 1,000 circles move smoothly for transitions.

There were several projects where I wrote the static version in SVG; then, when I moved on to transitions, I would bonk my head for realizing that I needed to switch to Canvas too late. Luckily, I found examples of hybrid approaches, where you could bind the data with D3 but draw with Canvas. This method saved me from completely overhauling my code.

The smooth transitions happening during scroll contribute to making this project particularly stunning! Did you use a JavaScript library other than D3 to create them?

Thanks! This was my first project using scroll events, so I did a lot of research on scroll-based and step-based transitions to figure out which library to use. The criteria I had were simplicity, ease of use, and relevancy. To answer the first two criteria, I read a few articles written by data visualists who already evaluated the options and described their firsthand experiences. To understand relevancy, I compared weekly downloads of my top choice libraries on NPM (a JavaScript package manager). I looked at when the last commit was made on GitHub to know if the code was maintained.

I treat the animation library Scrollama.js as the icing on the cake because I only add it after implementing all my D3 charts. My D3 charts and their transitions are all wrapped in functions, so Scrollama just needs to call the function when I scroll up or down past a section of the page.

Which tips would you share with our readers about learning D3 and creating personal projects?

Set goals for each personal project. On the learning front, my past goals included building my first network graph, using scrollytelling (this project), and building a responsive page. On the creative front, sometimes I have open-ended goals with prompts, such as drawing unconventional charts with multiple encodings or designing a fitting color palette.

Summary

- D3 layouts are functions that take a dataset as an input and produce a new, anno-tated dataset as an output. The annotated dataset contains the attributes neces-sary to draw a specific visualization. Layouts comprise a preprocessing step that formats your data so that it's ready to be displayed in the form you've chosen.
- Pie layout d3.pie() calculates the start and end angles of each slice of a pie or donut chart:
  - The pie layout expects the input data to be formatted as an array of numbers or an array of objects. Each element of the array corresponds to a slice of the pie.
  - If the data is formatted as an array of objects, we use the value() accessor function to tell the pie layout under which key of the objects the value that will determine the size of the slice is stored.
  - We obtain the annotated dataset by calling the pie layout function and pass-ing the input data as an argument.
  - The annotated dataset contains the start and end angles of each slice of the pie.
  - To draw the arcs of a pie or a donut chart, we need to declare an arc genera-tor function. This generator will use the start and end angles contained in the annotated dataset to calculate the d attribute of the SVG paths used to draw the arcs.
- Stack layout d3.stack() calculates the position of different series when "stacked" one over the other:
  - We tell the stack layout which keys from the input dataset contain the values we want to stack with the keys() accessor function.
  - We obtain the annotated dataset by calling the stack layout function and passing the input data as an argument.
  - The annotated dataset contains the value of the lower and upper boundaries of each series, accessible by index (respectively, d[0] and d[1]). It also con-tains a reference to the input data.
  - To draw a stacked bar chart, we use the data returned by the stack layout to append rectangles whose positions depends on the lower and upper bound-aries of each series.
  - To draw a streamgraph, we initialize an area generator function and use its accessor functions to specify how to access the values of the lower and upper boundaries in the annotated dataset. Then we use the annotated dataset to append SVG paths and calculate their d attribute with the area generator.
  - We control the order in which shapes are stacked by chaining the order() accessor function to the stack layout. D3 offers six built-in orders.
  - We control how shapes are positioned around the zero baseline of a stacked chart by chaining the offset() accessor function to the stack layout. D3 offers five built-in offsets.

- – Orders and offsets affect the domain of the chart, which should be taken into consideration when setting the scale responsible for calculating the position of the stacked shapes.
- D3's ordinal scales have both a discrete input and a discrete output. They are great for discrete color scales, where each element in an array is mapped to a specific color.
- Legends are a critical aspect of developing visualizations. When legends contain multiple elements, it's worth considering building them with traditional HTML elements and using CSS for the layout. This approach is usually easier than using SVG shapes and text.
- We can create complex SVG text layouts by breaking the text into multiple tspan elements. When positioning SVG text, the x and y attributes set the position of the text's baseline in reference to the origin of the SVG container, while dx and dy dictate the position in relation to the previous text element.

Visualizing distributions

6

This chapter covers

- Grouping data points into bins
- Drawing a histogram
- Comparing two distributions side by side with a pyramid chart
- Calculating the quartiles of a dataset and generating box plots
- Using violin plots to compare distributions of multiple categories

Visualizing distributions is a common request in data visualization. We use data distributions to assess how often data values occur within a specific bracket or the probability of data points appearing within a range.

In this chapter, we'll study the distribution of salaries for data visualization practitioners based in the United States. The data behind the report we'll build comes from the 2021 State of the Industry Survey hosted by the Data Visualization Society (DVS) (www.datavisualizationsociety.org). You can see this project in figure 6.1 or online at http://mng.bz/orvd.

For this project, we'll start by building the most common representation of data distribution, a histogram, to visualize the salary of the survey's 788 US-based and salaried respondents. We'll then compare the wages of respondents identifying as women and men using two types of visualizations: a pyramid chart and box plots. The first one is handy for comparing two categories side by side. The latter offers an extra layer of information compared to histograms, revealing the quartiles and median of a dataset.

We'll complete this chapter by investigating the distribution of earnings for different roles in data visualization, such as analysts, developers, and designers. We'll use violin charts showing the shape of the distribution for each role, to which we'll add the interquartile range and the average value.

To build the charts represented in figure 6.1, we'll introduce the concept of bins. *Bins* are groups of data points, generally of equal width. When creating distribution

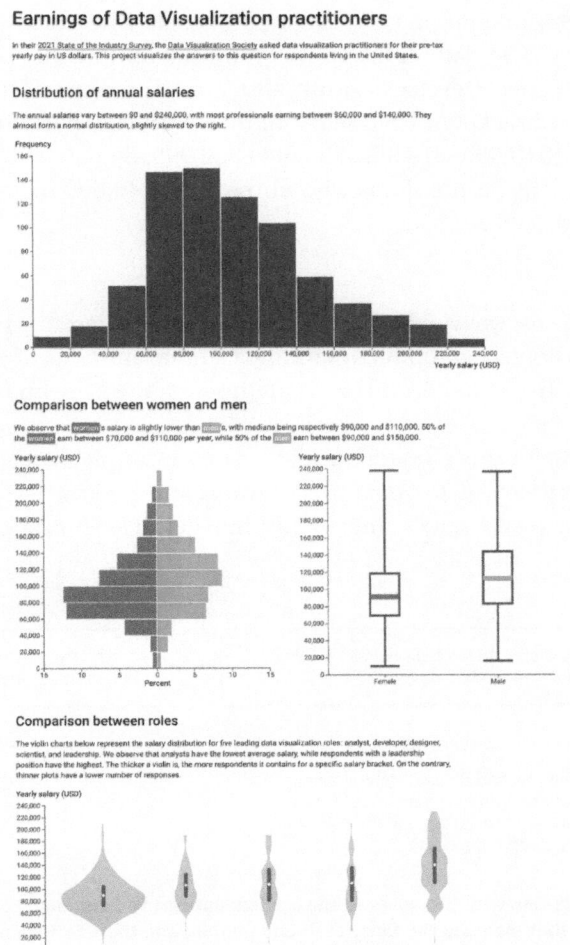

Figure 6.1   In this chapter, we'll build four charts to visualize the salary distribution among data visualization practitioners based in the United States.

visualizations with D3, we preprocess the data into bins and then use these bins to draw our charts.

Before we get started, go to the code files of chapter 6. If you haven't already, you can download them from the book's GitHub repository (http://mng.bz/Xqjv). In the chapter_06 folder, the code files are organized by section. To get started with this chapter's exercise, open the start folder inside 6.1-Binning_data in your code editor, and start your local web server. Refer to appendix A if you need help setting up your local development environment. You can find more details about the project's folder structure in the README file located at the root of this chapter's code files.

> **WARNING** When working with the chapter's code files, open only one start *or* one end folder in your code editor. If you open all the chapter's files at once and use the Live Server extension to serve the project, the path to the data file won't work as expected.

The project's data folder contains a CSV file where each row corresponds to a response to the DVS survey. The dataset has four columns: a unique identifier (UID), the respondent's role (Designer, Developer, Journalist, etc.), the respondent's gender, and the respondent's salary bracket in US dollars. In the survey, the participants could choose a bracket of $10K ($10,000–$19,999, $20,000–$39,999, $40,000–$59,999, etc.). For comparison purposes, the respondents who chose the $240,000 or more option won't be included in the visualizations.

6.1   *Binning data*

To visualize data distributions, we usually need to preprocess a dataset by grouping its data points into buckets or bins, each bin containing a similar number of data points, as explained in figure 6.2. In D3, we do this with method d3.bin() from the d3-array module.

Let's take the dataset from this chapter's project as an example (data.csv). This dataset contains the yearly salary of 788 data practitioners and is extracted from a survey where the respondent could select their salary bracket. These brackets cover a

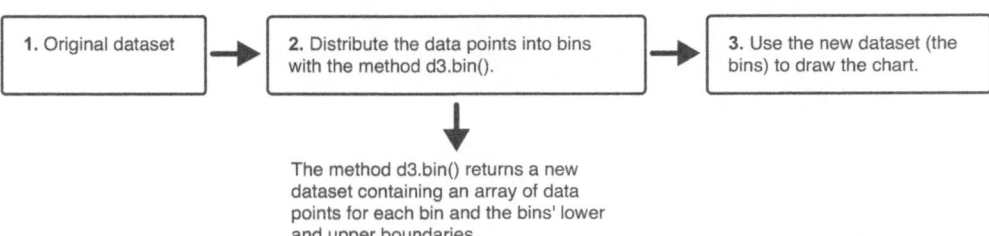

Figure 6.2   To visualize a distribution with D3, we pass the original dataset to function d3.bin()**. This function returns a new dataset that includes the bins, their boundaries, and their corresponding data points.**

range of $10K or $20K USD, for example $10,000–$19,999, $20,000–$39,999, $40,000–$59,000, $60,000–$79,999, and so on. Each salary bracket could be an example of how bins are used in data visualization. We know that the actual salary of the respondent exists within the boundaries of the bin, but we don't know the actual value.

To illustrate the concept of bins with an example, we'll start working on this chapter's project. Make sure that the start folder included in 6.1-Binning_data is open in your code editor and that your local web server is running. If you go to the load-data.js file, you'll see that the dataset is already loaded into the project using method d3.csv() discussed in chapter 3. You can see the related code in listing 6.1.

Because the survey dataset didn't list the actual salary of each respondent, we call function getRandomSalary() to get a random integer value located between the lower and upper boundaries of the salary bracket. This isn't something we would do in an actual dataviz project, but it will allow us to work with a realistic distribution.

> **WARNING**   Because we use function Math.random() to generate the salary values, the results you'll get while doing this chapter's project might differ slightly from the illustrations. But the overall trends revealed by the visualizations should remain the same.

While the data is loading, we filter out the earnings of $240,000 or more because we don't know the upper limit of this bracket. Once the random salaries are calculated and the data is done loading, we call functions drawHistogram(), drawBoxplot(), drawPyramid(), and drawViolinCharts(), where we'll build each visualization. These functions take the dataset as a parameter and are already declared in their corresponding JavaScript files.

Listing 6.1   Fetching and formatting the dataset (load-data.js)

> The function getRandomSalary() takes a salary bracket string as a parameter, for example, "$20,000–$39,999". It finds the lower and upper limits of the salary bracket and transforms them into numbers. It then returns a random integer number between the lower and the upper limits.

```
const getRandomSalary = (salary) => {
  const lowerLimit = +salary.slice(1, salary.indexOf(" -"))
    .replace(",","");
  const upperLimit = +salary.slice(
    salary.indexOf(" $") + 2)
    .replace(",", "");

  return Math.floor(Math.random() * (upperLimit -
    lowerLimit) + lowerLimit);
}

d3.csv("./data/earnings_per_role.csv", d => {
```

Fetch the dataset with method d3.csv().

```
if (d.pay_annual_USD !== "$240,000 or more") {
  return {
    role: d.role,
    gender: d.gender,
    salary: getRandomSalary(d.pay_annual_USD)
  };
}
```

Filter out the salary brackets of "$240,000 or more" with the if condition, and return the respondent's role, gender, and salary. Call function getRandomSalary() to obtain a random salary value between the salary bracket's lower and upper limits.

```
}).then(data => {

  drawHistogram(data);
  drawBoxplot(data);
  drawPyramid(data);
  drawViolinCharts(data);

});
```

Once the data is done loading, call the functions that build the visualizations, and pass the dataset as a parameter. Each of these functions is already declared in its corresponding JavaScript file.

Let's now open the histogram.js file and start working within function draw-Histogram(). You'll see that we've already declared the chart's margins, width, and height. We've also appended an SVG container to the DOM and an SVG group element translated into the position of the inner chart, following the strategy described in chapter 4, section 4.2.1. This group is saved into constant innerChart, to which we'll later append the elements constituting the histogram. This will be true for every chart in this chapter.

We then declare a bin generator with method d3.bin(). As you can see in the following snippet, this method can be chained with a few accessor functions. For example, because our data consists of an array of objects, we chain the value() function to tell D3 under which key the values we want to bin are stored. In our project, this key is salary. Finally, we generate the bins by calling the bin generator and passing the dataset as an argument. Note how the process is similar to the shape generators discussed in chapter 4:

```
const binGenerator = d3.bin()
  .value(d => d.salary);
const bins = binGenerator(data);
```

In the latest code snippet, we save the array returned by the bin generator into a constant named bins, which we'll reuse later to draw our histogram. If you log the bins into the console, you'll see that they are structured as a multidimensional array, as illustrated in figure 6.3. Each item in the top-level bin array contains an array of data points for that specific bin. The length property of a bin tells us how many data points it contains. Its lower and upper boundaries are found under the keys x0 and x1.

To illustrate the concept of bins, we drew the data points into their respective bins in figure 6.4. Each data point is a circle, in which its horizontal position corresponds to the salary, and its vertical position is arbitrarily attributed to reduce overlap between the circles. As you can see, there's a higher density of data points between $60K and $140K, while the density gets lower as we move toward the extremities. This

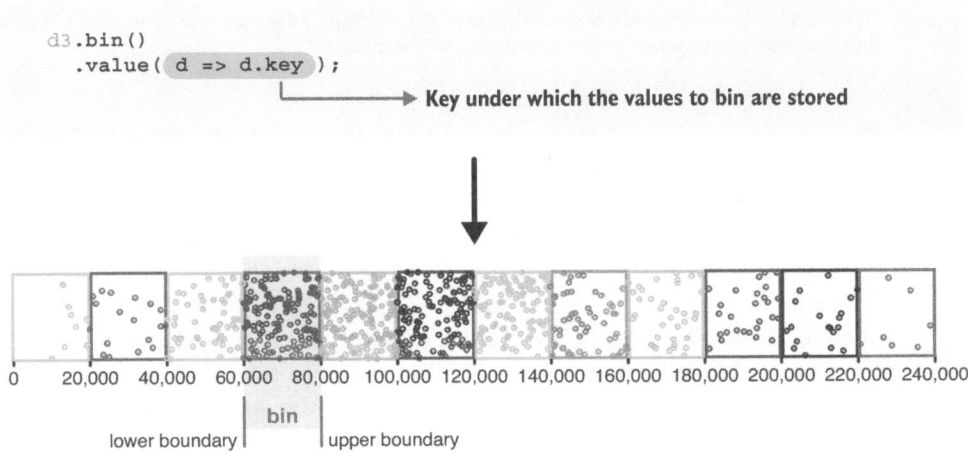

```
bins
▼Array(12) ⓘ
  ▶ 0: (9) [{…}, {…}, {…}, {…}, {…}, {…}, {…}, {…}, {…}, x0: 0, x1: 20000]
  ▶ 1: (18) [{…}, {…}, {…}, {…}, {…}, {…}, {…}, {…}, {…}, {…}, {…}, {…}, {…}, {…}, {…}, {…}, {…}, {…}, x0: 20000, x1: 40000]
  ▶ 2: (52) [{…}, {…}, {…}, {…}, {…}, {…}, {…}, {…}, {…}, {…}, {…}, {…}, {…}, {…}, {…}, {…}, {…}, {…}, {…}, {…}, {…}, …]
  ▶ 3: (147) [{…}, {…}, {…}, {…}, {…}, {…}, {…}, {…}, {…}, {…}, {…}, {…}, {…}, {…}, {…}, {…}, {…}, {…}, {…}, {…}, {…}, …]
  ▶ 4: (150) [{…}, {…}, {…}, {…}, {…}, {…}, {…}, {…}, {…}, {…}, {…}, {…}, {…}, {…}, {…}, {…}, {…}, {…}, {…}, {…}, {…}, …]
  ▶ 5: (126) [{…}, {…}, {…}, {…}, {…}, {…}, {…}, {…}, {…}, {…}, {…}, {…}, {…}, {…}, {…}, {…}, {…}, {…}, {…}, {…}, {…}, …]
  ▶ 6: (104) [{…}, {…}, {…}, {…}, {…}, {…}, {…}, {…}, {…}, {…}, {…}, {…}, {…}, {…}, {…}, {…}, {…}, {…}, {…}, {…}, {…}, …]
  ▶ 7: (59) [{…}, {…}, {…}, {…}, {…}, {…}, {…}, {…}, {…}, {…}, {…}, {…}, {…}, {…}, {…}, {…}, {…}, {…}, {…}, {…}, …]
  ▶ 8: (37) [{…}, {…}, {…}, {…}, {…}, {…}, {…}, {…}, {…}, {…}, {…}, {…}, {…}, {…}, {…}, {…}, {…}, {…}, {…}, {…}, …]
  ▶ 9: (27) [{…}, {…}, {…}, {…}, {…}, {…}, {…}, {…}, {…}, {…}, {…}, {…}, {…}, {…}, {…}, {…}, {…}, {…}, {…}, {…}, …]
  ▶ 10: (19) [{…}, {…}, {…}, {…}, {…}, {…}, {…}, {…}, {…}, {…}, {…}, {…}, {…}, {…}, {…}, {…}, {…}, x0: 200000, x1: 220000]
  ▶ 11: (7) [{…}, {…}, {…}, {…}, {…}, {…}, {…}, x0: 220000, x1: 240000]
```

Figure 6.3   In the multidimensional array returned by the bin generator, each bin is an array containing data points. In this figure, the data points, consisting of JavaScript objects, are represented by { . . . } for conciseness. A bin's lower and upper limits are accessible under the keys x0 and x1.

phenomenon will also be visible in the distribution visualizations we'll create later. Although figure 6.4 isn't a traditional way of visualizing distributions, it might help you better grasp the concept of bins.

Figure 6.4   Salary data points in their respective bins. The horizontal position of each circle corresponds to the salary, while their vertical positions are arbitrary to reduce overlap.

6.2   *Drawing a histogram*

Histograms provide an overview of how values are distributed within a dataset, allowing us to spot where the values are concentrated or if there are noticeable gaps between them. In this section, we'll build a histogram to visualize the salary distribution of 755 data visualization practitioners.

The completed histogram is shown in figure 6.1 and in the hosted project (http:// mng.bz/orvd). You'll notice that histograms are simply made of rectangles, one for each salary bracket. To build this graph with D3, all we have to do is append rectangle elements to an SVG container with the data-binding pattern via the bins generated in the previous section as data. We then calculate the position of each rectangle with D3 scales and set their height based on the number of data points they represent, as explained in figure 6.5.

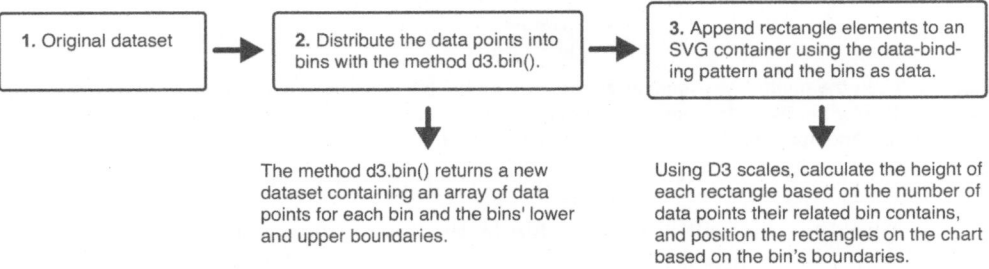

Figure 6.5   To generate a histogram, we first use method `d3.bin()` **to preprocess a dataset. This method returns a new dataset, where data points are distributed into bins (arrays), and each bin has a lower and an upper boundary. We then use this new dataset to append rectangles to an SVG container. The length of the rectangles is proportional to the number of data points the related bin contains, while their position corresponds to the boundaries of the bins.**

Let's start by declaring the scales for the histogram. As illustrated in figure 6.6, we'll need two scales: one to position the rectangles horizontally, which we'll name xScale, and one to calculate the rectangles' height and vertical position, named yScale. Because both scales' domains and ranges are continuous and we want the ranges to be linearly proportional to the domains, we'll use linear scales.

Still working in the drawHistogram() function within the histogram.js file, declare the horizontal and the vertical scales, as detailed in listing 6.2. The domain of the horizontal scale extends from the minimum to the maximum salaries covered by the bins. They can respectively be found with the lower boundary of the first bin (bins[0].x0) and the upper limit of the last bin (bins[bins.length - 1].x1). The range of this scale extends from 0 to innerWidth, covering the whole width of the inner chart. We save this scale into a constant named xScale.

On the other hand, the vertical scale is responsible for positioning and scaling the rectangles. Its domain extends from 0 to the number of data points contained in the tallest bin (d3.max(bins, d => d.length)). Its range covers the values between inner-Height, the height of the inner chart, and 0. Because in SVG the y-axis goes from top to bottom, innerHeight corresponds to the bottom of the histogram's rectangles, while 0 corresponds to the top of the chart. We save this scale in a constant named yScale and chain it with method nice() to ensure that the y-axis ends with a rounded value.

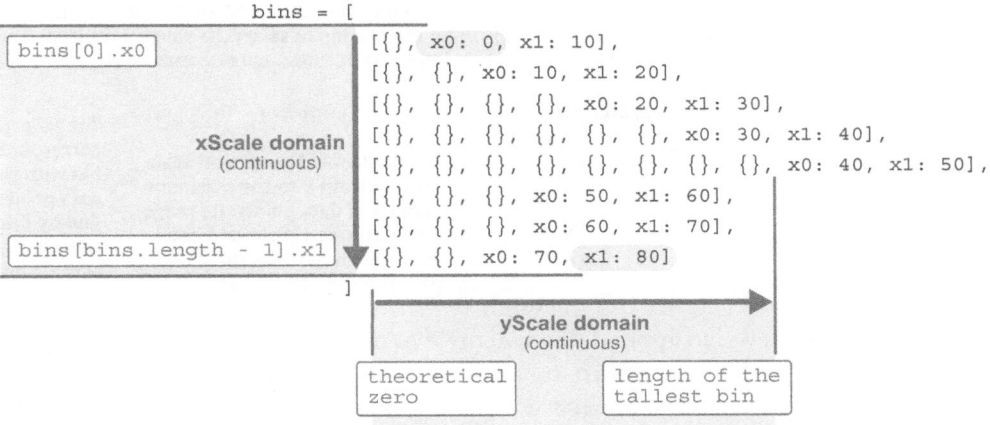

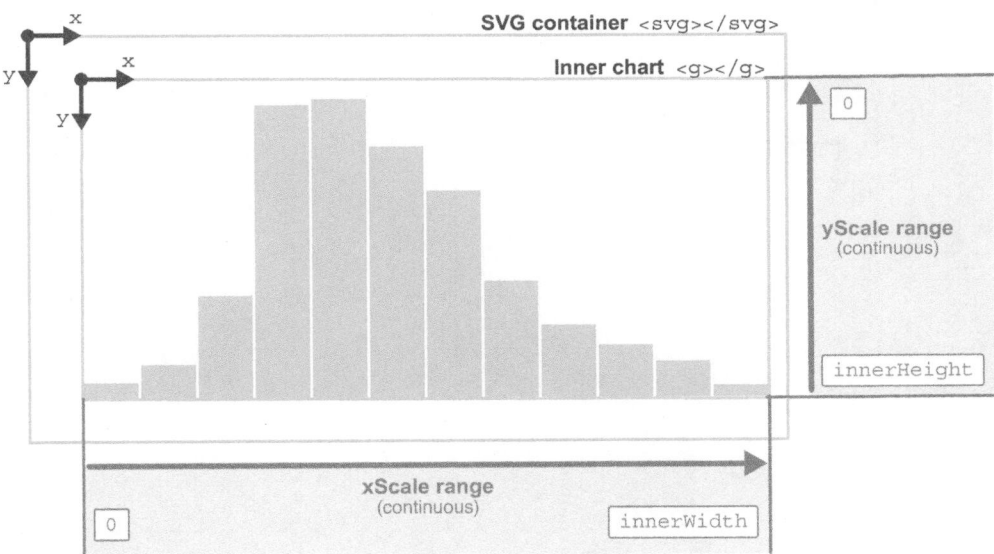

Figure 6.6 The horizontal scale is responsible for positioning rectangles along the x-axis. In contrast, the vertical scale arranges rectangles along the y-axis and calculates their height.

Listing 6.2   Declaring the scales (`histogram.js`)

```
const minSalary = bins[0].x0;
const maxSalary = bins[bins.length - 1].x1;
```

The minimum salary shown on the histogram corresponds to the first bin's lower limit (x0). The maximum wage is the last bin's upper limit (x1).

```
const xScale = d3.scaleLinear()
  .domain([minSalary, maxSalary])
  .range([0, innerWidth]);
```

The domain of the horizontal scale extends from the minimum to the maximum salary. Its range goes from 0 to the innerWidth, which corresponds to the width of the inner chart.

```
const binsMaxLength = d3.max(bins, d => d.length);
const yScale = d3.scaleLinear()
  .domain([0, binsMaxLength])
  .range([innerHeight, 0])
  .nice();
```

The domain of the vertical scale extends from 0 to the maximum number of data points. Its range starts at innerHeight and ends at 0; remember that the y-axis goes from top to bottom.

The tallest rectangle corresponds to the bin with the most data points, which we find by interrogating the length of each bin with d3.max().

The next step is to append one rectangle to the chart for each bin. To do so, we apply the data-binding pattern to `innerChart`, using the bins calculated in section 6.1 as data and asking D3 to append a rectangle element for each of them. As shown in figure 6.7, the x and y attributes of the rectangles correspond to the position of their top-left corner, while their `width` and `height` attributes control their dimensions.

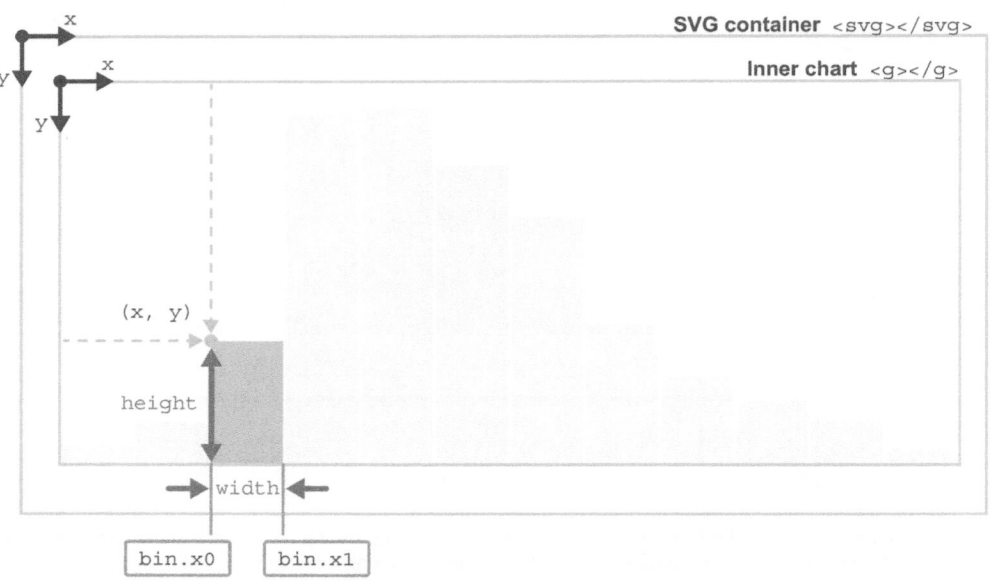

Figure 6.7   The position of the histogram's rectangles is controlled by their x and y attributes and their dimensions by their `width` and `height` attributes. The height of the rectangles is proportional to the number of data points contained in their related bin.

In listing 6.3, we use the data-binding pattern to append one rectangle for each bin inside the `innerChart` selection. We then set the rectangles' positional attributes:

- The x attribute of each rectangle corresponds to the position of their lower boundary, calculated with `xScale`.

- Their y attribute can be found by passing the length property of their bin to yScale.
- The width of the rectangles corresponds to the distance between their bin's upper and lower boundaries.
- The rectangles' height is equal to the difference between the height of the innerChart and the vertical position of their top-left corner.

Finally, we set the fill attribute of the rectangles to slateGray, a color variable already declared in the shared-constants.js file. We also add a white stroke to the rectangles to give the illusion of space between them.

Listing 6.3   Appending the rectangles (histogram.js)

```
innerChart
  .selectAll("rect")
  .data(bins)                        Use the data-binding pattern to
  .join("rect")                      append one rectangle for each bin.
    .attr("x", d => xScale(d.x0))
    .attr("y", d => yScale(d.length))
    .attr("width", d => xScale(d.x1) - xScale(d.x0))     Set the position and
    .attr("height", d => innerHeight - yScale(d.length)) size of the rectangles.
    .attr("fill", slateGray)
    .attr("stroke", white)           Set the look and feel
    .attr("stroke-width", 2);        of the rectangles.
```

As a final step, we add axes and labels to the histogram. We start by initializing the bottom axis constructor for the horizontal axis using method d3.axisBottom() and xScale as a reference, as detailed in listing 6.4. We then append an SVG group to the inner chart and translate it to the selection's bottom. By calling the axis constructor from this selection, we append all the elements that compose an axis inside the group: ticks, labels, and a horizontal line across the range. Finally, we append a text element to the SVG container to serve as the main label of the axis. This label has a text of "Yearly salary (USD)" and is positioned at the bottom-right corner of the container.

We proceed similarly for the left axis, using method d3.axisLeft() and yScale as a reference. Once the axis elements are appended, we add a label with the text "Frequency" to the top-left corner of the SVG container.

Listing 6.4   Adding the axes and labels (histogram.js)

```
                                               Initialize the bottom axis constructor
const bottomAxis = d3.axisBottom(xScale);  ←── using xScale as a reference.
innerChart
  .append("g")
    .attr("transform", `translate(0, ${innerHeight})`)
    .call(bottomAxis);
```

Append an SVG group to the inner chart, and translate this group to the bottom of the selection. Call the bottom axis constructor to generate the elements composing the axis.

```
svg
  .append("text")
    .text("Yearly salary (USD)")
    .attr("text-anchor", "end")
    .attr("x", width)
    .attr("y", height - 5);
```

Append a text element to the SVG container that will serve as the label for the bottom axis. Set its text to "Yearly salary (USD)", and position it in the bottom-right corner.

```
const leftAxis = d3.axisLeft(yScale);
innerChart
  .append("g")
    .call(leftAxis);
```

Append an SVG group to the inner chart and call the left axis constructor to generate the elements composing the axis.

Initialize the left axis constructor using yScale as a reference.

```
svg
  .append("text")
    .text("Frequency")
    .attr("x", 5)
    .attr("y", 20);
```

Append a text element to the SVG container that will serve as the label for the left axis. Set its text to "Frequency", and position it in the top-left corner.

You can see the completed histogram in figure 6.8. In the next chapter, we'll filter this visualization by gender.

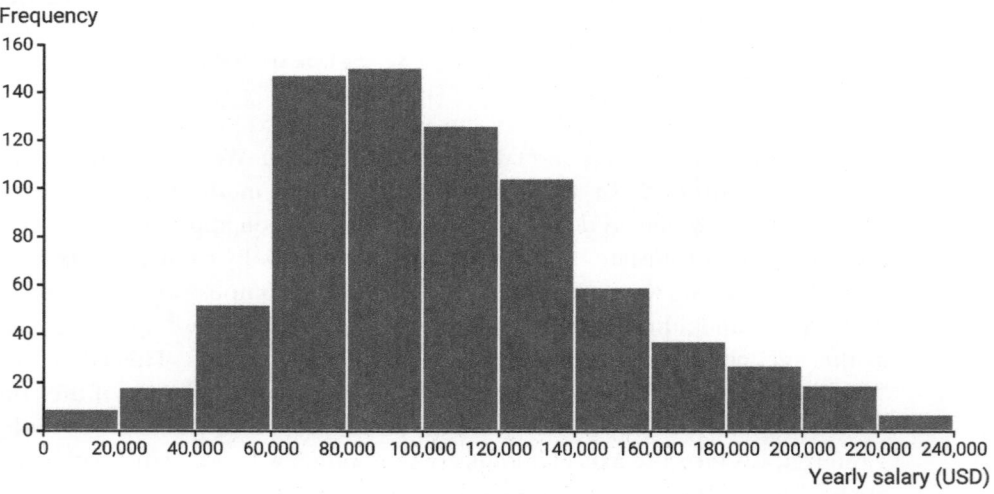

Figure 6.8 Completed histogram of the salary distribution among data visualization practitioners in the United States

6.3   *Creating a pyramid chart*

Another way to visualize distributions is with a pyramid chart. This chart consists of two vertical histograms standing back-to-back and is easy to build—thanks to D3 bins. We use pyramid charts to compare the distribution of two categories.

A common use case for pyramid charts is the age distribution between women and men, as in the example illustrated in figure 6.9. Such charts usually use bars to visualize the data, but lollipop or dumbbell shapes can also be employed. The x-axis of pyramid charts often uses percentages as units. For example, the following figure indicates that women between 20 and 24 years old represent about 3% of the total population, while men between 85 and 89 represent approximately 1%.

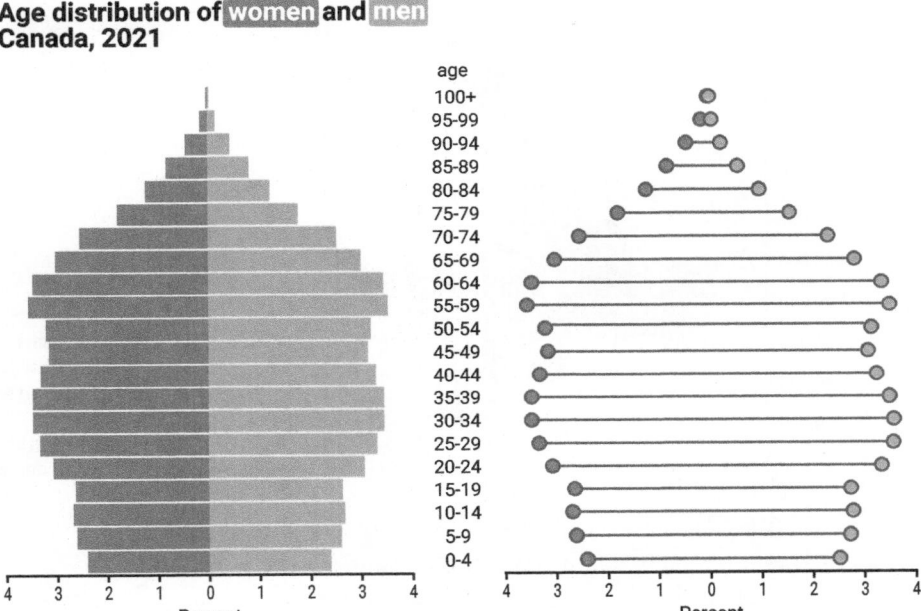

Data source: Statistics Canada

Figure 6.9   Pyramid charts of the age distribution of women and men in Canada in 2021. The chart on the left uses bars to visualize the data, while the chart on the right uses lollipop or dumbbell shapes.

Mini-project: Build a pyramid chart

Now that you're familiar with `d3.bin()` and know how to append rectangles to a chart, you have all the keys to building a pyramid chart. In this section, we challenge you to create the pyramid chart shown in the following figure, representing the earnings of US data visualization practitioners identifying as women and men.

On this chart, women's earnings are represented by purple bars and men's by orange bars. The length of the bars is proportional to the number of respondents in a salary bracket. For example, we observe that 12% of the respondents are women earning between $60K and $80K, while about 6.5% are men in the same salary bracket. The first half of the horizontal axis is reserved for women and extends from 15% to

(continued)

0%, while the second half is for men and extends from 0% to 15%. The vertical axis represents the salaries, from 0 to $240K.

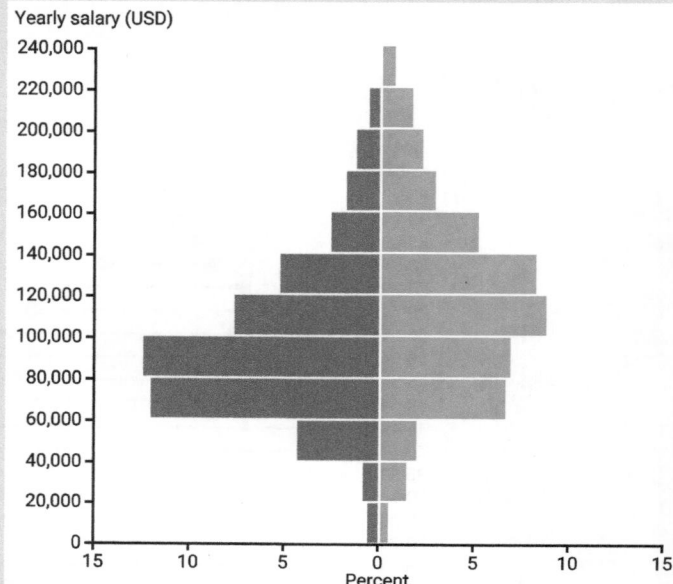

Pyramid chart visualizing the salary distribution of US data visualization practitioners identifying as women and men

Here are a few hints that might help you complete this exercise:

- Work in the `pyramid.js` file, inside function `drawPyramid()`. The SVG container and the inner chart (SVG group) have already been appended inside `div#pyramid`.
- Generate bins using `d3.bin()` and based on the salary. You'll need to generate separate bins for the women and the men.
- You can declare different horizontal scales for the women and the men. The women's scale extends on the first half of the x-axis, while the men's scale extends on the second half.
- The length of the bars is proportional to the percentage of the total respondents represented by each salary bracket. This percentage varies approximately between 0% and 15%.
- Each side of the pyramid chart is built exactly like the histogram created in section 6.2. Only the orientation is different!
- The color constants are available in `shared-constants.js`.

If you get stuck or want to compare your solution with ours, you'll find it in listing D.6.1 of appendix D and in the `6.3-Pyramid/end` folder of this chapter's code files. But we encourage you to try to complete it on your own; it's the best way to learn!

Note that your solution might differ slightly from ours. In development, there is often more than one way to achieve the same result.

6.4 Generating box plots

Box plots are another familiar way to visualize distributions. Their primary role is to highlight the median of a dataset and to illustrate quartiles, which divide the data points into four groups of more or less equal size. Box plots have the advantage of being more compact than histograms but might be harder to understand for readers who aren't familiar with statistics.

As shown in figure 6.10, a box plot is composed of a rectangle indicating where 50% of the data points are located. This rectangle covers the interquartile ranges, from the first quartile, or 25th percentile, to the third quartile, or 75th percentile. It also intersects with the median, that is, the threshold separating the data points' lower and higher halves.

The vertical lines extending from the bottom and the top of the rectangle are called whiskers. The lower one spreads from the minimum value in the dataset to the first quartile, while the upper one extends from the third quartile to the maximum value. Outliers may be plotted as dots outside the whiskers.

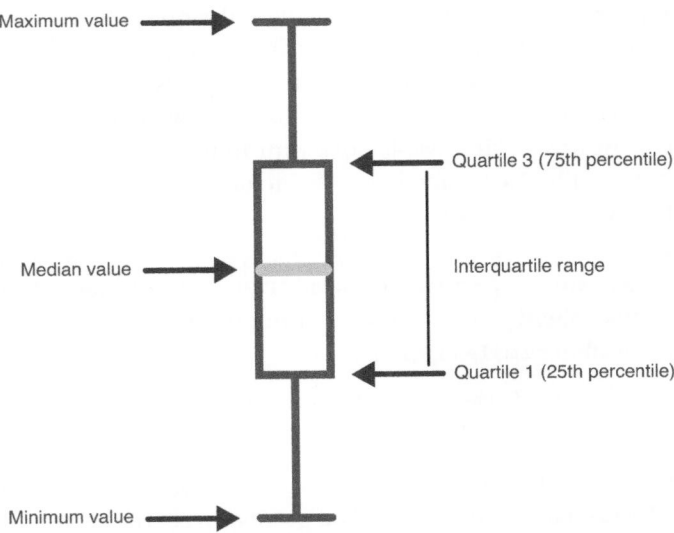

Figure 6.10   A box plot consists of five pieces of information encoded in a single shape: the minimum value in a dataset, the first quartile or the 25th percentile, the median or mean value, the third quartile or the 75th percentile, and the maximum value.

To generate a box plot with D3, we start by finding the minimum and maximum values in the dataset we're working with, as stated in figure 6.11. We then use a quantile scale to calculate the quartiles and median values. Finally, we append a rectangle and line elements to an SVG container and set their attributes to match the minimum, maximum, median, and quartile positions.

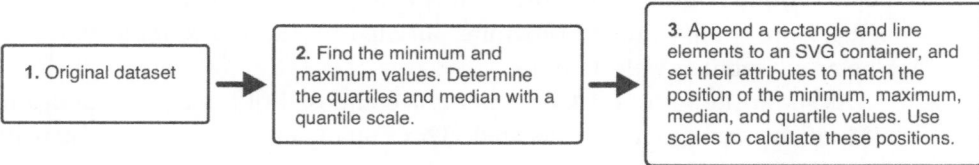

Figure 6.11   Steps to generate a box plot with D3

6.4.1   *Calculating quartiles with the quantile scale*

Quantiles are cut points splitting a data distribution into groups of similar sizes. *Quartiles*, on the other hand, are a type of quantile, dividing the data into exactly four groups. In D3, we use a quantile scale (https://d3js.org/d3-scale/quantile) to calculate both quantiles and quartiles.

Let's go back to this chapter's project and calculate the quartiles of the box plots illustrated in figure 6.1 and on the hosted project (http://mng.bz/orvd). In this project, box plots are used to compare women's and men's salaries, which means that we need to work with two datasets: one containing the wages of women and one containing the wages of men. In this section, we'll work with function `drawBoxplot()`, contained in the `box-plot.js` file. Note that it already includes the code that appends an SVG container to the DOM and an SVG group to hold the inner chart, per the strategy used since chapter 4.

In the following code snippet, we use the JavaScript `filter()` method to isolate women's salaries and map them into a new array using the JavaScript `map()` method. We save this array in constant `femalesSalaries`:

```
const femalesSalaries = data.filter(d => d.gender === "Female")
  .map(d => d.salary);
```

To calculate quartiles, we use D3's quantile scale, for which both the domain and the range are discrete. The domain is an array of data points (here, the salaries of women or men), while the range determines the number of quantiles that are computed. If we want to calculate quartiles, hence dividing the data into four groups, the range must be an array of four elements, such as `[0, 1, 2, 3]`.

In the following code snippet, we declare the quantile scale with `d3.scale-Quantile()`, passing the array of women's salaries as the domain and an array of four values as the range. We save this scale into constant `femalesQuartilesScale`:

```
const femalesQuartilesScale = d3.scaleQuantile()
  .domain(femalesSalaries)
  .range([0, 1, 2, 3]);
```

Finally, we compute the quartiles by calling the `quantiles()` accessor function of `femalesQuartilesScale`, which returns the quantile thresholds:

```
const femalesQuartiles = femalesQuartilesScale.quantiles();
```

If we save the thresholds into constant `femalesQuartiles` and log them into the console, we obtain an array of three values:

- The first quartile or 25th percentile
- The second quartile or 50th percentile, also known as the median
- The third quartile or 75th percentile

Note that we could also find the median directly with method `d3.median()` from the d3-array module. This method takes an array of values (here, the salaries) as an argument:

```
d3.median(femalesSalaries);
```

In listing 6.5, we repeat the same process for men's salaries. We also calculate the minimum and maximum values of both the women's and men's wages using `d3.extent()`, which returns an array of two values: the minimum and the maximum. We'll soon use the quartile, minimum, and maximum values to position the rectangle and line elements of the box plot on the chart.

Listing 6.5   Calculating quartile and min/max values (`box-plot.js`)

```
const femalesSalaries = data.filter(d => d.gender ===
  "Female").map(d => d.salary);
const femalesQuartilesScale = d3.scaleQuantile()
  .domain(femalesSalaries)
  .range([0, 1, 2, 3]);

const femalesQuartiles = femalesQuartilesScale
  .quantiles();
const femalesExtent = d3.extent(femalesSalaries);

const malesSalaries = data.filter(d => d.gender ===
  "Male").map(d => d.salary);
const malesQuartilesScale = d3.scaleQuantile()
  .domain(malesSalaries)
  .range([0, 1, 2, 3]);

const malesQuartiles = malesQuartilesScale.quantiles();
const malesExtent = d3.extent(malesSalaries);
```

Filter the dataset to keep only women's or men's data points, and map their salary values into a new array.

Get an array containing the quartile values by calling the quantiles() accessor function of the quantile scale. Calculate the minimum and maximum salary values with d3.extent().

Declare a quantile scale for women and men. Pass the salaries array as the domain and an array of four values as the range to generate quartiles.

6.4.2   Positioning multiple box plots on a chart

In our project, we want to position two box plots within a graph, one visualizing the salary distribution of women and one for men. As shown in figure 6.12 and on the hosted project (http://mng.bz/orvd), genders are positioned along the horizontal axis, while salaries are spread along the vertical axis. This means that for the horizontal axis, we need a scale that accepts discrete values for the domain, the genders, and outputs along a continuous range, that is, the horizontal space available. For the vertical scale, we need a scale that takes a continuous domain, that is, the salaries, and then outputs values along the vertical height of the chart, which is a continuous range.

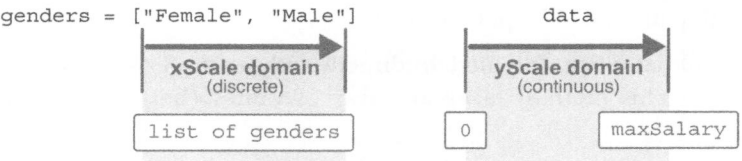

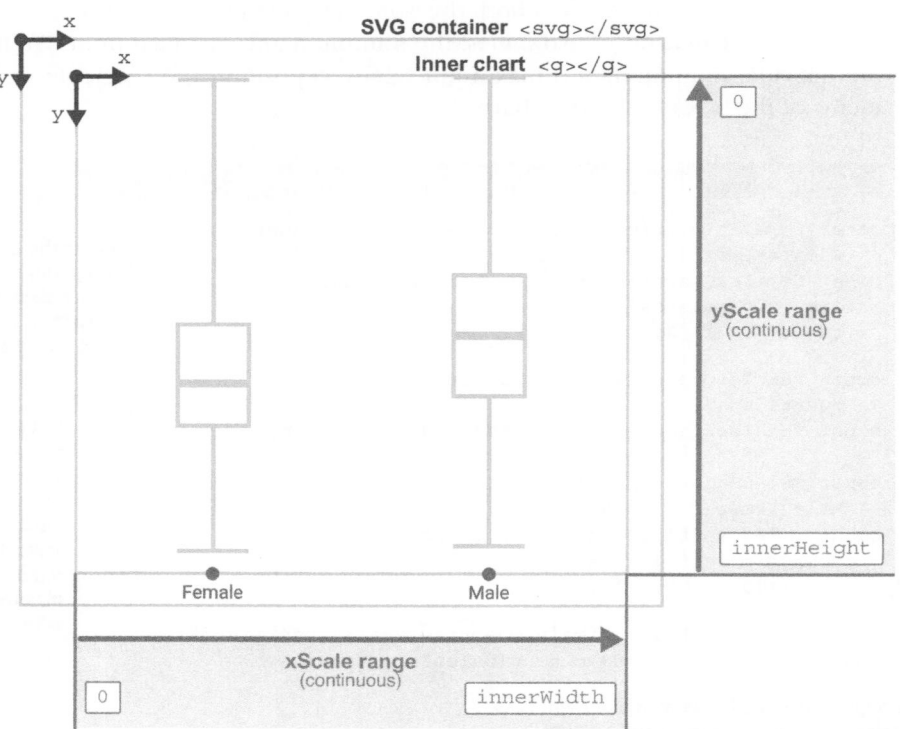

Figure 6.12   The horizontal scale will be responsible for positioning the women's and men's box plot along the x-axis. The vertical scale will distribute the salaries along the y-axis and allow calculation of the position of the minimum, maximum, median, and quartile values of the box plots.

6.4.3   *The point scale*

To position the genders along the x-axis, we'll use D3's point scale d3.scalePoint() (https://observablehq.com/@d3/d3-scalepoint). The point scale is very similar to the band scale used in chapters 3 and 5, except that the bandwidth is zero. This scale is used to distribute discrete elements along a continuous range.

In figure 6.13, we illustrate a point scale that uses an array of letters as the domain and that uses the horizontal space available as the range. We then chain the scale with method padding() to set its outer padding, which is the blank space at the two extremities. The padding() method accepts a factor between 0 and 1 as an argument. The outer padding is calculated as this factor multiplied by the size of the steps (padding factor * step); the steps are the spaces between adjacent points.

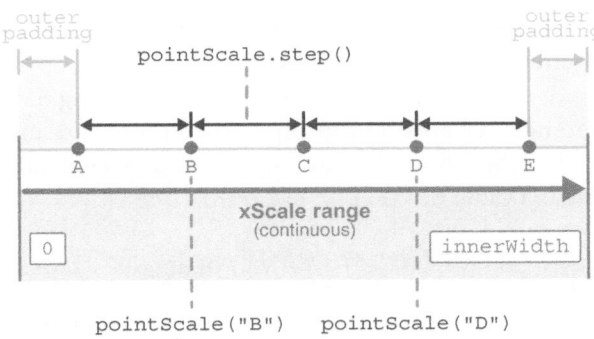

Figure 6.13   D3's point scale is similar to the band scale but with zero bandwidth. Its domain consists of a discrete list of elements distributed over a continuous range.

Before declaring the scales in listing 6.6, we create an array containing two strings, "Female" and "Male", and we name it genders. We then declare a point scale that will be used to distribute the genders uniformly along the x-axis. We pass the genders array as the scale's domain, set its range to extend from 0 to the inner width of the chart, and set its padding to 0.5, or 50%, of the distance between the position of the two box plots.

Like in the histogram we built in section 6.2, we want the salaries to be linearly proportional to their position along the y-axis. To do this, we declare a linear scale. Its domain extends from 0 to the maximum salary in the dataset, calculated with d3.max(). Its range extends from the inner height of the chart to 0 because the y-axis is positive in the top to bottom direction. Finally, we chain the nice() method to the linear scale to ensure that the axis ends with a round value.

Listing 6.6   Declaring the scales (box-plot.js)

```
const genders = ["Female", "Male"];
const xScale = d3.scalePoint()
  .domain(genders)
  .range([0, innerWidth])
  .padding(0.5);
```

Declare a point scale to distribute the genders (female and male) along the x-axis.

```
const maxSalary = d3.max(data, d => d.salary);
const yScale = d3.scaleLinear()
  .domain([0, maxSalary])
  .range([innerHeight, 0])
  .nice();
```

Use a linear scale to spread the salaries on the y-axis. Chain it with the nice() method to ensure that the axis ends with a round number.

We then use the scales to draw the axes of the box plots chart. In listing 6.7, we start by declaring a constructor for the bottom axis using method d3.axisBottom() and passing xScale as a reference. To hide the outer ticks of the axis, we chain the constructor with tickSizeOuter() (the method provided by the d3-axis module to set the size of the ticks at the beginning and the end of an axis), to which we give a value of 0. Then we append an SVG group to the inner chart, translate it to the bottom, and call the constructor to generate the axis elements.

Similarly, we declare a constructor for the left axis using d3.axisLeft() and pass yScale as a reference. We append a group to the inner chart and call the constructor. Finally, we display a label above the y-axis by appending a text element to the SVG container and giving it a value of "Yearly salaries (UDS)".

Listing 6.7   Drawing the axes (box-plot.js)

Initialize the bottom axis constructor, using xScale as a reference. Set the size of its outer ticks to 0.

```
const bottomAxis = d3.axisBottom(xScale)
  .tickSizeOuter(0);
innerChart
  .append("g")
    .attr("transform", `translate(0, ${innerHeight})`)
    .call(bottomAxis);
```

Append a group to the inner chart, translate it to the bottom, and generate the axis elements by calling the constructor.

```
const leftAxis = d3.axisLeft(yScale);
innerChart
  .append("g")
    .call(leftAxis);
```

Initialize the left axis constructor using yScale as a reference. Append a group to the inner chart, and generate the axis elements by calling the constructor.

```
svg
  .append("text")
    .text("Yearly salary (USD)")
    .attr("x", 0)
    .attr("y", 20);
```

Append a label for the y-axis with the text "Yearly salary (USD)".

6.4.4 Drawing a box plot

We're now ready to draw our box plots! As mentioned earlier, box plots are composed of three elements, illustrated in figure 6.14:

- A rectangle extending from the first to the third quartiles
- A line positioned at the median, corresponding to the second quartile
- The whiskers, or lines, extending from the minimum value to the first quartile and from the third quartile to the maximum value

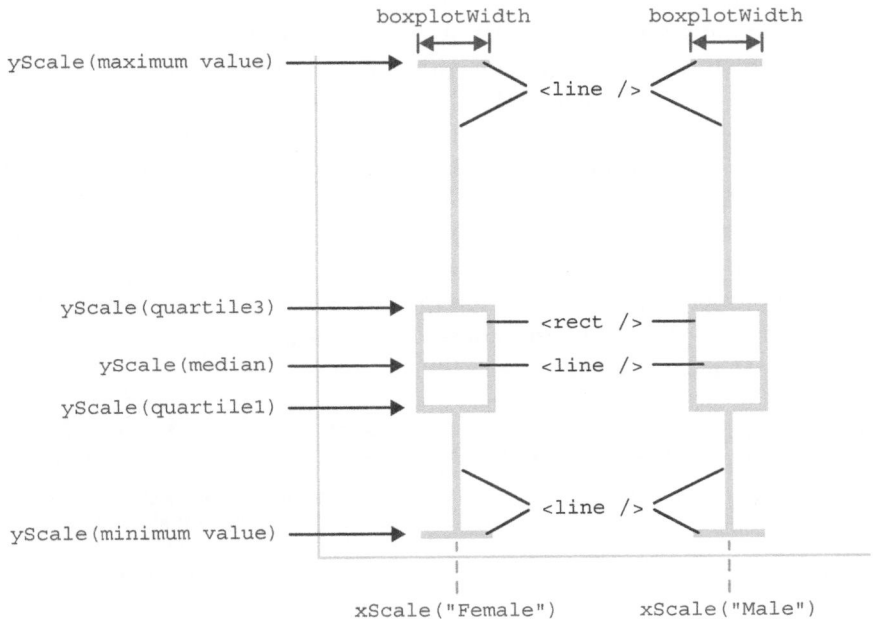

Figure 6.14 A box plot is composed of a rectangle extending from the first to the third quartile, a line positioned at the median, and whiskers extending from the minimum value to the first quartile and from the third quartile to the maximum value.

To draw the box plots, we start by declaring two constants, boxplotWidth and boxplotStrokeWidth, which are respectively responsible for holding the value of the width of the box plots and the width of their stroke. In listing 6.8, we give them values of 60 px and 3 px, respectively, but feel free to adjust them to your liking. These values will be used multiple times to draw the box plots, so saving them into constants facilitates future changes.

We then loop through the genders array declared in listing 6.8. For each gender, we append an SVG group to the inner chart. We set the stroke attribute to the color slateGray (#305252), declared in shared-constants.js, and the stroke-width attribute to constant `boxplotStrokeWidth` declared earlier. The elements appended into this group will inherit these attributes, so we won't have to set them multiple times.

Next, we append a rectangle element to the SVG group. To set its x attribute (the horizontal position of its top-left corner), we pass the current gender to `xScale`. Because `xScale` returns the position of the box plot's center, we need to subtract half of the box plot width to get the x attribute. The y attribute (the vertical position of the top-left corner) corresponds to the position of the third quartile, which we get by passing the third value in the `quartiles` array to `yScale`. The width of the rectangle is set with `boxplotWidth`. Its height is calculated by subtracting the position of the third quartile from the position of the first quartile (because the y-axis is positive in the top to bottom direction!). These last values are also returned by `yScale`. Finally, we set the `fill` attribute of the rectangle to the value `"transparent"`.

The position of the median is indicated with an SVG line. Horizontally, the line extends from the left to the right of the rectangle. These two values (x1 and x2) are calculated by finding the center of the rectangle (`xScale(gender)`) and adding or subtracting half of the width of the box plot. The vertical position of the line (y1 and y2) is found by passing the second quartile of each gender to `yScale`. To emphasize the median, we give its stroke a different color for women and men (#826C7F and #FA7E61, respectively, from the constants `womenColor` and `menColor` declared in `shared-constants.js`) and a stroke width of 10 px.

Listing 6.8   Drawing box plot rectangles and medians (`box-plot.js`)

```
const boxplotWidth = 60;
const boxplotStrokeWidth = 4;
```
Declare constants to hold the value of the width of the boxplots and the width of their strokes.

```
genders.forEach(gender => {
```
◁──| **Loop through the genders array.**

```
  const boxplotContainer = innerChart
    .append("g")
      .attr("stroke", slateGray)
      .attr("stroke-width", boxplotStrokeWidth);
```
Append an SVG group to the inner chart. Set its stroke and stroke-width attributes, which will be inherited by its children.

```
  boxplotContainer
    .append("rect")
      .attr("x", xScale(gender) - boxplotWidth/2)
      .attr("y", gender === "Female"
        ? yScale(femalesQuartiles[2])
        : yScale(malesQuartiles[2]))
      .attr("width", boxplotWidth)
      .attr("height", gender === "Female"
        ? yScale(femalesQuartiles[0]) -
            yScale(femalesQuartiles[2])
        : yScale(malesQuartiles[0]) -
            yScale(malesQuartiles[2]))
      .attr("fill", "transparent");
```
Append a rectangle element to the group. Calculate its position with the x and y attributes, width, and height using the scales declared earlier. Set the fill attribute to the value "transparent".

```
boxplotContainer
  .append("line")
    .attr("x1", xScale(gender) - boxplotWidth/2)
    .attr("x2", xScale(gender) + boxplotWidth/2)
    .attr("y1", gender === "Female"
      ? yScale(femalesQuartiles[1])
      : yScale(malesQuartiles[1]))
    .attr("y2", gender === "Female"
      ? yScale(femalesQuartiles[1])
      : yScale(malesQuartiles[1]))
    .attr("stroke", gender === "Female"
      ? womenColor
      : menColor)
    .attr("stroke-width", 10);
```

Append a horizontal line for the median. Set its x1, x2, y1, and y2 attributes.

```
});
```

In listing 6.9, we add whiskers at the bottom and the top of the rectangles using SVG lines. The bottom whisker consists of a vertical line going from the minimum salary value to the first quartile and a horizontal line at the position of the minimum salary. The top whisker comprises a vertical line from the third quartile to the maximum wage and a horizontal line at the position of the maximum salary.

Listing 6.9   Drawing the box plots' whiskers (`box-plot.js`)

```
genders.forEach(gender => {

  ...

  boxplotContainer
    .append("line")
      .attr("x1", xScale(gender))
      .attr("x2", xScale(gender))
      .attr("y1", gender === "Female"
        ? yScale(femalesExtent[1])
        : yScale(malesExtent[1]))
      .attr("y2", gender === "Female"
        ? yScale(femalesQuartiles[2])
        : yScale(malesQuartiles[2]));
```

Append the vertical line of the bottom whisker, spreading from the minimum salary to the first quartile.

```
  boxplotContainer
    .append("line")
      .attr("x1", xScale(gender) - boxplotWidth/2)
      .attr("x2", xScale(gender) + boxplotWidth/2)
      .attr("y1", gender === "Female"
        ? yScale(femalesExtent[0])
        : yScale(malesExtent[0]))
      .attr("y2", gender === "Female"
        ? yScale(femalesExtent[0])
        : yScale(malesExtent[0]));
```

Append the horizontal line of the bottom whisker, positioned at the minimum salary.

```
boxplotContainer
  .append("line")
    .attr("x1", xScale(gender))
    .attr("x2", xScale(gender))
    .attr("y1", gender === "Female"
      ? yScale(femalesQuartiles[0])
      : yScale(malesQuartiles[0]))
    .attr("y2", gender === "Female"
      ? yScale(femalesExtent[0])
      : yScale(malesExtent[0]));
```

Append the vertical line of the top whisker, spreading from the third quartile to the maximum salary.

```
boxplotContainer
  .append("line")
    .attr("x1", xScale(gender) - boxplotWidth/2)
    .attr("x2", xScale(gender) + boxplotWidth/2)
    .attr("y1", gender === "Female"
      ? yScale(femalesExtent[1])
      : yScale(malesExtent[1]))
    .attr("y2", gender === "Female"
      ? yScale(femalesExtent[1])
      : yScale(malesExtent[1]));
```

Append the horizontal line of the top whisker, positioned at the maximum salary.

```
});
```

Once completed, your box plots will look similar to the ones in figure 6.15. Note that there might be slight differences between the box plots shown in this chapter's figures and your results because the salary values are generated randomly in `load-data.js`.

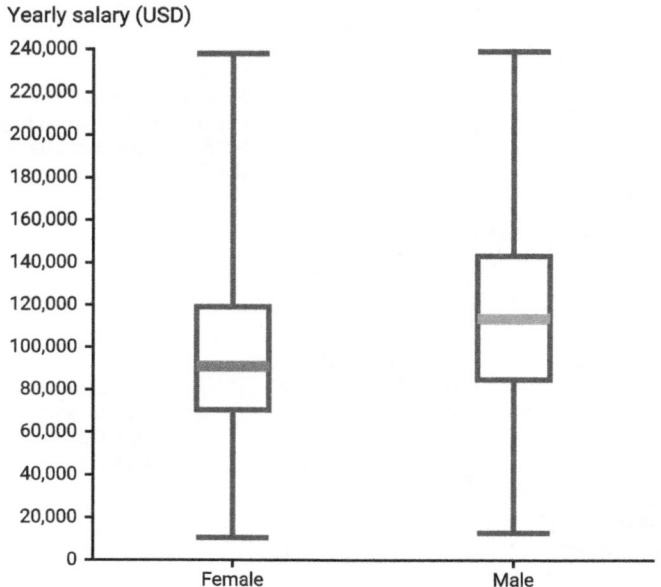

Yearly salary (USD)

Figure 6.15   Completed box plots of the salary distribution for women and men working in data visualization in the US

If you're still unsure about the meaning of a box plot, look at figure 6.16. It shows the actual data points visualized by the box plots. The vertical position of each circle corresponds to the salary it represents, while the horizontal position is attributed randomly to reduce overlap. Note how the circles' densities are higher within the rectangles, which contain 50% of the data points. These densities reduce as we move further from the rectangles along the whiskers.

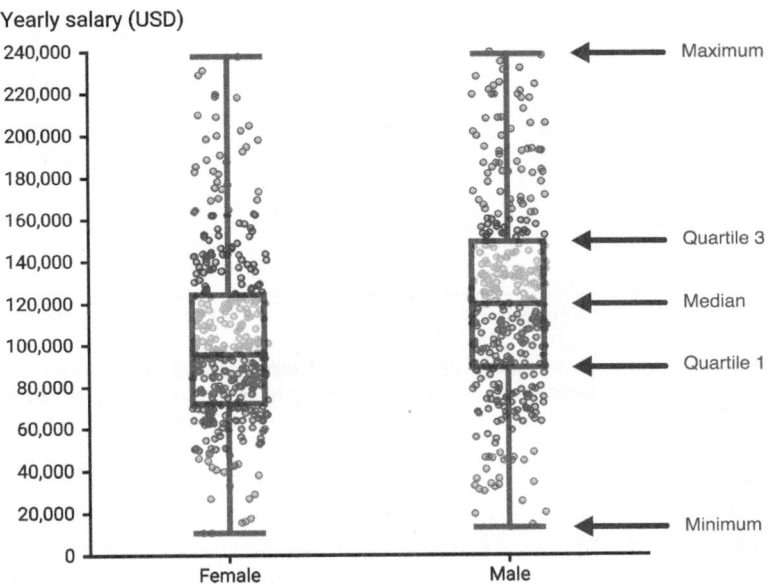

Figure 6.16   Salary data points visualized by the box plots. The vertical position of each circle corresponds to the salary it represents, while the horizontal position is calculated randomly to reduce overlap.

6.5   *Comparing distributions with violin plots*

We'll complete this chapter with a visualization that combines many of the notions we've discussed so far: a violin plot. Violin plots are mirrored, curved areas that bulge in regions containing multiple data points and taper where few exist. They're commonly seen in medical diagrams dealing with dosage and efficacy but are also used more generally to visualize distributions. Unlike box plots that only display predefined information (minimum, maximum, median, and quartiles), violin plots encode the entire distribution. They are often combined with additional information such as the position of the mean and the quartiles.

In this section, we'll compare the salary distribution of the dataset's leading five data visualization roles: analyst, developer, designer, scientist, and leadership. We chose not to visualize the other professions, such as cartographer and teacher, due to their low number of data points. Figure 6.17 shows the violin plots we'll build for each of the five roles. As you can see, they are combined with a line along the interquartile range and a dot at the position of the mean or average salary. We could also have chosen to represent the median instead of the mean, as both approaches are valid.

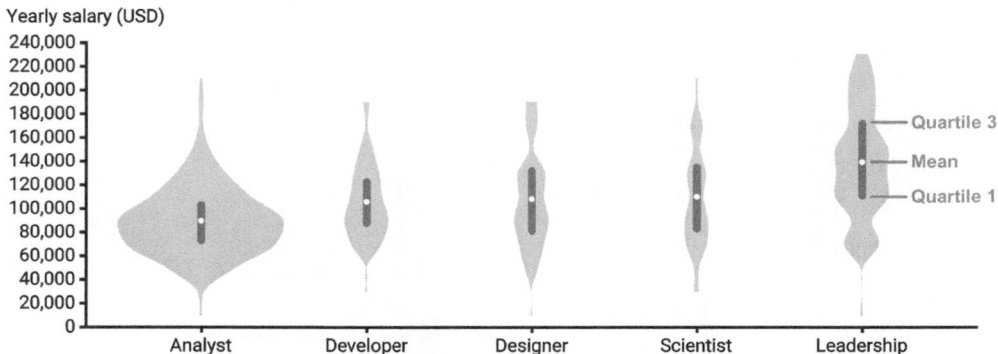

Figure 6.17   Violin plots of the salary distribution of the five leading data visualization roles. Each plot is combined with a gray line extending from the first to the third quartile and a white dot positioned at the mean value.

We'll start working in the `violins.js` file, inside function `drawViolinCharts()`. Note that the file already contains code adding an SVG container and the inner chart to the DOM. We've also declared the array named `roles`, which includes a list of objects with the ID of the professions we want to visualize.

To build the violin plots, we'll need to isolate the salaries for each role, calculate their mean or average value, organize them into bins, and calculate their quartiles. In listing 6.10, we perform these calculations while looping through the `roles` array. To isolate the data for the current role, we use JavaScript method `filter()` and chain the `map()` method to generate an array containing only the salary values. We store this array under the `salaries` key to make it accessible within the `roles` array.

We then calculate the mean value of the `salaries` array using method `d3.mean()`. This method is part of the d3-array module and works similarly to `d3.min()` and `d3.max()`.

We organize the salaries into bins using `d3.bin()` and the quartiles with D3's quantile scale by following the techniques used throughout this chapter. All of these values are also saved in the `roles` array.

Finally, we sort the roles to ensure that the mean values appear in ascending order using JavaScript method `sort()`. This will improve the readability of our chart and facilitate comparisons.

Listing 6.10   Extracting information for violin plots (`violins.js`)

```
const roles = [
  {id: "Designer" },
  {id: "Scientist" },
  {id: "Developer" },         Declare the roles array.
  {id: "Analyst" },
  {id: "Leadership" },
];
                                       Loop through
                                       the roles array.
roles.forEach(role => {                              Map the salaries for the current
                                                     role into an array. Store this
  role["salaries"] = data                            array under the "salaries" key.
    .filter(d => d.role === role.id)
    .map(d => d.salary);
                                                     Calculate the mean or average value of the
  role["mean"] = d3.mean(role.salaries);             salaries. Store it under the "mean" key.

                                                     Bin the salaries array with d3.bin().
  role["bins"] = d3.bin()(role.salaries);            Store the bins under the "bins" key.

  const quartilesScale = d3.scaleQuantile()          Calculate the quartiles of the
    .domain(role.salaries)                           salaries array using D3's
    .range([0, 1, 2, 3]);                            quantile scale. Store them
  role["quartiles"] = quartilesScale.quantiles();    under the "quartiles" key.

});
                                                     Sort the roles information in
                                                     ascending order of the mean value.
roles.sort((a, b) => a.mean - b.mean);
```

Figure 6.18 shows that we'll need three scales to build the violin charts:

- A point scale for spreading the roles along the x-axis
- A linear scale for the salary values along the y-axis
- A linear scale to calculate the width of the violin plots based on the number of data points within each bin

In listing 6.11, we declare a point scale responsible for spreading the roles along the x-axis and save it in a constant named `xScale`. As discussed in section 6.4.2, `d3.scalePoint()` accepts a discrete domain—here, an array of the roles created with the JavaScript `map()` method—and returns values from a continuous range, which is the space available on the width of the inner chart. We set the padding at the two extremities of the axis with method `padding()` and give it a value of `0.7`, or 70%, of the scale steps.

Then we declare the constant `yScale`, a linear scale used to distribute the salaries on the y-axis. The scale's domain is continuous and extends between 0 and the maximum wage in the dataset. The range is also continuous, returning values along the inner chart's vertical space. We chain this scale with method `nice()` to ensure that the y-axis ends with a round number.

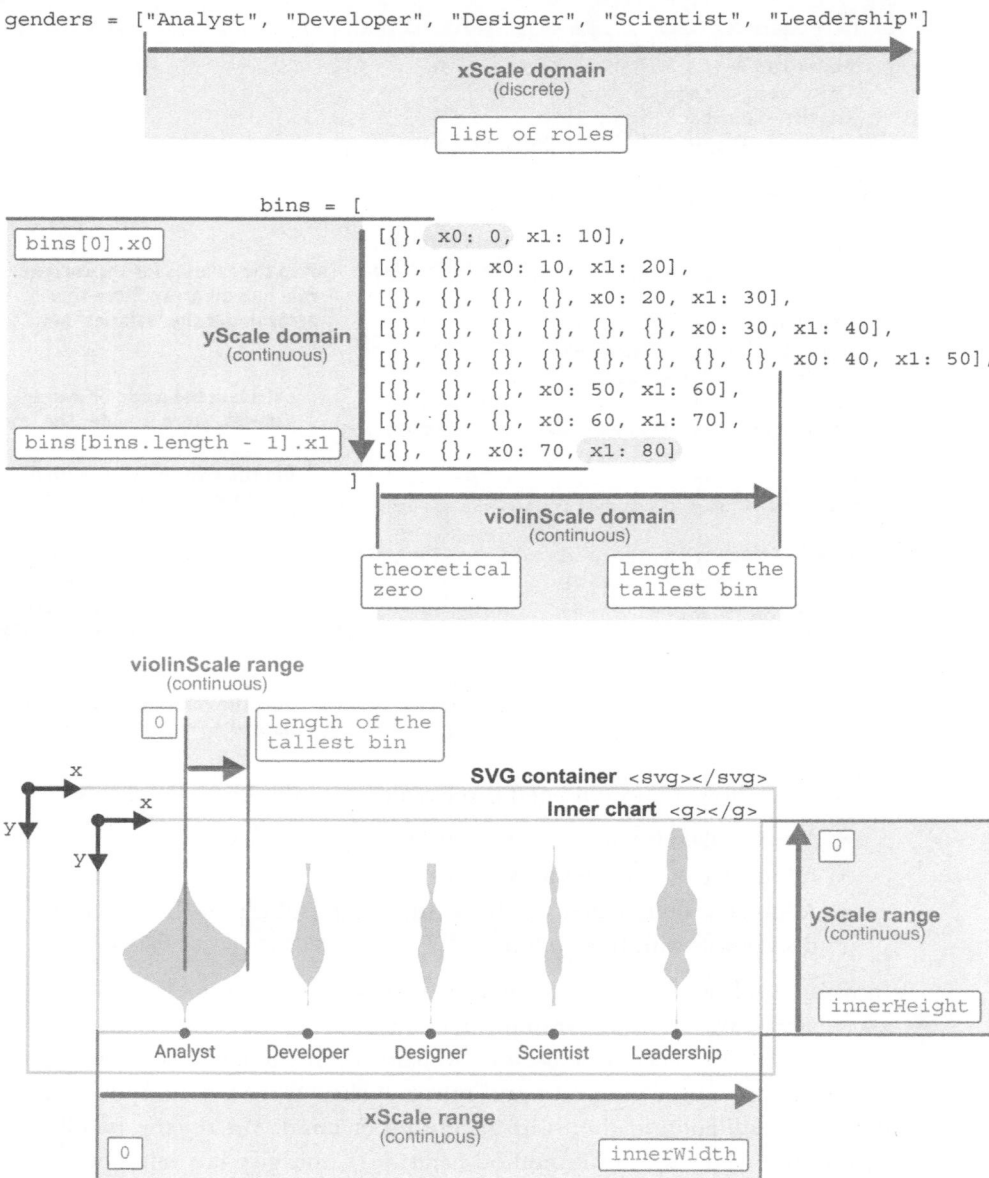

Figure 6.18   **To build the violin charts, we need three scales: a point scale responsible for spreading the roles along the x-axis, a linear scale for the salary values along the y-axis, and a linear scale to calculate the width of the violin plots based on the number of data points within each bin.**

Finally, we declare another linear scale, named `violinsScale`, that will be responsible for calculating the width of the violin plots. This width will vary along the y-axis, depending on the number of data points in each salary bracket.

Listing 6.11 Declaring the scales for the violin plots (`violins.js`)

```
const xScale = d3.scalePoint()
  .domain(roles.map(d => d.id))
  .range([0, innerWidth])
  .padding(0.7);
```
> Declare a point scale responsible for spreading the roles along the x-axis.

```
const maxSalary = d3.max(data, d => d.salary);
const yScale = d3.scaleLinear()
  .domain([0, maxSalary])
  .range([innerHeight, 0])
  .nice();
```
> Declare a linear scale to distribute the salaries on the y-axis.

```
let maxBinLength = 0;
roles.forEach(role => {
  const max = d3.max(role.bins, d => d.length);
  if (max > maxBinLength) {
    maxBinLength = max;
  }
});
```
> Find the length of the tallest bin among the roles.

```
const violinsScale = d3.scaleLinear()
  .domain([0, maxBinLength])
  .range([0, xScale.step()/2]);
```
> Declare a linear scale responsible for calculating the width of the violin plots for each salary bracket.

Exercise: Append the axes

You've witnessed how to append axes to a chart multiple times throughout the previous chapters. Now it's your turn! Use the scales declared in listing 6.11 to draw the axes for our violin charts. The roles should be displayed along the x-axis and the salaries along the y-axis. In addition, add a label to the y-axis with the text "Yearly salary (USD)."

Once completed, your axes should look similar to the ones in the following figure. If you get stuck or want to compare your solution with ours, refer to listing D.6.2 in appendix D or to the `6.5-Violins/end` folder in this chapter's code files.

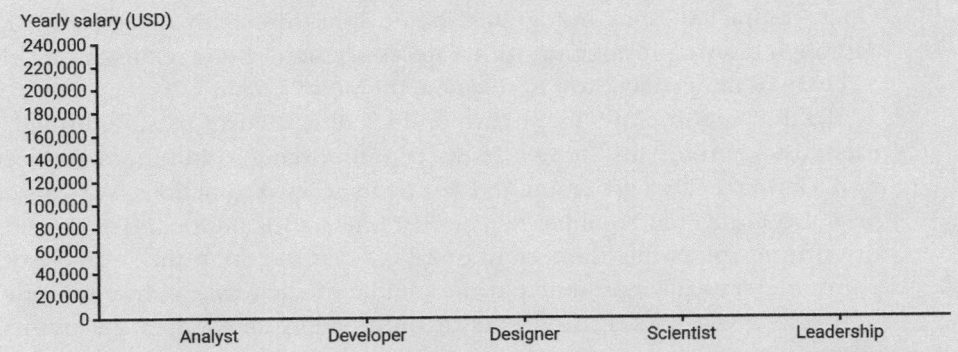

Axes for the violin charts. The roles are spread along the x-axis, while the salaries are represented along the y-axis.

Violin plots can be described as smoothed histograms mirrored around an invisible central axis. To illustrate this concept, we'll start by creating a vertically oriented histogram for each role.

In listing 6.12, we loop through the roles and append an SVG group to the inner chart for each one, which we save in a constant named `roleContainer`. This strategy will help us keep our markup tidy and easy to inspect.

Then we use the data-binding pattern to append a rectangle element for each bin within a role. The rectangles start at the current role's central axis, which is returned by `xScale`. Their width is proportional to the number of data points contained in the related bin and is calculated by `violinScale`. Finally, the vertical position and height of the rectangles depend on the salary brackets and are returned by `yScale`.

Listing 6.12   Drawing a histogram for each role (`violins.js`)

```
roles.forEach(role => {

    const roleContainer = innerChart        Append an SVG group to the inner chart.
      .append("g");                         Save it in a constant named roleContainer.

    roleContainer                                          Use the data-binding pattern
      .selectAll(`.bar-${role.id}`)                        to append a rectangle for each
      .data(role.bins)                                     bin of the current role. The
      .join("rect")                                        rectangles start at the current
        .attr("class", `bar-${role.id}`)                   role's central axis, returned by
        .attr("x", xScale(role.id))                        xScale. Their width is
        .attr("y", d => yScale(d.x1))                      proportional to the number of
        .attr("width", d => violinsScale(d.length))        data points inside each bin and
        .attr("height", d => yScale(d.x0) - yScale(d.x1))  is calculated by violinScale. The
        .attr("fill", slateGray)                           vertical position of the
        .attr("fill-opacity", 0.4)                         rectangles is proportional to
        .attr("stroke", white)                             the related salary and is
        .attr("stroke-width", 2);                          returned by yScale.

});
```

Loop through the roles.

Once completed, your histograms should look similar to the ones in figure 6.19. Although drawing histograms isn't a necessary step when creating violin charts, they will help us understand how to calculate the violin's paths.

To draw violin plots, all we have to do is draw a curve passing through the tip of each histogram bar. In listing 6.13, we're still working within the roles loop. We start by declaring an area generator and setting its accessor functions. We want the area to have two horizontal boundaries. The first one (`x0`) is positioned at the centerline of the current role, while the second one (`x1`) is at the tip of the related bar. The data points are vertically positioned at the middle of each bar, and we smooth the curve with `d3.curveCatmullRom`. For more information about area generators, refer to chapter 4.

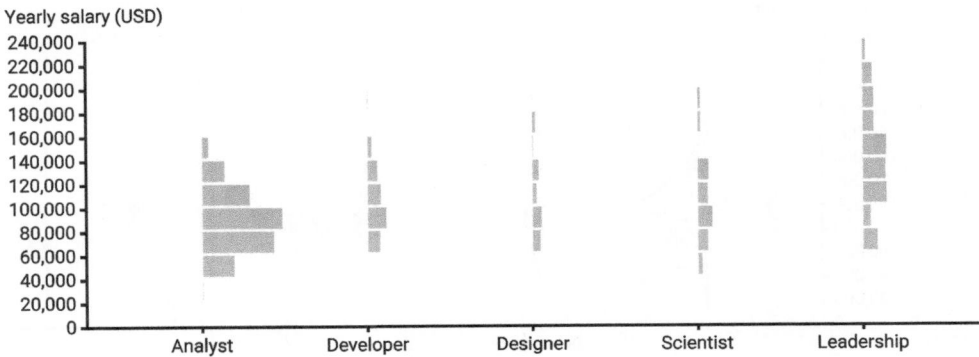

Figure 6.19   Histograms of the salary distribution for each role

We then append a path element to `roleContainer`. To calculate its d attribute, we call the area generator and pass the bins of the current role as an argument.

Listing 6.13   Drawing half-violin plots (`violins.js`)

```
roles.forEach(role => {

  ...

  const areaGenerator = d3.area()
    .x0(d => xScale(role.id))
    .x1(d => xScale(role.id) + violinsScale(d.length))
    .y(d => yScale(d.x1) + ((yScale(d.x0) -
      yScale(d.x1))/2))
    .curve(d3.curveCatmullRom);

  roleContainer
    .append("path")
      .attr("d", areaGenerator(role.bins))
      .attr("fill", "transparent")
      .attr("stroke", slateGray)
      .attr("stroke-width", 2);

};
```

Declare an area generator. The areas have two horizontal boundaries, the first (x0) located at the centerline of each role and the second (x1) at the tip of the histogram's bars. The data points are positioned vertically in the middle of each bar.

Append a path element to the roleContainer. To calculate its d attribute, call the area generator, and pass the bins of the current role as a parameter.

You should now have half-violin plots as in figure 6.20. The areas start at the center-line of each role and pass by the tips of the histogram's bars.

To finalize the violin plots, start by commenting out the lines of code that create the histogram. In JavaScript, single-line comments start with //, and multiline comments start with /* and end with */.

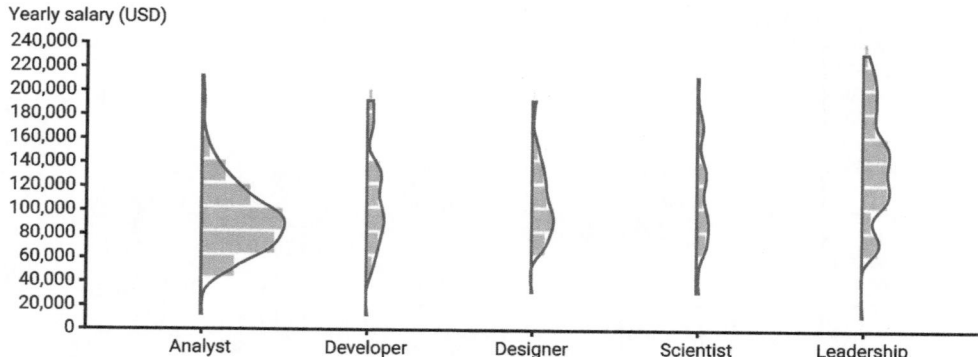

Figure 6.20   Half-violin plots drawn by passing a curve on the tip of each bar of the histograms

To complete the violin shapes, we simply have to mirror the right half of the violins. In the next listing,, we update the area generator's `x0()` accessor function to reflect `x1()`. Then we remove the path's stroke, set the fill to the color `slateGray` available in `shared-constants.js` (#305252), and change its opacity to 30%.

Listing 6.14   Drawing complete violin plots (`violins.js`)

```
roles.forEach(role => {

    ...

    const areaGenerator = d3.area()
      .x0(d => xScale(role.id) - violinsScale(d.length))
      .x1(d => xScale(role.id) + violinsScale(d.length))
      .y(d => yScale(d.x1) + ((yScale(d.x0) - yScale(d.x1))/2))
      .curve(d3.curveCatmullRom);

    roleContainer
      .append("path")
        .attr("d", areaGenerator(role.bins))
        .attr("fill", slateGray)
        .attr("fill-opacity", 0.3);

};
```

> **Complete the violin areas by mirroring the boundary x1.**

> **Remove the area's stroke, set the fill to the color slateGray, and set its opacity to 30%.**

Aa shown in figure 6.21, we now have violin plots! We only need to add a few details to complete this chapter's project, which you'll do in the following exercise.

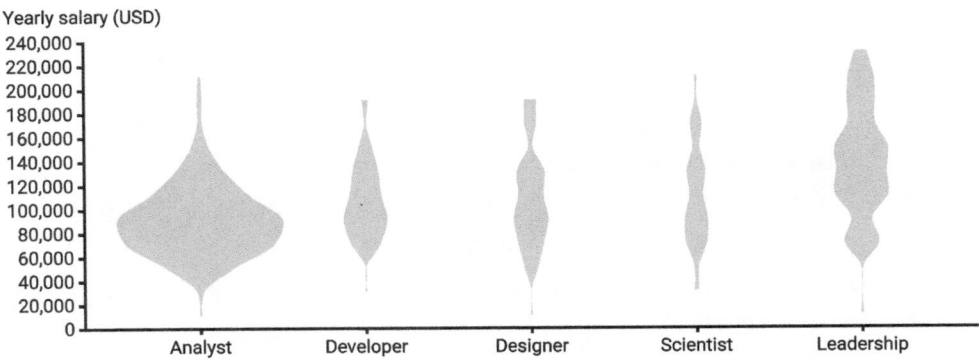

Yearly salary (USD)

Figure 6.21 Violin plots for each data visualization role

Exercise: Add the interquartile ranges and the mean values to the violin plots

To complete this chapter's project, indicate the interquartile ranges and the mean values on the violin charts, as shown in the following figure. The specifications are the following:

- The interquartile range is represented by rectangles spreading from the first to the third quartile. These values are available in the `roles` array.
- The rectangles have a width of 8 px, and their corners are rounded with a radius of 4 px. Their color is gray, for which you can use the variable `gray` available in `shared-constants.js` (#606464).
- The mean values are represented by circles.
- The circles have a radius of 3 px and a white color, for which you can use the variable `white` available in `shared-constants.js` (#faffff).

If you get stuck or want to compare your solution with ours, you'll find it in listing D.6.3 of appendix D and in the `6.5-Violins/end` folder of this chapter's code files. But as usual, we encourage you to try to complete it on your own. Your solution might differ slightly from ours, and that's all right!

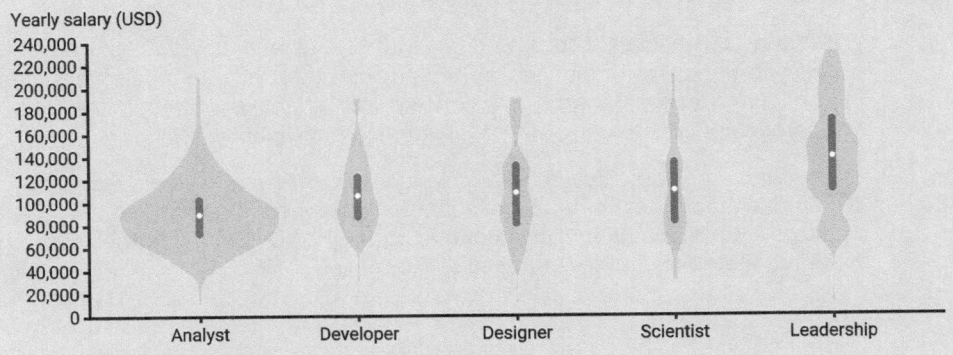

Yearly salary (USD)

Violin plots with interquartile ranges and mean values

This completes the first section of the book! You should now have a good grasp of D3's fundamental techniques. In the following chapters, we'll dive into more advanced topics and visualizations.

Interview with Moritz Stefaner and Fabian Ehmel

Stefaner is an independent data visualization designer and consultant.

Ehmel is a design technologist at Studio NAND.

Can you both tell us a little bit about your background and how you entered the field of data visualization?

Fabian: I initially studied geography and computer science and continued to study interaction design later. This combination of subjects led to my interest in data visualization, and I worked on several such projects during my studies. Before graduating, I spent a few months as a data visualization design intern at Accurat in Milan. Since graduation, I have worked as a design technologist at Studio NAND in Berlin on data visualization projects like the Impfdashboard.

Moritz: Prior to studying cognitive science and interface design, I worked in web design agencies in the early 2000s. Since 2007, I've worked as a self-employed "Truth & Beauty Operator" and have helped clients from industry, academia, and NGOs to find truthful and beautiful data representations. I have done some experimental projects—from data sculptures and interactive installation to using food as a medium—to explore how far we can push the dataviz envelope. Lately, I have been working mostly on larger design systems and ecosystems for visual data tools.

Which data visualization tools do you mainly use or have a preference for? What's the place of D3 in your current data visualization workflow?

Fabian: At Studio NAND, the web is our primary medium for data visualizations. We generally rely on one of the popular web frameworks for their development: React or Svelte. For both options, D3 is our go-to solution for data visualization, for both data preparation and visualization. We typically use it to generate scales, parse data, format dates and times, create force-directed layouts, project geo data, interpolate paths, and render chart axes. However, we don't use D3's functionalities for DOM updates but rely on React or Svelte's logic.

Moritz: Like Fabian, I love working with Svelte and d3. Lately, I have especially enjoyed working with plot.js from Observable. It provides a much more direct way to configure standard charts in a concise and effective way than the fairly low-level approach of constructing everything element individually.

Featured project: "Covid-19 Vaccination Dashboard - Impfdashboard" (https://impfdashboard.de/en/), a collaboration between Cosmonauts & Kings GmbH (https://cosmonautsandkings.com), Studio NAND GmbH (https://nand.io/), and Moritz Stefaner (https://truth-and-beauty.net/)

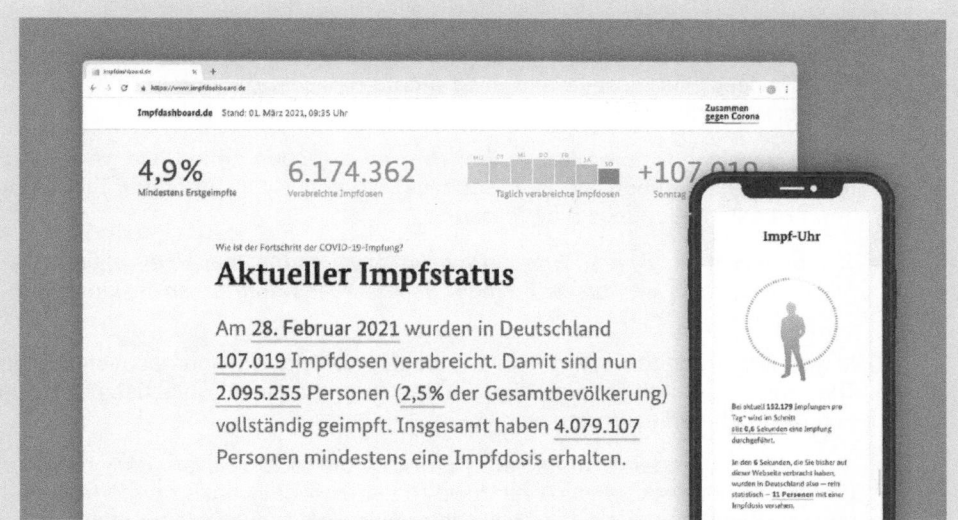

The Impfdashboard was the official German COVID-19 vaccination dashboard commissioned by the German Federal Ministry of Health. (Source: Cosmonauts & Kings GmbH with Studio NAND GmbH and Truth & Beauty)

The Impfdashboard was the official German COVID-19 vaccination dashboard commissioned by the German Federal Ministry of Health. We designed and developed it in cooperation with Cosmonauts & Kings.

The dashboard is based on a low-barrier approach. Visitors should be able to get the latest and most relevant information at first glance. Therefore, we communicated multiple vital indicators (such as vaccine doses administered, the daily vaccination rate, and the percentage of the overall vaccinated population) in a visual and written form at the very top of the page.

For visitors interested in more details, the Impfdashboard provides multiple visualizations with detailed information. These communicated the situation in different regions and age groups or about the historical progress of the vaccination campaign.

Can you explain the process of creating this project?

Due to the pandemic, our process was characterized by several dynamics and constraints. The dashboard's initial version had to be designed and developed in just a few weeks. Consequently, we used a very agile process, starting with identifying visitors' information needs and communicative goals, drafting wireframes and an initial visual design language, and implementing the first version. We continued using this method for the following development over the next two and a half years, prototyping new visualizations directly in our frontend setup using Svelte combined with D3.

The dashboard's data was provided by the Robert Koch Institute (RKI)—the German government's central scientific institution for biomedicine and public health. Initially,

(continued)

we had to run data updates to the site manually daily based on Excel sheets. Later, we enhanced this process and used a data pipeline to automatically release a new site version whenever new data became available.

As we developed the project further over an extended period, we were fortunate to receive a large amount of user feedback. We actively incorporated this feedback to improve existing or upcoming features.

This project is mobile-first. How did you work around the challenges of creating a dashboard that works well on both small touch screens and larger desktops with mouse interactions?

It was important to us to make the Impfdashboard as approachable as possible. Therefore, we opted for a mobile-first design and focused on accessibility, usability, and overall broad comprehensibility.

As mentioned, the site immediately provides the most relevant daily information, so visitors do not need to scroll far down to get their daily dose of information. In addition, we simplified some charts in the mobile view to make them easier to read and understand. We also designed UI components that adapt to the device. One example is a slider that allows seamless navigation inside a time-series chart on mobile without using complex touch gestures.

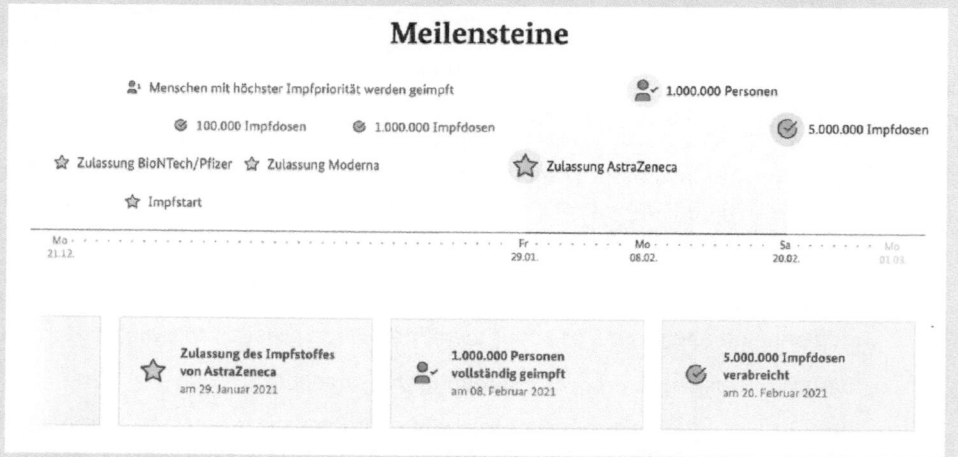

Text and badges are used to convey data and improve accessibility. (Source: Cosmonauts & Kings GmbH with Studio NAND GmbH and Truth & Beauty)

You also opted for "simplicity" by using text and badges to convey data. Moritz, on your website, you mention that text is a complement of choice for data visualization. That sounds obvious, but it is often neglected. Can you tell us a little more about that?

Sure! Thinking more about accessibility lately, I became more interested in the role of text in data visualization. Just like charts, text can also be automatically generated, based on the data, to convey information. Compared to a visual chart, text generated from data is potentially lower barrier, screen reader–friendly, easily shareable by copy-paste, and automatically translatable. So I think it's the perfect complement to charts and more visual elements.

Are you planning to collaborate again in the future? What types of projects would you like to work on?

The Impfdashboard was not the first collaboration between Studio NAND and Moritz. Previously, we worked on other data visualization projects, such as Peak Spotting, which we designed for the German railway company Deutsche Bahn. We'd love to collaborate again, as our skill sets complement each other quite nicely.

[a]If the project isn't available at this location, it can still be viewed via web archive (http://mng.bz/1GzR).

Summary

- To visualize data distributions, we often need to preprocess a dataset by grouping its data points into buckets or bins, which are groups of equal width along an axis. In D3, we do this with method `d3.bin()`.
- To draw a histogram, we use the data-binding pattern to append rectangle elements to a selection, using bins as data. The length of each rectangle is proportional to the number of data points contained in its related bin.
- The structure of a pyramid chart is similar to the one of a histogram, except that it is used to compare two distributions side by side.
- Box plots are composed of a rectangle spreading from the first to the third quartiles and whiskers or lines extending from the minimum value to the first quartile and the third quartile to the maximum value. The median is generally represented by a perpendicular line.
- In D3, we calculate quartiles with the quantile scale `d3.scaleQuantile()`, which accepts a discrete domain and a discrete range. If we want to calculate quartiles, hence dividing the data into four groups, the range must be an array of four elements, such as `[0, 1, 2, 3]`.
- To draw a box plot with D3, we simply need to append rectangle and line elements to a selection and set their attributes based on the positions of the minimum, maximum, median, and quartile values.
- D3's point scale `d3.scalePoint()` is similar to the band scale discussed in chapter 3, except it has zero bandwidth. Its domain consists of a discrete list of elements distributed over a continuous range.
- Violin plots are mirrored, curved areas that bulge in regions containing multiple data points and taper where few exist. They can be described as smoothed

histograms mirrored around an invisible central axis. To draw a violin plot, we need to generate an area passing through the tips of each bin. It can be helpful to draw histograms first to get situated.

- Violin plots are often combined with a rectangle showing the interquartile range and a circle positioned at the mean or the median value.

Part 2

Meeting the new standards

A lot has changed since D3 was first introduced in 2011! Today, more than half of digital content is consumed on phones. We also expect digital content to be interactive and even animated. As developers, our stack of tools has evolved, and most projects are now built with a JavaScript framework, like React or Svelte. We also finally came to the realization that not everyone accesses web content the same way, and we're (painfully) slowly adapting our development habits.

This section focuses on the new standards we're expected to meet when creating digital data visualizations. In chapter 7, we'll explore how to produce interactions and animations with D3. In chapter 8, we'll discuss three strategies to combine D3 with a framework. In chapter 9, we'll revisit data visualizations we built previously and make them responsive. In chapter 10, we'll conclude by improving the accessibility of a digital visualization.

Interactive visualizations

7

This chapter covers

- Adding event listeners to a D3 selection
- Creating smooth and reusable transitions
- Filtering a visualization
- Using tooltips to reveal additional information
- Animating the enter, update, and exit selections

One of D3's key selling points is how easy it is to create interactive visualizations that meet today's web standards. That's probably one of the primary reasons why so many data practitioners want to master this library.

In the first part of this book, you've worked hard to understand the philosophy behind D3 and its building blocks. Now it's time for a treat! In this chapter, we'll reuse previously built charts and make them interactive. We'll start by filtering the histogram created in chapter 6 by gender. This exercise will teach you how to listen to user events and create smooth transitions. Then we'll go back to the temperature line chart built in chapter 4 and display a tooltip when the mouse passes over a data point. We'll take this feature further in the following section with a composite

233

tooltip that reveals the sales breakdown for each music format as the mouse moves over the streamgraph from chapter 5. Finally, we'll create a scatterplot from scratch to explore how D3 offers granular control over the transitions when data enters or exits a visualization. We'll also introduce D3's logarithmic and radial scales.

Although it doesn't cover all the types of interactions available in D3, this chapter will give you a strong foundation for building interactive visualizations. Throughout the rest of the book, we'll cover other interactions such as brushing, zooming, and panning. But first, let's briefly discuss why we build interactive visualizations and the primary best practices.

7.1 Why use interactivity?

Interactive visualizations offer a wide range of opportunities compared to static ones. They allow users to explore rich datasets, highlight connections, or focus on a subset of data. Interactions can also make the information more easily accessible and easier to find. Instead of offering only an editorial perspective, interactive visualizations give the power back to the users. It is free to use them to explore a project, find outliers, and draw conclusions. As Andy Kirk puts it, "[Interactive visualizations] expand the physical limits of what can be consumed in a given space."[1] Interactivity is definitely an exciting subject. But it's good to remember that *not every visualization* can or *should* be interactive.

7.1.1 A few best practices for interactivity

Keeping the end user in mind when planning interactions is critical. By asking yourself the following questions, you increase the chances of creating interactions that are both relevant and intuitive:

- *How much time does the user have to explore the visualization?* The context can help us answer this question. If the visualization is part of a dashboard, critical information must be directly available, and interactions should allow the user to answer additional questions. On the other hand, if the work is part of a long-form online article, we can assume that the user has time to explore and get lost in the details.
- *Will the visualization be consumed mostly on desktops or mobile devices?* Desktops imply mouse events while mobiles use touch screens. On touch screens, we need to plan more space for touch interactions because our fingers are larger than the cursor of a mouse.
- *How much does the user already know about the subject?* This helps us decide whether we can display the foundational information directly or afford to "hide" it within interactive features.

---

[1] Andy Kirk, *Data Visualisation: A Handbook for Data Drive Design*, 2nd ed. (London: SAGE Publications Ltd, 2019), 203.

- *Is the user tech-savvy? Will they understand how to interact with the visualization?* Consider providing instructions when relevant.
- *What are the benefits of the interactions and animations?* We should determine whether they are enhancing the user experience, or if we're just adding them for the coolness factor.
- *Are the interactive features obstructing the visualization in any way?* If yes, consider modifying the type of interaction or use transparency to reduce obstruction.

7.2 Filtering a visualization

One of the typical use cases for interactivity is filtering a visualization. In this section, we'll work with the histogram built in chapter 6 and allow the user to filter data by gender. Take a look at the completed project at http://mng.bz/n1na, and click on the buttons above the histogram to see the transition happening. As you can see in figure 7.1, there are three buttons or filters: one to see all the data selected by default, one to see the data related to respondents identifying as women, and one for respondents identifying as men.

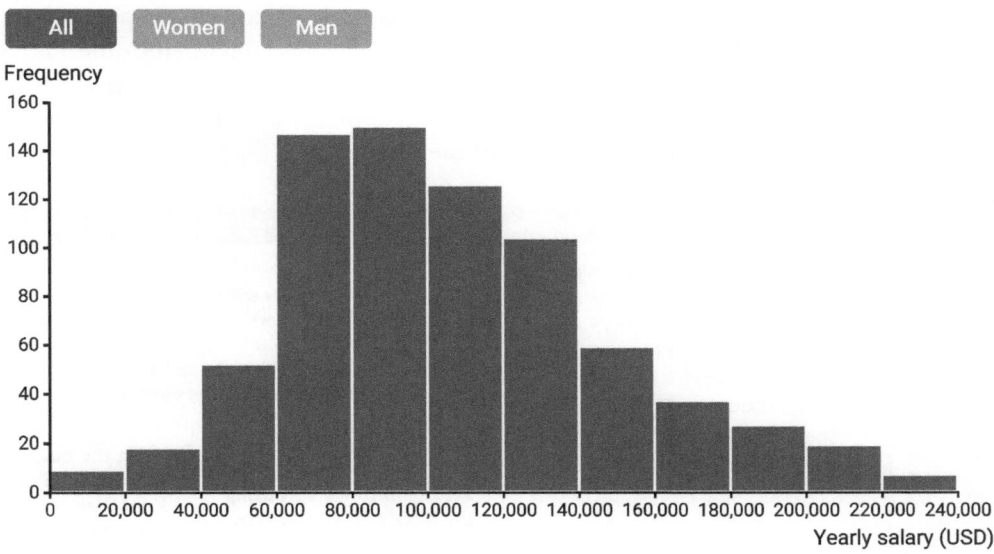

Figure 7.1 Histogram of the salary distribution among data visualization practitioners in the US with buttons to filter the chart by gender

NOTE To follow along with the instructions, download or clone the files from the book's GitHub repository (http://mng.bz/Xqjv). The chapter_07/7.2-Filtering folder contains two subfolders named start and end. Open the start folder in your code editor, and start your local web server. Refer to the solution in the end folder if you ever get stuck.

The code files for this project already contain the histogram built in chapter 6. Note that we moved the declaration of the scales to the `shared-constants.js` file to make them accessible globally.

First, let's add the filtering buttons to the histogram interface. The `shared-constants.js` file already contains an array named `filters`, with an ID, label, and status for each button. You can see this array in the following code snippet. Observe that the `isActive` property of the first filter is set to `true`, while the others are `false`. We'll use this property to track which filter is currently selected:

```
const filters = [
  { id: "all", label: "All", isActive: true },
  { id: "female", label: "Women", isActive: false },
  { id: "male", label: "Men", isActive: false },
];
```

To add the filters to the interface, we'll start working in the `interactions.js` file within function `populateFilters()`. This function is already called from `load-data.js` and gets the dataset as an argument.

In listing 7.1, we start by selecting the `div` with an ID of `"filters"` that already exists in `index.html`. We then use the data-binding pattern to append three button elements to the selection based on the three objects contained in the `filters` array. We give each button the class name `"filter"`. If the `isActive` property of the filter is `true`, we also add the class name `"active"`. Finally, we set the text of each button to correspond to the `label` property of the filter.

Listing 7.1   Adding filter buttons to the interface (`interactions.js`)

```
const populateFilters = (data) => {

  d3.select("#filters")              ← Select the div with
    .selectAll(".filter")              an ID of "filters".
    .data(filters)                   Use the data-binding pattern to add a
    .join("button")                  button for each object in the filters array.
      .attr("class", d => `filter ${d.isActive ?
        "active" : ""}`)                          Set the button's class
      .text(d => d.label);   ←   Set the buttons' text using    name to "filter". If the
};                                  the filter's label property.   isActive property of the
                                                                    related filter is true, add
                                                                    the class name "active".
```

Save your project, and look at it in the browser. You'll see that the three buttons are displayed above the histogram, as shown earlier in figure 7.1, and styled by the CSS styles listed in `visualization.css`. The active button is dark green, while the other buttons have a semitransparent background to suggest that they aren't selected.

If you click on the buttons, nothing happens because we aren't capturing the click event yet. You'll learn how to do that in the following section.

7.2.1 Capturing user events

For the histogram to react when we click on one of the buttons, we need to attach event listeners. *Event listeners* are simply strategies put in place to wait and detect when a predefined event happens. In JavaScript, we use the `addEventListener()` method. In D3, we attach event listeners to a selection with the `on()` method, which is part of the d3-selection module.

As illustrated in figure 7.2, the first argument accepted by the `on()` method is the name of the event we want to capture. Any DOM event type can be used, such as `click`, `mouseover`, `touch`, `keydown`, and so on. The second argument is a callback function in which we perform the desired action(s). This callback function receives two parameters: the event captured and the datum attached to the D3 selection on which the event occurred.

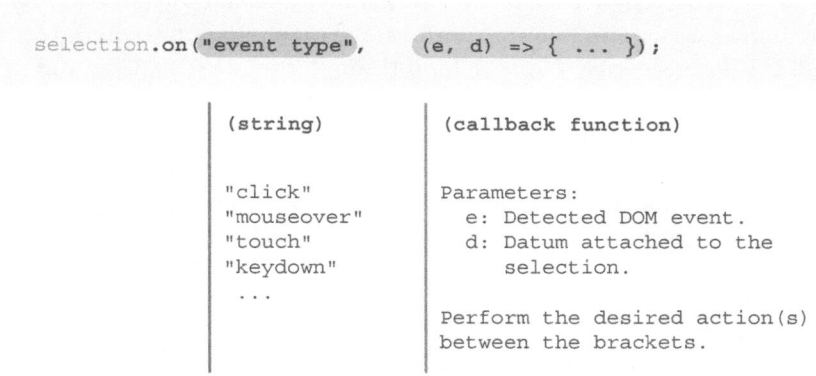

Figure 7.2 The `on()` **method attaches an event listener to a D3 selection and performs specific actions when the event occurs.**

Let's attach an event listener to our buttons. In the following snippet, we chain method `on()` to the filters selection. We pass event type `"click"` as the first argument, meaning that the callback function of `on()` (the second argument) will be executed every time a button is clicked:

```
d3.select("#filters")
  .selectAll(".filter")
  .data(filters)
  .join("button")
    .attr("class", d => `filter ${d.isActive ? "active" : ""}`)
    .text(d => d.label)
    .on("click", (e, d) => {
      console.log("DOM event", e);
      console.log("Attached datum", d);
    });
```

If you log the first parameter received by the callback function (e) in the console, you'll see that it consists of a comprehensive object. Properties such as clientX, clientY, offsetX, offsetY, pageX, and pageY provide the coordinates at which the event occurred relative to different elements on the page. The type of event can be confirmed by the type property, while the target property is probably the one we use most often. This property gives us the element on which the event took place—in this case, button.filter. It also includes the datum attached by D3 to the element under the __data__ key.

But we can access datum more directly with the second parameter received by the callback function (d). For example, if you log d into the console and click on the button with the label "Women", you'll get the object attached to the button:

```
{ id: "female", label: "Women", isActive: false }
```

We use the callback function of the on() method to perform actions based on the detected event. In listing 7.2, we first verify that the click that triggered the event wasn't an active button, as we don't want to perform the manipulations required for the chart update if it's not necessary. Then we loop through the filters array and update the isActive property of each filter based on the clicked button. Similarly, we select all the buttons with D3 and use the classed() method to add the "active" class name to or remove it from the buttons. Finally, we call function updateHistogram() and pass the clicked filter's ID and the complete dataset as arguments. This function is already declared in interactions.js, and this is where we'll update the histogram in a moment.

Listing 7.2   Handling the active state (interactions.js)

```
...
.on("click", (e, d) => {                          Verify that the clicked button
  if (!d.isActive) {          ◁───────┘           isn't currently active.

    filters.forEach(filter => {                    Loop though the filters array, and
      filter.isActive = d.id === filter.id ?       update the isActive property based
        true : false;                              on which button has been clicked.
    });

    d3.selectAll(".filter")                        Use the classed() method
      .classed("active", filter => filter.id ===   to add or remove the class
        d.id ? true : false);                      name "active" to the buttons.

    updateHistogram(d.id, data);      ◁───┐   Call function filterHistogram(), where
                                          │   the histogram will be updated.
  }

});
```

7.2.2   The classed method

So far in this book, we've handled class names with D3's attr() method, which takes the attribute's name as the first parameter and its value as the second. Let's say we want to give the class name `"filter"` to a selection. We simply use the `attr()` method, and we pass `"class"` as the name of the attribute and `"filter"` as its value:

```
filtersSelection
  .attr("class", "filter");
```

The `attr()` method only allows us to manipulate the class name(s) of a selection as a block. If we want to add the class name `"active"` to the selected filter, we could use the `attr()` method again, but because this method overwrites the entire class attribute, we would also need to include the initial class name, which was `"filter"`, with the two class names separated with a space:

```
myActiveFilter
  .attr("class", "filter active");
```

Fortunately, D3 lets us manipulate each class name separately with the `classed()` method. This method allows us to specify if a selection has a class name or not. It takes the class name as the first parameter and a Boolean (`true` or `false`) as the second, as illustrated in figure 7.3. In our example, instead of having to reapply the class name `"filter"` every time we add or remove the class name `"active"`, we can use the `classed()` method and control the class name `"active"` separately:

```
myActiveFilter
  .classed("active", true);
```

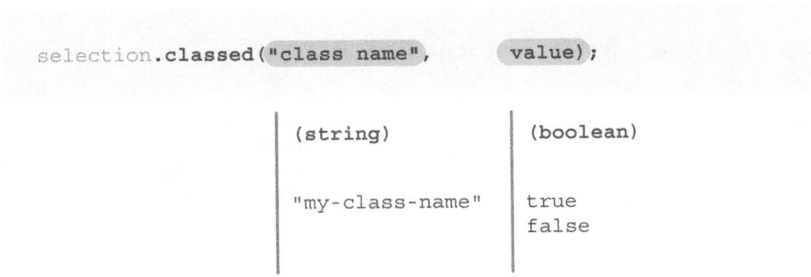

Figure 7.3 The `classed()` method provides control over each class name of a selection separately. Its first argument is the class name, and its second is true or false, indicating whether the selection should have the class name or not.

7.2.3 Updating the data in a visualization

Now that we can detect the clicks on the buttons, we're ready to update the histogram accordingly. We'll start working within function `updateHistogram()`, which we called earlier in listing 7.2.

If the user clicks on the Women button, we want the histogram to contain only the data of respondents identifying as women. Similarly, if the user clicks on the Men button, we want the histogram to include only the men's data. Finally, when selecting the All button, the histogram should visualize the whole dataset.

In listing 7.3, the first parameter that `updateHistogram()` receives is the `id` property of the data attached to the selected filter, which can have three different values: `"all"`, `"female"`, or `"male"`. If the `id` is `"all"`, we conserve the whole dataset (the second parameter received by the function). Otherwise, we filter the dataset to keep only the responses of people from the selected gender. We save the new data in constant `updatedData`.

Because our data changed, we must also recalculate the bins used to draw the histogram. To do that, we call the bin generator created when we made the original histogram and pass the updated dataset. We save the bins returned by the generator in constant `updatedBins`. Note that for the bin generator to be accessible from here, we added it to the global variables listed in `shared-constants.js`.

Finally, we select the rectangle elements that compose the histogram and attach the new bins as their data. We then only need to recalculate the `y` and the `height` attributes of the rectangles based on the new bins and using the `yScale` declared when we built the histogram.

Listing 7.3   Updating the data in the histogram (`interactions.js`)

```
const updateHistogram = (filterId, data) => {

  const updatedData = filterId === "all"
    ? data
    : data.filter(respondent => respondent.gender
      === filterId);

  const updatedBins = binGenerator(updatedData);

  d3.selectAll("#histogram rect")
    .data(updatedBins)
    .attr("y", d => yScale(d.length))
    .attr("height", d => innerHeight -
      yScale(d.length));

};
```

Filter the original dataset based on which button has been clicked.

Recalculate the bins by calling the bin generator function and passing the filtered dataset as an argument.

Bind the new bins to the histogram's rectangle elements, and update their y and height attributes.

You'll notice that the histogram now updates every time we click on one of the filter buttons, resulting in the visualizations shown in figure 7.4. But the shift happens abruptly, without a smooth transition. We'll address that in the following subsection.

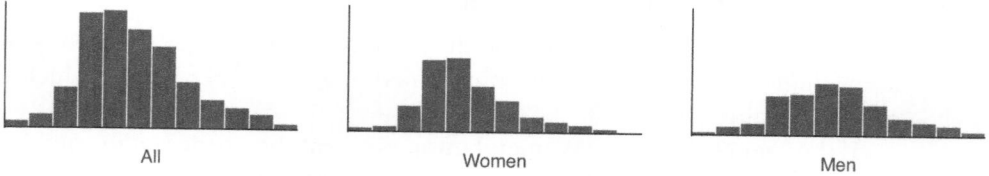

All   Women   Men

Figure 7.4   The three states of the histogram: with all the data, with women's data only, and with men's data only

7.2.4 *Creating smooth transitions*

Interactions generally imply that a change is happening between two or multiple states, for example, a blue element turning green or a tooltip going from hidden to visible. Ensuring that our transitions are smooth, meaning placing an animation between state A and state B, is important for more than esthetic purposes. Carefully crafted animations and transitions can actually reduce the users' cognitive load by helping them keep track of what changed, where it moved, and why. Animations literally help users understand what is happening.

In D3, we perform smooth transitions with the `transition()` method, which is part of the d3-transition module. We chain the `transition()` method just before changing the values of the attributes and styles on which we want to apply the animation. For example, the following snippet adds a transition to the histogram data update that is coded in listing 7.3. Because we chain the `transition()` method before updating the `y` and the `height` attributes, both of them will be animated. Transitions only affect the properties chained *after* the `transition()` method:

```
d3.selectAll("#histogram rect")
  .data(updatedBins)
  .transition()
    .attr("y", d => yScale(d.length))
    .attr("height", d => innerHeight - yScale(d.length));
```

Like in CSS, we can control the parameters of D3 transitions. First, we can set its duration with the `duration()` method, which accepts a value in milliseconds. If this method isn't set, a default duration of 250 ms is applied by D3.

We can also apply a delay before the transition happens with the `delay()` method, which also takes a value in milliseconds. The default delay is 0 ms.

Finally, we can specify the easing function of the transition or the rate of change over time. In real life, objects rarely move at a constant or linear speed. The movement rather starts slow and accelerates with time, or the movement starts quickly and gets slower or more controlled over time. These phenomena can be reproduced with easing functions. Because they mimic real-life action, carefully chosen easing functions can make transitions feel more natural. You've probably already used easing functions such as `ease-in`, `ease-out`, and `ease-in-out` in CSS.

Figure 7.5 shows the difference between a linear speed and the most common easing functions: quadratic, cubic, exponential, sinusoidal, circle, and polynomial. On each graph, the horizontal axis represents the time, while the vertical axis represents the change rate. For example, the change can be the position, color, or opacity of an element. The sinusoidal and quadratic functions offer a more subtle rate of change, while the exponential function creates the most dramatic one.

Note that the polynomial function is represented as an area in figure 7.5. This is because D3 allows us to change the value of the exponent applied to the time, providing a range of possibilities. The default value is 3, which corresponds to a cubic function.

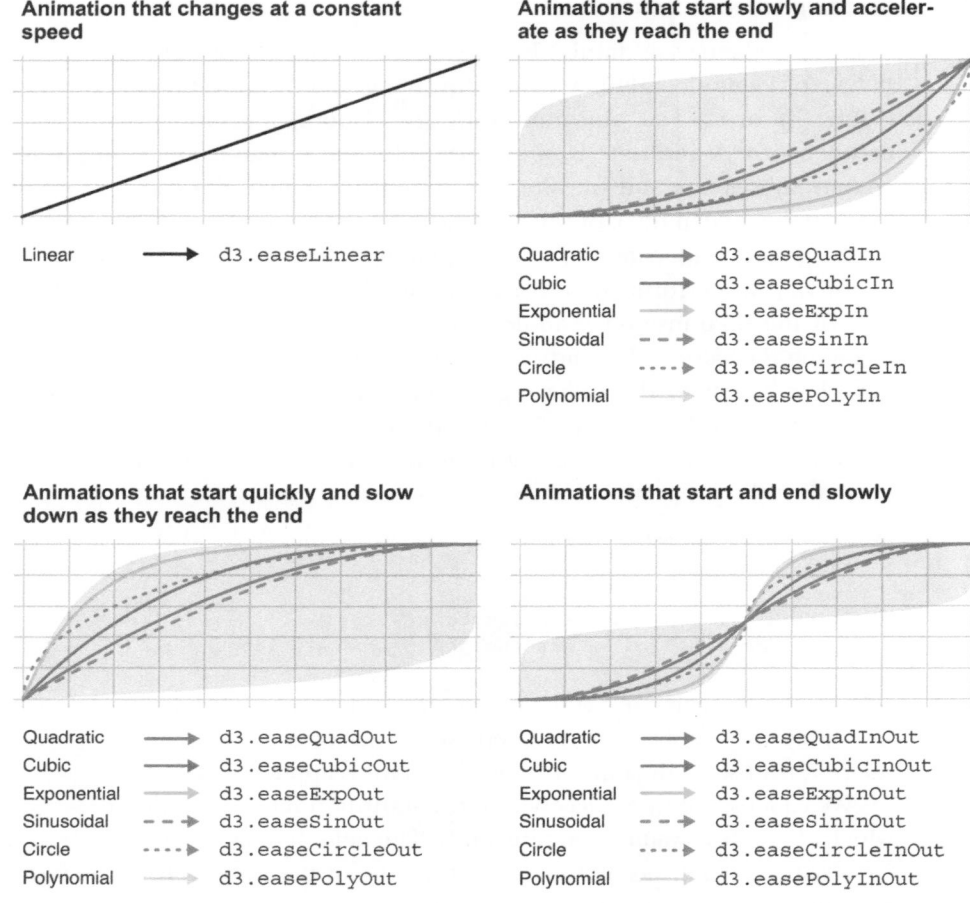

Figure 7.5   The most common easing functions in comparison to a linear rate of change. On each graph, the horizontal axis represents the time, while the vertical axis represents the change rate.

On the Observable "Easing Graphs" public notebook (https://observablehq.com/@d3/easing), you can test the effect of different exponents on the curve. Each easing function comes in three formats:

- *Animations that start slowly and accelerate as they reach the end.* These functions' names have the suffix "In," for example, d3.easeQuadIn, d3.easeExpIn, d3.easeCircleIn, and so on.

- *Animations that start quickly and slow down as they reach the end.* These functions' names have the suffix "Out," for example, d3.easeQuadOut, d3.easeExpOut, d3.easeCircleOut, and so on.

- *Animations that start and end slowly.* These functions' names have the suffix "InOut," for example, d3.easeQuadInOut, d3.easeExpInOut, d3.easeCircle-InOut, and so on.

If the ease method isn't set, D3 will use `d3.easeCubicInOut` by default. In addition to the more conventional ones, D3 gives us access to three easing functions that mimic specific physical reactions. These functions are described here and represented in figure 7.6:

- The elastic easing function reproduces a material that can be deformed and return to its original shape, like a rubber band. It accepts two parameters, the amplitude and the period, that can significantly affect the rate of change over time. You can see their effect at https://observablehq.com/@d3/easing.
- The back easing function produces an overshoot, which is adjustable. You can also test different overshoot values at https://observablehq.com/@d3/easing.
- The bounce easing is like a ball bouncing on the floor before reaching its full amplitude of movement. This function doesn't accept parameters.

These easing functions accept the three formats (in, out, and in-out) mentioned earlier.

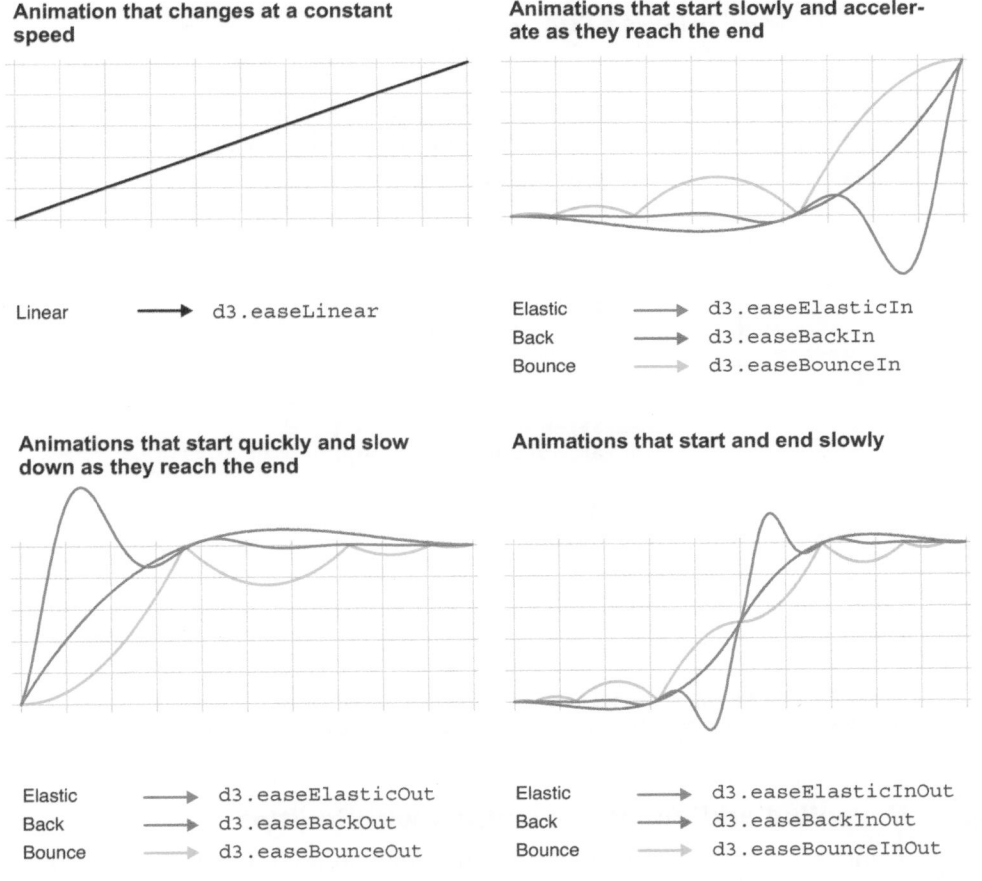

Figure 7.6 Easing function that mimic the elastic, overshoot, and bounce reactions. On each graph, the horizontal axis represents the time, while the vertical axis represents the change rate.

TIP You can see every easing function offered by D3 in action (applied to the horizontal translation of a circle) in the "Easing Animations" notebook created by Mike Bostock (http://mng.bz/vPg7). If the graphs in figures 7.5 and 7.6 are still a little unclear for you, this demo can help!

Let's go back to our project and tweak the histogram's animation. In the following snippet, we slow down the transition by giving it a duration of 500 ms and changing its easing function to `d3.easeCubicOut`. For such scenarios where the user clicks on a button and expects something to happen, it's preferable to choose a rate of change that starts quickly and slows down as it reaches the end because it provides immediate feedback to the user while conserving a natural feel. For this same reason, we won't apply a delay to the transition:

```
d3.selectAll("#histogram rect")
  .data(updatedBins)
  .transition()
    .duration(500)
    .ease(d3.easeCubicOut)
    .attr("y", d => yScale(d.length))
    .attr("height", d => innerHeight - yScale(d.length));
```

As you can see, smooth transitions are easy to apply in D3. The main rule to remember, highlighted in figure 7.7, is that the transition only affects the properties (attributes and styles) chained *after* the `transition()` method.

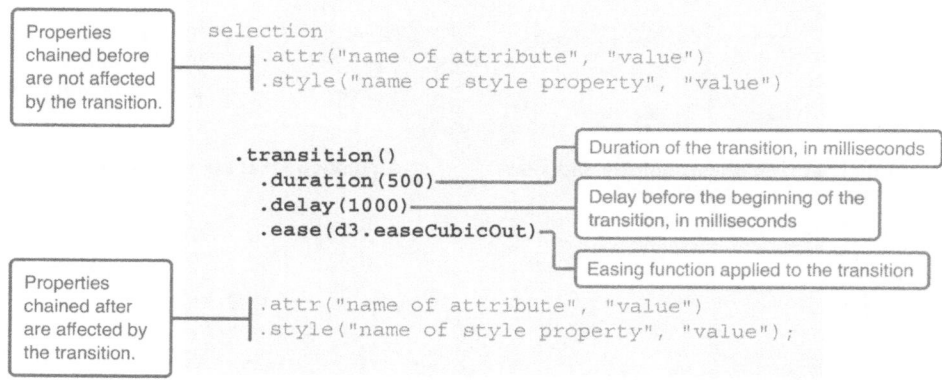

Figure 7.7 D3 transitions affect only the properties chained after the `transition` method. We can customize transitions by setting their duration, delay, and easing function.

7.3 *Revealing additional information with tooltips*

Tooltips are one of the first features that come to mind when we think about interactive visualizations. They allow adding annotations without overcrowding a chart.

Because they don't take up additional space, tooltips are a great way to reveal complementary information in a digital visualization.

In this section, we'll build two types of tooltips. We'll start with a simple, more classical tooltip to reveal the temperature points in the line chart made in chapter 4. Then we'll create a compound tooltip that follows the mouse over the streamgraph built in chapter 5 and provide the sales breakdown per music format for the corresponding year.

7.3.1 *Building a simple tooltip*

In this section, we'll work with the line chart of the 2021 New York City weather built in chapter 4. When the user passes the mouse over a circle, we'll display a tooltip with the exact temperature it represents. This chart is shown in figure 7.8, and the tooltip in action can be previewed at http://mng.bz/46dw.

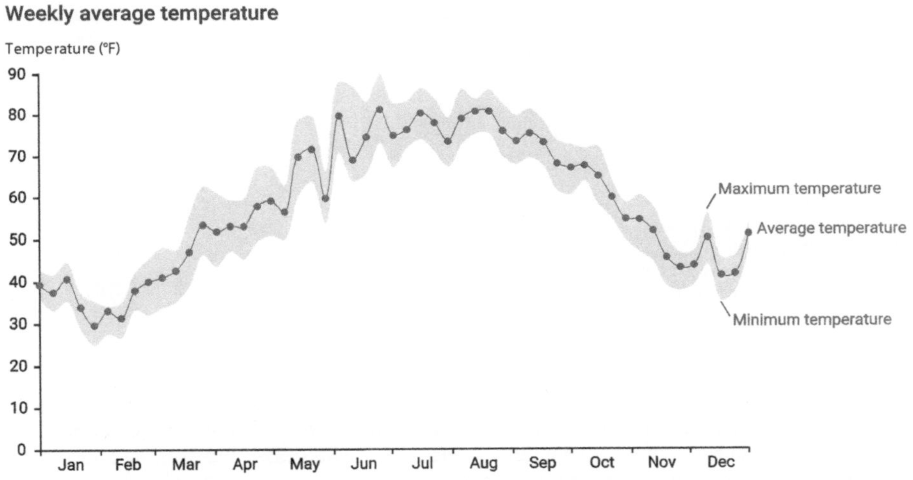

Figure 7.8 Line chart of the 2021 weekly average temperature in New York City built in chapter 4

> **NOTE** To follow along with the instructions, download or clone the files from the book's GitHub repository (http://mng.bz/Xqjv). The `chapter_07/7.3.1-Simple_tooltip` folder contains two subfolders named `start` and `end`. Open the `start` folder in your code editor, and start your local web server. Refer to the solution in the `end` folder if you ever get stuck.

There are many approaches to creating a tooltip with D3. In this project, we'll follow the steps illustrated in figure 7.9. First, we'll build the tooltip by appending a group element to the inner chart. This group will contain a rectangle element, which will act as the background of the tooltip, superposed with a text element, which we'll use to display the tooltip's text.

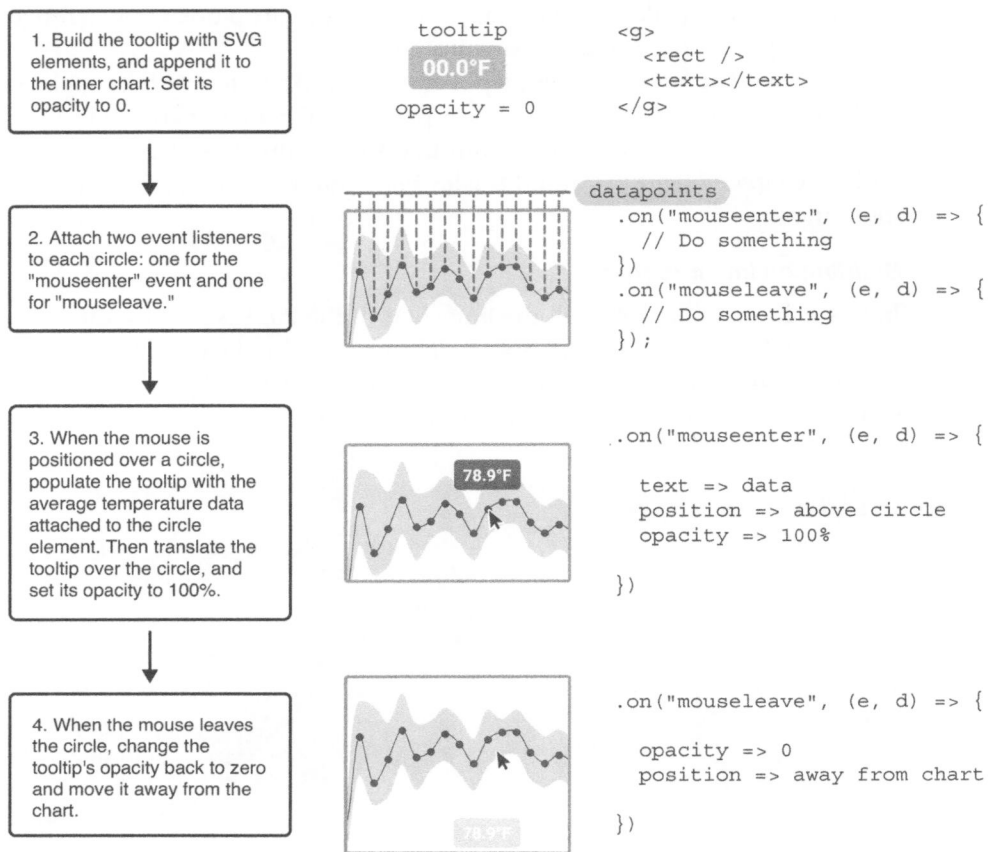

Figure 7.9   To create a tooltip, we first append a group element to the inner chart. In this group, we add a rectangle for the tooltip's background and a text element. We set the opacity of the tooltip to 0. Then we attach two mouse events to the chart's circles: "mouseenter" and "mouseleave". When the mouse enters a circle, we set the tooltip's text, translate it above the circle, and set its `opacity` to 100%. When the mouse leaves, we set the `opacity` to 0 and move the tooltip away from the chart.

To do so, start working inside function `createTooltip()`, which you'll find in `interactions.js`. Note that this function is already called after loading the data, so the code it contains will be executed.

As you can see in listing 7.4, we first append a group element to the inner chart and give it a class name of `"tooltip"`. The class name is important because we'll use it later to select the tooltip and change its position. We save the tooltip selection in a constant named `"tooltip"`.

Then we append a rectangle element to the tooltip selection, which will act as the background of the tooltip. We set its width and height with the constants `tooltip-Width` and `tooltipHeight`, as 65 px and 32 px, respectively, which have already been declared in `shared-constants.js`. With the attributes `rx` and `ry`, we give the tooltip's corners a radius of 3 px. We set its `fill` attribute to the color `"aubergine"`, another constant already saved in `shared-constants.js` and used for the stroke of the line chart. Finally, we make the rectangle semitransparent with a `fill-opacity` of `0.75`. This will ensure that the tooltip doesn't obstruct the chart completely when in view.

As the last step, we append a `text` element in the tooltip selection. We set its text to `"00.0°F"` as a test to ensure that the rectangle is big enough for the text, but this step isn't obligatory. We set the text's horizontal and vertical anchor to the value `"middle"`, and then position it at the center of the rectangle with the x and y attributes. We give the text a `"white"` color and a `"font-weight"` style property of `900` to help with readability.

Listing 7.4 Creating the elements of a tooltip (`interactions.js`)

```
const createTooltip = () => {

  const tooltip = innerChart          Append an SVG group to the inner chart, and
    .append("g")                      give it a class name of "tooltip". Save this
      .attr("class", "tooltip");      selection in a constant named "tooltip".

  tooltip
    .append("rect")                   Append a rectangle element to the tooltip
      .attr("width", tooltipWidth)    selection. Set its width, height, and fill
      .attr("height", tooltipHeight)  attributes with constants already declared in
      .attr("rx", 3)                  shared-constants.js. Give it rounded corners
      .attr("ry", 3)                  with the rx and ry attributes, and make it
      .attr("fill", aubergine)        semitransparent with a fill-opacity of 75%.
      .attr("fill-opacity", 0.75);

  tooltip
    .append("text")                          Append a text element to the tooltip
      .text("00.0°F")                        selection. Set its text to "00.0°F" (optional),
      .attr("x", tooltipWidth/2)             and center it with the rectangle element.
      .attr("y", tooltipHeight/2 + 1)        Give it a white color, and set its font-weight
      .attr("text-anchor", "middle")         to 900 to increase readability.
      .attr("alignment-baseline", "middle")
      .attr("fill", "white")
      .style("font-weight", 900);

}
```

After saving your project, you'll see the tooltip appearing in the top-left corner of the chart, as shown in figure 7.10.

We'll now set the tooltip's opacity to 0 to hide it from the user. In a few moments, we'll make it visible when the mouse passes over a circle on the chart:

```
const tooltip = innerChart
  .append("g")
    .attr("class", "tooltip")
    .style("opacity", 0);
```

Weekly average temperature

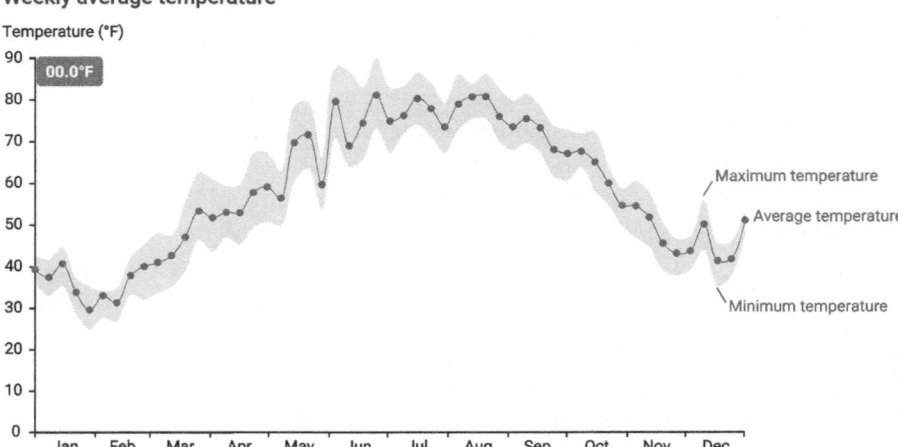

Figure 7.10   **Tooltip appended to the inner chart**

If we continue with the workflow illustrated in figure 7.9, the second step is to attach two event listeners to the line chart's circles. In listing 7.5, we add these event listeners inside function `handleMouseEvents()`, which is already declared in `interactions.js`.

First, we select all the circle elements from the inner chart and chain two `on()` methods. The DOM event detected by the first `on()` method is `mouseenter`, when the mouse enters a circle, while the second one is `mouseleave`, when the mouse leaves a circle. The callback function of the `on()` method receives two parameters: `e`, the DOM event, and `d`, the datum attached to the circle that triggered the event. Log them both into the console, and take a moment to explore their content. You'll notice that the datum attached to each circle corresponds to a row in the original dataset.

Listing 7.5   Adding the event listeners (`interactions.js`)

```
const handleMouseEvents = () => {

  innerChart.selectAll("circle")      ⟵ Select all the circles contained
    .on("mouseenter", (e, d) => {         by the inner chart.

      console.log("DOM event", e);     Attach an event listener to the
      console.log("Attached datum", d); circles to detect when the
                                        mouse enters one of them.
    })
    .on("mouseleave", (e, d) => {      Attach an event listener to the circles to
                                       detect when the mouse leaves one of them.
    });

}
```

Now that we know when the mouse enters a circle, we can make the tooltip appear by following these steps:

1. Set the tooltip's text to the average temperature found in the data attached to the circle element.
2. Move the tooltip above the circle using the DOM event.
3. Set the tooltip's opacity to 100%.

In listing 7.6, we select the text element inside the tooltip and set its text based on the average temperature in the datum returned by the callback function. We use method d3.format() to limit the number of digits to 3.

Then we get the position of the pointed circle via its cx and cy attributes. The target property of the DOM event returns the circle and cy attributes. We use these values to translate the tooltip above the pointed circle and center it horizontally. Finally, we apply the transition() method to the opacity of the tooltip, setting its duration to 200 ms.

Listing 7.6 Making the tooltip appear (`interactions.js`)

```
innerChart.selectAll("circle")
  .on("mouseenter", (e, d) => {

    d3.select(".tooltip text")
      .text(`${d3.format(".3")(d.avg_temp_F)}°F`);

    const cx = e.target.getAttribute("cx");
    const cy = e.target.getAttribute("cy");
    d3.select(".tooltip")
      .attr("transform", `translate(${cx -
        0.5*tooltipWidth},
        ${cy - 1.5*tooltipHeight})`)
      .transition()
      .duration(200)
      .style("opacity", 1);

});
```

Select the tooltip's text element, and change its text to the average temperature found in the datum attached to the circle. Use method d3.format() to limit the number to three digits.

Find the position of the pointed circle through its cx and cy attributes. Translate the tooltip above the circle using the transform attribute.

Change the opacity of the tooltip to 100% using a transition of 200 ms.

Save your project, and note how the tooltip now appears above the circles pointed with the mouse, as in figure 7.11.

> **TIP** When building tooltips, it's best to avoid obstructing the view of the adjacent markers, which are the neighboring circles in this case. One trick is to make the tooltip's background semitransparent, as we did in this project.

As the last step, we want the tooltip to disappear when the mouse leaves a circle. Within the callback function of the "mouseleave"" event listener, we select the tooltip and change its opacity back to 0. We then want to move the tooltip out of the way. If the tooltip is positioned above a circle, it will prevent mouse events from being

Weekly average temperature

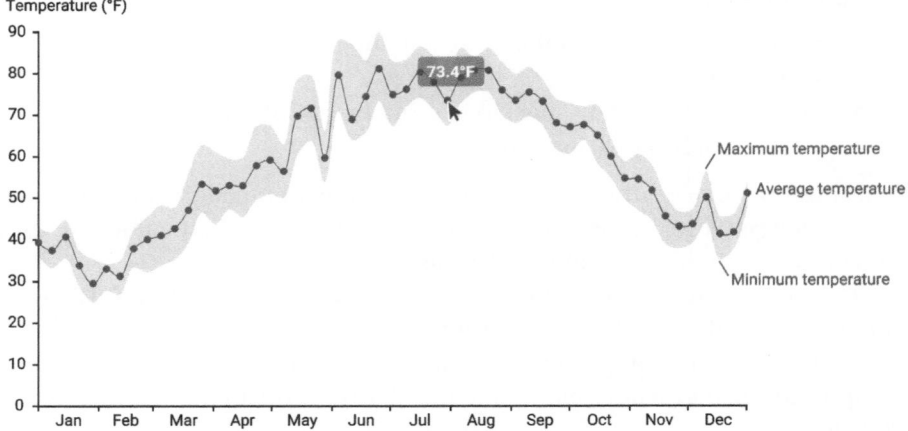

Figure 7.11   **When the mouse enters a circle, the tooltip appears above it and indicates the corresponding temperature.**

detected, even if the tooltip isn't visible. In the next listing, we simply translate it down by 500 px, but any translation away from the chart will do the trick.

Listing 7.7   **Making the tooltip disappear** (`interactions.js`)

```
...
.on("mouseleave", (e, d) => {

  d3.select(".tooltip")
    .style("opacity", 0)
    .attr("transform", `translate(0, 500)`);

});
```

And that's it—we now have a fully functional tooltip!

7.3.2 *Developing a compound tooltip*

Streamgraphs are built with areas stacked over a variable baseline and make exact values hard to read. A tooltip is a handy way to provide this additional information to the user. In this section, we'll build a compound tooltip that follows the mouse over the streamgraph made in chapter 5 and provide the breakdown of sales for each music format for the corresponding year. This tooltip can be seen in figure 7.12 and tried at http://mng.bz/QRGG.

> **TIP** You might observe that the stacking order of the streamgraph's paths is different than in chapter 5. We changed it to match the order in the tooltip. Such minor considerations can help the users map the information they see on the streamgraph to the tooltip labels.

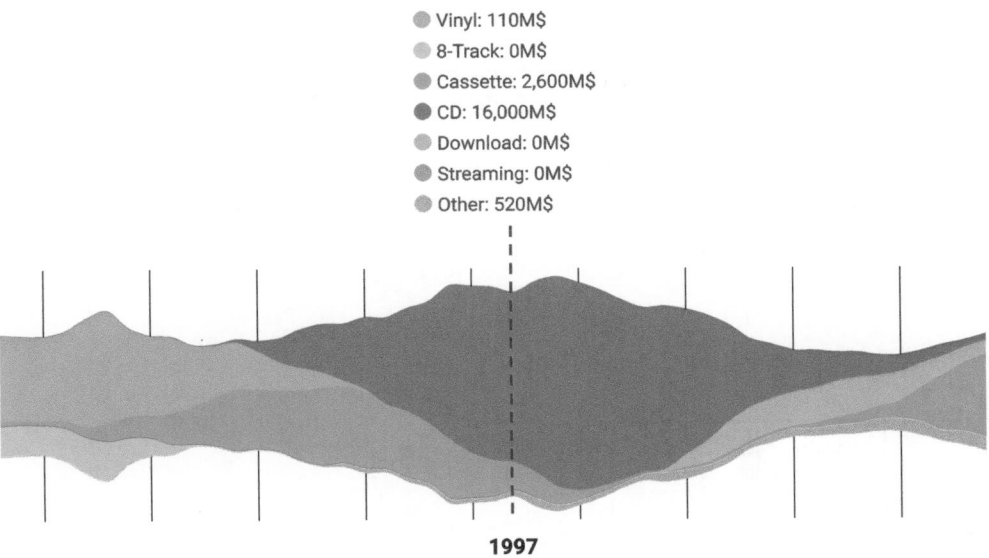

● Vinyl: 110M$
● 8-Track: 0M$
● Cassette: 2,600M$
● CD: 16,000M$
● Download: 0M$
● Streaming: 0M$
● Other: 520M$

1997

Figure 7.12 Streamgraph visualizing 40 years of music sales per format. The tooltip follows the mouse over the visualization, revealing the corresponding year and the breakdown of sales per format.

Again, there are many approaches to building a tooltip. In this project, we'll follow the steps illustrated in figure 7.13.

> **NOTE** To follow along with the instructions, download or clone the files from the book's GitHub repository (http://mng.bz/Xqjv). The `chapter_07/7.3.2-Compound_tooltip` folder contains two subfolders named `start` and `end`. Open the `start` folder in your code editor, and start your local web server. Refer to the solution in the `end` folder if you get stuck.

The first step, illustrated in figure 7.13, is to build the elements that comprise the tooltip. To do so, we'll start working within function `createTooltip()`, which is already declared in `interactions.js` and called from `load-data.js`. This function receives the dataset as an argument, and we've already declared a few handy constants for the tooltip's `width`, `height`, `color`, and `line-height` properties.

In listing 7.8, we first append a `group` element to the inner chart and give it a class name of `"tooltip"`. We'll use this class name later to select the tooltip and make it follow the mouse.

We then append a vertical line to the tooltip. The line's horizontal position is 0, extending vertically from the inner chart's bottom to 30 px above it. We give the line a `stroke-width` of 2 px and make it dashed with the `stroke-dasharray` attribute, to which we provide a value of `"6 4"`. The dashes will have a length of 6 px and 4 px of space in between.

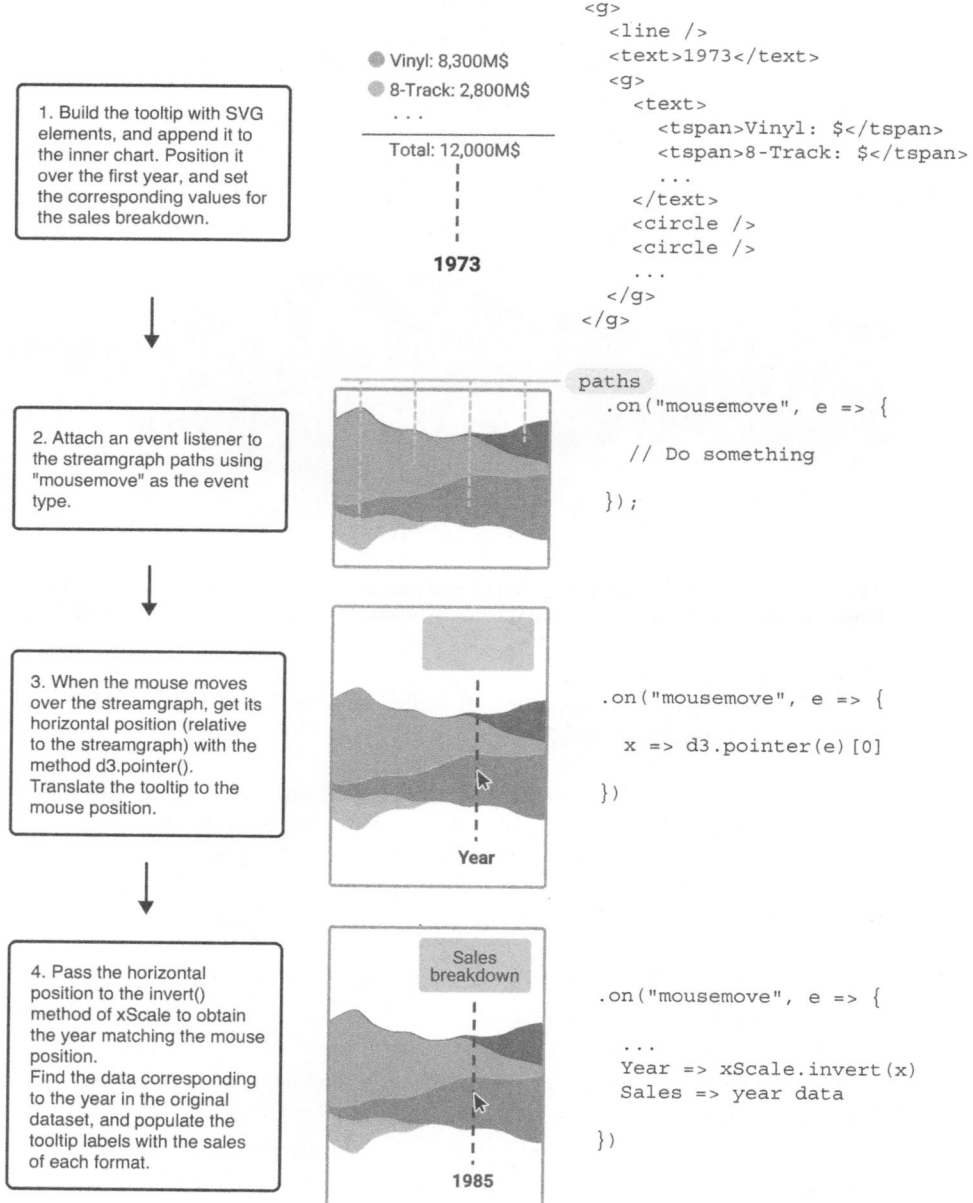

Figure 7.13 Steps to build our composite tooltip and its mouse interaction

We also append a text element and position it at the line's bottom. The text will display the year as the tooltip moves horizontally. For now, because the tooltip is positioned at the left extremity of the streamgraph, its year is the first one in the dataset,

1973, found with `d3.min()`. We give this text a class name of `"tooltip-year"` so that we can select it and update it as the tooltip moves.

Listing 7.8 Appending a vertical line and year (`interactions.js`)

```
const createTooltip = (data) => {

  ...

  const tooltip = innerChart
    .append("g")
      .attr("class", "tooltip");

  tooltip
    .append("line")
      .attr("x1", 0)
      .attr("x2", 0)
      .attr("y1", -30)
      .attr("y2", innerHeight)
      .attr("stroke", textColor)
      .attr("stroke-width", 2)
      .attr("stroke-dasharray", "6 4");

  const firstYear = d3.min(data, d => d.year);
  const tooltipYear = tooltip
    .append("text")
      .attr("class", "tooltip-year")
      .attr("x", 0)
      .attr("y", innerHeight + 25)
      .style("font-size", "16px")
      .style("font-weight", 700)
      .style("fill", textColor)
      .attr("text-anchor", "middle")
      .text(firstYear);

};
```

Append an SVG group to the inner chart, and give it a class name of "tooltip".

Append a dashed vertical line to the tooltip. Position it to the extreme left of the streamgraph.

Append a text element and position it below the vertical line. This is where we'll indicate the current year as the tooltip moves. For now, set its year to the first year in the dataset, 1973.

In listing 7.9, we handle the sales breakdown per music format and display it above the vertical line. First, we append an SVG group to the tooltip and translate it toward the left by half the tooltip's width and then upward. We save this group in a constant named `tooltipContent`. We append a `text` element inside the group, give it a class name of `"tooltip-content"`, and save it in constant `tooltipText`. It's in this element that we'll display the sales breakdown.

After retrieving the sales object for the first year (1973), we loop through the `formatsInfo` array declared in `shared-constants.js`. For each music format, we append a `tspan` element inside `tooltipText`. We set its text to the `label` property of the music format followed by the sales in M\$, formatted as grouped thousands with one significant digit (`d3.format(",.1r")`). Each `span` element is positioned below the previous one using its `y` attribute.

Finally, still inside the loop, we add a circle to the left of each `tspan`, giving it a radius of 6 px and a color corresponding to the music format. These circles will act as a legend and make the tooltip's content more digestible.

Listing 7.9   Appending the sales breakdown (`interactions.js`)

```
const createTooltip = (data) => {

  ...

  const tooltipContent = tooltip
    .append("g")
      .attr("transform", `translate(${-1 *
        tooltipWidth/2},
      ${-1 * margin.top + 30})`);          ◄── Append an SVG group to the tooltip. This group will contain both the text and the circles of the sales breakdown.

  const tooltipText = tooltipContent
    .append("text")
      .attr("class", "tooltip-content")
      .style("font-size", "14px")          ◄── Append a text element to the group.
      .style("font-weight", 500)
      .style("fill", textColor);

  const dataFirstYear = data.find(item => item.year === firstYear);

  formatsInfo.forEach((format, i) => {

    tooltipText
      .append("tspan")
        .attr("class", `sales-${format.id}`)
        .attr("x", 0)
        .attr("y", i * textLineHeight)
        .text(`${format.label}:          ◄── Loop through the music formats. For each format, append a tspan element to the tooltipText, and set its text to the label of the format followed by the sales for the first year. Append a circle also, giving it the color corresponding to the current format.
          ${d3.format(",.1r")(dataFirstYear[
          format.id])}M$`);

    tooltipContent
      .append("circle")
        .attr("cx", -10)
        .attr("cy", i * textLineHeight - 5)
        .attr("r", 6)
        .attr("fill", format.color);

  });

};
```

Once completed, your tooltip should look like the one in figure 7.14. Note how the vinyl format dominated the market in 1973, followed by 8-tracks.

With the tooltip in place, we're ready for the following steps: attaching an event listener to the streamgraph's paths and moving the tooltip along with the mouse! We'll start working inside function `handleMouseEvents()`, which is already declared in

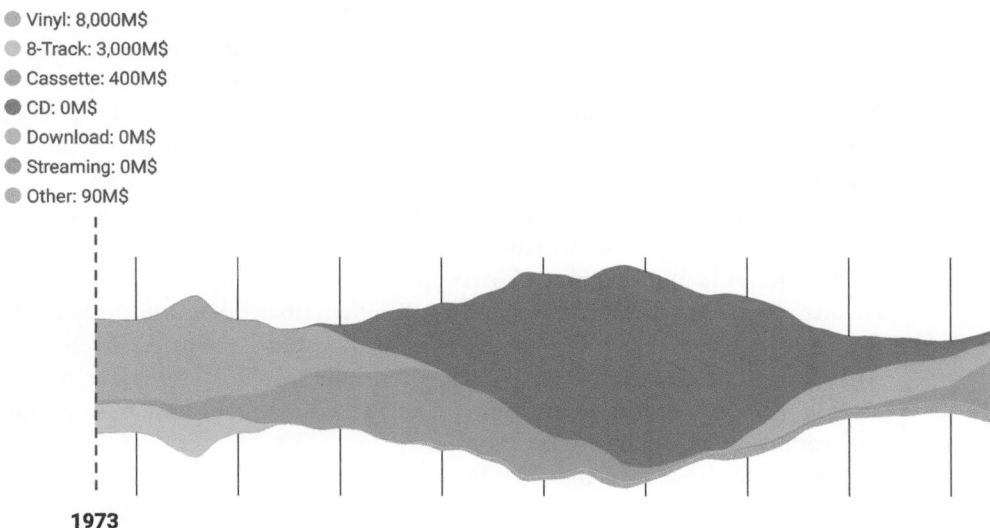

Figure 7.14   Tooltip positioned over the first year

`interactions.js`. In listing 7.10, we first select all the path elements in the stream-graph and use the `on()` method to attach an event listener. The DOM event we want to detect is `mousemove`, which will be triggered when the mouse moves over the streamgraph.

We then need to find the cursor's position and move the tooltip accordingly. D3 has a convenient method, `d3.pointer()`, that takes a DOM event as an argument and returns the coordinates of the event relative to the target—here, the streamgraph's paths. This method is part of the d3-selection module and provides the horizontal and vertical coordinates of the selection in an array. Because we're only interested in the horizontal coordinate, we can get it with `d3.pointer(e)[0]` and then translate the tooltip.

Listing 7.10   Translating the tooltip (`interactions.js`)

```
const handleMouseEvents = (data) => {

  d3.selectAll(".areas-container path")          Attach the "mousemove" event listener
    .on("mousemove", e => {                       to the streamgraph's path elements.

      const xPosition = d3.pointer(e)[0];         Get the horizontal position of the mouse
      d3.select(".tooltip")                        with d3.pointer(), and apply the
        .attr("transform", `translate(             corresponding translation to the tooltip.
          ${xPosition}, 0)`);

    });

};
```

If you move your mouse over the streamgraph, the tooltip should now follow it closely. How cool is that? Let's now update the tooltip's text as the mouse moves, starting with the year. To know the year corresponding to the mouse's position, we can use `xScale`, the scale responsible for positioning elements along the horizontal axis. So far in this book, we've always passed a value from the domain to the scales for them to return the corresponding value from the range. With continuous scales, we can also do the opposite! In listing 7.11, note how we call `xScale.invert(xPosition)`. By chaining `xScale` with the `invert()` method, we can pass a value from the range, a horizontal position on the streamgraph, and obtain the corresponding value from the domain, which is a year. Because `xScale` is a continuous scale, it will return floating-point numbers. Because we want the year to be an integer, we pass the value returned by `xScale.invert` `(xPosition)` to `Math.round()`. We can then select the `text` element responsible for holding the year (with the class name `"tooltip-year"`) and update its text to the year corresponding to the mouse position.

To update the text in the sales breakdown portion of the tooltip, we start by finding the data related to the mouse's position. We then loop through the music formats, and for each format, we select the corresponding `tspan` element and update the sales according to the year's data.

> ### Listing 7.11 Updating the tooltip's text (`interactions.js`)

```
const handleMouseEvents = (data) => {

  d3.selectAll(".areas-container path")
    .on("mousemove", e => {

      ...

      const year = Math.round(xScale.invert(xPosition));
      d3.select(".tooltip-year").text(year);

      const yearData = data.find(item =>
        item.year === year);
      formatsInfo.forEach(format => {
        d3.select(`.sales-${format.id}`)
          .text(`${format.label}:
            ${d3.format(",.1r")(yearData[format.id])}M$`);
      });

    });

};
```

Find the year corresponding to the horizontal position of the mouse with xScale.invert(), and set the year text of the tooltip accordingly.

Find the data corresponding to that year, and update the values in the sales breakdown.

TIP When an interaction isn't standard, give a little cue to your users. For example, we've added instructions above this project's streamgraph.

7.4   *Animating the enter, update, and exit selections*

Earlier in this chapter, we updated the data presented in a histogram with the click of a button. In that example, the number of SVG elements within the visualization invariably remained the same: 12 rectangles whose height changed depending on how many data points they represented. But what if a data update implies that new SVG elements must enter or exit the visualization? In this section, we'll build a scatterplot to answer this question.

The scatterplot we're about to create visualizes a dataset of cetacean species, as you can see in figure 7.15 and at http://mng.bz/Xq8v. Each circle in the scatterplot represents a cetacean species. The circles' horizontal position is relative to the species' estimated population, while the vertical position corresponds to the size of the cetacean in meters. The area of the circles is proportional to the weight of the cetacean, and their color symbolizes their conservation status according to the International

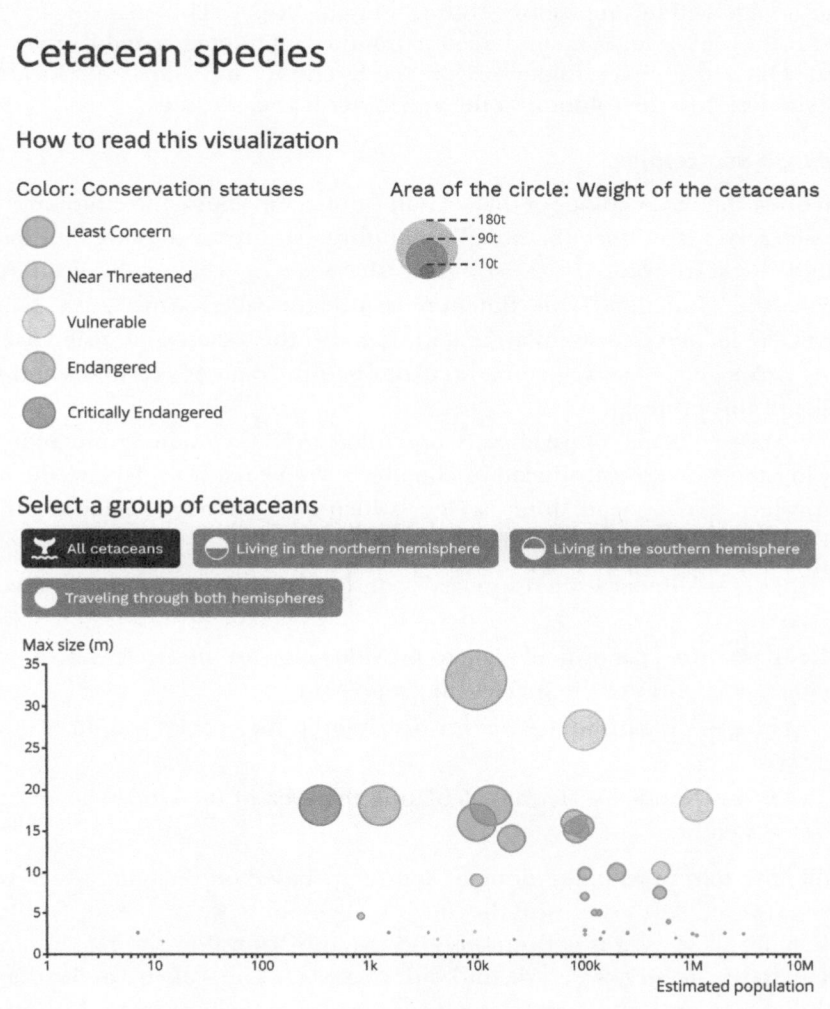

Figure 7.15   Visualization of cetacean species that we'll build in this section

Union for Conservation of Nature, from "Least Concern" in green to "Critically Endangered" in red.

Four buttons are displayed above the scatterplot to allow the scatterplot to be filtered. By default, all species are shown in the visualization, and the All Cetaceans button is selected. We can filter the cetaceans by the region where they live: in the northern hemisphere, in the southern hemisphere, or species traveling through both hemispheres. Every time we select a filter, the circles exiting the scatterplot slide downward, while the circles entering fall in from the top. We'll learn how to create this effect in a moment.

> **NOTE**   To follow along with the instructions, download or clone the files from the book's GitHub repository (http://mng.bz/Xqjv). The `chapter_07/7.4-Refining_data_updates` folder contains two subfolders named `start` and `end`. Open the `start` folder in your code editor, and start your local web server. Refer to the solution in the `end` folder if you get stuck.

7.4.1   *Building a scatterplot*

If you open the `start` folder of this section's project in your code editor and start your local web server, you'll see that the filter buttons are already in place, but we still need to build the scatterplot. To do so, go to the `scatterplot.js` file inside the `drawScatterplot()` function. This function is already called from `load-data.js` and receives the loaded data as an argument. Refer to the README file inside `chapter_07/7.4-Refining_data_updates` for a breakdown of the dataset's columns and the different files of this project.

In `scatterplot.js`, we've already appended an SVG container and an inner chart, following the strategy introduced in chapter 4. We're ready to declare the scales. For this project, we'll need four scales, which we already declared in `shared-constants.js` to make them globally accessible:

- `yScale`—A linear scale responsible for distributing the cetaceans' size along the y-axis
- `colorScale`—An ordinal scale to provide colors to the circles based on the conservation status of the species they represent
- `xScale`—A logarithmic scale for distributing the species' population along the x-axis
- `rScale`—A radial scale for calculating the area of the circles based on the species' weight

We still have to set the scales' domain and range based on the data, which we'll do in `scatterplot.js`. Let's start with the linear scale because we're already familiar with it. The domain of `yScale` is continuous and extends from 0 to the maximum size of a cetacean in the dataset, which we find with `d3.max()`. The scale maps the domain onto a continuous range that extends from `innerHeight` at the bottom of the inner chart to 0, at the top of the inner chart (you must know very well by now that, in the SVG world, the vertical axis is positive in the top-to-bottom direction!). Finally, we chain the scale with method `nice()` to ensure that the y-axis ends on a nice round value:

```
const maxSize = d3.max(data, d => d.max_size_m);
yScale = d3.scaleLinear()
  .domain([0, maxSize])
  .range([innerHeight, 0])
  .nice();
```

We can also set the color scale because we've already discussed ordinal scales in chapter 5. An ordinal scale maps a discrete domain over a discrete range. Here, the domain is an array of the conservation status IDs, created with JavaScript method `map()` and the `conservationStatuses` array already declared in `shared-constants.js`. We use the same method to generate an array of colors for the range:

```
colorScale = d3.scaleOrdinal()
  .domain(conservationStatuses.map(s => s.id))
  .range(conservationStatuses.map(s => s.color));
```

The two other scales will require a little more explanation because we'll use them for the first time. We'll do that in the following subsections.

THE LOG SCALE

In our project, the cetacean with the smallest population is the baiji, a dolphin whose population is currently estimated between 0 and 13 individuals (the latest expedition to estimate the population found none). On the other hand, the largest population is the Pantropical spotted dolphin, estimated to be 3 million individuals. That's a huge difference!

If we were to represent these populations on a linear scale, the species with smaller populations would be cramped together, and their actual values would be impossible to read. In figure 7.16, see how more clearly we can read the population values over a logarithmic axis, where the value at each marked location is increased by a factor of 10.

In D3, we create logarithmic axes with the log scale `d3.scaleLog()`, which returns the logarithmic transform of a continuous domain. This scale is especially handy when the data contains significant differences of magnitude.

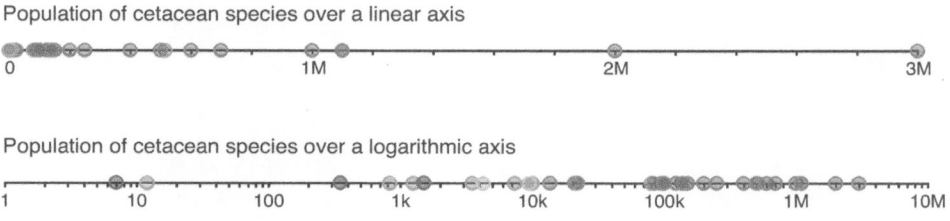

Figure 7.16   On a linear axis, the species with a smaller population appear cramped, and their values are almost impossible to read. The logarithmic scale helps solve this problem by presenting populations with a tenfold increase (1, 10, 100, 1k, 10k, 100k, 1M, and 10M).

TIP   The improvement in readability provided by logarithmic scales comes at the cost of losing the sense of how tiny some values are compared to the larger ones. Although log scales certainly have their place, it's important to be aware of this drawback.

In the following code snippet, we set the domain and the range of the log scale. The domain is continuous and accepts an array of the minimum and the maximum population. Note how we've set the minimum value to 1 rather than 0. If you remember your math classes, the logarithmic value of 0 is undefined (moving toward -∞, to be more precise). The range extends along the width of the inner chart, and we chain method `nice()` for the axis to end on a nice round value:

```
const maxPopulation = d3.max(data, d => d.global_population_estimate);
xScale = d3.scaleLog()
  .domain([1, maxPopulation])
  .range([0, innerWidth])
  .nice();
```

THE RADIAL SCALE

So far in this book, we've outputted data values onto one-dimensional graphical marks only, like the length of a bar in a bar chart or the horizontal position on a timeline. But in data visualization, we often use the area of a circle to represent the magnitude of data. If we want to map one-dimensional data—in our case, the weight of cetaceans onto a two-dimensional graphical mark, which is the area of a circle—we can't use a linear scale.

Let's first go back to the equation of the area of a circle (A), which is equal to pi (π = 3.1416. . .) multiplied by the radius squared. The radius is multiplied by itself; its effect on the area of a circle is quadratic, not linear:

$$A = \pi r^2$$

To map a linear value onto a graphical mark defined by its radius, like a circle, we can use a radial scale. As you can see in figure 7.17, circles sized with a linear scale create a visual distortion that exaggerates the difference in the area of circles representing 10,

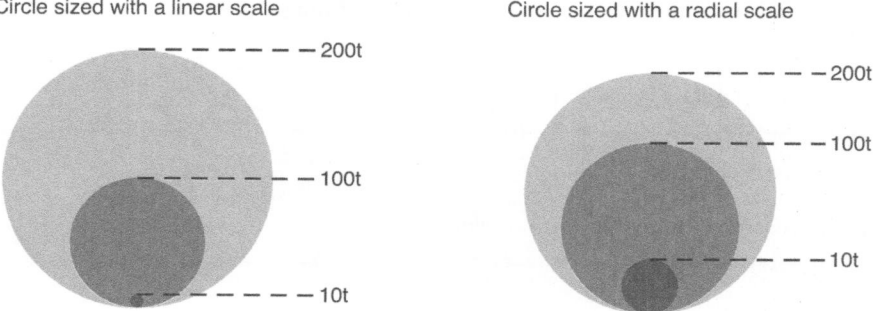

Figure 7.17   Weight of the cetacean represented by circles. On the left, the circles are sized with a linear scale, while on the right, we used a radial scale. Note how the linear scale creates a visual distortion by exaggerating the differences between the area of the circles for each weight.

100, and 200 tons. On the other hand, the radial scale internally squares the range and is better adapted for sizing circles.

In the following code snippet, we declare our radial scale. Both the domain and the range are continuous—the domain extends between 0 and the maximum weight found in the dataset, and the range extends between 0 and 45, the radius of the largest circle that will appear on the visualization:

```
const maxWeigth = d3.max(data, d => d.max_weight_t);
rScale = d3.scaleRadial()
  .domain([0, maxWeigth])
  .range([0, 45]);
```

Exercise: Create the axis, and append the circles to the scatterplot

Now that we've declared our scales, we're ready to build the scatterplot. You have all the knowledge required to do it. If you need more guidance, follow these steps:

1 Declare a generator for the bottom axis (`d3.axisBottom()`), and pass `xScale` as a reference. Append the axis to the inner chart.

2 Declare a generator for the left axis (`d3.axisLeft()`), and pass `yScale` as a reference. Append the axis to the inner chart.

3 Append two `text` elements to the SVG container, one for each axis label: "Estimated population" and "Max size (m)".

4 Using the data-binding pattern, append one circle to the inner chart for each cetacean in the dataset.

5 Set the circles' `cx`, `cy`, `r`, and `fill` attributes using the logarithmic, linear, radial, and color scales declared earlier.

6 If you wish, you can set the opacity of the fill attribute to 60% and add a stroke of 2 px to the circles.

Once completed, your scatterplot should look like the one in the following image.

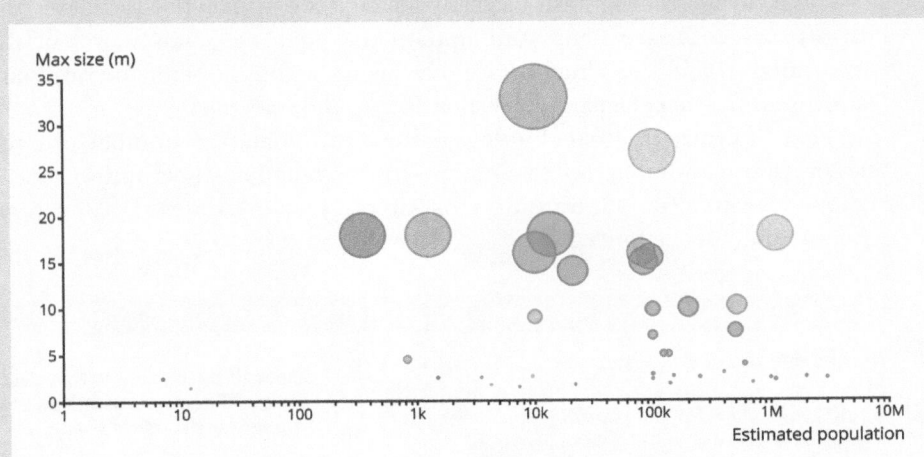

Completed scatterplot

(continued)

If you get stuck or want to compare your solution with ours, you'll find it in listing D.7.1 of appendix D and in the `7.4-Refining_data_updates/end` folder of this chapter's code files. But as usual, we encourage you to try to complete it on your own. Your solution might differ slightly from ours, and that's all right!

TIP For sizing our circles, we could also have used the square root scale, `d3.scaleSqrt()`, which is a power scale applying the exponent 0.5. The results would have been the same.

To generate the project legend, uncomment function `populateLegend()` in `load-data.js`. We encourage you to take a look at the code in `legend.js` because building legends is a request you'll meet as a D3 developer. We won't explain the legend code in detail here because it uses concepts you're already familiar with.

7.4.2 *Filtering a scatterplot*

We'll now enable the scatterplot filtering when the user clicks on one of the buttons above it. We'll also discuss how we can control the animations when circles enter or leave the chart.

First, let's go to the `interactions.js` file. The filter buttons have already been created in function `populateFilters()`. We'll handle the clicks on the filters inside function `handleClickOnFilter()`. In listing 7.12, we start by selecting all the buttons with the class name `"filter"` and attach an event listener to them. This listener waits for a `"click"` event and provides the datum attached to the clicked filter in the callback function. This datum is the corresponding object from array `cetaceanFilters`, which you can find in `shared-constants.js`.

If the clicked button wasn't already selected, we update the `isActive` properties in the `cetaceanFilters` array and update the `"active"` class name of the buttons accordingly. Based on which button has been clicked, we filter the original dataset to conserve only the cetaceans corresponding to the selection.

Finally, we use the data-binding pattern to update the number of circles on the screen, move these circles to their positions, calculate their radius, and find their color—all with a smooth transition. As you can see, the strategy is so far very similar to the one used in section 7.2.

Listing 7.12   Updating the scatterplot (`interactions.js`)

```
const handleClickOnFilter = (data) => {

  d3.selectAll(".filter")
    .on("click", (e, datum) => {

      if (!datum.isActive) {
```

Select all the buttons with a class name of "filter", and attach an event listener for the "click" event.

Check that the clicked button wasn't already selected.

```
cetaceanFilters.forEach(h => h.isActive =
  h.id === datum.id
    ? true : false);

d3.selectAll(".filter")
  .classed("active", d => d.id ===
    datum.id ? true : false);

const updatedData = datum.id === "all"
  ? data
  : data.filter(d => d.hemisphere === datum.id);

innerChart
  .selectAll("circle")
  .data(updatedData)
  .join("circle")
  .transition()
    .attr("class", "cetacean")
    .attr("cx", d => xScale(
      d.global_population_estimate))
    .attr("cy", d => yScale(d.max_size_m))
    .attr("r", d => rScale(d.max_weight_t))
    .attr("fill", d => colorScale(d.status))
    .attr('fill-opacity', 0.6)
    .attr("stroke", d => colorScale(d.status))
    .attr("stroke-width", 2);

      }

  });

};
```

Update the isActive properties in the cetaceanFilters array, and update the "active" class name of the buttons accordingly.

Filter the original dataset to conserve only the cetaceans corresponding to the selection.

Use the data-binding pattern to update the number of circles on the screen. Set their position, radius, and color.

If you save your project, go to your browser, and click on the filters, you'll see that the number of circles in the scatterplot adapts to the selected filter. As briefly mentioned in chapter 3, the `join()` method calculates how many circles need to enter or leave the visualizations and which ones need to be updated. It creates an interesting effect with little effort.

But there's a problem. When clicking on a filter, did you notice that circles not only enter and leave the screen but also move around in the scatterplot? The big orange circle at the top (representing blue whales) suddenly becomes a medium-size red circle (representing North Atlantic right whale), and so on. Although we all like seeing movement on the screen, that's not ideal from a storytelling perspective. What happens is that D3 automatically updates the number of circles in the DOM to match the filtered dataset. It then assigns the first circle element in the DOM to the first cetacean in the updated dataset, the second circle to the second cetacean, and so on.

Preferably, we want the circles that remain on the screen to keep representing the same cetacean. We can do this by adding a key function as the second argument of the `data()` method. With this key function, we tell D3 to maintain the datum assigned to each element remaining on the screen, as illustrated in figure 7.18. In the following snippet, we use the cetaceans' `uid` as a reference. If you're familiar with React, this is similar to giving key attributes to list elements that provide them with a stable identity:

```
innerChart
  .selectAll("circle")
  .data(updatedData, d => d.uid)
  .join("circle")
    ...
```

Save your project again, and play with the filters. That's much better!

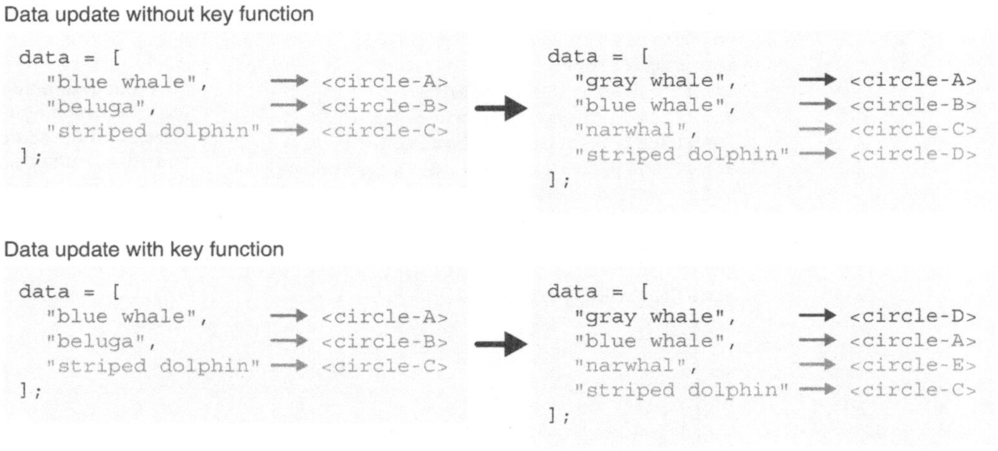

Data update without key function

```
data = [                                     data = [
  "blue whale",       ──▶ <circle-A>           "gray whale",      ──▶ <circle-A>
  "beluga",           ──▶ <circle-B>    ━━▶    "blue whale",      ──▶ <circle-B>
  "striped dolphin"   ──▶ <circle-C>           "narwhal",         ──▶ <circle-C>
];                                             "striped dolphin"  ──▶ <circle-D>
                                             ];
```

Data update with key function

```
data = [                                     data = [
  "blue whale",       ──▶ <circle-A>           "gray whale",      ──▶ <circle-D>
  "beluga",           ──▶ <circle-B>    ━━▶    "blue whale",      ──▶ <circle-A>
  "striped dolphin"   ──▶ <circle-C>           "narwhal",         ──▶ <circle-E>
];                                             "striped dolphin"  ──▶ <circle-C>
                                             ];
```

Figure 7.18 Without the key function, during data updates, D3 assigns the first circle element in the DOM to the first cetacean in the updated dataset, the second circle to the second cetacean, and so on. With a key function, the elements that remain on the screen keep the same data.

Currently, when we play with the filters of our scatterplot, the circles that enter the screen arrive from the left, while the circles that exit the screen simply disappear. How can we control these transitions? We've mentioned that when we update the data bound to our scatterplot, the circles (or the data attached to them) can enter, update, or exit, as explained here and in figure 7.19:

- The *enter selection* represents new elements that need to be created. For example, if the cetaceans living in the Northern Hemisphere are currently selected on the scatterplot, and we click the filter All Cetaceans, new circles will enter the screen.

- The *update selection* contains the elements that are already present on the screen and will remain on the screen. These elements might keep the same position and style, or they might change if the data bound to them has been updated. For example, if the cetaceans living in the Northern Hemisphere are currently selected on the scatterplot, and we click the filter All Cetaceans, the circles representing cetaceans from the Northern Hemisphere should remain as they are.

- The *exit selection* represents the elements that need to be removed. For example, suppose the cetaceans living in the Northern Hemisphere are currently selected on the scatterplot, and we click the filter Living in the Southern Hemisphere. In that case, the circles representing cetaceans from the Northern Hemisphere should leave the screen.

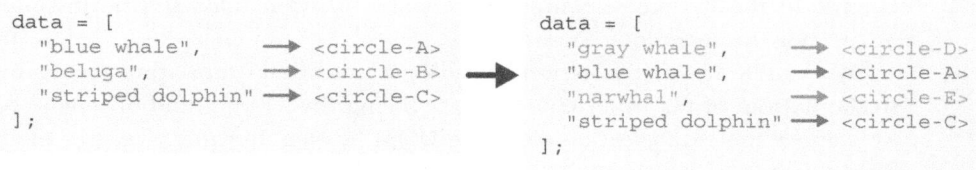

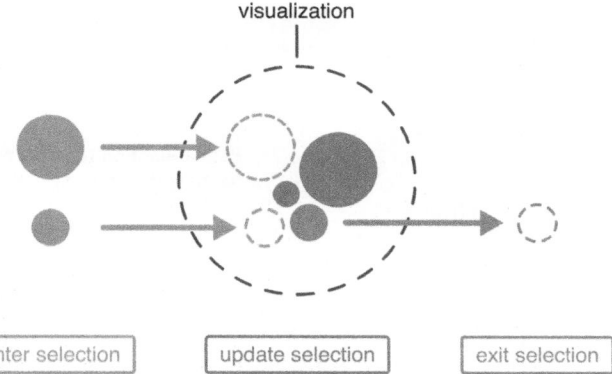

Figure 7.19 The enter selection represents new elements that need to be created, while the update selection contains the elements that are already displayed on the screen and will remain on the screen. The exit selection is made for elements that need to be removed from the DOM.

While the `join()` method makes our life easier by handling the enter, update, and exit selections for us, we can still access and control them separately. In the following snippet, instead of passing a string to the `join()` method as we've been doing so far, we pass separate functions for the enter, update, and exit selections, separated by a comma:

```
innerChart
  .selectAll("circle")
  .data(updatedData, d => d.uid)
  .join(
    enter => enter,
    update => update,
    exit => exit
  )
```

In listing 7.13, we specify what we want to happen with the enter, update, and exit selections. When new data is added to the scatterplot (the enter selection), we append the corresponding number of `circle` elements and set their attributes. Here we want to create an animation where circles enter from above, their radius increases from 0 to its final value, and their opacity goes from 0% to 100%. To do that, we first set the cy attribute to -50, r to 0, and the opacity style property to 0. Then we use the `call()` method to create a transition and set the cy, r, and opacity to their final values. Note that we don't chain the transition directly as we've been doing so far, but we perform the transition inside the `call()` method instead. Although we don't need to apply any change to the update selection, the update function must still be included inside `join()` for this technique to work.

We handle the exit selection by calling a transition, translating the exiting circles to the bottom of the inner chart, and reducing their radius and opacity to 0. Finally, we remove the exit selection from the DOM by chaining the `remove()` method, still inside `call()`.

Listing 7.13   Entering, updating, and exiting selections (`interactions.js`)

```
innerChart
  .selectAll("circle")
  .data(updatedData, d => d.uid)
  .join(
    enter => enter
      .append("circle")
        .attr("class", "cetacean")
        .attr("cx", d => xScale(
          d.global_population_estimate))
        .attr("cy", d => -50)
        .attr("r", 0)
        .attr("fill", d => colorScale(d.status))
        .attr('fill-opacity', 0.6)
        .attr("stroke", d => colorScale(d.status))
        .attr("stroke-width", 2)
        .style('opacity', 0)
      .call(enter => enter.transition()
        .attr("cy", d => yScale(d.max_size_m))
        .attr("r", d => rScale(d.max_weight_t))
        .style('opacity', 1)),
    update => update,
    exit => exit
      .call(exit => exit.transition()
        .attr("cy", d => innerHeight)
        .attr("r", 0)
        .style('opacity', 0)
        .remove())
  )
```

Pass a function to join() that handles the enter selection.

Append a circle for each datum in the enter selection, and apply these circles' initial attributes and styles. Set their vertical position to 50 px above the inner chart and their radius and opacity to 0.

Pass a function to join() that handles the update selection, even if we don't need to do anything with it.

Chain a call() method. Inside this method, apply a transition to the enter selection, and set the attributes and styles onto which we want the transition to happen: the final vertical position, radius, and opacity.

Pass one last function to join() that handles the exit selection.

Chain a call() method. Inside this method, apply a transition to the exit selection, and set the attributes and styles onto which we want the transition to happen: the final vertical position, radius, and opacity. Chain the remove() method as well to remove this selection from the DOM.

7.4.3   Creating a reusable transition

The default transition applied to the enter and exit selections is nice, but we would like to slow it down and change its easing function. If we want to use the same duration and easing function for both the enter and exit selections, we can create a reusable transition function.

In listing 7.14, we start by declaring a transition with method `d3.transition()`. We chain the `duration()` method and set its duration to 800 ms. We also chain the `ease()` method and set its easing function to `d3.easeExpOut`. Finally, we save this transition function into a constant named `t`.

Then all we have to do is pass this transition function to the `transition()` methods called for the enter and exit selections. Reusable transition functions help us avoid repetition, make our code easier to maintain, and keep the transition parameters consistent throughout our projects.

Listing 7.14   Adding a reusable transition (`interactions.js`)

```
const handleClickOnFilter = (data) => {

  d3.selectAll(".filter")
    .on("click", (e, datum) => {
      if (!datum.isActive) {

        ...

        const t = d3.transition()        Declare a transition function with
          .duration(800)                 d3.transition(). Set its duration and easing
          .ease(d3.easeExpOut);          function, and save it in a constant named t.

        innerChart
          .selectAll("circle")
          .data(updatedData, d => d.uid)
          .join(
            enter => enter
              .append("circle")
                .attr("class", "cetacean")
                ...
              .call(enter => enter.transition(t)     ◁┐
              ...,                                     │ Pass the transition
                                                       │ function t to the existing
            update => update,                          │ transition methods inside
            exit => exit                               │ the join() method.
              .call(exit => exit.transition(t)    ◁────┘
                ...)

          )

      }
    });

};
```

Exercise: Create a tooltip

Our scatterplot is pretty cool, but we have no idea which circle represents which ceta-cean species. To fix this, follow these steps:

1 Add a simple tooltip to the visualization that consists only of an SVG text element.
2 When the mouse is positioned over a circle, display the common name of the related cetacean.
3 When the mouse leaves the circle, hide the tooltip.

You can see an example in the following image. (Note that event listeners must be reattached when new elements enter the DOM!)

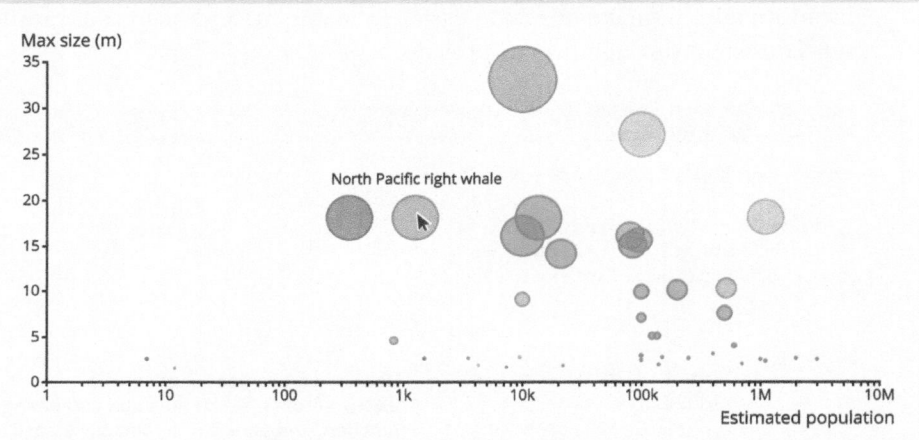

Tooltip displayed when the mouse is positioned over a circle

If you get stuck or want to compare your solution with ours, you'll find it in listings D.7.2, D.7.3, and D.7.4 of appendix D and in the `7.4-Refining_data_updates/end` folder of this chapter's code files. But as usual, we encourage you to try to complete it on your own. Your solution might differ slightly from ours, and that's all right!

Interview with Mohamad Waked

Mohamad Waked is a data visualization designer and data scientist.

Can you tell us a little bit about your background and how you entered the field of data visualization?

With pleasure. I will try to make my long story short. It started in my childhood. I've been passionate about exploring, drawing, designing, and building things since I was a child. It was one of my favorite moments when I held a pencil in my hand and saw my ideas and imaginations come to life on paper. I felt free, happy, and content. I also loved playing with numbers and was very good at math. I dreamed of being an engineer who was able to bring creative new things into the world, and this is what has happened. I graduated as a mechanical design and production engineer. My early career was as a process analytics engineer in an automotive manufacturing company. This was one of my early meetings with data. I had to deal with a huge amount of data on a daily basis with the aim of improving productivity and efficiency of the production line. This made me gradually shift my practical and postgraduate studies toward data science, where I had the opportunity to finish a specialization degree in data science from Johns Hopkins University. During my career, I was consciously observing my delight when it came to presenting the results of any analysis in a chart or graph. This is always the point where I feel that all my brain potential gets unleashed because I have to think and work using my whole brain power—the left logical and analytical side, together with the right creative and artistic side. This was the main driver behind my second shift toward data visualization. I still remember that day when I heard my internal voice saying: "This is my life task. This is where I can express my uniqueness. This is how I can serve others."

After a few years of studying, self-development, and practical experience, I decided to create Alhadaqa to be my personal DataViz Lab. There I can express part of my passion for data visualization to people and for people through a series of personal dataviz projects on a variety of topics: serious ones like migrants or natural disasters and light ones like movies or sports. My projects have won different awards on both regional and global levels, for example, Malofiej Awards, The Pudding Cup, and a gold medal from the Center For Global Data Visualization.

What brought you to D3? Did you meet challenges while learning this library? If yes, how did you overcome them?

During my career, I used to work with different software and tools to create charts and graphs. R plus its smart ggplot2 library brought me a step closer to freely creating custom charts. But when I discovered D3, I instantly knew that this is what I had been dreaming about. I love to design charts freely like holding a pencil and a paper. D3 somehow gives me this high degree of freedom over my designs, and not only in a static form but also in a dynamic form.

I have to admit that learning D3.js was a challenge. It is not easy to directly capture the logic behind its building blocks all at once. It requires time, patience, and a lot of practice. One of the main strategies I used during my learning journey was to think of D3 the same way it was created. It consists of modules, which, for me, are more like pieces of Lego™. You need to fully understand each piece alone, test its capability and features, and then try to combine and mix different pieces together piece after piece to examine how far and how creatively you can reach.

Do you use visualization tools other than D3? What's the place of D3 in your current data visualization workflow?

Yes, I'm a good user of most of the popular data visualization tools. But my personal preference in most cases is to use R during the data exploration phase, which might include some basic charts and graphs I need to create in order to better understand the data, and also to quickly test some of the initial design concepts. Then, during the data visualization phase, D3 becomes the most important tool inside my toolbox, where I use it heavily to test and validate the feasibility of some of the initial design concepts, and then I depend on it entirely while creating and building up my final designs.

(continued)

Featured project: "Migration between Search & Reality" (https://migrationinsearch.com/)

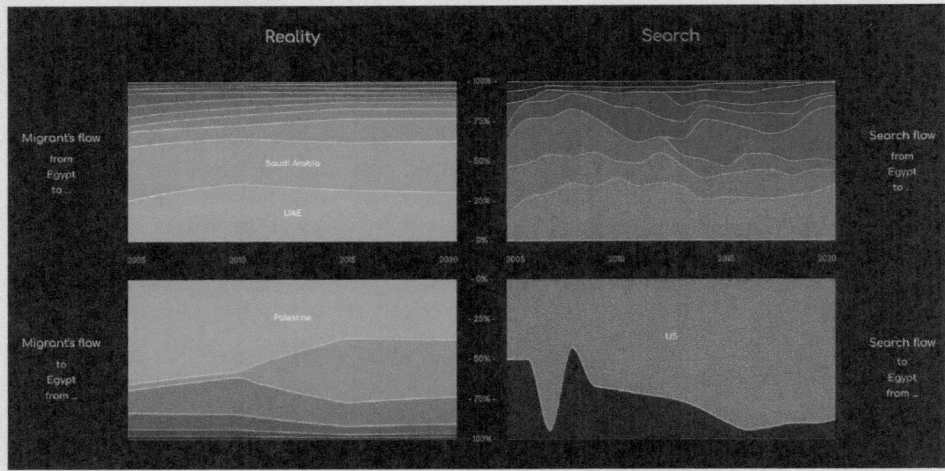

The project draws a parallel between the Google searches made by people who are embarking on a migration journey and the reality of their final destination.

Please describe your project, "Migration between Search & Reality." Using Google search statistics to draw a parallel between what migrants are looking for versus the reality of immigration is such a powerful concept!

"Migration between Search & Reality" is a data-driven visual exploration that tries to quantify how big the gap is between the reality of the world's migrants and their dreams, interests, and desires that could be measured by their search interests. It is an attempt to draw a whole, unified picture of the migration issue all over the world to have a better understanding of it and its related problems, such as migrants who get missed or die while they are trying to cross borders in an illegal way. The project looks at the issue from both sides of it: countries of origin and countries of destination.

Thanks for your kind words. I'm glad that you and many other people liked the idea. We are in the information age, and I believe that what was once impossible is possible today because of the huge amount of data we currently have access to and which should help us to better understand and solve our own problems. I also believe that data visualization designers are the messengers between the data world and the people world. They are the ones who can speak the language of both worlds, and they have a very serious role as the bridge between both worlds.

Can you explain the process of creating this project?

After agreeing on the project idea and creating the project concept note, the project started with a challenge of collecting this massive Google search data, but I successfully finished this part using variations of common search queries that have been translated into 10 of the world's most spoken languages to capture the most accurate results. Then I would be able to compare this search interest data against the world migration data that had been sourced from the United Nations (International Migrant Stock).

Preparing, normalizing, and analyzing the two datasets wasn't that easy. I can honestly say it was the most challenging data collecting, cleaning, and analysis project I had ever worked on. But after deep analysis, I had a clear understanding of the data and its attributes and a better vision of how this complicated dataset could be visualized and presented.

Some initial design concepts had been drafted and tested. Then it went through different iterations until it reached the current final design and shape that got the acceptance of Alberto and Simon [project supporters]. The design of data visualization is intended to take the viewer on a learning curve from conventional bar charts and stacked area charts to more complicated designs for "the bigger picture" circular interactive chart.

Here's one of my little secrets: there's always an inspiration behind my creative design decisions. It might take a while to find this inspiration at the beginning of the project, but once I do, it becomes my piece of gold. It's always next to me while I think through the different design decisions throughout the project.

When I was doing my research for this project, I got inspired by the golden jellyfish. What's amazing about these little creatures is that they spend much of their lives on daily migration—following the sun's arc across the sky. This echoes what migrants do too: they travel following this little spark of light at the end of the road. If you take a closer look at the large circular data visualization at the end of the story, you might notice how similar it is to a big, round jellyfish. The two inner maps imitate groups of jellyfish swimming together. Also, once you click on any of the countries, you'll see a clear front view of a jellyfish.

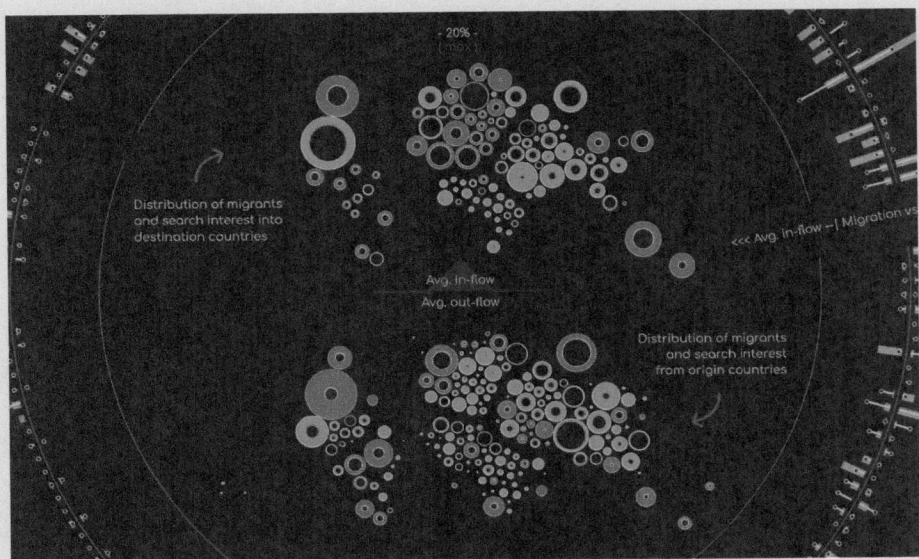

The main visualization clusters circles in a world map.

(continued)

Crafting a simple storyline that balanced data explanation and data exploration was a challenge. I selected the scene at Kabul Airport—when the United States was completing its withdrawal from Afghanistan—as an inciting incident. It was a popular event reported on in the news all over the world, so many people could relate to it. It also created a link between the East and the West in a single shot. I then followed Freytag's model, which is one of my favorite frameworks, and added a reader-customizable ending.

Data visualization is a critical craft that includes a large number of pitfalls that anyone can easily fall into. But one of the most common pitfalls I would like to highlight is thinking that there is a clear line between what is right and what is wrong, and there's a solid set of rules you have to follow. I believe this is a very wrong mindset that you have to change while working on any dataviz project because everything there is relative, and what could be right in one project could be wrong in another, and vice versa.

I love how the radial chart at the end of the project allows us to read the visualization two ways: the circles clustered as a geographical map in the middle and the radial bar chart on the outside. Both provide a different perspective on the data. Was creating this visualization an iterative process, or did you have a clear vision from the start?

Thanks so much. I was a bit worried about how people would receive or understand this complex unconventional chart type, taking into consideration that the previously used chart types before reaching this final one in the story are somewhat simple and common. But it happened that people weren't able to resist exploring it in different ways, according to the nice and different feedback I have received since publishing it.

I hadn't any clear idea about what the final design would be at the start of the project, but I had a vision of creating something that could summarize and visualize the full picture of those two parallel worlds (migrant's dreams versus migrant's reality) all together in a way that can allow users to freely explore and interact with it. Throughout the exploratory phase of the data, subconsciously some design concepts started to evolve throughout my mind. So once I reached the data visualization phase, those very basic concepts subconsciously became mature concepts that could be considered, sketched, and tested.

This is also one of my techniques: I depend heavily on my subconscious mind during the process of creating my data visualizations.

There is one other thing I would like to mention. This final design combines two basic concepts. The first is a bullet bar chart, and the second is a scatter bubble chart over two combined geographical maps. But after deep thinking, I found that adding the two concepts together would make a bigger impact.

This project was supported by Alberto Cairo, Simon Rogers, and Google Trends. This is a huge deal! Can you bring us behind the scene and tell us a little bit about how you came to collaborate with them?

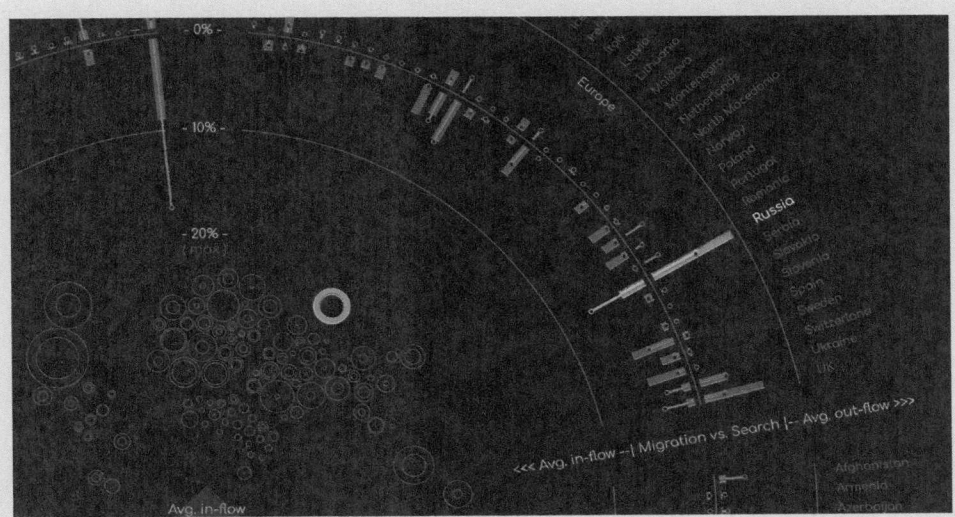

Each country is visualized two ways: with a radial bar chart and a cluster map, allowing readers to look at the data from two perspectives.

Everything started when I received an email from Alberto Cairo, asking me if I would like to create a project for Google under his management and art direction. The only constraint was that Google search/trends data had to be a part of it. Of course, I thought it a good opportunity to work closely with experts like Alberto Cairo and Simon Rogers and experience how they think. I was also excited by the freedom to select a topic that I cared about. Actually, this personal curiosity and freedom to explore is what connects all of my projects.

After my first meeting with Alberto and Simon, I was asked to suggest a few ideas. We eventually agreed that measuring the gap between the reality of the world's migrants and their search was the most interesting one. I was happy with the selection, as it built on one of my previous projects—"The Unwelcomed"—on migrants and refugees who are dying while attempting to cross international borders.

So the choice of topic was the starting point, and a very interesting journey of exploration and design unfolded afterword.

You recently specialized in data journalism. What types of projects do you want to work on in the future?

Yes, data journalism is an interesting field that I started to work in recently using my skills and knowledge. I see it as a personal and social responsibility rather than a job. As for the projects that I would like to work on in the future, I always prefer to work on projects that are meaningful and can have an effect—projects that can arouse interest in an issue, shed light on a case, or contribute to solving a problem.

Summary

- Keeping the end user in mind when planning interactions is critical. Always aim at creating interactions that are both relevant and intuitive.
- In D3, we capture user events with the `on()` method. This method takes the event's name as the first parameter (`click`, `mouseenter`, `mouseleave`, `mousemove`, etc.) and a callback function as the second. The callback function receives both the triggered DOM event and the datum attached to the selection.
- We can control the class names of a selection separately with the `classed()` method, which takes the class name as the first parameter and a Boolean (`true` or `false`) as the second.
- To create smooth animations between states, we use the `transition()` method.
- Any attribute or style chained after the transition method is affected by it.
- By default, D3 transitions have a duration of 250 ms, a delay of 0, and use easing function `d3.easeCubicInOut`. We can change these parameters respectively with the `duration()`, `delay()`, and `ease()` methods.
- We can declare transitions and their parameters separately and reuse them throughout our projects. To do so, we save our transition function into a constant and pass this constant to the `transition()` method chained to a selection.
- We use tooltips to add annotations to a chart and reveal additional information. We can build tooltips with SVG elements. We update their content and position from the callback function of an event listener.
- Method `d3.pointer()` takes a DOM event as an argument and returns the coordinates of the event relative to the target. It's useful to position elements on the screen based on a mouse event.
- Log scale `d3.scaleLog()` is a scale that returns the logarithmic transform of a continuous domain. It's especially handy when the data expands between significant differences of magnitude.
- Radial scale `d3.scaleRadial()` is used to map a linear value onto a graphical mark defined by its radius, such as a circle.
- On data updates, D3 automatically updates the number of elements in the DOM to match the new dataset. It then assigns the first element in the DOM to the first datum in the updated dataset, the second element to the second datum, and so on. If we want the data to stick to the elements that remain on the screen, we must add a key function to the `data()` method.
- The `join()` method takes care of the enter, update, and exit selections for us, but we can control them by passing their respective functions to the `join()` method instead of a string.
- The enter selection of the `join()` method represents new elements that need to be created.
- The update selection of the `join()` method contains the elements that are already present on the screen and will remain on the screen.
- The exit selection of the `join()` method represents the elements that need to be removed.

Integrating D3 in a frontend framework

This chapter covers

- Loading the D3 library in frontend frameworks
- Creating a dashboard with D3 and React
- Allowing D3 to manipulate the DOM with React hooks
- Using D3 as a utility library and letting React render and update the DOM
- Applying the same strategies in Angular and Svelte

So far in this book, we've been creating projects in a simple but old-fashioned way by using only HTML, CSS, and JavaScript files. But today's frontend projects are generally built with JavaScript frameworks. These tools facilitate the development of larger projects and optimize their performance.

With the help of JavaScript frameworks such as React, Angular, Svelte, and Vue.js, we can create projects where everything happens instantly and provide the feeling of a mobile application. We call such projects single-page applications (SPAs) because only one HTML file is loaded from the server and then updated dynamically, even for multipage websites.

According to the State of JavaScript 2021 survey, the most popular frameworks among frontend developers are React (80%), Angular (54%), Vue.js (51%), and Svelte (20%). Although the philosophy and syntax of these tools can vary broadly, using them in combination with D3 follows common principles. In this chapter, we'll discuss these principles and apply them to the interactive dashboard you can see in figure 8.1 and at http://mng.bz/yZlB. For this dashboard, we'll reproduce a visualization of the developers' satisfaction, interest, usage, and awareness of the different frontend frameworks between 2016 and 2021, created by the team behind the State of JavaScript 2021 survey (http://mng.bz/M9NW). We'll also build a scatterplot of the retention percentage (developers who would use the framework again) versus the number of users for each framework, as well as a bar chart of their awareness of each tool.

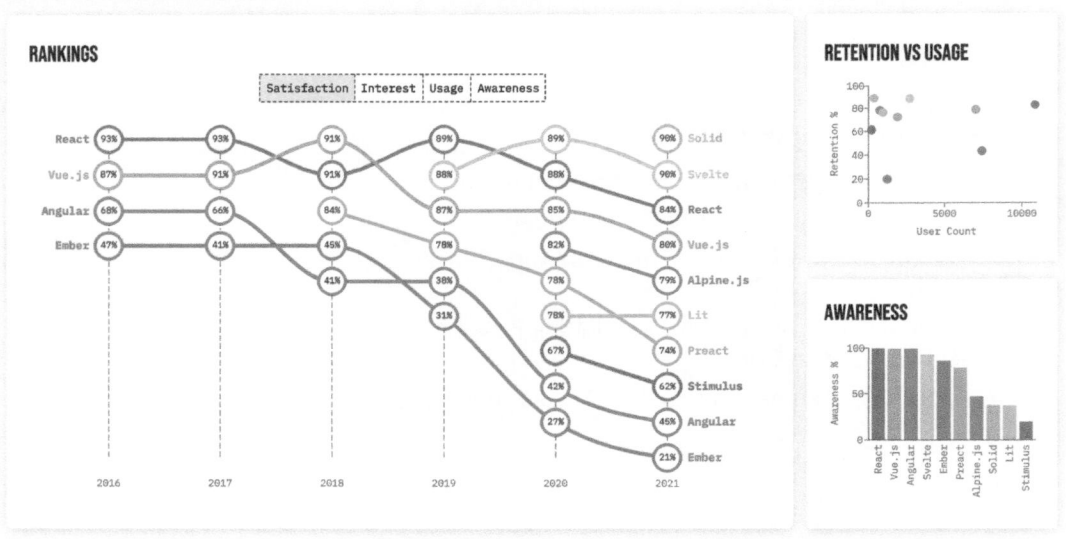

Figure 8.1   Dashboard about frontend frameworks that we'll build in this chapter

We'll build this dashboard by integrating D3 into a React application. React is the gold standard and by far the most popular framework. But because you'll likely also want to use D3 with other frameworks, we'll provide you with additional information regarding D3 integration in Angular and Svelte throughout this chapter. In this chapter's code files, you can find the dashboard built with these different frameworks at http://mng.bz/amW7. Later, in chapters 14 and 15, we'll build another project with D3 and Svelte.

NOTE React is technically a JavaScript library, and Svelte is a compiler rather than a framework. But for simplicity purposes, we'll assume that the term *framework* applies to React and Svelte.

Because we want to keep the focus of this book on D3, we recommend that you have a basic knowledge of React before reading this chapter. You should know how to build components, pass props to children and parent components, manage a component's state, and use React hooks. If you're new to React, here are a few resources that can help you get started:

- *React Quickly, Second Edition,* by Morten Barklund and Azat Mardan (Manning, 2023)
- *React.JS: The Complete Course for Beginners* (video), by Meta Brains (Manning, 2022)
- *React: The Complete Guide,* by Maximilian Schwarzmüller (Safari, 2021)

8.1 Approaches to using D3 in a frontend framework

The main job of a frontend framework is to manipulate the DOM based on the application state. Frameworks keep track of which pieces of the DOM need to be rendered or updated at any point in time. D3 was created before the arrival of such tools and was also meant to manipulate the DOM heavily. If we try to use D3 the way we have been so far within a framework, it can lead to conflicts when both the framework and D3 want to manipulate the same elements. For this reason, we need to be strategic and use one of the following approaches:

- Give D3 control over a portion of the DOM.
- Use D3 as a utility library.
- Apply a hybrid approach.

The first approach is to isolate an element of the DOM and give its control over to D3. The main benefit of this approach is its simplicity. It allows us to use D3 the same way we have been so far in this book. But it's often considered a bit of a hack, and we lose some of the optimization features that are an integral part of the JavaScript frameworks.

The second approach is the exact opposite: letting the framework handle the DOM alone and using D3 only as a utility library. This strategy implies forgetting about D3's data-binding pattern, axis generations, attributes and style manipulations, event detection, and transitions. Fortunately, many powerful D3 methods remain accessible, such as the scales and the shape generators. This approach is preferable for overall performance and allows us to create all the visualizations we've discussed so far, even though it requires a little more work.

With the hybrid approach, we let the framework control the DOM as much as possible and provide control to D3 with parsimony when there's a clear gain in development time or the workaround is too complex. For example, in chapter 7, we discussed how D3 transitions are powerful and easy to use, but they require that D3 manipulates the related elements in the DOM. In that case, we have to evaluate our options. To create transitions that imply only CSS properties, applying CSS transitions and animations or even using a React third-party library such as react-spring are usually the best approaches. But if we need to transition the d attribute of a path element, for example, D3 transitions are arguably the simplest and most effective way forward. Another example is the D3 brush() method, for which it can be acceptable to let D3 manipulate the DOM.

In this chapter, we'll use these three approaches to build our dashboard, and we'll proceed in the order shown in figure 8.2. First, we'll make the scatterplot of the frameworks' retention percentage versus user count using the first approach, where we let D3 control a portion of the DOM. Then we'll rebuild the same chart, using D3 as a utility library and giving DOM control only to React. Building the same chart with both approaches will enable you to appreciate the pros and cons of each one.

You'll then build the bar chart of the developers' awareness of the frameworks on your own, using the second approach. This exercise will be an excellent opportunity to consolidate what you've learned.

Finally, we'll build the interactive rankings visualization with the hybrid strategy. We'll make the chart itself with the second approach, but we'll allow D3 to control the DOM to smoothly transition the curves when the user clicks on one of the buttons above the visualization.

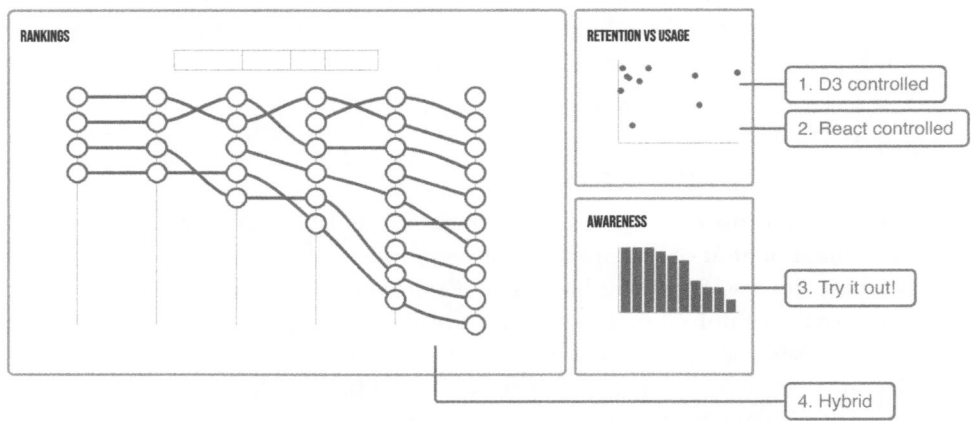

Figure 8.2 We'll build our dashboard with the three approaches described previously. First, we'll make the scatterplot with the first strategy by giving D3 access to the DOM. Then we'll rebuild the same chart with React, using D3 only as a utility library. You'll also use this approach to build the bar chart yourself. Finally, we'll make the rankings visualization with the hybrid strategy, building it with React but allowing D3 to access the DOM to transition the curves when the user clicks on one of the buttons.

8.2   Installing the D3 library in a React project

To perform this chapter's project, download the code files from the book's GitHub repository (http://mng.bz/Xqjv). Open the start folder contained in chapter_08/ 8.2-Installing_D3 in your code editor.

NOTE The `chapter_08` folder contains multiple subfolders, each named based on its related chapter section. Each of these subfolders has a `start` and an `end` folder. The `start` folder contains the code as it is at the beginning of a section, while the `end` folder contains the solution for that section.

If you have experience with frontend frameworks, then you're familiar with Node Package Manager (NPM), the registry of software from which we install libraries and tools into our projects. To install your project's dependencies, run the following command in your terminal. Ensure that your terminal's current directory is pointing to your project folder. If you use the integrated terminal in Visual Studio Code (VS Code), your current directory is your project root:

```
npm install
```

To add the D3 library to your project, install the `d3` package (www.npmjs.com/package/d3):

```
npm install d3
```

Finally, start the React project with

```
npm run start
```

The project should open automatically in your default browser. You can also access it at http://localhost:3000. We recommend that you use Chrome or Firefox for their handy inspector tools. All you should see on the screen at this point is the word "Loading . . ." because no data has been loaded yet into our project. We'll address that in the next section.

One of the key advantages of working with frameworks is that they encourage us to break down our code into small, reusable components. In the `src` folder of this chapter's project, the components of the dashboard are broken down into four subfolders:

- `ChartComponents`—Singular chart elements, such as circles, rectangles, and axes
- `Charts`—Complete charts such as the scatterplot or the bar chart
- `Interactions`—Where most of the interactions' code will live
- `UI`—For specific UI elements unrelated to charts, such as buttons and cards

Before we start using D3, we will import it into the components where we'll need it. Go to the `App.js` file, and at the top of the file, import D3 as follows:

```
import * as d3 from 'd3';
```

The previous code snippet is what we call a namespace import. Here, `d3` is a namespace object that contains all exports from the D3 library. We can then access any D3 method with the dot notation as we've been doing so far, such as `d3.scaleLinear()` and `d3.line()`. We need to import D3 into every file where we want to use it.

TIP   Instead of loading the entire D3 library, we could also choose to install only the D3 modules we need for a project, such as d3-scale or d3-shape. That's what we'll do from chapter 11 on.

In a React project, the vast majority of the files that we work with are located inside the src folder, where `index.js` is the root file and loads `App.js`. It's in `App.js` that we start writing our code and loading our components.

8.3   Loading data into a React project

If you take a closer look at `App.js`, you'll see that it consists of a functional component. In React, functional components are JavaScript functions that accept arguments, called *props*, and return the component's markup in JavaScript XML (JSX) format. In this chapter, we'll focus on functional components because this is the modern way of building React components and has been broadly adopted by the React community. The older way of building components, called class-based components, is still valid, though, and you'll find many examples of how to use D3 in class-based components on the web.

The `App` component has a state variable named `loading`, which is initialized to true, as in listing 8.1. It then returns a `div` element that contains a condition. If `loading` is `true`, the expression `"Loading..."` is returned and appears on the screen. If `loading` is `false`, it loads a component named `Charts`, which will later contain the three charts of the dashboard.

Listing 8.1   Initial state of `App.js`

```
import { useState } from 'react';        Import the React State hook, the D3
import * as d3 from 'd3';                library, and the Charts component.
import Charts from './Charts/Charts';

const App = () => {
  const [loading, setLoading] = useState(true);      Declare a state variable
                                                     named "loading", and
  return (                                           initialize its value to true.
    <div className="container">
      {loading && <div className="loading">          If loading is true, return a "Loading..."
        Loading...</div>}                            statement. If it's false, return the
      {!loading && <Charts />}                       Charts component.
    </div>
  );
};

export default App;
```

We've structured the `App` component this way because we need to load data into our application before we display the charts. And because fetching data is an asynchronous process, we need a strategy to wait for the data to be accessible before creating the charts.

In functional components, the effect hook is where we want to fetch data. In listing 8.2, we start by loading useEffect from the React library. Then we call the useEffect hook and pass an anonymous function as its first argument. In this function, we use method d3.json() to load data in the JSON format from a REST API accessible at http://mng.bz/g7ZV. So far, we've only loaded data from CSV files that were included in our project files, but fetching data from a REST API is more common in professional projects.

We chain the d3.json() method with the JavaScript then() method, which returns a Promise. Once the data is available, we call the setData() and the setLoading() functions to update the state of the component. Note that we've also declared the data state variable and set its initial value to an empty array.

The second argument of useEffect() is its dependencies, which tell React when the effect should be executed. Because we've set the dependencies to an empty array, the function will run only once, after the component is mounted. Finally, we pass the updated data state variable to the Charts component as a prop.

Listing 8.2 Loading data into App.js

```
import { useState, useEffect } from 'react';        ⟵ Import the effect hook
import * as d3 from 'd3';                              from the React library.
import Charts from './Charts/Charts';

const App = () => {
  const [loading, setLoading] = useState(true);
  const [data, setData] = useState([]);    ⟵ Declare a state variable named data, and
                                              set its initial value to an empty array.
  useEffect(() => {

    const dataURL = "https://d3js-in-action-third-edition.github.io/
      hosted-data/apis/front_end_frameworks.json";

    d3.json(dataURL).then(data => {          With method d3.json(), fetch data
      setData(data);                         from the API accessible via the URL
      setLoading(false);                     saved into constant dataURL. Once
    });                                      the data is available (returned by the
                           Pass an empty array as the second   chained then() method), set the data
                           argument of useEffect(). This will ensure   state variable to the loaded data, and
  }, []);     ⟵           that the function runs only once—after   set the loading state variable to false.
                           the component is mounted.
  return (
    <div className="container">
      {loading && <div className="loading">Loading...</div>}
      {!loading && <Charts data={data} />}    ⟵ Pass the data state variable
    </div>                                       as a prop to the Charts component.
  );
};

export default App;
```

The useEffect() cleanup function

Although this isn't likely for this project, the user might get impatient and browse to another page before D3 completes the data-fetching process. In that case, React will unmount the component where the data is being fetched. If the request is still going on behind the curtains, this might lead to unwanted behaviors such as memory leaks.

To avoid such problems, it's best to add a cleanup function inside the `useEffect` hook, which is the return function in the following example. If the component unmounts before the data fetching is completed, React will run the cleanup function.

There are many different ways to handle this situation, but here's a simple one. In the following example, we declare variable `mounted` inside the `useEffect` hook and set its initial value to `true`. In the cleanup function, which will be called when the component unmounts, we set `mounted` to `false`. Finally, we add a condition inside the `then()` method to update the state variables only if `mounted` is `true`. This way, we'll never try to update state variables on an unmounted component and avoid triggering errors:

```
useEffect(() => {
  ...

  let mounted = true
  d3.json(dataURL).then(data => {
    if (mounted) {
      setData(data);
      setLoading(false);
    }
  });

  return () => mounted = false;
}, []);
```

Inside the `then()` method, log the data into the console. You'll notice that it's composed of three arrays. The `ids` array contains a list of the frameworks addressed by the dataset, while the `years` array lists the years for which we have data. The `experience` array contains an object for each framework, with its ID, name, number of users (per the survey data collected by the State of JavaScript Survey 2021), and retention percentages. It also contains arrays accessible under the `satisfaction`, `interest`, `usage`, and `awareness` keys that provide the rank of the framework and the percentage of respondents that answered that they are satisfied, are interested in, use, or are aware of the framework for each year. Your data is now ready to use!

NOTE   You'll notice that the data is logged twice into the console although we told you that the anonymous function inside the effect hook would run only once. This feature of React, called `StrictMode`, is intentional and aims at helping us detect accidental side effects when we render our application. It only happens in development mode.

8.4   A reusable approach to SVG containers

From chapter 4 of this book, we've adopted an approach to building D3 charts that involves an SVG container and a group element, as illustrated in figure 8.3. This group is translated based on the chart's margins and becomes the parent of all the elements comprising the inner chart. Because children of an SVG group inherit the properties of their parent, they are all translated with the group.

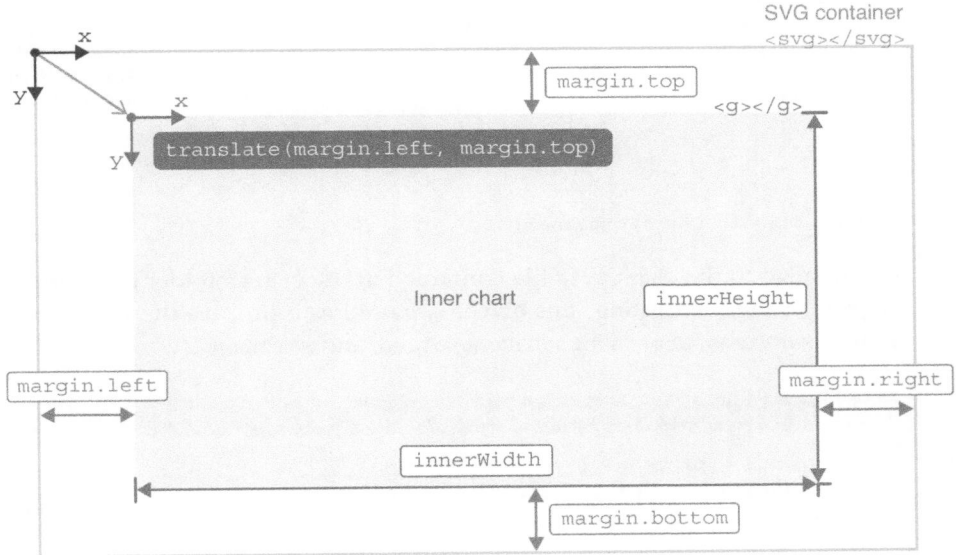

Figure 8.3   The strategy that we've been using since chapter 4 is to build charts with an SVG container to which we append a group element. This group is translated based on the chart's margins and becomes the parent of all the elements composing the inner chart. Those will inherit the translation.

Because our dashboard will contain three charts, creating a reusable SVG container component that holds both the SVG parent and the group wrapping the inner chart would be helpful. Let's go to the `ChartContainer.js` file contained in the `Chart-Components` folder. This file includes a functional component named `ChartContainer` that receives props and returns an SVG element.

To follow the strategy illustrated in figure 8.2, we add a group element inside the SVG container. In listing 8.3, we assume that this component receives three props: a `width`, a `height`, and a `margin` object. We apply the `width` and `height` props to the `viewBox` attribute of the SVG element. Then we set the transform attribute of the group and translate it horizontally with the left margin and vertically with the top margin.

Finally, knowing that in React, every component receives a prop named `children` that contains any child element defined within the parent component, we can return this prop between the brackets of the SVG group as follows: {props.children}.

Listing 8.3 **Creating the** `ChartContainer` (`ChartContainer.js`)

```
const ChartContainer = props => {
  return (
    <svg viewBox={`0 0 ${props.width} ${props.height}`}>
      <g transform={`translate(${props.margin.left},
        ${props.margin.top})`}>
        {props.children}
      </g>
    </svg>
  );
};

export default ChartContainer;
```

> **Set the viewBox attribute of the SVG container with the width and height props.**

> **Translate the SVG group with the left and the top margins.**

> **Return the children prop of the component.**

Then we go to the `Charts.js` file contained in the `Charts` folder and define a margin object. In the next listing, this object is passed as a prop to the three chart components (`Rankings`, `ScatterplotD3Controlled`, and `BarChart`).

Listing 8.4 **Passing a margin object as a prop** (`Charts.js`)

```
const Charts = props => {
  const margin = {top: 30, right: 10, bottom: 50,
    left: 60};

  return (
    <Fragment>
      <h1>Front-end Frameworks</h1>
      <div className='row'>
        <div className='col-9'>
          <Rankings margin={margin} />
        </div>
        <div className='col-3'>
          <div className='row'>
            <div className='col-12'>
              <ScatterplotD3Controlled margin={
                margin} />
            </div>
            <div className='col-12'>
              <BarChart margin={margin} />
            </div>
          </div>
        </div>
      </div>
        ...
    </Fragment>
  )
};
```

> **Declare a margin object.**

> **Pass the margin as props to the components Rankings, ScatterplotD3Controlled, and BarChart.**

To append the chart container, follow these steps:

1. Go to component `ScatterplotD3Controlled` located in the `Charts` folder.
2. At the top of the file, import the `ChartContainer` component.
3. Inside the component function, declare the `width` and `height` constants equal to `300` and `245`, respectively.
4. Calculate the `innerWidth` and `innerHeight` of the chart by subtracting the margins received as props from the dimensions, as shown in the next listing.
5. Just before the closing card tag (`</Card>`), call the `ChartContainer` component. Pass the `width`, `height`, and `margin` as props.

Listing 8.5 Calling `ChartContainer` (`ScatterplotD3Controlled.js`)

```
import Card from '../UI/Card';
import ChartContainer from '../ChartComponents/
  ChartContainer';
```
Import the ChartContainer component.

```
const ScatterplotD3Controlled = props => {
  const width = 300;
  const height = 245;
  const innerWidth = width - props.margin.left -
    props.margin.right;
  const innerHeight = height - props.margin.top -
    props.margin.bottom;
```
Declare the width and height constants. Calculate the innerWidth and the innerHeight of the chart by subtracting the margins received as props from the dimensions.

```
  return (
    <Card>
      <h2>Retention vs Usage</h2>
      <ChartContainer
        width={width}
        height={height}
        margin={props.margin}
      >
      </ChartContainer>
    </Card>
  )
};
```
Append the ChartContainer component. Pass the width, height, and margins as props. This component has an opening and closing bracket in between which we'll later add the chart.

```
export default ScatterplotD3Controlled;
```

Apply the same step to the `BarChart` and the `Rankings` component. The dimensions of the bar chart are the same as the scatterplot, while the rankings chart has a width of 1,000 px and a height of 542 px. We also increase the left and right margins of the rankings chart, as shown in the following snippet:

```
const width = 1000;
const height = 542;
const marginRight = 150;
const marginLeft = 110;
const innerWidth = width - props.marginLeft - props.marginRight;
const innerHeight = height - props.margin.top - props.margin.bottom;
```

Once all your files are updated and saved, take a look at your project in the browser. If you inspect the markup, you'll see that an SVG container and a group element have been added for each chart and that their attributes are set as expected. This is how we create a reusable SVG component in React!

8.5   Allowing D3 to control a portion of the DOM

We're now ready to draw a first visualization with the first approach, as shown in figure 8.4. In this section, we'll build the scatterplot shown in figure 8.1 and on the hosted project (http://mng.bz/yZlB) using the first approach: allowing D3 to control a portion of the DOM.

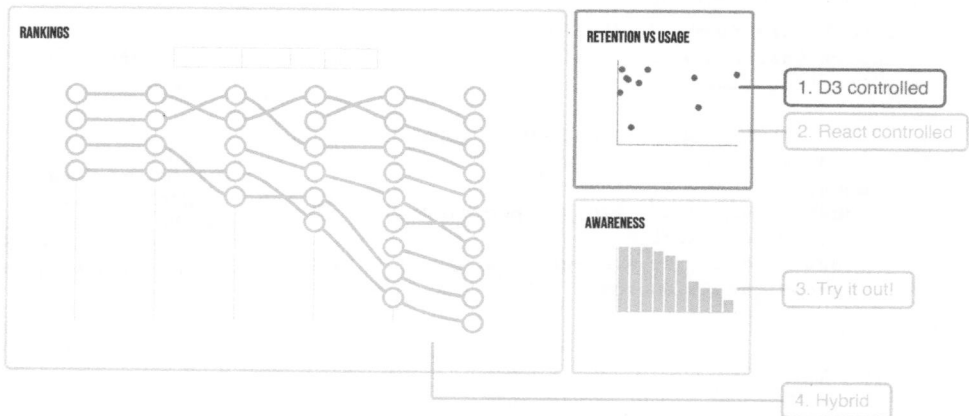

Figure 8.4   In this section, we'll build the scatterplot of the frameworks' retention versus user count by allowing D3 to control a portion of the DOM.

8.5.1   React

In React, we pass the control of an element with a reference, also called ref. We do so with the useRef() hook, as detailed in figure 8.5.

We first need to import the useRef and the useEffect hooks from React. Inside the component, we initialize useRef and save it in a constant called, for example, myRef. We then give a ref attribute to the element we want to control with D3 and point to the constant in which we saved the hook (myRef).

The second step is to use the effect hook to create a function where we'll be able to use D3. In the anonymous function passed as the first argument of useEffect, we select the current version of the ref with D3 (d3.select(myRef.current)). The current property ensures that the element we manipulate is up to date. From this point, we can use D3 as we have been so far, as long as it's inside the anonymous function of useEffect.

```
import { useRef, useEffect } from 'react';
```
1. Import the useRef and useEffect hooks.

```
const myComponent = props => {
  const myRef = useRef();
```
2. Inside the component, initialize the useRef() hook. Save it in a constant (myRef).

```
  useEffect(() => {

    const ref = d3.select(myRef.current)
      .append( ... )
      .style( ... )
      ...

  }, [ ... ]);

  return (
    <div ref={myRef}></div>
  );
};
```
3. Give a ref attribute to the element you want to control with D3, pointing to the useRef() hook initialized in step 2.

```
export default ScatterplotUncontrolled;
```

4. With D3, select the current instance of the ref inside a useEffect() hook.

5. Remaining inside the useEffect() hook, use D3 to append and style elements.

Figure 8.5   **To let D3 control a portion of the DOM in React, we first need to import the `useRef()` and the `useEffect()` hooks into our component. We then initialize a `ref` and attach it as an attribute to the element we want to control with D3. Finally, inside a `useEffect()` hook, we select the current instance of the `ref` and start using D3 as usual.**

To apply this strategy to the scatterplot, open the `ScatterplotD3Controlled.js` file located inside the `Charts` folder. At the top of the file, import the `useRef` and `useEffect` hooks from React, as well as the D3 library. Inside the component, initialize the `useRef` hook, and save it in a constant named `scatterplotRef`, as detailed in the next listing. Append a group element inside the `ChartContainer`, and set its ref attribute to `scatterplotRef`. Finally, create a `useEffect` hook and use D3 to select the current property of the ref.

> **Listing 8.6   D3 controlled approach (`ScatterplotD3Controlled.js`)**

```
import { useRef, useEffect } from 'react';
import * as d3 from 'd3';
```
Import the useRef and useEffect hooks from React. Import the D3 library.

```
const ScatterplotD3Controlled = props => {
  ...

  const scatterplotRef = useRef();
```
Initialize a useRef hook, and save it into a constant named scatterplotRef.

```
useEffect(() => {
  const scatterplotContainer = d3.select(
    scatterplotRef.current);
}, []);
```

Inside the anonymous function of a useEffect hook, select the current property of the ref with D3.

```
return (
  <Card>
    <h2>Retention vs Usage</h2>
    <ChartContainer
      ...
    >
      <g ref={scatterplotRef}></g>
    </ChartContainer>
  </Card>
)
};
```

Append a group element inside ChartContainer, and set its ref attribute to scatterplotRef.

```
export default ScatterplotD3Controlled;
```

Before we build our scatterplot, let's go back to the Charts component and declare the color scale we'll use throughout the project. We chose D3's ordinal scale, which maps a discrete domain onto a discrete range. The domain is the array of framework IDs available in the data, while for the range, we use one of D3's predefined color palettes, d3.schemeTableau10, available in the d3-scale-chromatic module:

```
import * as d3 from 'd3';

const colorScale = d3.scaleOrdinal()
  .domain(props.data.ids)
  .range(d3.schemeTableau10);
```

We pass the color scale as props to component ScatterplotD3Controlled, as well as the experience array as data:

```
<ScatterplotD3Controlled
  margin={margin}
  data={props.data.experience}
  colorScale={colorScale}
/>
```

We're now ready to build our scatterplot with D3. The horizontal axis of the scatterplot represents the number of users, while the vertical axis is their retention percentage. Back in ScatterplotD3Controlled and inside the anonymous function of the useEffect hook, we can declare scales, generate axes, and use the data-binding pattern to append a circle element for each framework, as demonstrated in listing 8.7. If you read the previous chapters, you should be familiar with these steps by now.

Note how we pass the dependencies innerWidth, innerHeight, and props to the useEffect hook. These variables are used inside the useEffect function, and if we don't add them to the dependencies array, React will throw a warning. But because these variables won't change, the useEffect function will still run only once.

Listing 8.7 Building a scatterplot (`ScatterplotD3Controlled.js`)

```
const ScatterplotD3Controlled = props => {
  ...

  const scatterplotRef = useRef();
  useEffect(() => {
    const scatterplotContainer = d3.select(scatterplotRef.current);

    const xScale = d3.scaleLinear()
      .domain([0, d3.max(props.data, d =>
        d.user_count)])
      .range([0, innerWidth])
      .nice();
    const yScale = d3.scaleLinear()
      .domain([0, 100])
      .range([innerHeight, 0]);

    const bottomAxis = d3.axisBottom(xScale)
      .ticks([3])
      .tickFormat(d3.format("d"));
    scatterplotContainer
      .append("g")
        .attr("class", "axis")
        .attr("transform", `translate(0,
          ${innerHeight})`)
        .call(bottomAxis);
    const leftAxis = d3.axisLeft(yScale)
      .ticks([5]);
    scatterplotContainer
      .append("g")
        .attr("class", "axis")
        .call(leftAxis);

    scatterplotContainer
      .selectAll(".scatterplot-circle")
      .data(props.data)
      .join("circle")
        .attr("class", "scatterplot-circle")
        .attr("cx", d => xScale(d.user_count))
        .attr("cy", d => yScale(d.retention_percentage))
        .attr("r", 6)
        .attr("fill", d => props.colorScale(d.id));
  }, [innerWidth, innerHeight, props]);

  return (
    <Card>
      <h2>Retention vs Usage</h2>
      <ChartContainer ... >
        <g ref={scatterplotRef}></g>
      </ChartContainer>
    </Card>
  )
};
```

Declare two linear scales, one for the horizontal and one for the vertical axis. The domain of the horizontal axis extends from 0 to the maximum number of users for a framework. The domain of the vertical axis extends from 0 to 100 and covers the retention percentage.

Initialize the axes generators, and append the axes to the inner chart.

Use the data-binding pattern to append one circle for each framework. The horizontal position of the circles represents the number of users, while their vertical position is their retention percentage. To set their fill attribute, we call the color scale received as a prop and pass the framework's ID.

Add the required dependencies. Because these variables won't change, the function inside the useEffect hook will run only once.

Once completed, your scatterplot should look similar to the one in figure 8.6. Note that we won't spend time styling the axes and giving them labels at this stage, but feel free to do so if you want.

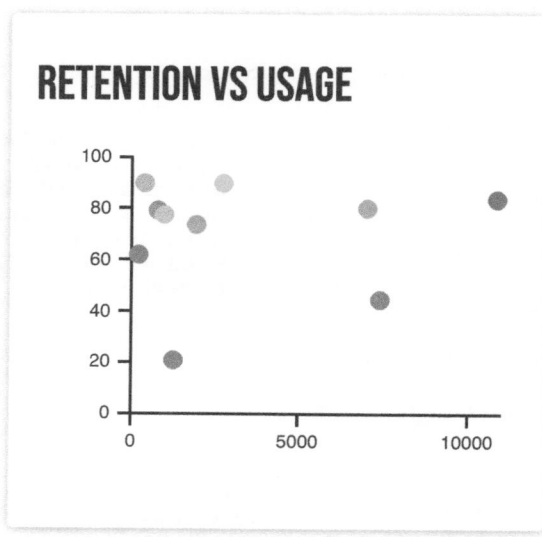

Figure 8.6   Scatterplot built by letting D3 control a portion of the DOM

Building a visualization by allowing D3 to control a portion of the DOM is relatively simple. From the moment the ref attribute is handled, we can use D3 the same way we have been in the first part of this book. This approach is advantageous when you're short on time or want to build a quick demo. But it's important to remember that it can affect your project's performance because we prevent React from using its optimization features on the part of the DOM that D3 controls. On a small project containing few visualizations, the effect is probably unnoticeable, but on larger, more complex projects, it's crucial to take performance into consideration.

In the next section, we'll discuss how we can use D3 while maintaining React's total control over the DOM. First, however, here are a few tips to implement the same strategy in Angular and Svelte.

8.5.2   Angular

To apply the same strategy in Angular, we use an ElementRef, which is Angular's way of providing direct access to the DOM. We first need to import ElementRef and ViewChild from Angular's core module, as shown in figure 8.7. Then, in the HTML template, we give a direct reference to an element with a hash symbol (#) followed by the name of your choice, for example, #myRef.

Inside the component's JavaScript class, we use property decorator ViewChild and pass the name of the reference. This decorator returns an ElementRef, and we specify that the reference is applied to an SVG element (<SVGElement>).

We then need to wait for the component to be fully initialized before we try to manipulate the referenced element. To do so, we call the function where we'll use D3 inside Angular's lifecycle hook ngAfterViewInit(). Finally, we select the nativeElement property of the reference with D3 and start using D3 as usual. To see this strategy applied inside an actual Angular application, look at component scatterplot-d3-controlled in the d3-with-angular folder of this chapter's code files.

```
import { ElementRef, ViewChild } from '@angular/core';

@Component({
  selector: '...',
  template: '<svg:g #myRef></svg:g>',
})

export class MyComponent {
  @ViewChild('myRef')
  myRef!: ElementRef<SVGElement>;

  ngAfterViewInit(): void {
    this.buildChart();
  }

  buildChart() {
    d3.select(this.myRef.nativeElement)
      .append( ... )
      .style( ... )
      ...
  }
}
```

1. Import ElementRef and ViewChild from Angular's core module.

2. Inside the HTML template, give a direct reference to an element with a hash (#) symbol followed by the name of your choice (myRef).

3. Use the property decorator ViewChild to access the reference. It returns an ElementRef on an SVG element.

4. Wait for the component to be fully initialized before calling the function where you will build the chart; otherwise, the reference won't be available.

5. Select the nativeElement property of the reference with D3.

6. Use D3 to append and style elements.

Figure 8.7 To allow D3 to control a portion of the DOM in Angular, we use an `ElementRef`. We give a reference to an element from the HTML template using a hash followed by the name of our choice. Then, inside the component's JavaScript class, we pass the reference to the `ViewChild` property decorator. Finally, once the component is initialized, we select the `nativeElement` property of the reference with D3 and start using D3 as usual.

Although this strategy allows us to use D3 in the way we're familiar with, it isn't recommended by Angular. We should use it cautiously because it interferes with Angular's rendering of the DOM and can make your application more vulnerable to cross-site scripting (XSS) attacks. We'll discuss a better approach in the next section.

When working with SVG elements in Angular, you should also be aware of a few syntax specificities. First, SVG elements other than the SVG container require an `svg:` prefix, for example, `<svg:g></svg:g>`, `<svg:circle />`, or `<svg:text></svg:text>`:

```
<svg>
  <svg:g>
    <svg:circle />
  </svg:g>
</svg>
```

In addition, SVG attributes must be prefixed with `attr`:

```
<svg:circle
  [attr.cx]="10"
  [attr.cy]="15"
  [attr.r]="5"
/>
```

Finally, it's helpful to know that Angular uses TypeScript, so we must declare types as we code. You can install type definitions for D3 with the NPM package @types/d3.

8.5.3   *Svelte*

Svelte is all the rage in the data visualization world at the time of writing this book. Its lightweight, slim architecture makes it easier to learn for new coders, and it's an efficient tool for shipping small, standalone projects.

Like in React and Angular, we can let D3 control a portion of the DOM in Svelte using a reference. We apply a reference to a DOM element with `bind:this`, to which we pass the name of our reference. Then, once the component has mounted, we select the reference with D3 and start using it as usual, as shown in figure 8.8.

To see this strategy applied inside a real Svelte application, look at component `scatterplotD3Controlled` in the `d3-with-svelte` folder of this chapter's code files.

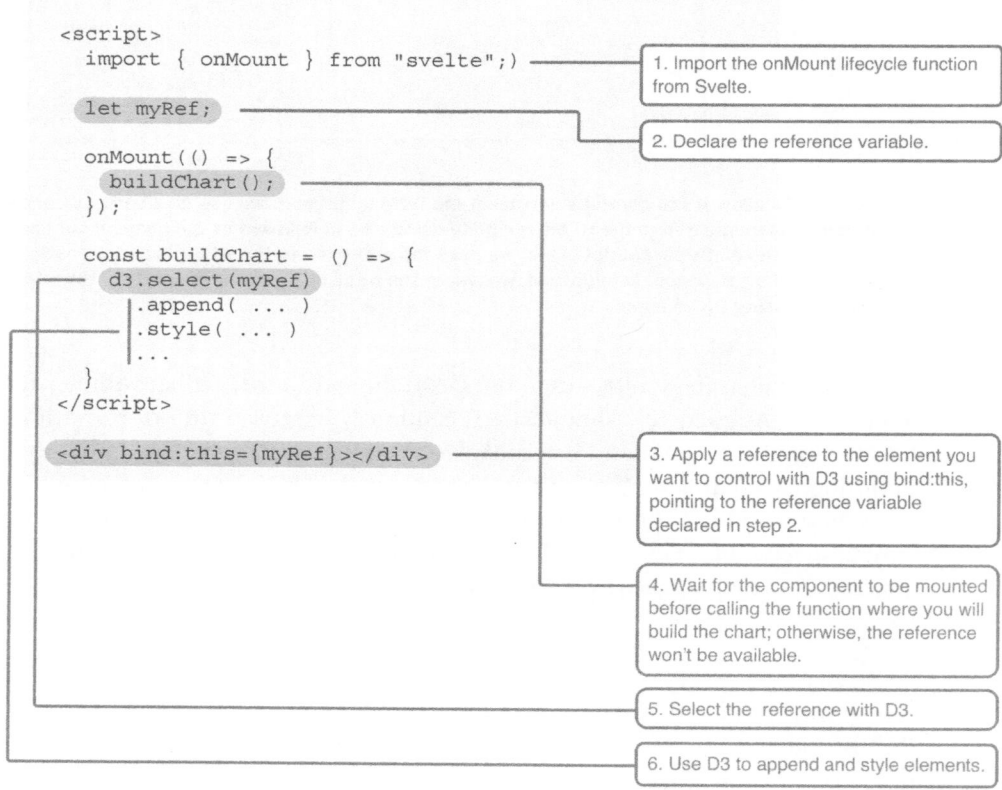

Figure 8.8   To allow D3 to control a portion of the DOM in Svelte, we declare a reference variable within the `<script>` tags and point to this variable from the DOM element we want to control using `bind:this`. Then we wait for the component to be mounted, using the `onMount()` lifecycle function, and call another function, where we'll build the chart. Inside this function, we select the reference with D3 and start using it as usual.

8.6   Using D3 as a utility library

In this section, we'll discuss a better approach to using D3 within a framework: letting the framework fully control the DOM and using D3 only as a utility library. This strategy implies that D3 won't append elements to the DOM, set their attributes, or set their style properties. When following this approach, we can't use methods from the d3-selection, d3-axis, or d3-transition modules, for example.

This might sound discouraging, and you might wonder, what's the point of using D3, then? Actually, a lot of powerful D3 methods are still available! As a rule of thumb, we can still perform all the background calculations with which we create visualizations, with scales or shape generators, for example. We then generate the markup, or SVG elements, that compose our visualizations with the framework.

If we take the scatterplot we've built in the preceding section as an example, shown in figure 8.9, can you mentally list the SVG elements required to draw it? There's a circle for each framework, a line for each axis, and a bunch of axis labels built with SVG text elements. Not that bad! In the following subsection, we'll rebuild the scatterplot with this approach in mind.

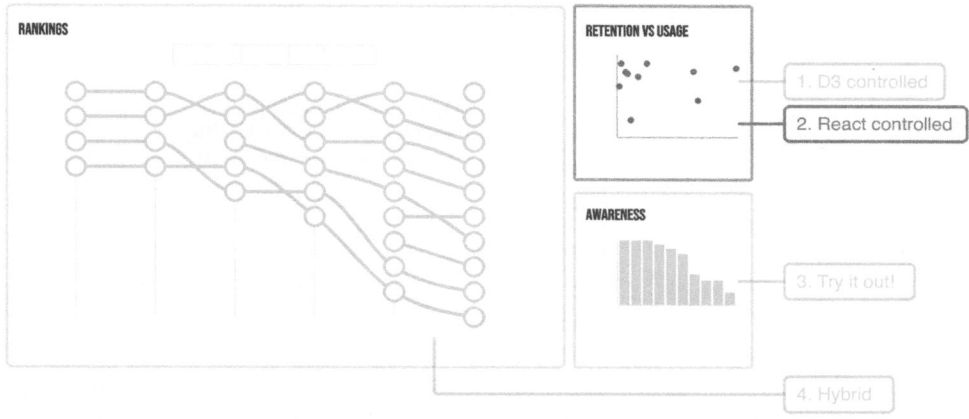

Figure 8.9   We'll rebuild the scatterplot of the frameworks' retention versus user count by controlling the DOM only with React and using D3 as a utility library.

8.6.1   React

To build the scatterplot with the second approach, go to `Charts.js`, and comment out the `ScatterplotD3Controlled` component. Import the `ScatterplotReactControlled` component into the file, and display this one instead, passing the same props as before:

```
<ScatterplotReactControlled
  margin={margin}
  data={props.data.experience}
  colorScale={colorScale}
/>
```

Now go into `ScatterplotReactControlled.js`, and import the `ChartContainer` component. Declare constants for a width of 300 px and a height of 245 px. Calculate the related `innerWidth` and `innerHeight`, as in the next listing. Finally, append the `ChartContainer` component after the `h2` title, and pass its required props (`width`, `height`, and `margin`).

Listing 8.8   Preparing `ScatterplotReactControlled`

```
import Card from '../UI/Card';
import ChartContainer from '../ChartComponents/          Import the ChartContainer
  ChartContainer';                                       component.

const ScatterplotReactControlled = props => {
  const width = 300;
  const height = 245;
  const innerWidth = width - props.margin.left -         Initialize width and height
    props.margin.right;                                  constants of 300 px and 245 px,
  const innerHeight = height - props.margin.top -        and calculate the related
    props.margin.bottom;                                 innerWidth and innerHeight.

  return (
    <Card>
      <h2>Retention vs Usage</h2>
      <ChartContainer
        width={width}
        height={height}                                  Append the ChartContainer
        margin={props.margin}                            component after the h2 title,
      >                                                   and pass its required props.
      </ChartContainer>
    </Card>
  )
};

export default ScatterplotReactControlled;
```

To create our scatterplot, we want to append a circle element to the chart for each framework in the dataset. With our previous approach, we would have used the data-binding pattern, but because we don't want to let D3 manipulate the DOM, we'll do it manually.

Because circles are primary chart elements that are likely to be used at more than one place in a project, and because it's best to create small, reusable components, we'll have a separate component whose only job is to return a circle element. Open the `Circle.js` file inside the `ChartComponents` folder. Currently, this component returns a circle element (`<circle />`), but its attributes aren't set. It would be useful to pass the required attributes of the circle element via props. In listing 8.9, we set the `cx`, `cy`, `r`, and `fill` attributes of the circle with the props we expect it to receive. To make this component even more generic, we set the `stroke` and `stroke-width` attributes but make them optional, with a ternary operator that sets the `stroke` property to `"none"` and the `stroke-width` to `0` if they aren't passed as props.

Listing 8.9   Preparing the `Circle` component (`Circle.js`)

```
const Circle = props => {
  return (
    <circle
      cx={props.cx}
      cy={props.cy}
      r={props.r}
      fill={props.fill}
      stroke={props.stroke ? props.stroke : "none"}
      strokeWidth={props.strokeWidth ? props.strokeWidth : 0}
    />
  )
};

export default Circle;
```

Back to the `ScatterplotReactControlled` component; we import the `Circle` component and the `d3` library at the top of the file. We also declare a horizontal and a vertical linear scale, responsible for calculating the position of the circles based on the
number of users and the retention percentage.

To create the circles, we use the JavaScript `map()` method to append a `Circle` component for each framework in the dataset. To help React keep track of which item to
update in the DOM (in the eventuality that the circles are updated), we pass a unique
key to each `Circle` component. We calculate their `cx` attribute with `xScale`, `cy` with
`yScale`, and `fill` with the `colorScale`, and then pass them as props. The `r` attribute is
a static value of `6`. If you save your project, you should see the circles on the screen.

Listing 8.10   Appending circles (`ScatterplotReactControlled.js`)

```
...
import * as d3 from 'd3';                                    │ Import the d3 library and
import Circle from '../ChartComponents/Circle';             │ the Circle component.

const ScatterplotReactControlled = props => {
  ...

  const xScale = d3.scaleLinear()                            │ Declare two linear scales,
    .domain([0, d3.max(props.data, d => d.user_count)])      │ one to position the
    .range([0, innerWidth])                                  │ circles horizontally based
    .nice();                                                 │ on the number of users,
  const yScale = d3.scaleLinear()                            │ and one to position them
    .domain([0, 100])                                        │ vertically based on the
    .range([innerHeight, 0]);                                │ retention percentage,
                                                             │ which can vary between
  return (                                                   │ 0% and 100%.
    <Card>
      <h2>Retention vs Usage</h2>
      <ChartContainer ... >
        {props.data.map(framework => (
          <Circle
```

```
            key={`circle-${framework.id}`}
            cx={xScale(framework.user_count)}
            cy={yScale(framework.retention_percentage)}
            r={6}
            fill={props.colorScale(framework.id)}
        />
    ))}
  </ChartContainer>
 </Card>
 )
};

export default ScatterplotReactControlled;
```

> With the JavaScript map() method, append a Circle component for each framework in the dataset. Give them a unique key, and set their attributes.

To complete our scatterplot, we need to create the axes without the help of D3's axis generator. We'll have two axes: a bottom axis and a left axis. Go to the `Axis.js` file inside the `ChartComponents` folder. The `Axis` component declared at the bottom of the file receives a `type` props that can have the value `"bottom"`, `"left"`, or `"band"`. If the type is `"bottom"`, we call the function `AxisBottom` and pass our props, while if the type is `"left"`, we call the function `Axisleft`. With this strategy, our different axes will be created inside the same file, but we could also decide to create them in separate files.

In `ScatterplotReactControlled`, let's import the `Axis` component and render it twice inside the chart container, as shown in listing 8.11. The first axis has a type of `"bottom"`, its scale is `xScale`, and its label is `"User Count"`. We also need to pass the `innerWidth` and `innerHeight` as props, which we'll use to position the axis properly. For the second axis, the type is `"left"`, the scale is `yScale`, and the label is `"Retention %"`. We'll see how these props will be used to draw the axis in a moment.

Listing 8.11   Calling Axis (ScatterplotReactControlled.js)

```
...
import Axis from '../ChartComponents/Axis';        ◁──  Import the Axis
                                                         component.
const ScatterplotReactControlled = props => {
  ...

  return (
    <Card>
      <h2>Retention vs Usage</h2>
      <ChartContainer ... >
        <Axis
          type="bottom"
          scale={xScale}
          innerWidth={innerWidth}
          innerHeight={innerHeight}
          label={"User Count"}
        />
        <Axis
          type="left"
          scale={yScale}
          innerWidth={innerWidth}
```

> Display the Axis component twice, the first one for the bottom axis and the second for the left axis. Pass the related scale, label, innerWidth, and innerHeight as props.

```
        innerHeight={innerHeight}
        label={"Retention %"}
      />
      {props.data.map(framework => (
        <Circle
            ...
        />
      ))}
    </ChartContainer>
  </Card>
 )
};
```

```
export default ScatterplotReactControlled;
```

In chapter 4, we explained that D3 generates three kinds of elements when it creates an axis: a line (or a path) that extends along the axis, a text element accompanied by a short line for each tick, or labels that are displayed with the axis. Figure 8.10 shows the bottom axis from the scatterplot created in section 8.5. This is something we can easily reproduce manually.

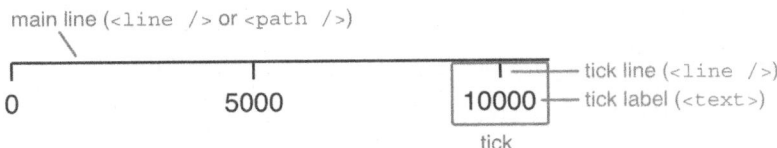

Figure 8.10   The axes generated by D3 are composed of a main line or path that extends along the length of the axis, and then each axis label is accompanied by a short line. The combination of the two is called a tick.

Back to `Axis.js`; we'll start by creating the bottom axis inside function `AxisBottom`. First, we need to determine how many ticks, or axis labels, we want to display. In listing 8.12, we specify that we want to show a tick every 100 px. If we divide the `innerWidth`, which is 300 px, by 100, we'll have three ticks. We save this number in constant `numberOfTicks`.

In D3, continuous scales have a `ticks()` property to which we pass a number, and that returns an array with the ticks and their value from the domain. Still in listing 8.12, we call this method with `props.scale.ticks(numberOfTicks)`, and it returns array `[0, 5000, 10000]` that we save in constant `ticks`.

To draw the axis, we translate the group element that already exists in the return statement to the bottom of the chart and give it a class name of `"axis"`. In the `Axis.css` file, we've already declared a few styles for the axis. Then we append a line element extending from the axis's left to the right.

For the labels, for each tick inside the `ticks` array, we append a group, a short vertical line, and a text element that displays the tick label. Finally, if a label is passed as a prop, we show it below the axis.

Listing 8.12   Generating the bottom axis (`Axis.js`)

```
const AxisBottom = props => {
  const numberOfTicks = props.innerWidth / 100;
  const ticks = props.scale.ticks(numberOfTicks);

  return (
    <g className="axis" transform={`translate(0,
    ${props.innerHeight})`} >
      <line x1={0} y1={0} x2={props.innerWidth}
      y2={0} />
      {ticks.map(tick => (
        <g key={tick} transform={`translate(
        ${props.scale(tick)}, 0)`}>
          <line x1={0} y1={0} x2={0} y2={5} />
          <text x={0} y={20} textAnchor="middle" >
          {tick}
          </text>
        </g>
      ))}
      {props.label &&
        <text
          className="axis-label"
          textAnchor="middle"
          transform={`translate(${props.innerWidth /
          2}, 45)`}
        >
          {props.label}
        </text>
      }
    </g>
  );
};
```

Calculate the number of ticks to display. Create an array containing the label for each tick by calling the tick() method, which can be applied to any continuous D3 scale.

Translate the group element to the bottom of the chart, and give it a class name of "axis".

Append a horizontal line extending from the axis's left to the right.

For each label in the ticks array, append a short vertical line and a text element that displays the label.

If a label prop is passed to the component, display this label below the axis.

In the next listing, we proceed similarly for the left axis. The main difference is that we display an axis label every 50 px and rotate the main label 90 degrees.

Listing 8.13   Generating the left axis (`Axis.js`)

```
const AxisLeft = props => {
  const numberOfTicks = props.innerHeight / 50;
  const ticks = props.scale.ticks(numberOfTicks);

  return (
    <g className="axis">
```

Calculate the number of ticks to display. Create an array containing the label for each tick by calling the tick() method, which can be applied to any continuous D3 scale.

```
<line x1={0} y1={props.innerHeight} x2={0}
  y2={0} />
{ticks.map(tick => (
  <g key={tick} transform={`translate(0,
    ${props.scale(tick)})`}>
    <line x1={-5} y1={0} x2={0} y2={0} />
    <text x={-10} y={0} textAnchor="end"
    ➥ alignmentBaseline="middle">
      {tick}
    </text>
  </g>
))}
{props.label &&
  <text
    textAnchor="middle"
    transform={`translate(-42,
      ${props.innerHeight / 2})
      ➥ rotate(-90)`}
  >
    {props.label}
  </text>
}
  </g>
 );
};
```

Append a vertical line that extends from the bottom to the top of the axis.

For each tick inside the ticks array, append a short horizontal line and a text element that displays the label.

If a label prop is passed to the component, display this label to the left of the chart, rotated 90 degrees.

Once completed, your scatterplot should look like the one in figure 8.11.

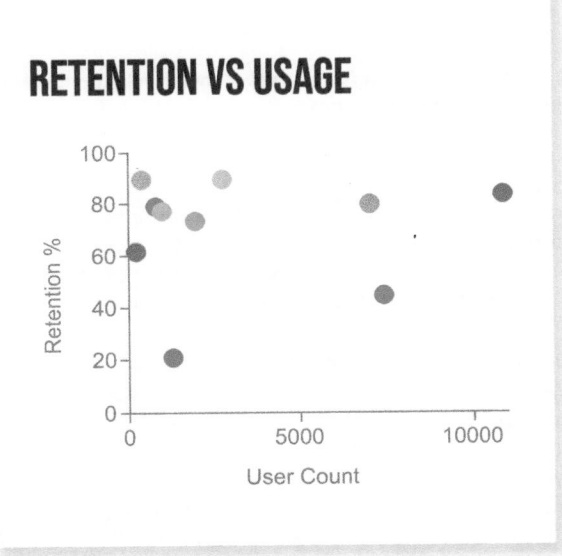

Figure 8.11 Scatterplot built by using D3 solely as a utility library

8.6.2   Angular and Svelte

When letting the framework handle the DOM and using D3 as a utility library, there is no specific strategy to apply, whether we use React, Angular, or Svelte. Once you know your framework and its syntax, you can build any chart as we've been doing in this section. For examples of how to build the scatterplot with the second strategy in Angular and Svelte, refer to components `scatterplot-angular-controlled` and `Scatter-plotSvelteControlled` in the `d3-with-angular` and `d3-with-svelte` folders of this chapter's code files.

Exercise: Create a bar chart

Let's consolidate your knowledge by building the bar chart of the developer's aware-ness of each framework, as shown in the following image.

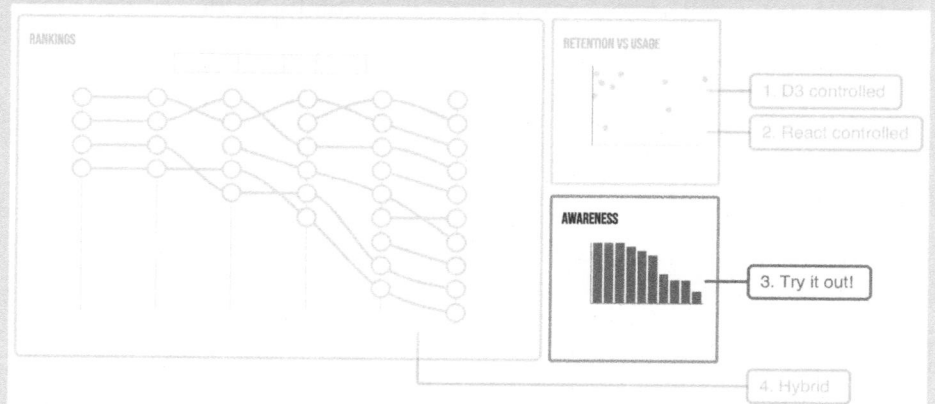

Now it's your turn to try! Creating the chart elements and axes manually might not seem easy at first, but this exercise should help you clarify the process.

Here are a few tips:

1. Create a component responsible only for drawing a rectangle (`Rectangle.js`) and call it for each rectangle in the bar chart (call it from `BarChart.js`).
2. Give the bar chart a width of 300 px and a height of 245 px. You should increase its bottom margin to accommodate the framework labels (we applied 85 px).
3. Use a band scale to calculate the horizontal position of each bar.
4. To improve the readability of this visualization, sort the bars in descending order using the JavaScript method `sort()`.
5. For the bottom axis, pass a type prop with the value `"band"`, and generate the axis in the function `AxisBandBottom()` available in `Axis.js`.
6. Because the band scale isn't continuous, it doesn't have a `ticks()` method. To generate a label for each framework, pass an array of their names to the `Axis` component.

---

7 You'll need to rotate the labels on the bottom axis. To do so, you can use the
   `transform` attribute with a translation followed by a rotation.

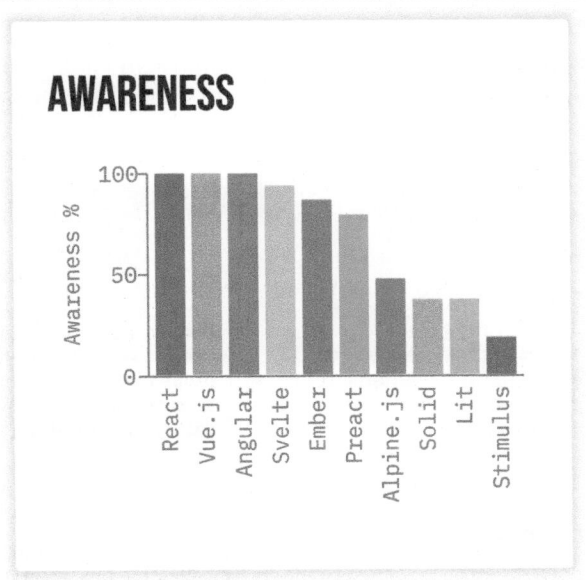

**Completed bar chart of the
developers' awareness of
each framework**

If you get stuck or want to compare your solution with ours, you'll find it in section
D.8.1 of appendix D and in the `8.6.b-Bar_chart/end` folder of this chapter's code
files. But as usual, we encourage you to try to complete it on your own. Your solution
might differ slightly from ours, and that's all right!

8.6.3 Generating curves

So far, we've been rendering simple shapes such as circles, rectangles, and lines. But
what if we need to use D3's shape generator to create a curve? Well, because the shape
generator's only job is to return the d attribute of a path element, we can use it while
applying the second strategy. We'll demonstrate this by building the rankings chart
from figure 8.1 and the hosted project (http://mng.bz/yZlB). This chart shows the
ranking of each framework in terms of user satisfaction. The framework that ranks
first is positioned at the top, and the one that ranks last is at the bottom. First, in
`Charts.js`, let's pass the data and the color scale to the `Rankings` component:

```
<Rankings
  margin={margin}
  data={props.data}
  colorScale={colorScale}
/>
```

Then let's go to the `Curve` component and declare a line generator, as shown in listing 8.14. We assume that we receive `xScale` and `yScale` as props, as well as the key accessors for the `x()` and the `y()` functions, which in our case are `"year"` and `"rank"`.

Because not every framework has data for the first years, we need to use the `defined()` accessor function, which will handle the years without data. We also set the curve to `d3.curveMonotoneX`.

When appending the path element, we set the d attribute by calling the line generator (`lineGenerator(props.data)`). The `stroke` and `strokeWidth` attributes are passed as props.

Listing 8.14 Preparing the curve generator (`Curve.js`)

```
import * as d3 from "d3";

const Curve = props => {
  const lineGenerator = d3.line()        // Declare a line generator function.
    .x(d => props.xScale(d[props.xAccessor]))   // Use the scales and keys passed as
    .y(d => props.yScale(d[props.yAccessor]))   // props to set the x() and y()
    .defined(d => d[props.yAccessor] !== null)  // accessor functions. Handle missing
    .curve(d3.curveMonotoneX);          // data with the defined() method.

  return (
    <path
      d={lineGenerator(props.data)}    // Append a path element, and set its d
      fill="none"                      // attribute by calling the line generator
      stroke={props.stroke}            // function and passing the path's data prop.
      strokeWidth={props.strokeWidth}
    />
  );
};

export default Curve;
```

We'll call the `Curve` component from `Rankings.js`. Note that this file already has an array named `rankingFilters` that contains the information for each button displayed above the chart. In the component, we also have a state variable named `activeFilter`, which is initialized to `satisfaction`. In the next section, we'll make these filters usable and update the rankings visualization accordingly.

But for now, we need to declare our scales. If you refer to figure 8.1 or to the hosted project (http://mng.bz/yZlB), you'll see that the years 2016 to 2021 are spread horizontally, and the frameworks are distributed vertically by rank. We can use a point scale in both cases, as in listing 8.15.

For each framework, we call the `Curve` component and pass the required props. Note how the data passed to the `Curve` component is determined with the `activeFilter` state variable, which means that currently we're passing the array available under the key `satisfaction`, which provides the rank of the current framework in terms of user satisfaction for the years 2016 to 2021.

Listing 8.15 Displaying the rank curves (`Rankings.js`)

```
import * as d3 from 'd3';
import Curve from '../ChartComponents/Curve';

const Rankings = props => {
  ...

  const xScale = d3.scalePoint()
    .domain(props.data.years)
    .range([0, innerWidth]);
  const yScale = d3.scalePoint()
    .domain(d3.range(1, props.data.ids.length + 1))
    .range([0, innerHeight]);

  return (
    <Card>
      <h2>Rankings</h2>
      <RankingFilters ... />
      <ChartContainer ... >
        {props.data.experience.map((framework, i) => (
          <g key={`curve-${framework.id}`}>
            <Curve
              data={framework[activeFilter]}
              xScale={xScale}
              yScale={yScale}
              xAccessor="year"
              yAccessor="rank"
              stroke={props.colorScale(framework.id)}
              strokeWidth={5}
            />
          </g>
        ))}
      </ChartContainer>
    </Card>
  )
};
```

> **Declare two point scales: one that distributes the years horizontally and one that positions the ranks vertically.**

> **Call the Curve component for each framework, and pass the data related to the activeFilter as a prop, as well as the other required props. Note that we wrap the Curve component into a group element. In a moment, we'll add labels to these groups.**

To clarify which curve represents which framework, we'll add labels to the left and right sides of the chart. In listing 8.16, we go to the `Label` component and set the attributes of a `text` element based on its props. Because we'll have labels on both sides, we'll need to set the `textAnchor`, which is also done via the labels' props. We also give it a `fontWeight` of `"bold"` to improve readability.

Listing 8.16 Preparing the `Label` component (`Label.js`)

```
const Label = props => {
  return (
    <text
      x={props.x}
      y={props.y}
      fill={props.color}
      textAnchor={props.textAnchor}
```

```
        alignmentBaseline="middle"
        style={{ fontWeight: "bold" }}
      >
        {props.label}
    </text>
  );
};

export default Label;
```

In listing 8.17, we call the `Label` component twice if a framework has data for the first year (2016) and once otherwise. The first framework label is displayed to the left of the chart, with a `textAnchor` of `"end"`, and the second framework is displayed on the right, with a `textAnchor` of `"start"`.

Listing 8.17 Adding labels to the sides of the chart (`Rankings.js`)

```
...
import Label from '../ChartComponents/Label';

const Rankings = props => {
  ...

  return (
    <Card>
      <h2>Rankings</h2>
      <RankingFilters ... />
      <ChartContainer ... >
        {props.data.experience.map((framework, i) => (
          <g key={`curve-${framework.id}`}>
            <Curve ... />
            {framework[activeFilter][0].rank &&
              <Label
                x={-25}
                y={yScale(framework[activeFilter][0]
                  .rank)}
                color={props.colorScale(framework.id)}
                label={framework.name}
                textAnchor={"end"}
              />
            }
            <Label
              x={innerWidth + 25}
              y={yScale(framework[activeFilter]
                [framework[activeFilter].length -
                  1].rank)}
              color={props.colorScale(framework.id)}
              label={framework.name}
              textAnchor={"start"}
            />
          </g>
        ))}
```

If the framework has data for the first year (2016), display a label to the left of the chart with a textAnchor attribute of "end".

Display a label for each framework to the right of the chart.

```
        </ChartContainer>
      </Card>
   )
};
```

Finally, behind the curves, we append a dashed vertical line for each year. In listing 8.18, we add the text element for the year labels manually for simplicity, but we could also have tweaked the `Axis` component. We wrap those two elements with a group that has a class of `"axis"` to apply the styles already declared in `Axis.css`.

Listing 8.18   Adding grid and labels (`Rankings.js`)

```
const Rankings = props => {
   ...

   return (
      <Card>
        <h2>Rankings</h2>
        <RankingFilters ... />
        <ChartContainer ... >
          {props.data.years.map(year => (          ◁── For each year in the
            <g                                           dataset, append a
              key={`line-year-${year}`}                  group element. Give it
              className="axis"                           a class of "axis" to
              transform={`translate(${xScale(year)}, 0)`}   reuse the styles already
            >                                              declared in Axis.css,
              <line                                        and translate each
                x1={0}                                     group to the horizontal
                y1={innerHeight}                           position of the year.
                x2={0}
                y2={0}                       ◁── For each year, append
                strokeDasharray={"6 4"}          a dashed vertical line.
              />
              <text
                x={0}
                y={innerHeight + 30}       ◁── For each year, append
                textAnchor="middle"            a label to the bottom
              >                                of the chart.
                {year}
              </text>
            </g>
          ))}
          {props.data.experience.map((framework, i) => (
            <g key={`curve-${framework.id}`}>
              <Curve ... />
              ...
            </g>
          ))}
        </ChartContainer>
      </Card>
   )
};
```

Once completed, your rankings chart should look like the one in figure 8.12.

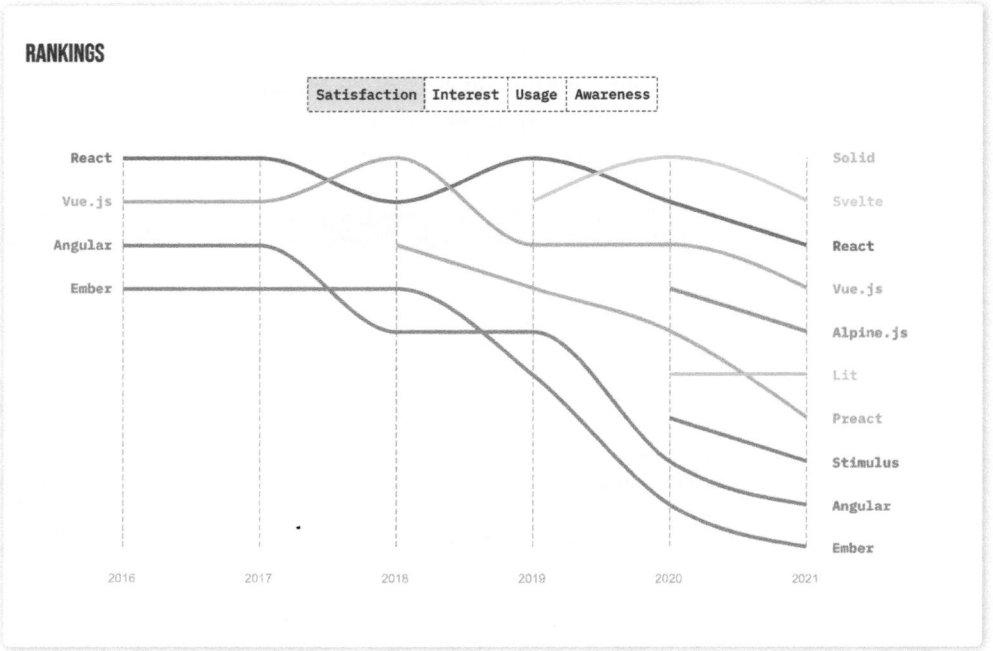

Figure 8.12   Rankings chart with framework labels

Exercise: Add badges to the rankings visualization

Only one element needs to be added to complete the static version of our dashboard: badges that communicate the percentage of developers who answered that they are satisfied with a framework for each year. You can see the result in the following image. Try to implement these badges on your own by following these instructions:

1   Each badge consists of three elements:
     a   A group element that is translated to the proper position using the CSS transform property.
     b   A white circle with a stroke of 3 px. The color of the stroke corresponds to one of the related frameworks.
     c   A text element that displays the percentage for the selected filter. Currently, the selected filter is Satisfaction, but in the next section, that will vary based on which filter is selected. Make sure to take this into consideration when passing the text to the badge.
4   We suggest that you create the badges in the `Badge` component, available in the `/UI` folder.

5   To display the circles, use the `Circle` component that we used to draw the scatterplot. The circles have a radius of 18 px.
6   You might want to round the percentages to integers by using the JavaScript `Math.round()`.
7   For the text, we used a color of #374f5e, a font size of 12 px, and a font weight of bold.

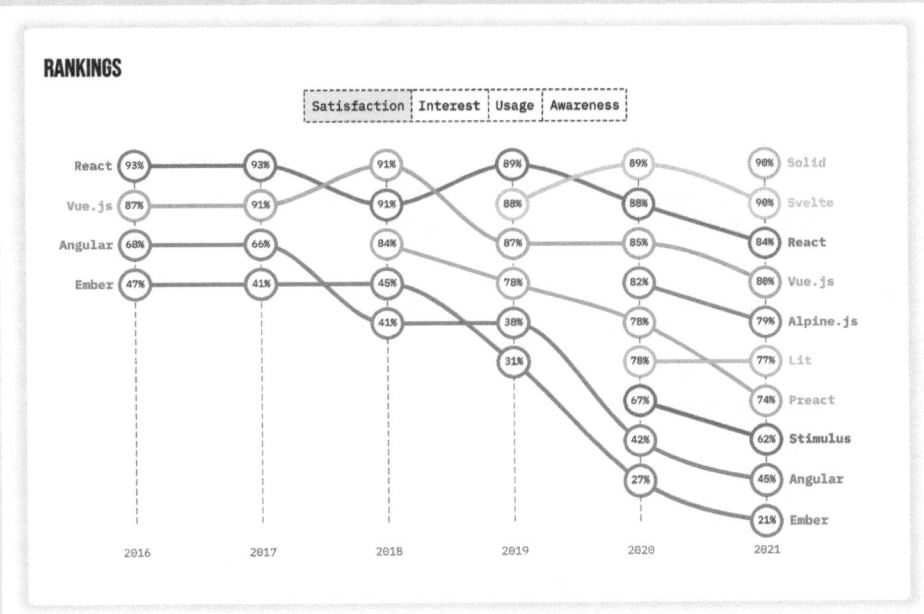

Completed rankings visualization with badges

If you get stuck or want to compare your solution with ours, you'll find it in section D.8.2 of appendix D and in the `8.6.d-Rankings_with_badges/end` folder of this chapter's code files. But as usual, we encourage you to try to complete it on your own. Your solution might differ slightly from ours, and that's all right!

8.7   *Hybrid approach*

To complete our dashboard, we'll listen to click events on the buttons at the top of the rankings visualization and update it accordingly. As we implement the solution, we'll discuss one last strategy for using D3 with a framework: the hybrid approach mentioned in figure 8.13.

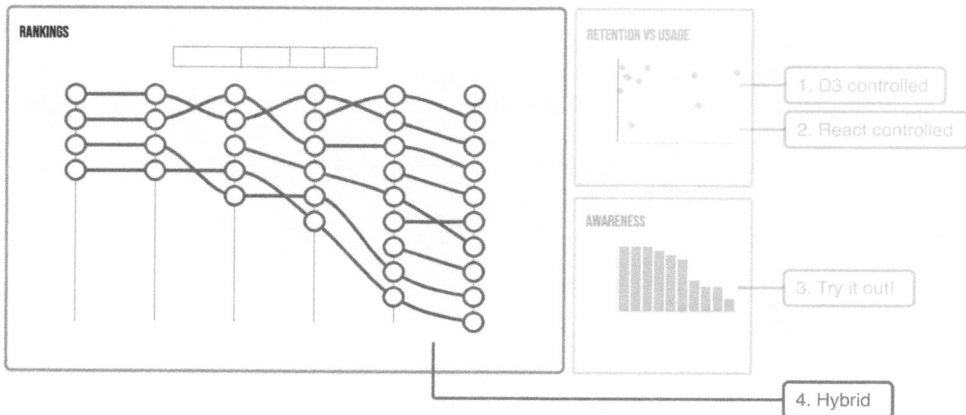

Figure 8.13   For the rankings visualization, we'll use the hybrid approach. We built the chart entirely with React but will allow D3 to control the d **attribute of the curves to provide smooth transitions.**

But first, go to `RankingFilters.js`, and add an `onClick` event to the `Button` component, as in the following snippet. When the click event is detected, point to the prop `onFilterSelection`, sent from the parent component. Note that the `Button` component already returns its `id` when clicked (see `Button.js`):

```
<Button
  key={filter.id}
  id={filter.id}
  label={filter.label}
  isActive={props.activeFilter === filter.id ? true : false}
  onClick={props.onFilterSelection}
/>
```

Then go to the parent component in `Rankings.js`, and add the prop `onFilter-Selection` to the `RankingFilters` component. This prop points to a function named `filterSelectionHandler`:

```
<RankingFilters
  filters={rankingFilters}
  activeFilter={activeFilter}
  onFilterSelection={filterSelectionHandler}
/>
```

Still in the `Rankings` component, declare the function `filterSelectionHandler` that receives the ID of the clicked filter as an argument. If the `activeFilter` state variable isn't equal to the received ID, update the state with the passed ID, using `setActive-Filter()`:

```
const filterSelectionHandler = (id) => {
  if (activeFilter !== id) {
    setActiveFilter(id);
  }
};
```

Save your project, and click on the buttons. The rankings visualization should update accordingly.

The filtering is working fine, but we lack a smooth transition of the curves and the position of their labels and badges. Because D3 allows us to easily animate shapes, we could argue that it makes sense to allow D3 to control these paths only and use the `transition()` method over their `d` attributes. Because this is a small project, it shouldn't significantly affect its performance. But this decision highly depends on your project, team, and priorities.

In listing 8.19, we import the `useRef` and `useEffect` hooks from React. We then initialize a `useRef` hook and save it in a constant named `pathRef`. We give a `ref` attribute to the `path` element and point to that constant. Note that we also removed the `d` attribute from the `path` element.

Finally, in a `useEffect` hook, we pass an anonymous function where D3 selects the current instance of `pathRef`, applies a transition function, and updates the `d` attribute by calling the line generator. Because this anonymous function depends on the data received as props and the line generator, we need to pass them as dependencies. The last two won't change, but every time the data passed as a prop to the `Curve` component updates, the anonymous function in `useEffect` will be executed.

Listing 8.19 Applying a smooth transition to the curves (`Curve.js`)

```
import { useRef, useEffect } from "react";     ⟵┐  Import the useRef and the
import * as d3 from "d3";                           useEffect hooks from React.

const Curve = props => {
  const lineGenerator = d3.line()
    .x(d => props.xScale(d[props.xAccessor]))
    .y(d => props.yScale(d[props.yAccessor]))
    .defined(d => d[props.yAccessor] !== null)
    .curve(d3.curveMonotoneX);
                                              Declare a useRef hook, and save
  const pathRef = useRef();           ⟵      it in a constant named pathRef.
  useEffect(() => {                               Create a useEffect hook, and
    const path = pathRef.current;                 pass an anonymous function
    d3.select(path)                               where the current instance
      .transition()                               of pathRef is selected. Apply
      .duration(400)                              a transition to the path, and
      .ease(d3.easeCubicOut)                      update its d attribute by
        .attr("d", lineGenerator(props.data));    calling the line generator.
  }, [props.data, lineGenerator]);     ⟵   Because the anonymous function depends on the
                                           data passed as the prop, the transition function,
  return (                                 and the line generator, they all need to be passed
    <path                                  as dependencies. The last two won't change, but
      ref={pathRef}          ⟵             every time the data updates, the anonymous
      fill="none"                          function inside useEffect() will run.
      stroke={props.stroke}
      strokeWidth={props.strokeWidth}      Apply a ref attribute on the path
    />                                     element that points to pathRef.
  );                                       Remove the d attribute.
};

export default Curve;
```

CHAPTER 8 *Integrating D3 in a frontend framework*

We must still apply a smooth transition to the framework labels and badges. Although using a D3 transition would work, it's worth considering if there is a better approach. For example, we could move them around with the transform CSS property and apply a CSS transition. Not only is this simpler, but it's likely better for performance, given that there are multiple labels and badges.

In the following snippet, we update the text element returned by the `Label` component. We set its `x` and `y` attributes to `0`, wrap it in a group element, and position the group with the transform CSS property. We also give the group a class name of `"label"`:

```
import "./Label.css";

<g
  className="label"
  style={{ transform: `translate(${props.x}px, ${props.y}px)` }}
>
  <text
    x={0}
    y={0}
    fill={props.color}
    textAnchor={props.textAnchor}
    alignmentBaseline="middle"
    style={{ fontWeight: "bold" }}
  >
    {props.label}
  </text>
</g>
```

NOTE We apply the CSS transform property to a group rather than the text element because the Safari browser doesn't apply this property correctly to the text element. In other browsers, applying the transform directly to the text element works fine.

Then we create a file named `Label.css` and import it into our component. In this file, we set the `transition` property of the labels as follows:

```
.label {
  transition: transform 400ms cubic-bezier(0.33, 1, 0.68, 1);
}
```

Finally, because the group element that wraps the badges is already positioned with a transformed property, all we have to do is to give it a class name of `"label"`, as in the previous snippet. Because styles are global by default in React, the transition will apply.

Now that we've had an overview of the three approaches to integrating D3 in a frontend framework, you might still wonder which one to use. Although the correct answer highly depends on the type of projects you work on and your priorities, here are a few guidelines:

1 The first approach, where we allow D3 to control a portion of the DOM, is mainly adapted to quick internal demos and small projects that contain few visualizations and where performance isn't the primary concern.

2 The second approach, where the framework solely manipulates the DOM and we use D3 as a utility library, is preferred whenever possible. This approach not only enhances performance on large projects but also makes maintenance easier across broad teams. In such teams, most developers won't know D3. They will find it easier to understand the code where the SVG elements are built manually rather than with the data-binding pattern or with axis generators.

3 The hybrid approach is to be used with care when there's a clear advantage to letting D3 manipulate a portion of the DOM. If you plan to use D3 to perform transitions, ask yourself if you could use a CSS transition or animation instead or even an animation library built specifically for your framework of choice.

We're now done with our dashboard! In the next chapter, we'll make it responsive.

Interview with Connor Rothschild

Rothschild is a data visualization engineer.

Can you tell us a little bit about your background and how you entered the field of data visualization?

In college, I actually majored in political science! It wasn't until my third year that I decided to try my hand at data visualization. Inspired by publications like *The Pudding* and the *New York Times*, I wanted to know how to make engaging visual stories. I had started making static charts using R and ggplot2 and adding them to reports for a thinktank housed at my university.

Eventually, I entered the interactive space by learning the tools of the web (HTML, CSS, JavaScript). I was first introduced to D3 when I read *Fullstack D3 and Data Visualization* by Amelia Wattenberger, and *Interactive Data Visualization for the Web* by Scott Murray.

After (painfully) teaching myself D3, I tried my hand at creating a few data-driven stories on the web, like "How Much Does Kid Cudi Hum?" [https://connorrothschild .github.io/cudi-hums/] and "The Bob Ross Virtual Art Gallery" [https://connorroth schild.github.io/bob-ross-art-gallery/]. Those projects ended up garnering some attention, the former winning the Pudding Cup in 2020, and the latter getting me a cease and desist from Bob Ross, Inc.! (Really . . . ask me over coffee sometime.)

After graduating college, I worked for a brief stint as a visual journalist at Axios, and in 2021, I cofounded Moksha Data Studio [https://mokshadata.studio/]. We work with nonprofits, newsrooms, and impact-driven companies to tell visually compelling stories on the web.

Do you use visualization tools other than D3? What place does D3 have in your current data visualization workflow?

Yes! I am a staunch advocate of using D3 in combination with a JavaScript framework. My tool of choice is Svelte. In this workflow, D3 plays the part of doing math, manipulating arrays, and scaling data, while Svelte plays the part of rendering items on the screen.

(continued)

You created a course with Newline called "Better Data Visualization with Svelte," which I enjoyed a ton. Can you tell us a little bit more about why you like combining those two technologies?

Thank you! As a self-taught developer, I found D3's selection syntax (`.enter`, `.exit`, `.join`, etc.) to be a bit intimidating. Other parts, like D3 scales and D3 array manipulation, were very intuitive and easy to debug. Svelte removes the need for more imperative document object model (DOM) manipulation and allows you to write your markup directly (using built-in tools like `{#each}` blocks, and inline data binding). In my view, we're able to get the best of both worlds, using D3 for math and data manipulation, and Svelte for handling the DOM.

Featured project: "In the Dark" (https://restofworld.org/2022/blackouts/)

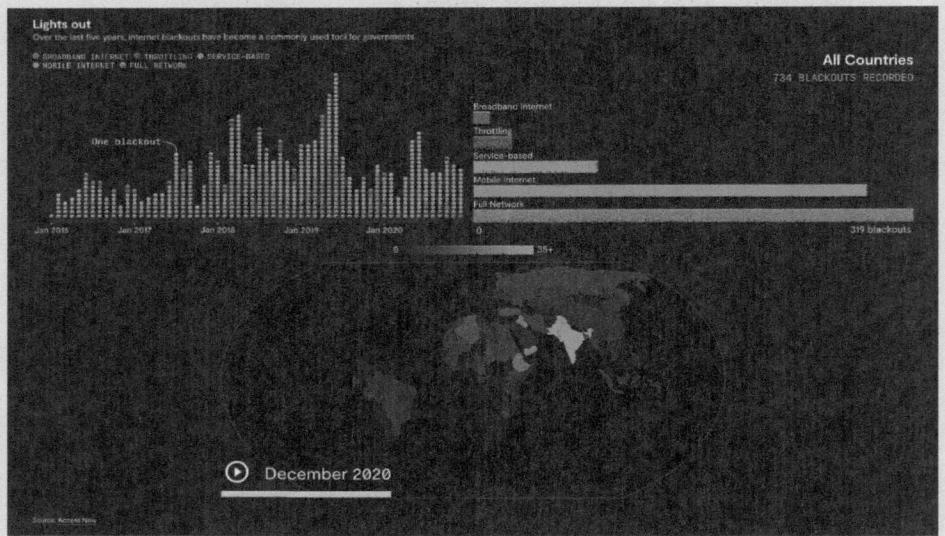

The project explores the number of internet blackouts between 2016 and 2020, by type and country.

Please describe your project "In the Dark," which you created for the Rest of World website (https://restofworld.org).

This was a really engaging project we worked on with Rest of World, telling the story of government-sponsored blackouts across the world. We were given a variety of datasets, covering the types and frequencies of blackouts by country over time.

Can you explain the process of creating this project?

We collaborated closely with the story author and the Rest of World designer to build a series of thematically aligned data visualizations for the story. We met weekly with these stakeholders to show progress on each chart and update them accordingly. The data was already provided, and we had creative liberty in design and development, choosing which chart types and interactions would be used.

You used a dot plot to visualize each blackout event individually. Did you create your own function to calculate the vertical position of each dot, or did you use D3's force layout with a strong constraint for the horizontal position?

We created linear and point scales for the x and y positions of each dot, and positioned them accordingly! We considered force layout, but given that this chart was static, for example, circles could be hovered or highlighted, but not moved, we opted for this rigid positioning approach.

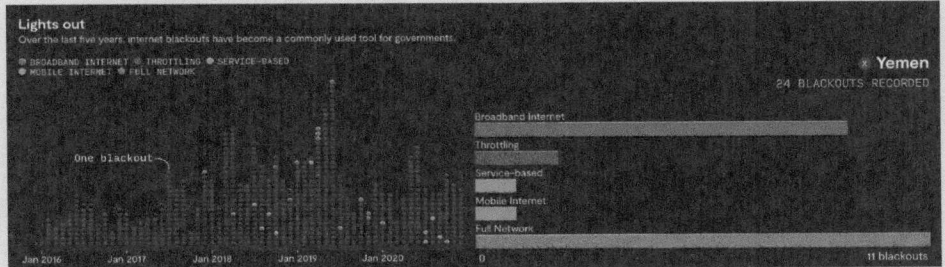

Thanks to cross-highlighting, we can explore the events that happened in a specific country.

In this project, the map acts as a filter, allowing the user to explore the internet blackouts that happened in specific countries. The flexibility to create such cross-highlighting effects is one of the things I love the most about D3. Is it one of the reasons you opted for D3 for this project?

Yes! As a note, the main interaction here was actually thanks to Svelte "stores," but the logic is similar. We wanted to maximize explorability beyond the first page load, which is why the chart offers filtering, highlighting, and forward animation via the Play button.

What types of projects are you hoping to work on in the future?

We've had the privilege of working with Rest of World on other projects since then, including a recent project showcasing the global tech downturn of 2022. Moving forward, my studio hopes to continue to work with impact-driven organizations to tell stories with data visualization.

Summary

- Modern frontend development projects are usually built with frameworks such as React, Angular, or Svelte. If you ship professional D3 projects, you'll likely need to integrate D3 into one of those frameworks.

- There are three approaches to using D3 with a framework: giving D3 access to a portion of the DOM, manipulating the DOM with the framework only and using D3 as a utility library, and a hybrid approach where we give D3 access to the DOM occasionally when there's a clear benefit.
- Frameworks allow us to manipulate portions of the DOM with references. Once a reference is set, we can use D3, as we have in the earlier chapters of this book.
- When following the second strategy and manipulating the DOM only with a framework, we can't use D3's data-binding pattern, axes generators, event listeners, and transitions, for example. But we still have access to a plethora of useful methods to build visualizations such as scales and shape generators.
- A case scenario for the hybrid approach is when we need to animate the d attribute of an element. D3's transition method is advantageous in this case and might not significantly affect the performance of a project.

Responsive visualizations

This chapter covers

- Understanding the main approaches to responsive design
- Dynamically adapting the size of text elements to fit smaller screens
- Using a responsive grid layout
- Adapting the density of information to different screen sizes
- Changing the orientation of a chart

In web design, deciding whether a website or a web application should be responsive is no longer a question. We take it for granted that users will access our projects from phones, tablets, and desktop screens. We have clear guidelines and best practices, and adapting standard digital features to different screen sizes is straightforward. But when it comes to digital data visualizations, the process is more challenging and often highly dependent on the type of visualization that we're working on and our target audience.

In this chapter, we'll transform the line chart from chapter 4 and the dashboard from chapter 8 to make them responsive. As we progress, we'll introduce key tips and ideas for making responsive digital visualizations with D3.

9.1   *What is responsive design?*

A responsive design is a design that adapts to the most common screen sizes and modalities: from desktop to tablet and mobile and from mouse to touch interactions. According to Statcounter (https://gs.statcounter.com/), in July 2023, mobile devices accounted for 56% of the overall internet traffic, desktops 42%, and tablets 2%, as visualized in figure 9.1. Therefore, adapting our data visualizations for mobile users significantly increases their potential reach. For example, visualizations from news articles or storytelling pieces shared on social media are highly likely to be consumed on mobile devices.

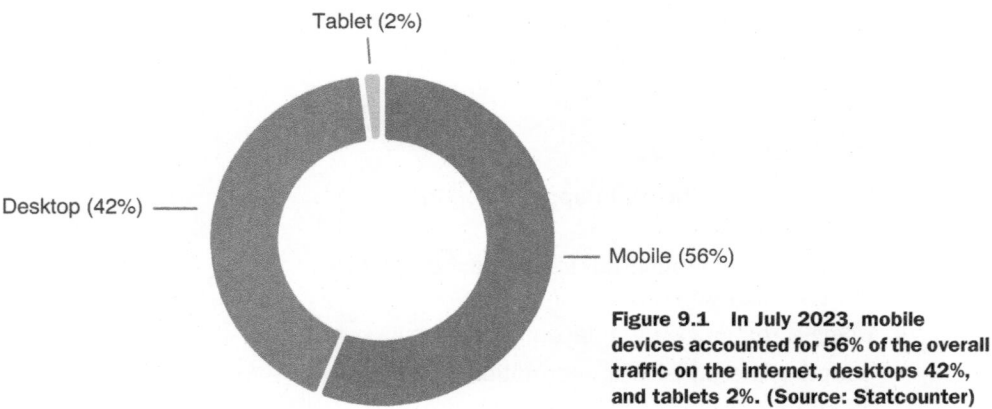

Figure 9.1   In July 2023, mobile devices accounted for 56% of the overall traffic on the internet, desktops 42%, and tablets 2%. (Source: Statcounter)

Although techniques for developing responsive websites are well established, responsive data visualizations are different. As Hoffswell, Wilmot, and Liu point out,

> *Techniques for responsive web design [...] are not directly transferable to visualization: webpages primarily employ text wrapping, image resizing, and document reflow to achieve responsiveness; these approaches offer little insight on visualization challenges such as data encoding, scale adjustment, or annotation placement.*[1]

Because the process isn't straightforward and can be time-consuming, it's crucial to plan additional time and budget to make our data visualizations responsive.

Two fundamental approaches to responsive web design still need to be considered when working with digital data visualizations: mobile-first and desktop-first. We'll look at both in the following subsections.

---

[1]   Jane Hoffswell, Wilmot Li, and Zhicheng Liu, "Techniques for Flexible Responsive Visualization Design," in *CHI*, 2020.

9.1.1 Mobile-first approach

With the mobile-first approach, we first create a design with a mobile layout in mind. This process often implies simpler visualizations adapted to the phones' portrait orientation. Once the mobile design is complete, we can expand it to larger screens by modifying the layout and adding supplementary information and features.

During the implementation phase, we code the mobile version first. We also ensure that we load only the styles and code that apply to the mobile version on phones, which can enhance performance. CSS media queries are of type `min-width`, allowing us to progressively add styles and features that only apply to larger screens:

```
@media (min-width: 600px) { ... }
```

9.1.2 Desktop-first approach

With the desktop-first approach, we start by creating a design with the desktop layout in mind. This design can be more intricate and include multiple details and interactions. We then adapt it to smaller screens, sometimes by simplifying the layout and focusing the story on the most critical information.

During the implementation phase, we code the desktop version first. CSS media queries are of type `max-width`, allowing us to progressively add styles that apply to smaller screens only:

```
@media (max-width: 600px) { ... }
```

9.2 A responsive line chart

In this section, we'll revisit the temperature line chart built in chapter 4 and make it responsive. As we proceed, we'll introduce a few tips and ideas for making responsive charts. You can see the responsive layout in figure 9.2 and at http://mng.bz/5orB.

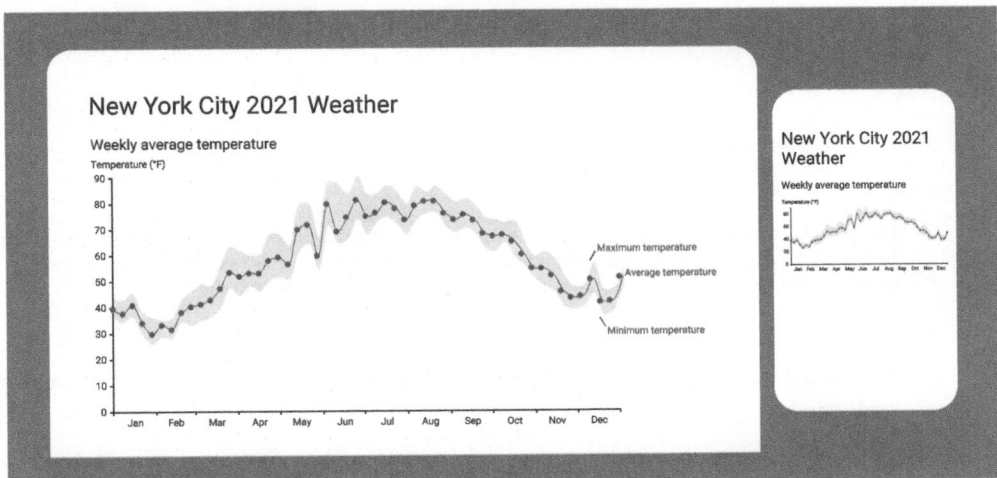

Figure 9.2 Responsive line chart

First, open the `9.2-Responsive_line_chart/start` folder in your code editor, and start your local web server. Refer to appendix A if you need a refresher on how to proceed.

NOTE   This chapter's code file can be found on the book's GitHub repository at http://mng.bz/Xqjv.

Open the project in your browser, and play with the window size. We suggest you open the inspector tool and dock it to the right side of your screen because it's easier to resize the inspector tool than the entire screen. If you use Chrome or Firefox, you can simulate mobile devices with Device Mode.

We already did a good job of making our chart responsive by setting the `viewBox` attribute of the SVG container and avoiding setting its width and height attributes. Refer to chapter 1, section 1.1.5, for an in-depth discussion about this strategy. But you may have noticed a few problems on smaller screens, as in figure 9.3. The first one is that the labels get way too small to be readable. This happens because SVG text acts like any other graphical element and scales down with the rest of the chart. The second problem is that the line chart doesn't have enough horizontal space to spread correctly. The dots and axis labels become very close to each other.

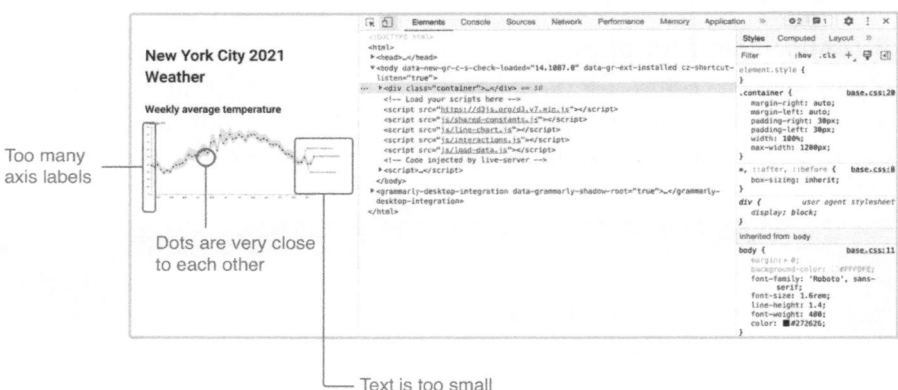

Figure 9.3   Although the visualization is responsive, thanks to the `viewBox` attribute applied to the SVG container, there are still a few problems to address: the text labels are too small, there are too many axis labels, and the dots are very close to each other.

As we adapt a visualization to make it responsive, we want to address two case scenarios:

1   *The size of the screen on which the project is initially loaded.* Whether we open the visualization on a phone, a tablet, or a desktop, it should be easy to read and adapted to the screen layout.

2   *The user might resize the screen.* On desktops, users might resize their browser window, while on phones and tablets, they might change the orientation of their device. The visualization should adapt dynamically to these changes with CSS media queries or by listening to the window `resize` event in Java Script.

9.2.1   *Adapting the size of the text labels*

Let's first address the size of the text labels. Currently, the axis labels have a size of 14 px, while the other labels have a size of 16 px. The SVG container of the line chart has a `viewBox` attribute of `0, 0, 1200, 500`. On desktops, where the SVG container can expand to its full size (1200 px × 500 px), the labels match their CSS `font-size` property and are easily readable. But as we reduce the window width, the whole SVG graphic scales down, including its `text` elements, making them tiny on phone screens.

To solve this problem, we need to apply a larger font size on smaller screens. To make that happen, we'll use a trick shared by Nadieh Bremer in her blog article "Techniques for Data Visualization on Both Mobile & Desktop" (www.visualcinnamon .com/2019/04/mobile-vs-desktop-dataviz/) and use a linear scale to calculate the font size based on the screen width.

Go to the `shared-constants.js` file, and declare the following `fontSizeScale`. Its domain extends from a screen width of 600 px to 1,000 px, while its range goes from a font size of 26 px to 16 px. Note how we also enable the `clamp()` property to keep D3 from extrapolating the values outside the range. If the screen has a width of 600 px or smaller, the font size will be 26 px. If it's 1,000 px or larger, the font size will be 16 px. In between, the font size varies:

```
const fontSizeScale = d3.scaleLinear()
  .domain([600, 1000])
  .range([26, 16])
  .clamp(true);
```

To apply this scale to our visualization, we need to know the screen's width. At the top of `shared-constants.js`, add the following snippet. It declares function `getWindow-Width()`, which returns the `innerWidth` property of the JavaScript `window` object. We then call this function and store its value in the constant `windowWidth`:

```
const getWindowWidth = () => {
  return window.innerWidth;
};
let windowWidth = getWindowWidth();
```

In `line-chart.js`, at the end of function `drawLineChart()`, we call the `font-SizeScale` to set the `font-size` style property of each text element contained in the `div` with an ID of `"line-chart"`:

```
d3.selectAll("#line-chart text")
  .style("font-size", `${fontSizeScale(windowWidth)}px`);
```

This strategy works fine but adapts the font size only once: on page load. If we resize the screen, nothing happens, and the text labels still end up with a suboptimal size. To solve this problem, let's go to the resize.js file and add an event listener for the JavaScript window resize event. When the resize event is detected, update the value of windowWidth, and call function resizeChart(), where we update the font size of each text element with fontSizeScale:

```
const resizeChart = () => {
  d3.selectAll("#line-chart text")
    .style("font-size", `${fontSizeScale(
      windowWidth)}px`);
};
```
> Adapt the font size of each text element within the chart using fontSizeScale.

```
window.addEventListener("resize", () => {
  windowWidth = getWindowWidth();
  resizeChart();
});
```
> Listen to the window resize event. When the event is detected, update the value of windowWidth, and call function resizeChart().

Finally, to avoid code duplicates, go back to function drawLineChart() in line-chart.js, and instead of updating the font-size properties directly, call resizeChart(). This way, the code inside resizeChart() will run both at page load and on screen resize.

In your browser, open the inspector tool, and select one of the text labels on the chart. Play with the size of the window. You should see the font size update dynamically!

9.2.2 *Adjusting the axes labels*

Because the labels are now larger on phone screens, you could argue that there are too many axis labels on the y-axis. Currently, there's a label every 10°F. Let's see how we can reduce it dynamically.

First, let's distinguish what we'll call our desktop layout and our mobile layout. In the shared-constants.js file, declare a new constant named isDesktopLayout. If the window width is greater than or equal to 700 px, set it to true; otherwise, set it to false:

```
let isDesktopLayout = windowWidth >= 700 ? true : false;
```

Then, in line-chart.js, specify the number of ticks on the y-axis based on the current layout. On desktop, we want 10 ticks; on mobile, we want 5 ticks:

```
leftAxis = d3.axisLeft(yScale)
  .ticks(isDesktopLayout ? 10 : 5);
```

Finally, to handle window resizing, we go back to resize.js. To update the number of ticks only if we cross the boundary of 700 px, where the layout changes from desktop to mobile, we add a condition inside resizeChart(). If the window width is greater than or equal to 700 px and isDesktopLayout is false, or if the window width is smaller than 700 px and isDesktopLayout is true, we update the value of isDesktopLayout.

We call the leftAxis generator, which we made available by declaring it inside shared-constant.js, and update its number of ticks. We then select the group that contains the y-axis elements (with a class name of "axis-y") and call leftAxis while applying a smooth transition:

```
const resizeChart = () => {

  ...

  if ((windowWidth >= 700 && !isDesktopLayout) ||
      (windowWidth < 700 && isDesktopLayout)) {

    isDesktopLayout = !isDesktopLayout;

    leftAxis
      .ticks(isDesktopLayout ? 10 : 5);
    d3.select(".axis-y")
      .transition()
        .call(leftAxis);
  }

};
```

If the window width is greater than or equal to 700 px and isDesktopLayout is false, or if the window width is smaller than 700 px and isDesktopLayout is true, enter the conditional statement.

Update the value of isDesktopLayout.

Update the number of ticks of the leftAxis.

Call the leftAxis generator to update the y-axis.

The number of ticks on your left axis should now update dynamically!

9.2.3 *Adopting a minimalistic approach*

Working with small screens often means adopting a minimalistic approach. We focus on the critical pieces of information and remove what is secondary to the understanding of our story.

An example is the annotations displayed on the right side of the visualization. They are helpful but not necessary to understand what the chart is about. In addition, they take up a lot of horizontal real estate, which we lack on phones (assuming a portrait orientation).

At the bottom of line-chart.js, we already call function appendAnnotations(), located in annotations.js. Let's call this function only if isDesktopLayout is true. This condition will ensure that these annotations don't appear on a phone's page load:

```
if (isDesktopLayout) {
  appendAnnotations();
}
```

In shared-constants.js, let's also set the right margin based on the current layout. If we're on a desktop layout, the right margin is 200 px, while it's 10 px for smaller screens:

```
const margin = {
  top: 35,
  right: isDesktopLayout ? 200 : 10,
  bottom: 35,
  left: 45
};
```

In annotations.js, we then add a new function named removeAnnotations(). In this function, D3 selects the group with a class name of ".annotations" and removes it from the DOM with method remove():

```
const removeAnnotations = () => {
  d3.select(".annotations").remove();
};
```

Finally, let's get back to `resize.js` inside function `resizeChart()`. Within the condition where `isDesktopLayout` is updated, we recalculate the right margin and the chart's inner width. Then, as shown in the next listing, we update the range of `xScale`, the bottom axis, and the chart's elements. We also add or remove the annotations.

Listing 9.1   Updating the curve and right margin (`resize.js`)

```
const resizeChart = () => {

  ...

  if ((windowWidth >= 700 && !isDesktopLayout) ||
      (windowWidth < 700 && isDesktopLayout)) {

    ...

    margin.right = isDesktopLayout ? 250 : 10;          Update the right margin
    innerWidth = width - margin.left - margin.right;     and the chart's inner width.

    xScale.range([0, innerWidth]);          ⟵──────      Update the range
                                                          of xScale.
    bottomAxis = d3.axisBottom(xScale)
      .tickFormat(d3.timeFormat("%b"));                  Update the bottom axis,
    d3.select(".axis-x")                                 and recalculate the
      .transition()                                      position of the axis labels.
        .call(bottomAxis);
    positionXaxisLabels();

    if (isDesktopLayout) {                   If on a desktop layout, call
      appendAnnotations();                   the function that appends
    } else {                                 annotations; otherwise,
      removeAnnotations();                    remove the annotations.
    }

    d3.select(".temperature-area")
      .transition()
        .attr("d", areaGenerator(data));

    d3.select(".temperature-curve")
      .transition()
        .attr("d", curveGenerator(data));
                                             Update the temperature area,
    d3.selectAll("circle")                   curve, and data points.
      .data(data)
      .join("circle")
      .transition()
        .attr("r", 5)
        .attr("cx", d => xScale(d.date))
        .attr("cy", d => yScale(d.avg_temp_F))
        .attr("fill", aubergine);

  }

};
```

Once completed, your line chart should be better adapted to mobile screens, as in figure 9.4. As you can tell, the changes we've performed are minor. We increased the size of labels, adjusted the number of axis ticks, and removed secondary information. But if you compare the initial project (http://mng.bz/46dw) with the final layout (http://mng.bz/wxBg) on an actual phone, you'll see a significant improvement of legibility. In the next section, we'll discuss a slightly more complex use case.

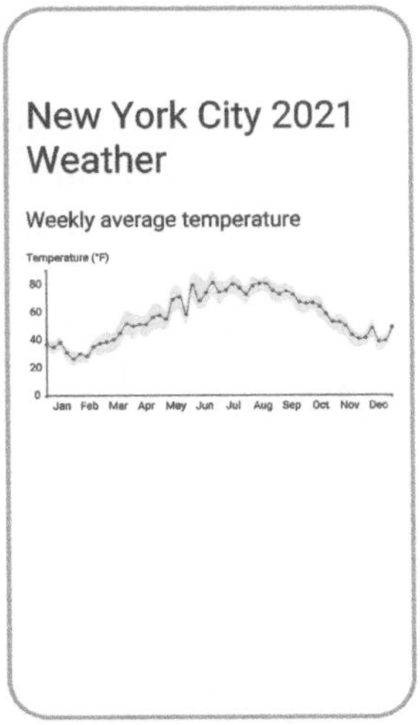

Figure 9.4   Completed responsive line chart

9.3   *A responsive dashboard*

In chapter 8, we created a dashboard of the top Java-Script frameworks and built it with React. In this section, we'll make this dashboard responsive, as shown in figure 9.5, while introducing additional considerations for responsive visualizations.

Because the dashboard is built in React, you'll need a basic knowledge of this framework to follow along with the instructions. You should know how to build components, pass props to children and parent components, manage a component's state, and use React hooks. But if you're unfamiliar with React or don't want to use it, you can keep reading this section because the tips we share for responsive visualization design apply to any digital project.

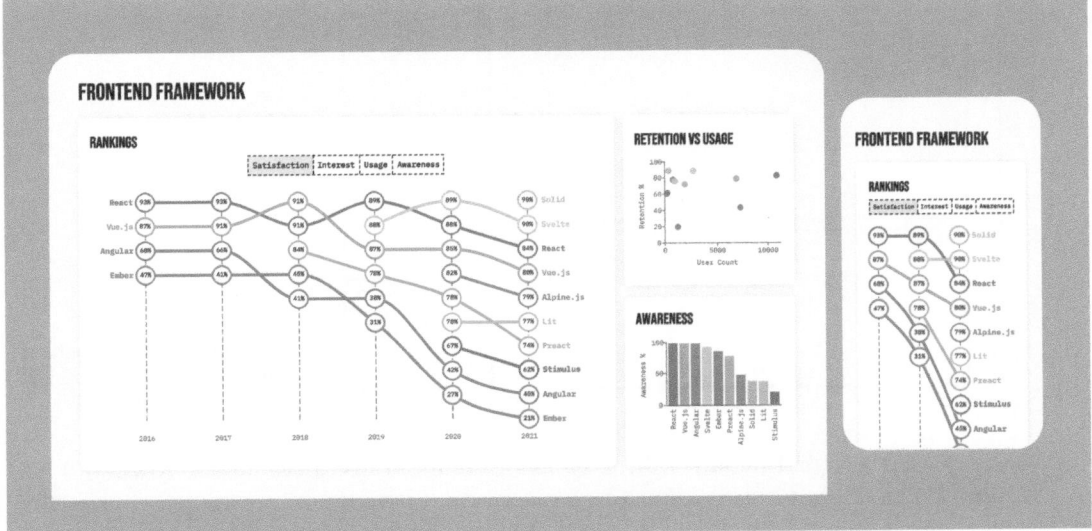

Figure 9.5   Responsive dashboard

9.3.1   *Using a responsive grid*

A responsive CSS grid is a great place to start when working with a more complex layout that may contain multiple visualizations or a mix of visualizations and text. For example, our dashboard uses a 12-column flexbox grid inspired by Bootstrap's grid system. With the help of CSS media queries and a strategy for class names, we can generate three layouts for our dashboard: one for desktop, one for tablet, and one for mobile. In figure 9.6, each rectangle contains a visualization in this order: rankings visualization, scatterplot, and bar chart.

Desktop layout (large)

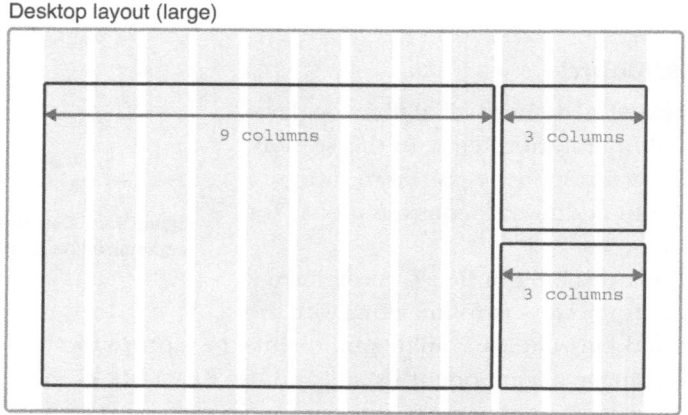

Tablet layout (medium)   Mobile layout (small)

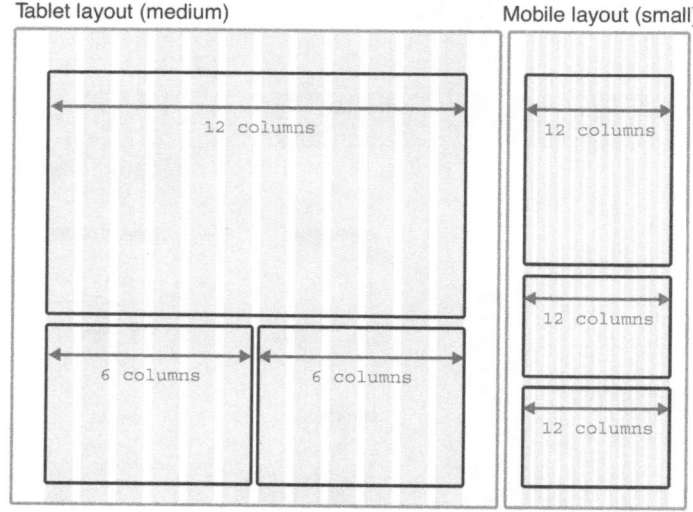

Figure 9.6   Using a responsive grid to position the visualizations based on the screen width

A CSS flexbox grid includes three types of components: a container, rows, and columns. The container is responsible for centering the content on the page, providing horizontal padding, and ensuring that the content doesn't get larger than the specified maximum width. If you open the code files for this section (the `start` folder in `9.3-Responsive_dashboard`) and go to the `grid.css` file, you'll find the following style declaration for the element with a class name of `container`. The `margin-right` and `margin-left` properties are set to `auto`, which centers the `div`. We also apply 20 px of padding on both sides and set the `max-width` property to 1,400 px:

```
.container {
  margin-right: auto;
  margin-left: auto;
  padding-right: 20px;
  padding-left: 20px;
  width: 100%;
  max-width: 1400px;
}
```

In figure 9.7, the container `div` corresponds to the green rectangle. As you can see, it encompasses all the content of the dashboard.

Desktop layout (large)

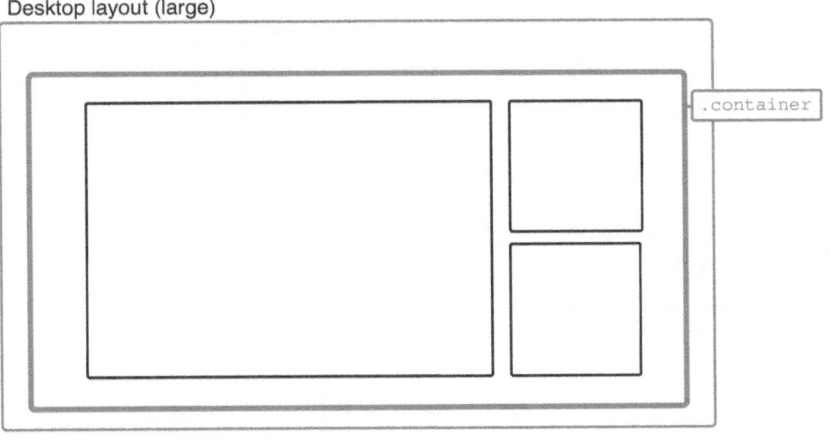

Tablet layout (medium)

Mobile layout (small)

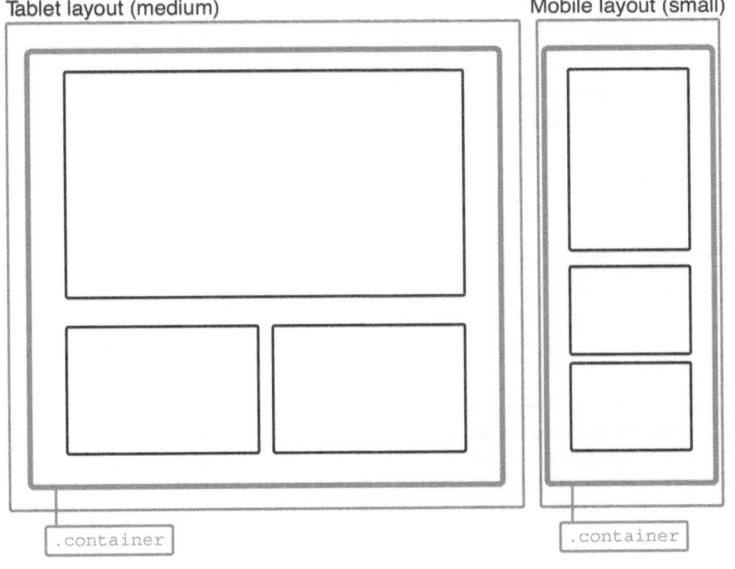

**Figure 9.7
The container is responsible for centering the content on the page, providing horizontal padding, and ensuring that the content doesn't get larger than the specified maximum width. It encompasses all the visualizations and text of the dashboard.**

As their name suggests, we use rows to enclose horizontal blocks of content. To generate our responsive layout, we need two `divs` with a class of `row`, shown as the yellow rectangles in figure 9.8. On the desktop layout, the outer row creates a block that contains the rankings visualization on the left and the stacked scatterplot and bar chart on the right. On the tablet layout, the inner row creates a second horizontal block

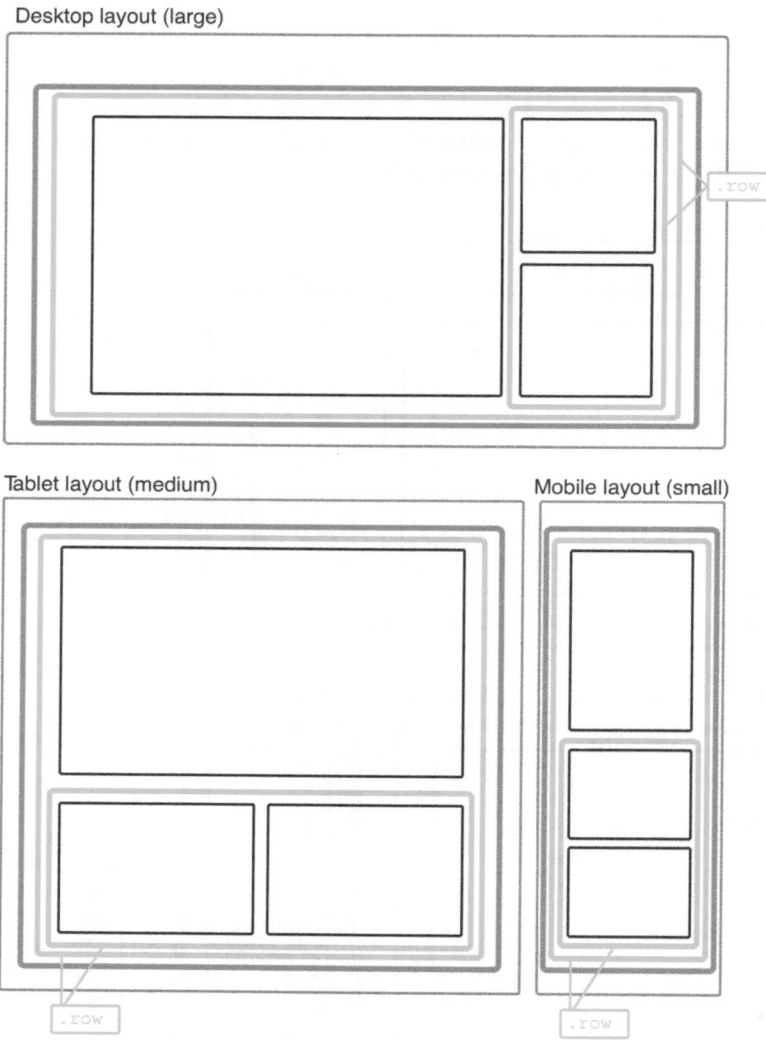

Figure 9.8   Rows enclose horizontal blocks of content. For our responsive layout, we need two rows: one for the desktop layout with the rankings chart on the left and the other charts on the right, and one for the tablet layout with a second horizontal block that includes the scatterplot and the bar chart.

where the scatterplot is displayed on the left and the bar chart on the right. Both rows remain present on all screen sizes.

In the following snippet, we give the rows a `display` property of `flex`, which will allow us to generate the desired layout in a moment. The `flex-wrap` ensures that children can wrap onto multiple lines, and the negative margins account for the gutter, or horizontal space between elements, that will be created with the columns:

```css
.row {
  display: flex;
  flex-wrap: wrap;
  margin-left: -10px;
  margin-right: -10px;
}
```

In this grid system, the word *column* has two meanings, which can be confusing. First, the *column elements* are actual `divs` in the markup with a class name starting with `col-`. Then there's the *12-column grid system* that we use as a design reference to distribute our content horizontally.

In figure 9.9, we see the column elements as blue rectangles. They dictate the width of their content and need to be the immediate children of a row element for the styles to work as expected.

We handle the columns layout with two sets of properties. The first one applies to all the elements with a class name starting with the term `"col-"`. Such elements have a left and right padding of 10 px, creating the gutter, and a width of 100% of their parent:

```css
[class^="col-"] {
  position: relative;
  width: 100%;
  min-height: 1px;
  padding-right: 10px;
  padding-left: 10px;
}
```

As mentioned previously, we base our design on a 12-column grid system. Using such a grid of 12 columns is very common because this number can easily be subdivided (by 12, 6, 4, 3, 2, and 1). We also have three screen sizes: small, medium, and large. To use a mobile-first approach, we first give the class names that apply to small screens, then to medium screens, and finally to large screens.

Let's take the scatterplot and bar chart visualizations as examples. On small screens (e.g., phones), we want them to take the entire width of the screen. We'll give them a class of `col-12` to spread them over all the 12 columns. On medium screens (e.g., tablets), we want them to take 50% of the screen's width, or 6 columns. Their class names will be `col-md-6`. It's like saying, "From the medium screen width, take up six columns." Finally, on large screens (e.g., desktop), we want them to take all the width available in their row parent (12 columns). We'll give them a class name of

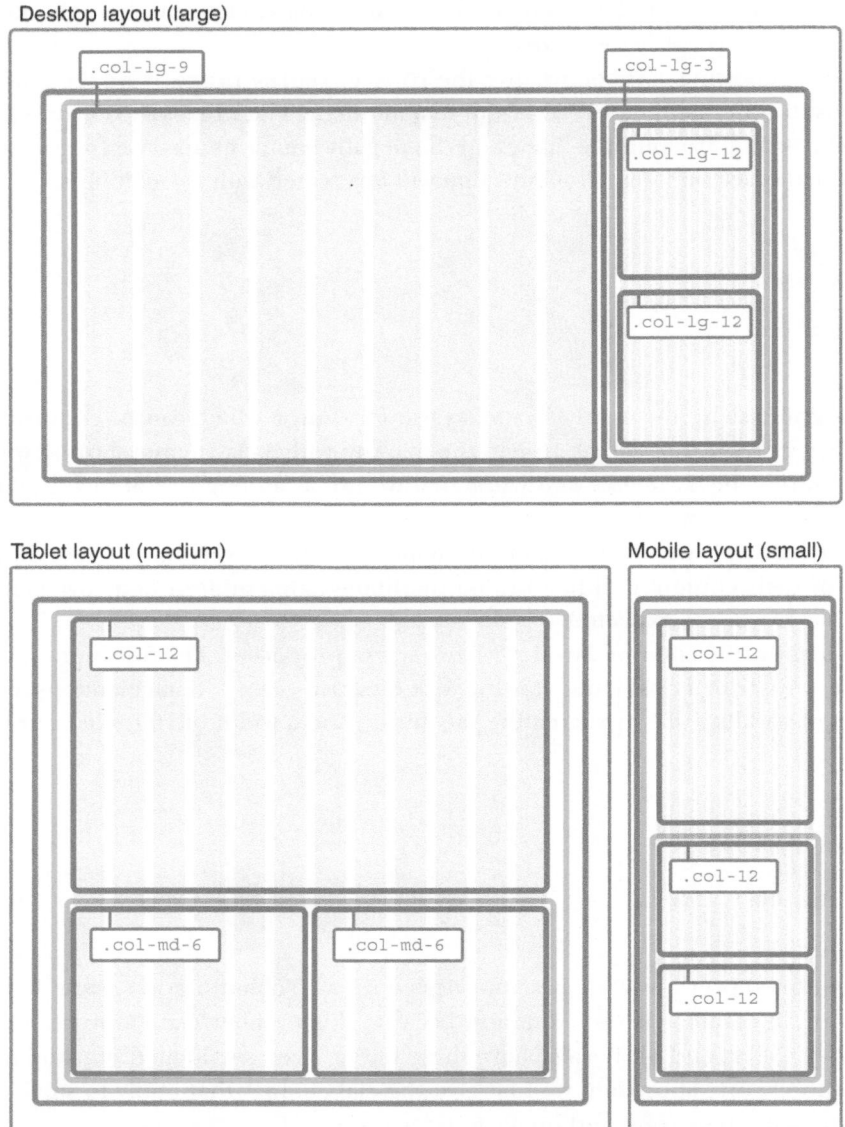

Figure 9.9   Column elements dictate the width of their content. They must be immediate children of a row element.

col-lg-12, which means "from large screens, take up 12 columns." Note that every row element creates a new grid layout of 12 columns. On the desktop layout, the outer row encompasses the rankings chart, which spreads over 9 columns, and the right part of the screen, which takes 3 columns. The right part of the screen contains a second row element, from which we start a new 12-column layout. The scatterplot and bar chart it contains both spread along these 12 columns.

In the following snippet, you can see how we handle these class names. For 12 columns, we give a `flex` shorthand property of `0 0 100%` (flex-grow flex-shrink flex-basis) and a `max-width` of `100%`. In the `flex` shorthand property, we apply a flex-grow and flex-shrink of `0` to ensure that the columns' desired width is respected while the flex-basis handles the actual width of the column.

We also handle the different screen sizes with CSS media queries: the medium screen has a `min-width` of `600px`, and the large screen has a `min-width` of `1100px`. These numbers will vary from project to project and are chosen to ensure that the dashboard looks good on any screen size:

```
.col-12 {
  flex: 0 0 100%;
  max-width: 100%;
}
.col-3 {
  flex: 0 0 25%;
  max-width: 25%;
}
@media (min-width: 600px) {
  .col-md-6 {
    flex: 0 0 50%;
    max-width: 50%;
  }
}
@media (min-width: 1100px) {
  .col-lg-12 {
    flex: 0 0 100%;
    max-width: 100%;
  }
}
```

If you're new to the CSS flex property, it might be a lot of information to assimilate. For more details, refer to the "A Complete Guide to Flexbox" article by Chris Coyier (http://mng.bz/qOMz).

NOTE We can also create a responsive grid with the CSS `grid` property.

Let's see this strategy in action for our dashboard. With the project open in your code editor, open your terminal, and run command `npm install`, followed by `npm run start`.

In your browser, you'll see that the desktop layout of 9 by 3 columns is already in place. But if you resize your screen, the same layout remains, which isn't ideal for phones and tablets. In the `App.js` file, we already have a `div` with a class name of `container`. Then, in `Charts.js`, we have two `div`s with a class name of `row`, as illustrated in figure 9.7. In listing 9.2, we only have to change the class names applied to the chart columns (the ones starting with `col-`).

We give the wrapper of the rankings chart the class names `col-12` and `col-lg-9`. These classes mean "On small screens, spread over 12 columns and from large screens, take up 9 columns." Similarly, for the `div` that wraps both the scatterplot and the bar chart, we give the classes `col-12` and `col-lg-3`. Finally, the individual wrappers of the scatterplot and the bar chart take the class names `col-12`, `col-md-6`, and `col-lg-12`. On small screens, they'll spread over 12 columns; on medium screens, they'll take up 6 columns; and on large screens, 12 columns, or the entire width available in their parent with a class of `row`.

Listing 9.2   Creating the responsive layout (`Charts.js`)

```
<Fragment>
  <h1>Front-end Frameworks</h1>
  <div className='row'>
    <div className='col-12 col-lg-9'>      ◁── On small screens, spread
      <Rankings ... />                            over 12 columns. On large
    </div>                                        screens, take up 9 columns.
    <div className='col-12 col-lg-3'>      ◁── On small screens, spread over 12 columns.
      <div className='row'>                       On large screens, take up 3 columns.
        <div className='col-12 col-md-6 col-lg-12'>   ◁──┐
          <ScatterplotReactControlled ... />               On small screens, spread
        </div>                                             over 12 columns. On
        <div className='col-12 col-md-6 col-lg-12'>   ◁──  medium screens, take
          <BarChart ... />                                 up 6 columns, and on
        </div>                                             large screens, take up
      </div>                                               12 columns.
    </div>
  </div>
  ...
</Fragment>
```

Because all the required styles are already declared in `grid.css`, if you resize your screen, the dashboard should adapt to the three layouts illustrated in figures 9.6 to 9.9.

9.3.2   *Adapting the density of information*

Now that we have handled the responsive grid, let's focus on the rankings chart. On small screens, you'll notice that the badges get tiny, and the labels are hard to read. A strategy for mobile design is to reduce the density of information by focusing on the essentials. For example, instead of showing the rankings for all the years between 2016 and 2021, we could focus only on 2016, 2019, and 2021. Our story would still work but would focus on the main shifts that occurred between those years.

First, we need to know the current layout based on the screen width. Let's say we want the rankings visualization to have a desktop layout on screens larger or equal to 600 px and a mobile layout on smaller screens. In listing 9.3, we declare a constant named `breakpoint` and set its value to `600`. Then we declare a function named `getLayout()` that returns `"desktop"` or `"mobile"` based on the `innerWidth` property of the JavaScript `window` object. Note that we've declared this constant and function outside the `Charts` component because they don't need any related props or variables. Then, inside the `Charts` component, we declare a state variable named `layout` and initialize its value by calling `getLayout()`.

Inside the anonymous function passed to a `useEffect` hook, we attach an event listener to the JavaScript `window` object. Every time the window is resized, we call a function named `handleWindowResize()` that gets the `innerWidth` of the window. If the width is greater than or equal to the breakpoint and the layout is mobile, or if the width is smaller than the breakpoint and the layout is desktop, we update the `layout` state variable by calling `getLayout()`.

Note that we also define a cleanup function in the return statement of the `useEffect` hook that removes the event listener when the component is unmounted. We also pass the layout state variable as a dependency.

Listing 9.3   Listening to the window resize event (`Charts.js`)

```
import { Fragment, useState, useEffect } from 'react';          ⬅  Import the useState
import * as d3 from 'd3';                                           and the useEffect hooks.

const breakPoint = 600;                                         Declare a constant named
const getLayout = () => {                                       breakpoint, and set its value to 600.
  const layout = window.innerWidth >= breakPoint                Declare a function named getLayout()
    ? "desktop" : "mobile";                                     that returns "desktop" if the window
  return layout;                                                innerWidth is greater than or equal
};                                                              to 600 and "mobile" if it's smaller.

const Charts = props => {
  const [layout, setLayout] = useState(getLayout());     ⬅
  const margin = {top: 30, right: 10, bottom: 50, left: 60};
                                                                Declare a state
                                                                variable named layout, and initialize its
  useEffect(() => {                                             value by calling the getLayout() function.

    const handleWindowResize = () => {
      const windowWidth = window.innerWidth;                    Inside a useEffect hook, attach
      if ((windowWidth >= breakPoint && layout ===              an event listener to the window
        "mobile") || (windowWidth < breakPoint &&               object. When the window is
        layout === "desktop")) {                                resized, call function
        setLayout(getLayout());                                 handleWindowResize() where
      }                                                         the window innerWidth is
    };                                                          compared to the current layout.
                                                                When needed, update the
    window.addEventListener('resize',                           layout variable.
      handleWindowResize);

    return () => {
      window.removeEventListener('resize',                      Add a cleanup function that
        handleWindowResize);                                    removes the event listener when
    };                                                          the component is unmounted.

  }, [layout]);      ⬅  Add the layout state variable as a
                        dependency of the useEffect hook.
```

```
    return (
      <Fragment>
        ...
      </Fragment>
    )
};
```

```
export default Charts;
```

In a moment, we'll create a second rankings component, named RankingsMobile, that we'll use to display the mobile version of the rankings visualization. In listing 9.4, if the layout state variable is equal to "desktop", we call the Rankings component; otherwise, we call RankingsMobile. Note that we've moved the rankingFilters array to the Charts component to make it available to both Rankings and RankingsMobile. We've also moved the functions that handle the filter selection to Charts.

Listing 9.4   Calling the Rankings (Charts.js)

```
...
const rankingFilters = [
  { id: "satisfaction", label: "Satisfaction" },          Declare the rankingFilters
  { id: "interest", label: "Interest" },                  array in Charts.js instead
  { id: "usage", label: "Usage" },                        of Rankings.js.
  { id: "awareness", label: "Awareness" },
];

const Charts = props => {
  ...

  const [activeFilter, setActiveFilter] =
    useState("satisfaction");
  const filterSelectionHandler = (id) => {                Handle the activeFilter
    if (activeFilter !== id) {                            state variable in Charts.js
      setActiveFilter(id);                                instead of Rankings.js.
    }
  };

  return (
    <Fragment>
      <h1>Front-end Frameworks</h1>
      <div className='row'>
        <div className='col-12 col-lg-9'>
          {layout === "desktop"
            ? <Rankings                                   If the layout state variable is equal
                margin={margin}                           to "desktop", display the Rankings
                data={props.data}                         component; otherwise, display
                colorScale={colorScale}                   RankingsMobile. Pass the margin,
                rankingFilters={rankingFilters}           data, colorScale, and filters-related
                activeFilter={activeFilter}               variables as props.
                onFilterSelection={
```

```
                              filterSelectionHandler}
                  />
              : <RankingsMobile
                    margin={margin}
                    data={props.data}
                    colorScale={colorScale}
                    rankingFilters={rankingFilters}
                    activeFilter={activeFilter}
                    onFilterSelection={
                        filterSelectionHandler}
                  />
          }
        </div>
        <div className='col-12 col-lg-3'>
            ...
        </div>
      </div>
      ...
    </Fragment>
  )
};
```

> If the layout state variable is equal to "desktop", display the Rankings component; otherwise, display RankingsMobile. Pass the margin, data, colorScale, and filters-related variables as props.

```
export default Charts;
```

Finally, in listing 9.5, we create the `RankingsMobile` component. It's very similar to the `Rankings` component created in the previous chapter, but with the following differences:

- The chart's width, height, right margin, and left margin are different.
- We create an array with the years we want to display on the visualization. We opt for the dataset's first, last, and median years. Showing only the first and last years would also be a good choice.
- We make a deep copy of the experience data received as props and save it in a constant named `mobileData`. Then we loop through `mobileData` and keep only the data included in the years array.
- We render the visualization exactly like we've been doing in `Rankings.js`, the only difference being that no framework labels are displayed to the left of the chart.

Listing 9.5 Creating the `RankingsMobile` component (`RankingsMobile.js`)

```
...
const RankingsMobile = props => {
  const width = 300;
  const height = 550;
  const marginRight = 120;
  const marginLeft = 30;
  const innerWidth = width - marginRight - marginLeft;
  const innerHeight = height - props.margin.top - props.margin.bottom;
```

> Change the chart's width, height, right margin, and left margin values.

```
const firstYear = props.data.years[0];
const lastYear = props.data.years[props.data.
  years.length - 1];
const middleYear = Math.round(d3.median([firstYear,
  lastYear]));
const years = [firstYear, middleYear, lastYear];
```

Create an array of the years we want to display on the chart: the first, last, and median years from the dataset.

```
const mobileData = JSON.parse(JSON.stringify(
  props.data.experience));
mobileData.forEach(framework => {
  framework.awareness = framework.awareness.
    filter(d =>
    ➥ years.includes(d.year));
  framework.interest = framework.interest.filter(d =>
    ➥ years.includes(d.year));
  framework.satisfaction = framework.satisfaction.
    filter(d =>
    ➥ years.includes(d.year));
  framework.usage = framework.usage.filter(d =>
  ➥ years.includes(d.year));
});
```

Make a deep copy of the experience data received as a prop, and save it in a constant named mobileData. Loop through mobileData, and keep only the data included in the years array.

```
const xScale = d3.scalePoint()
  .domain(years)
  .range([0, innerWidth]);
const yScale = d3.scalePoint()
  .domain(d3.range(1, props.data.ids.length + 1))
  .range([0, innerHeight]);

return (
  <Card>
    <h2>Rankings</h2>
    <RankingFilters
      filters={props.rankingFilters}
      activeFilter={props.activeFilter}
      onFilterSelection={props.onFilterSelection}
    />
    <ChartContainer
      width={width}
      height={height}
      margin={{ top: props.margin.top, right: marginRight, bottom:
      ➥    props.margin.bottom, left: marginLeft }}
    >
      ...
    </ChartContainer>
  </Card>
);
};

export default RankingsMobile;
```

Once completed, your mobile version of the rankings visualization should look like the one in figure 9.10.

Desktop and tablet layouts   Mobile layout

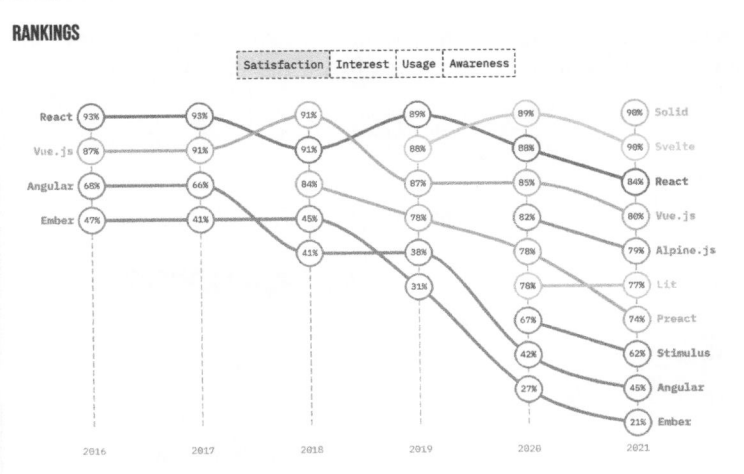
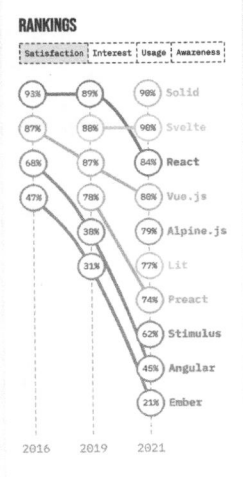

Figure 9.10 On the mobile layout of the rankings chart, we reduced the number of years we display to three. Reducing information density allows us to adapt to the screen's width while still showing the main trends. We also removed the framework labels on the left of the chart.

9.3.3 Changing the orientation of a chart

Some types of visualizations take up lots of horizontal space, such as line charts and streamgraphs. But phones are primarily used in portrait mode, where the height is much larger than the width. Changing the orientation of a chart can be a handy way to accommodate such layouts.

An example is the bar chart on our dashboard. On a desktop layout, the name of the frameworks are displayed along the x-axis, and the percentage of awareness is displayed on the y-axis. If we look at this chart on a mobile layout, the framework names are cramped together and hard to read.

> **Exercise: Change the orientation of the bar chart on a mobile layout**
>
> Change the orientation of the bar chart on a mobile layout by making the bars horizontal and displaying the framework names along the y-axis. Follow these steps for a little additional help:
>
> 1 Create a new component named `BarChartMobile` that will render the mobile layout of the bar chart.
> 2 In `Charts.js`, if the layout is `"desktop"`, call the `BarChart` component; otherwise, call `BarChartMobile`.
> 3 To render the names of the frameworks along the y-axis, you can create a new axis generator function for vertical band scales in `Axis.js`.

(continued)

4 Instead of displaying an axis for the awareness percentages, show the rounded values at the tip of each bar. Check figure 9.9 for an example.

Desktop and tablet layouts

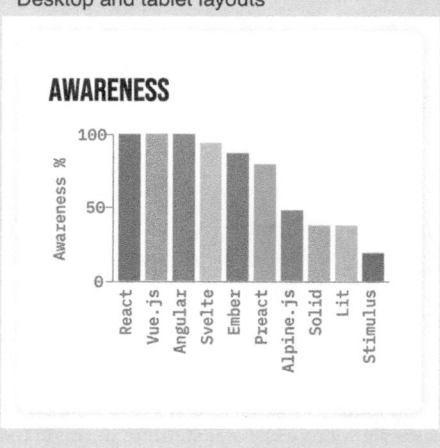

Mobile layout

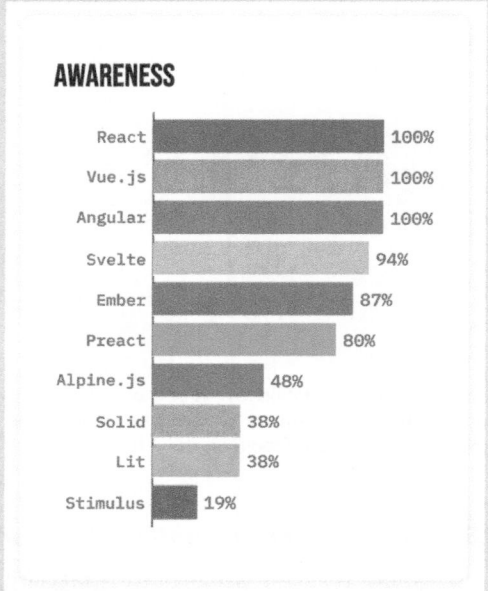

Changing the orientation of a chart can be a handy strategy for responsive visualizations. Here, the framework labels of our bar chart get cramped together on a mobile layout. We can take up more space by displaying them vertically instead of horizontally. We also show the awareness percentages as labels instead of on an axis, making the information readily available.

If you get stuck or want to compare your solution with ours, you'll find it in section D.9.1 of appendix D and folder `9.3-Responsive_dashboard/end` of this chapter's code files. But as usual, we encourage you to try to complete it on your own. Your solution might differ slightly from ours, and that's all right!

9.4 Additional tips

This chapter covered many concrete tips for transposing digital visualizations onto small screens. But this was far from an exhaustive discussion. Here are additional ideas to help you adapt your projects:

- Certain types of visualizations don't adapt well to mobile screens, for example, intricate radial visualizations. For such projects, it might be worth opting for a completely different type of chart on mobile layouts.
- Some projects, such as internal business intelligent (BI) dashboards, might not be accessed on phones at all. In that case, desktop design might be enough.

- Complex visualizations that contain hundreds, if not thousands, of elements can require a lot of resources, especially on mobile layouts. Unstable connectivity can also be a problem when loading large datasets on mobile layouts. If a visualization won't change over time and isn't interactive, it might make sense to serve it only as a static image on mobile layouts.
- When relevant, ensure that users can zoom and pan mobile visualizations. This is especially true for maps and network layouts.
- Make the primary information readily accessible. On mobile layouts, interacting with visualizations can be cumbersome, and tooltips don't work very well. Ensure all the information essential to your story is displayed directly on the screen or is easy to access.
- Fingers are way bigger than cursors! If you plan to make your project interactive on mobile layouts, ensure that the user can comfortably trigger touch events.
- For visualizations that take a lot of horizontal real estate and where we don't want to change the chart's orientation, we can consider allowing users to scroll horizontally. This approach allows the chart to be bigger while making it relatively easy to explore.

Here are resources to dig deeper into responsive visualizations:

- "Techniques for Data Visualization on Both Mobile & Desktop" by Nadieh Bremer, http://mng.bz/PZA5
- "Designing for Small Screens: Responsive Data Viz, Resizing, and Aspect Ratios" by Diana MacDonald, http://mng.bz/7dX4
- *Building Responsive Data Visualization for the Web* by Bill Hinderman (Wiley, 2015)

Interview with Mihály Minkó

Minkó is a data visualization expert.

Can you tell us a little bit about your background and how you entered the field of data visualization?

After my philosophy studies at the University of Szeged, I became interested in information graphics and data visualization. I started to work on a dashboard project for the director of finance of the university, which basically started my data visualization career. I continued with designing dashboards in different tools, but I also became interested in other tools, like Processing and D3.js. This was more than 10 years ago, and these are still my favorite. Currently I'm a researcher at the Data Storytelling Hub at Moholy-Nagy University of Art and Design, where we are researching different visualization-related topics and are also involved in project-based work for companies and public organizations.

Which data visualization tools do you use on a regular basis? Any favorites among those?

I use dashboard development tools mostly, and often D3.js, Processing, and Gephi. Lately, I've started to use Blender as a tool because it enables me to quickly prototype

(continued)

data physicalizations and add lights and textures. When I work alone, my favorite tool is Tableau because it enables me to quickly connect to a wide variety of data sources and to create design prototypes. When I work in a team, I mostly use D3.js because it can be customized very easily and can be embedded into different publishing systems or exported for offline media. D3.js also enables a great level of custom interactivity, which other tools can't provide.

Which role does D3.js play in the spectrum of data visualization tools you use? What place does it play in your workflow?

D3.js plays an important role in my workflow because it is the only tool that properly fits my needs when I have to deploy work to online media. Since I mainly work in collaboration with others, it enables us to do fast prototyping and finalization in a cooperative way. We can work together on different layers of a visualization and can see the result instantly. It is also the most versatile tool that I know of, enabling me to try out new types of visualizations quickly. I often use it as an intermediary step when I publish something to print media because I can export complex visualizations to a desktop publishing software and finalize it there.

Featured project: "The Metaverse of the Hungarian National Cooperation System" (https://atlo.team/ner-metaverzum/)

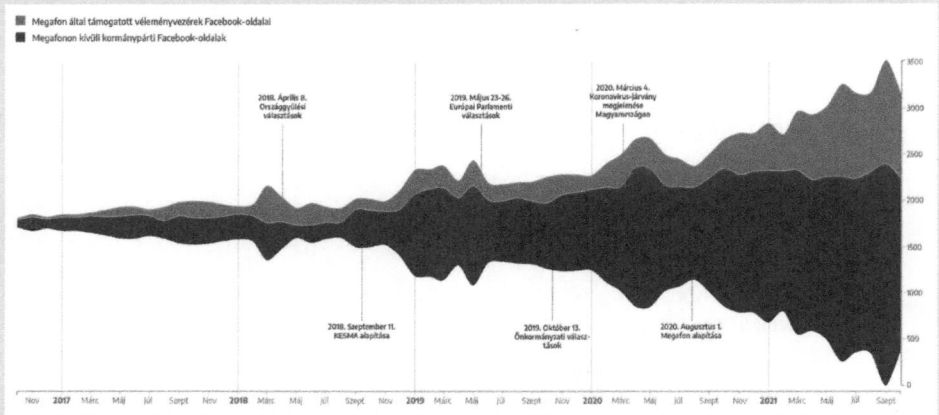

A streamgraph visualizing the number of Facebook pages of opinion leaders supported by Megafon (in red) and the number of non-Megafon pro-government Facebook pages (in black)

Please describe your project, "NER Metaverzum," which was published on atlo.team, a Hungarian site specializing in data journalism, and created in collaboration with Eszter Katona and Szilvi Német.

Facebook started to become popular in Hungary in 2010. It was the year the current governing party, FIDESZ (Hungarian Civic Alliance), won the parliamentary elections, and they have been in power ever since. However, their recognition of the importance of social media has been lagging until 2020. This is why we chose it as our research topic: who makes up the pro-government information ecosystem on the social network in a given period in 2021. As they understood the importance of social media, several dozen new pro-government Facebook pages were started. The government indirectly supports their influencers. A training program called Megafon has also been launched to spread pro-government messages. It turned out that the formation of Megafon has had a massive effect on the Hungarian social media universe. This possibly also helped FIDESZ to win the 2022 elections.

We used network analysis methods and visualizations to unfold the possible connections between the right-wing actors of this space. We measured the quantitative changes in the number of published posts by Megafon-related outlets. Based on this analysis, we identified the most important actors of this information space. We managed to collect their Facebook posts before they were part of Megafon, and it can be clearly seen that the number of posts increased significantly after they joined.

Can you explain the process of creating this project?

We used CrowdTangle to obtain the posts from the selected influencers. One important thing is that it is always good to define the scope of the data that one would like to get because handling it can get overwhelming without that in later steps. After getting them, we applied some data preprocessing and cleaning steps in order to have a standardized dataset. We decided to use a streamgraph visualization metaphor because we wanted to show the volume of these posts, and possibly this is the best representation for that. We used D3.js to visualize it, and surprisingly the shape of the data showed us a megaphone. It was very easy to actually implement the graph because there are hundreds of good examples out there to learn from. At the beginning, we agreed that we would like to create static data visualizations so that interaction doesn't distract the user. We also wanted to enable visitors to download and use these images as standalone pictures. That's why as a final step, we imported the SVG file from D3.js to Adobe Illustrator to add some little details to it, and also because this was showcased in a print media outlet *Átlátszó*, which means "transparent."

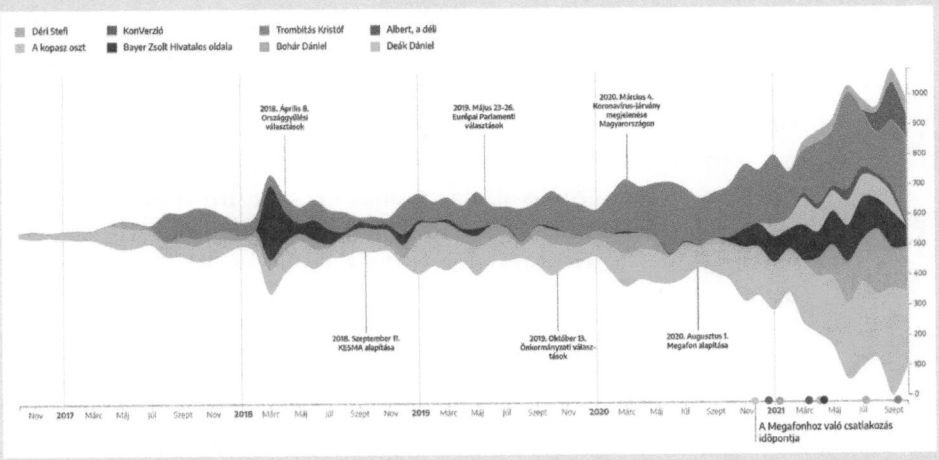

Number of posts on pro-government influencers' Facebook pages

(continued)

You developed the streamgraph with D3.js and then exported it to Adobe Illustrator to refine the visuals and add annotations. Do you often use such a hybrid approach in your work? What's the advantage?

Yes, I use this approach often. This gives me the possibility to control each step during the process and also to prepare the final visualization for printing. I use different systems or frameworks together quite often because in this way, I can combine the strengths of these frameworks. I sometimes also create physical objects, and for that, I use laser engraving or cutting, which requires a different type of preparation. I think if someone knows how these tools can work together, a whole new world opens up.

You teach data visualization. Which tips would you share with people who are taking their first steps in the field? Are there specific roadblocks you often witness your students struggling with?

My first tip would be—the one that I missed at the time, unfortunately—to draw. Sketch. Draw more and sketch more. It is a whole lot easier and can be a thousand times more creative if one uses pen (colors, maybe) and paper. It only requires one additional thing, though: being aware how one can convert their data into visual attributes on the paper. This can be a roadblock, but with patience and practice, the connection between those two will come. Implementation of drawings or sketches can be done in D3.js, which I think is the most supportive framework for standard and custom data visualizations.

Summary

- Today, a majority of internet content is consumed on phones. Hence, adapting our data visualizations for smaller screens is critical to reaching a larger audience.
- Although techniques for developing responsive websites are well established, approaches to responsive data visualizations aren't. The strategy depends on the type of chart you're working with and your audience.
- Depending on our priorities or preferences, we can create responsive designs in two ways: with a mobile-first or a desktop-first approach.
- There is no one-size-fits-all way to make responsive visualizations. In this chapter, we've used a linear scale to dynamically adapt the size of labels based on screen width. We've also reduced the number of ticks on an axis and removed secondary information.
- Responsive grids make responsive layouts easy to develop. Such layouts can include multiple visualizations or a mix of visualizations and texts.
- For charts that mainly take horizontal space, we can consider changing their orientation on phones (assuming the phone is used in portrait mode).

Accessible visualizations 10

This chapter covers

- Understanding how people with disabilities navigate web content
- Providing easy-to-read text and instructions
- Ensuring sufficient color contrast and using double-encoding
- Allowing proper navigation to screen reader users
- Accessing interactions with a keyboard

When designing and developing data visualizations, we tend to focus on the fun stuff, such as selecting a color palette and a font that match a specific look-and-feel or developing delightful, out-of-the-box interactions and animations. But many of us fail to give accessibility the consideration it deserves.

In the United States, 26% of adults live with a disability and 4.9% have a vision disability that requires screen readers (see Geoff Cudd, "57 Web Accessibiity Statistics," https://ddiy.co/web-accessibility-statistics). But in 2022, only 3% of the internet is accessible to people with disabilities (see David Moradi, "What's Next for Digital Accessibility," http://mng.bz/X10M).

In the field of data visualization, we face an additional challenge because visualizations are, by nature, highly visual, and the structure of our projects is less predictable than traditional websites. The good news is that we don't have to create an identical experience for people with disabilities, but rather an *equivalent* experience. This means giving them access to the main conclusions people without disabilities can draw from looking at and interacting with our projects. It can also mean providing easy access to the underlying data.

We often hear that making our projects accessible requires a lot of additional time, budget, and knowledge. But by paying attention to a few key considerations during the development phase, we can significantly improve accessibility at no extra cost. It's actually way easier and cheaper to consider accessibility as we create a project than to try to make a project accessible once it's already built. And the strategies used to improve accessibility often enhance a project in a way that is useful to everyone. You'll see how in this chapter!

10.1 *How people with disabilities access web content*

People with disabilities browse the web using adaptive strategies and assistive technologies. Adaptive strategies include increasing the size of the text, zooming into images, reducing the mouse speed, accessing content with the keyboard, and turning on video captions.

Assistive technologies imply screen readers, screen magnifiers, speech recognition software, and switch controls. *Screen readers* render web content as speech or braille. They are primarily used by people who are blind or have very limited vision. On the other hand, people with reduced vision tend to use *screen magnifiers*, which are devices or software that enlarge the information displayed on the screen. Such tools may also improve color contrast, increase the size of icons, or enhance the cursor. *Speech recognition software* can navigate a web page, activate links and buttons, or fill text fields with voice commands. This type of software is helpful to people who can't use a keyboard or mouse due to injuries, handicaps, chronic conditions, or even cognitive disabilities. Recently, they also became popular among people without disabilities with the introduction of Siri and Google Assistant. Finally, *switch controls* look like one or multiple big buttons that send a keystroke signal to a device to navigate the internet.

10.2 *Meeting the accessibility standards*

The Web Accessibility Initiative (WAI) of the World Wide Web Consortium (W3C) has developed accessibility guidelines called the Web Content Accessibility Guidelines (WCAG). These guidelines encourage us to create Perceivable, Operable, Understandable, and Robust projects. *Perceivable* means that nontext content, such as images and videos, has a text alternative. Colors offer enough contrast, and sufficient cues are given to the user when content is hoverable or is under focus. *Operable* projects ensure that all the content is navigable with a keyboard, that we provide enough time for the user to read and use our content, or that buttons are big enough to be targeted by people with limited motor skills. To make our content *understandable*, we ensure that the text content can be understood by most people, that the web features operate in predictable ways, and that our forms help users avoid and correct mistakes. Finally, we make our projects *robust* by ensuring that they can be interpreted by various user agents, such as browsers and assistive technologies. These were only a few examples, and we recommend you read the WCAG's Quick Reference for more details (www.w3.org/WAI/WCAG22/quickref/).

In this chapter, we'll use a list of criteria created by Chartability (https://chartability .fizz.studio/) as a reference to improve the accessibility of the cetacean scatterplot built in chapter 7 and shown in figure 10.1. Chartability is a set of testable questions for ensuring accessible data visualizations. Their list includes 50 tests, 14 of which are con-

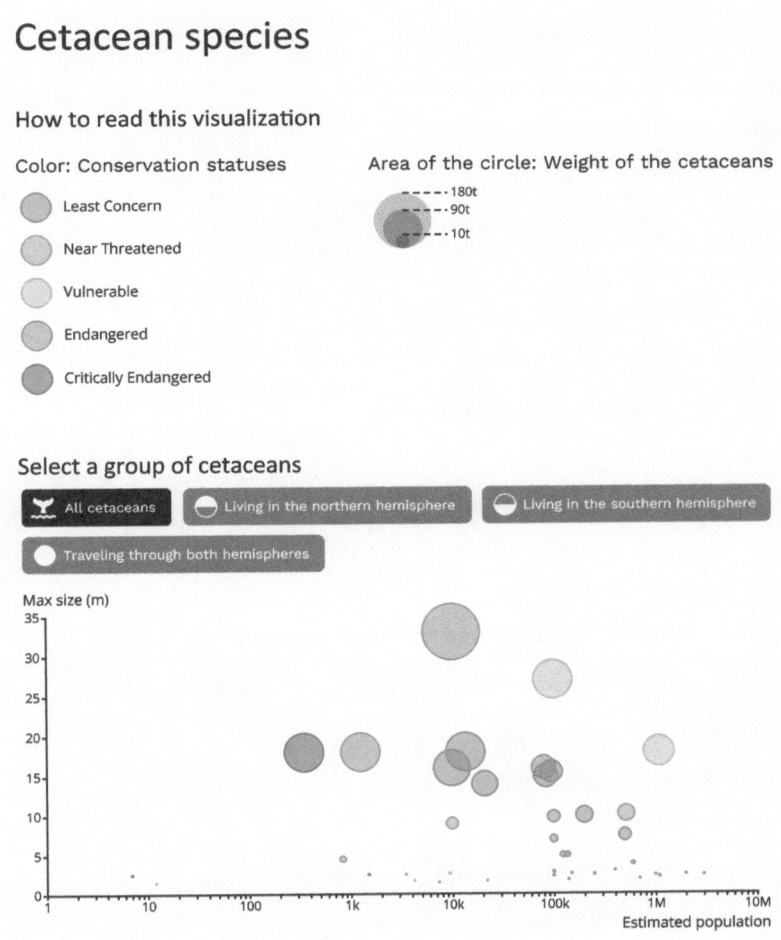

Figure 10.1   Scatterplot of the cetacean population, size, and weight built in chapter 7. In this chapter, we'll improve its accessibility.

sidered critical. In this chapter, we'll primarily focus on those 14 critical tests. As you get more comfortable with accessibility principles, we encourage you to keep building up your list of tests until you meet all of them. This subject deserves a book of its own, and we can't be exhaustive in one single chapter. But by paying attention to the critical tests suggested by Chartability, we can significantly improve the experience of users with disabilities.

Table 10.1 presents the list of tests we'll perform throughout this chapter. We broke down this list into five sections: textual information, visual information, screen reader access, interactions, and other considerations. You can find the completed project at http://mng.bz/maB0.

Table 10.1   Accessibility checklist for D3.js projects

Textual information
The chart's purpose and how to read, use, and interpret it are explained.
All text targets a reading grade level of 9 or lower.
Text size is at least 12 px, ideally larger.

Visual information
Colors provide sufficient contrast.
Information isn't communicated with color alone.
Data is presented at an appropriate density.

Screen readers access
The markup is semantic.
The SVG container provides additional context.
The visualized data is read by screen readers.
A data table is provided as an alternative.
Custom keyboard and touch controls don't override screen reader settings.

Interactions
Users can operate interactions with a keyboard.
Navigation and interaction are easy and not labor-intensive.
Interaction cues are provided.

Other considerations
The project offers an equivalent experience on all screen sizes.
Style changes made by the user aren't overridden.
Visuals don't present a risk of seizure.

10.2.1   *Textual information*

The data visualizations we develop rarely live alone on the page. We generally accompany them with text providing context and instructions. In this section, we'll discuss the type of information we should add to our projects to improve their accessibility, how a vast audience should be able to read the text easily, and how to format it correctly.

THE CHART'S PURPOSE AND HOW TO READ, USE, AND INTERPRET IT ARE EXPLAINED

The first principle on our accessibility list is to explain the chart's purpose and how to read, use, and interpret it. In the project's introduction section, shown in figure 10.2, we explain what the visualization is about, what the circles represent, and the meaning of their position, size, and color. There's also a legend for the circles' color and size.

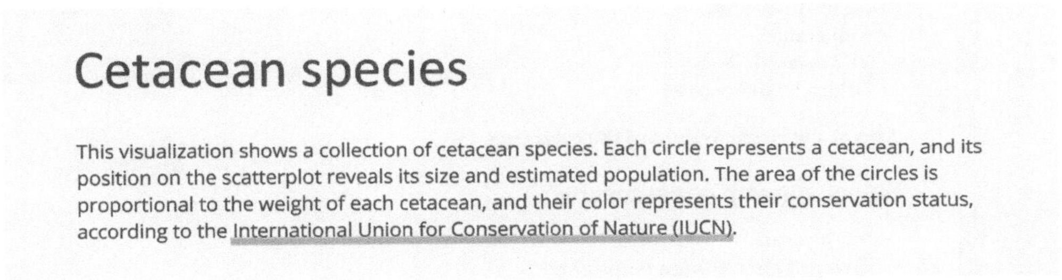

Cetacean species

This visualization shows a collection of cetacean species. Each circle represents a cetacean, and its position on the scatterplot reveals its size and estimated population. The area of the circles is proportional to the weight of each cetacean, and their color represents their conservation status, according to the International Union for Conservation of Nature (IUCN).

Figure 10.2   The project's introduction explains the chart's topic and how to read it.

The Select a Group of Cetaceans label provides instructions on how to use the buttons above the visualizations, and the axes have labels. So we already did a decent job at helping users interpret our project.

ALL TEXT TARGETS A READING GRADE LEVEL OF 9 OR LOWER

We must also ensure that all the text on our project has a reading grade level of 9 or lower. Some projects require complex terminology, but we should provide an easy-to-understand definition for such terms. To assess the reading level of our content, Chartability suggests using the Hemingway app (https://hemingwayapp.com/). In figure 10.3, you can see that we've entered the main chunks of text from the project into the app interface. The Hemingway app tells us that our overall content meets a reading grade level of 9, which is great. But it also points out that the introduction contains one sentence that is hard to read and one that is very hard to read. Actually, if we provide only the introduction to the app, the reading grade level climbs to 14.

To improve the readability of our text, let's simplify the introduction. The sentence "Each circle represents a cetacean, and its position on the scatterplot reveals its size and estimated population" is considered hard to read and can be broken down into two sentences. We proceed similarly with the second problematic sentence: "The

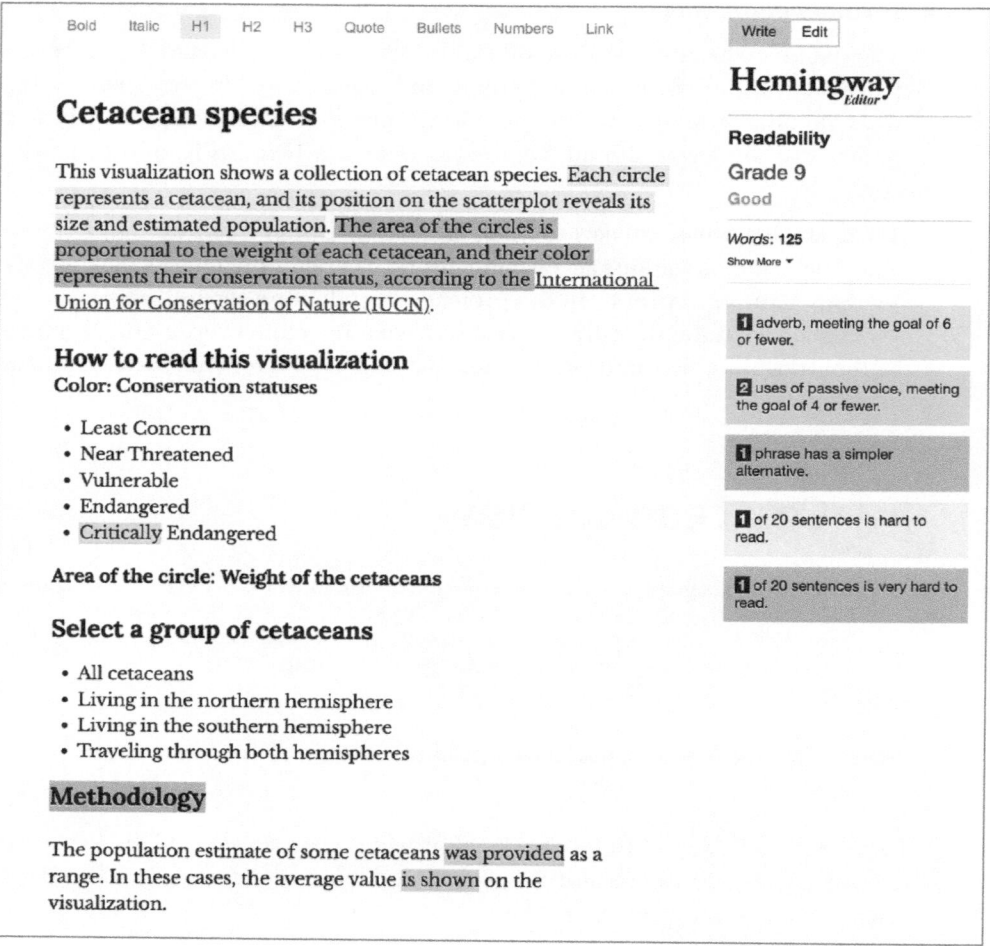

Figure 10.3   According to the Hemingway app, the texts of our project meet a reading level of grade 9, which is what we want. But it also points out that one sentence in the introduction is hard to read, and another is very hard to read. (https://hemingwayapp.com/)

area of the circles is proportional to the weight of each cetacean, and their color represents their conservation status, according to the International Union for Conservation of Nature (IUCN)." In figure 10.4, you'll observe that we moved the reference to IUCN to the Methodology section to simplify the text even more. The introduction is now straightforward to read and understand.

Per Heminway's suggestion, we also changed the subtitle Methodology to Method, which is a simpler alternative. The overall changes brought down the reading grade level to 8. Note that such adjustments will also depend on your audience and your organization's style. But it's good to remember that clarity always wins over literary style.

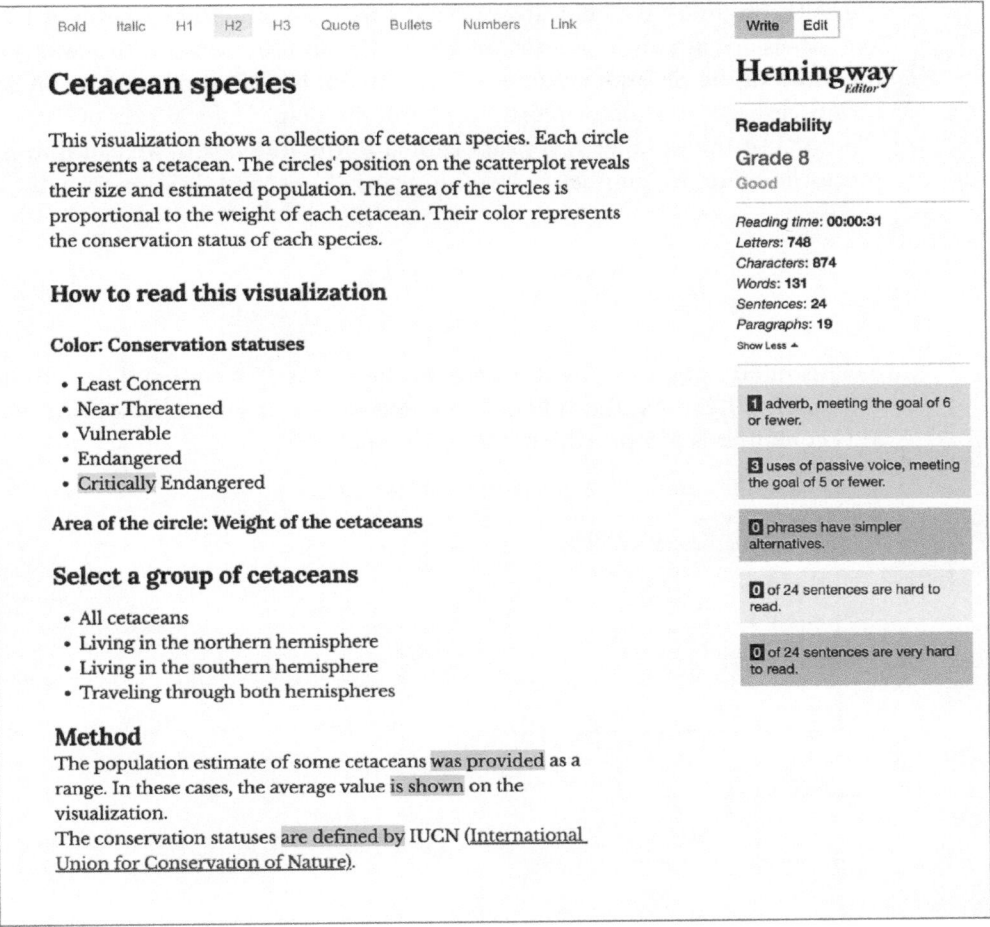

Figure 10.4   After a few minor modifications, our text has a reading grade level of 8.

In the `index.js` file, available in the `10.2.1-Textual_information/start` folder of this chapter's code files, we update the text accordingly. You can find the final text on the completed project at http://mng.bz/maB0.

TEXT SIZE IS AT LEAST 12 PX, IDEALLY LARGER

Chartability recommends that all text elements in our project should use a font size of at least 12 px. They also explain that 12 px should only apply to text that is secondary to the comprehension of the project and that most text should be larger. On the desktop version of the project, the main body of text uses a font size of 16 px, while the axis labels use 15 px. But if we reduce the screen size, all SVG elements become smaller, including the text.

To ensure that the axis labels are large enough on small screens, we'll need to calculate the actual font size to apply to the text because it's proportional to the width of the SVG container. We know that when the SVG container has a width of 1,200 px, the axis labels are displayed at a size of 15 px. On an iPhone SE, with a width of 375 px, the width of the SVG container is 315 px (we remove 30 px of padding on each side).

An easy way to scale proportions is with the mathematical rule of three. This rule states that if the number A is proportional to the number B, we can find X, which is proportional to the number C, by multiplying B by C and dividing with A:

$$A \sim B$$

$$C \sim X$$

$$X = B \times C \div A$$

As illustrated in figure 10.5, if the size of the text is 15 px when the width of the SVG container is 1,200 px, the rule of three tells us that it will be 4 px if the width of the SVG container is 315 px, which is way too small:

$$315 \times 15 \div 1{,}200 \approx 4$$

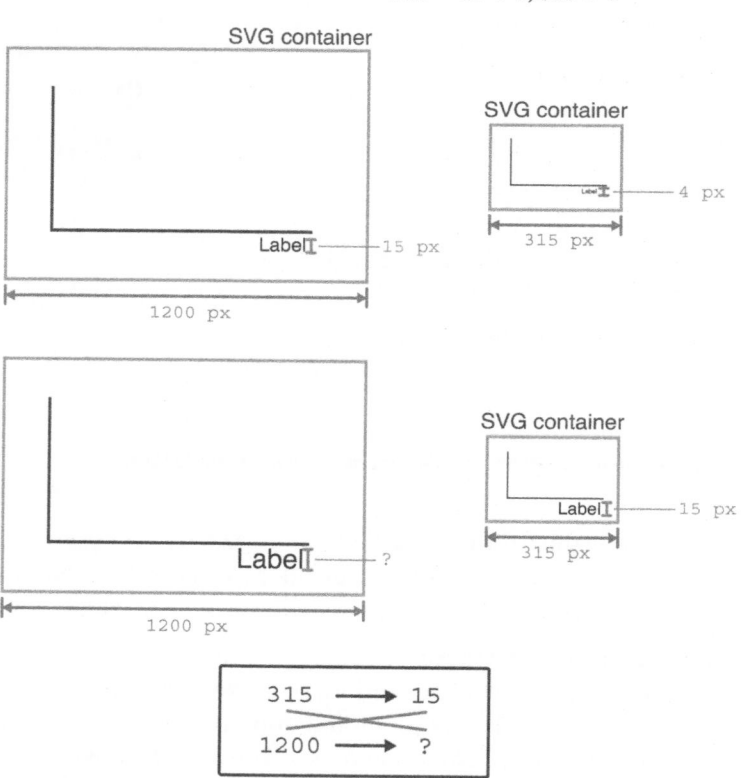

Figure 10.5   Because the `viewBox` attribute of the SVG container is set and its `width` and `height` attributes are not, all the graphical elements resize with the screen. If the font size of the axis label is set to 15 px, they will look much smaller on phone screens. We can use a rule of three to find the actual font size that we need to apply on phone screens.

If we want the labels to look like they are 15 px high on phones, their actual size, in relation to the SVG container, should be about 57 px:

$$15 \times 1,200 \div 315 \approx 57$$

As discussed in chapter 9, we can use a linear scale to adjust the text size dynamically based on the screen width. In `shared-constants.js`, we declare a linear scale and name it `fontSizeScale`. The domain is related to the width of the SVG container, which varies from 315 px on an iPhone SE to 1,200 px on desktop screens. We set the range based on the font size we want to apply on different screen widths. On a desktop layout, we want to stick with a font size of 15 px, whereas on phones, we'll increase it to 57 px, as calculated previously. We also enable the `clamp()` property to keep D3 from extrapolating the values outside the range:

```
const fontSizeScale = d3.scaleLinear()
  .domain([315, 1200])
  .range([57, 15])
  .clamp(true);
```

Then, in `resize.js`, we listen to the window `resize` event and call the function `resizeChart()`, as shown in listing 10.1. We get the `innerWidth` property of the `window` object and call the `fontSizeScale` to adjust the `font-size` style property of the axis ticks and labels. We also change the vertical position of the axis labels with the `y` attribute.

> ### Listing 10.1 Adjusting the font size of axis labels (`resize.js`)
>
> ```
> const resizeChart = () => {
>
>   windowWidth = window.innerWidth;        ⟵   Get the innerWidth property of the
>                                                window object, and save it in a
>                                                constant named windowWidth.
>
>   d3.selectAll(".tick text, .axis-label")      Call fontSizeScale to adjust
>     .style("font-size", `${fontSizeScale(      the font-size style property of
>       windowWidth)}px`);                       the axis ticks and labels.
>   d3.select(".axis-label-left")
>     .attr("y", margin.top - fontSizeScale(windowWidth));    Adjust the vertical
>   d3.select(".axis-label-bottom")                           position of the
>     .attr("y", height - margin.bottom +                     axis labels.
>       2.2*fontSizeScale(windowWidth));
>
> };
>
> window.addEventListener("resize", () => {      Listen to the window resize event,
>   resizeChart();                               and call the function resizeChart().
> });
> ```

To have enough room for the larger axis ticks and labels, we also increase the margins applied to the chart, as well as the total height:

```
const margin = {top: 110, right: 55, bottom: 130, left: 70};
const height = 800;
```

Once the change is completed, save your project, and resize the window of your browser; you'll see that the text size is now sufficient on all screen sizes. If you take a look at the completed project on your phone (http://mng.bz/maB0) or in figure 10.6, the text on the chart is sufficiently large to meet the accessibility standard.

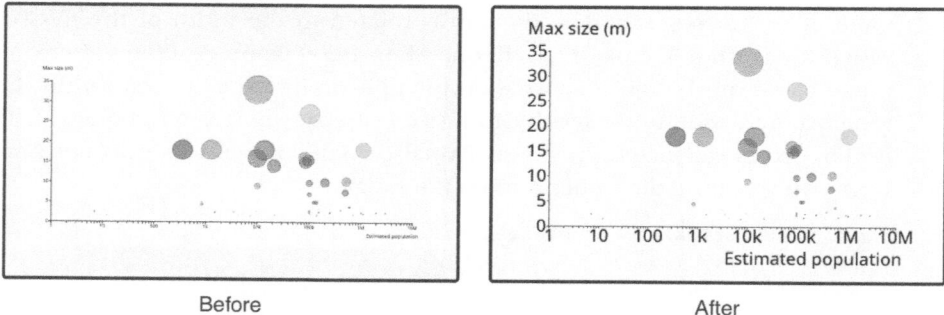

Before   After

Figure 10.6 Because the text acts like any other graphical element, the axis labels looked tiny on small screens. With the help of a linear scale, the text is dynamically resized based on the screen's width.

We've completed the tests related to the accessibility of the textual information:

- The chart's purpose and how to read, use, and interpret it are explained.
- All text targets are reading grade level of 9 or lower.
- Text size is at least 12 px, ideally larger.

10.2.2 *Visual information*

In this section, we'll take a look at how we carry visual information in our project. We'll ensure that colors provide sufficient contrast, that information isn't communicated with color alone, and that data is presented at an appropriate density.

COLORS PROVIDE SUFFICIENT CONTRAST

Per the WCAG standard, Chartability recommends that all geometric shapes and large text must have a contrast of at least 3:1 against the background, while regular text should have a contrast of at least 4.5:1. To measure the contrast of the text elements, we can use the WCAG Color contrast checker Chrome extension. For the geometric elements, such as the circles on our scatterplot and the legend for the circle areas, we need to enter their color manually into the WebAIM contrast checker (https://webaim.org/resources/contrastchecker/).

In figure 10.7, we see the results of these contrast verifications. The text on the page and the text on the active button have a contrast ratio of 12.91:1, which is well above the minimum of 4.5:1. The text displayed on the inactive buttons, on the other hand, has a contrast ratio of 3.84:1, which isn't sufficient. For the geometric shapes used in the visualization, we want a contrast ratio of at least 3:1 between the color of

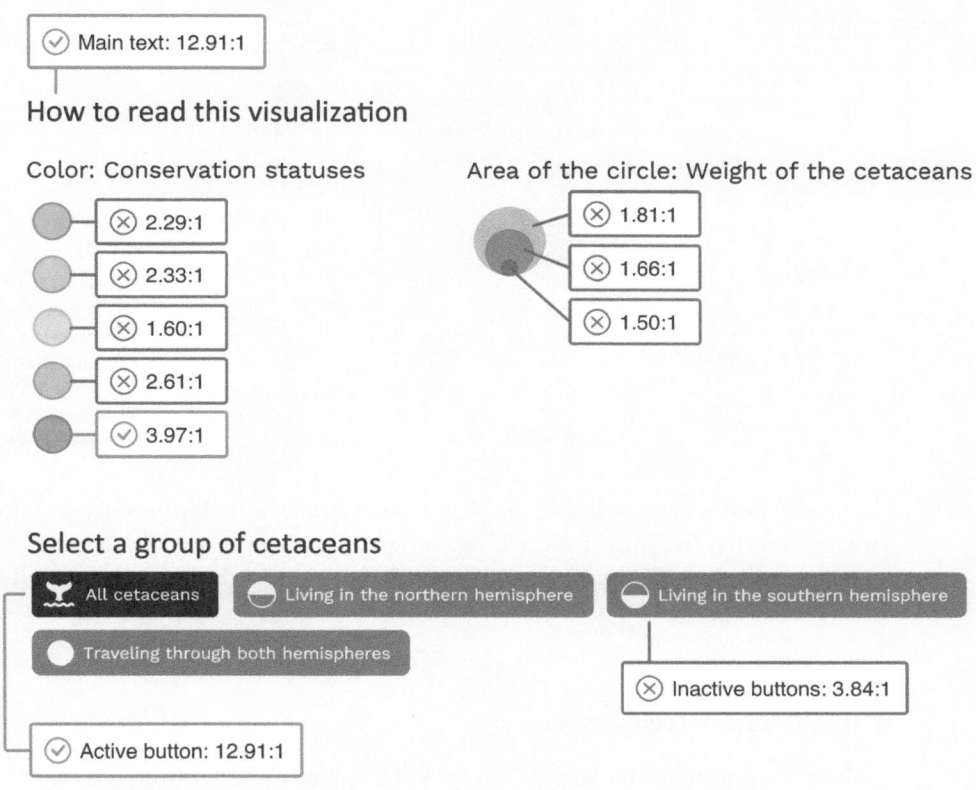

Figure 10.7   According to the WCAG Color contrast checker extension, the text and active button on our chart present sufficient contrast. But the contrast of the text on the inactive buttons isn't high enough to meet the standards. The colors selected to represent the conservation statuses and the legend for the area of the circle all fail to create a sufficient contrast with their background.

their border and the background. Unfortunately, most of the colors chosen to represent the conservation statuses fail the test, as do the geometric shapes used in the legend of the circles' areas.

To improve the contrast of the circles representing the conservation statuses, we'll start by changing the background color to pure white (#ffffff). Then the WebAIM contrast checker has a slider to darken the entered color. It dynamically calculates the new contrast ratio and lets us know once we reach a sufficient contrast. But darkening the colors can make them feel flat. Instead, we can search for accessible color palettes. In figure 10.8, we see a new categorical color palette inspired by the accessible colors suggested by the Data Visualization Standards of the US government (http://mng.bz/ 5laq). These colors offer a slightly higher contrast.

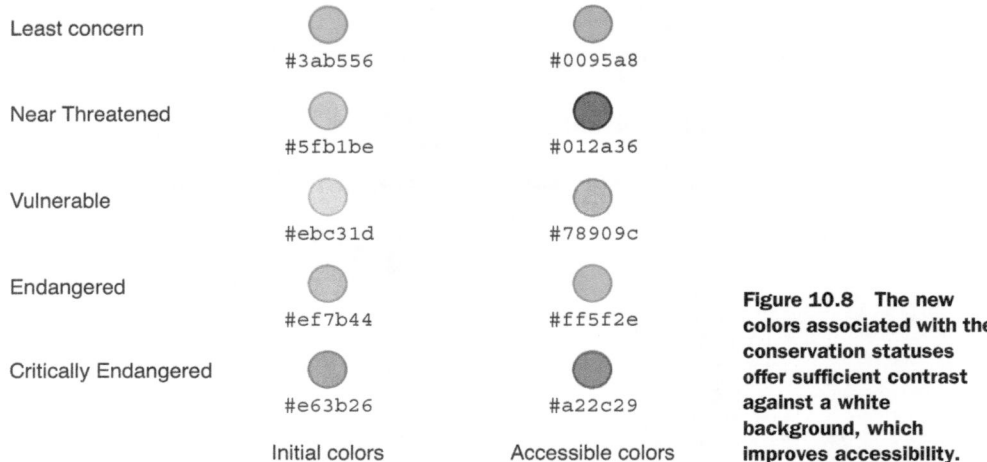

Figure 10.8   The new colors associated with the conservation statuses offer sufficient contrast against a white background, which improves accessibility.

We now have a categorical color palette that offers sufficient contrast. The new contrasts are listed in figure 10.9. We've also increased the opacity of the inactive buttons' backgrounds to 65% instead of 60% and have added a dark stroke around the circles

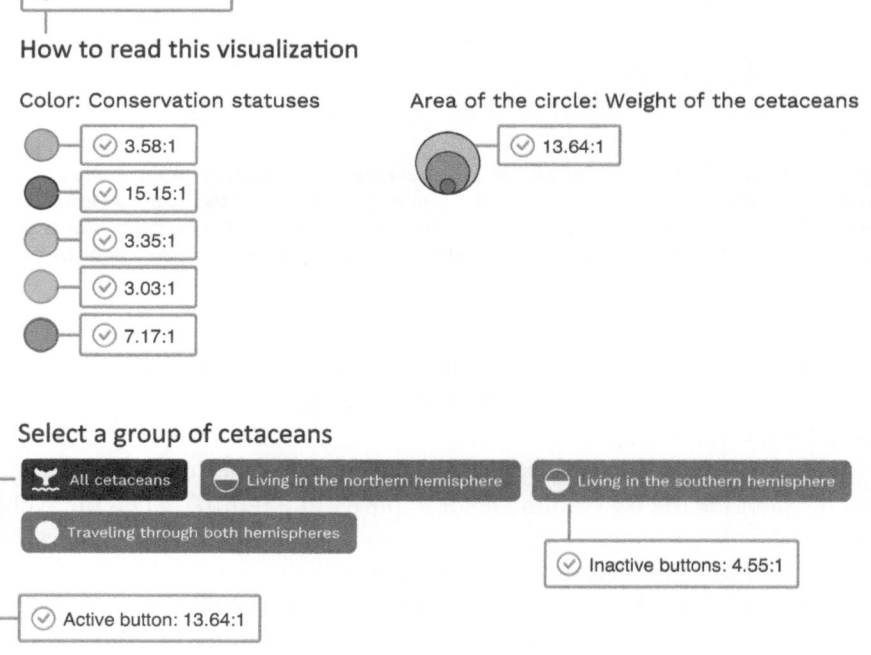

Figure 10.9   The new colors chosen for the conservation statuses palette offer sufficient contrast against a white background. We've also applied a dark stroke around the circles used in the cetaceans' weight legend and increased the inactive buttons' opacity.

in the cetaceans' weight legend. Adding a darker stroke is a helpful strategy when we can't or don't want to change the fill color of a shape.

INFORMATION ISN'T COMMUNICATED WITH COLOR ALONE

Although our colors now have sufficient contrast with the background, they might be difficult to differentiate for people with color blindness, who see colors differently than most of the population. The symptoms of color blindness can vary between difficulties seeing the difference between colors or between different shades of the same color. It can also affect one's capacity to see how bright colors are. In figure 10.10, we see our conservation status color palette from the perspective of people with different types of color blindness. We can reproduce this effect with the WCAG Color contrast checker Chrome extension.

To ensure that people with color blindness can differentiate the conservation statuses, we'll use a strategy called *double encoding*. With double encoding, we combine a categorical color palette with another way to convey information. For example, we could give a different shape to every conservation status or superpose a different pattern to each color. Because the size of the circles in the scatterplot already carries

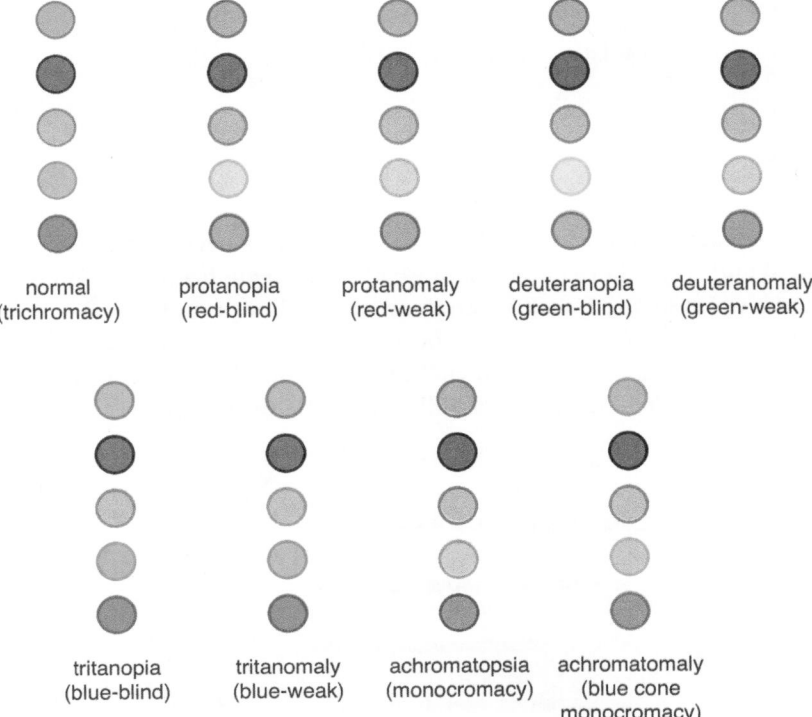

Figure 10.10 Colors are perceived differently by people with color blindness, often making the colors hard to differentiate. Ideally, we don't want to communicate information with color alone. This figure shows how people with different types of color blindness perceive the categorical palette of the conservation statuses.

information (the weight of the cetacean species), using different shapes would be challenging to apply. Instead, we'll opt for the second option: adding patterns on the scatterplot circles.

To create an SVG pattern, we first need to append a `<defs>` element to the SVG container. The `defs` element stores graphical objects that will be used later within the SVG. It can contain gradients, blurs, or, in our case, patterns. We append a `<pattern>` element inside the `defs` element and start creating the shapes that will constitute the pattern.

Let's make the first pattern horizontal lines. At the end of function `draw-Scatterplot()` inside `scatterplot.js`, we append a `defs` element to the SVG container. In the following snippet, we then append a pattern element inside `defs` and save it in a constant named `horizontalLinesPattern`. We give it an ID of `"pattern-horizontal-lines"`. Later, we'll use this ID to apply the pattern on the desired shape, so it must be unique. We give the pattern a width and a height of 4 px and set its `patternUnits` attribute to `userSpaceOnUse`, which means that geometry properties are relative to the SVG parent:

```
const defs = d3.select("#scatterplot svg")
  .append("defs");

const horizontalLinesPattern = defs
  .append("pattern")
    .attr("id", "pattern-horizontal-lines")
    .attr("width", 4)
    .attr("height", 4)
    .attr("patternUnits", "userSpaceOnUse");
```

The SVG shapes defined inside the `pattern` element become tiles repeated in the horizontal and vertical directions. So if we want to create horizontal lines, our tile can consist of a white square on which we draw an SVG line, as in figure 10.11.

In the following snippet, we start by appending a white `rect` element to the pattern. We set its width and height to 100% to cover the entire region. We then append a horizontal line element in the middle of the pattern container and set its stroke

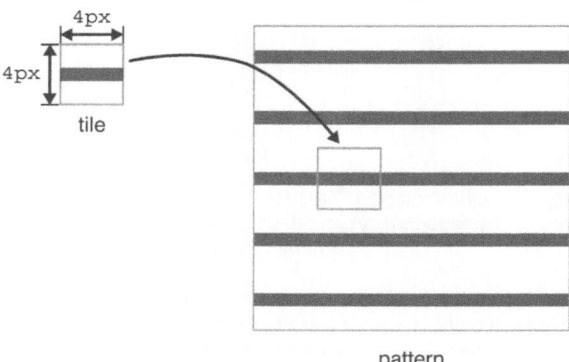

Figure 10.11 To create a pattern consisting of horizontal lines, we can make a tile with a white square and a horizontal SVG line. This tile will be repeated horizontally and vertically, creating the desired pattern.

attribute to the color associated with the Near Threatened (NT) species. To do so, we call the color scale created in chapter 7 and available in `scatterplot.js`:

```
horizontalLinesPattern
  .append("rect")
    .attr("x", 0)
    .attr("y", 0)
    .attr("width", "100%")
    .attr("height", "100%")
    .attr("fill", "#fff");
horizontalLinesPattern
  .append("line")
    .attr("x1", 0)
    .attr("y1", 2)
    .attr("x2", 4)
    .attr("y2", 2)
    .attr("stroke", colorScale("NT"));
```

To apply the desired pattern, we need to be able to select the scatterplot circles by conservation status. Let's go up in `scatterplot.js` and find the code where the circles are appended to the scatterplot with the data-binding pattern. We give two class names to each circle: `"cetacean"` and `"cetacean-"` followed by the conservation status in the datum attached to each element. The statuses are LC for Least Concern, NT for Near Threatened, VU for Vulnerable, EN for Endangered, and CE for Critically Endangered:

```
innerChart
  .selectAll(".cetacean")
  .data(data)
  .join("circle")
    .attr("class", d => `cetacean cetacean-${d.status}`)
    ...
```

Finally, we select all the circles with a class name of `"cetacean-NT"` and replace their fill attributes with `url(#pattern-horizontal-lines)`, which is the ID applied to the pattern container earlier:

```
d3.selectAll(".cetacean-NT")
  .attr("fill", "url(#pattern-horizontal-lines)");
```

Once completed, the circles of species with a Near Threatened conservation status will look like the corresponding one in figure 10.12.

| Least Concern | Near Threatened | Vulnerable | Endangered | Critically Endangered |

Figure 10.12   We'll apply a different pattern to each conservation status. Combining a color with a pattern is an example of the double encoding strategy.

The other patterns we'll create are the white dots associated with the Least Concern conservation status and the stars related to Endangered. In listing 10.2, we append a new pattern container to the `defs` element. We give this container an ID of "pattern-circles" and a width and height of 5 px. As we did previously, we set the `pattern-Units` attribute to `userSpaceOnUse`, which means that geometry properties are relative to the SVG parent. We also set the `patternTransform` attribute to a translation of 2 px and a rotation of 45 degrees to create a more interesting layout.

Then we append a `rect` element to the pattern container and set its `fill` attribute to the color associated with the Least Concern conservation status. Finally, we append a white circle with a radius of 1.5 px and position it in the middle of the tile.

Listing 10.2   Creating the pattern of white dots (`scatterplot.js`)

```
const circlesPattern = defs
  .append("pattern")
    .attr("id", "pattern-circles")
    .attr("width", 5)
    .attr("height", 5)
    .attr("patternUnits", "userSpaceOnUse")
    .attr("patternTransform", "translate(2)
      rotate(45)");
circlesPattern
  .append("rect")
    .attr("x", 0)
    .attr("y", 0)
    .attr("width", "100%")
    .attr("height", "100%")
    .attr("fill", colorScale("LC"));
circlesPattern
  .append("circle")
    .attr("cx", 2)
    .attr("cy", 2)
    .attr("r", 1.5)
    .attr("fill", "#fff");
```

Append a new pattern to the defs element. Set its width and height to 5 px. Apply a transformation with the patternTransform attribute.

Append a rect element to the pattern, and set its fill attribute to the color associated with the Least Concern conservation status.

Append a white circle with a radius of 1.5 px to the middle of the tile.

In listing 10.3, we proceed similarly for the star pattern associated with the Endangered conservation status. We first append a new pattern to the `defs` element and give it a width and height of 10 px. We apply a translation of 2 px and a rotation of 45 degrees.

We then append a white rectangle into the pattern to serve as the background. Finally, we use an SVG polygon element to create the star. The polygon element is a closed shape made of straight lines. These lines connect at the coordinates defined in the `points` attribute. We set the `fill` attribute of the star to the orange color associated with endangered species.

Listing 10.3 Creating the pattern of orange stars (`scatterplot.js`)

```
const starPattern = defs
  .append("pattern")
    .attr("id", "pattern-stars")
    .attr("width", 10)
    .attr("height", 10)
    .attr("patternUnits", "userSpaceOnUse")
    .attr("patternTransform", "translate(2)
      rotate(45)");
starPattern
  .append("rect")
    .attr("x", 0)
    .attr("y", 0)
    .attr("width", "100%")
    .attr("height", "100%")
    .attr("fill", "#fff");
starPattern
  .append("polygon")
    .attr("points", "0,0 2,5 0,10 5,8 10,10
      8,5 10,0 5,2")
    .attr("fill", colorScale("EN"));
```

Append a new pattern to the defs element. Set its width and height to 10 px. Apply a transformation with the patternTransform attribute.

Append a white rect element to the pattern.

Append a polygon element whose points attribute creates the shape of a star. Set its fill attribute to the color associated with endangered species.

Exercise: Create SVG patterns

Now it's your turn! Create two new SVG patterns that will be associated with the Vulnerable and Critically Endangered conservation statuses. For vulnerable species, the pattern consists of vertical gray lines over a white background. For critically endangered species, draw white crosses over a red background. The crosses can be created with two lines or with a polygon. You can access the colors associated with each conservation status by calling `colorScale()` and passing the status abbreviation as a parameter (`"VU"` for vulnerable and `"CR"` for critically endangered).

Feel free to explore different patterns if you prefer! You can get inspired at https://pattern.monster/. You'll find the solution in section D.10.1 of appendix D and folder `10.2.2-Visual_information/end` of this chapter's code files. But as usual, we encourage you to try to complete it on your own. Your solution might differ slightly from ours, and that's all right!

Once all the SVG patterns are created, we simply have to apply them as the `fill` attribute of each circle in the scatterplot. In listing 10.4, we create function `getPattern()` that receives a status code and returns the associated pattern ID. Then, inside `drawScatterplot()`, we select all the elements with a class name of `"cetacean"` and set their fill attributes by calling `getPattern()` and passing the status from the data attached to each circle.

Listing 10.4 Applying the patterns (`scatterplot.js`)

```
const drawScatterplot = (data) => {

  ...

  d3.selectAll(".cetacean")
    .attr("fill", d => getPattern(d.status))

};
```

Select all the elements with a class name of "cetacean", and set their fill attributes by calling function getPattern() and passing the status from the data attached to each circle.

```
const getPattern = (status) => {
  switch(status) {
    case "LC":
      return "url(#pattern-circles)";
    case "NT":
      return "url(#pattern-horizontal-lines)";
    case "VU":
      return "url(#pattern-vertical-lines)";
    case "EN":
      return "url(#pattern-stars)";
    case "CR":
      return "url(#pattern-cross)";
  };
};
```

Declare a function that receives a status and returns the associated pattern ID.

When we click on the filters above the scatterplot, new circles are generated and enter the visualization. In the following snippet, we call `getPattern()` to set the `fill` attribute on the entering circles (in `interactions.js`):

```
innerChart
  .selectAll("circle")
  .data(updatedData, d => d.uid)
  .join(
    enter => enter
      .append("circle")
        ...
        .attr("fill", d => getPattern(d.status))
        ...
    )
```

In `legend.js`, we proceed similarly for the circles displayed in the conservation status legend:

```
statuses
  .append("svg")
    .attr("width", 32)
    .attr("height", 32)
  .append("circle")
    ...
    .attr("fill", d => getPattern(d.id))
    ...
```

Once the patterns are completed, your scatterplot should look like the one in figure 10.13 and in the completed project (http://mng.bz/maB0).

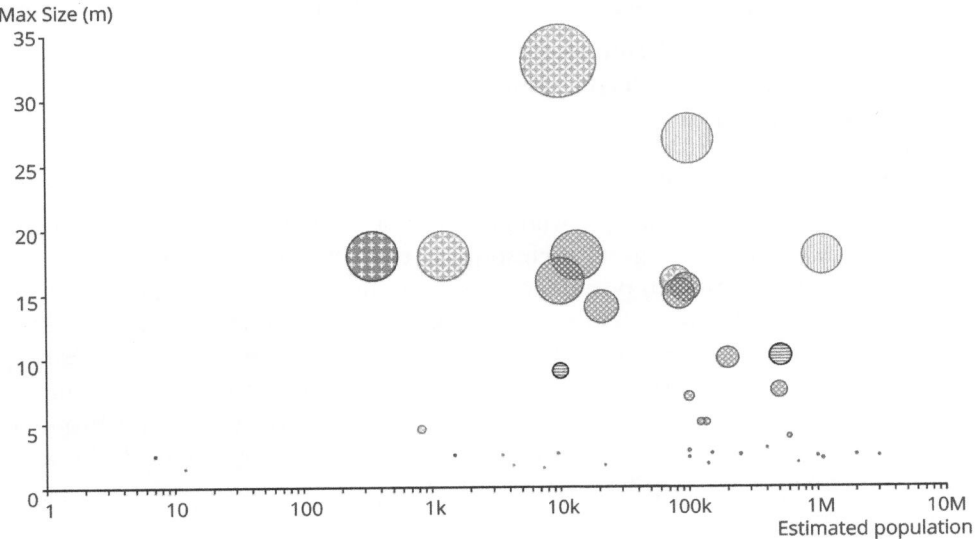

Figure 10.13   We've applied a different SVG pattern to the various conservation statuses represented on the scatterplot in addition to the categorical color palette. This is another example of the double encoding strategy, which helps users with color blindness differentiate the categories.

DATA IS PRESENTED AT AN APPROPRIATE DENSITY

There isn't much overlapping in our scatterplot, which allows us to say that the data is represented at an appropriate density. Chartability suggests that when too many data visualization elements compete for the same space, we must provide additional explanations for the clustering patterns or aggregate the chart to a level with fewer elements, as illustrated in figure 10.14.

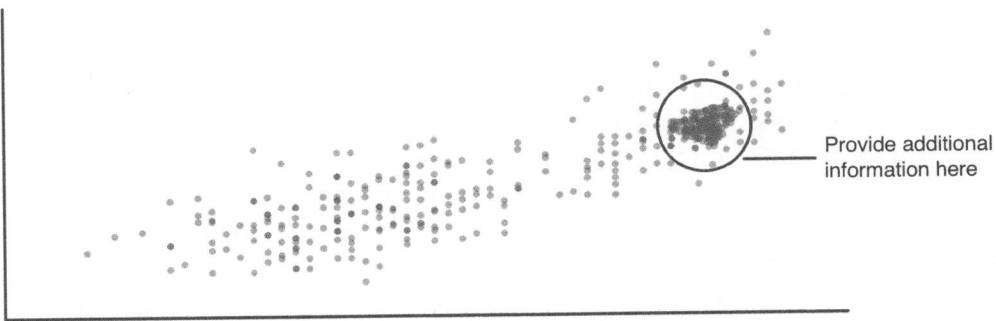

Figure 10.14   When too many elements compete for the same space on a data visualization, it's recommended to provide additional information that explains the pattern or to aggregate the chart to a level with fewer elements.

We've completed the tests related to the accessibility of the visual information:

- Colors provide sufficient contrast.
- Information isn't communicated with color alone.
- Data is presented at an appropriate density.

10.2.3 *Screen reader access*

Screen readers help people who are blind or have very limited vision access web content. As the name suggests, such software reads the content out loud to the users. For screen reader users to be able to access the information carried by our data visualizations, we need to pay attention to a few key aspects. However, it's important to remember that the goal isn't to provide an identical experience but an *equivalent* experience.

A few different software applications can be used as screen readers, including Narrator on PC and VoiceOver on Mac. In this chapter, we'll use a Chrome extension called ChromeVox because we can use it on any operating system. To install the extension, follow these steps:

1. Open Chrome.
2. Go to http://mng.bz/aMvX.
3. Click on Add to Chrome to install ChromeVox as an extension.
4. ChromeVox will be automatically turned on. To turn it off, go to Settings > Extensions, and uncheck Enabled.

When we land on a new tab in Chrome, the ChromeVox extension reads out loud the HTML `<title>` tag of the project, in our case, "Cetacean species | D3.js in Action." You can find it at the top of `index.html`, inside the `<head>` tag. Because this is the first thing people using screen readers hear when they land on a page, it should be descriptive enough to provide context.

There are different ways to navigate the page with ChromeVox. If we click on elements on the page, the screen reader will read them out loud. We can also use the Tab key to move to the next selectable item, such as a button or link. To explore all the content on the page, we can navigate with Control-Alt on Windows and Control-Cmd on Mac, followed by the up and down arrows.

After using a screen reader to navigate the cetaceans project, we notice that we don't tell the users when they navigate through graphical elements, such as the legend or the scatterplot. The screen reader can reach the numbers and labels of the axes, but they don't make sense at all if your eyes don't allow you to see the scatterplot. In addition, the information carried by the circles of the scatterplot is completely omitted. In this section, we'll aim to improve the user experience for screen readers.

THE MARKUP IS SEMANTIC

For screen readers to be able to interpret a web page, it's essential to ensure that our markup is structured semantically, meaning HTML elements are used for their intended purpose. Semantic HTML is sometimes called Plain Old Semantic HTML (POSH). Not only are proper semantic elements helpful to screen reader users, but they also improve search engine optimization (SEO)!

Here are a few key points to pay attention to:

- Use heading elements (`<h1>`, `<h2>`, `<h3>`, etc.) for titles and subtitles. A web page should have only one `<h1>` element. Screen readers notify users when a header is present and can bring up a list of all heading elements to create a navigable table of contents.
- Use semantic elements such as `<header>`, `<nav>`, `<main>`, `<article>`, `<section>`, and `<footer>` to structure your page layout. This way, the layout will make logical sense when read by the screen reader.
- Use semantic elements for UI control such as buttons (`<button>`), links (`<a>`), and forms (`<form>`). Give them meaningful labels. Avoid using `<div>` elements for UI control.
- Group collections of items into unordered (`<ul>`) or ordered (`<ol>`) lists. When meeting a list, screen readers notify the user in advance of how many items they contain, helping them make sense of the collection of items.

In our project, we correctly use heading elements, and the screen reader mentions those. But semantic layout elements such as `<header>`, `<main>`, `<section>`, and `<footer>` are missing. The `<header>` element is meant to be a container for the introductory section. In listing 10.5, we add a `<header>` element around the `<h1>` title and the introduction paragraph. Then we open a `<main>` element and move the legend and the scatterplot into it. The `<main>` element specifies the main content of the page. We break down this content into two sections: the legend and the visualization. We use `<section>` elements. Finally, we wrap the sources and methodology into a `<footer>` element.

Listing 10.5 Adding semantic layout elements (`index.html`)

```html
<body>
  <div class="container">
    <header>
      <h1>Cetacean species</h1>
      <div class="intro">...</div>
    </header>
    <main>
      <section>
        <div class="legend-container">
          ...
        </div>
      </section>
      <section>
        <div class="filters-container">
          ...
        </div>
        <div class="responsive-svg-container">
          <div id="scatterplot"></div>
        </div>
      </section>
    </main>
```

```
<footer>
  <div class="sources">
    ...
  </div>
  <div class="methodology">
    ...
  </div>
</footer>
</div>
...
</body>
```

In our project, we've grouped the conservation status legend items and the sources into unordered lists, which is good. But we should also do it for the buttons displayed above the chart because they are a distinct collection of items. Doing so will help screen reader users anticipate that a group of similar items is present.

In addition, to improve the accessibility of the buttons, we set their `type` attribute to `button`, and we set their `aria-pressed` attribute to `true` if the filter is active and `false` otherwise. This will let screen reader users know which of the buttons is currently selected.

Listing 10.6   Grouping filters (`interactions.js`)

```
const populateFilters = () => {

  const filters = d3.select("#filters")
    .append("ul")
    .selectAll(".filter")
    .data(cetaceanFilters)
    .join("li")
    .append("button")
      .attr("class", d => `filter filter-${d.id} ${d.isActive ?
      ➥ "active" : ""}`)
      .attr("type", "button")
      .attr("aria-pressed", d => d.isActive ? true : false);

  ...

};
```

Then, in `visualization.css`, we need to modify the styles applied to the filters slightly:

```
#filters ul {
  display: flex;
  flex-wrap: wrap;
  margin: 0;
  padding-left: 0;
  list-style: none;
}
```

Figure 10.15 shows how the semantic elements are distributed on the page.

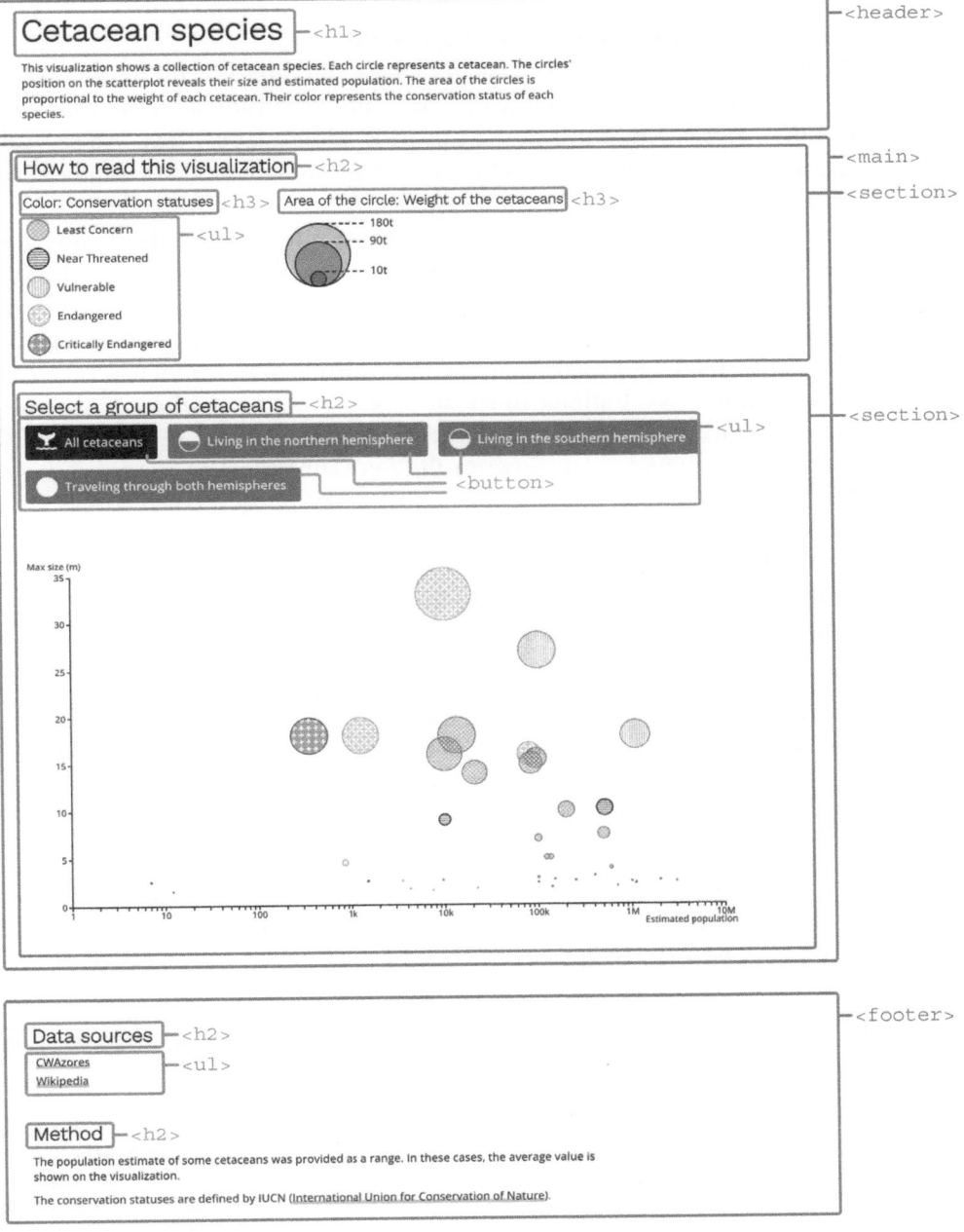

Figure 10.15   Proper semantic HTML elements help screen reader users understand the page's layout and are great for SEO.

If you access the project with the screen reader again, you'll notice that the semantic layout elements such as `<header>` and `<section>` are mentioned and that the collection of buttons is announced properly.

THE SVG CONTAINER PROVIDES ADDITIONAL CONTEXT

Because SVG graphics are similar to images, they are difficult to interpret for screen readers. Currently, the screen reader reads the text inside the scatterplot SVG, like the axis ticks and labels, but it doesn't provide additional context. We can solve this by adding a `<title>` and a `<desc>` tag to the SVG container. Those will be read out loud to the user.

In listing 10.7, we start by giving a role attribute of `img` to the SVG container. This role provides a semantic meaning and will let screen readers know how to interact with the SVG. The `img` role attribute also prevents the screen reader from reading the text labels inside the SVG container. Depending on the context, this might be preferable because reading the axis ticks one by one isn't always useful to screen reader users. But sometimes, you'll prefer to let the screen reader read those text elements, especially on charts that contain few elements.

We then append a `title` tag to the SVG container. The `<title>` tag contains a short title of the SVG graphic—here, "Visualization of a collection of cetacean species"—and it must be the first child of the SVG container. When the mouse is positioned over the SVG, it will also be used as a tooltip.

For the `desc` tag, we aim at providing information per what the chart is about, the main conclusions we can draw by looking at it, and its significant trends. Here's the description we'll use for our scatterplot:

> *This scatterplot provides information about 39 cetacean species. The biggest cetacean is the blue whale, with a length of 33 meters and a weight of 173 tons. The Pantropical Spotted dolphin has the largest population, with 3 million individuals. The Baiji dolphin, the North Atlantic Right whale, and the Atlantic Humpback dolphin are in danger of extinction.*

We give a unique ID attribute to both the `title` and the `desc` tags and pass these IDs as the `"aria-labelledby"` attribute of the SVG container. Those IDs provide the screen readers with recognizable, accessible names.

Listing 10.7   Making the SVG container accessible (`scatterplot.js`)

```
const svg = d3.select("#scatterplot")
  .append("svg")
    .attr("viewBox", `0, 0, ${width}, ${height}`)
    .attr("role", "img")                              ◁── Give a role attribute of
    .attr("aria-labelledby", "scatterplotTitle            img to the SVG container.
      scatterplotDescription");
```

Set the aria-labelledby attribute of the SVG container to the ID of the title tag, followed by the ID of the desc tag.

```
svg
  .append("title")
    .attr("id", "scatterplotTitle")
    .text("Visualization of a collection of
      cetacean species");
svg
  .append("desc")
    .attr("id", "scatterplotDescription")
    .text("...");
```

Append a title tag as the first child of the SVG container, and give it a unique ID. Set its text to a short title that tells what the graphic is about.

Append a desc tag to the SVG container, and give it a unique ID. Set its text to what the chart is about, the main conclusions we can draw by looking at it, and its significant trends.

We'll use a similar process for the legend of the project. In listing 10.8, we add a title of "Legend for the area of the circles" and a description of "Three circles representing a weight of 180, 90 and 10 tons." We also set the role attribute of the SVG container to img, and its "aria-labelledby" attribute to the unique IDs of the <title> and the <desc> tags.

Listing 10.8 Making an accessible legend (`legend.js`)

```
const legendArea = d3.select(".legend-weight")
  .append("svg")
    .attr("width", 180)
    .attr("height", 120)
    .attr("role", "img")
    .attr("aria-labelledby", "legendAreasTitle
      legendAreasDescription");
legendArea
  .append("title")
    .attr("id", "legendAreasTitle")
    .text("Legend for the area of the circles");
legendArea
  .append("desc")
    .attr("id", "legendAreasDescription")
    .text("Three circles representing a weight of
      180, 90 and 10 tons.");
const sizes = legendArea
  .append("g")
    .attr("transform", "translate(0, 10)");
```

Set the role and the aria-labelledby attributes of the SVG container.

Append a title tag as the first child of the SVG container. Give it a unique ID, and set its text.

Append a desc tag to the SVG container. Give it a unique ID, and set its text.

For the color legend of the conservation statuses, a description isn't necessary, and in the next listing, we give only a title to the SVG container of each status.

Listing 10.9 Making the color legend accessible (`legend.js`)

```
const legendConservationStatuses = statuses
  .append("svg")
    .attr("width", 32)
    .attr("height", 32)
    .attr("role", "img")
    .attr("aria-labelledby", d => `legendCS-${d.id}`);
```

Set the role and the aria-labelledby attributes of each SVG container.

```
legendConservationStatuses
  .append("title")
    .attr("id", d => `legendCS-${d.id}`)
    .text(d => `Color legend for the conservation
      status ${d.label}`);
legendConservationStatuses
  .append("circle")
    .attr("cx", 16)
    .attr("cy", 16)
    .attr("r", 15)
    ...
```

> Append a title tag as the first child of the SVG containers. Give it a unique ID, and set its text.

Once completed, navigate the project with the screen reader extension. Try closing your eyes to experience the navigation like someone who is blind or has very low vision.

THE VISUALIZED DATA IS READ BY SCREEN READERS

Screen reader users can now have a global idea of what our visualization is about and the main conclusion we can draw from looking at it. But what if they would also like to interpret the data attached to each circle in the scatterplot?

There are two main approaches to revealing visualized data to screen readers. The first one is to omit giving `role` and `aria-labelledby` attributes to the SVG container, which will expose the text element inside the SVG to screen readers. Because the text elements are read in the order in which they are appended to the DOM, we need to adjust this order so that it makes sense to screen reader users. If we want to add text elements that will be read by screen readers but will be invisible on the screen, we can set their x and y attributes so that they are visually positioned outside of the SVG container.

The second approach, which we'll use for this project, is to provide a more specific `desc` attribute by dynamically adding the desired data values. In listing 10.10, we declare a function named `generateDescription()`. We then declare an array and save it in a constant named `desc`. As the first item in this array, we push the description we wrote in the previous section. This will provide the most important information to the users right at the beginning. We then loop through our data, and for each cetacean species, we push a string consisting of the name of the cetacean and its population, size, weight, and conservation status. Finally, when setting the text of the SVG container's `desc` attribute, we call `generateDescription()`.

Listing 10.10 Exposing the underlying data (`scatterplot.js`)

```
const generateDescription = () => {
  const desc = [];
  desc.push("... Introductory text ...");
  desc.push("Cetacean species:");
  data.forEach(d => {
    const cetacean = `
      ${d.common_name},
      population estimate:
      ➡  ${d3.format(".2s")
          (d.global_population_estimate)},
      maximum size: ${d.max_size_m} meter,
```

> Declare an empty array named desc, and push the description text written earlier into it.

> Loop through the data, and, for each cetacean, create a string containing the name of the cetacean and its population, size, weight, and conservation status.

```
        maximum weight: ${d.max_weight_t} ton,
        conservation status: ${conservationStatuses
          .find(status =>
            status.id === d.status).label}
    `;
    desc.push(cetacean);
  });
  return desc;
};
```

> Loop through the data, and, for each cetacean, create a string containing the name of the cetacean and its population, size, weight, and conservation status.

```
svg
  .append("desc")
  .attr("id", "scatterplotDescription")
  .text(generateDescription());
```

> Call the generateDescription() function to set the text of the SVG container's desc attribute.

If you listen to the new description, you'll hear a long list of the cetacean species and their related data. This approach is mostly adapted to visualizations that contain a limited amount of data, but at least it does expose the underlying data to screen reader users. In the next section, we'll discuss a better approach for charts that contain a lot of data points.

A DATA TABLE IS PROVIDED AS AN ALTERNATIVE

Even with the best efforts, data visualizations can still be difficult to interpret via screen readers. As an alternative, it's recommended to provide a human-readable and accessible data table containing the data used to create the visualization. This strategy is beneficial not only to screen reader users but also to any user who wants to extract data from your work.

As mentioned previously, this approach is mainly suitable for visualizations containing a large amount of data. In smaller visualization, providing the data within the chart's description might be sufficient.

To make the data table accessible to the user, we can add two buttons above the chart: one to see the chart and the other to display the data table instead. This way, the users can select whichever mode they prefer. In listing 10.11, we add these buttons to the markup as the first children of the `<main>` tag. The first button has a text of "Display Chart" and an `aria-pressed` label of `true` so that screen readers can inform the user that this button is selected by default. The second button has a text of "Display Data Table" and an `aria-pressed` label of `false`. We've also wrapped the legend, filters, and SVG container inside a `div` with a class of `"chart-container"`. In the next listing, we create another `div` with a class of `"data-table-container"`.

Listing 10.11   Adding buttons (index.html)

```
<body>
  <div class="container">
    <header>
      <h1>Cetacean species</h1>
      <div class="intro">...</div>
    </header>
    <main>
```

```
<div class="mode-selector">
  <button
    type="button"
    aria-pressed="true"
  ➥ class="toggle toggle-chart active">
    Display Chart
  </button>
  <button
    type="button"
    aria-pressed="false"
  ➥ class="toggle toggle-table">
    Display Data table
  </button>
</div>
<div class="chart-container">
  <section>
    <div class="legend-container">
      ...
    </div>
  </section>
  <section>
    <div class="filters-container">
      ...
    </div>
    <div class="responsive-svg-container">
      <div id="scatterplot"></div>
    </div>
  </section>
</div>
<section>
  <div class="data-table-container"></div>
</section>
</main>
<footer>
  ...
</footer>
</div>

...
</body>
```

Add two buttons to the markup: one to display the chart and one to display the data table. The first button is selected by default.

Wrap the legend, filters, and SVG container in a div with the class name "chart-container".

Create a new div with the class name "data-table-container".

Then we create a new JavaScript file and name it data-table.js. In this file, we declare function createDataTable() that receives the dataset. We call this function from load-data.js once the data is available. Inside createDataTable(), we append a table element inside the div with a class name of "data-table-container". In listing 10.12, we append a caption tag as the first child of the table and set its text to "Cetacean species data". We also append a link to the caption to allow the users to download the dataset. Allowing the users to read the data in a table format is good, but letting them download the dataset is better!

We then append a table row element (tr) into which we add a table header (th) for each column: Common name, Population estimate, Maximum size (meter), Maximum weight (ton), and Conservation status. We give each table header a scope attribute of col to define the direction of the header cells for screen readers. Finally, we loop through the data, append a table row for each cetacean, and populate the columns with data cell elements (td).

```
const createDataTable = (data) => {

  const table = d3.select(".data-table-container")
    .append("table");

  table
    .append("caption")
      .text("Cetacean species data")
    .append("a")
      .attr("href", "./data/data.csv")
      .attr("download", "cetaceans_data")
      .text("Download the data in CSV format");

  const tableHeader = table
    .append("tr");
  tableHeader
    .append("th")
      .attr("scope", "col")
      .text("Common name");
  tableHeader
    .append("th")
      .attr("scope", "col")
      .text("Population estimate");
  tableHeader
    .append("th")
      .attr("scope", "col")
      .text("Maximum size (meter)");
  tableHeader
    .append("th")
      .attr("scope", "col")
      .text("Maximum weight (ton)");
  tableHeader
    .append("th")
      .attr("scope", "col")
      .text("Conservation status");

  data.forEach(d => {
    const tableRow = table
      .append("tr");
    tableRow
      .append("td")
        .text(d.common_name);
    tableRow
      .append("td")
        .text(d3.format(".2s")
          (d.global_population_estimate));
    tableRow
      .append("td")
        .text(d.max_size_m);
    tableRow
      .append("td")
        .text(d.max_weight_t);
```

Append a table element to the div with a class name of "data-table-container".

Append a caption element to the table, and add a link to download the dataset.

Append header elements, and set their scope attribute to col.

Loop through the data, and append a table row for each cetacean. Fill the columns with the data.

```
      tableRow
        .append("td")
          .text(conservationStatuses.find(status =>
            status.id === d.status).label);
  });
};
```

Loop through the data, and append a table row for each cetacean. Fill the columns with the data.

All we have to do now is handle the clicks on the buttons to display the chart or the table. In listing 10.13, we select the div with a class name of `"data-table-container"` and set its `display` style property to "none".

Then we add a click event listener to the button with the class `"toggle-table"` (the second button added earlier). When a click happens, we change the `aria-pressed` attribute of this button to `true` and add the class name `"active"`. We do the reverse for the button with the class `"toggle-chart"`. We set the `display` style property of the table container to `"block"`, and the one of the chart container to `"none"`. We also add a click event listener to the other button and execute the reverse actions: set this button as active, set the other button as inactive, hide the table, and show the chart.

Listing 10.13 Handling clicks on buttons (`data-table.js`)

```
const createDataTable = (data) => {

  ...

  d3.select(".data-table-container")
    .style("display", "none");

  d3.select(".toggle-table")
    .on("click", () => {
      d3.select(".toggle-table")
        .attr("aria-pressed", true)
        .classed("active", true);
      d3.select(".toggle-chart")
        .attr("aria-pressed", false)
        .classed("active", false);
      d3.select(".data-table-container")
        .style("display", "block");
      d3.select(".chart-container")
        .style("display", "none");
    });

  d3.select(".toggle-chart")
    .on("click", () => {
      d3.select(".toggle-table")
        .attr("aria-pressed", false)
        .classed("active", false);
      d3.select(".toggle-chart")
        .attr("aria-pressed", true)
        .classed("active", true);
      d3.select(".data-table-container")
        .style("display", "none");
      d3.select(".chart-container")
        .style("display", "block");
    });

};
```

Set the display style property of the table container to "none". This will hide the table.

Attach a click event listener to the button responsible for showing the table. When a click is detected, set this button as active, set the other button as inactive, show the data table, and hide the chart.

Attach a click event listener to the button responsible for showing the chart. When a click is detected, set this button as active, set the other button as inactive, show the chart, and hide the data table.

Figure 10.16 shows the buttons to select between the chart and the data table. In this example, the table button is selected, and the data table is displayed below. Note that we've added custom styles to the buttons and the table. You'll find them in `table.css`.

Cetacean species

This visualization shows a collection of cetacean species. Each circle represents a cetacean. The circles' position on the scatterplot reveals their size and estimated population. The area of the circles is proportional to the weight of each cetacean. Their color represents the conservation status of each species.

[≁ Display Chart]   [⊞ Display Data table]

Cetacean species data ⤓

Common name	Population estimate	Maximum size (meter)	Maximum weight (ton)	Conservation status
Blue whale	10k	33	173	Endangered
Fin whale	100k	27	80	Vulnerable
north Atlantic right whale	350	18	80	Critically Endangered
north Pacific right whale	1.3k	18	80	Endangered
southern right whale	14k	18	80	Least Concern
Sperm whale	1.1M	18	50	Vulnerable
Bowhead whale	10k	16	70	Least Concern
Sei whale	80k	16	30	Endangered
Bryde's whale	95k	15.5	26	Least Concern
Humpback whale	84k	15	30	Least Concern
Gray whale	21k	14	35	Least Concern
Antarctic minke whale	520k	10.2	15	Near Threatened
Common minke whale	200k	10	15	Least Concern
northern bottlenose whale	10k	9	7.5	Near Threatened
southern bottlenose whale	500k	7.5	8	Least Concern
Cuvier's beaked whale	100k	7	3	Least Concern
Beluga	140k	5	1.5	Least Concern
Narwhal	120k	5	1.6	Least Concern
Perrin's beaked whale	830	4.5	2	Endangered
Common bottlenose dolphin	600k	3.9	0.65	Least Concern
northern right whale dolphin	400k	3	0.1	Least Concern
White-beaked dolphin	100k	2.8	0.275	Least Concern
Australian snubfin dolphin	9.5k	2.6	0.15	Vulnerable
Rough-toothed dolphin	150k	2.6	0.15	Least Concern
Atlantic humpback dolphin	1.5k	2.5	0.15	Critically Endangered
Atlantic white-sided dolphin	250k	2.5	0.2	Least Concern
Baiji	7.0	2.5	0.16	Critically Endangered
south Asian river dolphin	3.5k	2.5	0.09	Endangered
Striped dolphin	2.0M	2.5	0.15	Least Concern
Pacific white-sided dolphin	1.0M	2.4	0.15	Least Concern
Pantropical spotted dolphin	3.0M	2.4	0.115	Least Concern
Atlantic spotted dolphin	100k	2.3	0.14	Least Concern
Dall's porpoise	1.1M	2.2	0.22	Least Concern
Harbour porpoise	700k	1.9	0.065	Least Concern
Hourglass dolphin	140k	1.8	0.12	Least Concern
Commerson's dolphin	22k	1.7	0.06	Least Concern
Franciscana	4.3k	1.7	0.053	Vulnerable
Hector's dolphin	7.4k	1.5	0.06	Endangered
Vaquita	12	1.5	0.055	Critically Endangered

Figure 10.16   When the related button is selected, the data table is displayed instead of the chart. Its caption includes a link to download the dataset.

Not only can data tables be easier to understand for screen reader users, they are also helpful to all users who want to access and read the data. Take a moment to explore the project with the ChromeVox screen reader extension, and compare the experience of listening to the content of the chart versus the table.

CUSTOM KEYBOARD AND TOUCH CONTROLS DON'T OVERRIDE SCREEN READER SETTINGS

Most screen readers use a combination of Shift, Ctrl, Option, arrow, and Tab keys. It's crucial not to override these keys with custom JavaScript events. Overriding those can create significant problems for screen reader users.

We've completed the tests related to the accessibility for screen readers:

- The markup is semantic.
- The SVG container provides additional context.
- The visualized data is read by screen readers.
- A data table is provided as an alternative.
- Custom keyboard and touch controls don't override screen reader settings.

10.2.4 *Interactions*

Users with motricity limitations, whether due to a handicap or a temporary condition, might find it challenging to use a mouse to navigate or interact with our content. Such users will likely use the arrow and Tab keys on their keyboard instead. In this section, we'll discuss how we can make our interactions accessible to these users.

USERS CAN OPERATE INTERACTIONS WITH A KEYBOARD

In our project, the name of the corresponding cetacean is shown as a tooltip when the mouse enters one of the circles on the scatterplot. If you try to navigate this chapter's project with the Tab key on your keyboard, you'll be able to focus on all the buttons and links but not the circles in the visualization. For accessibility purposes, we want all users to have access to our interactions, whether they use a mouse or a keyboard.

We can make SVG elements focusable by setting their `tabindex` attribute. This attribute accepts any integer as a value, which defines the order in which the elements will be focused on in the page. In the following snippet, we go to `scatterplot.js` and go to the code that uses the data-binding pattern to add circles to the scatterplot. We sort the cetacean data in ascending order of population and add a `tabindex` attribute of 0 to the circles. By sorting the data, we choose the order in which the circles will appear in the DOM and hence the focus order. With the `tabindex` attribute, we tell the browser that the circles can be focused with the Tab key:

```
innerChart
  .selectAll(".cetacean")
  .data(data.sort((a, b) => a.global_population_estimate -
  ⮑ b.global_population_estimate))
  .join("circle")
    .attr("class", d => `cetacean cetacean-${d.status}`)
    ...
    .attr("tabindex", 0);
```

Then, to show the tooltip on focus, all we have to know is that the focus event fires when an element has received focus, and the blur event fires when the element has lost focus. In the following snippet, we add the focus event to the event listener that handles the reveal of the tooltip and blur to the one that handles hiding the tooltip. When listening to multiple events with the on() method, we need to separate the event names with a space:

```
innerChart
  .selectAll(".cetacean")
  .data(data.sort((a, b) => a.global_population_estimate -
➡ b.global_population_estimate))
  .join("circle")
    .attr("class", d => `cetacean cetacean-${d.status}`)
    ...
    .attr("tabindex", 0)
    .on("mouseenter focus", showTooltip)
    .on("mouseleave blur", hideTooltip);
```

And voilà—we can now access the tooltip with the keyboard. As we discussed in chapter 7, when we click on the filters above the scatterplot, some circles exit the visualization, and others enter. Because the circles that enter are brand-new DOM elements, we need to repeat the same process of sorting the data, adding the tabindex attribute, and handling the focus and blur events. In the following snippet, we make these modifications in interactions.js:

```
const updatedData = datum.id === "all"
  ? data
  : data.filter(d => d.hemisphere === datum.id)
        .sort((a, b) => a.global_population_estimate -
        ➡ b.global_population_estimate);

innerChart
  .selectAll("circle")
  .data(updatedData, d => d.uid)
  .join(
    enter => enter
      .append("circle")
      ...
      .attr("tabindex", 0)
      .on("mouseenter focus", showTooltip)
      .on("mouseleave blur", hideTooltip)
      ...
```

NAVIGATION AND INTERACTIONS ARE EASY AND NOT LABOR-INTENSIVE

The tooltip interaction in our scatterplot is simple and not labor-intensive. Still, it can be hard to execute on the tiny circles representing smaller cetaceans, especially for people whose mobility is challenged but who can still use a mouse. To facilitate the tooltip interaction on small circles, we'll add larger but invisible circles behind them that will also capture the mouse event and display the tooltip.

In listing 10.14, we append a new set of circles behind the original ones. The cx and cy attributes of the circles remain the same, but their radius is 30 px. We set their `fill` attribute to `"transparent"`. Because we only want to make the mouse event easier, we only attach a listener for the `mouseenter` and `mouseleave` events and show or hide the tooltip accordingly. Note that we still listen to the mouse and the focus events on the original circles.

Listing 10.14   Adding larger invisible circles (`scatterplot.js`)

```
innerChart
  .selectAll("interaction-circles")          Append a set of new circles
  .data(data)                                 behind the original ones.
  .join("circle")
    .attr("class", "interaction-circles")
    .attr("cx", d => xScale(d.global_population_estimate))
    .attr("cy", d => yScale(d.max_size_m))
    .attr("r", 30)                            Set their radius to a fixed value of 30
    .attr("fill", "transparent")              px and their fill to "transparent".
    .on("mouseenter", showTooltip)
    .on("mouseleave", hideTooltip);           Attach listeners for mouse
                                              events. Display and hide
innerChart                                    the tooltip accordingly.
  .selectAll(".cetacean")
  .data(data.sort((a, b) => a.global_population_estimate -
➥ b.global_population_estimate))
  .join("circle")
    .attr("class", d => `cetacean cetacean-${d.status}`)
    .attr("cx", d => xScale(d.global_population_estimate))
    .attr("cy", d => yScale(d.max_size_m))
    .attr("r", d => rScale(d.max_weight_t))
    .attr('fill-opacity', 0.6)
    .attr("stroke", d => colorScale(d.status))
    .attr("stroke-width", 2)
    .attr("tabindex", 0)
    .on("mouseenter focus", showTooltip)
    .on("mouseleave blur", hideTooltip);
```

We now have a tooltip that is much easier to access with the mouse. Whenever we listen to mouse events, it's important to cover a large enough area for people who struggle to be precise with the mouse.

INTERACTION CUES ARE PROVIDED

As developers, we spend so much time working on our projects that how to trigger the interactions can seem obvious to us. But for users who discover a project for the first time, additional cues can help indicate how to interact with a chart. We can achieve this simply by adding instructions at the chart's top.

In the following snippet, we add an instruction section above the chart in `index.html`. As discussed in section 10.2.1, we should ensure that the text has a reading grade level of 9 or lower:

```
<div class="filters-container">
  <h2>Select a group of cetaceans</h2>
    <div id="filters"></div>
</div>
```

```
<div class="instructions">Pass your mouse over the circles or access them
  with the tab key to discover the cetacean they represent.</div>
<div class="responsive-svg-container">
  <div id="scatterplot"></div>
</div>
```

We can see the instructions in figure 10.17. Note that we've also added custom styles in base.css. Adding instructions is a simple step that can significantly improve the experience for all of your users!

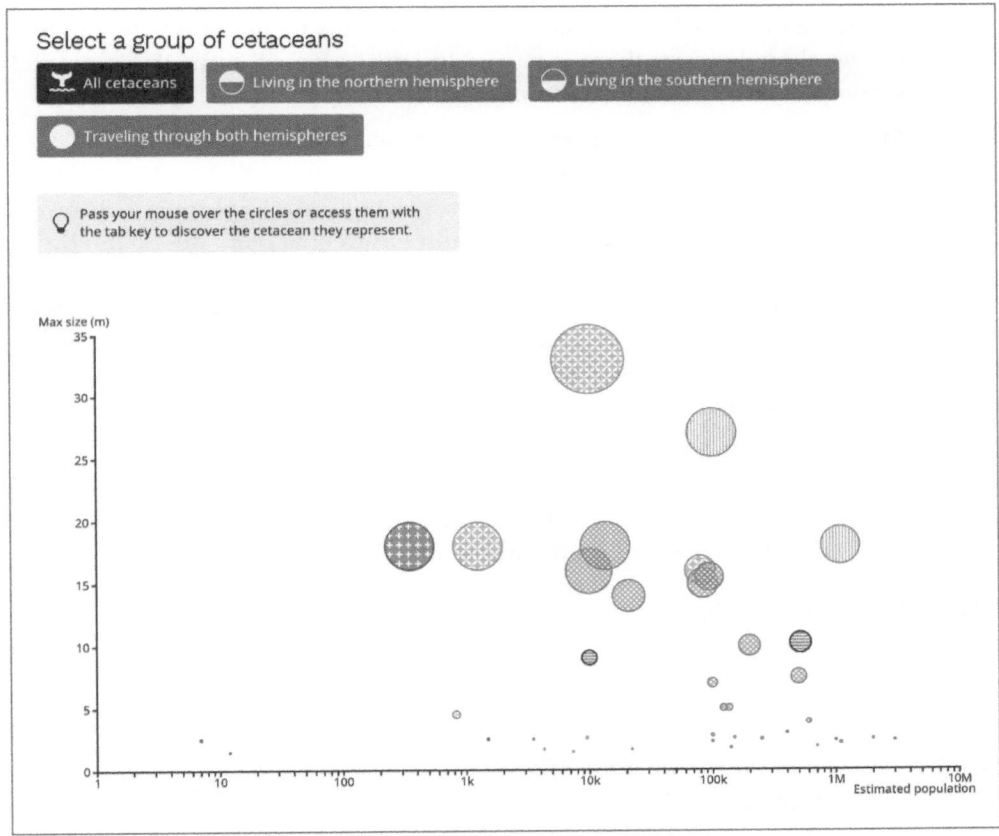

Figure 10.17   We've added instructions above the chart to let the users know how to access the tooltip.

We've completed the tests related to the accessibility of our interactions for mouse and keyboard users:

- Users can operate interactions with a keyboard.
- Navigation and interactions are easy and not labor-intensive.
- Interaction cues are provided.

10.2.5 *Other considerations*

In this section, we'll discuss three additional accessibility considerations related to the responsiveness of the project, user custom styles, and the risk of seizure.

THE PROJECT OFFERS AN EQUIVALENT EXPERIENCE ON ALL SCREEN SIZES

Providing users with an equivalent experience on all screen sizes, aka responsive design, is essential from an accessibility perspective. We want to ensure that users can access our project from the device they are most comfortable with or have access to. In chapter 9, we've discussed in detail multiple strategies for responsive data visualizations, such as using a grid layout, adapting the number of ticks on the axes, and changing the chart's orientation. We won't discuss them again here, but for this project, we should ensure that the legend layout is adapted to small screens and that the scatterplot remains comfortable to read.

STYLE CHANGES MADE BY THE USER AREN'T OVERRIDDEN

Some users need to change the styles on a web page to improve their reading comfort. They can do so with extensions such as Stylebot or by importing their own stylesheet with the browser developer tools. We must ensure that our styles do not override those applied by the user. This implies being careful with inline styles like the ones we can apply with the `style()` method in D3. Inline styles will overwrite most CSS styles provided via a stylesheet. Using them on data visualization elements, for which the user isn't likely to have preset styles, is fine. But we should avoid setting styles for the generic layout of the page this way, such as the font family, font size, color, and such.

VISUALS DO NOT PRESENT A RISK OF SEIZURE

Specific colors, such as red, and large patterns with parallel stripes can inadvertently induce epileptic seizures. To reduce the risk of seizures, avoid red flashes, animating with red, or having a significant portion of the display use the color red in your projects.

10.2.6 *Additional resources*

Here are some resources to learn more about accessibility and data visualizations:

- Dataviz Accessibility Resources: https://github.com/datavizally/resources
- "An Introduction to Accessible Data Visualizations with D3.js" by Sarah L. Fossheim (http://mng.bz/67Q5)
- "Making Data Visualization Accessible," by Bill Shander (http://mng.bz/oePj)
- MDN Web Docs, Accessibility: http://mng.bz/ngP8

Data visualization accessibility is a broad and crucial topic that deserves its own book. Although we discussed some of the most important aspects of accessibility in this chapter, there's still much more to learn. Once the habits from this chapter are integrated, we encourage you to work your way through the 57 accessibility tests listed by Chartability (https://chartability.fizz.studio/).

As was the case for responsive visualizations, the strategies used to make accessible visualizations may vary significantly from one project to another. It's even possible to add a toggle that allows users to choose between a "regular" and an "accessible" mode. Although these strategies imply a little more work on our end, they can make a whole world of difference to our users.

Interview with Eszter Katona, PhD

Katona is a researcher and assistant professor at Eötvös Loránd University (ELTE).

You have a background in computer science, statistics, and social sciences. That's an unconventional mix! Can you tell us a little bit about your fields of interest and how they intertwine?

First of all, thank you for featuring our visualization and for the possibility to introduce myself and our research group.

I am a statistician by profession, but I like to describe myself as a computational social scientist. I studied Social Sciences BA at ELTE, and my favorite subjects in the first semester were already methodology and social statistics. I also studied German Studies BA, where I first heard about computational linguistics. Natural language processing was not yet widespread, but I was immediately fascinated by it. Then I graduated in Survey Statistics MSc and received a PhD in Interdisciplinary Social Research. My research interests include natural language processing, research methodology, and data visualization.

I look with admiration at researchers who spend years, decades, researching the same area and really going deep into it, dedicating themselves to one research topic. I, as a methodological researcher, don't follow this path; instead, I work with domain experts to gain insights into a wide range of fields. I am involved in various research projects like the analysis of depression forums, public procurements, politicians' speeches, or Holocaust survivors' testimonies. Mostly I do the coding, modeling, and visualization part of the different research projects.

I believe that interdisciplinary collaborations are the future. As a computational social scientist, I work on answering social questions by analyzing large datasets and text corpora. Of course, in finding answers, interpreting, and communicating results, data visualization also plays a key role in my work.

How did you enter the field of data visualization?

I first met reporting during an internship at an advertising agency where I worked as a junior data analyst. We were using Power BI, but everything I did was based on intuition. I stayed at the agency for six months because I didn't feel like I was doing anything exciting or creative at all. After that I got much more exciting jobs. I became part of a great team where I learned a lot: one of my first mentors in the data science field, Zoltán Varjú, involved me in projects where I could get familiar with different open source data visualization tools.

I am in love with design, colors, typography, and graphics. If you combine it with my profession, you get my passion: data visualization. Somehow, for a long time, data visualization was just a hobby, but in recent years I have had more and more opportunities to apply what I have always loved to do on a professional level.

(continued)

Which tools do you use the most to create data visualizations? What's the role of D3 in this spectrum of tools?

Lately I've been using Tableau the most. One of my jobs is at the Government Transparency Institute, where I develop dashboards that display data on public procurement. That's why I also frequently turn to Tableau in my academic work. It's the tool I teach in my Sociology BA course, but for students in Statistics and Data Analytics MSc—where programming is not at all new—I've been using Python's Altair package as an introduction for the last few semesters. Besides Tableau and Altair, I prefer D3.js in my everyday life because I can customize the charts without any constraints. D3.js is a great tool for me to use to create standalone visualizations. I like it also because it is easy to export and modify for static prints, which is great because most journals publish static charts.

Featured project: ELTE Digital Lens (http://mng.bz/4JAg)

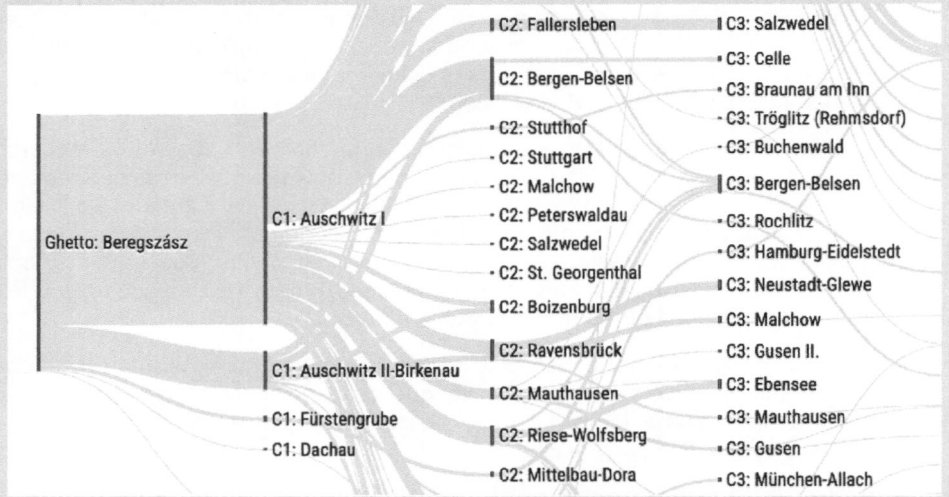

Close-up of the Sankey diagram visualizing the routes of Hungarian Holocaust survivors

Your project visualizes the routes of Jews who were deported from the Hungarian ghetto Beregszász during World War II. Can you describe this project and the context in which it's taking place?

Our research group, Digital Lens, is part of the ELTE Research Center for Computational Social Science. Digital Lens is an interdisciplinary cooperation: we use computational tools, natural language processing, machine learning, and data visualization to analyze historical sources. We investigate written sources: early testimonies of Jewish Holocaust survivors recorded by the National Committee for Attending Deportees (DEGOB for short in Hungarian). We complement the computational analysis with qualitative methods. Our research questions address three aspects: gendered experiences, language usage, and topography. We also deal with the overarching topic of ethics in Holocaust representation. Visualizations shown in this material focus on topography.

Can you explain the process of creating this project?

The most difficult part of the project so far has been the cleaning and standardization of the data. The original protocols were typed with typewriters. Later, they were digitized (we have a scanned photo of each protocol) and transcribed into textual format. But the transcription process of the data was not carried out accurately; corrections were needed.

The DEGOB protocols consist of two parts: the "hard" data on the header and an interview section describing the experiences of the survivors. The former contains metadata: demographic characteristics of the survivors, the ghetto where they were concentrated in, and the camps they were forcibly transported to. The interview section describes the experiences of the survivors. The selected visualizations are based on the first part of the protocols, concerning the metadata.

First of all, we had to extract, check, and correct the names of the camps in the protocols selected for the visualization. This was necessary mainly because different spellings were used in different protocols, and in some cases, the names of camps had probably been misunderstood and misspelled to such an extent that it was not possible to identify them accurately.

This is a step in data preprocessing that we have done manually; a lot of undergrad students helped us with this work.

I find tree visualizations and Sankey diagrams to be especially captivating, maybe because the story they tell is so literal. What made you opt for those charts?

We knew from the start we'd use flow maps to show the routes of Holocaust survivors based on the standardized, hard data extracted from the protocols.

But I also wanted to experiment a bit, and created a Sankey diagram that displays the number of survivors who made the same routes. Nodes represent the camps they were deported to.

Of course, we know that spatiality is missing from this representation (we also have maps, but those weren't created in D3.js.), but our aim is to have different approaches. We use the radial tree to show how widespread the camp system was. And with the Sankey, we present that for many survivors, Auschwitz was not the final destination of deportations as historiography has many times suggested. Moreover, the visualization also shows that many Hungarian Jews were deported through various camps. The charts are built around the same topic: the decentralization of Auschwitz. It is important to note, however, that only the route of the survivors is shown here; most Hungarian Jews were killed upon arrival at Auschwitz.

Which tips would you share with people who want to start using D3 in an academic setup?

Perhaps my most important suggestion is to dare to do it! In my community, Python and R are the most common programming languages; JS can seem scary. However, there are countless tutorials and templates available, which are much more friendly

(continued)

to customize than implementing a new figure from scratch. D3.js is also a good choice for scholars because most journals prefer static charts. From this aspect, D3.js is also a great tool, as it can be easily exported in SVG format, which even allows for additional editing in graphic design software.

Summary

- We should always aim at providing an equivalent experience for users with disabilities.
- To make our text content accessible, it should have a font size of at least 12 px on all screen sizes.
- The purpose of the chart and how to read it should be explained.
- The text on our project should have a reading grade level of 9 or lower. We can test the reading level with the Hemingway app (https://hemingwayapp.com/).
- All geometries and large text must have a contrast of at least 3:1 against the background, while regular text should have a contrast of at least 4.5:1. We can test the contrast with the WCAG Color contrast checker and the WebAIM contrast checker (https://webaim.org/resources/contrastchecker/).
- People with color blindness can struggle to differentiate colors in a categorical color palette. It's recommended to use double encoding (adding patterns or using a variety of shapes in addition to the color palette) to avoid carrying information with color alone.
- We can create SVG patterns with the `<pattern>` element appended inside a `<defs>`. Inside the pattern, we create a tile that will be repeated horizontally and vertically by the browser.
- For screen readers to be able to interpret our content, we should always use semantic HTML elements.
- Adding a `<title>` and `<desc>` elements to SVG containers, in addition to the `img` role attribute, is a great way to help screen reader users gather more information about our visualizations. A data table should also be provided as an alternative.
- Users should be able to access interactions with a keyboard. We make SVG shapes accessible via the Tab key with the `tabindex` attribute.
- The `focus` event fires when an element has received focus, and the `blur` event fires when the element has lost focus.
- Responsive design is important from an accessibility perspective.
- We should use inline styles with caution because they might overwrite the stylesheets uploaded by the user.
- We should be aware of the risk of seizure presented by the color red.

Part 3

Intricate data visualizations

So far in this book, we've been exploring relatively simple types of data visualizations: bar charts, scatterplots, donut charts, and so on. Because of the philosophy behind it, D3 allows us to build much more complex data visualizations. The huge advantage this gives us is that we don't need to learn a new library for networks and another one for maps. Instead, the techniques you've learned so far will still be helpful for those data representation types.

In chapter 11, we'll work with hierarchical data of the most common languages spoken today and visualize them with a circle pack and a tree chart. In chapter 12, we'll look at the dynamics between the characters from the play *Romeo and Juliet* with network visualizations. Finally, in chapter 13, we'll ask ourselves if the country in which you were born is correlated with your chances of ever winning a Nobel Prize by creating maps.

Hierarchical visualizations

11

In the early chapters of this book, we used data visualizations to encode numerical data. For example, the length of the bars in the bar chart from chapter 3 represented the number of related survey responses. Similarly, the position of data points in chapter 4's line chart depicted temperature. In this chapter, we'll discuss hierarchical visualizations, which encode parent-child relationships and can reveal patterns that would go unnoticed with the simpler visualizations we've worked with so far.

Hierarchical visualizations communicate parent-child relationships via *enclosure*, *connections*, or *adjacency*. Figure 11.1 shows two examples of hierarchical visualizations that use enclosure: the circle pack and the treemap. As its name says, the circle pack is a group of circles. There's a root parent, the most outer circle, and subsequent levels of children called nodes. All children of a node are "packed" into that node, and the size of the circles is proportional to the number of nodes they contain. The size of the leaf nodes, the children at the lowest level, can represent an arbitrary property. The treemap works similarly but uses nested rectangles instead of circles. Treemaps can be more space efficient than circle packs, and we often meet them in visualizations related to finances.

Another familiar and intuitive way to visualize parent-child relationships is via connections, like in tree charts. Tree charts can be linear, like a genealogy tree, or radial, as shown in figure 11.1. Linear tree maps are easier to read but can take up a

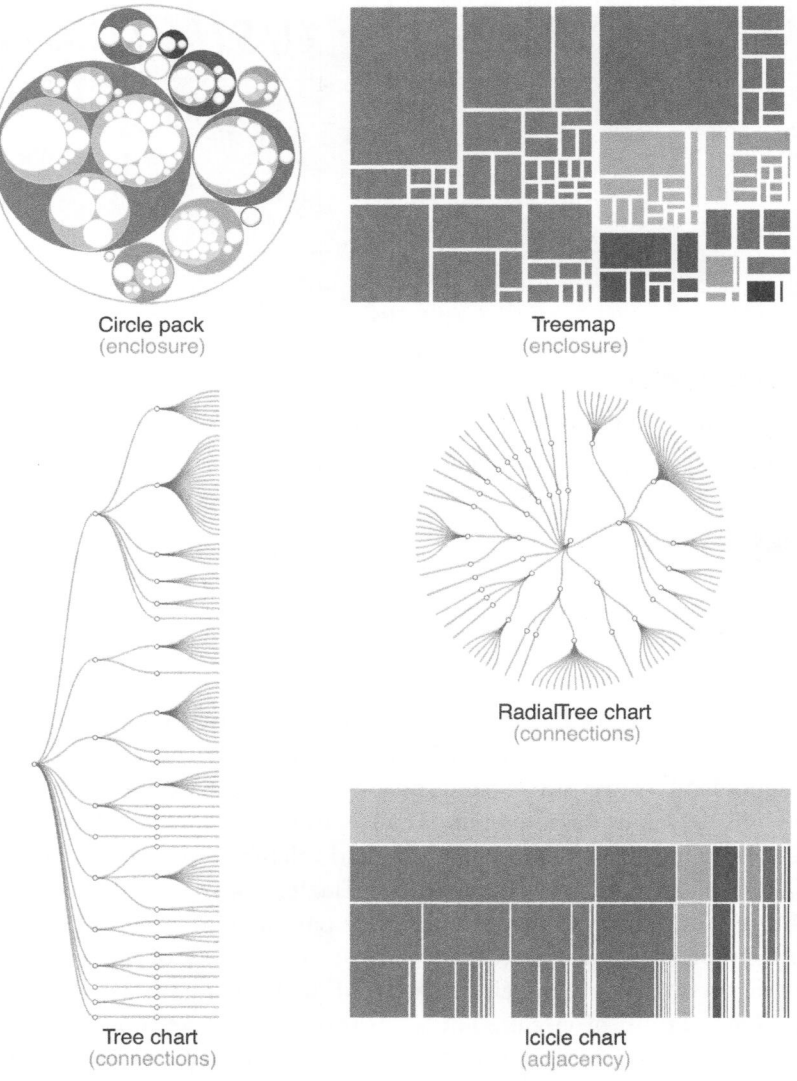

Figure 11.1   In hierarchical visualizations, the parent-child relationship can be communicated via enclosure (e.g., a circle pack or a treemap), connections (e.g., a tree chart), or with adjacency (e.g., an icicle chart).

lot of space, while radial trees are more compact but require a little more effort to decipher.

Finally, we can visualize hierarchical patterns via adjacency with icicle charts, also called partition layer charts. We often meet such charts in information technologies.

The charts presented in figure 11.1 may look diverse, but building them with D3 implies a similar process that involves layout generator functions. In chapter 5, we learned how D3's layout generator functions add information to an existing dataset and that we can use this information to append the desired shapes to an SVG container. Creating hierarchical visualizations is no different.

In this chapter, we'll build two hierarchical visualizations: a circle pack and a linear tree chart. We'll base our visualizations on a dataset of the 100 most spoken languages in the world. You can see the charts that we'll build at http://mng.bz/QZye.

Each language in our dataset belongs to a language family or a group of related languages that developed from common ancestors. Such families can be subdivided into smaller groups called branches. Let's take the five most spoken languages as an example. In table 11.1, we see how we might store the information about each language in a spreadsheet. The left column contains the languages: English, Mandarin Chinese, Hindi, Spanish, and French. The following columns include the related language families, Indo-European and Sino-Tibetan, and the language branches, Germanic, Sinitic, Indo-Aryan, and Romance. We complete the table with the total number of speakers and the number of native speakers for each language.

Table 11.1   Top five most spoken languages in the world

Language	Family	Branch	Total Speakers	Native Speakers
English	Indo-European	Germanic	1,132 M	379 M
Mandarin Chinese	Sino-Tibetan	Sinitic	1,117 M	918 M
Hindi	Indo-European	Indo-Aryan	615 M	341 M
Spanish	Indo-European	Romance	534 M	460 M
French	Indo-European	Romance	280 M	77 M

Hierarchical visualizations have a single root node that separates into multiple branches that end with *leaves*. In the sample dataset of table 11.1, the *root* node could be called "Languages", as in figure 11.2. The root divides into two language families—Indo-European and Sino-Tibetan—which also separate into branches: Germanic, Indo-Aryan, Romance, and Sinitic. Finally, the leaves appear to the right of the figure: the English, Hindi, Spanish, French, and Mandarin Chinese languages. Each language, branch, family, and root is called a *node*.

In the first half of this book, we primarily have been working with a legacy-like project structure. The main goal was to have a simple setup and focus solely on D3. But if you ship D3 projects, there's a high chance that you'll work with JavaScript

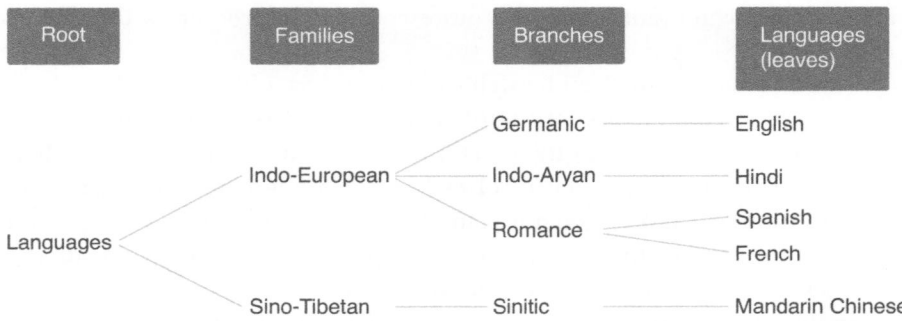

Figure 11.2   A hierarchical visualization has one single root that separates into one or more branches. It ends with leaf nodes, which in this example are the languages.

module imports. In this chapter, we'll modernize our project structure to allow importing D3 modules separately. It will make our project files smaller, hence faster to load, and will be an excellent opportunity to review which D3 modules contain which method. Such knowledge will make it easier for you to search through D3 documentation in the future.

To combine our JavaScript files and Node Package Manager (NPM) modules into one that is readable by the browser, we need a bundler. You might already be familiar with Webpack or Rollup. Because such tools can require quite a bit of configuration, we'll turn to Parcel (https://parceljs.org/), a bundler that is very easy to use and requires near-to-zero configuration.

If Parcel isn't already installed on your computer, you can install it globally with the following command, where -g stands for *global.* Run this command in a terminal window:

```
npm install -g parcel
```

We recommend such a global installation because it will make Parcel available to all your projects. Note that depending on your computer's configuration, you might need to add the term sudo on Mac and Linux or runas on Windows at the beginning of the command.

Once Parcel is installed on your machine, open the start folder of this chapter's code files in your code editor (http://mng.bz/X1PM). If you're using Visual Studio Code (VS Code), open the integrated terminal, and run the npm install command to install the project dependencies. At this stage, the only dependencies we have are to allow us to load the CSV data files later.

To start the project, run the parcel command, followed by the path to the root file:

```
parcel src/index.html
```

Open http://localhost:1234/ in your browser to see your project. The project displayed in the browser will automatically update every time you save your files. Once you finish your working session, you can stop Parcel by pressing Ctrl-C in your terminal.

In the `index.html` file, we're already loading the `main.js` file with a script tag. Because we'll work with modules, we've set the `type` attribute of the script tag to `module`. The nice thing about JavaScript modules is that we won't need to load additional scripts into `index.html`; everything will happen from `main.js`. Note how we didn't need to load the D3 library with a script tag either. We'll install and import the D3 modules we need, starting in the next section.

11.1   Formatting hierarchical data

To create hierarchical visualizations, D3 expects us to format data in a specific way. We have two main options: working with a CSV file or with a hierarchical JSON.

11.1.1   Working with a CSV file

Most of our data comes in a tabular form, often as spreadsheets. Such files must indicate the parent-child relationships via columns. In table 11.2, we've reorganized our sample dataset of the five most spoken languages into Child and Parent columns. We'll use these column names later to let D3 know how to establish the parent-child relationships. In the first row, we have the root node, "Languages," in the Child column. Because this is the root node, it has no parent. Then, in the following rows, we list the direct children of the root: the Indo-European and Sino-Tibetan families. Both of them have "Languages" as a parent. We follow with the language branches (Germanic, Sinitic, Indo-Aryan, and Romance) and declare which language family is their parent. Finally, we have one row for each language (English, Mandarin Chinese, Hindi, Spanish, and French), and we set their parent, the related language branch. We also set the `"total_speakers"` and `"native_speakers"` columns for each language because we can use this information in our visualizations, but those aren't essential to hierarchical layouts.

Table 11.2 shows how we structure a spreadsheet before building a hierarchical visualization with D3. We then export it as a CSV file and add it to our project. Note that you don't have to make your own spreadsheet for this chapter's exercise. You can find a properly formatted CSV file of the 100 most spoken languages, named `flat_data.csv`, in the `/data` folder.

Table 11.2   The parent-child relationships communicated via columns in a CSV file

child	parent	total_speakers	native_speakers
Languages			
Indo-European	Languages		
Sino-Tibetan	Languages		

Table 11.2   The parent-child relationships communicated via columns in a CSV file *(continued)*

child	parent	total_speakers	native_speakers
Germanic	Indo-European		
Sinitic	Sino-Tibetan		
Indo-Aryan	Indo-European		
Romance	Indo-European		
Romance	Indo-European		
English	Germanic	1,132 M	379 M
Mandarin Chinese	Sinitic	1,117 M	918 M
Hindi	Indo-Aryan	615 M	341 M
Spanish	Romance	534 M	460 M
French	Romance	280 M	77 M

Let's load `flat_data.csv` into our project! First, create a new JavaScript file in the `/js` folder. Name it `load-data.js` because this is where we'll load our dataset. In listing 11.1, we create a function named `loadCSVData()`. We add an `export` declaration to the function to make it accessible to other JavaScript modules in our project.

To load the CSV file into our project, we'll need to take a different route than using method `d3.csv()`. Parcel needs a proper transformer to load a CSV file. We've done all the configuration for you in the project by installing modules allowing Parcel to parse a CSV file (see the `.parcelrc` and `.parcel-transformer-csv.json` files for more details). All we have to do now is load the CSV file with the JavaScript `require()` function and save it into constant `csvData`. If you log `csvData` into the console, you'll see that it consists of an array of objects, each object corresponding to a row from the CSV file. We loop through `csvData` to format the number of speakers into numbers and return `csvData`.

Listing 11.1   Loading a CSV file into the project (`load-data.js`)

```
export const loadCSVData = () => {

  const csvData = require("../data/flat_data.csv");

  csvData.forEach(d => {
    d.total_speakers = +d.total_speakers;
    d.native_speakers = +d.native_speakers;
  });

  return csvData;

};
```

Import flat_data.csv into the project. With the require() function, we tell Parcel that flat_data.csv is an external file that will need to be included in the dist folder.

Convert the number of speakers into numbers.

In `main.js`, we use an `import` statement to access function `loadCSVData()`, as shown in the next listing. Then we save the array returned by `loadCSVData()` into a constant named `flatData`.

Listing 11.2 Importing the flat data into `main.js` (`main.js`)

```
import { loadCSVData } from "./load-data.js";          ◁───────  Import function
                                                                  loadCSVData().
const flatData = loadCSVData();   ◁──┐ Save the array returned
                                     │ by loadCSVData() into a
                                     │ constant named flatData.
```

Our next step is to convert the flat CSV data into a *hierarchical* format, or a root node with its children. The d3-hierarchy module contains a method called `d3.stratify()` that does just that. It also includes all the other methods we'll need to build hierarchical visualizations.

To maximize our project performance, we won't install the entire D3 library but only the modules we need. Let's start with `d3-hierarchy`. In VS Code, open a new terminal window, and run the following command:

```
npm install d3-hierarchy
```

Then create a new JavaScript file named `hierarchy.js`. At the top of the file, import the `stratify()` method from `d3-hierarchy`, as in listing 11.3. Then create a function named `CSVToHierarchy()` that takes the CSV data as a parameter. Note that we make this function available with an export declaration.

Inside `CSVToHierarchy()`, we declare a hierarchy generator by calling method `stratify()`. In our previous setup, we would have called this method with `d3.stratify()`. Because we've installed only the d3-hierarchy module, we no longer need to call methods upon the `d3` object and treat `stratify()` as a standalone function.

To convert our CSV data into a hierarchical structure, the `stratify()` function needs to know how to establish the parent-child relationship. With the `id()` accessor function, we indicate under which key the children can be found, in our case, `child` (the children were stored in the Child column in the original CSV file). With the `parentId()` accessor function, we indicate under which key the parent can be found, in our case, `parent` (the parents were stored in the Parent column in the original CSV file).

We pass the data to the hierarchy generator and save it in a constant named `root`, our hierarchical data structure. This nested data structure comes with a few methods such as `descendants()`, which returns an array of all the nodes in the tree (`"Languages"`, `"Indo-European"`, `"Germanic"`, `"English"`, etc.), and `leaves()`, which returns an array of all the nodes that don't have children (`"English"`, `"Mandarin Chinese"`, `"Hindi"`, etc.). We save the descendant and leaf nodes into constants and return them with the root data structure.

Listing 11.3 Converting CSV data into a hierarchy (`hierarchy.js`)

```
import { stratify } from "d3-hierarchy";          ⟵⎯  Import the stratify() function
                                                          from d3-hierarchy.
export const CSVToHierarchy = (data) => {

  const hierarchyGenerator = stratify()                  Create a hierarchy generator with
    .id(d => d.child)                                    function stratify(). Use the id() and
    .parentId(d => d.parent);                            parentId() accessor functions to indicate
  const root = hierarchyGenerator(data);     ⟵⎯         under which key the children and parents
                                                          can be found in the original CSV data.

  const descendants = root.descendants();
  const leaves = root.leaves();
                                                         Pass the CSV data to the hierarchy
  return [root, descendants, leaves];                    generator, and save the data structure
                                                          it returns in a constant named root.
};              Extract the tree nodes with
                root.descendants() and the nodes
                without children with root.leaves().
```

In `main.js`, we import function `CSVToHierarchy()` and call it to obtain the `root`, `descendants`, and `leaves`, as shown in the next listing. We'll use this hierarchy data structure in the following sections to build visualizations.

Listing 11.4 Importing the CSV hierarchy data (`main.js`)

```
import { loadCSVData } from "./load-data.js";
import { CSVToHierarchy } from "./hierarchy.js";

const flatData = loadCSVData();
const [root, descendants, leaves] = CSVToHierarchy(flatData);
```

11.1.2 Working with a hierarchical JSON file

Our dataset can also be stored as a hierarchical JSON file. JSON inherently supports hierarchical data structures and makes them easy to understand. The following JSON object shows how to structure the data for our sample dataset. At the root of the file, we have an object wrapped with curly braces (`{}`). The `"name"` property of the root is `"Languages"`, and its `"children"` property is an array of objects. Every direct child of the root is a language family that contains a `"children"` array of language branches, which also includes a `"children"` array with the language leaves. Note that each child is stored within an object. We can add additional data related to the languages within the leaf objects, such as the total number of speakers and native speakers, but this is optional:

```
{
  "name": "Languages",
  "children": [
    {
      "name": "Indo-European",
      "children": [
        {
          "name": "Germanic",
          "children": [
```

```
          {
            "name": "English"
          }
        ]
      },
      {
        "name": "Indo-Aryan",
        "children": [
          {
            "name": "Hindi"
          }
        ]
      },
      {
        "name": "Romance",
        "children": [
          {
            "name": "Spanish"
          },
          {
            "name": "French"
          }
        ]
      },
    ]
  },
  {
    "name": "Sino-Tibetan",
    "children": [
      {
        "name": "Sinitic",
        "children": [
          {
            "name": "Mandarin Chinese"
          }
        ]
      }
    ]
  }
]
}
```

A hierarchical JSON file is already available in the data folder (hierarchical-data.json). We'll proceed similarly to the CSV file to load it into our project. In listing 11.5, we go back into load-data.js and create a function called loadJSONData(). This function uses the JavaScript require() method to fetch the dataset and store it in a constant named jsonData. The constant jsonData is returned by the function.

Listing 11.5   Loading JSON data into the project (load-data.js)

```
export const loadJSONData = () => {

  const jsonData = require("../data/hierarchical-data.json");
```

```
    return jsonData;

};
```

Back to `main.js`. We import `loadJSONData()`, call it, and store the object it returns into a constant named `jsonData`, as shown in the following listing.

Listing 11.6   Importing the JSON data into `main.js` (`main.js`)

```
import { loadCSVData, loadJSONData } from "./load-data.js";
import { CSVToHierarchy } from "./hierarchy.js";

const flatData = loadCSVData();
const [root, descendants, leaves] = CSVToHierarchy(flatData);

const jsonData = loadJSONData();
```

To generate a hierarchical data structure from a JSON file, we use method `d3.hierarchy()`. In listing 11.7, we import the `hierarchy` function from `d3-hierarchy`. Then we create a function named `JSONToHierarchy()` that takes the JSON data as a parameter.

We call the `hierarchy()` function and pass the data as an argument. We store the nested data structure it returns in a constant named `root`. Like the data structure returned earlier by the `stratify()` function, `root` has a `descendants()` method that returns an array of all the nodes in the tree (`"Languages"`, `"Indo-European"`, `"Germanic"`, `"English"`, etc.), and a `leaves()` method that returns an array of all the nodes that don't have children (`"English"`, `"Mandarin Chinese"`, `"Hindi"`, etc.). We save the descendant and leaf nodes into constants and return them with the root data structure.

Listing 11.7   Converting JSON data into a hierarchy (`hierarchy.js`)

```
import { stratify, hierarchy } from "d3-hierarchy";

...

export const JSONToHierarchy = (data) => {

  const root = hierarchy(data);

  const descendants = root.descendants();
  const leaves = root.leaves();

  return [root, descendants, leaves];

};
```

Finally, in `main.js`, we import the `root`, `descendants`, and `leaves` data structures, as shown in the following listing. To differentiate them from the ones imported from the CSV data, we add the `_j` suffix.

Listing 11.8 Importing the JSON hierarchy data (`main.js`)

```
import { loadCSVData, loadJSONData } from "./load-data.js";
import { CSVToHierarchy, JSONToHierarchy } from "./hierarchy.js";

const flatData = loadCSVData();
const [root, descendants, leaves] = CSVToHierarchy(flatData);

const jsonData = loadJSONData();
const [root_j, descendants_j, leaves_j] = JSONToHierarchy(jsonData);
```

NOTE In a real-life project, we would not need to load both the CSV and the JSON data; it would be one or the other. We did this for pedagogical purposes only.

There are two main ways we can load hierarchical data into a D3 project: from a CSV file or a hierarchical JSON file. As illustrated in figure 11.3, if we use data from a CSV file, we pass it to `d3.stratify()` to generate the hierarchy data structure. If we work with a JSON file, we use method `d3.hierarchy()` instead. Both methods return the same nested data structure, often called `root`. This root has a `descendants()` method that returns all the nodes in the hierarchy and a `leaves()` method that returns the nodes without children.

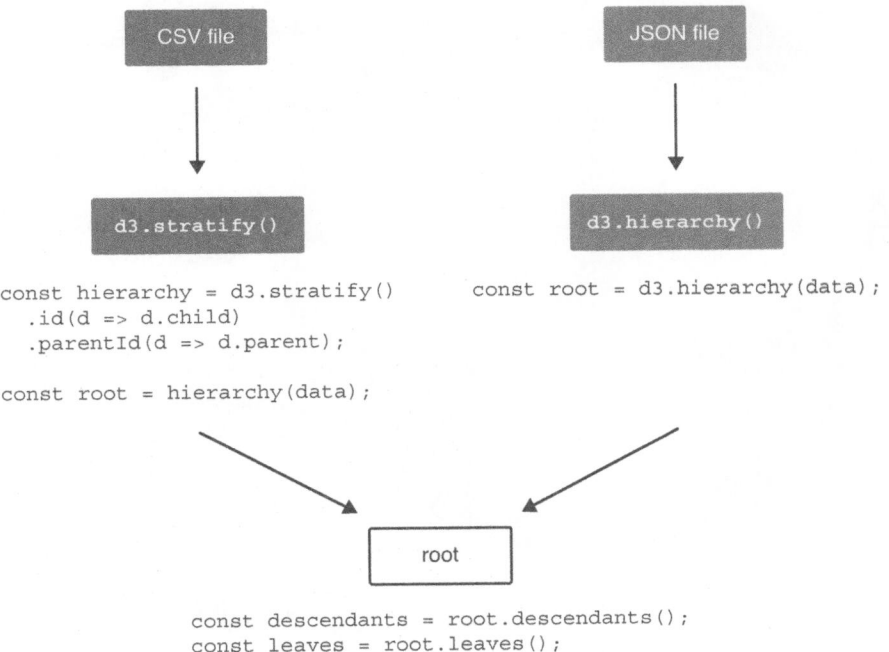

Figure 11.3 We get hierarchical data as a CSV or a JSON file. If we work with a CSV file, we pass the data to `d3.stratify()` to generate a hierarchy. If we work with a JSON file, we use method `d3.hierarchy()` instead. The nested data structure generated by these methods is the same and is often stored in a constant named `root`. It has method `descendants()` that returns all the nodes in the hierarchy and method `leaves()` that returns all the nodes with no children.

Now that our hierarchical data is ready, we can get to the fun part and build visualizations! That's what we'll do in the following sections.

11.2 *Building a circle pack chart*

In circle packs, we represent each node with a circle, and child nodes are nested inside their parent. Such visualization is helpful when we want to apprehend an overall hierarchical organization with one glance. It's easy to understand and has a pleasant look.

In this section, we'll visualize our 100 most spoken languages dataset with the circle pack shown in figure 11.4. In this visualization, the outermost circle is the root node, which we named "Languages". The circles with a darker color are the language

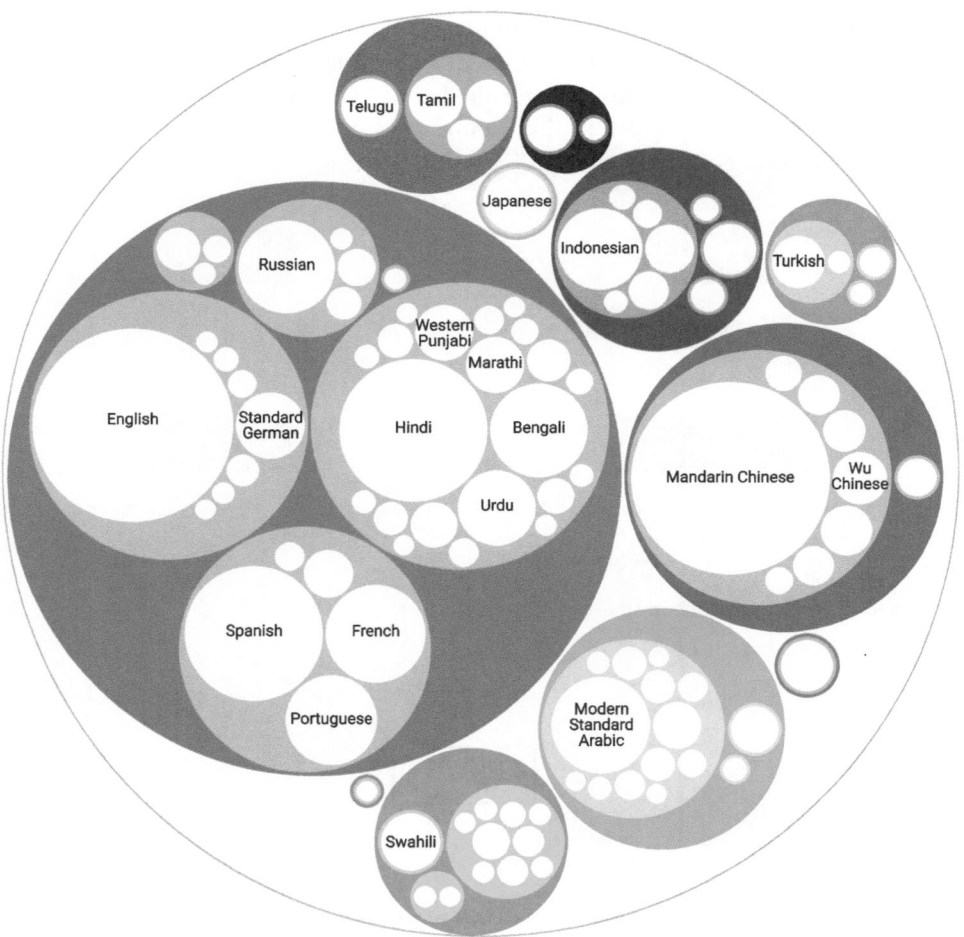

Figure 11.4   Circle pack visualization of the 100 most spoken languages that we'll build in this section

families, and the ones with a paler color are the language branches. The white circles depict the languages, and their size represents the number of speakers.

11.2.1   Generating the pack layout

To create a circle pack visualization with D3, we need to use a layout generator. Similar to the ones discussed in chapter 5, such generators append an existing dataset with the information required to build the chart, such as the position and the radius of each circle and node, as explained in figure 11.5.

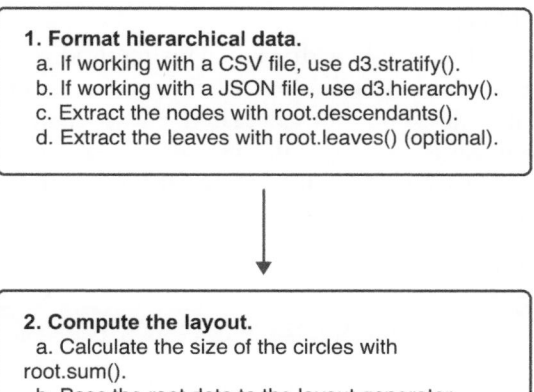

1. Format hierarchical data.
a. If working with a CSV file, use d3.stratify().
b. If working with a JSON file, use d3.hierarchy().
c. Extract the nodes with root.descendants().
d. Extract the leaves with root.leaves() (optional).

2. Compute the layout.
a. Calculate the size of the circles with root.sum().
b. Pass the root data to the layout generator d3.pack(). It calculates the layout and appends the data with the nodes' position and radius.

3. Draw the visualization.
a. Create an SVG container.
b. Append a circle for each node in the hierarchical data (aka the descendants).
c. Set the circles' position and radii based on the data appended to the dataset in step 2.

Figure 11.5   To create a circle pack visualization with D3, we start with hierarchical data, often named `root`. To compute the layout, we call the root `sum()` method to calculate the size of the circles. Then we pass the `root` data structure to D3's `pack()` layout generator. This generator appends each circle's position and radius into the data. Finally, we append circles to an SVG container and set their position and size with the appended data.

We already have our hierarchical data structure, called root, and are ready to jump to the second step from figure 11.5. First, let's create a new JavaScript file in the js/ folder called `circle-pack.js` and declare a function called `drawCirclePack()`. This function takes the root, descendants, and leaves data structures created in the previous section as parameters:

```
export const drawCirclePack = (root, descendants, leaves) => {};
```

In `main.js`, we import `drawCirclePack()` and call it, passing the `root`, `descendants`, and `leaves` as arguments:

```
import { drawCirclePack } from "./circle-pack.js";

drawCirclePack(root, descendants, leaves);
```

Back to `circle-pack.js`. Inside function `drawCirclePack()`, we'll start computing our layout. In listing 11.9, we begin by declaring the dimensions of the chart. We set both the width and the height to 800 px. Then we declare a margin object where the top, right, bottom, and left margins are equal to 1 px. We'll need this margin to see the visualization's outermost circle. Finally, we calculate the chart's inner width and height with the strategy adopted in chapter 4.

Then we call the `sum()` method, available with `root`. This method is responsible for calculating the aggregated size of the visualization. We also indicate to D3 the key from which the radius of the leaf nodes should be calculated: `total_speakers`.

To initialize the pack layout generator, we call D3 method `pack()`, which we imported from `"d3-hierarchy"` at the top of the file. We use its `size()` accessor function to set the overall size of the circle pack and the `padding()` function to set the space between circles to 3 px.

Listing 11.9   Computing the pack layout (`circle-pack.js`)

```
import { pack } from "d3-hierarchy";

export const drawCirclePack = (root, descendants, leaves) => {
  const width = 800;
  const height = 800;
  const margin = { top: 1, right: 1, bottom: 1,
    left: 1 };
  const innerWidth = width - margin.right - margin.left;
  const innerHeight = height - margin.top -
    margin.bottom;

  root.sum(d => d.total_speakers);

  const packLayoutGenerator = pack()
    .size([innerWidth, innerHeight])
    .padding(3);
  packLayoutGenerator(root);

};
```

Declare the constants that hold the dimensions of the chart.

Compute the aggregated sum of all nodes, and let d3 know that the size of the leaf nodes is proportional to the total number of speakers for each language.

Initialize a pack layout generator with method d3.pack(). Set its size with the innerWidth and innerHeight constants, and set the padding between the circles to 3.

Call the pack layout generator function, and pass the root data structure as an argument.

If you log the `descendants` array into the console, you'll see that the pack layout generator appended the following information for each node:

- `id`—The label of the node
- `depth`—0 for the root node, 1 for the language families, 2 for the language branches, and 3 for the languages

- r—The radius of the node's circle
- x—The horizontal position of the node's circle center
- y—The vertical position of the node's circle center
- data—An object containing the name of the node parent, the total number of speakers, and the number of native speakers

We'll use this information in the following section to draw the circle pack.

11.2.2 *Drawing the circle pack*

We're now ready to draw our circle pack! To select and append elements to the DOM, we need to install the d3-selection module by running `npm install d3-selection` in the terminal. This module contains the D3 methods responsible for manipulating the DOM, applying the data-binding pattern, and listening to events. At the top of `circle-pack.js`, we import the `select()` function from `"d3-selection"`.

Inside `drawCirclePack()`, we append an SVG container to the `div` with an ID of `"circle-pack"` that already exists in `index.html`. We set its `viewBox` attribute and append a group to contain the inner chart, following the strategy explained in chapter 4.

Then we append a circle for each node in the `descendants` array. We set their `cx` and `cy` attributes with the x and y values appended to the data by the pack layout generator, as in the next listing. We do the same for the radius. For now, we set the `fill` attribute of the circles to `"none"`, and their stroke to `"black"`. We'll change that in a moment.

Listing 11.10 Drawing the circle pack (`circle-pack.js`)

```
import { pack } from "d3-hierarchy";
import { select } from "d3-selection";

export const drawCirclePack = (root, descendants, leaves) => {

  ...

  const svg = select("#circle-pack")
    .append("svg")
      .attr("viewBox", `0 0 ${width} ${height}`)
      .append("g")
      .attr("transform", `translate(${margin.left},
        ${margin.top})`);
```

> Append an SVG element to the div with an ID of "circle-pack" that already exists in index.html. Set its viewBox attribute, and add a group that will contain the inner chart.

```
  svg
  .selectAll(".pack-circle")
  .data(descendants)
  .join("circle")
    .attr("class", "pack-circle")
    .attr("cx", d => d.x)
    .attr("cy", d => d.y)
    .attr("r", d => d.r)
```

> Use the data-binding pattern to append a circle for each node in the descendants array.

> Set the position and the radius of the circles with the data appended by the pack layout generator into the data.

```
    .attr("fill", "none")
    .attr("stroke", "black");

};
```

Once this step is completed, your circle pack should look like the one in figure 11.6. Our visualization is taking shape!

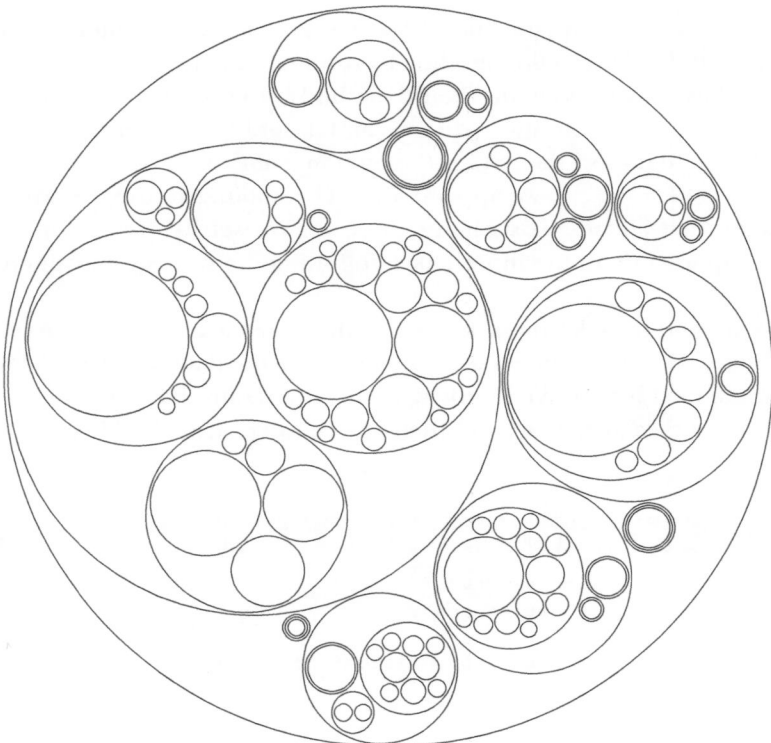

Figure 11.6   At this stage, the shape of our circle pack is ready. We'll add color and labels next.

We want each language family in our circle pack to have its own color. If you open the `helper.js` file, you'll see an array named `languageFamilies`. It contains a list of language families and their associated colors, as in the following snippet. We can use this array to create a color scale and use it to set the `fill` attribute of each circle:

```
export const languageFamilies = [
  { label: "Indo-European", color: "#4E86A5" },
  { label: "Sino-Tibetan", color: "#9E4E9E" },
  { label: "Afro-Asiatic", color: "#59C8DC" },
```

```
    { label: "Austronesian", color: "#3E527B" },
    { label: "Japanic", color: "#F99E23" },
    { label: "Niger-Congo", color: "#F36F5E" },
    { label: "Dravidian", color: "#C33D54" },
    { label: "Turkic", color: "#D57AB1" },
    { label: "Koreanic", color: "#33936F" },
    { label: "Kra-Dai", color: "#36311F" },
    { label: "Uralic", color: "#B59930" },
];
```

To use D3 scales, we need to install the d3-scale module with `npm install d3-scale`. For our color scale, we'll use an ordinal scale, which takes a discrete array as the domain (i.e., the language families) and a discrete array as the range (i.e., the associated colors). In listing 11.11, we create a new file in the js/ folder named `scales.js`. At the top of the file, we import `scaleOrdinal` from "d3-scale" and our `languageFamilies` array from `helper.js`. Then we declare an ordinal scale, named `colorScale`, passing an array of the language family labels as the domain and an array of the associated colors as the range. We generate these arrays with the JavaScript `map()` method.

> **Listing 11.11 Creating the color scale (`scales.js`)**

```
import { scaleOrdinal } from "d3-scale";
import { languageFamilies } from "./helper";

export const colorScale = scaleOrdinal()
  .domain(languageFamilies.map(d => d.label))
  .range(languageFamilies.map(d => d.color));
```

At the end of section 11.2.1, we discussed how the D3 pack layout generator appended multiple pieces of information to the descendants dataset (aka the nodes), including their depth. Figure 11.7 shows that our circle pack has depths varying from 0 to 3. The outermost circle, representing the "Languages" root node, is assigned a depth of 0. This circle has a gray border and a transparent fill. The following circles are the language families with a depth of 1. Their fill attribute corresponds to the color returned by the color scale we just declared. Then the language branches have a depth of 2. They inherit a paler version of their parent's color. Finally, the leaf nodes, or the languages, have a depth of 3 and a white color. This color gradation doesn't follow any specific rule but aims at making the parent-child relationships as explicit as possible.

Back to `circle-pack.js`; we'll set the fill attribute of the circles with the color scale. At the top of the file, we import the color scale created earlier in `scales.js`. To generate the lighter colors of the language branches (the circles of depth 2), we'll use a D3 method called interpolate, which is available in the d3-interpolate module. Install this module with `npm install d3-interpolate`, and import this method at the top of `circle-pack.js`.

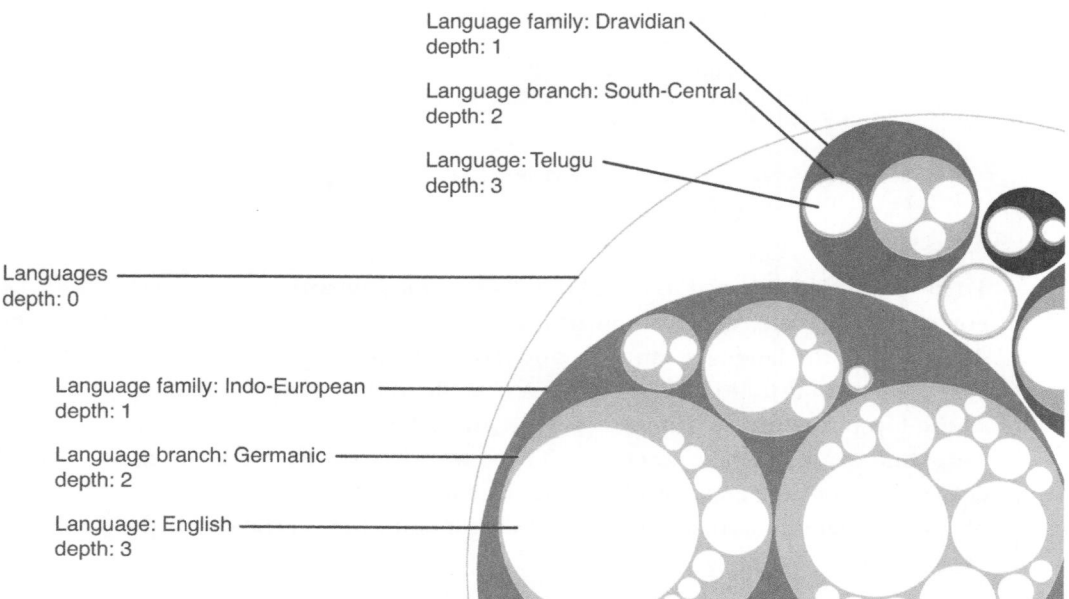

Language family: Dravidian
depth: 1

Language branch: South-Central
depth: 2

Language: Telugu
depth: 3

Languages
depth: 0

Language family: Indo-European
depth: 1

Language branch: Germanic
depth: 2

Language: English
depth: 3

Figure 11.7   On our circle pack, the outermost circle is the languages, with a depth of 0. Follow the language families with a depth of 1, the language branches with a depth of 2, and the languages with a depth of 3.

In listing 11.12, we then go back to the code where we set the circles' fill attribute. We use a JavaScript `switch()` statement to evaluate the value of the depth number attached to each node. If the depth is 1, the node is a language family. We pass its id to the color scale, which returns the associated color. For the language branches, we still call the color scale, but on the value of their parent node (`d.parent.id`). We then pass the color returned by the scale as the first argument of the D3 `interpolate()` function. The second argument is `"white"`, the color with which we want to interpolate the initial value. We also pass the value `0.5` to the `interpolate()` function to indicate that we want a value that is 50% in between the original color and the color white. Finally, we return a default fill attribute of `"white"` for all the remaining nodes.

We also change the `stroke` attribute of the circles. If the depth is 0, hence the node is the outermost circle, we give it a gray stroke. Otherwise, no stroke is applied.

Listing 11.12   Applying color to the circles (`circle-pack.js`)

```
...
import { colorScale } from "./scales";
import { interpolate } from "d3-interpolate";

export const drawCirclePack = (root, descendants, leaves) => {

  ...
```

```
svg
  .selectAll(".pack-circle")
  .data(descendants)
  .join("circle")
    .attr("class", "pack-circle")
    ...
    .attr("fill", d => {
      switch (d.depth) {
        case 1:
          return colorScale(d.id);
        case 2:
          return interpolate(colorScale(
            d.parent.id), "white")(0.5);
        default:
          return "white";
      };
    })
    .attr("stroke", d => d.depth === 0 ? "gray" : "none");

};
```

Evaluate the depth of each node with a JavaScript switch() statement.

If the depth is 1, this is a language family node, and the fill color is returned by the color scale.

If the depth is 2, this is a language branch node. The fill color corresponds to the fill of its parent (a language family), lightened with the D3 interpolate method to a value located at 50% between the original color and the color white.

All the other nodes have a white fill.

If the node has a depth of 0, we give the circle a gray stroke. Otherwise, no stroke is applied.

Once completed, your colored circle pack should look like the one in figure 11.8.

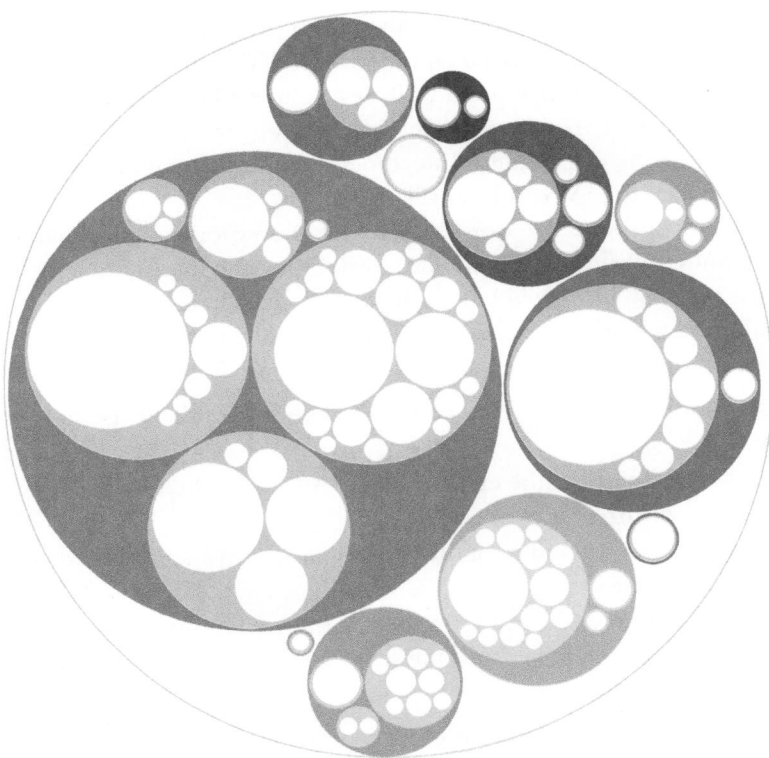

Figure 11.8 Circle pack after the colors are applied

11.2.3 *Adding labels*

Our circle pack definitely looks nice, but it doesn't provide any clue about which circle represents which language, branch, or family. One of the main disadvantages of circle packs is that putting labels on them while maintaining their readability isn't easy. But because we're working on a digital project, we can provide additional information to the reader via mouse interactions.

In this section, we'll start by adding labels to the larger language circles. Then we'll build an interactive tool that provides additional information when the mouse is positioned over a leaf node.

APPLYING LABELS WITH HTML DIVS

In our visualizations, we're dealing with languages with relatively short names, such as French or German, and others with long ones, such as Modern Standard Arabic or Western Punjabi. To display these longer labels within their corresponding circles, we need to let them break into multiple lines. But if you remember our earlier discussions about SVG text elements, displaying them over multiple lines is possible but requires a lot of work. It's so much easier with regular HTML text that automatically breaks lines when needed! Guess what: we can use regular HTML elements inside an SVG element, and this is exactly what we'll do here.

The SVG element `foreignObject` allows us to include regular HTML elements inside an SVG container, such as a `div`, for example. This `div` can then be styled like any other `div`, and its text will automatically break lines when needed.

In D3, we append `foreignObject` elements the same way as any other. Then, inside these `foreignObject` elements, we append the `div`s we need. You can see those as a gateway between the SVG and the HTML worlds.

For readability purposes, we won't apply a label on every language circle but only on the larger ones. In listing 11.13, we start by defining the minimum radius of the circles on which we want to apply a label, which is 22 px. Then we use the data-binding pattern to append a `foreignObject` element for each leaf node that meets the minimum radius requirement. `foreignObject` elements have four required attributes:

- `width`—The width of the elements, which corresponds to the diameter of the circle (`2 * d.r`).
- `height`—The height of the element. Here we apply a height of 40 px, which will leave room for three lines of text.
- `x:`—The horizontal position of the top-left corner. We want this corner to match the left side of the circle (`d.x - d.r`).
- `y`—The vertical position of the top-left corner. We want this to be 20 px above the center of the circle because the total height of the `foreignObject` element is 40 px (`d.y - 20`).

Then we need to specify the XML namespace of the element we want to append into the `foreignObject`. This is why we append an `xhtml:div` rather than only a `div`. We give this `div` a class name of `"leaf-label"` and set its text to the ID of the node. The `visualization.css` file already contains the styles required to center the label both horizontally and vertically within the `foreignObject` element.

```
export const drawCirclePack = (root, descendants, leaves) => {

  ...

  const minRadius = 22;
  svg
    .selectAll(".leaf-label-container")
    .data(leaves.filter(leave => leave.r ===
      minRadius))
    .join("foreignObject")
      .attr("class", "leaf-label-container")
      .attr("width", d => 2 * d.r)
      .attr("height", 40)
      .attr("x", d => d.x - d.r)
      .attr("y", d => d.y - 20)
    .append("xhtml:div")
      .attr("class", "leaf-label")
      .text(d => d.id);

};
```

Use the data-binding pattern to append a foreignObject element for each circle that meets the minimum radius requirement.

Set the width, height, x and y attributes of foreignObject. Note that elements overflowing the width and height of foreignObject won't be visible.

Append a div element inside foreignObject while specifying its namespace ("xhtml:div"). Set its class name to "leaf-label" and its text to the node's ID.

Once the labels are applied, your circle pack should look like the one in figure 11.4 and on the hosted project (http://mng.bz/QZye). We can now locate the main languages in the visualization.

PROVIDING ADDITIONAL INFORMATION WITH A TOOLTIP

In chapter 7, we discussed how to listen to mouse events with D3, for example, for displaying a tooltip. In this section, we'll build something similar, but instead of displaying the tooltip over the visualization, we'll move it to the side. This is a great option whenever you have more than a few lines of information to show to the user. Because such a tooltip is built with HTML elements, it's also easier to style.

In the `index.html` file, uncomment the `div` with an ID of `"info-container"`. This `div` contains two main elements:

- A `div` with an ID of `"instructions"` that is displayed by default and that indicates to the users to pass their mouse over the circles to show additional information.
- A `div` with an ID of `"info"` that will display the information about the hovered node's language, branch, family, and number of speakers. This `div` also has a class of `"hidden"`, which sets its `max-height` and `opacity` properties to `0`, making it invisible. You can find the related styles in `visualization.css`.

In listing 11.14, we're back in `circle-pack.js`. At the top of the file, we import the `selectAll` function from `"d3-selection"`. We also need to install the d3-format module and import its `format` function.

To differentiate the node levels, in listing 11.14, we add their depth value to their class names. Then we use the `selectAll()` function to select all the circles with a class name of `"pack-circle-depth-3"` and all the `foreignObject` elements. We attach a `mouseenter` event listener with the D3 `on()` method to the leaf nodes and their labels. Within the callback function of this event listener, we use the data attached to the element to fill the tooltip information about the corresponding language, branch, family, and number of speakers. Note that we use the `format()` function to display the number of speakers with three significant digits and a suffix such as "M" for "millions" (`".3s"`).

We then hide the instructions and show the tooltip by adding and removing the class name `"hidden"`. We also apply an event listener for when the mouse leaves a language node or its label. In its callback function, we hide the tooltip and show the instructions.

Listing 11.14   Listening to mouse events (`circle-pack.js`)

```
import { select, selectAll } from "d3-selection";
import { format } from "d3-format";

export const drawCirclePack = (root, descendants, leaves) => {

  ...

  svg
    .selectAll(".pack-circle")
    .data(descendants)
    .join("circle")
      .attr("class", d => `pack-circle
      pack-circle-depth-${d.depth}`)
    ...

  selectAll(".pack-circle-depth-3, foreignObject")
    .on("mouseenter", (e, d) => {

      select("#info .info-language").text(d.id);
      select("#info .info-branch .information")
        .text(d.parent.id);
      select("#info .info-family .information")
        .text(d.parent.data.parent);
      select("#info .info-total-speakers .information")
        .text(format(".3s")(d.data.total_speakers));
      select("#info .info-native-speakers .information")
        .text(format(".3s")(d.data.native_speakers));

      select("#instructions").classed("hidden", true);
      select("#info").classed("hidden", false);

    })
    .on("mouseleave", () => {
```

Select all the elements with a class of pack-circle-depth-3 and the foreignObject elements. We want the event to be triggered when the mouse is positioned over a circle or one of the foreignObjects that contain the labels.

Add a class name to each circle that contains the circle's depth.

Attach an event listener for when the mouse enters a circle or a label.

Fill the tooltip divs with the information related to the corresponding language, branch, family, and number of speakers.

Hide the instructions and show the tooltip.

Attach an event listener for when the mouse leaves a circle or a label.

```
    select("#instructions").classed("hidden", false);
    select("#info").classed("hidden", true);

  });

};
```

**Show the instructions
and hide the tooltip.**

When you pass your mouse over a language node, you should now see additional information about the branch, family, and number of speakers displayed to the right of the visualization, as shown in figure 11.9.

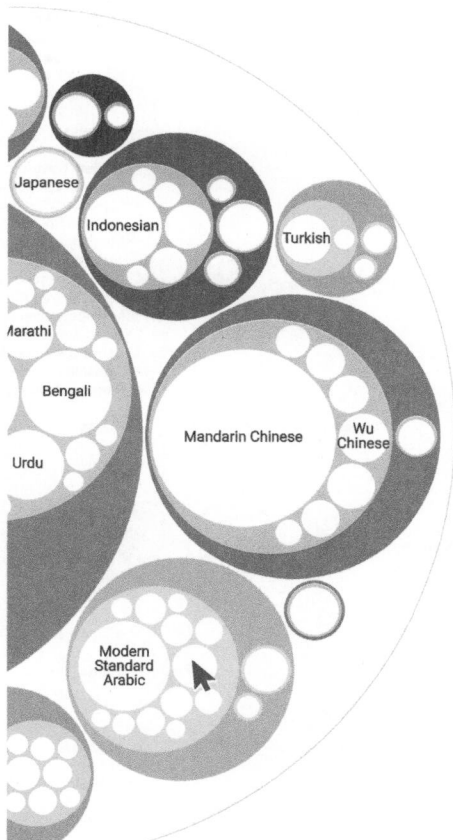

Egyptian Spoken Arabic

Branch: Semitic
Family: Afro-Asiatic
Total speakers: 64.6M
Native speakers: 64.6M

**Figure 11.9 When we pass our mouse over a
language node, information about the language
name, branch, family, and number of speakers is
displayed on the right side of the visualization.**

A disadvantage of circle packs is that they are tricky to render on mobile screens. Although the circles still provide a good overview of the parent-children relationships on small screens, labels become even harder to make readable. In addition, because the language circles can become small, using the touch event to display information can be tricky. To work around these disadvantages, we could stack the language families over one another or opt for a different type of visualization on mobile.

11.3   *Building a tree chart*

A familiar and intuitive way to visualize parent-child relationships is with a tree chart. Tree charts are similar to genealogical trees. Like the circle pack, they are composed of nodes but also show the links between them. In this section, we'll build a tree chart of the 100 most spoken languages, like the one shown in figure 11.10. On the left is

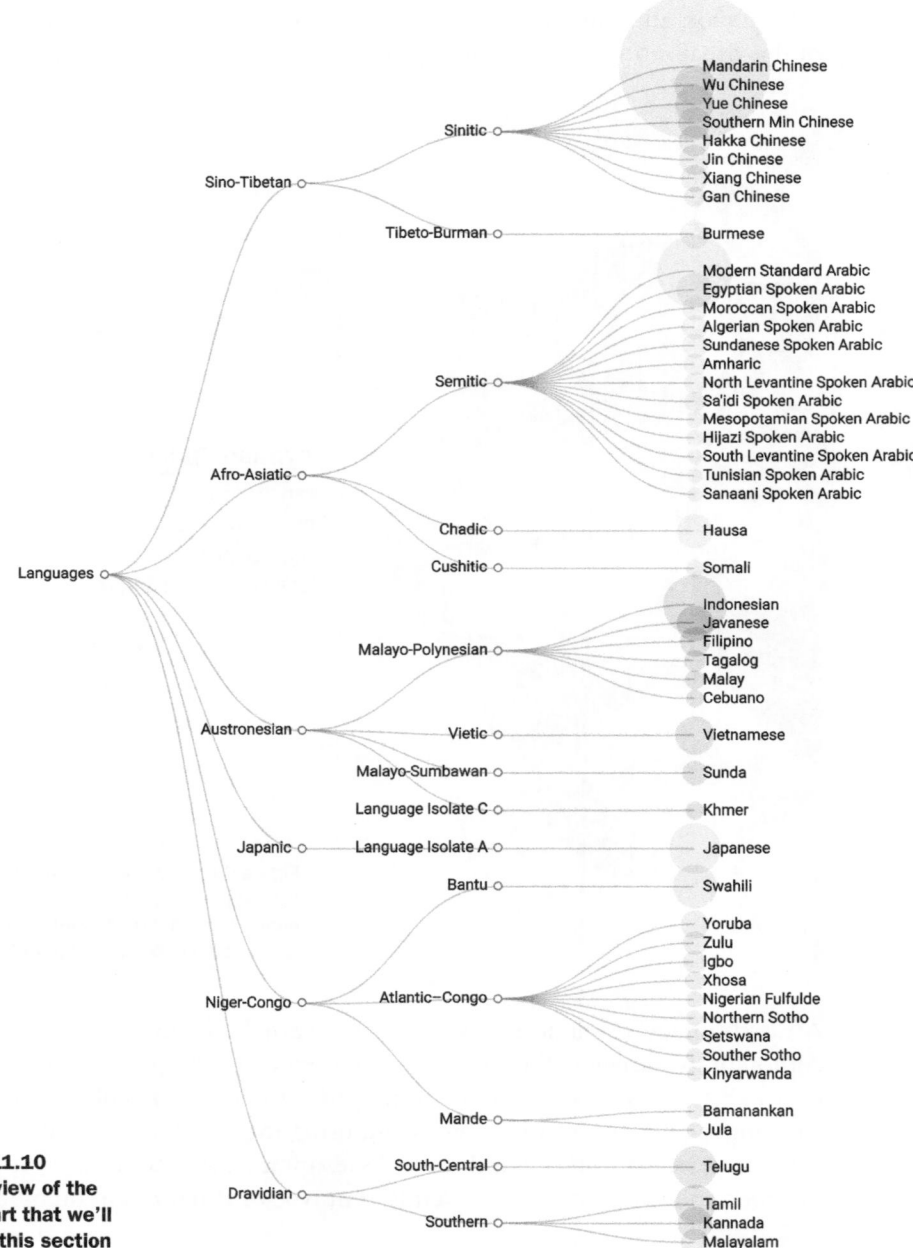

**Figure 11.10
Partial view of the
tree chart that we'll
build in this section**

the root node, the "Languages". It divides into language families that also subdivide into language branches and, finally, languages. We visualize the total number of speakers for each language with the size of a circle. As for the circle pack, the color of these circles represents the language family they belong to.

11.3.1 Generating the tree layout

Similar to the circle pack built in the previous section, D3 tree charts are created with a layout generator, as explained in figure 11.11. The d3.tree() layout generator is part of the d3-hierarchy module, and we use the information provided by the layout to draw the links and nodes.

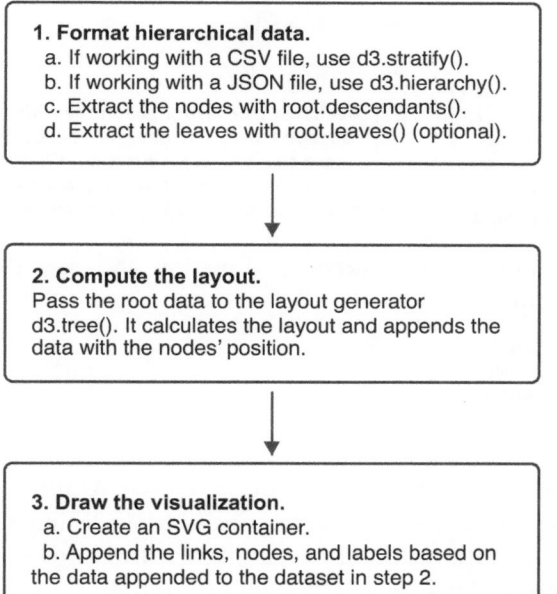

Figure 11.11   To create a tree chart with D3, we start with hierarchical data, often called root. To compute the layout, we pass the root data structure to D3's tree() layout generator. This generator appends the position of each node to the data. Finally, we append links, nodes, and labels to an SVG container and set their position and size with the appended data.

To generate our tree layout, let's start by creating a new file and naming it tree.js. Inside this file, we create a function called drawTree() that takes the hierarchical data (aka the root, the descendants, and the leaves) as parameters. In listing 11.15, we declare the dimensions of the chart. We give it a width of 1,200 px, the width of the chart's HTML container, and a height of 3,000 px. Note that the height is proportional to the number of leaf nodes in the chart and was found with trial and error. When you work on a tree visualization, start with a ballpark value, and adjust it once the visualization is displayed on the screen.

To generate the layout, we call D3's tree() function, which we imported from "d3-hierarchy" at the top of the file, and set its size() accessor function, which takes an array of the width and the height of the chart as arguments. Because we want our tree to deploy from left to right, we pass the innerHeight first, followed by the `innerWidth`. We'd do the reverse if we wanted the tree to deploy from top to bottom. Finally, we pass the hierarchical data (`root`) to the tree layout generator.

Listing 11.15   **Generating the tree layout (`tree.js`)**

```
import { tree } from "d3-hierarchy";

export const drawTree = (root, descendants, leaves) => {

  const width = 1200;
  const height = 3000;
  const margin = {top:60, right: 200, bottom: 0,
    left: 100};
  const innerWidth = width - margin.left -
    margin.right;
  const innerHeight = height - margin.top -
    margin.bottom;

  const treeLayoutGenerator = tree()
    .size([innerHeight, innerWidth]);
  treeLayoutGenerator(root);   ◄─────

};
```

Set the dimensions of the chart.

Declare a tree layout generator with the function tree(), and pass the chart's dimensions to the size() accessor function. We pass the innerHeight followed by the innerWidth for the tree branches to deploy from left to right.

Pass the hierarchical data (root) to the tree layout generator.

In `main.js`, we also need to import the `drawTree()` function and pass the `root`, `descendants`, and `leaves` as arguments:

```
import { drawTree } from "./tree.js";

drawTree(root, descendants, leaves);
```

11.3.2 *Drawing the tree chart*

Once the layout is generated, drawing a tree chart is pretty simple. As usual, we first need to append an SVG container and set its `viewBox` attribute. In listing 11.16, we append this container to the `div` with an ID of `"tree"` that already exists in `index .html`. Note that we had to import the `select()` function from the `"d3-selection"` module at the top of the file. We also append an SVG group to this container and translate it according to the left and top margins defined earlier, following the strategy used since chapter 4.

To create links, we need the `d3.link()` link generator function. This function works exactly like the line generator introduced in chapter 3. It's part of the d3-shape module, which we install with the command `npm install d3-shape`. At the top of the file, we import the `link()` function from `"d3-shape"`, as well as the `curveBumpX()` function, which we'll use to determine the shape of the links.

We then declare a link generator named `linkGenerator` that passes the curve function `curveBumpX` to D3's `link()` function. We set its `x()` and `y()` accessor functions to use the values stored in the `y` and `x` keys by the tree layout generator. Like when we prepared the tree layout generator, the `x` and the `y` values are inversed because we want the tree to be drawn from right to left instead of top to bottom.

To draw the links, we use the data-binding patterns to append path elements from the data provided by `root.links()`. This method returns an array of the tree's links, with their source and target points. The link generator is then called to calculate the `d` attribute of each link or path. Finally, we style the links and set their opacity to 60%.

Listing 11.16   Drawing the links (`tree.js`)

```
...
import { select } from "d3-selection";
import { link, curveBumpX } from "d3-shape";

export const drawTree = (root, descendants) => {

  ...

  const svg = select("#tree")
    .append("svg")
      .attr("viewBox", `0 0 ${width} ${height}`)
    .append("g")
      .attr("transform", `translate(${margin.left},
        ${margin.top})`);

  const linkGenerator = link(curveBumpX)
    .x(d => d.y)
    .y(d => d.x);
  svg
    .selectAll(".tree-link")
    .data(root.links())
    .join("path")
      .attr("class", "tree-link")
      .attr("d", d => linkGenerator(d))
      .attr("fill", "none")
      .attr("stroke", "gray")
      .attr("stroke-opacity", 0.6);

};
```

Append an SVG container to the div with an id of "tree". Set its viewBox attribute, and append a group element that will act as the inner chart.

Declare a link generator with function d3.link(), and set its curve function to curveBumpX. Set its x() and y() attributes to retrieve the y and x keys in the data calculated earlier by the tree layout generator. Note that the x and y are reversed to generate a tree that expands from left to right rather than top to bottom.

Use the data-binding pattern to append a path element for each link returned by method root.link(). Call the link generator to set its d attribute.

Once ready, your links will look similar to the ones from figure 11.12. Note that this figure only shows a partial view because our tree is very tall!

To highlight the position of each node, we'll append circles to the tree chart. Small circles with a gray stroke will represent the root, language family, and language branch nodes. In contrast, the language node circles will have a size proportional to the total number of speakers and a color associated with their language family.

To calculate the size of the language nodes, we'll need a scale. In listing 11.17, we go to `scales.js` and import `scaleRadial()` from "d3-scale". The scale's domain is continuous and extends from 0 to the maximum number of people speaking one of the languages in the dataset. Its range can vary between 0 px and 83 px, the radius of the largest circle from the circle pack created in the previous section.

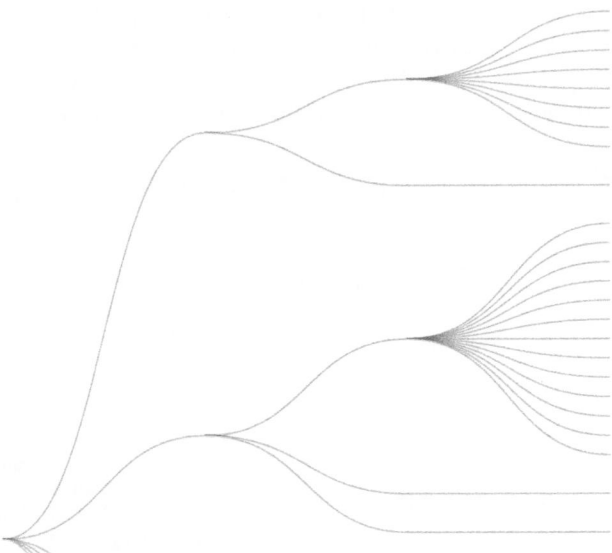

Figure 11.12   Partial view of the tree chart links

Because the maximum number of speakers is only available once we've retrieved the data and created the hierarchy (`root`), we need to wrap the radial scale into a function named `getRadius()`. When we need to calculate the radius of a circle, we'll pass the number of speakers for the current language as well as the maximum number of speakers, and this function will return the radius.

Listing 11.17   Retrieving values from a radial scale (`scales.js`)

```
import { scaleOrdinal, scaleRadial } from "d3-scale";
...

export const getRadius = (maxSpeakers, speakers) => {
  const radialScale = scaleRadial()
    .domain([0, maxSpeakers])
    .range([0, 83]);

  return radialScale(speakers);
};
```

Back to `tree.js`; we calculate the maximum number of speakers with method `d3.max()`. To use this method, we need to install the d3-array module with `npm install d3-array` and import the `max()` function at the top of the file. We also import function `getRadius()` and the color scale from `scales.js`.

Then, in listing 11.18, we use the data-binding pattern to append one circle to the inner chart for each descendant node. We set these circles' `cx` and `cy` attributes with the `x` and `y` keys appended to the data by the tree layout generator. If the circle is a leaf node, we set its radius based on the number of speakers for the associated language and with the `getRadius()` function. We set its color with the color scale, `fill-opacity` to 30%, and `stroke` to `"none"`. The other circles have a radius of 4 px, a white fill, and a gray stroke.

Listing 11.18   Appending the nodes (`tree.js`)

```
...
import { max } from "d3-array";
import { getRadius, colorScale } from "./scales";

export const drawTree = (root, descendants) => {

  ...

  const maxSpeakers = max(leaves, d => d.data.total_speakers);
  svg
    .selectAll(".node-tree")
    .data(descendants)
    .join("circle")
      .attr("class", "node-tree")
      .attr("cx", d => d.y)
      .attr("cy", d => d.x)
      .attr("r", d => d.depth === 3
        ? getRadius(maxSpeakers, d.data.total_speakers)
        : 4
      )
      .attr("fill", d => d.depth === 3
        ? colorScale(d.parent.data.parent)
        : "white"
      )
      .attr("fill-opacity", d => d.depth === 3
        ? 0.3
        : 1
      )
      .attr("stroke", d => d.depth === 3
        ? "none"
        : "gray"
      );
};
```

Calculate the maximum number of speakers for a language with method d3.max().

Use the data-binding pattern to append a circle element for each node. Set their position with the x and y keys appended to the data by the tree layout generator.

If the circle is a leaf node, set the radius with getRadius(), passing the maximum number of speakers and the number of speakers associated with the current language. Otherwise, set its radius to 4 px.

If the circle is a leaf node, set its fill attribute with the color scale. Otherwise, return the color white.

If the circle is a leaf node, set its fill-opacity to 30% and its stroke to "none". Otherwise, set the fill-opacity to 100% and the stroke to the color gray.

To complete the tree chart, we add a label to each node. In listing 11.19, we use the data-binding pattern to append a text element for each node in the dataset. We display the label on the right if it's associated with a leaf node. Otherwise, the label is positioned on the left side of its node. We also give a white stroke to the labels so that they are easier to read when positioned over the links. By setting the `paint-order` attribute to `"stroke"`, we ensure that the stroke is drawn before the text fill color. This also helps with readability.

Listing 11.19   Appending a label for each node (`tree.js`)

```
export const drawTree = (root, descendants) => {

  ...
```

```
svg
  .selectAll(".label-tree")
  .data(descendants)
  .join("text")
    .attr("class", "label-tree")
    .attr("x", d => d.children ? d.y - 8 : d.y + 8)
    .attr("y", d => d.x)
    .attr("text-anchor", d => d.children ?
      "end" : "start")
    .attr("alignment-baseline", "middle")
    .attr("paint-order", "stroke")
    .attr("stroke", d => d.depth ===3 ?
      "none" : "white")
    .attr("stroke-width", 2)
    .style("font-size", "16px")
    .text(d => d.id);

};
```

Use the data-binding pattern to append a text element for each node in the dataset.

If the label is associated with a leaf node, position it to the right. Otherwise, move it to the left side of the node. As mentioned previously, the x and y values are reversed because we draw the tree from left to right.

Add a white stroke to the text, and set its paint-order attribute to "stroke". This improves the readability of the labels positioned over links.

Once completed, your tree chart should look similar to the one on the hosted project (http://mng.bz/QZye) and in figure 11.13.

The linear layout of this tree chart makes it relatively easy to translate to mobile screens, as long as we increase the labels' font size and ensure enough vertical space between them. Refer to chapter 9 for tips on building responsive charts.

For this project to be complete, we need to add a legend for the language family colors and the size of the circles. We've already built it for you. To display the legend, go to index.html, and uncomment the div with a class of "legend". Then, in main.js, import function createLegend() from legend.js, and call it to generate the

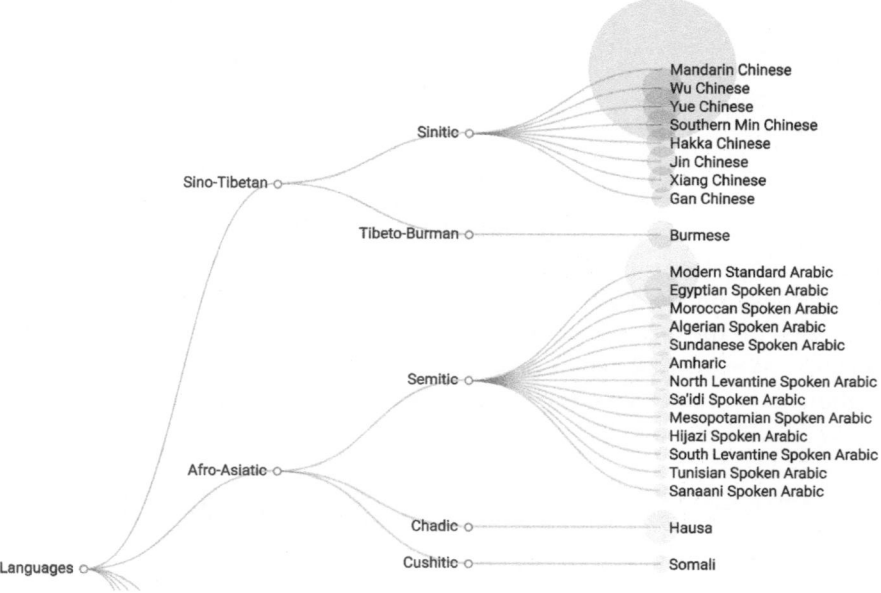

Figure 11.13   Partial view of the completed tree chart

legend. Refer to the cetacean visualization from chapter 7 for more explanations on how we built this legend. Take a look at the code in `legend.js`, or even better, try to build it yourself!

11.4 *Building other hierarchical visualizations*

In this chapter, we've discussed how to build a circle pack and a tree chart visualization. Making other hierarchy representations such as treemaps and icicle charts with D3 is very similar.

Figure 11.14 illustrates how we start from CSV or JSON data, which we format into a hierarchical data structure named `root`. With this data structure, we can build any

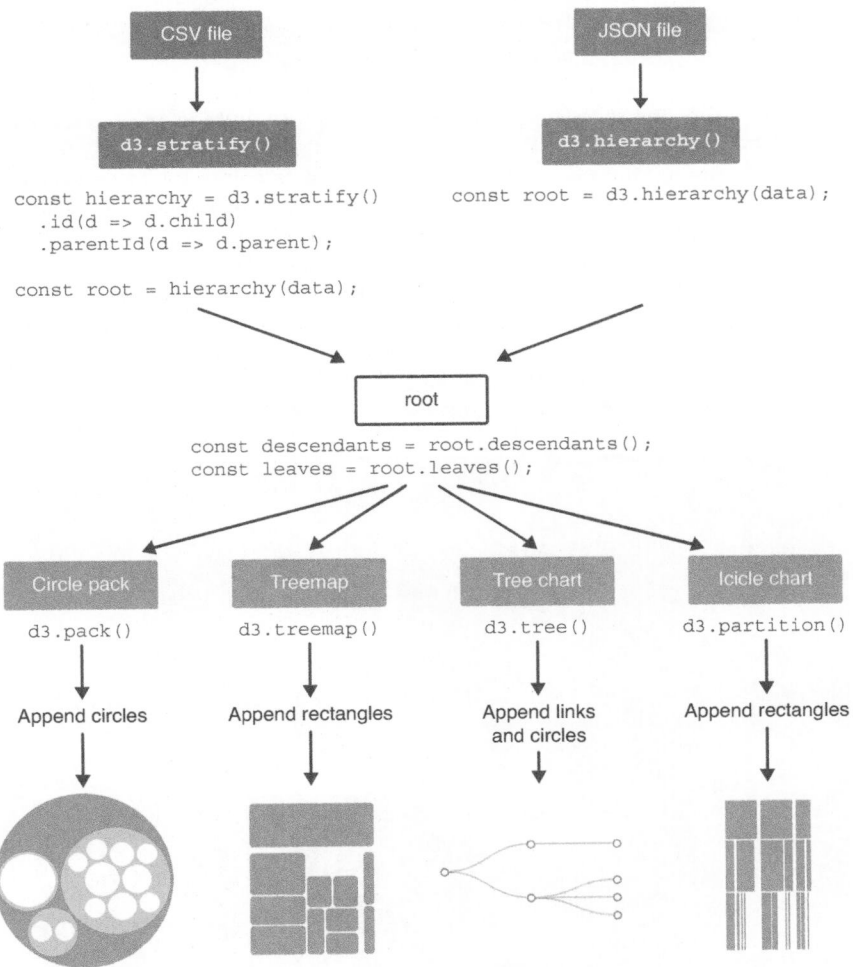

Figure 11.14   To create a hierarchical visualization with D3, we start by formatting CSV or JSON data into a hierarchical data structure called `root`. From this root, we can generate a circle pack, a treemap, a tree chart, or an icicle chart. Each chart has its own layout generator that calculates the layout and appends the information required to build it into the dataset. We then use this information to draw the shapes we need: circles, rectangles, or links.

hierarchical visualization, the only difference being the function used as a layout generator. For circle packs, the layout generator function is `d3.pack()`; for treemaps, it's `d3.treemap()`; for tree charts, it's `d3.tree()`; and for icicle charts, it's `d3.partition()`. We can find these layout generators in the d3-hierarchy module.

Exercise: Create a treemap

You now have all the knowledge required to build a treemap of the 100 most spoken languages, like the one in the following figure and the hosted project (http://mng.bz/QZye). Treemaps visualize hierarchical data as a set of nested rectangles. Traditionally, treemaps only show the leaf nodes, which in our case, are the languages. The size of the rectangles, or leaf nodes, is proportional to the total number of speakers for each language. Here are a few guidelines:

1. In `index.html`, add a `div` with an id of `"treemap"`.
2. Create a new file named `treemap.js` with a function called `drawTreemap()`. This function receives the `Root` data structure and the `leaves` as parameters and is called from `main.js`.
3. Use the `d3.Treemap()` layout generator to calculate the treemap layout. With the `size()` accessor function, set the width and height of the chart. You can also specify the padding between rectangles with `paddingInner()` and `paddingOuter()`. Refer to the d3-hierarchy module for more in-depth documentation.
4. Append an SVG container to the `div` with an id of `"treemap"`.
5. Append a rectangle for each leaf node. Set its position and size with the information added to the dataset by the layout generator.
6. Append a label for each language on the corresponding rectangle. You might also want to hide labels that are displayed over smaller rectangles.

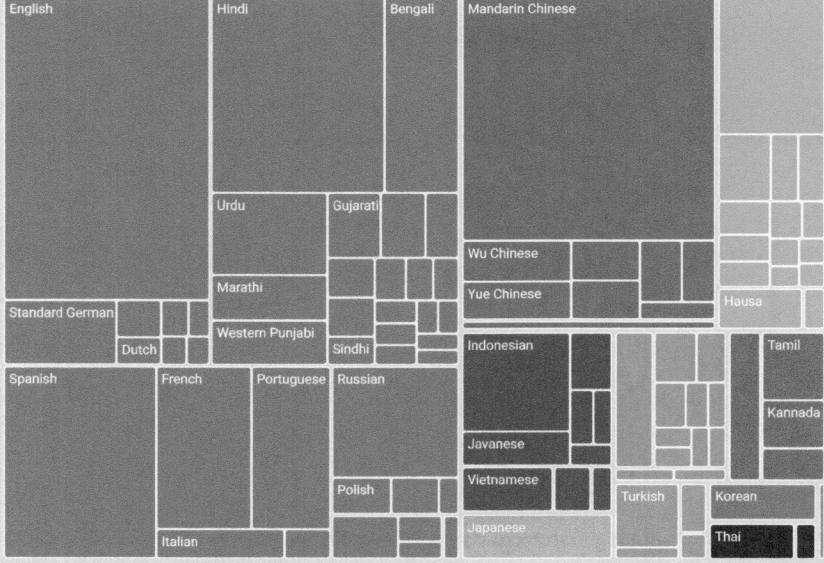

Treemap of the 100 most spoken languages

If you get stuck or want to compare your solution with ours, you'll find it in section D.11 of appendix D and in the `11.4-Treemap/end` folder of this chapter's code files. But as usual, we encourage you to try to complete it on your own. Your solution might differ slightly from ours, and that's all right!

Interview with Shirley Wu

Wu asked for her professional title to be listed as "human being" for this interview.

Can you tell us a little bit about your background and how you entered the world of data visualization?

I landed my first job after university at a company where we were building dashboards using tools like Highcharts, but the company was interested in going beyond traditional charts. It was about one year after D3 came out, and my manager at the time asked me if I would be interested in learning D3 and using it to build our dashboards.

While learning D3, I attended multiple meetups in the San Francisco Bay area where people who knew it well took the time to explain the parts I was struggling with, like the enter-update-exit pattern.

Do you use visualization tools other than D3? What's the place of D3 in your current data visualization workflow?

For building digital visualizations, I use D3 with Vue.js and GreenSock for the animations. Because Vue.js prioritizes animations, I find that it plays really nicely with D3. GreenSock also allows me to create animations that are more complex than D3 transitions, like in scrollytelling projects.

Lately, I've started creating static visualizations for *Scientific American*, for example, for which I extract the SVG created with D3 and export it to Adobe Illustrator.

Featured project: "~~wonder~~ & hope" (www.wonder-and-hope.art/)

"Pre-pandemic, I used to love being outside. I loved looking up at a bright blue sky and feeling the wind on my skin and the sun on my face. I'd see the flowers blooming or hear the birds chirping and be overcome with a sense of wonder." (Photo courtesy of Tuan Huang, https://tuan-h.com/).

(continued)

Please describe your project "~~wonder~~ & hope".

One of the things I love is being outside. I also take a lot of photos and take most of them while I'm outdoors. During the pandemic, I developed a fear of going outside on my own, mainly due to hatred events targeted at Asian people. What was previously a source of wonder (being outside) was not anymore.

Once I got vaccinated, I started slowly to go out on my own again but realized how much I needed to heal my relationship with being outside. I looked for a way to reflect on my experience through the photos I took during the years prior, during, and after the pandemic. I used the photo's metadata (data and location), as well as a script I wrote to extract the primary color in each photo (I wrote this script for the project "Four Years in Vacations in 20,000 Colors," which I built for the Data Sketches project [https://shirleywu.studio/travel/]). I used this data to create a visualization with D3.

I then built different physical layers to print the different elements of the visualization: the support, the circles representing each photo, the labels, etc. The number of layers is actually the same as the one I would have used to build this project digitally! Those were used to walk the visitors through how to read the visualization.

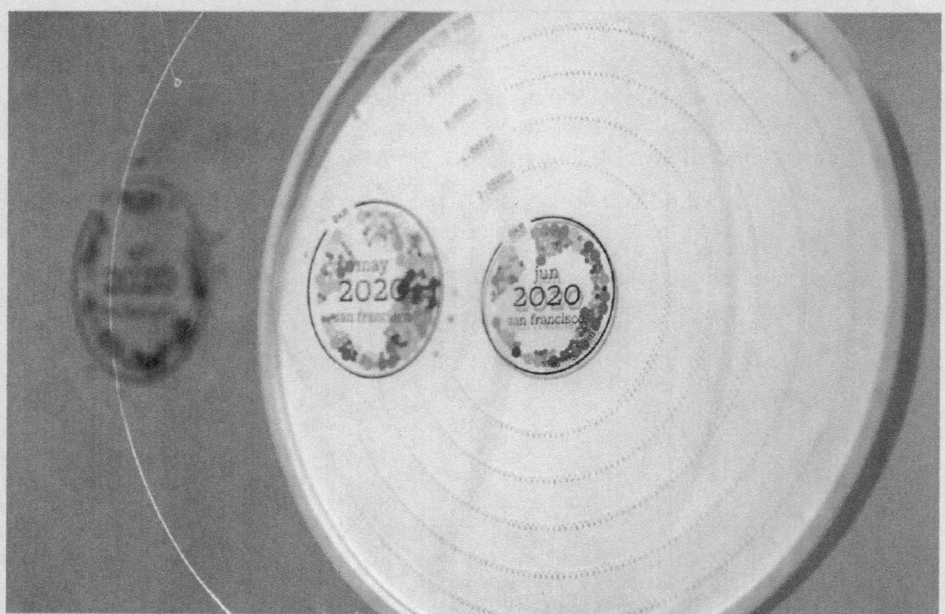

"San Francisco issues the first stay-at-home order on March 16, and it lasts well into May. [...] In those same months, we read article after report after personal anecdote of anti-Asian hate crimes. We don't go outside for weeks at a time, and in the rare times we go out for errands, we never go out by ourselves." (Photo courtesy of Tuan Huang, https://tuan-h.com/)

The visualization is also projected onto water, into which drops fall to represent the number of people who died in the pandemic. In the future, it will become the number of victims of hatred events targeted toward Asians during the pandemic.

Finally, there are physical flowers at the beginning of the exhibition that represent each flower photo I took before the pandemic, and one flower at the end of the exhibition, representing one specific flower photo I took after I started again to go out on my own.

When I create digital projects, I might know how many people visited the page, but there's no direct contact with the users. With such a physical exhibition, I got to see people reading their way through it, and they could tell me how they were touched by the installation. There's something very different from scrolling through an article on your phone versus making the effort of going to a specific installation to see a project.

Based on this experience, which tips would you share with new data visualization practitioners who are hesitating to "take up space" in this field?

It's interesting because I'm currently redirecting my career into arts, a field that is new for me, and I get to feel again what it means to start in a new professional area and be a beginner. But every time I put work out there, I get feedback from people who are more advanced on the path. This feedback helps me iterate my work. And even when there are no reactions online, at least I know that I'm documenting my work, and there's value in this process.

Summary

- Hierarchical visualizations communicate parent-child relationships via *enclosure*, *connections*, or *adjacency*.
- They can be created from CSV or JSON data.
- If we work with CSV data, we need two columns: one for the child nodes and one for their parents. Once the dataset is loaded into our project, we use method `d3.stratify()` to generate a hierarchical data structure named `root`.
- If we work with hierarchical JSON data, we use method `d3.hierarchy()` to generate the hierarchical data structure named `root`.
- The `root` hierarchical data structure has a `descendants()` method that returns an array of all the nodes and a `leaves()` method that returns an array of all the leaf nodes (the nodes without children).
- To create a circle pack visualization, we pass the `root` hierarchical data to the layout generator `d3.pack()`. This generator calculates the position and size of each circle and appends this information to the dataset. We then use it to draw the circles that compose the visualization.
- To draw a tree chart, we pass the `root` hierarchical data to layout generator `d3.tree()`. This generator calculates the position of each node and appends this information to the dataset. We then use it to draw the links and circles that compose the visualization.

Network visualizations

This chapter covers

- Manipulating nodes and link datasets
- Drawing an adjacency matrix
- Creating an arc diagram
- Running a simulation with the d3-force layout
- Applying positioning, collision, centering, many-body, and link forces

Network analysis and network visualizations are standard now in the age of social networks and big data. They are particularly interesting because they focus on how things are related and represent systems more accurately than the traditional flat data seen in more common data visualizations. While in the hierarchical visualizations (discussed in chapter 11), a node can have many children but only one parent, networks present the possibility of many-to-many connections.

In general, when dealing with networks, you refer to the things being connected (e.g., people) as *nodes* and the connections between them (e.g., following someone on X, formerly Twitter) as *edges* or *links*. Networks may also be referred to as *graphs* because that's what they're called in mathematics. They can represent many different data structures, such as transportation networks and linked open data.

Networks aren't just a data format: they're a perspective on data. When you work with network data, you typically try to discover and display patterns of the network or parts of the network rather than individual nodes in the network. In general, you'll find that the typical information visualization techniques are designed to showcase the network structure rather than individual nodes.

In this chapter, we'll look at four common forms of network visualizations: adjacency matrices, arc diagrams, beeswarm plots, and network graphs, as shown in figure 12.1. We'll create the last two visualizations with D3's force-directed layout.

12.1 Preparing network data

In this chapter, we'll build a project based on data from Shakespeare's play *Romeo and Juliet*. You can see this project at http://mng.bz/y8yE and download the code files from the book's GitHub repository (http://mng.bz/Xqjv).

You'll find the main dataset in the `romeo_and_juliet.json` file. In this JSON file, each object is a line from the play, accompanied by the name of the character that performs this line, the act, and the scene numbers. Table 12.1 shows a sample of lines from this dataset, specifically from act 1, scenes 3 and 5.

Table 12.1 Sample of lines from the play *Romeo and Juliet*

Act-Scene-Line	Character	Line
1.3.1	Lady Capulet	Nurse, where's my daughter? call her forth to me.
1.3.2	Nurse	Now, by my maidenhead, at twelve year old,
1.3.3	Nurse	I bade her come. What, lamb! what, ladybird!
1.3.4	Nurse	God forbid! Where's this girl? What, Juliet!
1.3.5	Juliet Capulet	How now! who calls?
1.5.115	Romeo Montague	Give me my sin again.
1.5.116	Juliet Capulet	You kiss by the book.
1.5.117	Nurse	Madam, your mother craves a word with you.
1.5.118	Romeo Montague	What is her mother?

To build network visualizations, we need to create two separate data files from the original dataset: one that contains the nodes and one with the edges. In our project, the nodes will be the characters from the play. Whenever two characters share at least one scene in the play, there will be an edge, or link, between them. The weight of this edge will be the number of scenes in which they appear together.

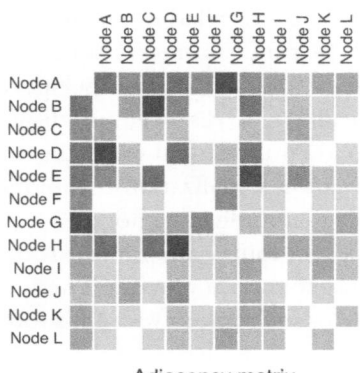

Adjacency matrix

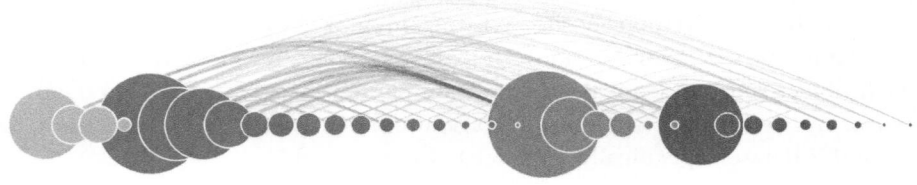

Arc diagram

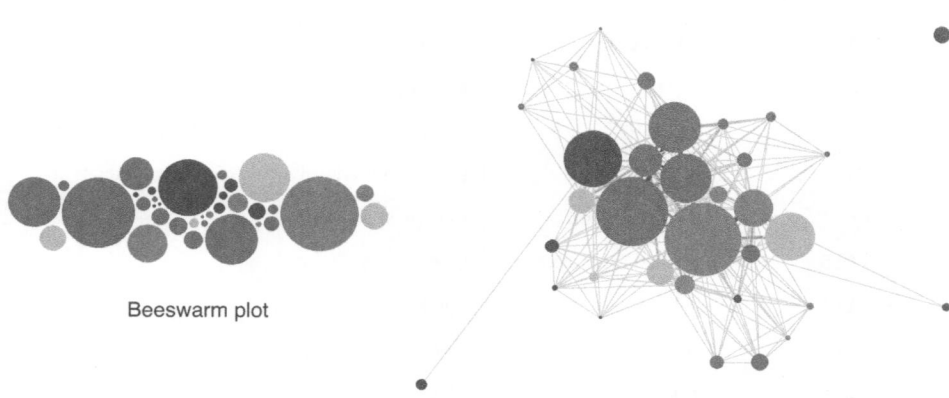

Beeswarm plot

Network graph

Figure 12.1 Adjacency matrices, arc diagrams, beeswarm plots, and network graphs are four common ways to visualize network data. While beeswarm plots focus on the nodes, adjacency matrices use a grid to represent the links between those nodes. Arc diagrams and network graphs display both the nodes and their connections.

If we take our sample dataset from table 12.1, the nodes data file could look like table 12.2. It contains any relevant information about each node. In our case, those are the characters' names, the house to which they belong, their description, and the number of lines they perform in the play.

Table 12.2 Nodes list for the sample dataset

Name	House	Description	Number of Lines
Lady Capulet	House of Capulet	Matriarch of the house of Capulet	115
Nurse	House of Capulet	Juliet's personal attendant and confidante	281
Juliet Capulet	House of Capulet	13-year-old daughter of Capulet, the play's female protagonist	544
Romeo Montague	House of Montague	Son of Montague, the play's male protagonist	614

A complete node list is already available in this chapter's code file named `nodes.json`. We'll use this information as we build our project.

The second file we need is an edge list. A list of edges has two primary columns named *source* and *target*. As their name suggests, they represent the source and target of each link. Figure 12.2 shows two types of network edges: directed and undirected. *Directed edges* have a meaningful direction from the source node to the target node. An arrow can represent this direction. For example, you might be following Lady Gaga on X, but Lady Gaga isn't necessarily following you. In *undirected edges*, the connection is valid in both directions. For our *Romeo and Juliet* project, the edges are undirected.

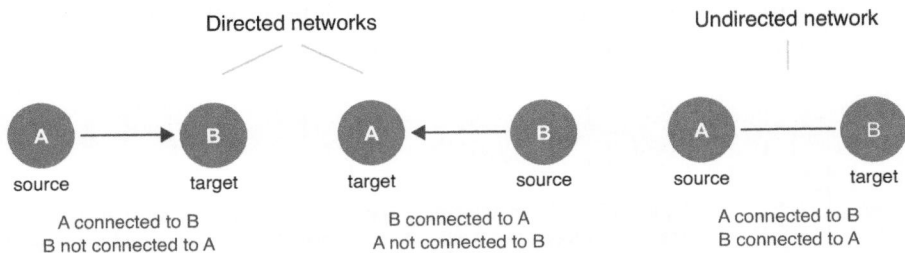

Figure 12.2 Network edges have a source and a target. In directed networks, the direction of the connection is meaningful and often represented by an arrow. In undirected networks, there's no specific direction to the relationship.

Table 12.3 shows an example of how an edge list would look for our sample dataset. In this small sample of lines, Lady Capulet and the Nurse share only one scene (1.3), while the Nurse and Juliet are present together in two scenes (1.3 and 1.5). Because the edges in our example are undirected, it doesn't matter which character is associated with the source or the target as long as they appear on the same line in the table.

Then we use the *weight* attribute to indicate how many scenes the characters share. This weight will later influence how close two nodes appear in the network graph.

Table 12.3   Links list for the sample dataset

Source	Target	Weight
Lady Capulet	Nurse	1
Nurse	Juliet Capulet	2
Romeo Montague	Juliet Capulet	1

A complete list of edges is already available in this chapter's code file named edges.json. It contains every pair of characters that appear together in at least one scene. The weight attributes indicate the number of scenes in which they appear side by side. In the edges.json file, this number represents the total number of scenes two characters share throughout the play. We'll use this information to build our visualizations in the following sections.

12.2   *Creating an adjacency matrix*

It may surprise you that one of the most effective network visualizations has no connecting lines at all. Instead, the adjacency matrix uses a grid to represent connections between nodes. The principle of an adjacency matrix is simple: you place the nodes along the x-axis and then place them again along the y-axis. If a node from the x-axis is connected to a node from the y-axis, the corresponding grid square is filled. Otherwise, it's left blank, as shown in figure 12.3. Because our network is also weighted, we can use saturation or opacity to designate the weight, with lighter colors indicating a weaker connection, and darker colors indicating a stronger connection.

B and D are connected.

Figure 12.3   In an adjacency matrix, the nodes are placed along the x-axis and then again along the y-axis. If two nodes are connected, the corresponding grid square is filled. We can communicate the strength of this connection with color saturation or opacity.

Figure 12.4 shows the adjacency matrix that we'll build in this section. Note how the matrix is symmetric. This is because our network links are undirected. If Romeo shares a scene with Juliet, then Juliet also shares a scene with Romeo! Because characters can't be connected to themselves, the spaces along the diagonal of the matrix are blank.

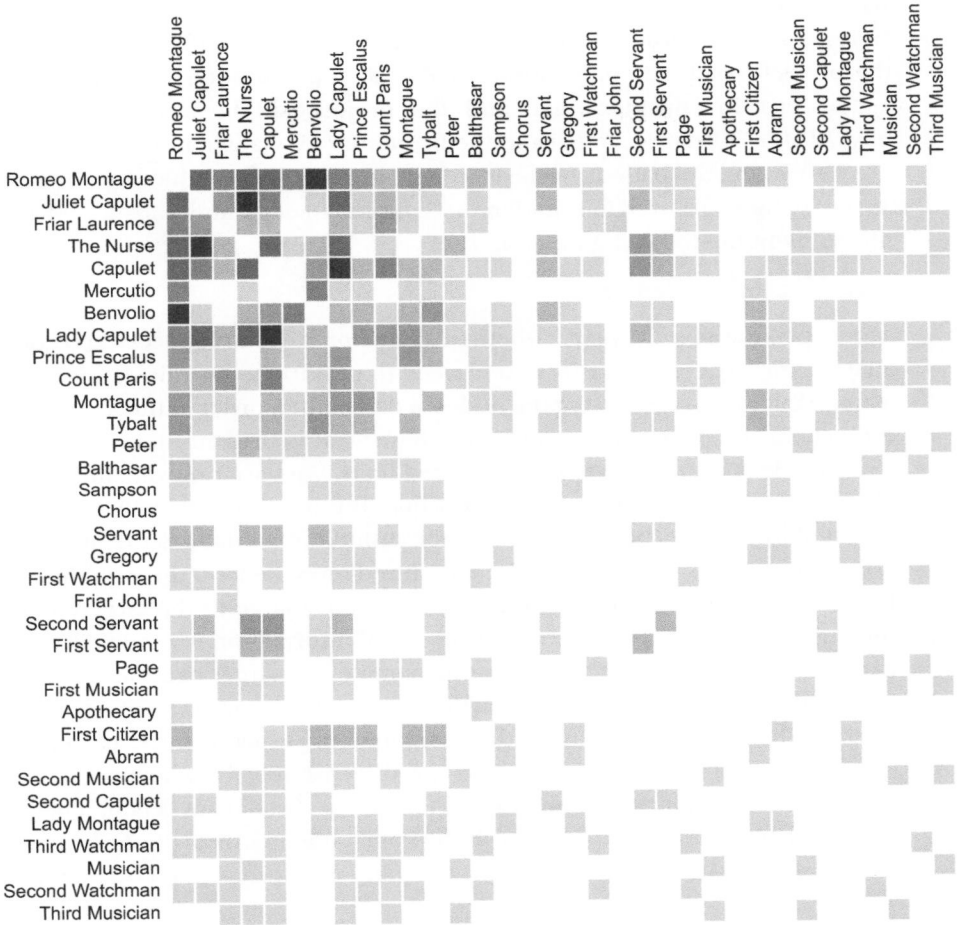

Figure 12.4   Adjacency matrix of Romeo and Juliet. The characters, or nodes, are listed along the x-axis and y-axis, while the number of scenes they share, the edges, are communicated by the filled grid squares. The darker the square, the more scenes the two characters share. Adjacency matrices of undirected networks are symmetric, but they can also visualize directed networks, for which they become asymmetric.

Building an adjacency matrix with D3.js is relatively simple because this visualization is only made of rectangle and text elements. In this section, we'll explain how to manipulate the network data (the nodes and the links data files) to achieve this chart. We'll also make it interactive to improve its readability.

To get started with this exercise, open the `start` folder from the `chapter_12/ 12.2-Adjacency_matrix` code files in your code editor. This project is built with ES6 JavaScript modules, and we've already added the relevant D3 dependencies for you.

You can see them in `package.json`. To install those dependencies, run command `npm install` in your terminal. As explained in chapter 11, you'll need a bundler to run the project locally. If you've installed Parcel, you can enter command `parcel src/index.html` in your terminal, and the project will be available at http://localhost:1234/. Otherwise, go back to the beginning of chapter 11 for instructions.

We've already loaded the `nodes.json` and `edges.json` files into the project. In `main.js`, they are available under the constants `nodes` and `edges`. Still in `main.js`, uncomment the following function call:

```
drawMatrix(nodes, edges);
```

Then open the `matrix.js` file, where this function is declared. Because D3 doesn't have a layout for adjacency matrices, we'll need to perform a few calculations ourselves. In listing 12.1, we start by sorting the nodes in descending order of the number of lines for each character. This is the order in which we want to present them on our matrix.

Our `edges` array is made of undirected links. We have only one link between each character pair that shares at least one scene. But in adjacency matrices, links are represented in two directions: from the nodes listed horizontally to the nodes listed vertically, and vice versa. To extract all the required links, we loop through the `edges` array. For each edge, we create two links: one from the source to the target, and one from the target to the source. We store these edges' information in an object named `edgeHash`, under a key corresponding to their source and target names.

Finally, we create all the possible source-target connections by looping twice through the nodes. We calculate the position of the top-left corner of the corresponding grid square with the indexes and the dimensions of the squares and save those under the keys x and y. By doing so, we create our own layout. Then, if `edgeHash` contains the corresponding link, we push the item to the matrix array. Once complete, the matrix array contains one item for every square that will be filled on our visualization.

Listing 12.1   Preparing the data matrix (`matrix.js`)

```
export const drawMatrix = (nodes, edges) => {

  nodes.sort((a, b) => b.totalLinesNumber -     Sort the nodes in descending
    a.totalLinesNumber);                         order of line number.

  const edgeHash = {};
  edges.forEach(edge => {

    const link1 = {
      source: edge.source,                       Extract all the existing links (in both
      target: edge.target,                       directions), and store them by ID in
      weight: edge.weight                        an array named edgeHash. This
    };                                            object will help us test whether a
    const id1 = `${edge.source}-${edge.target}`; source-target pair has a link.
    edgeHash[id1] = link1;

    const link2 = {
```

```
      source: edge.target,
      target: edge.source,
      weight: edge.weight
    };
    const id2 = `${edge.target}-${edge.source}`;
    edgeHash[id2] = link2;

  });

  const matrix = [];
  const squareWidth = 16;
  const padding = 2;
  nodes.forEach((charA, i) => {
    nodes.forEach((charB, j) => {
      if (charA !== charB) {
        const id = `${charA.id}-${charB.id}`;
        const item = {
          id: id,
          source: charA.id,
          target: charB.id,
          x: i * (squareWidth + padding),
          y: j * (squareWidth + padding)
        };

        if (edgeHash[id]) {
          item.weight = edgeHash[id].weight;
          matrix.push(item);
        }
      }
    }
  });
};
```

Extract all the existing links (in both directions), and store them by ID in an array named edgeHash. This object will help us test whether a source-target pair has a link.

Create all possible source-target connections by looping twice through the nodes.

Set the xy coordinates based on the source-target array indexes. We'll use this information later to set the position of the grid's squares.

If there's a corresponding edge in our edge list, give the item the related weight, and push it to the matrix array.

Exercise: Draw the adjacency matrix

Now that we've preprocessed the data, you have all the knowledge required to draw an adjacency matrix like the one from figure 12.4 and from the hosted project (http://mng.bz/y8yE). Follow these steps:

1. Keep working in `matrix.js`, inside function `drawMatrix()`.
2. Calculate the chart's dimensions based on the number of nodes and the size and padding of each square.
3. Append an SVG element in the `div` with an ID of `matrix` that already exists in `index.html`.
4. Append a `rectangle` element for each item in the `matrix` array. Use the `x` and `y` keys to set the position of the squares. Set their `fill` attribute to the color `"#364652"`, and make their `fill-opacity` proportional to the weight of the link (the greater the weight, the higher the opacity).
5. Append a label for each node on the left side of the matrix.
6. Append a label for each node on the top of the matrix. Use the `transform` attribute to rotate the text elements.

(continued)

If you get stuck or want to compare your solution with ours, you'll find it in section D.12 of appendix D and in the `12.1-Adjacency_matrix/end` folder of this chapter's code files. But as usual, we encourage you to try to complete it on your own. Your solution might differ slightly from ours, and that's all right!

Once completed, your adjacency matrix should look similar to the one in the hosted project. To help the user interpret the opacity of the squares, we'll create a legend. In listing 12.2, we start by declaring an array called `weights`, containing a list of integers between 1 and 7. Those correspond to the possible weights or number of scenes two characters share.

We use this `weights` array to create an unordered list of the possible weights. Each list item contains a `div` responsible for displaying the color and another for displaying the labels. We've already written styles for this legend in `visualization.css`. Make sure to use the same class names as in the code snippet for these styles to be effective.

Listing 12.2 Adding a legend for the squares' opacity (`matrix.js`)

```
import { select, selectAll } from "d3-selection";
import { max, range } from "d3-array";
import { scaleLinear } from "d3-scale";

export const drawMatrix = (nodes, edges) => {

  ...

  const weights = range(1, maxWeight + 1);     ⟵  Create an array containing
                                                   all the possible weights.

  const legend = select(".matrix-legend")
    .append("ul")
    .selectAll(".legend-color-item")             Append an unordered list to the div with
    .data(weights)                               a class of "matrix-legend". Use the
    .join("li")                                  data-binding pattern to append a list
      .attr("class", "legend-color-item");       item for each weight in the weights array.
  legend
    .append("div")                               Inside each list item, append a
      .attr("class", "legend-color")             div responsible for displaying the
      .style("background-color", "#364652")      opacity related to each weight.
      .style("opacity", d => opacityScale(d));
  legend
    .append("div")                               Inside each list item, append a div
      .attr("class", "legend-color-label")       responsible for displaying the number of
      .text(d => d);                             shared scenes corresponding to each weight.

});
```

Adjacency matrices can be hard to read without something to highlight the row and column of a square. By adding such interactivity, as in the next listing, we make our visualization easier to read.

Listing 12.3 Highlighting related nodes on mouse over (`matrix.js`)

```
...
import { transition } from "d3-transition";

export const drawMatrix = (nodes, edges) => {

  ...

  selectAll(".grid-quare")
    .on("mouseenter", (e, d) => {

      const t = transition()
        .duration(150);

      selectAll(".label-left")
        .transition(t)
          .style("opacity", label => label.id ===
          d.source ? 1 : 0.1);

      selectAll(".label-top")
        .transition(t)
          .style("opacity", label => label.id ===
          d.target ? 1 : 0.1);

      const charA = nodes.find(char => char.id ===
        d.source).name;
      const charB = nodes.find(char => char.id ===
        d.target).name;
      select(".matrix-tooltip-charA").text(charA);
      select(".matrix-tooltip-charB").text(charB);
      select(".matrix-tooltip-scenes").text(d.weight);
      select(".matrix-tooltip").classed("hidden", false);

    })
    .on("mouseleave", (e, d) => {

      selectAll(".label-top, .label-left")
        .style("opacity", 1);

      select(".matrix-tooltip").classed("hidden", true);

    });

});
```

Annotations:
- Add an event listener for when the mouse enters a square from the matrix.
- Set the opacity of all the characters' node labels to 10%, except for the ones corresponding to the edge's source and target.
- Populate and display a tooltip detailing the number of scenes shared by the two characters.
- Add an event listener for when the mouse leaves a square from the matrix.
- Set the opacity of all the characters' node labels to 100%.
- Hide the tooltip.

You can see in figure 12.5 how moving your cursor over a square from the matrix highlights the corresponding nodes and displays a tooltip with the number of scenes shared by the characters.

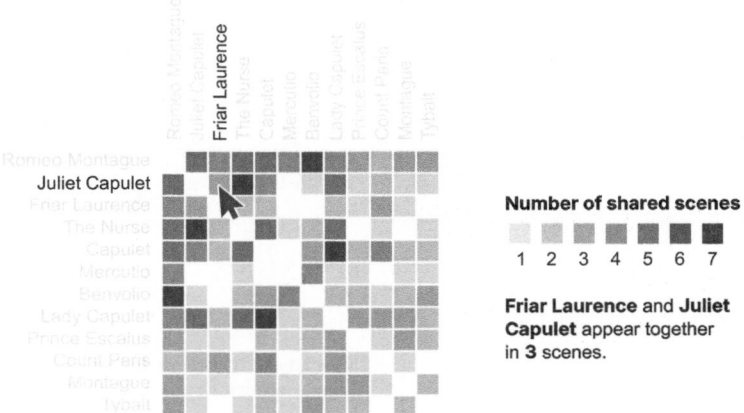

Figure 12.5   When the cursor is positioned over a square from the adjacency matrix, the corresponding characters' node labels are highlighted, and a tooltip with the number of scenes they share is displayed (partial view).

12.3   *Drawing an arc diagram*

Another way to graphically represent networks is by using an arc diagram. An arc diagram arranges the nodes along a line and draws the links as arcs above or below that line. Whereas adjacency matrices focus on edge dynamics, arc diagrams concentrate on node dynamics, allowing you to see which nodes are isolated and which ones have many connections. Figure 12.6 shows that node A is connected to nodes B and C, node B is connected to nodes A and C, node C is connected to nodes A and B, and node D is isolated.

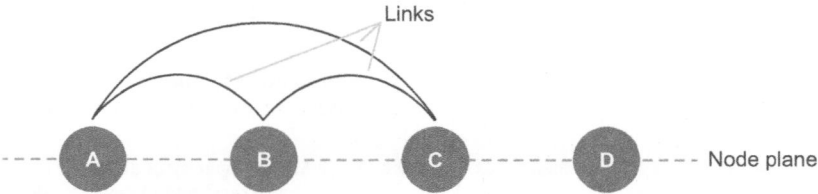

Figure 12.6   On arc diagrams, the nodes are positioned along a line, and the links are displayed as arcs between the nodes. In this example, node A is connected to nodes B and C, node B is connected to nodes A and C, node C is connected to nodes A and B, and node D is isolated.

In this section, we'll build the arc diagram shown in figure 12.7. The character nodes are represented by circles and positioned along the horizontal axis. The color of the nodes represents the family to which they belong (yellow for the Ruling House of

Verona, red for the House of Capulet, green for the House of Montague, and purple for other characters). The size of the circles is proportional to the number of lines they say throughout the play. A link is drawn between the characters sharing at least one scene. The higher the number of shared scenes, the thicker the link.

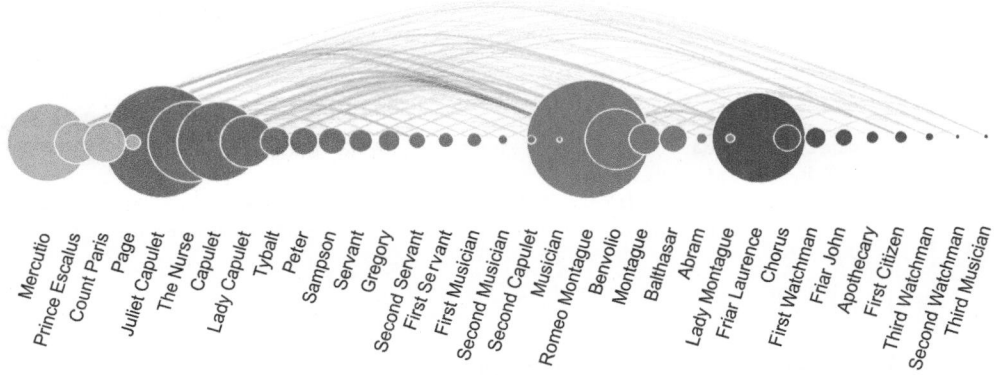

Figure 12.7   Arc diagram showing the connections between characters from *Romeo and Juliet*. The thicker a link, the more scenes two characters share.

To get started, go to `main.js`, and uncomment function call `drawArcDiagram(nodes, edges)`. Then open `arc.js.`, where we'll work inside function `drawArcDiagram()`. We've already declared the chart's dimensions.

As we did for the adjacency matrix, we must preprocess the node and edge data before drawing an arc diagram. In listing 12.4, we create a deep copy of the `nodes` and `edges` array. This copy will allow us to append information related to the arc diagram without affecting the original arrays.

We build a pseudo layout by setting the horizontal position of each node with a point scale. We also make the `edges` source and target point to the whole node object rather than only the node ID. This trick will allow us later to easily have access to the starting and ending position of the edges.

Listing 12.4   Preprocessing the arc diagram data (`arc.js`)

```
import { scalePoint } from "d3-scale";
import { houses } from "./helper";

export const drawArcDiagram = (nodes, edges) => {

  ...

  const nodeHash = {};
  const arcNodes = JSON.parse(JSON.stringify(nodes));
```
⟵┘ **Make a deep copy of the nodes array.**

```
arcNodes.sort((a, b) => houses.find(h =>
  h.house === a.house).order - houses.find(h =>
  h.house === b.house).order);
```
Sort the nodes to the order set in the houses array (predefined in helper.js).

```
const xScale = scalePoint()
  .domain(arcNodes.map(node => node.id))
  .range([0, innerWidth]);
```
Declare a point scale responsible for calculating the position of the nodes along the horizontal axis.

```
arcNodes.forEach((node, i) => {
  nodeHash[node.id] = node;
  node.x = xScale(node.id);
});
```
Create a hash that associates each node with its ID value.

Set the x position of each node.

Make a deep copy of the edges array.

```
const arcEdges = JSON.parse(JSON.stringify(edges));
arcEdges.forEach(edge => {
  edge.source = nodeHash[edge.source];
  edge.target = nodeHash[edge.target];
});
```
Replace the ID of the nodes with a pointer to the node object.

```
};
```

With the data preprocessing step completed, we can append the shapes composing an arc diagram. To draw the arcs, we use `path` elements. In listing 12.5, we pass the coordinates of the arc's source node, computed middle point, and target node to D3's line generator to get the path's `d` attribute. We also set the `stroke-width` attribute of each arc based on its weight. Finally, we call the color scale already declared in `scales.js` to set the color of the character nodes.

Listing 12.5   Appending the arcs and the nodes (`arc.js`)

```
...
import { line, curveCardinal } from "d3-shape";
import { max } from "d3-array";
import { getRadius, colorScale } from "./scales";

export const drawArcDiagram = (nodes, edges) => {

  ...

  const svg = select("#arc")
    .append("svg")
      .attr("viewBox", `0 0 ${width} ${height}`)
    .append("g")
      .attr("transform", `translate(${margin.left},
        ${margin.top})`);
```
Append the SVG container and the inner chart.

```
  const getArc = d => {
    const arcGenerator = line().curve(curveCardinal);
    const midX = (d.source.x + d.target.x) / 2;
    const midY = -Math.abs((d.source.x -
      d.target.x) / 6);
```
Calculate the d attribute of a curve starting at the source node, passing through a computed middle point above the nodes, and ending at the target node.

```
  const path = arcGenerator([
    [d.source.x, 0],
    [midX, midY],
    [d.target.x, 0]
  ]);

  return path;
};
```

Calculate the d attribute of a curve starting at the source node, passing through a computed middle point above the nodes, and ending at the target node.

```
svg
  .selectAll(".arc-link")
  .data(arcEdges)
  .join("path")
    .attr("class", "arc-link")
    .attr("d", d => getArc(d))
    .attr("fill", "none")
    .attr("stroke", "#364652")
    .attr("stroke-width", d => d.weight)
    .attr("stroke-opacity", 0.1)
    .attr("stroke-linecap", "round");
```

Use the data-binding pattern to append a path element for each edge. Call the getArc() function to set the d attribute, and set the stroke-width to the weight of the link.

```
const maxLines = max(arcNodes, d =>
  d.totalLinesNumber);
svg
  .selectAll(".arc-node")
  .data(arcNodes.sort((a, b) => b.totalLinesNumber -
    a.totalLinesNumber))
  .join("circle")
    .attr("class", "arc-node")
    .attr("cx", d => d.x)
    .attr("cy", 0)
    .attr("r", d => getRadius(maxLines,
      d.totalLinesNumber))
    .attr("fill", d => colorScale(d.house))
    .attr("stroke", d => "#FAFBFF")
    .attr("stroke-width", 2);
```

Use the data-binding pattern to append a circle element for each node, sorted in descending line number. Set their fill attribute based on the characters' house, with the color scale already declared in scales.js.

```
  svg
    .selectAll(".arc-label")
    .data(arcNodes)
    .join("text")
      .attr("class", "arc-label")
      .attr("text-anchor", "end")
      .attr("dominant-baseline", "middle")
      .attr("transform", d => `translate(${d.x}, 70),
        rotate(-70)`)
      .text(d => d.name)
      .style("font-size", "14px");

};
```

Use the data-binding pattern to append a text label for each node. Rotate the text to facilitate readability.

After this step, your arc diagram will look like the one from the hosted project (http://mng.bz/y8yE). With such an abstract chart, interactivity is no longer optional to help determine who is connected to whom. For example, when the mouse is positioned over a node, we can reveal only the characters that share a link with that node and the corresponding edges. This is what we do in the next listing.

```
...
import { transition } from "d3-transition";

export const drawArcDiagram = (nodes, edges) => {

  ...
  selectAll(".arc-node")
    .on("mouseenter", (e, d) => {          ⟵  Attach event listeners for when
                                              the cursor enters a node.
      const t = transition()
        .duration(150);

      const isLinked = char => {
        return arcEdges.find(edge =>
          (edge.source.id === d.id && edge.target.id      Check whether a character
            === char.id) || (edge.source.id              shares a link with the node
            === char.id && edge.target.id === d.id))      that triggered the event.
          ? true
          : false;
      };

      selectAll(".arc-link")
        .transition(t)
        .attr("stroke-opacity", link =>
          link.source.id === d.id || link.target.id
            === d.id ? 0.1 : 0);

      selectAll(".arc-node")
        .transition(t)
        .attr("fill-opacity", char => char.id === d.id     Show only the nodes and
          || isLinked(char) ? 1 : 0 )                      edges related to the node
        .attr("stroke-opacity", char => char.id ===        that triggered the event.
          d.id || isLinked(char) ? 1 : 0 );

      selectAll(".arc-label")
        .transition(t)
        .style("opacity", char => char.id === d.id
          || isLinked(char) ? 1 : 0 )
        .style("font-weight", char => char.id === d.id
          ? 700
          : 400);

    })
    .on("mouseleave", (e, d) => {          ⟵  Attach event listeners for when
                                              the cursor leaves a node.
      selectAll(".arc-link")
        .attr("stroke-opacity", 0.1);            Revert the opacity of the links
                                                 and nodes to their initial state.
      selectAll(".arc-node")
        .attr("fill-opacity", 1)
```

```
        .attr("stroke-opacity", 1);

    selectAll(".arc-label")
        .style("opacity", 1)
        .style("font-weight", 400);

    });

});
```

Revert the opacity of the links and nodes to their initial state.

In figure 12.8, we see how the interaction reveals the nodes' dynamics. We can conclude that Romeo shares at least one scene with almost every character from the play, while Friar John shares a scene only with Friar Laurence.

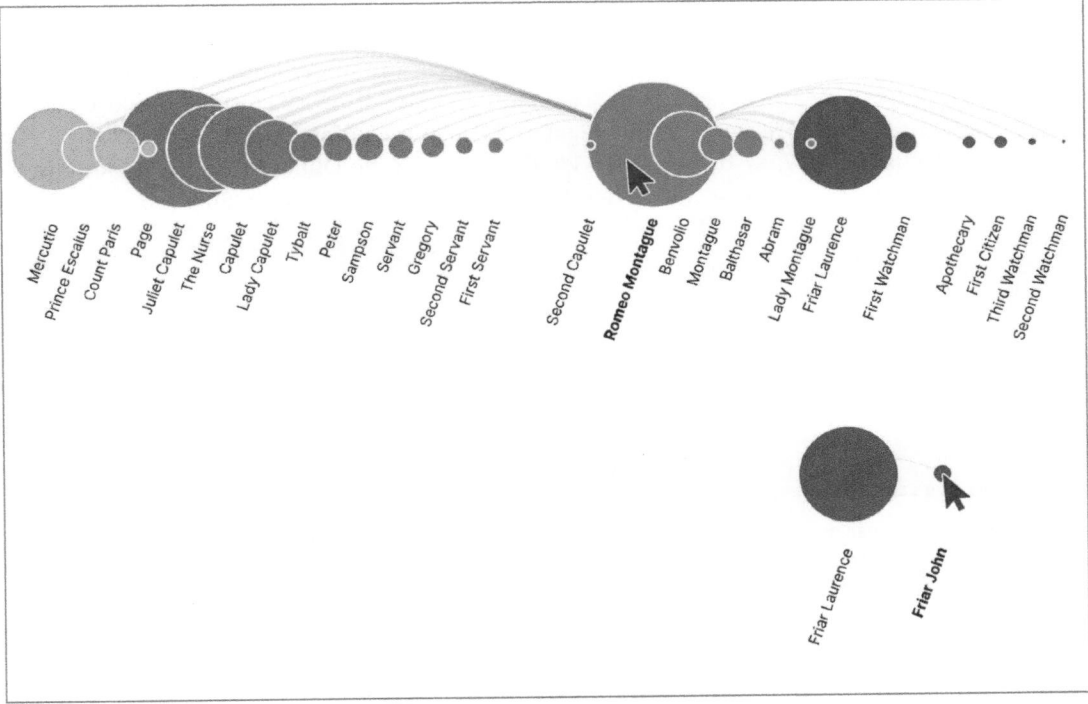

Figure 12.8 The interaction helps reveal the nodes' dynamics. We observe that Romeo shares scenes with almost every character from the play while Friar John shares the stage with Friar Laurence only.

12.4 Playing with forces

The force layout inherited its name from the method by which it determines a network's most optimal graphical representation. It dynamically updates the positions of its elements to find the best fit. Unlike the D3 layouts discussed previously, the force layout does it in real time rather than as a preprocessing step before rendering.

The principle behind a force layout is the interplay between positioning, collision, centering, many-body, and link forces. By mixing and matching these forces, we can attract nodes toward a specific position, ensure that they don't overlap, make nodes repel each other, and so on. In this section, we'll play with these different forces and see how they affect a visualization. We'll also build a beeswarm plot and a network diagram.

12.4.1   *Running a force simulation*

To run a D3 simulation, we call method `d3.forceSimulation()` from the d3-force module. Based on the forces applied to the simulation, D3 appends two types of information to each node: their next position (x and y) and their next velocity (vx and vy). Every time D3 completes an iteration of the simulation, called a tick, we call a custom function where we change the position of the circle according to the data appended by D3. We perform this cycle, illustrated in figure 12.9, until the simulation converges, meaning that the nodes found an optimal position according to the bound forces.

To set up your first simulation, go to `main.js`, and uncomment function call `draw-Beeswarm(nodes)`. Then open `beeswarm.js`. We'll work inside function `draw-Beeswarm()`, where we've already declared the chart's dimensions.

In listing 12.7, we append an SVG container to the DOM and a circle element for each node. Note that we don't need to set the circles' `cx` and `cy` attributes. We'll handle this during the simulation.

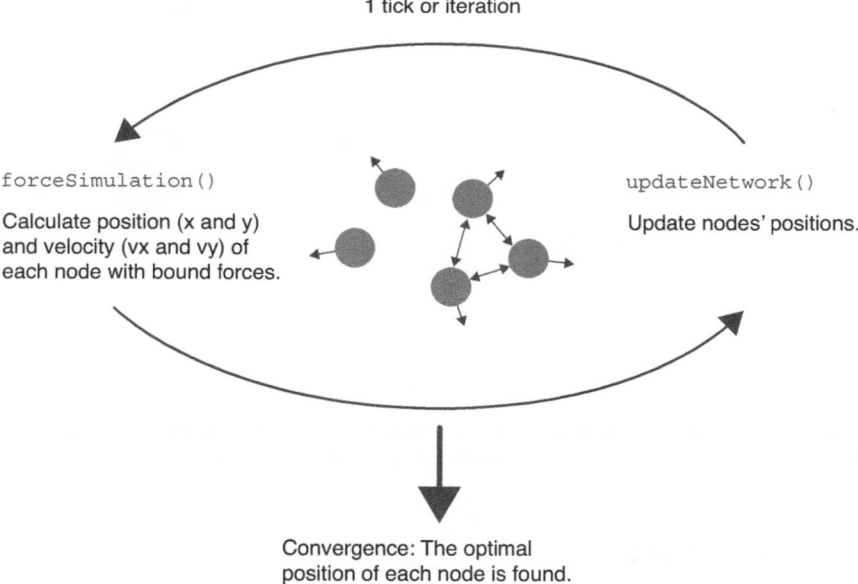

Figure 12.9   When running a force layout simulation, D3 makes a series of real-time ticks, or iterations, where it calculates the position and velocity of each node according to the bound forces. We can then update the nodes' positions in the tick's callback function. The simulation stops once an optimal position has been found for each node.

We then declare a function named `updateNetwork()`, where we select all the nodes and set their position based on the `x` and `y` attributes appended by the simulation. To run the simulation, we call D3 method `forceSimulation()`. We set the `nodes()` accessor function and call `updateNetwork()` after each tick.

Listing 12.7   Running a force simulation (`beeswarm.js`)

```js
import { select, selectAll } from "d3-selection";
import { forceSimulation } from "d3-force";
import { colorScale } from "./scales";

export const drawBeeswarm = (nodes) => {

  ...

  const svg = select("#beeswarm")
    .append("svg")
      .attr("viewBox", `0 0 ${width} ${height}`)
    .append("g")
      .attr("transform", `translate(${width/2},
        ${height/2})`);

  svg
    .selectAll(".beeswarm-circle")
    .data(nodes)
    .join("circle")
      .attr("class", "beeswarm-circle")
      .attr("r", 8)
      .attr("fill", d => colorScale(d.house))
      .attr("stroke", "#FAFBFF")
      .attr("stroke-width", 1);

  const updateNetwork = () => {
    selectAll(".beeswarm-circle")
      .attr("cx", d => d.x)
      .attr("cy", d => d.y);
  };

  const simulation = forceSimulation()
    .nodes(nodes)
    .on("tick", updateNetwork);

};
```

Append an SVG container and a group element for the inner chart. Translate this group to the center of the SVG container.

Use the data-binding pattern to append a circle for each node. Set their color based on the characters' houses.

Declare a function that updates the position of each node based on their x and y attributes.

Use method d3.forceSimulation() to run the simulation. Set the nodes accessor function, and after each tick, call function updateNetwork().

If you save this code and take a look in the browser, you'll see that the nodes are clustered nicely in the middle of the SVG container, as shown in figure 12.10. In listing 12.7, we translated the inner chart to the center of the SVG container for that purpose. In the following subsections, we'll apply different forces to the simulation and see how they affect the nodes' positions.

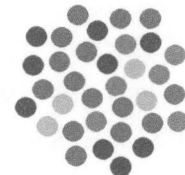

Figure 12.10 If we apply no force to the simulation, the nodes form a cluster without overlapping.

POSITIONING FORCES

The first forces we'll discuss are the positioning forces d3.forceX() and d3.forceY(). As their names suggest, forceX() makes the nodes move toward a specific horizontal position, while forceY() does the same with a vertical position. Figure 12.11 shows that applying forceX(0) sets the nodes' x-position to 0 and lets the nodes loosely find a place along the y-axis. forceY(0) does precisely the reverse: it sets the nodes' y-position to 0 and positions the nodes loosely along the x-axis. If we apply both forceX(0) and forceY(0), all the nodes are stacked upon each other at (0, 0).

```
forceSimulation()
  .force("x", d3.forceX(0) )
```

```
forceSimulation()
  .force("y", d3.forceY(0) )
```

```
forceSimulation()
  .force("x", d3.forceX(0) )
  .force("y", d3.forceY(0) )
```

Figure 12.11 d3.forceX() **makes the nodes move toward a specific horizontal position, while** d3.forceY() **does the same with a vertical position.**

We can also control how strong a force is with the strength() accessor function. When not specified, the strength of the forces defaults to 1. Suppose we apply both an x positioning force and a y positioning force while reducing the strength of the x-force to 0.01. In that case, the attraction toward the coordinate (0,0) will be stronger vertically than horizontally. Figure 12.12 shows that this results in the node being loosely positioned on the x-axis. If we do the reverse and set the strength applied by the y-force to 0.01, the attraction of the nodes toward a y-position of zero is weaker. Note that we can use the strength accessor function with any of the D3 forces.

> **NOTE** There's another positioning force, d3.forceRadial() (not covered here), that you'll want to use to position nodes on the circumference of a circle.

We can also use positioning forces to create clusters. For example, in figure 12.13, we call a D3 point scale that returns the horizontal or vertical position of the nodes based on the character's house. By passing this value to the positioning force, we create a distinct cluster, or grouping, for each house.

```
forceSimulation()
  .force("x", d3.forceX(0) )
  .force("y", d3.forceY(0) )
```

```
forceSimulation()
  .force("x", d3.forceX(0).strength(0.01) )
  .force("y", d3.forceY(0) )
```

```
forceSimulation()
  .force("x", d3.forceX(0) )
  .force("y", d3.forceY(0).strength(0.01) )
```

Figure 12.12 We can control the strength with which a force is applied with the strength() accessor function. By default, this strength is set to 1. If we apply both an x-force and a y-force but weaken the x-force, the attraction toward the coordinate (0,0) will be stronger vertically than horizontally. If we do the reverse, the attraction toward the center will be stronger horizontally than vertically.

```
forceSimulation()
  .force("x", d3.forceX(d => xScale(d.house)) )
```

```
forceSimulation()
  .force("y", d3.forceY(d => yScale(d.house)) )
```

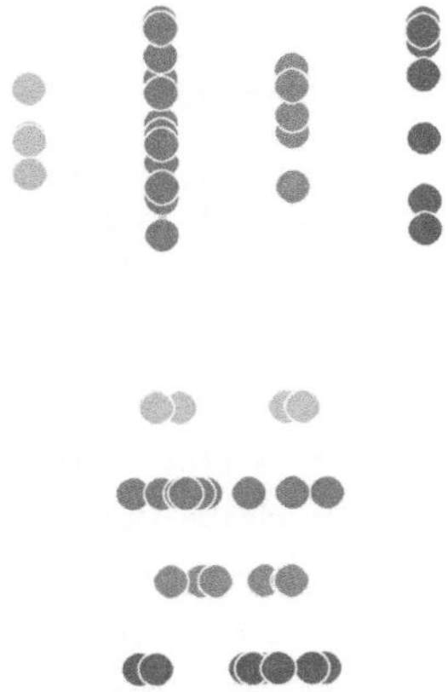

Figure 12.13 We can use positioning forces to create clusters. By passing the value returned by a point scale to forceX() or forceY(), we create a distinct group for each house.

COLLISION FORCE

To prevent nodes from overlapping, we can use collision force d3.forceCollide(). This force takes a given radius to set a minimum distance between the nodes. In the example illustrated in figure 12.14, each node has a radius of 10 px, and the value passed to the radius() accessor function is 12. This means that the collision force will ensure that there are always at least 12 px between the centers of two nodes, creating a padding of 2 px.

If we don't set any positioning force, the nodes naturally group into a circular shape. If we apply `forceX()` or `forceY()` in addition to the collision force, we obtain a beeswarm-like shape.

```
forceSimulation()
  .force("collide", d3.forceCollide().radius(12) )
```

```
forceSimulation()
  .force("x", d3.forceX(0) )
  .force("collide", d3.forceCollide().radius(12) )
```

```
forceSimulation()
  .force("y", d3.forceY(0) )
  .force("collide", d3.forceCollide().radius(12) )
```

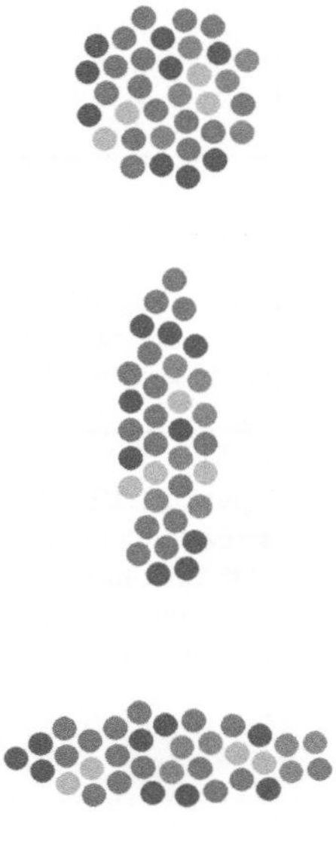

Figure 12.14   The collision force `d3.forceCollide()` prevents the nodes from overlapping. By setting its `radius()` accessor function, we impose a minimum distance between the center of each node. Without positioning forces, the nodes naturally aggregate into a circle. If we combine the collision force with a positioning force, we obtain a flattened shape that resembles a beeswarm chart.

Let's take a moment to explore our new ability to create a beeswarm visualization. Beeswarm charts are popular for showing distributions while maintaining individual points. For the purpose of this demonstration, we'll create 300 nodes and use method `d3.randomNormal()` to set their `value` attribute to a random number that follows a normal distribution, also called Gaussian distribution:

```
const sampleArray = range(300);
sampleNodes = [];
sampleArray.forEach(() => {
  const randomNumberGenerator = randomNormal();
  sampleNodes.push({ value: randomNumberGenerator() * 10 });
});
```

Suppose we append those nodes to an SVG container and run a force simulation using `forceX()` to position the nodes toward the horizontal position corresponding to their value (the `value` attribute set in the previous code snippet). In that case, `forceY()` moves the nodes toward the vertical center, and the collision force ensures that there's no overlapping. We end up with a beeswarm chart:

```
forceSimulation()
    .force("x", forceX(d => xScale(d.value)) )
    .force("y", forceY(0) )
    .force("collide", forceCollide().radius(7) )
    .nodes(sampleNodes)
    .on("tick", updateNetwork);
```

In figure 12.15, we observe that we indeed get a normal distribution. Although the horizontal position of each node should be pretty close to the one corresponding to its `value` attribute, it's good to know that D3 tries to find the positions that balance all the forces applied in the simulation. The final horizontal positions might not correspond exactly to the `value` attribute.

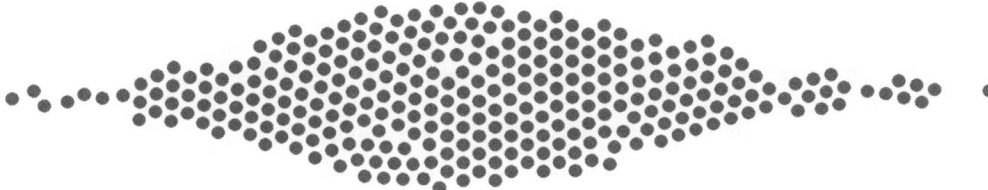

Figure 12.15   Beeswarm plot representing normally distributed values

CENTERING FORCE

Centering force `d3.forceCenter()` moves an entire cluster of nodes toward a specific position. While the x and y positioning forces move particles individually and might flatten a system of particles, the centering force translates the entire particle system, which keeps its original shape. In figure 12.16, we start by applying a collision force to

```
forceSimulation()
    .force("collide", d3.forceCollide().radius(12) )
```

(0, 0)

```
forceSimulation()
    .force("center", forceCenter().x(-10).y(5) )
    .force("collide", d3.forceCollide().radius(12) )
```

(-10, 5)

Figure 12.16   The centering force moves an entire system of particles, or nodes, toward the coordinates passed to the `x()` and `y()` accessor functions.

a group of nodes. By default, the nodes will center around the coordinate (0,0). If we apply a centering force with d3.forceCenter() and set the coordinates around which we want the system to move with the x() and y() accessor functions, all the nodes move altogether to the defined coordinate.

MANY-BODY FORCE

So far, we've only discussed forces that attract nodes toward a position. Many-body force d3.forceManyBody() is different in the sense that it influences how nodes interact with each other. A negative many-body force mimics repulsion, while a positive many-body force simulates attraction, as shown in figure 12.17.

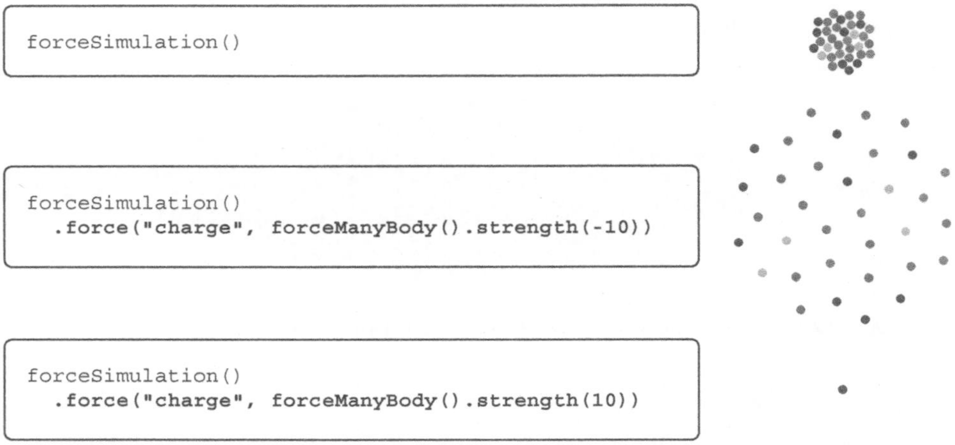

```
forceSimulation()
```

```
forceSimulation()
    .force("charge", forceManyBody().strength(-10))
```

```
forceSimulation()
    .force("charge", forceManyBody().strength(10))
```

Figure 12.17 The many-body force influences how nodes interact with each other. A negative many-body force creates repulsion, while a positive one mimics attraction.

To create a beeswarm-like visualization of Romeo and Juliet's characters, like the one shown in the hosted project (http://mng.bz/y8yE), we scale the radius of the nodes based on the number of lines said by the related character. To do so, we call function getRadius(), already available in scales.js. We also store the radius of each node in the bound data. We'll use it in a moment to set the collision force between the nodes. Note how we also made a deep copy of the nodes array and used it in our simulation. This will keep us from getting into trouble when running two force simulations from the same data (a beeswarm and a network diagram):

```
const beeswarmNodes = JSON.parse(JSON.stringify(nodes));

const maxLines = max(nodes, d => d.totalLinesNumber)
svg
  .selectAll(".beeswarm-circle")
  .data(beeswarmNodes)
```

```
.join("circle")
  .attr("class", "beeswarm-circle")
  .attr("r", d => {
    d.radius = getRadius(maxLines, d.totalLinesNumber);
    return d.radius;
  })
  .attr("fill", d => colorScale(d.house))
  .attr("stroke", "#FAFBFF")
  .attr("stroke-width", 1);
```

Then we apply a y-positioning force to the simulation, attracting the nodes toward the vertical center of the SVG container. We also use a collision force to avoid overlap. Finally, we set the `radius` accessor function to the `radius` attribute we appended to the nodes' data plus 2 px:

```
forceSimulation()
  .force("y", forceY(0) )
  .force("collide", forceCollide().radius(d => d.radius + 2) )
  .nodes(beeswarmNodes)
  .on("tick", updateNetwork);
```

The final beeswarm chart looks like the one in figure 12.18.

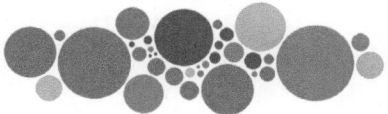

LINKS

The last force available in the d3-force module is link force `d3.forceLink()`, which applies a force between connected nodes. The more strongly two nodes are connected, the closer the link force will pull them together. It's with the link force, in combination with the other forces discussed previously, that we can create a network diagram.

Figure 12.18   Beeswarm-like chart of the characters from Romeo and Juliet. The color of the characters corresponds to their house, and their size corresponds to the number of lines they have in the play.

Still working with our *Romeo and Juliet* dataset, we'll create a network diagram where the links represent the number of scenes two characters share. We can go to `main.js` and uncomment function call `drawNetwork(nodes, edges)`. Then we open the `network.js` file and start working inside function `drawNetwork()`.

In the following code snippet, we use the `id()` accessor function to let D3 know how to recognize the source and target nodes. Note that the ID used to identify nodes must be unique. We also use the `strength()` accessor function to specify that the force the links apply on the nodes is proportional to their `weight` attribute (the number of scenes shared by two characters).

The code in listing 12.8 is similar to the one used to create the beeswarm-like chart in the previous section. The main difference is that we append a line element for each edge in addition to the node circles. Then function `updateNetwork()`, called after each tick, not only updates the positions of the nodes but also the positions of the links.

We combine the link force with a centering force that moves the visualization toward the center of the SVG container, a strong negative many-body force to create repulsion between the nodes so that there's some distance between them, and a collision force to avoid overlapping.

Listing 12.8 Creating a network diagram (`network.js`)

```
import { select, selectAll } from "d3-selection";
import { max } from "d3-array";
import { forceSimulation, forceCollide, forceCenter, forceManyBody,
        forceLink } from "d3-force";
import { colorScale, getRadius } from "./scales";

export const drawNetwork = (nodes, edges) => {

  const width = 850;
  const height = 600;

  const svg = select("#network")
    .append("svg")
      .attr("viewBox", `0 0 ${width} ${height}`)
    .append("g")
      .attr("transform", `translate(${width/2}, ${height/2})`);

  svg
    .selectAll(".network-link")
    .data(edges)
    .join("line")
      .attr("class", "network-link")
      .attr("stroke", "#364652")
      .attr("stroke-opacity", 0.1)
      .attr("stroke-width", d => d.weight);

  const maxLines = max(nodes, d => d.totalLinesNumber)
  svg
    .selectAll(".network-node")
    .data(nodes)
    .join("circle")
      .attr("class", "network-node")
      .attr("r", d => {
        d.radius = getRadius(maxLines, d.totalLinesNumber);
        return d.radius;
      })
      .attr("fill", d => colorScale(d.house))
      .attr("stroke", "#FAFBFF")
      .attr("stroke-width", 1);

  const updateNetwork = () => {
    selectAll(".network-link")
      .attr("x1", d => d.source.x)
      .attr("y1", d => d.source.y)
      .attr("x2", d => d.target.x)
      .attr("y2", d => d.target.y);
```

Use the data-binding pattern to append a line element for each edge. Don't set their position yet.

Update the positions of the links after each tick.

```
    selectAll(".network-node")
      .attr("cx", d => d.x)
      .attr("cy", d => d.y);
  };

  const simulation = forceSimulation()
    .force("charge", forceManyBody()
      .strength(-1000))
    .force("collide", forceCollide()
      .radius(d => d.radius + 2) )
    .force("center", forceCenter().x(0).y(0))
    .force("link", forceLink()
      .id(d => d.id)
      .strength(d => d.weight/10))
    .nodes(nodes)
    .on("tick", updateNetwork);

  simulation
    .force("link")
    .links(edges);
```

Combine the link force with a centering force that moves the visualization toward the center of the SVG container, a negative many-body force to create repulsion between the nodes so that there's some distance between them, and a collision force to avoid overlapping.

Set the array of edges associated with the link force.

```
};
```

CUSTOM BOUNDING FORCE

If you look at the network in your browser, you'll notice that the node representing the chorus is nowhere to be seen. This is because this node has no link attaching it to another one (the chorus has its own scenes and doesn't share the stage with other characters), and the many-body force applies a strong repulsion. If you look for the chorus node with the inspector tool, you'll see it ended up outside the SVG container. We'll create our custom bounding force to bring it back inside. Because D3 forces are simply callback functions, nothing keeps us from writing one of our own!

In the following snippet, we write a custom force named `"bounding"`. In the callback function, we loop through each node, and if the node is currently outside of the SVG container, we change its velocity (vx or vy) so that it's redirected toward the SVG container:

```
const simulation = forceSimulation()
  ...
  .force("bounding", () => {
    nodes.forEach(node => {
      if (node.x < -width/2 + node.radius) {
        node.vx = 1;
      }
      if (node.y < -height/2 + node.radius) {
        node.vy = 1;
      }
      if (node.x > width/2 - node.radius) {
        node.vx = -1;
      }
      if (node.y > height/2 - node.radius) {
        node.vy = -1;
      }
    });
  })
```

Figure 12.19 shows the final network visualization. The main characters (the larger circles) are close to each other because they share multiple scenes. Secondary characters (smaller circles) are on the periphery of the visualization because the links that attach them to others are weaker.

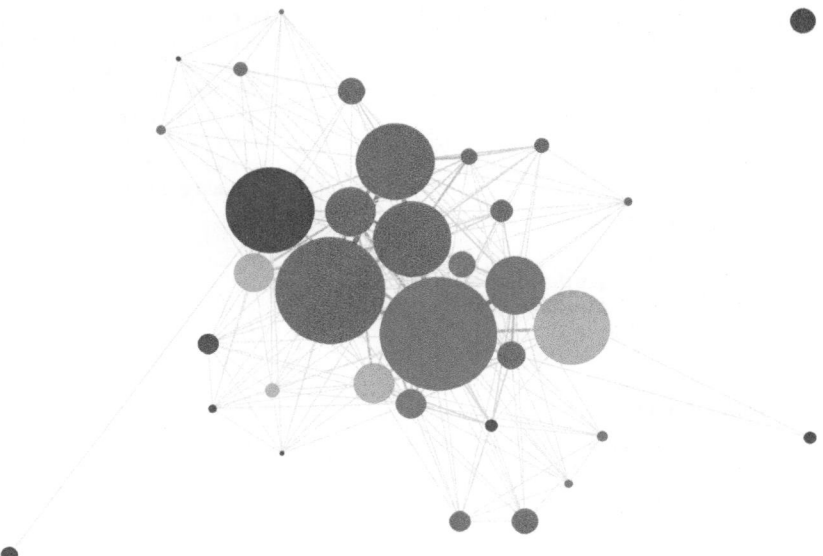

Figure 12.19   **Network visualization of the *Romeo and Juliet* characters. Each circle represents a character, and their size is proportional to the number of lines they have in the play. The links between the nodes represent the number of scenes they share. The closer two nodes are to each other, the more scenes they share in the play.**

To complete this project, we'll add an interaction to highlight relationships on mouse over. The technique is similar to the one used earlier to make the arc diagram interactive. When the mouse is positioned over a node, we set the opacity of all the nodes and links to 0, except the ones related to the selected node, as in the next listing. We also display the character's name and description in a tooltip on the right side of the visualization.

Listing 12.9   Adding interactivity (`network.js`)

```
export const drawNetwork = (nodes, edges) => {

  ...

  selectAll(".network-node")
    .on("mouseenter", (e, d) => {

      const t = transition()
        .duration(150);
```

```
        const isLinked = char => {
          return edges.find(edge =>
            (edge.source.id === d.id && edge.target.id === char.id) ||
            (edge.source.id === char.id && edge.target.id === d.id))
            ? true
            : false;
        };

        selectAll(".network-link")
          .transition(t)
          .attr("stroke-opacity", link =>
            link.source.id === d.id || link.target.id === d.id ? 0.1 : 0);

        selectAll(".network-node")
          .transition(t)
          .attr("fill-opacity", char =>
            char.id === d.id || isLinked(char) ? 1 : 0 );

        select(".network-character")
          .text(d.name);
        select(".network-description")
          .text(d.description);
        select(".network-sidebar")
          .classed("hidden", false);

    })
    .on("mouseleave", () => {

      selectAll(".network-link")
        .attr("stroke-opacity", 0.1);

      selectAll(".network-node")
        .attr("fill-opacity", 1);

      select(".network-sidebar")
        .classed("hidden", true);

    });

}));
```

> **Display the selected character's name and description in a tooltip on the right side of the visualization. The markup is already available in index.html, and the styles are available in visualization.css.**

> **Hide the tooltip.**

When the mouse is positioned over a node, only the characters sharing at least one scene with that node are displayed, as in figure 12.20.

Apothecary
Reluctantly sells Romeo
poison.

Figure 12.20 When the cursor is positioned over a node, only the characters that share at least one scene and their related links are displayed.

STOPPING AND RESTARTING THE FORCE LAYOUT

The force layout is designed to "cool off" and eventually stop after the network is laid out well enough that the nodes no longer move to new positions. When the layout has stopped like this, you'll need to restart it if you want it to animate again. In addition, if you've made any changes to the force settings or want to add or remove parts of the network, you'll need to stop and restart it.

You can stop a simulation by using `simulation.stop()`. It's good to stop the network when there's an interaction with a component elsewhere on your web page or a change in the styling of the network and then restart it once that interaction is over.

To begin or restart the layout animation, use `simulation.restart()`. You don't have to start the simulation when you first create it; it starts automatically.

Finally, if you want to move the layout forward with one step, you can use `simulation.tick()`. You can also precalculate your chart if you don't need the fancy animation. For example, you could run `simulation.tick(120)` to perform 120 iterations before laying out the visualization. Simulating the network without graphically animating it is much faster, and you can use D3 transitions to animate the movement of the nodes to their final precalculated position.

OPTIMIZATION

The force layout is highly resource-intensive. That's why it cools off and stops running by design. And if you have a large network running with the force layout, you can tax a user's computer until it becomes practically unusable. The first tip for optimization is to limit the number of nodes and edges in your network. A general rule of thumb is no more than 1,000 nodes. Still, that limit used to be 100 and gets higher as browsers increase in performance, so use profiling, and understand the minimum performance of the browsers that your audience will likely be using.

But if you have to present more nodes and want to improve the performance, you can use `forceManyBody.chargeDistance()` to set a maximum distance when computing the repulsive charge for each node. The lower this setting, the less structured the force layout will be, but the faster it will run. Because networks vary so much, you'll have to experiment with different values for `chargeDistance()` to find the best one for your network.

Finally, consider delegating the force layout calculation to a web worker or rendering parts of the graph with canvas if there are no expected interactions with the user. We'll discuss how to use canvas in chapter 15.

Interview with Matthias Stahl

Stahl is a data visualization designer/developer and is currently head of data and visualizations at *DER SPIEGEL*.

Can you tell us a little bit about your background and how you entered the field of data visualization?

The passion for data visualization came late into my life. Until 2020, I was a natural sciences researcher originally trained in biochemistry. During my PhD, I studied bacteria that are resistant against a multitude of antibiotics. On a molecular level, we sought to understand why these parasites get resistant and how we could design new drugs to circumvent them.

In order to be able to look into the machine room of bacteria, we conducted a lot of experiments, resulting in huge datasets. Suddenly, there was a need to analyze this data, which made me learn R and data visualization. Later, I discovered data visualization as a whole toolkit, which enabled us as researchers to succeed: the right visualization was often the key to a new breakthrough.

At the same time, I got a bit tired of my research in the lab. Although we tackled important medical questions, it was too abstract and too far away from people's lives. I started considering moving into data visualization consulting. It took me roughly a year to think this through and to eventually leave academia. In the end, it was the best decision I could make. I had the chance to work on exciting projects with various topics, not only science. Also publishing data visualizations immediately had an effect: people reacted, commented, and talked about the pieces. Ultimately, my interest in data and statistics met the exciting domains of art and design while involving a lot of psychology, and I have never regretted taking this path.

Do you use visualization tools other than D3? What's the place of D3 in your current data visualization workflow?

I almost exclusively design and build interactive visualizations for the web. Thus, HTML, CSS, and JavaScript are my best friends. Of course, writing vanilla, plain JavaScript can be quite cumbersome. That's where I bring in Svelte as a sophisticated platform to abstract most of the boilerplate. It also allows me to divide visualizations into components that can be reused, which is quite important in the fast-paced newsroom setting. Within these components, I use D3 as a collection of useful functions. As a rule of thumb, I apply D3 functions for the math and the paths, that is, for the mathematical transformations such as scales or geo projections and for the handling of geometries. My friend Connor Rothschild once said "D3 for the data and Svelte for the DOM"; I couldn't agree more. That being said, I don't use D3's general update pattern anymore. Rather, I combine Svelte and D3 in a way that allows me to write declarative instead of imperative code. As an example, I always set up SVGs as HTML (<svg>) elements in Svelte and then apply D3 functions to bring in the data.

You work with DER SPIEGEL. *How is your experience creating data visualizations and scrollytelling projects for a news magazine?*

I have been working with Der SPIEGEL for 2.5 years—first as deputy head of the graphics desk and later as head of the newly formed data and visualizations department. My experience as a data visualization designer, developer, and manager in the newsroom is double-edged. On the one hand, we have a very large and interested audience and we are usually free to come up with whatever topic and story idea we like. On the other hand, in our setting, stories are most often coupled to the current news. Thus, our projects have very short turnaround times, which could restrict the

(continued)

creative space. The latter can be countered by thoroughly elaborated frameworks and libraries. For our large visual stories, for example, we use Svelte plus D3 as a robust framework to support building apps in no time. On top, we assembled a collection of Svelte components and patterns that we can easily integrate into growing projects.

After all, it's on us to shape the future of data journalism and data visualization in the newsrooms. We, and I know it's similar in other newsrooms, have the freedom to test innovative ideas, and—most importantly—our audiences are open to these experiments as well.

Featured project: "Visualizing Censorship in Iran" created for "Journalism is Not a Crime" (https://journalismisnotacrime.com)

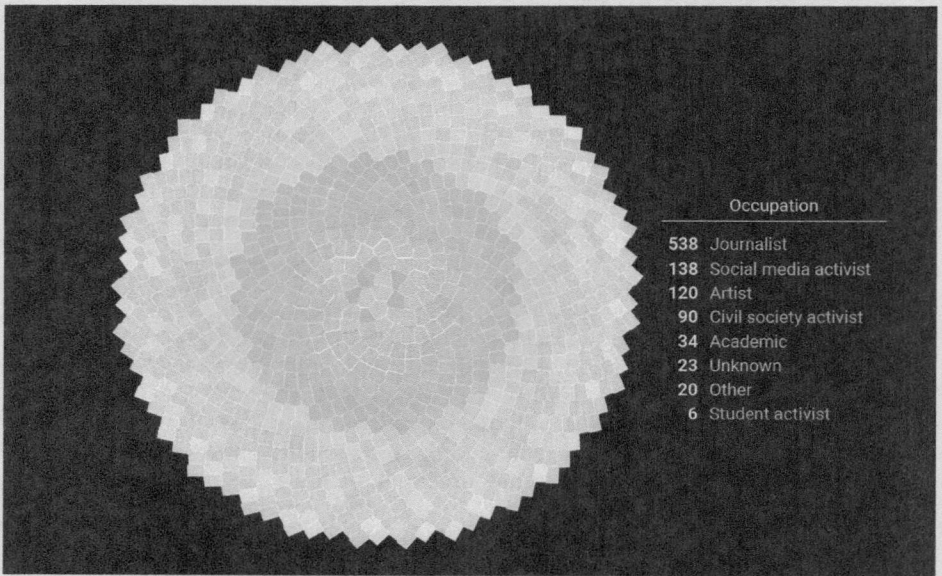

Occupation

538	Journalist
138	Social media activist
120	Artist
90	Civil society activist
34	Academic
23	Unknown
20	Other
6	Student activist

This project is a visualization of Iranian journalists and activists censored in Iran.

"Visualizing Censorship in Iran" is a visualization of Iranian journalists and activists who have been harassed, detained, jailed, exiled, and, in some cases, killed by the government. "Journalism Is not a Crime" documents these atrocities and maintains a detailed database. The visualization takes the data and tells the stories of all of these people.

Can you explain the process of creating this project?

When I got into the project, the data was ready to be visualized, which is a dream condition. Then I started a design exploration phase and used just pen and paper to probe different visualization ideas.

In parallel, I collected different impressions from Iran on a mood board. I soon got attracted to Persian architecture and its colorful, glazed mosaic tiles. The project came with the challenge to visualize the sheer mass of people in the database (around 700 at that time) on the one hand, but also needed to highlight the individual biographies behind the data points. Using the tiles metaphor was a good solution to cover both interests: they are unique on their own and have a different effect when seen in community with other tiles.

Admittedly, the tiles idea was hard to sketch, as it immediately needed to use the real data points. So I started right away and designed by coding with Svelte and D3—with a lot of code inspiration from Observable notebooks.

As we wanted to show the statistics and the biographies, I designed an explorative tool to gain different perspectives on the full dataset, but also to be able to dive into the individual stories of people in the data. It quickly turned out that animation would do the trick to connect the different states and let the readers follow the story.

After a couple of weeks, the final product was ready to be published. You can find its code here: https://github.com/higsch/censorship-in-iran.

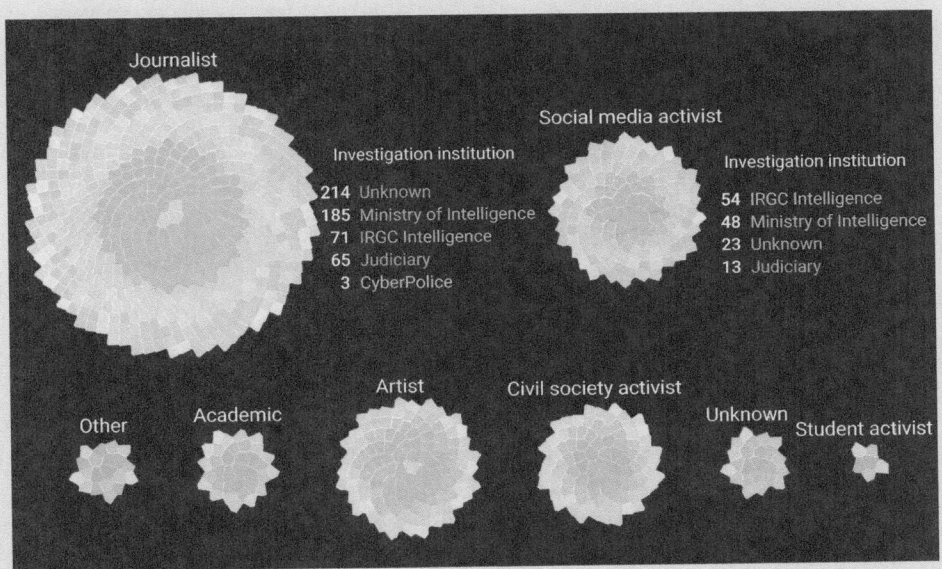

Each tile represents a journalist or activist that the user can aggregate based on investigation institution, occupation, or gender, for example.

The mosaic tiles design is stunning! Was it difficult to generate those programmatically and to render them with canvas?

Thank you! The tiles indeed look unique and consist of individual geometries. However, it is less complicated than you might think. I built them by first rendering a

(continued)

number of dots in the form of a phyllotaxis layout. Then I used the dot centers to construct a Voronoi diagram. The latter can easily be built by using the Delaunay library within D3. That's everything to craft a rosette of tiles.

As the tiles can appear in different rosettes, they need to be animated from one state to another. With more than 700 tiles, this calls for HTML canvas as the best device to draw them in the browser. SVG would just be too slow to handle the parallel movements. Drawing custom paths on canvas can be a pain—but it is not when you use the D3-generated Voronoi tiles in combination with Svelte renderless components. With this concept (which also exists in other frontend frameworks), we have one parent canvas component, which takes care of the drawing routines. This component takes the tiles as children. These components are called "renderless" because they do not appear on the frontend themselves. They only send their individual drawing information to the parent where everything is eventually drawn onto the canvas.

What's your perspective on how D3 development evolved between when you started as a data visualization developer, when you worked on this project in 2020–2021, and now? Has your workflow changed?

Now and then, I use D3 as a library of functions from which I cherry-pick what I need to solve a specific task. So my workflow, as I outlined it above, did not change. But I am still amazed when—from time to time—I find D3 functions that I did not know before.

What types of projects are you hoping to work on in the future?

My absolute dream project is an installation with a very large screen or canvas in a museum. It would be a pleasure to work on the specially adapted design and to tweak the high-resolution interactions to perfection.

Of course, it would be built with Svelte and D3.

Summary

- There are many ways to represent a network, such as with adjacency matrices, arc diagrams, and force-directed diagrams. Make sure you use the method that suits your network structure and your audience.
- To build network visualizations, we need to create two separate data files from the original dataset: one that contains the nodes and one with the edges.
- Adjacency matrices focus on the relationships between nodes, while arc diagrams emphasize the nodes' dynamics.
- Force layout `d3.forceSimulation()` dynamically updates the positions of its elements to find the best fit.
- To control the layout of a force layout, we use a combination of positioning, collision, centering, many-body, and link forces.
- Positioning forces make the nodes move toward a specific position. They can also be used to create clusters of nodes.

- We use the collision force to set a minimum distance between nodes and avoid overlap.
- The centering force moves an entire cluster of nodes toward a specific position.
- The many-body force influences how nodes interact with each other. A negative many-body force mimics repulsion, while a positive many-body force simulates attraction.
- The link force applies a force between connected nodes. The more strongly two nodes are connected, the closer the link force will pull them together.
- We can also write custom forces, for example, to keep nodes from spreading outside a specific area.
- The force layout is highly resource-intensive, and you'll want to use optimization techniques whenever it might tax your user's computer.

13

Geospatial information visualizations

This chapter covers

- Manipulating GeoJSON and TopoJSON data
- Comparing projections and their effect on map layouts
- Drawing points on a map
- Enabling a zoom and pan functionality
- Listening to the brushing event

The last type of visualization that we'll discuss in this section is maps. Maps are a symbolic interpretation of geospatial data. They use different projections to draw the surface of the globe we live on onto a flat 2D plane.

Because mapmaking and geographic information systems (GIS) and geographic information science (GIScience) have been in practice for so long, well-developed methods exist for representing this kind of data. D3 has robust built-in functions to load and display geospatial data, and most of them are included in the d3-geo module.

In this chapter, we'll use two types of geographic data: GeoJSON and TopoJSON. We'll study different projections from which we'll create maps. We'll also add standard functionalities, such as allowing users to zoom and pan the map, and less common ones, such as listening to a brushing event to filter the data visualized by the map.

To create those visualizations, we'll work with a dataset containing all the Nobel Prize laureates between 1901 and 2022 and try to answer the following question: "How does your birthplace influence your chances of earning a Nobel Prize?" We'll build a world map visualizing the countries and cities where Nobel Prize laureates were born and a more detailed map of France, like the ones in figure 13.1. You can see the final project at http://mng.bz/MZdm.

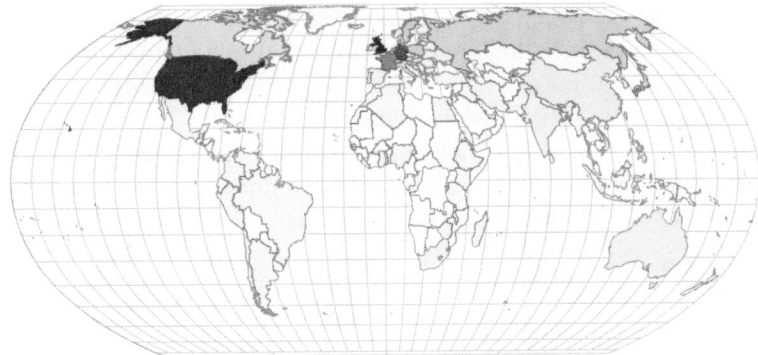

World choropleth map with an Equal Earth projection

World proportional symbol map with an Equal Earth projection

Proportional symbol map of France with a Mercator projection

Figure 13.1 In this chapter, we'll build a world map using an Equal Earth projection from GeoJSON data and a map of France using a Mercator projection from TopoJSON data.

13.1   *Geographical data*

Geographical data can come in several forms, from simple latitude and longitude coordinates to more complex geodata such as shapes or lines found in GeoJSON or TopoJSON files. We'll explore both in this chapter.

13.1.1   *GeoJSON*

GeoJSON is a way of encoding geodata in JSON format. It consists of a collection of geometries such as points, lines, and polygons and is used to draw simple geographic features. Each object in a GeoJSON file must contain three pieces of information: `type`, `properties`, and `geometry`. The two possible values for the `type` are `Feature` and `FeatureCollection`, where the latter organizes multiple features into one group.

Each feature contains a `properties` object with relevant meta-information about the geometry, such as its name. It also includes the `geometry` object with a geometry type and its coordinates. The following snippet provides the GeoJSON code for drawing the polygon illustrated in figure 13.2. Each coordinate is a point corresponding to a longitude and a latitude, such as (x, y), in a Cartesian coordinate system:

```
{
  "type":"Feature",
  "geometry":{
    "type":"Polygon",
    "coordinates":[
      [
        [25,56],
        [23,55],
        [22,54],
        [26,54],
        [25,56]
      ]
    ]
  },
  "properties":{"name":"Country Name"},
  "id":"Country Code"
}
```

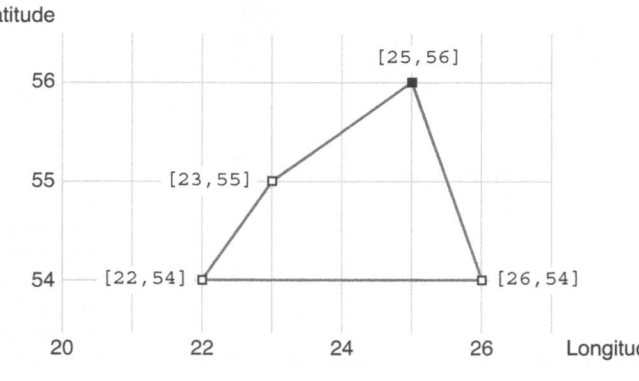

Figure 13.2   **Polygon and its latitude and longitude coordinates, similar to what we find in a GeoJSON file**

NOTE Longitudes are vertical lines that measure distance east or west of the Greenwich meridian, while latitudes are horizontal lines that indicate distance north or south from the equator.

If a shape is closed, the starting and ending points of the geometry appear twice in the coordinates list, such as the coordinate `[25,56]` in our example.

In the GeoJSON file from which we'll build a world map in a moment (`world.json` in this chapter's code files), each feature corresponds to a country, and the geometries are called multipolygons. But GeoJSON geometries can also consist of simple points and lines.

We won't go into the details of GeoJSON geometries because there's a good chance you'll never have to build your own GeoJSON file. But if you want to dive deeper, take a look at the GeoJSON article on Wikipedia, which contains useful examples for each geometry (https://en.wikipedia.org/wiki/GeoJSON).

The main advantage of GeoJSON is that this format is relatively easy to create, read, and understand. But such files can quickly become large because the format isn't optimized for file size due to it keeping all lines of a feature even if they are duplicated. This is especially true when mapping large areas in great detail. In such a case, we turn to the TopoJSON format.

13.1.2 *TopoJSON*

The main difference between GeoJSON and TopoJSON is that whereas GeoJSON records an array of coordinates for each feature that describes a point, line, or polygon, TopoJSON stores only an array of arcs. An arc is any distinct segment of a line shared by one or more features in your dataset.

Most datasets have shared segments, like the border between two countries. While in GeoJSON, those shared borders appear twice, TopoJSON reduces redundancy by merging them into one single arc, as illustrated in figure 13.3. It produces significantly smaller files that are optimized for the web and that allow data to be held for more detailed geographic features. In addition, if you know what segments are shared, you can do exciting things with the data, such as quickly calculating the shared border or merging features.

But while GeoJSON is easy to read and can be interpreted directly by D3, TopoJSON is hard to decipher and requires an additional library called `topojson-client` to decode TopoJSON back to GeoJSON before treating it with D3.

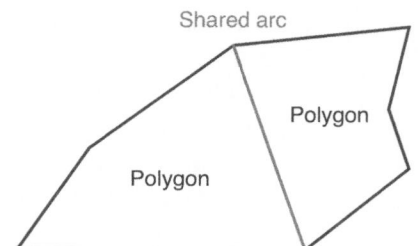

Figure 13.3 While shared borders appear twice in GeoJSON, TopoJSON reduces redundancy by merging them into a single arc.

Finding geographical data

Although a simple Google search is often enough to find the data files you need to create maps, Dea Bankova, a graphics journalist at Reuters, created a practical Observable notebook with links to different resources and helpful D3 code snippets (http://mng.bz/aERY).

13.2 Drawing a map from GeoJSON data

In this section, we'll draw a world map from GeoJSON data. We'll then use this map to visualize the countries and cities Nobel Prize laureates come from.

13.2.1 Choosing a projection

Entire books have been written on creating web maps, and an entire book could be written on using D3.js for crafting maps. Because this is only one chapter, we'll gloss over many deep problems. One of these is projection. In GIS, projection refers to the process of rendering points on a globe, like the earth, onto a flat plane like your computer monitor. Projections inevitably distort geographical data to some degree.

D3 provides methods for four common types of projections: azimuthal, conic, cylindrical, and composite. *Azimuthal projections*, such as the Equal Earth projection shown in figure 13.4, project the sphere directly onto a plane. The center of the projection is tangent to the earth, and the distortion increases as we move further from this central point.

Conic projections project the earth onto a cone and then unroll this cone onto a plane. They are best suited for mapping long east-west distances because the distortion is constant along horizontal parallel lines.

Cylindrical projections project the earth onto a cylinder, and then unroll this cylinder onto a plane. This makes countries that are closer to the poles larger than they are in reality. The Mercator projection, shown in figure 13.4, is a standard cylindrical projection. Note how Greenland and Antarctica are exaggeratedly large. This projection was used in the early versions of Google Maps and is the default in Tableau and Power BI.

Finally, *composite projections* consist of several projections grouped into one single display. Those are particularly useful for showing the distant lands of a country together, such as Alaska and Hawaii with the continental United States. Note the effect of the projection on this example. Although Alaska is more than twice the size of Texas, it seems smaller.

Creating a map with D3 requires three steps:

1 Defining a projection
2 Initializing the geo path generator function
3 Appending the paths to the SVG container

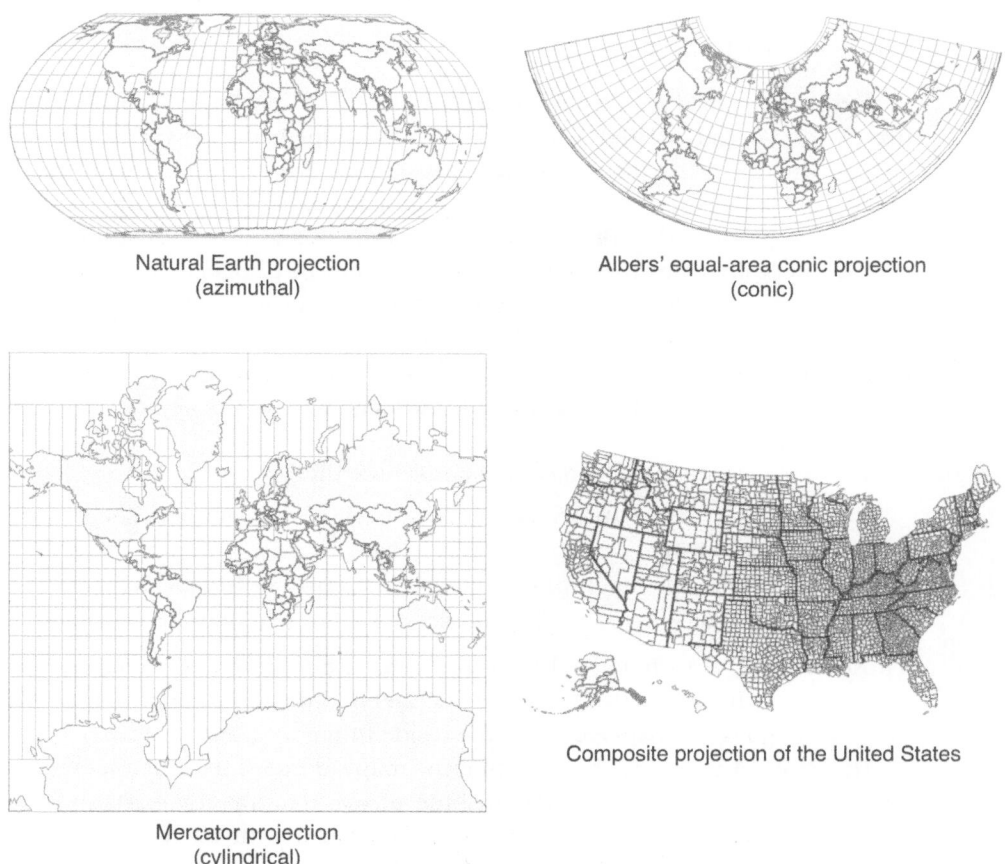

Natural Earth projection
(azimuthal)

Albers' equal-area conic projection
(conic)

Mercator projection
(cylindrical)

Composite projection of the United States

Figure 13.4   D3 provides methods for four common types of projections: azimuthal, conic, cylindrical, and composite. This figure shows an example of each.

The following snippet illustrates the first two steps. First, we declare a projection type and save it in a constant named `projection`. In this example, we used `d3.geoEqual-Earth()`, but we can call any of the projections available in the d3-geo module. Note how we chain it with the `transition()` and `scale()` accessor functions, which are used to scale the map and center it inside the SVG container.

Then we initialize a geo path generator function with `d3.geoPath()` and pass the projection defined previously to the `projection()` accessor function. This generator acts like the shape generators introduced in chapter 5—we pass it a GeoJSON feature (geometry), and it returns the `d` attribute of the corresponding path element:

```
const projection = d3.geoEqualEarth()
  .translate([translationX, translationY])
  .scale(factor);
```

```
const geoPathGenerator = d3.geoPath()
  .projection(projection);
```

Let's draw the world map from the hosted project (http://mng.bz/MZdm) and in figure 13.1. To get started with this exercise, open the `start` folder from the `chapter_13/13.2-GeoJSON` code files in your code editor. You can find the code files in the book's GitHub repository at http://mng.bz/Xqjv.

This project is built with ES6 JavaScript modules, and we've already added the relevant D3 dependencies for you. You can see them in `package.json`. To install those dependencies, run command `npm install` in your terminal. As explained in chapter 11, you'll need a bundler to run the project locally. If you've installed Parcel, you can enter command `parcel src/index.html` in your terminal, and the project will be available at http://localhost:1234/. Otherwise, go back to the beginning of chapter 11 for instructions.

The `data` folder of the project contains three files:

- `laureates.json`—Information about each Nobel laureate, such as their birth city and country
- `world.json`—A geographic dataset of the world in GeoJSON format
- `france.json`—A geographic dataset of France in TopoJSON format

Those files are already loaded in `main.js`, where we also call function `drawWorldMap()`, to which we pass the `laureates` dataset and the `world` map GeoJSON data. To get started, go to the `map-world.js` file inside function `drawWorldMap()`.

In listing 13.1, we start by declaring the map's dimensions and appending an SVG container to the `div` with an ID attribute of `map` that already exists in `index.html`. Then we declare a projection of type Equal Earth with `d3.geoEqualEarth()` and save it in a constant named `projection`. Note that we didn't set its `scale()` and `translate()` accessor functions yet. We'll play with those parameters in a moment.

We also declare a path generator function with `d3.geoPath()` and pass the projection to its `projection()` accessor function. Finally, we use the data-binding pattern to append a path element for each feature in the GeoJSON dataset, found in `world.features`, and we call the path generator function to set their `d` attribute.

Listing 13.1 Drawing a world map (`map-world.js`)

```
import { select } from "d3-selection";          Import the required D3 methods.
import { geoPath, geoEqualEarth } from "d3-geo";

export const drawWorldMap = (laureates, world) => {

  const width = 1230;          Declare the map's dimensions.
  const height = 620;

  const svg = select("#map")          Append an SVG
    .append("svg")                    container.
    .attr("viewBox", `0 0 ${width} ${height}`);
```

```
const projection = geoEqualEarth();

const geoPathGenerator = geoPath()
  .projection(projection);

svg
  .selectAll(".country-path")
  .data(world.features)
  .join("path")
    .attr("class", "country-path")
    .attr("d", geoPathGenerator)
    .attr("fill", "#f8fcff")
    .attr("stroke", "#09131b")
    .attr("stroke-opacity", 0.4);

};
```

◁— **Define a projection using D3's Natural Earth projection function.**

Initialize the path generator function d3.geoPath(). Pass the projection declared previously to the projection() accessor function.

Use the data-binding pattern to append a path element for each feature in the GeoJSON dataset.

◁— **Call the path generator function to get the d attribute of each country shape.**

If you save your project and take a look in the browser, you should see a world map! But you'll notice that it doesn't take all the space available in the SVG container and isn't centered. That's what the projection's `transition()` and `scale()` accessor functions are for.

To center the map, we start by applying a horizontal transition of half the width of the SVG container and a vertical transition of half its height, as in the following snippet. Note that we pass these values in an array. Depending on the geographical data you're working with and the size of your SVG container, the transition required to position a map correctly can vary and demands a trial-and-error approach:

```
const projection = geoEqualEarth()
  .translate([width/2, height/2])
```

When it comes to scaling the map, there's no strict rule to apply, and you need to try different scaling factors until you find the right one. In the next piece of code, we use a scaling factor of 220. Afterward, your world map should look like the one in figure 13.5:

```
const projection = geoEqualEarth()
  .translate([width/2, height/2])
  .scale(220);
```

Figure 13.5 Equal Earth projection of a world map drawn from GeoJSON data

As you can see, drawing a map from GeoJSON data with D3 is pretty simple! Figure 13.6 recapitulates the three main steps.

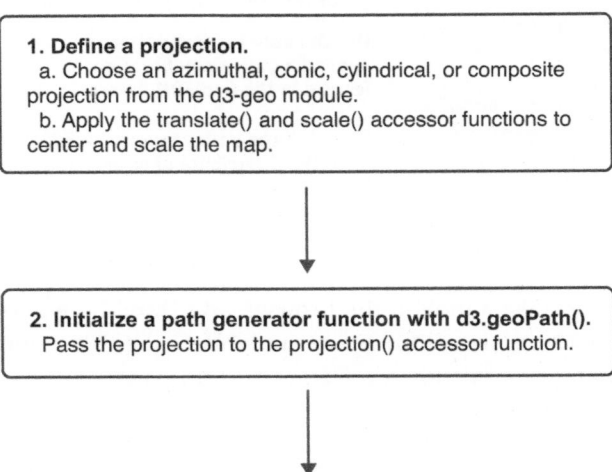

1. **Define a projection.**
   a. Choose an azimuthal, conic, cylindrical, or composite projection from the d3-geo module.
   b. Apply the translate() and scale() accessor functions to center and scale the map.

2. **Initialize a path generator function with d3.geoPath().**
   Pass the projection to the projection() accessor function.

3. **Append the paths to the SVG container.**
   a. Append one path element for each feature (geometry) in the GeoJSON data.
   b. Call the path generator function to get the d attribute of each path.

Figure 13.6   Creating a map from GeoJSON data with D3 requires three main steps: defining a projection, initializing a path generator function, and appending the geometry paths to the SVG container.

13.2.2 Improving readability with graticules

Graticules are grid lines representing latitudes and longitudes on a map. They help users better understand the projection and its effect on the 2D map representation. They can also help users estimate the coordinates of locations.

Unsurprisingly, D3 has a generator function for graticules, d3.geoGraticule(), that returns a GeoJSON geometry object. By default, it creates a uniform grid of meridians and parallels every 10°, except at the poles, where it draws meridians every 90°. Figure 13.7 shows the default graticules on projection d3.geoOrthographic(), which resembles a 3D globe.

To draw graticules on our world map, we first need to declare a graticule generator function using d3.geoGraticule(). In listing 13.2, we save this function in a constant named graticuleGenerator.

We then append a group element to the SVG container and save it in a constant named graticules. This group is responsible for propagating the styles of the graticules, such as their transparent fill, stroke color, and stroke width.

The grid of graticules is drawn with one single path element. In the code, we append this path element to graticules. You'll notice that we use method datum() to

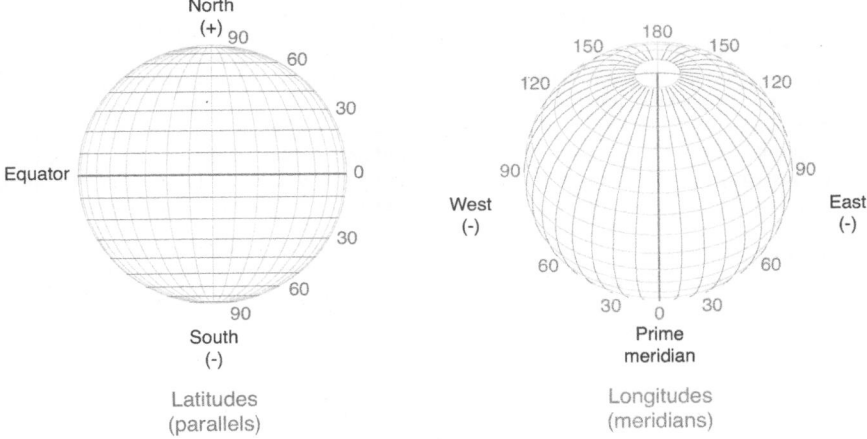

Figure 13.7   Graticules are lines representing latitudes and longitudes, also known as parallels and meridians. Lines of latitude are parallel to the equator and cover 180 degrees from the South Pole to the North Pole. Lines of longitude are perpendicular to the equator and cover 360 degrees around the earth. The prime meridian, or Greenwich meridian, is defined to be 0°.

bind data to this path element instead of `data()`. The word *datum* being the singular of *data*, this method is used to bind a piece of data to a single element. We then pass the graticule generator to this method.

Finally, we append a second path element to draw a border around the map. The required datum is accessible with `graticuleGenerator.outline`. In both cases, the `d` attribute is calculated by the `geoPathGenerator` initialized earlier.

Because we want the graticules to appear behind the countries, their paths need to be appended before the country paths but after declaring the `geoPathGenerator` because we need it for the graticules' `d` attribute.

Listing 13.2   Adding graticules to the world map (`map-world.js`)

```
import { select } from "d3-selection";
import { geoPath, geoEqualEarth, geoGraticule } from "d3-geo";

export const drawWorldMap = (laureates, world) => {

  ...

  const projection = geoEqualEarth()

  const geoPathGenerator = geoPath()
    .projection(projection);

  const graticuleGenerator = geoGraticule();          Declare a graticule
                                                       generator.
```

```
const graticules = svg
  .append("g")
    .attr("fill", "transparent")
    .attr("stroke", "#09131b")
    .attr("stroke-opacity", 0.2);
graticules
  .append("path")
  .datum(graticuleGenerator)
    .attr("d", geoPathGenerator);
graticules
  .append("path")
  .datum(graticuleGenerator.outline)
    .attr("d", geoPathGenerator);

svg
  .selectAll(".country-path")
  .data(world.features)
  .join("path")
    .attr("class", "country-path")
    .attr("d", geoPathGenerator)
    .attr("fill", "#f8fcff")
    .attr("stroke", "#09131b")
    .attr("stroke-opacity", 0.4);
```

```
};
```

Append a group element that will contain the graticules' paths. Use it to set their fill, stroke, and stroke-opacity attributes.

Append a single path element for the graticules' grid. Bind data to this element with the datum() method, calling the graticuleGenerator. Set its d attribute by calling the geographical path generator declared earlier.

Append a path element for the graticules' outline, calling the outline() method of the graticule generator as data.

After this step, we can appreciate how the 3D globe is projected onto a 2D surface, as in figure 13.8.

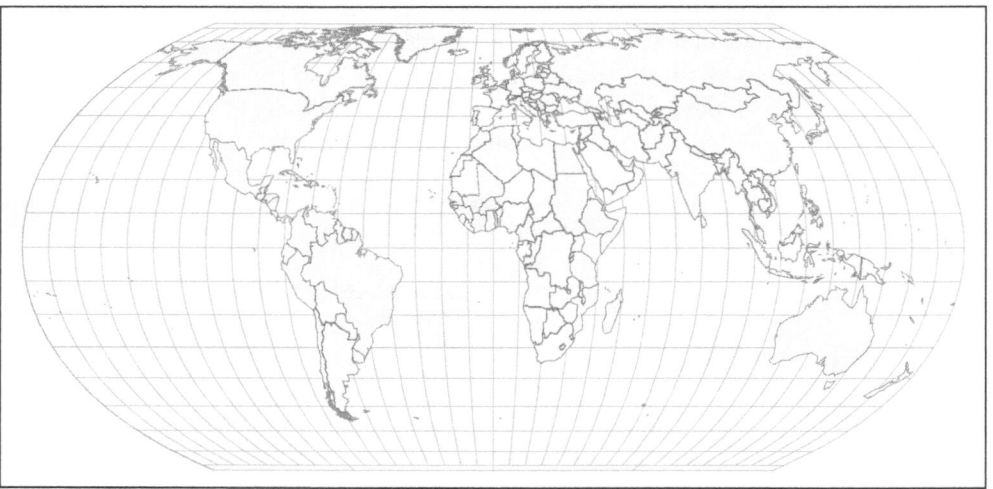

Figure 13.8   With the addition of graticules, the reader can estimate the coordinates of locations in terms of latitude (horizontal lines) and longitude (vertical lines) and appreciate how the 3D globe is projected onto a 2D surface.

13.2.3 *Making a choropleth map*

A *choropleth map* is a map that encodes data using the color of regions, such as countries. We use it to compare statistical data such as countries' GDP, population, or number of Nobel laureates!

To create a choropleth map, we need a color scale. In our project, the number of Nobel laureates born in a country can vary between 0 and 289. We want countries where no Nobel laureates were born to remain white, so we'll need colors that cover a range of 1 to almost 300. Sequential color scales are super handy in such a situation. They take a continuous domain as an input (the number of laureates born in any country) and return a continuous range of outputs, the related colors. D3 has prebuilt sequential color functions available in the d3-scale-chromatic module. For our project, we'll use the sequential multi-hue color scheme `d3.interpolateYlGnBu`, where `YlGnBu` stands for yellow-green-blue.

Figure 13.9 shows this color scale. Countries with a low number of Nobel laureates will appear in a shade of yellow, countries with around 50 laureates will be turquoise, and countries with the most will be dark blue. We'll cap the upper limit of the domain at 100 Nobel laureates. Because only one country has significantly more than 100 laureates (the United States), using the actual value of 289 as an upper limit would cause almost all other countries to appear yellow in comparison, making the differences between the countries practically unreadable.

1   100

Figure 13.9 We'll use the `d3.interpolateYlGnBu` sequential multi-hue color scale to represent the number of Nobel laureates born in each country.

In listing 13.3, we open the `scales.js` file and initialize a sequential color scale with method `d3.scaleSequential()`. We save it in a constant named `countryColorScale`, which we export for future use. We set the scale's domain to an array of two values: 1, the lowest value for which we want to apply color, and 100, the value at which we want to cap the color scale.

Note that we don't set the range of the scale. Instead, we pass function `interpolateYlGnBu` to `scaleSequential()`, which will take care of returning the desired colors.

Listing 13.3 Declaring the color scale (`scales.js`)

```
import { scaleSequential } from "d3-scale";
import { interpolateYlGnBu } from "d3-scale-chromatic";

export const countryColorScale = scaleSequential(interpolateYlGnBu)
  .domain([1, 100]);
```

To make the colors appear on the map, we need to calculate the number of Nobel laureates born in each country. In listing 13.4, we go back to `map-world.js` and loop through the countries contained in the `features` object of the GeoJSON data. As mentioned earlier, each country has an object named `properties` that can include relevant information about the country, such as its name. That's a perfect place to store an array of Nobel laureates related to that country. To do so, we filter the `laureates`' array and keep only the ones whose birthplace corresponds to the name of the current country.

Listing 13.4 Adding a `laureates` array to each country (`map-world.js`)

```
export const drawWorldMap = (laureates, world) => {

  world.features.forEach(country => {
    const props = country.properties;
    props.laureates = laureates.filter(laureate =>
      laureate.birth_country === props.name);
  });

  ...

};
```

Then, after importing the color scale into the file, we go back to the code where we appended the countries' paths. Instead of giving them all a fill of #f8fcff, we use a ternary operator to call the color scale when the number of laureates is higher than zero, as in the next listing. We pass the number of laureates to the scale function, which returns the corresponding color.

Listing 13.5 Applying a color to each country (`map-world.js`)

```
import { countryColorScale } from "./scales";

export const drawWorldMap = (laureates, world) => {

  ...

  svg
    .selectAll(".country-path")
    .data(world.features)
    .join("path")
      .attr("class", "country-path")
      .attr("d", geoPathGenerator)
      .attr("fill", d => d.properties.laureates.length > 0
        ? countryColorScale(d.properties.laureates.length)
        : "#f8fcff")
      .attr("stroke", "#09131b")
      .attr("stroke-opacity", 0.4);

};
```

We now have a choropleth map, like the one shown in figure 13.10. You'll observe that the country with the most Nobel laureates is the United States, followed by the United Kingdom, Germany, and France. In `index.html`, you can uncomment the `div` with a class of `legend-container`, which will make a color legend appear on the left side of the map. We have created this legend with a CSS background property and a linear gradient, which you can find in `visualization.css`.

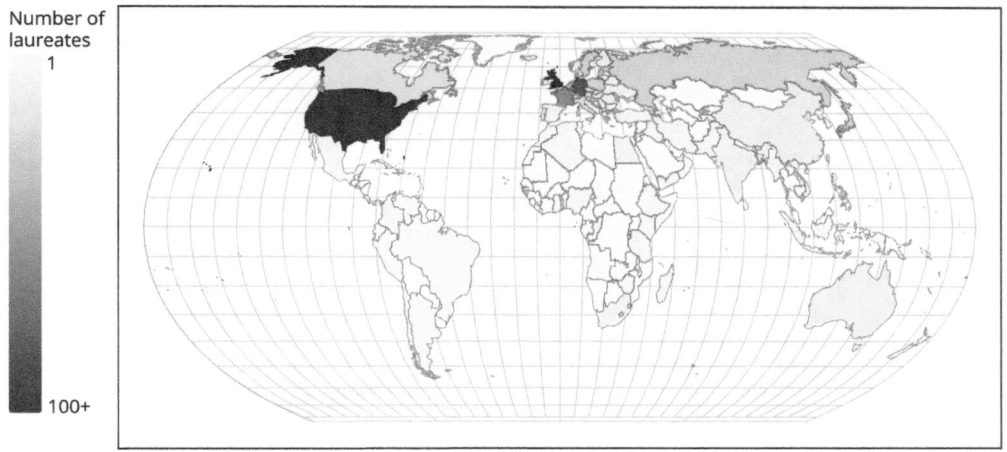

Figure 13.10   Choropleth map of the number of Nobel laureates born in each country

> **NOTE**   Keep in mind that choropleth maps, though useful, are subject to what's known as the *areal unit problem,* which is what happens when you draw boundaries or select existing features in such a way that they disproportionately represent your statistics. The size of a geographic area may be way larger than its data value, creating overrepresentation. For example, Russia's territory is gigantic compared to Japan. Although both countries have a similar population, any color applied to Russia will draw more attention than the one used on the smaller territory.

Our choropleth map provides a good overview of countries where more or fewer Nobel laureates were born. But we can't know precisely how many laureates were born in each country from the color only. Because we work with digital visualizations, we can solve this problem easily with an interaction! When the mouse is positioned over a country, we'll display a tooltip with its name and the number of laureates born there. The `index.html` file already contains a `div` with an ID of `"map-tooltip"`, which is absolutely positioned on the top-right corner of the map. This is where we'll inject the tooltip's text.

In listing 13.6, we create two functions: showTooltip(), which makes the tooltip appear with the desired text, and hideTooltip(), which hides the tooltip. We also add event listeners to the countries' paths. When the mouse enters one of them, we extract the desired text and call showTooltip(). When the mouse leaves, we call hideTooltip().

Listing 13.6 Adding a tooltip (`map-world.js`)

```
...
import { transition } from "d3-transition";

export const drawWorldMap = (laureates, world) => {

  ...

  const showTooltip = (text) => {
    select("#map-tooltip")
      .text(text)                        Make the tooltip appear
      .transition()                      with the related text.
      .style("opacity", 1);
  };

  const hideTooltip = () => {
    select("#map-tooltip")
      .transition()                      Hide the tooltip.
      .style("opacity", 0);
  };

  svg
    .selectAll(".country-path")
    .data(world.features)
    .join("path")
      .attr("class", "country-path")
      .attr("d", geoPathGenerator)
      .attr("fill", d => d.properties.laureates.length > 0
        ? countryColorScale(d.properties.laureates.length)
        : "#f8fcff")
      .attr("stroke", "#09131b")
      .attr("stroke-opacity", 0.4)
      .on("mouseenter", (e, d) => {
        const p = d.properties;              When the mouse enters a
        const lastWord = p.laureates.length > 1     country path, extract the
          ? "laureates"                      desired tooltip text, and
          : "laureate"                       pass it to the
        const text = `${p.name}, ${p.laureates.length}   showTooltip() function.
          ${lastWord}`
        showTooltip(text);
      })
      .on("mouseleave", hideTooltip);    When the mouse leaves a country
};                                        path, call the function hideTooltip().
```

Figure 13.11 shows the tooltip when the mouse is positioned over India.

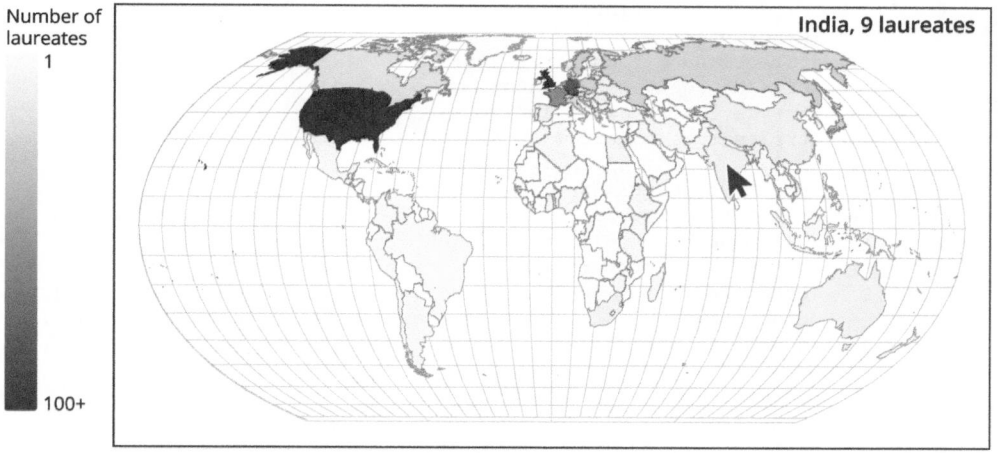

Figure 13.11 Although the color scale helps identify which countries have a lot of Nobel laureates and which have fewer, it doesn't allow us to know the exact number. With a simple tooltip, we make this information accessible to the user.

13.2.4 Locating cities on a map

Projections aren't used just to display areas; they're also used to place individual points on a map. Typically, you think of cities or people as represented not by their spatial footprint (though you do this with particularly large cities) but with a single point on a map, which is sized based on a variable such as population. We can use a D3 projection to calculate the position of a city by passing it an array containing longitude and latitude coordinates. It then returns the corresponding coordinates of that point inside the SVG container.

Let's say we want our map to also show the cities where Nobel laureates were born. Uncomment the `div` with an ID of `"filters-container"` in `index.html` to reveal radio buttons to select the laureates' countries or cities map.

In listing 13.7, we listen to the selection of the radio buttons and call a function that displays the countries or the cities. We also refactor the earlier code to allow us to switch between the two map states. When the page loads, we call function `display-Countries()`, which is responsible for applying the color scale to the countries.

Listing 13.7 Refactoring to allow dynamic selection (`map-world.js`)

```
export const drawWorldMap = (laureates, world) => {

  ...

  let isCountryMap = true;          ◁─┐  Initialize a state variable responsible
                                       │  for tracking if the map is showing the
  svg                                  │  laureates' countries or cities.
    .selectAll(".country-path")
```

```
      .data(world.features)
      .join("path")
        .attr("class", "country-path")
        .attr("d", geoPathGenerator)
        .attr("stroke", "#09131b")
        .attr("stroke-opacity", 0.4);

  const updateCountryFills = () => {
    selectAll(".country-path")
      .on("mouseenter", (e, d) => {
        const p = d.properties;
        const lastWord = p.laureates.length > 1 ? "laureates" : "laureate";
        const text = `${p.name}, ${p.laureates.length} ${lastWord}`;
        showTooltip(text);
      })
      .on("mouseleave", hideTooltip)
      .transition()
      .attr("fill", d => d.properties.laureates.length > 0
        ? countryColorScale(d.properties.laureates.length)
        : "#f8fcff");
  };

  const displayCountries = () => {
    isCountryMap = true;
    updateCountryFills();
  };

  const displayCities = () => {};

  selectAll("input#countries, input#cities")
    .on("click", e => {
      if (e.target.id === "countries") {
        displayCountries();
      } else if (e.target.id === "cities") {
        displayCities();
      }
    });

  displayCountries();
};
```

Listen to the selection of the radio buttons, and call the related function.

On page load, call the function where the laureates' countries are displayed.

The city of birth of each Nobel laureate is available in the `laureates` array under the `birth_city` key. It also contains the latitude and longitude of that city under `birth_city_latitude` and `birth_city_longitude`. Before we display these cities on the map, we'll create a new array, called `cities`, that contains every city where a Nobel laureate was born and its latitude, longitude, and an array of related laureates. The following listing shows how we proceed.

Listing 13.8   Creating the `cities` array (`map-world.js`)

```
export const drawWorldMap = (laureates, world) => {

  const cities = [];
```

Create an empty array named cities.

```
laureates.forEach(laureate => {
  if (laureate.birth_country !== "" &&
      laureate.birth_city !== "") {

    const relatedCity = cities.find(city =>
      city.city === laureate.birth_city &&
      city.country === laureate.birth_country);

    if (relatedCity) {
      relatedCity.laureates.push(laureate);
    } else {
      cities.push({
        city: laureate.birth_city,
        country: laureate.birth_country,
        latitude: laureate.birth_city_latitude,
        longitude: laureate.birth_city_longitude,
        laureates: [laureate]
      });
    }

  }
});

...

};
```

Loop through the laureates array and check if it has a birth city and country. Some laureates are international organizations that aren't bound to a specific birthplace.

If the cities array already contains an object corresponding to the birth city of the current laureate, add the laureate to the laureates array. Otherwise, create a new city object, and push it into the cities array.

We're now ready to show the cities on the map! We'll append a circle to the SVG container for each city in the `cities` array and scale its radius based on the number of candidates born in that city. In listing 13.9, we open `scales.js` and declare a function, `getCityRadius()`, that receives two numbers: the number of laureates and the maximum possible number of laureates for a city. We use the second number to initialize a radial scale and return the radius corresponding to the number of laureates.

Listing 13.9   Declaring a radial scale (`scales.js`)

```
import { scaleSequential, scaleRadial } from "d3-scale";
import { interpolateYlGnBu } from "d3-scale-chromatic";

export const countryColorScale = scaleSequential(interpolateYlGnBu)
  .domain([1, 100]);

export const getCityRadius = (numLaureates, maxLaureates) => {
  const cityRadiusScale = scaleRadial()
    .domain([0, maxLaureates])
    .range([0, 25]);

  return cityRadiusScale(numLaureates);
};
```

To calculate the position of each city on the map, we can call the projection created in section 13.2.1. The following code snippet provides an example. Let's say we have a projection function saved in a constant named `projection`. If we pass an array containing a longitude and a latitude, the projection function returns an array of the corresponding coordinates within the SVG container:

```
const projection = d3.geoEqualEarth();

[x, y] = projection([longitude, latitude]);
```

Listing 13.10 is long but fairly simple once we break it down. It contains four main functions:

- `updateCountryFills()` is responsible for adding an event listener to the countries and setting their fill color.
- `updateCityCircles()` adds event listeners to the city circles and sets their radii.
- `displayCountries()` is called on page load and when the laureates' countries radio button is selected. It removes the city circles and calls `updateCountry-Fills()`.
- `displayCities()` is called when the laureates' cities radio button is selected. It removes the event listeners from the country paths and reverts their fill attribute to white. It then appends the city circles, sets their positions by passing the longitude and latitude to the projection, and calls `updateCityCircles()`.

The first two functions might seem unnecessary at this point, but we'll need them later when we add the brush functionality.

Listing 13.10   Displaying the countries or cities (`map-world.js`)

```
...
import { select, selectAll } from "d3-selection";
import { max } from "d3-array";
import { countryColorScale, getCityRadius } from "./scales";

export const drawWorldMap = (laureates, world) => {

  ...

  const updateCountryFills = () => {          ◁─┐  Add the country event
    selectAll(".country-path")                   │  listeners, and set their colors.
      .on("mouseenter", (e, d) => {
        const p = d.properties;
        const lastWord = p.laureates.length > 1 ? "laureates" : "laureate";
        const text = `${p.name}, ${p.laureates.length} ${lastWord}`;
        showTooltip(text);
      })
      .on("mouseleave", hideTooltip)
      .transition()
      .attr("fill", d => d.properties.laureates.length > 0
        ? countryColorScale(d.properties.laureates.length)
        : "#f8fcff");
  };
```

```
const maxLaureatesPerCity = max(cities, d => d.laureates.length);
const updateCityCircles = () => {                      ⟵⎤ Add the city circles and
  selectAll(".circle-city")                               ⎦ their event listeners.
    .on("mouseenter", (e, d) => {
      const lastWord = d.laureates.length > 1 ? "laureates" : "laureate";
      const text = `${d.city}, ${d.laureates.length} ${lastWord}`;
      showTooltip(text);
    })
    .on("mouseleave", hideTooltip)
    .transition()
    .attr("r", d => getCityRadius(d.laureates.length,
      maxLaureatesPerCity));
};

const displayCountries = () => {
  isCountryMap = true;

  selectAll(".circle-city")
    .transition()
    .attr("fill-opacity", 0)
    .attr("stroke-opacity", 0)
    .remove();

  updateCountryFills();
};

const displayCities = () => {
  isCountryMap = false;

  selectAll(".country-path")
    .on("mouseenter", null)
    .on("leave", null)
    .transition()
    .attr("fill", "#f8fcff");

  selectAll(".circle-city")
    .data(cities)
    .join("circle")
      .attr("class", "circle-city")
      .attr("cx", d => projection([d.longitude,
        d.latitude])[0])
      .attr("cy", d => projection([d.longitude,
        d.latitude])[1])
      .attr("fill", "#35a7c2")
      .attr("fill-opacity", 0.5)
      .attr("stroke", "#35a7c2");

  updateCityCircles();
};

  selectAll("input#countries, input#cities")
    .on("click", e => {
      if (e.target.id === "countries") {
        displayCountries();
```

When a laureate's country map is selected, hide the city circles, and call the function responsible for setting the country colors.

When a laureate's city map is selected, remove the event listeners from the country paths, and revert their fill to white.

Use the data-binding pattern to append a circle for each city.

Get the position of the circles by calling the projection function and passing the city's longitude and latitude in an array.

```
        } else if (e.target.id === "cities") {
          displayCities();
        }
    });

  displayCountries();

};
```

To complete this visualization, we display the color legend when the laureates' countries option is selected and the radius legend for the laureates' cities option. We have already created the radius legend for you. All we have to do in the next listing is call function `drawLegend()` and pass it the maximum number of laureates per city.

> **Listing 13.11   Dynamically displaying the legends (`map-world.js`)**

```
...
import { drawLegend } from "./legend";

export const drawWorldMap = (laureates, world) => {

  ...

  const displayCountries = () => {

    ...

    select(".legend-cities")
      .style("display", "none");
    select(".legend-countries")
      .style("display", "flex");
  };

  const displayCities = () => {

    ...

    select(".legend-countries")
      .style("display", "none");
    select(".legend-cities")
      .style("display", "block");
  };

drawLegend(maxLaureatesPerCity);

};
```

We're done showing cities on a map by using their longitude and latitude! You should now be able to switch between the two states of the map with the radio buttons. You might notice on figure 13.12 that the city circles are very dense, especially in Europe. The brushing feature we'll add later will help make it more readable.

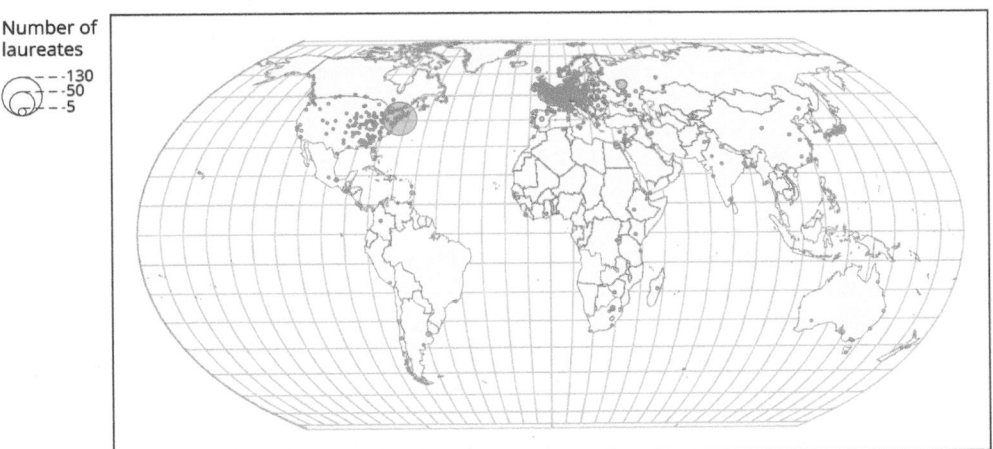

Figure 13.12 Laureates' birth cities

13.3 *Zooming and panning*

Maps are widespread on the web, and users expect them to have a certain level of interactivity—the ability to zoom and pan the map around being the first that comes to mind. Zooming and panning allow users to focus on a region of interest and see more details. In this section, we'll implement a zoom feature while controlling how much the user can scale and translate the map.

D3 has a module dedicated to the zooming and panning functionalities, d3-zoom, and implementing such a feature is deceivingly simple. In listing 13.12, we declare a new zoom behavior with method d3.zoom() and save it in a constant named zoom-Handler. We also attach a listener to zoomHandler that detects the "zoom" event. When this event is detected, we log it into the console.

For the zoom behavior to be operational, we select the div with a "map-container" class (the first parent of the SVG container) and use the call() method to attach zoomHandler to this selection.

Listing 13.12 Implementing zooming and panning (`map-world.js`)

```
...
import { zoom } from "d3-zoom";

export const drawWorldMap = (laureates, world) => {

  ...

  const zoomHandler = zoom()          ⟵─┐  Create a new zoom
    .on("zoom", (e) => {                 │  behavior function.
      console.log(e);
    });                                     Add a listener for the zoom event,
                                            and log it into the console.
```

```
select(".map-container")
  .call(zoomHandler);

};
```

> Apply the zoom behavior to
> the map-container selection
> with the call() method.

Now save your project, and position your cursor over the map. Start zooming the map by turning your mouse wheel or pinching out with your trackpad. Nothing will happen, which is expected because we haven't applied any transformation to the map yet. But if you open the console of your browser's inspector, you should see the zoom event being logged in, as in figure 13.13. This event contains a `transform` object with k, the zooming factor; x, the horizontal translation; and y, the vertical translation.

```
▼ ZoomEvent {type: 'zoom', sourceEvent: WheelEvent, transform: Transform, _: Dispatch, target: ƒ} ⓘ
  ▶ sourceEvent: WheelEvent {isTrusted: true, deltaX: −0, deltaY: −2.7549855709075928, deltaZ: 0, deltaMode: 0, …}
  ▶ target: ƒ zoom(selection)
  ▶ transform: Transform {k: 1.8420359696923372, x: 272610.815749858, y: −308257.07603286544}
    type: "zoom"
```

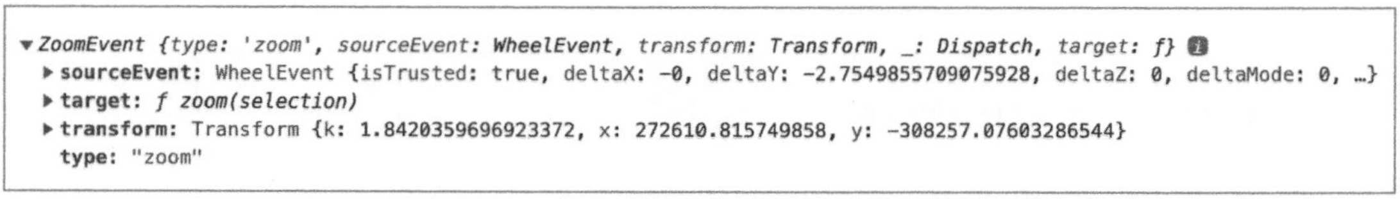

Figure 13.13 The zoom event contains a transform object with k, the zooming factor; x, the horizontal translation; and y, the vertical translation.

We can then use the `transform` object to scale and move the map based on the detected event. In the next listing, we update the `transform` attribute of the SVG container based on this event.

Listing 13.13 Transforming the map on zoom (map-world.js)

```
export const drawWorldMap = (laureates, world) => {

  ...

  const zoomHandler = zoom()
    .on("zoom", (e) => {
      console.log(e);
      svg.attr("transform", e.transform);
    });
  select(".map-container")
    .call(zoomHandler);

};
```

> Use the detected zoom event
> to update the transform
> attribute of the SVG container.

If you return to your browser, the zooming and panning functionality should now work as expected. But we can see the map overflowing the region delimited by the black border, which doesn't look neat. Fortunately, that's an easy fix! Go to `visualization.css`, and find the styles applied to the `.map-container` selection, which is the first parent of the SVG container. Set its `overflow` property to `hidden`, and voilà, no more overflow:

```
.map-container {
  position: relative;
  border: 1px solid #09131b;
  overflow: hidden;
}
```

We should also limit how much the user can scale and translate the map to avoid the situation where the map is entirely out of view. The zoom behavior has two handy accessor functions, `scaleExtent()` and `translateExtent()`, that, as their names suggest, allow us to set the extent to which users can scale and translate the selection. Those functions take an array of minimum and maximum values. In listing 13.14, we set the minimum scale of the zoom to 1, or 100%, and the maximum to 5, or 500%. We also set the translation extent to half the width of the map horizontally and half its height vertically.

Listing 13.14   Setting scale and translation extent (`map-world.js`)

```
export const drawWorldMap = (laureates, world) => {

  ...

  const zoomHandler = zoom()
    .scaleExtent([1, 5])          ◁──┐  Allow the user to zoom
    .translateExtent([[-width/2, -height/2],   between 1 and 5 times the
      [3*width/2, 3*height/2]])             original size of the map.
    .on("zoom", (e) => {
      console.log(e);                    Limit the translation of the map
      svg.attr("transform", e.transform);   so that half its width and height
    });                                  are always within the frame.

  select(".map-container")
    .call(zoomHandler);

};
```

It would also be nice to allow the user to easily reset the map to its initial state. In `index.html`, start by uncommenting the button with the ID `"map-reset"`. You'll see a blue button with the text Reset Zoom appear on the top-right corner of the map.

Because it doesn't make sense to show the reset button before any zoom has been performed, we'll add and remove the class name `"hidden"` to the `reset` button whenever relevant. This class name sets its `opacity` to 0 and prevents it from detecting clicks (see `visualization.css`). We do that by adding the class name `"hidden"` to the `reset` button on page load. Then, when a `zoom` event is detected, we check if the `reset` button has the class name `"hidden"`. If this is the case, we remove it.

The actual reset happens when the button is clicked. In listing 13.15, we attach a listener for the `click` event on the `reset` button. When a click is detected, we call the `transform()` accessor function of the `zoomHandler()` attached to the `.map-container` selection. As a second parameter, we pass the transformation value we want, for which we can use function `d3.zoomIdentity`. This function refers to a transformation where the scale is 1, or 100%, and the translations are 0, hence the reset.

Listing 13.15   Enabling the reset button (`map-world.js`)

```
...
import { zoom, zoomIdentity } from "d3-zoom";

export const drawWorldMap = (laureates, world) => {

  ...

  const zoomHandler = zoom()
    .scaleExtent([1, 5])
    .translateExtent([[-width/2, -height/2], [3*width/2, 3*height/2]])
    .on("zoom", (e) => {
      console.log(e);
      svg.attr("transform", e.transform);

      if (select("#map-reset").classed("hidden")) {     ◁── If the reset button has the class
        select("#map-reset")                                   name "hidden", remove that
          .classed("hidden", false);                           class to make the button visible.
      }
      if (e.transform.k === 1 &&
          e.transform.x === 0 &&
          e.transform.y === 0) {          ◁── If the map returns to its initial
        select("#map-reset")                    state, hide the reset button.
          .classed("hidden", true);
        }
    });

  select(".map-container")
    .call(zoomHandler);

  select("#map-reset")
    .attr("class", "hidden")        ◁── Hide the reset button.
    .on("click", () => {
      select(".map-container")              ◁── When the reset button is
        .transition()                            clicked, reverse the zoom
        .call(zoomHandler.transform, zoomIdentity);   to its initial state.
    });

};
```

If you click the Reset Zoom button after zooming, the map should revert to its initial state.

> **Semantic zoom**
>
> When you picture yourself zooming in on things, you naturally think about increasing their size. But when working with mapping, you can do more than merely increase the size or resolution as you zoom in; you can also change the kind of data that you present to the reader. Such functionality is known as semantic zoom in contrast to the graphical zoom we have implemented in this section.
>
> It's most evident when you look at a zoomed-out map and see only country boundaries and a few major cities, but as you zoom in, you see roads, smaller towns, parks, and so on. Maps on mobile devices often use such semantic zoom. You can even apply semantic zoom whenever you let your user zoom in and out of any data visualization, not just maps. It allows you to present strategic or global information when zoomed out and high-resolution data when zoomed in.

13.4 Adding a brushing functionality

Another type of interactivity that combines nicely with maps is brushing. *Brushing* is a one- or two-dimensional selection created with a click and drag of the mouse. It's often used to select elements, zoom onto a region, or filter data over a timeline.

Our project visualizes data from 1901 to 2022. But what if we want to know if the origin of the Nobel laureates was similar at the beginning of the 20th century versus today? By listening to a brush event, we can let users select a specific year range on a timeline. To do so, we'll use methods from the d3-brush module. In the next listing, we simply use a D3 axis to create a timeline that will serve as a base for our brushing feature.

Listing 13.16 Adding a timeline (`map-world.js`)

```
...
import { max, min } from "d3-array";
import { scaleLinear } from "d3-scale";
import { axisBottom } from "d3-axis";
import { format } from "d3-format";

export const drawWorldMap = (laureates, world) => {

  ...

  const tlWidth = 1000;
  const tlHeight = 80;                                          Set the dimensions
  const tlMargin= { top: 0, right: 10, bottom: 0, left: 0 };    of the timeline.
  const tlInnerWidth = tlWidth - tlMargin.right -
    tlMargin.left;

  const minYear = min(laureates, d => d.year);       Declare a linear scale responsible
  const maxYear = max(laureates, d => d.year);       for spreading the years on the
  const xScale = scaleLinear()                       horizontal space available.
    .domain([minYear, maxYear])
    .range([0, tlInnerWidth]);
```

```
const yearsSelector = select("#years-selector")
  .append("svg")
    .attr("viewBox", `0 0 ${tlWidth} ${tlHeight}`);
```

Append an SVG container to the div with an ID of "years-selector".

```
const xAxisGenerator = axisBottom(xScale)
  .tickFormat(format(""))
  .tickSizeOuter(0);
```

Declare a bottom-axis generator.

```
yearsSelector
  .append("g")
    .attr("class", "axis-x")
    .attr("transform", `translate(0, 30)`)
    .call(xAxisGenerator);
```

Append the axis to the SVG container.

```
};
```

Once created, your timeline should look like the one in figure 13.14.

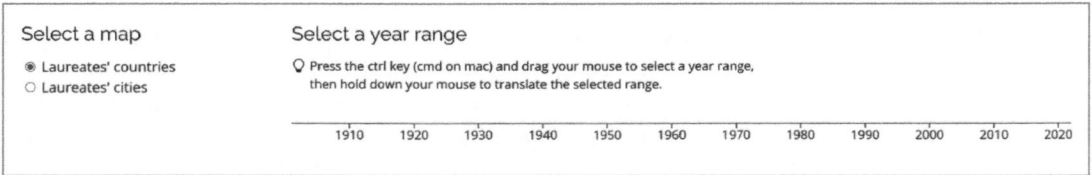

Figure 13.14   Timeline added to the year range selector

As you can see in listing 13.17, D3's brush functionality is set in a manner similar to the zoom discussed in the previous section. First, we create a one-dimensional brush with `d3.brushX()` and save it in a constant named `brushHandler`. With accessor function `extent()`, we let D3 know which area is brushable: from the upper-left to the bottom-right corner of the timeline. We then attach a listener for the `"brush"` event that calls function `handleBrush()`. For now, `handleBrush()` only logs the event in the console, but that's where we'll perform manipulations later. We also need to attach the `brushHandler` function to the timeline selection, and we initialize the default brush so that it covers the whole timeline.

Listing 13.17   Adding the brushing functionality (`map-world.js`)

```
...
import { brushX } from "d3-brush";

export const drawWorldMap = (laureates, world) => {

  ...

  const handleBrush = (e) => {
    console.log(e);
  };
```

This function is called when a brush event is detected.

Create a new one-dimensional
brush along the x-dimension.

Set the extent to which the brush
event can be detected, from the
upper-left corner to the bottom-
right corner of the timeline.

```
const brushHandler = brushX()
  .extent([[0, 0], [tlInnerWidth, tlHeight]])
  .on("brush", handleBrush);
```

When a brush event is detected,
call the brushHandler function.

```
yearsSelector
  .call(brushHandler)
  .call(brushHandler.move, [xScale(minYear),
    xScale(maxYear)]);
```

Apply the brush behavior to the timeline selection.

Initialize the default brushed
area to cover the whole timeline.

```
};
```

At this point, you should see a rectangle over the timeline and gray rectangles over the handles of the brushed area, as in figure 13.15.

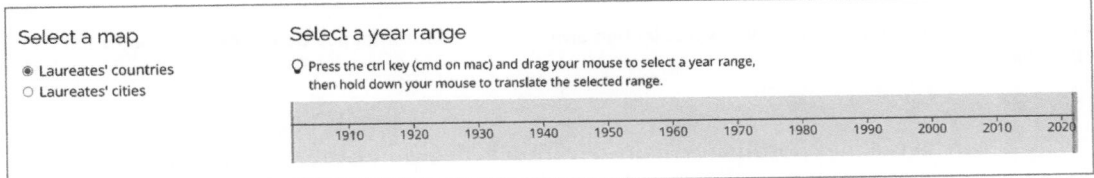

Figure 13.15   Rectangle covering the default year range and gray rectangle over the handles of the brushed area

This blue rectangle represents the selected year range or brushed area. If you open your inspector tool and take a look at the markup, you'll see that D3 added four rectangles on top of the timeline:

- `rect.overlay` covers the whole brushable area.
- `rect.selection` covers the current selection. We have set the default selection, but if you brush a section of the timeline, this rectangle will resize (press the Ctrl key [Cmd on Mac], and drag your mouse over the timeline).
- `rect.handle--w` is a handle on the left side of the selection.
- `rect.handle--e` is a handle on the right side of the selection.

The `visualization.css` file contains the following styles to make the last three rectangles recognizable:

```css
.selection {
  fill: #35a7c2;
  fill-opacity: 0.3;
  stroke: none;
}
.handle {
  fill: #09131b;
  fill-opacity: 0.3;
}
```

Now trigger the brushing event by pressing the Ctrl key (Cmd on Mac) and dragging your mouse over the timeline. You can also resize the selected area with the handles or drag the whole selection left and right. Take a look at the brushing event logged in to the console. As shown in figure 13.16, you'll observe that the brushing event contains a `selection` array of the horizontal position of the left and the right borders of the selection. If we were using `d3.brush()` instead of `d3.brushX()`, we would get the x and y coordinates of the upper-left corner and the bottom-right corner of the selection.

```
▼BrushEvent {type: 'brush', sourceEvent: MouseEvent, selection: Array(2), mode: 'handle', target: f, …} ℹ
   mode: "handle"
 ▶selection: (2) [153.87115478515625, 404.5075378417969]
 ▶sourceEvent: MouseEvent {isTrusted: true, screenX: 796, screenY: 432, clientX: 796, clientY: 296, …}
 ▶target: f brush(group)
   type: "brush"
```

Figure 13.16 The brush event includes a selection array with the horizontal position of the selection's left and right borders.

We can use the coordinates of the selection to determine the corresponding years. Continuous scales such as the linear scale we used to draw the timeline have an `invert()` method that accepts a value from the range and returns the corresponding value from the domain, as used in listing 13.18. This method inverts how we usually use scales. We round the minimum and maximum values of the selection because we don't want years to be floating numbers, and we update two variables named `brushMin` and `brushMax`. We'll use those variables in a moment to update the country colors or the city circles based on the selection. But when the page loads, those variables are set to the minimum and the maximum years of the timeline, which is the default selection.

Listing 13.18   Adding the brushing functionality (`map-world.js`)

```
...
import { brushX } from "d3-brush";

export const drawWorldMap = (laureates, world) => {

  ...

const minYear = min(laureates, d => d.year);
const maxYear = max(laureates, d => d.year);
let brushMin = minYear;
let brushMax = maxYear;

  const handleBrush = (e) => {
    console.log(e);

    brushMin = Math.round(xScale.invert(e.selection[0]));
    brushMax = Math.round(xScale.invert(e.selection[1]));
```

Use the invert() function of xScale to determine the minimum and maximum years of the selection.

```
  if (isCountryMap) {
    updateCountryFills();
  } else {
    updateCityCircles();
  }
};
```

> If a laureate's country map is currently selected, update the country colors. Otherwise, update the city circles.

```
const brushHandler = brushX()
  .extent([[0, 0], [tlInnerWidth, tlHeight]])
  .on("brush", handleBrush);

yearsSelector
  .call(brushHandler)
  .call(brushHandler.move, [xScale(minYear), xScale(maxYear)]);

};
```

In listing 13.19, we call the `updateCountryFills()` or `updateCityCircles()` functions declared earlier to update the country colors or the city circles based on the selection. When updating the country colors, we first make a deep copy of the GeoJSON dataset to avoid modifying the original. Then we filter out the laureates that aren't included in the selection and update the data bound to the country paths. We proceed similarly in the function that updates the city circles by making a deep copy and filtering the `cities` array.

Listing 13.19   Updating country colors/city circles (`map-world.js`)

```
...
import { brushX } from "d3-brush";

export const drawWorldMap = (laureates, world) => {

  ...

  const updateCountryFills = () => {
    const selectedData = JSON.parse(
      JSON.stringify(world.features));
    selectedData.forEach(d => {
      if (d.properties.laureates) {
        d.properties.laureates = d.properties
          .laureates.filter(l => l.year >= brushMin &&
          l.year <= brushMax);
      }
    });

    selectAll(".country-path")
      .data(selectedData)
      .on("mouseenter", (e, d) => {
        const p = d.properties;
        const lastWord = p.laureates.length > 1 ? "laureates" : "laureate";
        const text = `${p.name}, ${p.laureates.length} ${lastWord}`;
        showTooltip(text);
```

> Make a deep copy of the GeoJSON data to avoid modifying the original.

> Filter out the laureates that aren't included in the years' selection.

> Update the data bound to the country paths.

```
    })
    .on("mouseleave", hideTooltip)
    .transition()
    .attr("fill", d => d.properties.laureates.length > 0
      ? countryColorScale(d.properties.laureates.length)
      : "#f8fcff");
};

const maxLaureatesPerCity = max(cities, d => d.laureates.length);
const updateCityCircles = () => {
  const selectedData = JSON.parse(          Make a deep copy of the cities array
    JSON.stringify(cities));                to avoid modifying the original.
  selectedData.forEach(city => {
    city.laureates = city.laureates.filter(l =>        Filter out the laureates
      l.year >= brushMin && l.year <= brushMax);       that aren't included in
  });                                                  the years' selection.

  selectAll(".circle-city")         Update the data bound
    .data(selectedData)          ◁─┘  to the city circles.
    .on("mouseenter", (e, d) => {
      const lastWord = d.laureates.length > 1 ? "laureates" : "laureate";
      const text = `${d.city}, ${d.laureates.length} ${lastWord}`;
      showTooltip(text);
    })
    .on("mouseleave", hideTooltip)
    .transition()
    .attr("r", d => getCityRadius(d.laureates.length,
      maxLaureatesPerCity));
};

};
```

Our brushing feature is now fully operational! Test it out with both the laureates' country and the laureates' city options.

13.5 *Drawing a map from TopoJSON data*

We have already discussed the fact that the two main types of files that store geographical data are GeoJSON and TopoJSON. So far, we have only worked with GeoJSON, but in this section, we'll use TopoJSON data to draw a map of the 96 France departments.

To draw a map from TopoJSON data, we must install the TopoJSON client library (www.npmjs.com/package/topojson-client), which transforms the data into a format D3 can read and manipulate. To install the library into the project, open your integrated terminal, and run command `npm i topojson-client`. Then open the `map-france.js` file. We'll work inside function `drawFranceMap()`.

In listing 13.20, we convert the TopoJSON data into GeoJSON features by calling the `feature()` method of the `topojson-client` library. This method takes two arguments: the `topojson` dataset, also called *topology*, and the object containing the geometries in the dataset, which can be found under the keys `object.FRA_adm2`. We save these extracted GeoJSON features into a constant named `departments`.

We also need to extract the borders separately by using `topojson-client`'s `mesh()` method, which returns a GeoJSON `MultiLineString` geometry object. We'll use it in a moment to draw the borders.

Listing 13.20 Extracting TopoJSON data (`map-france.js`)

```
import * as topojson from "topojson-client";

export const drawFranceMap = (laureates, france) => {

  let departments = topojson.feature(france,
    france.objects.FRA_adm2).features;

  let borders = topojson.mesh(france,
    france.objects.FRA_adm2);

};
```

- `let departments = topojson.feature(france, france.objects.FRA_adm2).features;` → **Convert the TopoJSON data into GeoJSON features.**
- `let borders = topojson.mesh(france, france.objects.FRA_adm2);` → **Extract the departments' borders.**

After that, drawing the map is very similar to what we did earlier with GeoJSON data. In listing 13.21, we declare a new Mercator projection with `d3.geoMercator()`, followed by a geo path generator. Then we use the `departments` object generated in the previous step to append the departments paths to the SVG container. We don't give a `stroke` attribute to these paths. Instead, we append an additional path element and set its `d` attribute by passing the `borders` object to the geo path generator, creating the borders. This way, the borders will be drawn with a single path, avoiding overlap.

Listing 13.21 Drawing the map (`map-france.js`)

```
import * as topojson from "topojson-client";
import { select } from "d3-selection";
import { geoMercator, geoPath } from "d3-geo";

export const drawFranceMap = (laureates, france) => {

  let departments = topojson.feature(france,
    france.objects.FRA_adm2).features;

  let borders = topojson.mesh(france, france.objects.FRA_adm2);

  const width = 800;
  const height = 800;

  const projection = geoMercator()
    .scale(3000)
    .translate([280, 3150]);

  const geoPathGenerator = geoPath()
    .projection(projection);

  const svg = select("#map-france")
    .append("svg")
      .attr("viewBox", `0 0 ${width} ${height}`);
```

- `const width = 800; const height = 800;` → **Initialize the map's dimensions.**
- `const projection = geoMercator() .scale(3000) .translate([280, 3150]);` → **Create a Mercator projection.**
- `const geoPathGenerator = geoPath() .projection(projection);` → **Initialize the geo path generator.**
- `const svg = select("#map-france") .append("svg") .attr("viewBox", \`0 0 ${width} ${height}\`);` → **Append an SVG container to the div with an ID of "map-france".**

```
svg
  .selectAll(".department")
  .data(departments)
  .join("path")
    .attr("class", "department")
    .attr("d", d => geoPathGenerator(d))
    .attr("fill", "#f8fcff");

svg
  .append("path")
    .attr("class", "departments-borders")
    .attr("d", geoPathGenerator(borders))
    .attr("fill", "none")
    .attr("stroke", "#09131b")
    .attr("stroke-opacity", 0.4);
};
```

Use the data-binding pattern to append a
path for each department in the data. Call
geoPathGenerator() to set the d attribute.

Append a single path for the borders,
and pass the borders object to
geoPathGenerator() to set its d attribute.

Your map of France should now look like the one in figure 13.17.

**Figure 13.17   Map of
France's 96 departments
drawn with TopoJSON data**

As explained at the beginning of this chapter, one of the advantages of TopoJSON is
the absence of redundancy in the data. Every shared border is an arc instead of two
separate strokes. This approach not only creates smaller files but also makes maps
look much cleaner: the duplicated borders aren't drawn twice. Figure 13.18 shows the
borders duplication in our GeoJSON world map compared to the neat borders we
obtained for the map of France.

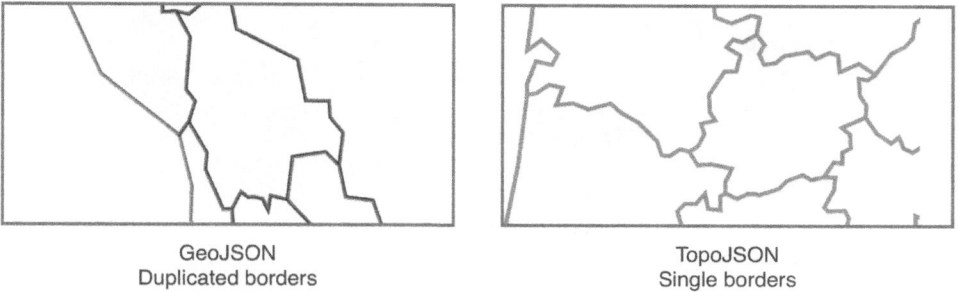

GeoJSON
Duplicated borders

TopoJSON
Single borders

Figure 13.18 In a TopoJSON dataset, every shared border is stored as a single arc, generating smaller files and neater maps.

Exercise: Visualize French cities where Nobel laureates were born

To complete this project, let's draw circles over French cities where Nobel laureates were born. The process is exactly the same as when we did it on the world map. Here are a few guidelines:

1 Filter the laureates' dataset to keep only the ones born in France.
2 Extract their birth cities and the information you'll need to draw the circles.
3 Append a circle for each city where a Nobel laureate was born. Get the circle radius by calling the `getCityRadius()` function from `scales.js`, and use the cities' latitude and longitude to calculate the circles' positions.
4 Once completed, your map will look like the one in the following figure.

Map of France visualizing the cities where Nobel laureates were born

(continued)

If you get stuck or want to compare your solution with ours, you'll find it in section D.13 of appendix D and in the `13.5-TopoJSON/end` folder of this chapter's code files. But as usual, we encourage you to try to complete it on your own. Your solution might differ slightly from ours, and that's all right!

13.6 Further concepts

As mentioned earlier, the things you can do with D3's mapping capabilities would fill an entire book. This section touches on a few other capabilities we didn't cover in this chapter.

13.6.1 Tile mapping

We can build maps with tiles: individual images joined seamlessly to produce a map, such as the ones used by Google Maps. We can use d3-geo with the d3-tile module to overlay vector features on raster tiles. If you're serious about developing tile-based maps, you'll probably want to dig into dedicated libraries such as Mapbox GL (www.mapbox.com/mapbox-gl-js/api/).

13.6.2 Canvas drawing

The `path.context` function of `d3.geoPath()` allows you to easily draw your vector data to a `<canvas>` element. This can dramatically improve performance because with Canvas, you're not adding DOM elements but instead drawing the image as pixels, which takes less computational power. The tradeoff is that you can't interact with the image as you can with DOM elements.

13.6.3 Raster reprojection

You can use raster reprojection to show a satellite-projected terrain map or terrain map on one of the projections offered by the d3-geo module. You can see an example created by Mike Bostock at http://mng.bz/gvyn.

13.6.4 Hexbins

The d3-hexbin module allows you to easily create hexbin overlays for your maps like the one shown in figure 13.19. This option is interesting when you have quantitative data in point form and want to aggregate it by area.

13.6.5 Voronoi diagrams

As with hexbins, if you only have point data and want to create area data from it, you can use the d3-delaunay module to derive polygons from points such as the state capitals shown in figure 13.20. A Voronoi diagram is a partition of a plane into cells that defines regions closest to predefined points.

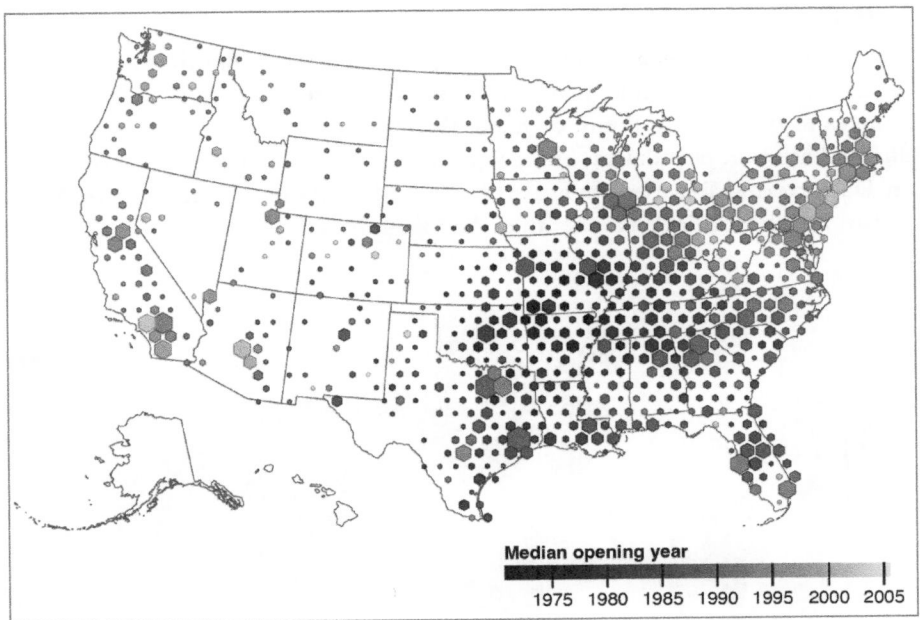

Figure 13.19   An example of hexbinning by Mike Bostok showing the locations of Walmart stores in the United States(Source: https://observablehq.com/@d3/hexbin-map)

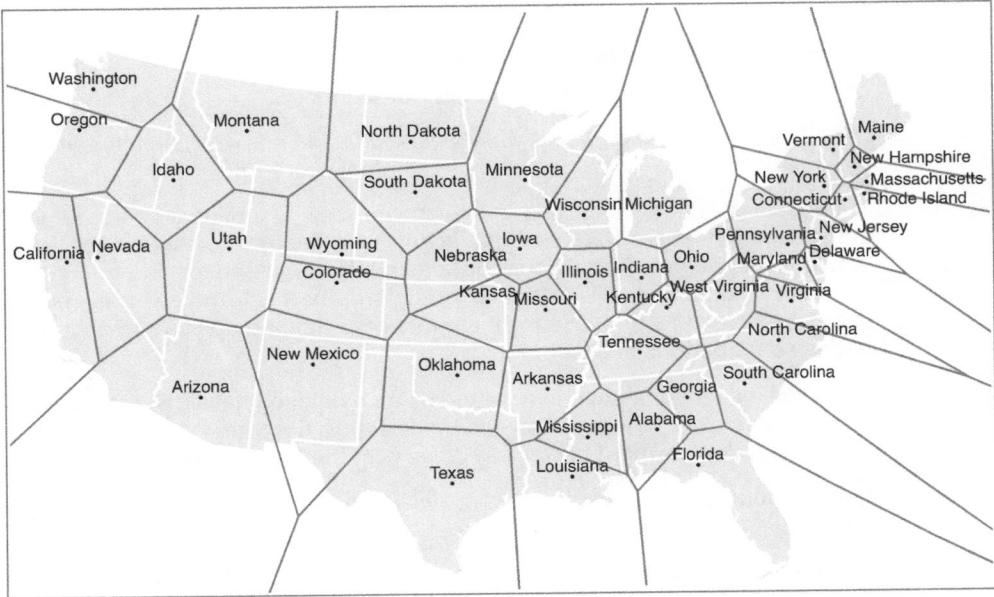

Figure 13.20   An example of a Voronoi diagram used to split the United States into polygons based on the closest state capital, created by Mike Bostock (Source: http://mng.bz/OZMO)

13.6.6 Cartograms

Distorting the area or length of a geographic object to show other information creates a cartogram. For example, you could distort the streets of your city based on the time it takes to drive along them, or make the size of countries on a world map bulge or shrink based on population. Although no simple functions exist to create cartograms in D3, external libraries such as the World Population Cartogram by Matt Dzugan (http://mng.bz/Y7rQ) can be used. An example is shown in figure 13.21.

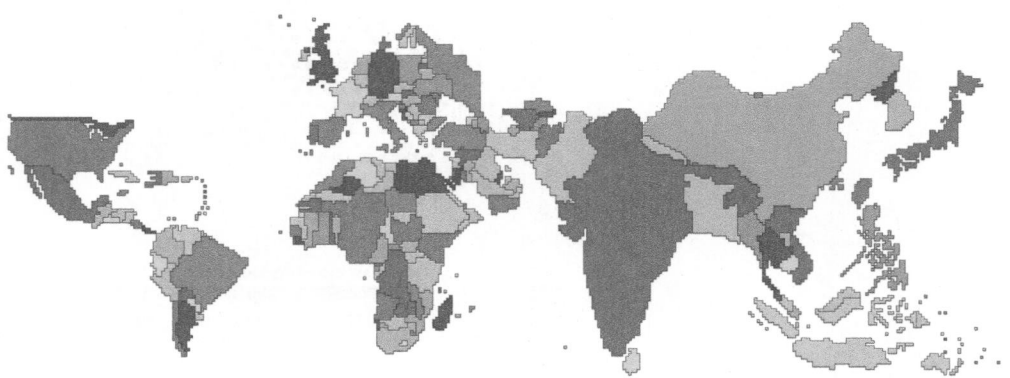

Figure 13.21   Cartogram created by Matt Dzugan where the countries are sized by their population (Source: http://mng.bz/GZd8)

Interview with Maarten Lambrechts

Lambrechts is a data visualization engineer at Planet.

Can you tell us a little bit about your background and how you came to data visualization?

Sure. I am a bio engineer, and in university I took an optional course in GIS (Geographical Information Systems). That is how I first learned to make maps. After graduating, I had many different jobs, but one constant was that I had to communicate numbers to others. And like for many others in the field, the eye-openers were the books by Edward Tufte: they taught me that data visualization can be a lot more than hitting some buttons in Excel.

After working for some time in newsrooms as a data journalist, where data visualization was already a big part of my job, I decided to become a data visualization freelancer, and that is what I have been doing over the last couple of years.

How did you learn D3? What were your main challenges, and how did you overcome them?

I entered the field of interactive data visualization just at the time that Flash was dying and that D3 was taking over. I tried to get a grip on it through duplicating and editing blocks (bl.ocks.org was a platform on which people shared pieces of code, made by Mike Bostock, the creator of D3), but my breakthrough came through a knee injury. I had to go through a knee surgery, which immobilized me for six weeks, and I decided to use that time to learn proper web development and D3. During that period, I made the Weather Browser (www.maartenlambrechts.be/vis/weatherbrowser/), my first big dataviz project and an entry to a dataviz competition. It won silver in that competition, so that encouraged me to keep going.

My main challenge was that I had no background in programming. So in the beginning, I was copying a lot of code, but didn't know how it worked. I learned that it pays to learn the basics of JavaScript and to read through the D3 documentation to clearly understand all the code you are writing.

Do you use visualization tools other than D3? What's the place of D3 in your current data visualization workflow?

I used to use all the DOM interaction features of D3, but today I use the Svelte framework for that, and I mainly use all the helper functions to build visualizations, like scales, shape generators, data fetching, and d3-geo for maps.

For data processing, I rely on the R tidyverse packages. I usually export CSV files out of R, which I then load in my D3 applications.

Featured project: "Why Budapest, Warsaw, and Lithuania Split Themselves in Two" (https://pudding.cool/2019/04/eu-regions/)

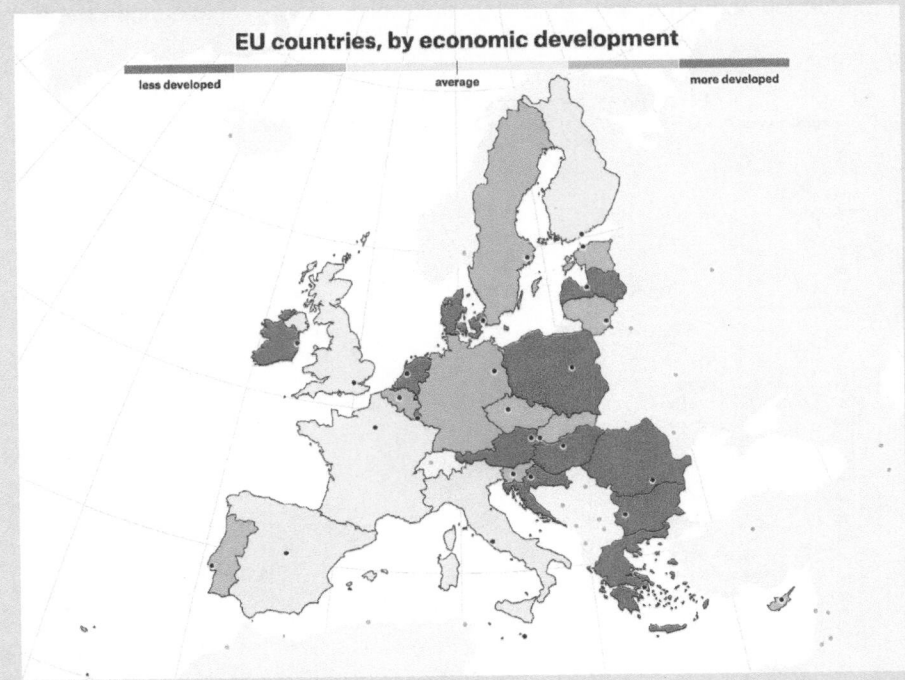

EU countries, by economic development

(continued)

Please describe your project "Why Budapest, Warsaw, and Lithuania Split Themselves in Two."

I had the initial idea while I was still working in the newsroom of Flemish newspaper *De Tijd*. But my programming skills were still too basic back then, and there was not enough interest from my editors to pursue the story.

But I did develop a basic prototype that I could show when I pitched it a couple of years later to *The Pudding*. I thought the way the EU was redistributing money from richer to poorer regions was not very well known, and so I tried to find an angle to make it newsworthy. At first, I thought I saw some indications of fraud: it looked like regions were fiddling with their GDP numbers to stay below certain thresholds. After talking to some statisticians at the European Commission, this proved not to be the case. But by talking to these people, I learned that some regions were redrawing their boundaries to optimize the distribution of funds to them. And that was an interesting enough story that also lent itself very well to be explained visually.

Can you describe the process of creating this project?

I started by gathering the data and making some exploratory visualizations with ggplot2 in R. That was how I saw some suspicious spikes in some histograms, which in the end proved not to indicate fraud. I kept going back and forth with Matt, my editor at *The Pudding* (https://pudding.cool/), until we found the right angle. Then we brainstormed about the flow of the story and which visuals could support the story best.

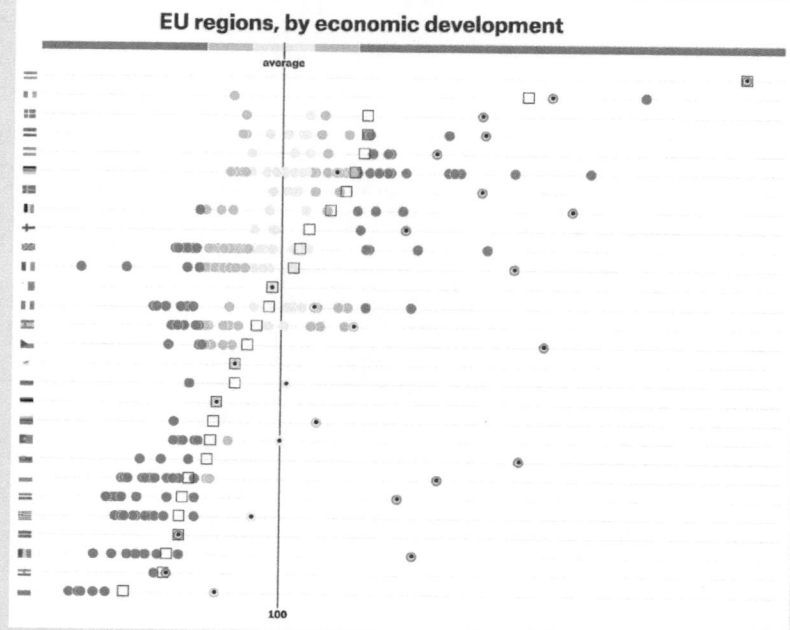

EU regions, by economic development

For the development, I could rely on a web development boilerplate that the developers of *The Pudding* were using. This had all the necessary features built in, like D3 and a scrollytelling component. Then it took some months to build the story because I was developing it in parallel with some other projects. But this also allowed me and Matt to go back and forth a lot, and to really take the story to the next level, both in content and in design.

One thing I love about this project is how purposeful the animations and transitions are. They undeniably support the story and our comprehension. Did you know from the start the type of scrollytelling you wanted to create, or was it an iterative process?

The main animation and scrollytelling were already part of the basic prototype I made some time earlier. The animation transitions regions on a map to a dot plot to make sure the reader understands that each dot on the plot represents a region they were seeing on the map just before. So this was already part of the very first idea.

Let's discuss the shape-shifting transition where the countries' SVG paths become circles in a strip plot. Did you use a library other than D3 to generate that effect?

The morphing of regions to circles is done with Flubber (https://github.com/veltman/flubber). I met Flubber's creator, Noah Veltman, at the OpenVis Conference in 2018, where he launched his library to interpolate SVG shapes. One of the examples he showed was how the shapes of the US states could morph into each other, and I think that was what inspired me.

Which tips would you share with our readers who are interested in entering the field of data journalism?

I always say that you have to just do it. You can read many books and articles about how to do it, but you can only learn it by doing it. Start small, and apply a technique you learned about elsewhere to your own local data and local environment, and run with it.

On a technical level, I can highly recommend learning R and the tidyverse packages ggplot2 (for visualization), dplyr, and tidyr (for data cleaning and reshaping). They make you think methodically about the structure of your data and about how you can visualize it.

To learn interactive data visualization, the best resource today is probably Observable. It's an interactive notebook environment, cofounded by Mike Bostock. Many people use it to experiment with visualizations, and a lot of notebooks use different parts of D3.

Summary

- Geographical data comes in different forms, from simple latitude and longitude coordinates to GeoJSON and TopoJSON datasets.
- The main difference between GeoJSON and TopoJSON is that whereas GeoJSON records an array of coordinates for each feature that describes a point, line, or polygon, TopoJSON stores an array of arcs.

- GeoJSON data is relatively easy to create, read, and understand, but such files can quickly become heavy.
- TopoJSON data allows for rendering detailed features with smaller files, making it particularly well adapted to web projects.
- While GeoJSON data can be manipulated directly by D3, an external library is required to decode TopoJSON before treating it with D3.
- Projections refer to rendering points from a 3D globe onto a flat 2D surface. They inevitably distort geographical data to some degree. D3 provides methods for four common types of projections: azimuthal, conic, cylindrical, and composite.
- Creating a map with D3 requires three main steps: defining a projection, initializing the geo path generator with `d3.geoPath()`, and appending the paths to the SVG container.
- A grid of longitude and latitude lines can be drawn with the `d3.geoGraticule()` functionality.
- To draw points on a map, we pass their longitude and latitude to the projection function, which returns the corresponding (x, y) coordinates in the SVG container.
- D3 has modules dedicated to the zooming and brushing functionalities.

Part 4

Advanced techniques

Now that you've used D3 to create a bunch of different visualizations, it's time for the fun part! In chapter 14, we'll create a fully customized project by combining multiple D3 modules. We'll discuss a strategy to produce unique work and create engaging stories. Then, in chapter 15, we'll talk about performance and when we might want to render our work with Canvas instead of SVG. With those pieces of knowledge in your toolbox, you'll be ready to tackle advanced projects.

Creating a custom visualization

This chapter covers

- Exploring visual channels for quantitative and qualitative data
- Breaking down a complex project
- Combining D3 methods to create a custom visualization
- Creating a responsive SVG grid
- Positioning visual elements on a radial layout

In the first three sections of this book, we've been applying diverse D3 techniques to develop well-known visualization layouts, such as bar charts, streamgraphs, histograms, maps, and so on. But if you picked D3 as a data visualization tool, there's a good chance that you also want to build intricate and unusual visualizations. To create unique projects, you need to understand the different methods and layouts that D3 has at your disposal. It's not so much about knowing every single method in detail but instead mastering the philosophy behind D3 and knowing where to find information when needed. Appendix C, where we mapped all the D3 modules and what they are about, can help you with that. Another skill you'll need in order to create custom layouts is the ability to break down ideas and geometries into code, which we'll do in this chapter's project.

This project will bring you behind the scenes of creating a fully customized visualization, from sketching ideas to breaking down the project into components to rendering visual elements onto a radial layout. The project we'll build explores Vincent van Gogh's artistic legacy produced during the last decade of his life. You can find the completed project at http://mng.bz/z8rg.

We'll follow a six-step process to bring this project to life. Although this isn't set in stone, this is roughly the methodology you can expect to follow for any data visualization project:

1 Gathering data
2 Exploring the data
3 Sketching the layout
4 Building the project skeleton
5 Creating the visualizations
6 Planning meaningful interactions

14.1 *Gathering data*

Gathering and cleaning data is the most critical step of any data visualization project. If lucky, we get ready-to-use datasets and can start working directly on the visualization, as with this book's previous projects. But more often than not, we need to gather data from different sources, and analyze, clean, and format it. Data gathering and manipulation can take an impressive amount of time. It requires patience and diligence. In this section, we'll discuss the different steps we went through to prepare the data for this chapter's project.

But before we look for data, let's take a moment to define what type of information we want to visualize. The inspiration for this project comes from a data visualization workshop with Frederica Fragapane (www.behance.net/FedericaFragapane), during which we worked with a dataset of the letters Vincent van Gogh wrote to his brother Theo. We were awestruck by the richness of Van Gogh's literary legacy and thought it would be interesting to combine it with his well-known paintings and drawings to offer an insight into his whole artistic heritage.

So we know that we want to gather data about Van Gogh's paintings, drawings, and letters. Ideally, we would like to situate those in time to visualize the ebbs and flows of his artistic production. After a few Google searches, we found the following resources:

- *List of works by Vincent van Gogh*—A Wikipedia page listing every painting produced by Van Gogh, as well as sketches he sent with his letters, grouped by medium and period
- *List of drawings by Vincent van Gogh*—A Wikipedia page listing every drawing produced by Van Gogh, other than his letter sketches
- *Vincent van Gogh: The Letters*—A website dedicated to Van Gogh's letters, grouped by period

- *Vincent van Gogh*—A Wikipedia page about Van Gogh's life, which can help us better understand the events that shaped his artistic production

By exploring these resources, we also noted that we can break down Van Gogh's life into phases based on the cities he lived in. For example, he moved from the Netherlands to Paris in 1886, where he met Paul Gauguin and Henri de Toulouse-Lautrec, to name just those two. Those artistic encounters undoubtedly influenced Van Gogh's work. We also know that he was hospitalized at the Saint-Paul de Mausole asylum from May 1889 until May 1890. During this period, he started incorporating swirls into his depictions of the hospital's garden. Finally, Van Gogh died by suicide in July 1890, marking an abrupt end to a prolific 10 years of artistic production. Being aware of those events, we want our visualization to constitute a timeline of Van Gogh's last 10 years.

Now we need to extract data from the resources we found. Let's take the paintings as an example (http://mng.bz/0GZW). This Wikipedia page contains a series of tables listing a little more than a thousand paintings—not something we want to extract manually! You can find online services that extract tables from a web page and convert them into CSV files, such as TableConvert (https://tableconvert.com). Such tools are convenient and quick to use. But if we want more fine-grain control, we can write a simple script to do the work.

Listing 14.1 contains a script that you can use to extract the title, image URL, and medium of each painting from the Wikipedia page. To use this script, open your browser's console, copy and paste the entire snippet, and press Enter.

If we look at the page structure, we observe that it consists of a series of HTML tables, each table containing a list of paintings made with the same medium. The first six tables are about oil paintings; the seventh contains watercolors; the eighth and the ninth are about lithographs and etchings, which we'll group under the "print" medium. The last table contains letter sketches, which we don't want to extract yet. In listing 14.1, we declare an array containing the index of the tables we're interested in and their related mediums.

We then extract all the HTML tables from the page using the document method `querySelectorAll()` and the classes `"wikitable"` and `"sortable"` as a selector. We found this selector by opening our browser inspector and taking a closer look at the markup to find a unique and common selector for the tables we're interested in.

While looping through those tables, we check to see if they already exist in the tables array declared at the beginning of the script. This verification allows us to avoid extracting information from the letter sketches table. We can then loop through each table row and extract the title and URL of the painting image. Note that we had to accommodate different DOM structures in the code because the table rows aren't consistently formatted the same way. The paintings that don't match those HTML structures are given a title and an image URL of `null` and will be completed by hand later. Dealing with real-life data is often messy! You'll also see that we extract the image URL from the `srcset` attribute instead of the `src` because this image is smaller and will require less loading time in our project.

Finally, we structure the painting information into an object and push it into an array named `"paintings"`. By logging this array into the console, we can copy and paste it into our code editor and create a JSON file.

This script is tailored to this specific example and won't be helpful on another web page. But you can see how valuable your JavaScript skills can be for extracting any information from a web page.

Listing 14.1   Extracting data from Van Gogh's paintings on Wikipedia

```
const tables = [
  { index: 0, medium: "oil" },
  { index: 1, medium: "oil" },
  { index: 2, medium: "oil" },
  { index: 3, medium: "oil" },
  { index: 4, medium: "oil" },
  { index: 5, medium: "oil" },
  { index: 6, medium: "watercolor" },
  { index: 7, medium: "print" },
  { index: 8, medium: "print" },
];

const domTables = document.querySelectorAll(
  ".wikitable.sortable"
);
const paintings = [];

domTables.forEach((table, i) => {
  if (i <= tables.length - 1) {
    const medium = tables[i].medium;

    const rows = table.querySelectorAll("tbody tr");
    rows.forEach(row => {
      let title;
      if (row.querySelector(".thumbcaption i a")) {
        title = row.querySelector(".thumbcaption i a")
          .textContent;
      } else if (row.querySelector(".thumbcaption i")) {
        title = row.querySelector(".thumbcaption i")
          .textContent;
      } else {
        title = null;
      }

      let imageLink;
      if (row.querySelector(".thumbinner img")) {
        const image = row.querySelector(
          ".thumbinner img"
        ).srcset;
        imageLink = `https${image.slice(
          image.indexOf("1.5x, ")+6,-3
        )}`;
      } else {
        imageLink = null;
      }
```

Create a list of the tables from which we want to extract paintings and their related medium.

Initialize an empty array and save it in a constant named "paintings". This is where we'll store the information about each painting.

Select all the HTML tables with a class of "sortable".

Loop through the tables extracted from the DOM. If a table is part of the tables array, save the related medium in a constant, and loop through the table rows.

Extract the title of the painting, and save it in a constant.

Extract the URL of the painting image, and save it in a constant.

```
    paintings.push({
      title: title,
      imageLink: imageLink,
      medium: medium
    });
  })
  }
});
console.log(paintings);
```

Add the title, image URL, and medium to an object, and push it into the paintings array.

Log the paintings array into the console.

The script example from listing 14.1 is incomplete. We still need to extract the date, dimension, current location, and creation location for each painting. We won't do it here to avoid making this section too long, but give it a try if you want to practice extracting data from a web page! Note that we also had to manipulate the extracted data to store the width and height of the paintings separately, as well as the month and year of creation. Some additional research was required to find the month of creation of some paintings and to find their subject (portrait, still life, landscape, etc.).

If you want to jump directly to using the data, this chapter's code files contain ready-to-use datasets for Van Gogh's paintings, drawings, letters, and the timeline of the cities he lived in (see http://mng.bz/KZ5E).

14.2 Exploring the data

In chapter 3, we defined two main categories of data: *quantitative* and *qualitative* (illustrated in figure 14.1). Quantitative data consists of numerical information, such as the

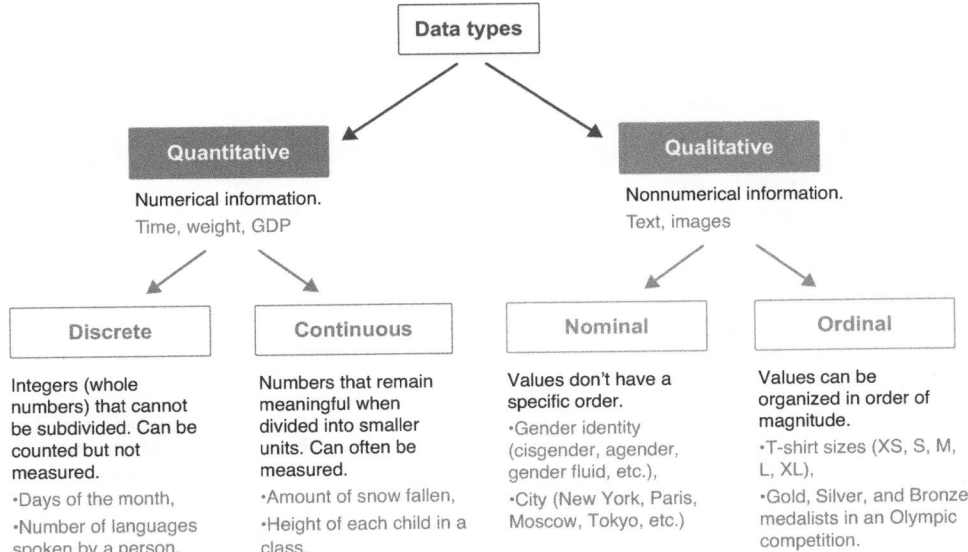

Figure 14.1 We can group data into two main categories: quantitative (numerical information) and qualitative (nonnumerical information). Quantitative data is discrete or continuous, while qualitative data is nominal or ordinal.

ebbs and flows of stock market action values or the number of students in a classroom. Quantitative data can be *discrete*, that is, made of whole numbers that can't be subdivided, or *continuous*, where numbers remain meaningful when subdivided into smaller units. Qualitative data, on the other hand, is nonnumerical information, such as a list of countries or the available sizes for coffee orders at Starbucks (short, tall, grande, venti, etc.). Qualitative data can be *nominal*, where values don't have a specific order, or *ordinal*, where the order matters.

Because we won't use the same channels to visualize different data types, it's often helpful to write a list of the variables we have at our disposal for a project and organize them by data types. This step can help us identify the different visual channels or ways to encode data that we can use. Figure 14.2 illustrates that quantitative data is often visualized with *position*, such as in a scatterplot; *length*, such as in a bar chart; *area*, such as the size of the nodes in our Romeo and Juliet project (refer to chapter 12); *angle*, such as in a pie chart; or with a *continuous color scale*. Qualitative data, on the other hand, is often translated with a *categorical color scale, patterns, symbols, connections*, as in a network graph; or *enclosure* for hierarchical data, as in circle packs. Such a list can only be incomplete because with a bit of creativity, we can devise new ways to visualize data. But it provides an overview of the primary visual encodings at our disposal.

At this point, a helpful exercise consists of listing the different data attributes included in our datasets, identifying quantitative and qualitative data, and

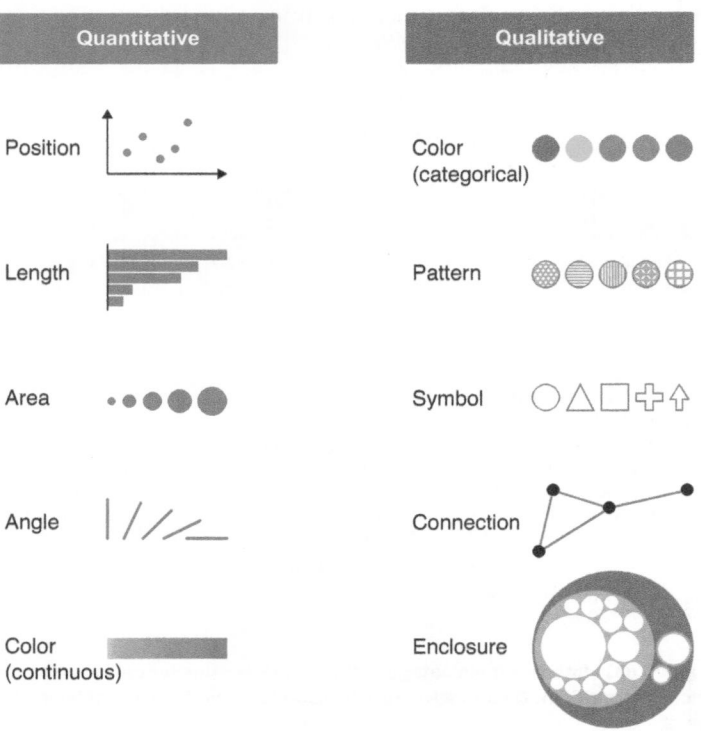

Figure 14.2 Quantitative data is often visualized with position, length, area, angle, and continuous color scales, while qualitative data uses categorical color scales, patterns, symbols, connections, and enclosure.

brainstorming how we would like to visualize the main attributes. In figure 14.3, we list the four datasets that we have for this project (a list of Van Gogh's paintings, a list of his drawings, the number of letters he wrote each month, and a timeline of the cities where he lived during his career) and identify if the data attributes are quantitative (blue dots) or qualitative (red dots). Based on this information, we can start thinking about the visualization we want to create.

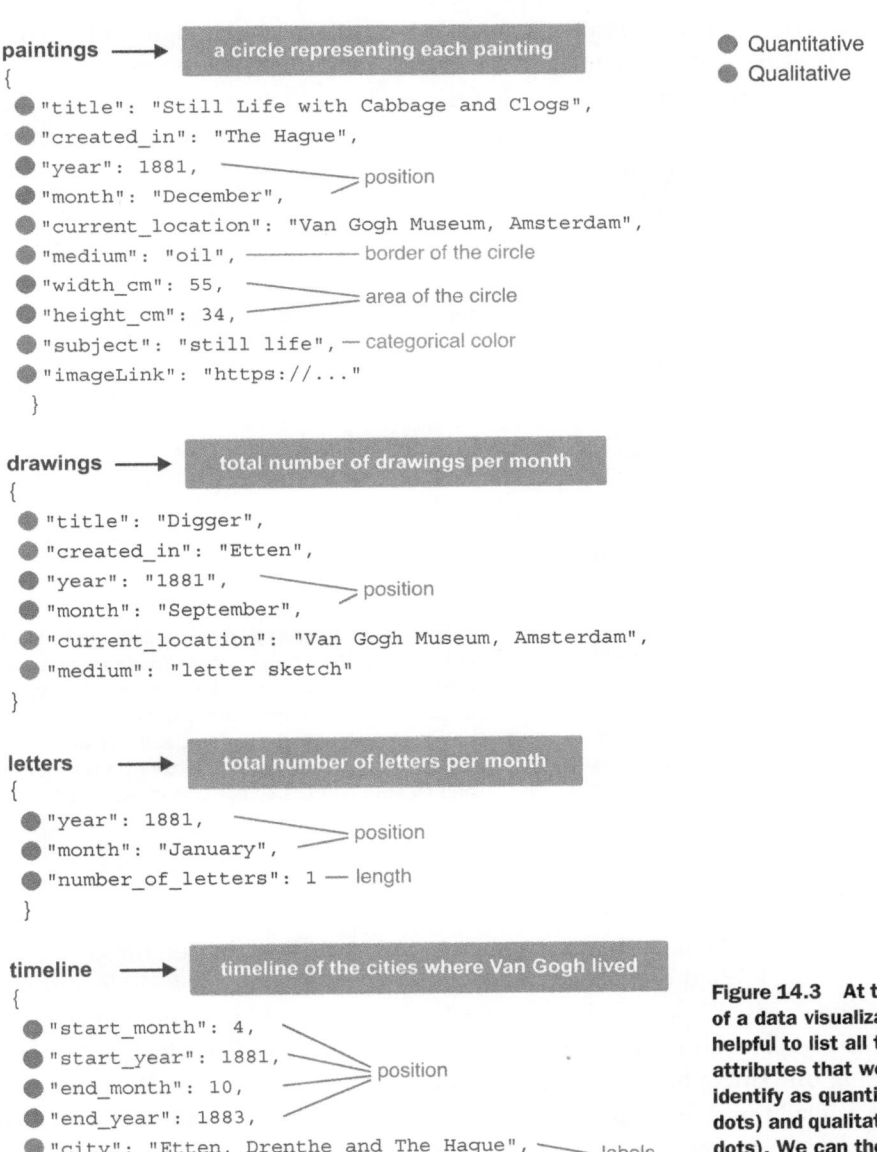

Figure 14.3   At the beginning of a data visualization, it's helpful to list all the data attributes that we have to identify as quantitative (blue dots) and qualitative data (red dots). We can then start to brainstorm how we'd like to visualize those data attributes.

In this project, we want to present Van Gogh's artistic production (paintings, drawings, and letters) over a timeline to explore the correlation between the use of each mode of expression and how those evolved as the artist moved throughout the Netherlands and France. We want to focus more on the paintings and allow users to explore them individually. If a circle represents each painting, we could use the color of the circles to communicate the subject of the painting (portrait, still life, landscape, etc.), use their size for the dimensions of the piece, and highlight the medium (oil, watercolor, or print) with the circle's border, as illustrated in figure 14.4. Those circles will be positioned over some kind of timeline.

The number of drawings and letters produced each month could be added as secondary information via the length of bars or an area chart. Finally, we know that we need some clickable timeline to select and highlight Van Gogh's production over different periods of his life.

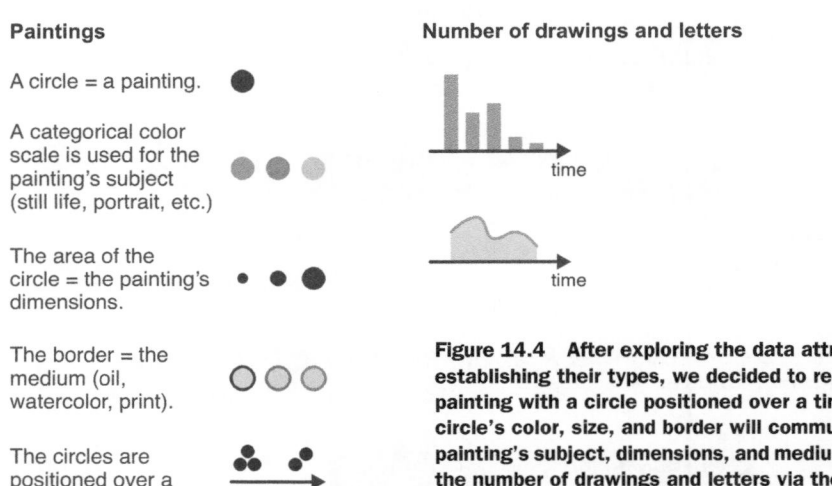

Figure 14.4   **After exploring the data attributes and establishing their types, we decided to represent each painting with a circle positioned over a timeline. The circle's color, size, and border will communicate the painting's subject, dimensions, and medium. We'll visualize the number of drawings and letters via the length of bars and an area chart, also positioned over a timeline.**

14.3   *Sketching the layout*

Once the visual channels are chosen, we can start sketching the project's layout. We already established that each painting will be represented by a circle and positioned on a time axis. A horizontal or a vertical axis could work, although it may get too large for the screen. An interesting workaround could be a radial time axis. And instead of having one single big circle, which can be hard to adapt to mobile screens, we could use a small multiples approach. Small multiples are composed of a series of visualizations using the same scale and axes but representing a different aspect of the data. With this approach, we could have a wheel for every year, allowing us to position them into a grid, as in figure 14.5. On desktop layouts, we would have a clickable timeline on the left and the small multiples visualization laid out in a three-column grid on the right. On tablets, the grid would be reduced to two columns, while on mobile devices, we would use a one-column grid without the timeline functionality.

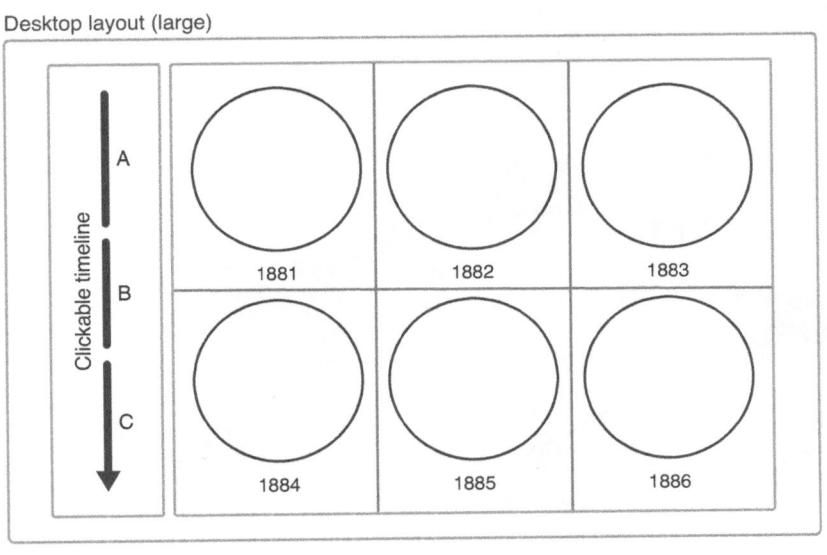

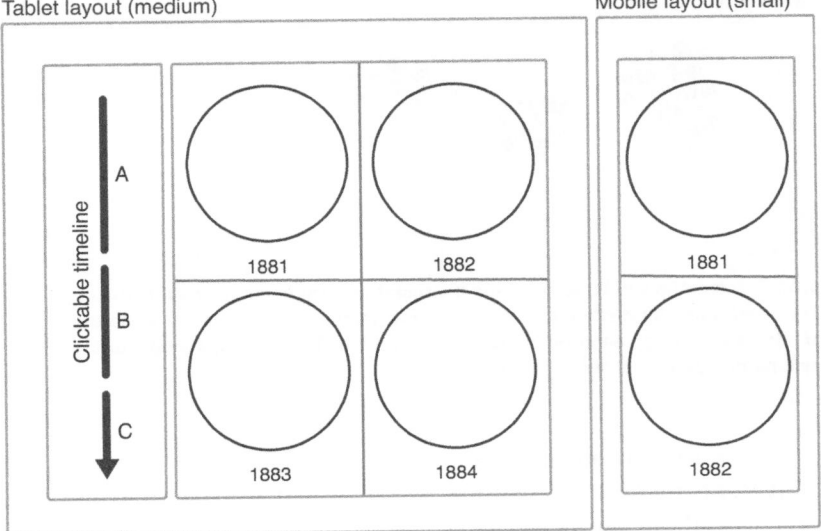

Figure 14.5   Small multiples visualizations are composed of a series of charts sharing the same scale and axes. They are usually laid out into a grid, making them easy to adapt to different screen sizes.

Each small multiple will visualize an entire year, the months being distributed along the circumference of a circle. For each month, the number of drawings will be represented by an area chart, and the number of letters will be represented with the length of a bar. The circles representing the paintings made during a month will be clustered together, as in figure 14.6.

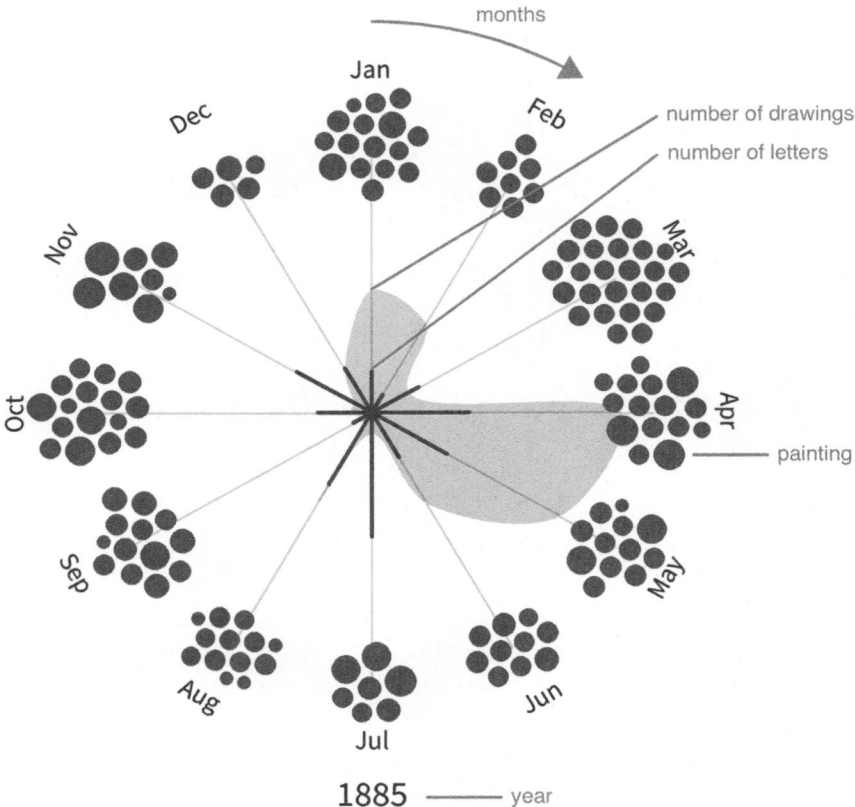

Figure 14.6 The months will be arranged in a circular pattern in each small multiple. The number of drawings for each month will be shown through an area chart, while the number of letters will be represented by the length of a bar. The paintings made during a month will be grouped together in a cluster.

The next step is creating a color palette and choosing fonts. We'll need a categorical color palette for eight different painting subjects—self-portraits, portraits, peasant life, interior scene, still life, landscape, cityscape-building, and others—and another color for the letters and drawings. When creating any color palette, think about the ambiance you want to install in your project. For example, here we'd like to go with a cheerful color palette inspired by the hues found in Van Gogh's paintings from the last few years of his life. We created the categorical color palette from figure 14.7 by extracting a golden color from a painting and using the Coolors website (https://coolors.co) to generate matching colors. Eight colors are already a lot for a categorical palette, so we had to use similar hues for some categories. For example, we selected an old rose color for the portraits (#c16e70) and a brighter version of that same color for the self-portraits (#f7a3a6). You can also find inspiration for your color palettes on Adobe Color (https://color.adobe.com) and Color Hunt (https://colorhunt.co).

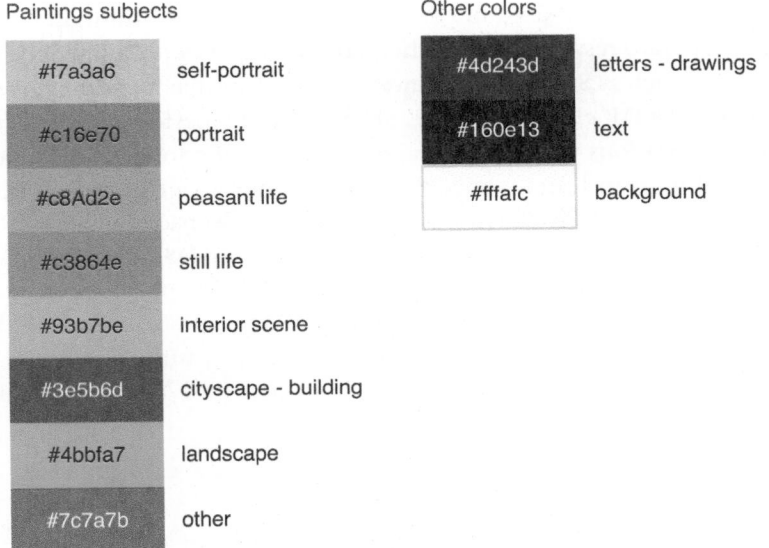

Paintings subjects

#f7a3a6	self-portrait
#c16e70	portrait
#c8Ad2e	peasant life
#c3864e	still life
#93b7be	interior scene
#3e5b6d	cityscape - building
#4bbfa7	landscape
#7c7a7b	other

Other colors

#4d243d	letters - drawings
#160e13	text
#fffafc	background

Figure 14.7   For this project, we'll need a categorical palette of eight colors for the painting subjects and an additional color for the letters and drawings. By playing with the brightness, we generate two other variations of this last color that we'll use for the text and the project's background.

For the font, we find Google Fonts (https://fonts.google.com) to be a great resource for free web fonts. Generally, you'll want to stick to a maximum of two font families per project, one for the headings and one for the body of text. A simple Google search will provide plenty of ideas for Google font combinations. For this project, we opted for Libre Baskerville Bold for the headings, a serif font that echoes the 19th century, with Source Sans Pro for the text and labels, a sans serif font that has excellent readability for user interfaces.

14.4   Building the project skeleton

Once we know what we want to build, we must decide on the infrastructure we want to use. Because this project is more complex than the ones we've created earlier in this book, we'll turn to a JavaScript framework. Working with a framework will allow us to break down our project into small components, making it easier to develop and maintain. We've already built a project with React in chapter 8, so this time, we'll opt for Svelte, a simple compiler that the data visualization community particularly loves. Don't worry if you're not familiar with Svelte yet. The focus of this chapter will remain on the general principles behind creating a complex data visualization project. You can read along and gather little nuggets of wisdom without having to dive into Svelte. If you've played with Svelte before or are curious to give it a try, you'll see that it's pretty intuitive and plays very well with D3. You can find a brief introduction to Svelte in appendix E and handy bite-sized tutorials at https://svelte.dev/tutorial.

We want to separate responsibilities when combining D3 with a JavaScript framework or a compiler such as Svelte. The framework is responsible for adding, removing, and manipulating DOM elements, while D3 is used to perform the calculations related to the visualizations with scales, shape generators, the force layout, and so on. Simply put, you'll want to forget about the data-binding pattern and use D3 transitions sparingly to avoid conflicts between D3 and Svelte. Go back to chapter 8 for an in-depth discussion of the possible approaches to combining D3 with a framework.

To start working on this chapter's project, open the `start` folder from http://mng.bz/9dA0 in your code editor. Open the integrated terminal, and install the project dependencies with `npm install`. Then start the project with `npm run dev`. The project will be available in your browser at http://localhost:5173/. You'll find all the files we'll work with inside the `src/` folder:

- `App.svelte` is the root component of our project and calls the child components that create the page layout.
- The `/data` folder contains the four datasets we'll use for this project: `drawings.json`, `letters.json`, `paintings.json`, and `timeline.json`.
- `global_styles/` contains four Sass CSS (SCSS) files that are then loaded into `styles.scss`. Using SCSS instead of CSS allows us to declare style variables (e.g., `$text: #160E13`) that we can reuse throughout the project, making it easier to maintain.
- `layout/` contains the main components of the project layout, such as the header and the legend.
- `chart_component/` contains components related to specific visualization components, such as the paintings or the letters.
- `/UI` is for interface components, such as the tooltip.
- `utils/` contains utility functions and constants.

14.4.1 *Another approach to responsive SVG containers*

From chapter 1, we adopted a simple yet effective way to make our SVG graphics responsive: by setting the `viewBox` attribute of the SVG container and leaving the `width` and `height` attributes blank. This approach is super easy to implement and works out of the box. The only real drawback is that when the SVG container gets smaller, the text elements it contains get proportionally smaller, making them potentially hard to read.

In this project, we'll take a different approach by setting the `width` and `height` attributes of the SVG container and leaving the `viewBox` empty. We'll use an event listener to update these attributes whenever the screen size changes. Although this approach requires more effort from us as programmers and for the browser, it enables us to adjust the layout of our visualization according to the screen width. Additionally, it maintains the size of text labels as the screen size decreases.

In our previous project discussion, we decided to display a grid of small multiple visualizations. All of these visualizations will be enclosed in a single SVG element. Additionally, we'll be using a 12-column flexbox grid, similar to the one discussed in chapter 9, for the overall page layout that includes the timeline and the visualizations.

In figure 14.8, you can see the page layout at three different screen widths: larger than or equal to 1,400 px (the width of the flexbox grid container), smaller than 1,400 px but larger than 748 px, and smaller than 748 px. For each of these three screen sizes, the calculation of the width of the SVG container is slightly different. When the screen is larger than or equal to 748 px, the timeline is displayed on the left, taking 2 columns out of the 12-column grid, and the visualization, or the SVG container, is displayed on the right over the 10 remaining columns. When the screen is smaller than 748 px, we remove the timeline, and the visualization can extend over the 12 columns. The flexbox grid container also has a padding of 30 px applied to the left and right.

The flexbox grid is limited to a `max-width` of 1,400 px in its CSS property. This means that even on larger screens, the content won't exceed this width. To calculate the width of the SVG container on screens wider than 1,400 px, we can subtract the padding on each side of the flexbox grid container, multiply it by 10, and then divide it by 12. This is because the SVG container spans across 10 out of the 12 columns:

$$\texttt{svgWidth} = 10 \div 12 \times (\texttt{gridContainer} - 2 \times \text{padding})$$

When the screen is smaller than 1,400 px, the size of the SVG container gets proportionally smaller. In the equation of the `svgWidth`, we only need to change the `gridContainer` for the window width:

$$\texttt{svgWidth} = 10 \div 12 \times (\texttt{windowWidth} - 2 \times \text{padding})$$

Finally, when the screen is smaller than 768 px, the SVG container spreads over the entire width of the screen minus the padding:

$$\texttt{svgWidth} = \texttt{windowWidth} - 2 \times \text{padding}$$

In listing 14.2, we use those equations to dynamically calculate the SVG container's width. For that, we work in the `Grid.svelte` file. We first declare two variables, one for the `windowWidth` and one for the SVG width. With a switch statement, we set the value of the SVG `width` variable based on the screen's width with the equations discussed a

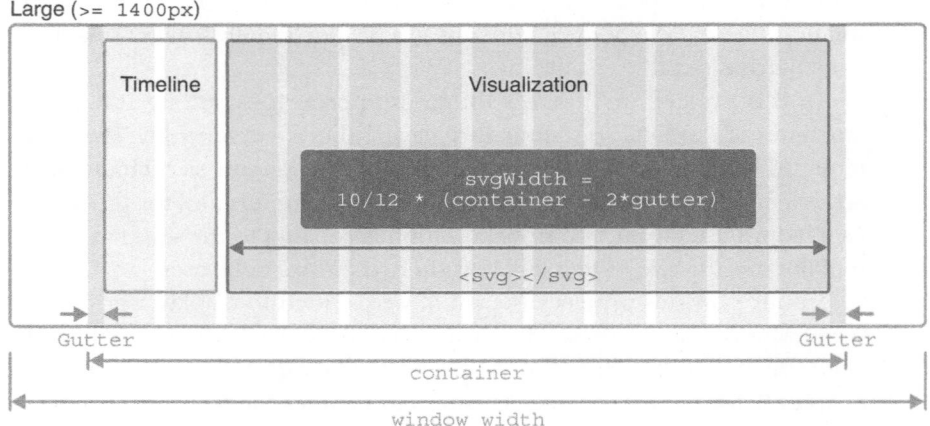

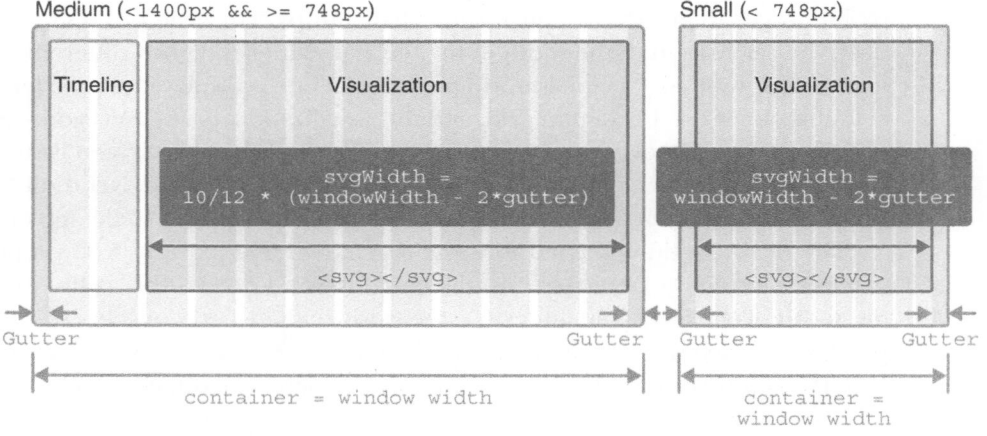

Figure 14.8   The width of the SVG container is proportional to the screen width and the page's responsive layout. On screens larger than 748 px, the SVG spreads over 10 columns in the 12-column flexbox grid, while on smaller screens, it takes all 12 columns.

moment ago. Because the switch statement is declared with the Svelte reactivity sign ($), it runs anytime a variable it contains changes.

Note that we bound the `windowWidth` variable to the `innerWidth` property of the window object. In Svelte, we can access the window object from any component with `<svelte:window />`.

Finally, we dynamically set the width attribute of the SVG container with the `svgWidth` variable. Because we're working with a JavaScript framework, we don't use D3 to append an SVG element to the DOM but rather add it directly to the component's markup.

Listing 14.2 Dynamically updating the width (`Grid.svelte`)

```
<script>
   let windowWidth;
   const gridContainer = 1400;
   const padding = 30;
   let svgWidth;
   $: switch (true) {
      case windowWidth >= gridContainer:
        svgWidth = (10 / 12) * (gridContainer -
          2 * padding);
        break;
      case windowWidth < gridContainer &&
        windowWidth >= 768:
        svgWidth = (10 / 12) * (windowWidth -
          2 * padding);
        break;
      default:
        svgWidth = windowWidth - 2 * padding;
      }
</script>

<svelte:window bind:innerWidth={windowWidth} />

<svg width={svgWidth} />

<style>
  svg {
    border: 1px solid magenta;
  }
</style>
```

> **Whenever the windowWidth variable change, calculate svgWidth. This update can happen because of the reactive block created with the $ sign.**

> **Bind the value of the windowWidth variable to the innerWidth property of the window object. You can access the window object inside any Svelte component!**

> **Dynamically set the width attribute of the SVG container with the value of svgWidth.**

In the `"styles"` section, a magenta border has been added to the SVG element. You can experiment with resizing your screen to see how it affects the width of the SVG element.

Now that the width of the SVG container is handled, we need to set its height. Because the SVG element will contain a grid of small multiple visualizations, we can calculate its height if we know the following: the number of visualizations, their height, and the number of columns in the grid. In listing 14.3, we start by declaring an array of the years for which we want to visualize Van Gogh's work. We do that with D3's range method. Then we set the grid's number of columns based on the width of the screen. If the screen is larger than 900 px, we want three columns; if it's smaller than 600 px, we want one column; and if it's in between, we want two columns. We use ballpark numbers for now, and we'll adjust them later if needed.

Once we know the number of columns, we can calculate the number of rows by dividing the number of small multiple visualizations by the number of columns and rounding up the result. The width of each of the small multiples is found by dividing the width of the SVG element by the number of columns. We also arbitrarily set their height to their width plus 40 px. Finally, we find the total height of the SVG element by multiplying the number of rows by the height of each small multiple.

Because the `svgWidth` and `svgHeight` variables are null when the component mounts, the browser will throw an error. This is why we use a conditional statement to add the SVG element to the markup only after those two variables are defined. Note how the switch statement and the dimension variables are made reactive with the `$` symbol. They will be updated every time the screen width changes.

We now have a responsive SVG element! This implementation required much more work than our previous strategy, but it will be helpful in the next section when we play with the responsive SVG grid.

Listing 14.3   Dynamically updating the height (`Grid.svelte`)

```
<script>
  import { range } from "d3-array";

  ...

  const years = range(1881, 1891);          ◁──┐  Create an array of the years each
  let numColumns;                                   small multiple will visualize.
  $: switch (true) {
    case windowWidth > 900:
      numColumns = 3;
      break;
    case windowWidth <= 900 && windowWidth > 600:         Set the number of SVG
      numColumns = 2;                                      grid columns based on
      break;                                               the screen width.
    default:
      numColumns = 1;
  }
  $: numRows = Math.ceil(years.length / numColumns);    ◁──  Calculate the number of grid rows by dividing the number of visualizations by the number of columns.
  $: smWidth = svgWidth / numColumns;         Calculate each grid element's width
  $: smHeight = smWidth + 40;                 and height (sm => small multiple).
  $: svgHeight = numRows * smHeight;       ◁──┐
</script>                                        Calculate the height of the SVG container
                                                 by multiplying the number of rows by
<svelte:window bind:innerWidth={windowWidth} />  the height of each grid element.

{#if svgWidth && svgHeight}
    <svg width={svgWidth} height={svgHeight} />         Set the height attribute of the SVG
{/if}                                                    element. Add the SVG element to
                                                         the markup only if both the
<style>                                                  svgWidth and the svgHeight
  svg {                                                  variables are defined.
    border: 1px solid magenta;
  }
</style>
```

14.4.2   Creating a responsive SVG grid

In the previous listing, we determined the width and height of every grid item using the variables `smWidth` and `smHeight`. Using these values, we'll construct the grid that will hold all visualizations. Because we're working within an SVG container, we'll use group elements to enclose each small multiple.

To begin with, in listing 14.4, we insert an each block within the SVG container that iterates through the previously created years array. It's worth noting that we can access the index (i) for each year as the second argument. We create a group element for each year, and then use the transform attribute to apply a translation. To determine which column each group belongs to, we use the remainder, also known as the modulo (%), of the index divided by the number of columns. The following equations illustrate the remainder for indexes between zero and five in a three-column layout, and we then calculate the horizontal translation by multiplying the remainder by smWidth:

$$0 \% 3 = 0$$

$$1 \% 3 = 1$$

$$2 \% 3 = 2$$

$$3 \% 3 = 0$$

$$4 \% 3 = 1$$

$$5 \% 3 = 2$$

. . .

For the vertical translation, we round the index divided by the number of columns to know which row we are in and multiply the result by the height of a grid element. We then append a rect element inside the group, set its dimensions to the width and height of the grid item, and give it a blue stroke. We add this rectangle to ensure that our grid is working as expected and resizes properly when the screen width changes, but we won't keep it in the final visualization.

Listing 14.4 Adding a responsive grid (Grid.svelte)

```
{#if svgWidth && svgHeight}
  <svg width={svgWidth} height={svgHeight}>          Add a Svelte each block to
    {#each years as year, i}                          loop through the years array.
      <g transform="translate(
        {(i % numColumns) * smWidth},                 Append a group element for each
        {Math.floor(i / numColumns) * smHeight})"     year, and translate it to its
      >                                               position within the grid.
        <rect x={0} y={0} width={smWidth}             Append a rect to the group, and
          height={smHeight} />                        set its dimensions with smWidth
      </g>                                            and smHeight. This element will
    {/each}                                           allow us to confirm that our grid is
  </svg>                                              working as expected. We'll remove
{/if}                                                 it once the visualization is ready.

<style>
  svg {
    border: 1px solid magenta;
  }
  rect {
```

```
    fill: none;
    stroke: cyan;
  }
</style>
```

Once the grid is implemented, resize your screen to ensure that the number of columns and the position of the grid items adjust as expected. The grid should have three columns when the screen is larger than 900 px, two columns between 600 px and 900 px, and one column if smaller than 600 px, as illustrated in figure 14.9.

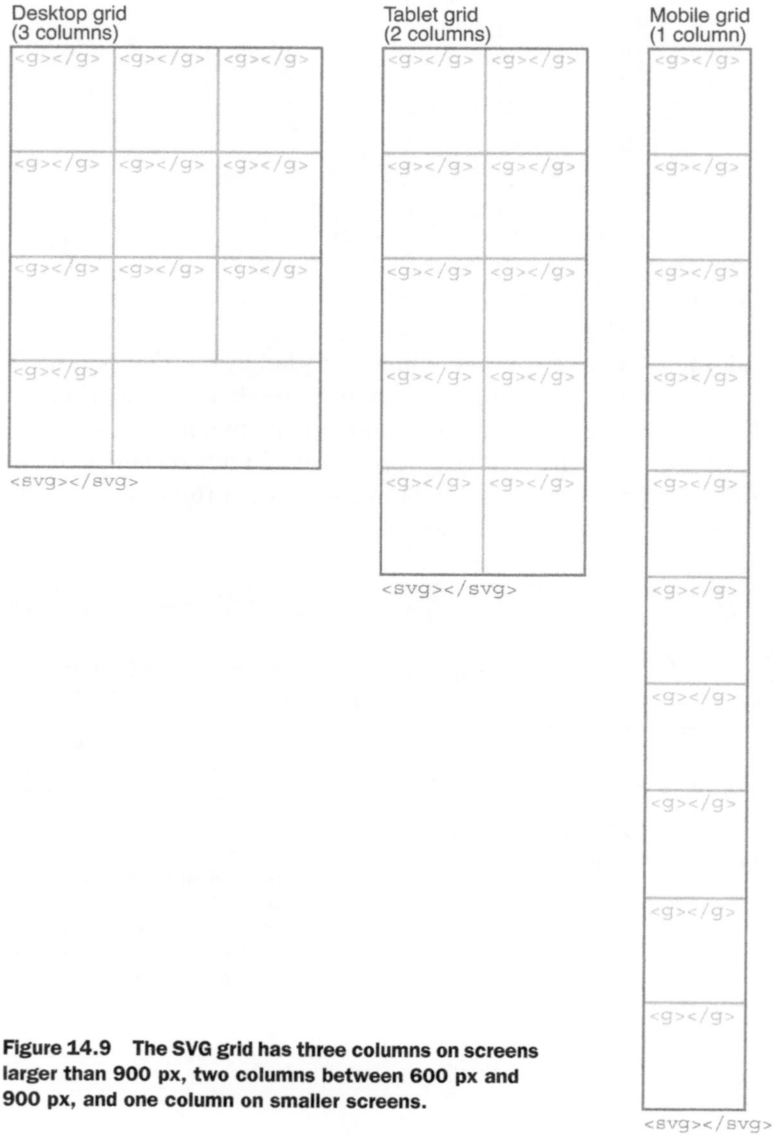

Figure 14.9   The SVG grid has three columns on screens larger than 900 px, two columns between 600 px and 900 px, and one column on smaller screens.

14.5 Creating radial visualizations

With the skeleton of our project ready, we can start using D3 to create our visualizations of Van Gogh's work! In this section, we'll build our small multiples visualizations, starting with the axes and labels, continuing with the paintings, and finishing with the drawings and letters.

14.5.1 Adding radial axes

The backbone of our small multiples visualizations can be simplified to a background circle and a year label. But before implementing those elements, we need to define their exact positions. Figure 14.10 shows a sketch of the different parameters that need to be taken into account before positioning the circle and the year label. We already calculated the width (smWidth) and height (smHeight) of each small multiple. To ensure that there will be enough space between the visualizations and to leave space for the month labels, we can define the padding that we want to apply around each circle, let's say 60 px. From this value and the width of the grid elements, we can calculate the radius of the background circles.

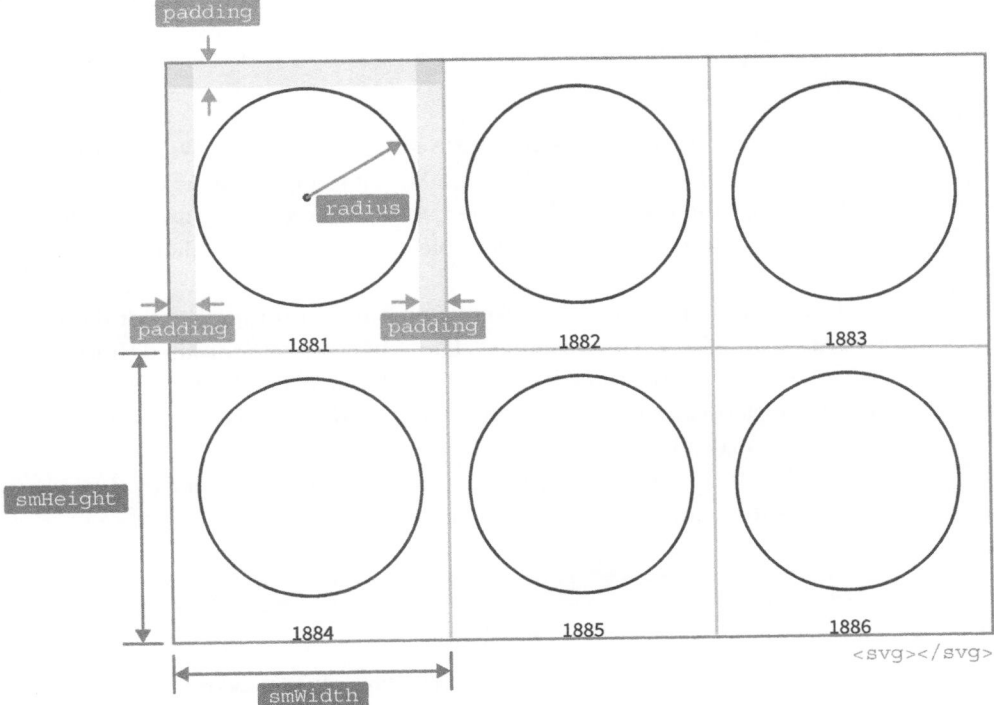

Figure 14.10 We already calculated the width and the height of the grid elements. If we set a fixed padding value around the background circles, we can calculate their radius.

We'll start building our visualization in a child component of `Grid.svelte` named `GridItem.svelte`. In listing 14.5, we start by importing this component into `Grid.svelte`. Then we append the `GridItem` inside the `each` block, which will result in a `GridItem` for each year from the `years` array. We pass `smWidth`, `smHeight`, and the current `year` as props to this child component.

Listing 14.5 Importing the `GridItem` component (`Grid.svelte`)

```
<script>
  import GridItem from "./GridItem.svelte";        ←┐ Import the GridItem
                                                      component.
  ...
</script>

{#if svgWidth && svgHeight}                                    Append a GridItem
  <svg width={svgWidth} height={svgHeight}>              component for each year
    {#each years as year, i}                                inside the related SVG
      <g transform="translate(                           group. Pass smWidth,
          {(i % numColumns) * smWidth},                     smHeight, and the
          {Math.floor(i / numColumns) * smHeight})"       current year as props.
      >
        <rect x={0} y={0} width={smWidth} height={smHeight} />
        <GridItem {smWidth} {smHeight} {year} />        ←
      </g>
    {/each}
  </svg>
{/if}
```

In listing 14.6, we start working inside `GridItem.svelte`. We import props `smWidth`, `smHeight`, and `year` in the `script` tags. We then set a `padding` constant to a value of `60` and calculate the radius of the circle based on the `padding` and `smWidth`. Because the radius is declared as a reactive variable (`$`), it will be recalculated anytime `smWidth` changes.

In the markup, we use two group elements to set the origin of the relative coordinate system of the visualizations. The first one is translated horizontally to half `smWidth`. It serves as a reference point for the `year` label, which then only needs to be translated vertically to the bottom of the grid item. The second group element is translated vertically to the center of the background circle. This strategy will come in especially handy when we start appending additional shapes to the visualizations to represent the paintings, drawings, and letters.

Listing 14.6 Adding the circle and the year (`GridItem.svelte`)

```
<script>
  export let smWidth;
  export let smHeight;              Import smWidth, smHeight, and the
  export let year;                  related year from the parent component.

  const padding = 60;               Set the padding, and
  $: radius = (smWidth - 2 * padding) / 2;    calculate the circle's radius.
```

```
</script>

<g transform="translate({smWidth / 2}, 0)">
  <g transform="translate(0, {padding + radius})">
    <circle cx={0} cy={0} r={radius} />
  </g>
  <text x={0} y={smHeight - 5} text-anchor="middle">{year}</text>
</g>

<style lang="scss">
  circle {
    fill: none;
    stroke: $text;
  }
</style>
```

Translate SVG groups to serve as reference points for the elements that they will contain.

The next step is adding an axis and label for each month, as shown in figure 14.11. This figure shows that the origin of the circle's coordinate system is at its center, thanks to the SVG groups translated previously. Each month's axis will be a line starting at the origin and reaching the circle's circumference with the angle being different for each month.

To calculate the position of the axes' endpoints, we'll need to do a little bit of trigonometry. Let's take February's axis as an example. On the right side of figure 14.11, you see that we can form a right-angled triangle (a triangle in which one corner has a 90° angle) by joining the axis with its horizontal (x) and vertical (y) side lengths. Let's also call theta (θ) the angle between twelve o'clock (at 0 degrees) and February's axis.

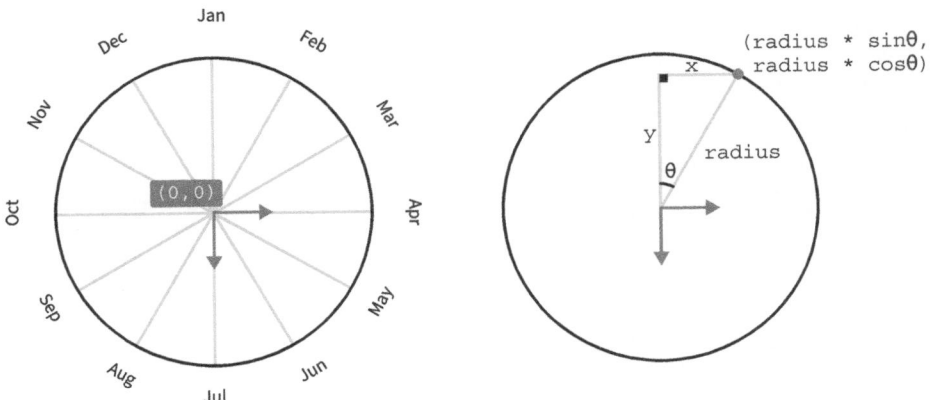

Figure 14.11   We want to draw an axis for each month inside the circle. The starting point of those axes is the origin of the visualization's coordinate system, while the endpoints' positions can be determined with basic trigonometry.

The trigonometric functions tell us that the sine of θ is equal to x divided by the length of February's axis or the background circle's radius. So we can calculate the endpoint's horizontal position by multiplying the radius by sinθ. Similarly, the cosine

516 Chapter 14 Creating a custom visualization

of θ equals y divided by the length of February's axis. So we can calculate the end-point's vertical position by multiplying the radius by $\cos\theta$ and by -1 because we're going in the negative direction of the vertical axis:

$$\sin\theta = x \div radius \Rightarrow x = radius \times \sin\theta$$

$$\cos\theta = y \div radius \Rightarrow y = radius \times \cos\theta$$

To draw the month axis, we keep working in `GridItem.svelte`. In listing 14.7, we first declare a point scale that takes an array of the months as an input (this array is available in the `/utils/months.jsv` file) and returns the corresponding angle. We want the month of January to be displayed at twelve o'clock, corresponding to an angle of 0. We know that a full circle covers 360° or 2π radians. Because there are 12 months in a year, we set the last angle in our scale to be $2\pi - 2\pi/12$ radians, or a full circle minus one-twelfth of a circle.

In the markup, we use an `each` block to append one line element for each month. The starting point of each line is $(0, 0)$, while its endpoints are calculated with the trigonometric functions discussed a moment ago.

> ### Listing 14.7 Adding the month axes (`GridItem.svelte`)

```
<script>
  import { scalePoint } from "d3-scale";
  import { months } from "../utils/months";

  export let smWidth;
  export let smHeight;
  export let year;

  const padding = 60;
  $: radius = (smWidth - 2 * padding) / 2;

  const monthScale = scalePoint()
    .domain(months)
    .range([0, 2 * Math.PI - (2 * Math.PI) / 12]);
</script>
```

Declare a point scale that takes an array of the months as an input and returns the corresponding angle.

```
<g transform="translate({smWidth / 2}, 0)">
  <g transform="translate(0, {padding + radius})">
    <circle cx={0} cy={0} r={radius} />
    {#each months as month}
      <line
        x1="0"
        y1="0"
        x2={radius * Math.sin(monthScale(month))}
        y2={-1 * radius * Math.cos(monthScale(month))}
        stroke-linecap="round"
      />
    {/each}
  </g>
```

Append a line element for each month. The starting point of each line is (0, 0), while the endpoint is calculated with trigonometric functions.

```
<text x={0} y={smHeight - 5} text-anchor="middle">{year}</text>
</g>

<style lang="scss">
  circle {
    fill: none;
    stroke: $text;
  }
  line {
    stroke: $text;
    stroke-opacity: 0.2;
  }
</style>
```

As a last step, we'll add a label to each month's axis at 30 px outside of the circle. In listing 14.8, we append a text element for each month, and with the JavaScript slice() method, we set the text to be the month's first three letters. To position the text label properly, we perform a translation followed by a rotation. We find the translation with trigonometric functions, similarly to how we calculated the axes' endpoint. For the labels displayed on the top half of the circle (between nine o'clock and three o'clock), the rotation is the same as their axis. For the labels on the bottom half (between three o'clock and nine o'clock), we give them an additional 180° of rotation so that they are easier to read.

While we use radians inside the JavaScript Math.sin() and Math.cos() functions, the rotation's transform attribute requires degrees. To facilitate the translation from radians to degrees, we created a helper function named radiansToDegrees() that you can find in /utils/helper.js. It takes an angle in radians as an input and returns the same angle in radians.

> ### Listing 14.8 Adding the month labels (GridItem.svelte)

```
<script>
  import { scalePoint } from "d3-scale";
  import { months } from "../utils/months";
  import { radiansToDegrees } from "../utils/helpers";

  export let smWidth;
  export let smHeight;
  export let year;

  const padding = 60;
  $: radius = (smWidth - 2 * padding) / 2;

  const monthScale = scalePoint()
    .domain(months)
    .range([0, 2 * Math.PI - (2 * Math.PI) / 12]);
</script>

<g transform="translate({smWidth / 2}, 0)">
  <g transform="translate(0, {padding + radius})">
```

```
  <circle cx={0} cy={0} r={radius} />
  {#each months as month}
    <line
      x1="0"
      y1="0"
      x2={radius * Math.sin(monthScale(month))}
      y2={-1 * radius * Math.cos(monthScale(month))}
      stroke-linecap="round"
    />
    <text
      class="month-label"
      transform="translate(
        {(radius + 30) * Math.sin(monthScale(month))},
        {-1*(radius+30) * Math.cos(monthScale(month))}
      )
      rotate({
        monthScale(month) <= Math.PI / 2 ||
        monthScale(month) >= (3 * Math.PI) / 2
         ? radiansToDegrees(monthScale(month))
         : radiansToDegrees(monthScale(month)) - 180
      })"
      text-anchor="middle"
      dominant-baseline="middle">
        {month.slice(0, 3)}
      </text>
    >
  {/each}
</g>
<text x={0} y={smHeight - 5} text-anchor="middle">{year}</text>
</g>

<style lang="scss">
  circle {
    fill: none;
    stroke: $text;
  }
  line {
    stroke: $text;
    stroke-opacity: 0.2;
  }
  .month-label {
    font-size: 1.4rem;
  }
</style>
```

Append a text element for each month.

Translate the label 30 px outside the circle's radius, using the same trigonometric functions as for the axes' endpoints.

Rotate the top-half labels to the same angle as their corresponding axis. Do the same with the bottom-half labels, but add 180° for readability.

Conserve only the first three letters of the month.

14.5.2 *Applying the force layout on a circle's circumference*

With our axis ready, we can start drawing the visualizations. We'll begin by representing every one of Van Gogh's paintings with a circle. Those circles will be grouped by year and then by month of creation, around the endpoints of the corresponding months' axes. As mentioned in section 14.3, the color of the circles will be based on the subject of the painting and the border of the circles on the medium. Finally, we'll set the area of the circles to be proportional to the dimensions of the related artwork.

Figure 14.12 shows the effect we're after. To generate the clusters of circles while avoiding overlap, we'll use D3's force layout.

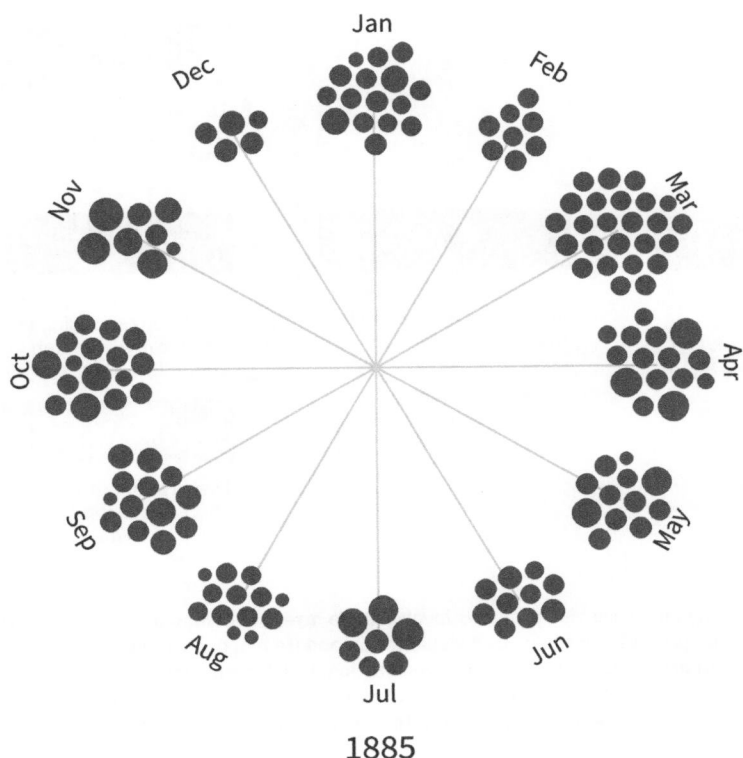

Figure 14.12 Each painting created by Van Gogh will be represented by a circle. Those circles will be positioned on the small multiple visualization corresponding to their year of creation, clustered at the tip of the month axes. We'll use D3's force layout to create those clusters.

Before jumping further into the code, let's take a moment to reflect on the architecture of our components and strategize on the best way forward. Our small multiple visualization is made of three layers of components, as shown in figure 14.13. The first one is held by the Grid.svelte component, which is responsible for adding the SVG container to the markup and for breaking down the years into a grid-like layout. This component is "aware" of all the years for which we'll produce a visualization.

The second layer is handled by GridItem.svelte. This component is only aware of a single year of data and displays its corresponding year label and month axes. Finally, there are components Paintings.svelte, Drawings.svelte, and Letters.svelte. We haven't dealt with these files yet, but they are contained in the chart_components/ folder. As their name suggests, these components are responsible for visualizing the paintings, drawings, and letters produced during a year. Because they will be called from `GridItem.svelte`, they also will be aware of one single year of data.

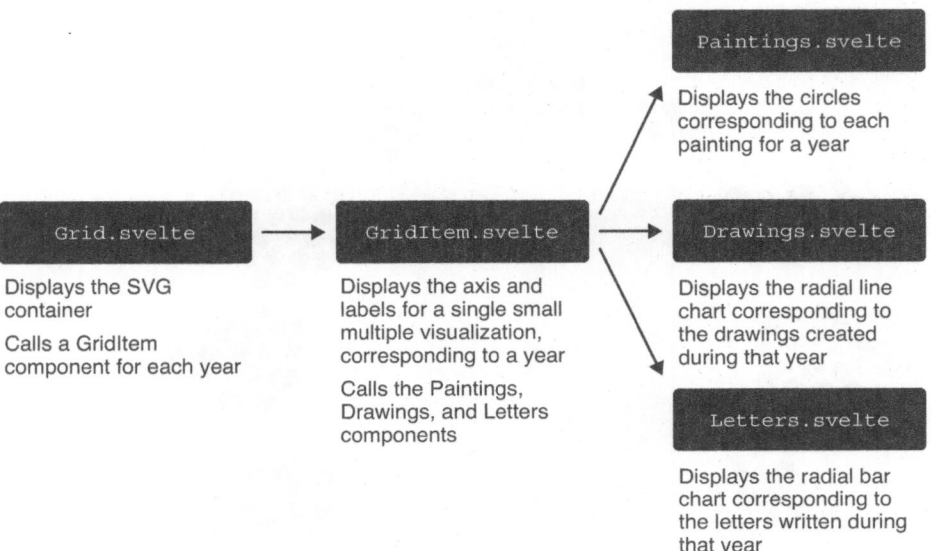

Figure 14.13 Our small multiple visualizations involve three layers of components. The first one (`Grid.svelte`) is responsible for the overall visualization and its responsive grid. The second (`GridItem.svelte`) holds each small multiple visualization, which corresponds to a year, and displays the month axes. The last one (`Paintings.svelte`, `Drawings.svelte`, and `Letters.svelte`) is responsible for the visualization elements related to the paintings, drawings, and letters.

With this layered architecture in mind, we see that the best place for loading the entire dataset of paintings is `Grid.svelte` because this component oversees the totality of the visualization and is loaded only once in the application. This component will then pass the paintings corresponding to each year as props to `GridItem.svelte`, which will then pass them to `Paintings.svelte`.

Based on this logic, in listing 14.9, we go back to `Grid.svelte` and import the paintings dataset. Because we'll later want to size the circles representing the paintings based on the paintings' dimensions, we calculate the area of those works and use this information to find the largest painting dimensions in the dataset. Note that there are a few paintings in the dataset for which the dimensions aren't available. When this is the case, we'll set the radius of the corresponding circle to 3 px.

To scale the area of a painting (in cm^2) into the area of a circle on the screen (in px^2), we can use a linear scale. We call this scale `paintingAreaScale` and find the maximum area covered by the range with the formula of the area of a circle:

$$a = \pi r^2$$

Finally, we pass to `GridItem` the data and functions that we'll need to display the paintings. Note how we filter the paintings dataset to pass only the paintings corresponding to the current year.

Listing 14.9 Making a scale for the paintings' area (`Grid.svelte`)

```
<script>
  import { range, max } from "d3-array";
  import { scaleLinear } from "d3-scale";
  import paintings from "../data/paintings.json";

  ...

  paintings.forEach((painting) => {
    if (painting.width_cm && painting.height_cm) {      Calculate the area of each
      painting["area_cm2"] = painting.width_cm *        painting and the maximum
        painting.height_cm;                             painting area in the dataset.
    }
  });
  const maxPaintingArea = max(paintings, (d) =>
    d.area_cm2);

  const maxPaintingRadius = 8;                          Declare a linear scale responsible
  const paintingDefaultRadius = 3;                      for receiving the area of a painting
  const paintingAreaScale = scaleLinear()               as an input and providing the
    .domain([0, maxPaintingArea])                       corresponding area of the SVG
    .range([0,Math.PI*Math.pow(maxPaintingRadius,2)]);  circle to display on the screen.
</script>

<svelte:window bind:innerWidth={windowWidth} />

{#if svgWidth && svgHeight}
  <svg width={svgWidth} height={svgHeight}>
    {#each years as year, i}
      <g
        transform="translate(
            {(i % numColumns) * smWidth},
            {Math.floor(i / numColumns) * smHeight})"
      >
        <rect x={0} y={0} width={smWidth} height={smHeight} />
        <GridItem
          {smWidth}
          {smHeight}
          {year}
          {paintingAreaScale}                           Pass the data and functions
          {paintingDefaultRadius}                       that we'll need to display
          paintings={paintings.filter((painting) =>     the paintings to GridItem.
            painting.year === year)}                    Filter the paintings dataset
        />                                               to pass only the paintings
      </g>                                               corresponding to the
    {/each}                                              current year.
  </svg>
{/if}
```

In `GridItem.svelte`, all we have to do is declare the props received from `Grid.svelte`, import the `Paintings` component, add the `Paintings` component to the markup, and pass the same props, as shown in the next listing.

Listing 14.10   Calling the `Paintings` component (`GridItem.svelte`)

```
<script>
  import Paintings from "../chart_components/      | Import the Paintings
    Paintings.svelte";                             | component.

  export let paintingAreaScale;
  export let paintingDefaultRadius;          | Declare the new props
  export let paintings;                      | received from Grid.svelte.

  ...
</script>

<g transform="translate({smWidth / 2}, 0)">
  <g transform="translate(0, {padding + radius})">
    <circle ... />
    {#each months as month}
      <line ... />
      <text ... >{month.slice(0, 3)}</text>
    {/each}
    <Paintings
      {paintingAreaScale}
      {paintingDefaultRadius}          | Call the Paintings
      {paintings}                      | component, and pass
      {monthScale}                     | the required props.
      {radius}
    />
  </g>
  <text ... >{year}</text>
</g>
```

Finally, the real action happens in `Paintings.svelte`. For now, we loop through the paintings received as props and add a circle to the markup for each one of them. The initial position of those circles is the tip of their related month axis, which can be found with the trigonometric functions we used earlier. We also have to take into account the paintings for which we don't know during which month they were created. We'll position them in the center of the visualization.

To calculate the circles' radius in listing 14.11, we call `paintingAreaScale`. Because this scale returns an area, we need to calculate the corresponding radius with the following formula:

$$r = \sqrt{(a \div \pi)}$$

Listing 14.11   Appending the paintings' circles (`Paintings.svelte`)

```
<script>
  export let paintingAreaScale;          | Declare the props received
  export let paintingDefaultRadius;      | from GridItem.svelte.
```

```
    export let paintings;
    export let monthScale;
    export let radius;
</script>
```

Declare the props received
from GridItem.svelte.

```
{#each paintings as painting}
  <circle
    cx={painting.month !== ""
      ? radius * Math.sin(monthScale(painting.month))
      : 0}
    cy={painting.month !== ""
      ? -1 * radius * Math.cos(monthScale(
        painting.month))
      : 0}
    r={painting.area_cm2
      ? Math.sqrt(paintingAreaScale(painting.area_cm2)
          / Math.PI)
      : paintingDefaultRadius}
  />
{/each}
```

Loop through the paintings, and
append a circle for each one.

Position the circles to the tip
of their corresponding month
axis using the trigonometric
functions discussed earlier. If a
painting has no corresponding
month, position it in the
center of the visualization.

Call paintingAreaScale to get
the circle's area corresponding
to the painting's dimensions,
and calculate the radius of the
circle. If the painting's
dimensions aren't available,
set the radius of the circle to
the default value.

At this stage, the paintings' circles overlap at the tip of their month axis, as shown in figure 14.14. We'll fix that in a minute with D3's force layout.

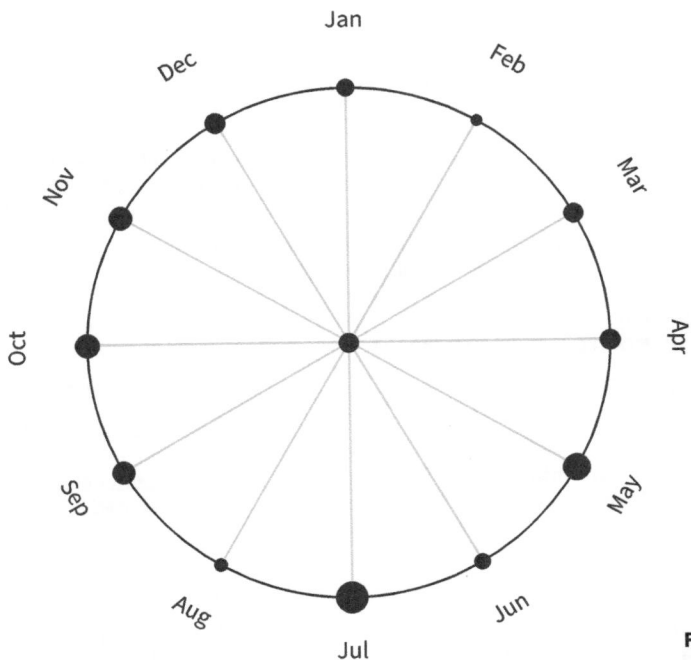

1887

Figure 14.14 At this stage, the paintings' circles overlap at the tip of their month axis, which we'll fix with D3's force layout.

To create clusters of nodes around the tip of each month axis, we'll use D3's force layout. This layout is somewhat complex, so if you need a more in-depth introduction, we recommend reading chapter 12. In listing 14.12, we initialize a new force simulation with the `forceSimulation()` method, to which we pass our `paintings` array. We also declare an empty `nodes` array which we update with the simulation's nodes after each tick. We then loop through this `nodes` array instead of the `paintings` array to append the circles to the markup.

We calculate the forces applied to the nodes inside a reactive block (`$`) to trigger a recalculation when the related variables change. Inside this block, the positioning forces (`forceX` and `forceY`) push the nodes toward the tip of their month axes, while the collision force (`forceCollide`) ensures there's no overlap between the nodes.

We also reduce the `alpha` (the "temperature" of the simulation) and increase the `alpha decay` rate to help the simulation converge faster. This adjustment requires a trial-and-error approach to find the proper settings. Finally, we use the x and y properties added to the nodes by the simulation to set the `cx` and `cy` attributes of the corresponding circles.

Listing 14.12   Getting the circles' positions (`Paintings.svelte`)

```
<script>
  import { forceSimulation, forceX, forceY, forceCollide } from "d3-force";

  ...

  let simulation = forceSimulation(paintings);
  let nodes = [];
  simulation.on("tick", () => {
    nodes = simulation.nodes();
  });

  $: {
    simulation
      .force("x",
        forceX((d) => d.month !== ""
          ? radius * Math.sin(monthScale(d.month))
          : 0
        ).strength(0.5)
      )
      .force("y",
        forceY((d) => d.month !== ""
          ? -1 * radius * Math.cos(monthScale(d.month))
          : 0
        ).strength(0.5)
      )
      .force("collide",
        forceCollide()
          .radius((d) => d.width_cm === null
            && d.height_cm === null
              ? paintingDefaultRadius + 1
```

Initialize a new force simulation and an empty array of nodes.

After each simulation tick, update the nodes array with the latest calculated positions.

Use a reactive block to trigger the application of the forces anytime a related variable changes.

Apply positioning forces toward the tip of the month axes. When the month isn't defined, the center of the visualization is used instead.

Apply a collision force to avoid overlap between the nodes.

```
          : Math.sqrt(paintingAreaScale(d.area_cm2)
            / Math.PI) + 1
      ).strength(1)
    )
    .alpha(0.5)
    .alphaDecay(0.1);
}
</script>
```

Apply a collision force to avoid overlap between the nodes.

Reduce the alpha and increase the alpha decay rate to help the simulation converge faster.

```
{#each nodes as node}
  <circle
    cx={node.x}
    cy={node.y}
    r={node.area_cm2
       ? Math.sqrt(paintingAreaScale(node.area_cm2) / Math.PI)
       : paintingDefaultRadius}
  />
{/each}
```

Use the x and y properties applied by the simulation to each node to set their cx and cy attributes.

You should now see node clusters appearing at the month axes' tip. To complete the painting visualization, we'll set the color of the circles based on the subject of their corresponding painting. The `utils/subjects.js` file contains an array of the available painting subjects and their colors. In the next listing, we declare an ordinal scale that takes a subject as an input and returns the corresponding circles. All we have to do then is to set the `fill` attribute of the circles by calling this scale.

Listing 14.13 Setting the circles' color (`Paintings.svelte`)

```
<script>
  import { scaleOrdinal } from "d3-scale";
  import { subjects } from "../utils/subjects";

  ...

  const colorScale = scaleOrdinal()
    .domain(subjects.map((d) => d.subject))
    .range(subjects.map((d) => d.color));
</script>
```

Declare an ordinal scale that takes a subject as an input and returns the corresponding color.

```
{#each nodes as node}
  <circle
    cx={node.x}
    cy={node.y}
    r={node.area_cm2
       ? Math.sqrt(paintingAreaScale(node.area_cm2) / Math.PI)
       : paintingDefaultRadius}
    fill={colorScale(node.subject)}
  />
{/each}
```

Set the fill attribute of the circles by calling the color scale.

We're done visualizing the paintings! At this point, your visualization will look similar to the one in figure 14.15.

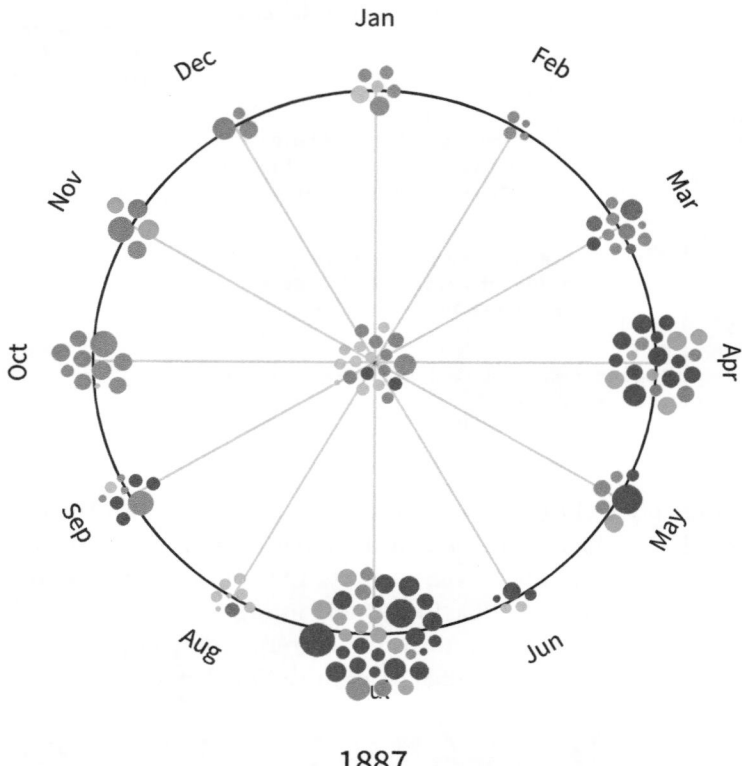

Figure 14.15   Visualization of the paintings created by Van Gogh over the course of 1887

14.5.3 Drawing a radial area chart

Our next step is to draw an area chart that visualizes the number of drawings per-formed by Van Gogh over the course of each year. In chapter 4, we learned how to use D3's shape generator to calculate the d attribute of path elements for line charts and area charts. Here we'll use a similar strategy with shape generator lineRadial(), available in the d3-shape module.

As in the previous section, we want to take into account the three layers of Svelte components used to render the visualizations. We'll load the entire drawings dataset in Grid.svelte and calculate the maximum number of drawings for a month. We'll also reorganize the dataset to split the information on a yearly basis, as in listing 14.14. We'll pass this information to GridItem.svelte, initialize a scale responsible for calculating the radial position along the month axes corresponding to a number of drawings (see listing 14.15), and pass all of this information to Drawings.svelte, which will draw the area chart.

Listing 14.14   Importing drawings and reorganize data (`Grid.svelte`)

```
<script>
  import drawings from "../data/drawings.json";
  import { months } from "../utils/months";

  ...

  const yearlyDrawings = [];
  years.forEach((year) => {
    const relatedDrawings = { year: year, months: [] };
    months.forEach((month) => {
      relatedDrawings.months.push({
        month: month,
        drawings: drawings.filter(drawing =>
          drawing.year === year.toString() &&
          drawing.month === month),
      });
    });
    yearlyDrawings.push(relatedDrawings);
  });

  const maxDrawings = max(yearlyDrawings, d =>
    max(d.months, (i) => i.drawings.length)
  );
</script>
```

Reorganize the
drawings dataset
structure to
group them per
year and month.

Find the maximum number
of drawings for a month.

```
<svelte:window bind:innerWidth={windowWidth} />

{#if svgWidth && svgHeight}
  <svg width={svgWidth} height={svgHeight}>
    {#each years as year, i}
      <g
        transform="translate(
          {(i % numColumns) * smWidth},
          {Math.floor(i / numColumns) * smHeight})"
      >
        <rect x={0} y={0} width={smWidth} height={smHeight} />
        <GridItem
          {smWidth}
          {smHeight}
          {year}
          {paintingAreaScale}
          {paintingDefaultRadius}
          paintings={paintings.filter((painting) =>
            painting.year === year)}
          {maxDrawings}
          drawings={yearlyDrawings.find((d) =>
            d.year === year).months}
        />
      </g>
    {/each}
  </svg>
{/if}
```

Pass maxDrawings and the drawings
of the current year to GridItem.

In the next listing, we then initialize a scale responsible for positioning the number of drawings along the month axis.

Listing 14.15   A scale for the drawings (`GridItem.svelte`)

```
<script>
  import { scaleLinear } from "d3-scale";
  import Drawings from "../chart_components/Drawings.svelte";

  export let maxDrawings;
  export let drawings;

  ...

  $: radialScale = scaleLinear()
    .domain([0, maxDrawings])
    .range([0, 2 * radius]);
</script>
```

> Initialize a linear scale that takes a number of drawings as an input and returns the corresponding position on the month axes.

```
<g transform="translate({smWidth / 2}, 0)">
  <g transform="translate(0, {padding + radius})">
    <circle ... />
    ...
    <Drawings {drawings} {monthScale} {radialScale} />
  </g>
  <text ... >{year}</text>
</g>
```

> Append the Drawings components and pass the required props.

In listing 14.16, we use D3's `lineRadial()` method to initialize a line generator. As explained in chapter 4, we set its accessor functions to calculate the position of each data point. But this time, we're working in polar coordinates rather than Cartesian, hence the necessity to use the `angle()` and `radius()` functions. When we append the `path` element to the markup, we call the line generator to set its `d` attribute. In the styles, we give it a semi-transparent fill property. Figure 14.16 shows the area chart for the year 1885.

Listing 14.16   Drawing the radial area charts (`Drawings.svelte`)

```
<script>
  import { lineRadial, curveCatmullRomClosed } from "d3-shape";

  export let drawings;
  export let monthScale;
  export let radialScale;

  const lineGenerator = lineRadial()
    .angle((d) => monthScale(d.month))
    .radius((d) => radialScale(d.drawings.length))
    .curve(curveCatmullRomClosed);
</script>
```

> Use the lineRadial() method to initialize a line generator. Set the angle and radius accessor functions to calculate the position of each data point in polar coordinates.

```
<path d={lineGenerator(drawings)} />

<style lang="scss">
  path {
```

> Call the line generator to set the d attribute of the path used to draw the areas.

```
        fill: rgba($secondary, 0.25);
        pointer-events: none;
    }
</style>
```

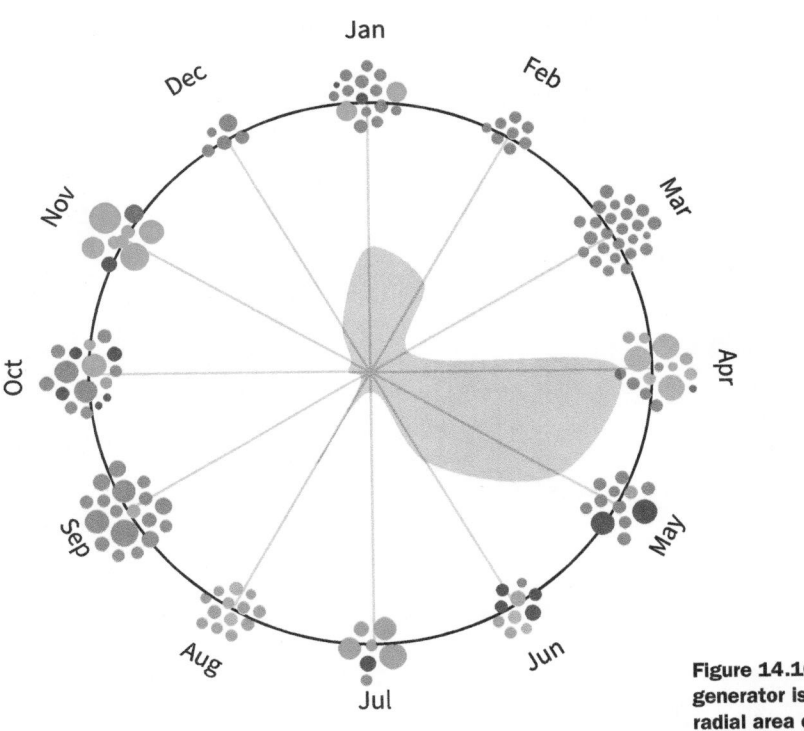

Figure 14.16   D3's radial line generator is used to draw a radial area chart of the number of drawings created by Van Gogh over the course of each year.

14.5.4   *Drawing a radial bar chart*

The last portion of Van Gogh's work we'll visualize is the number of letters he wrote each month. Because you now have all the required knowledge, give it a go on your own!

> **Exercise: Visualize the number of letters written by Van Gogh each month with a radial bar chart**
>
> You can go through this project on your own or follow these instructions:
>
> 1 Load the letters dataset in `Grid.svelte`. This dataset contains the total number of letters written every month.
> 2 Pass the letters corresponding to the current year to `GridItem.svelte` via a prop.

(continued)

3 In `GridItem.svelte`, import the `Letters` component. Add it to the markup, and pass the letters data and the scales as props.

4 In `Letters.svelte`, append a line for each month, and then set the endpoint of the lines based on the number of related letters and using trigonometric functions.

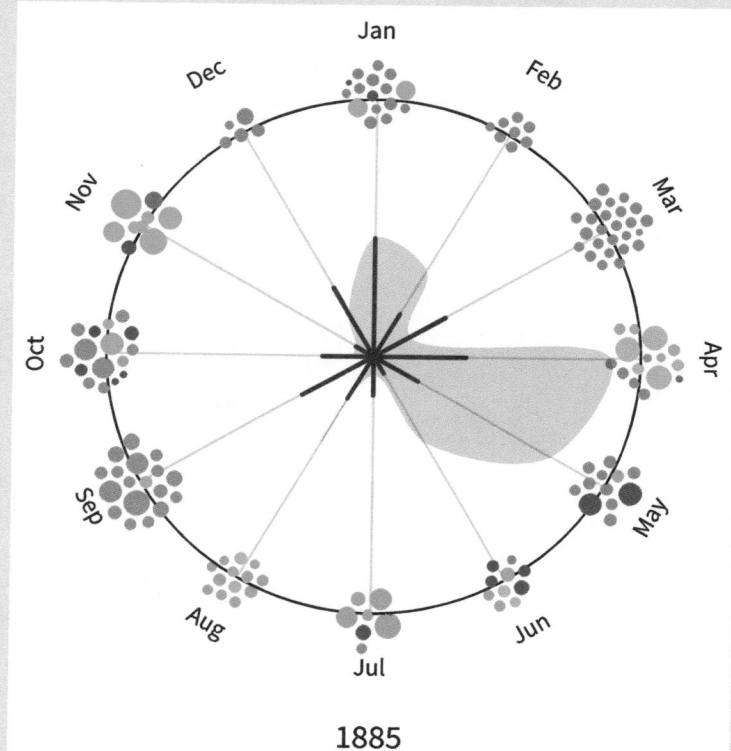

1885

Number of letters written by Van Gogh over the course of the year 1885

If you get stuck or want to compare your solution with ours, you'll find it in section D.14 of appendix D and in the `14.5.4-Radial_bar_chart/end` folder of this chapter's code files. But as usual, we encourage you to try to complete it on your own. Your solution might differ slightly from ours, and that's all right!

To complete the static version of the visualization, we comment out the rectangles and circles used earlier to see our grid layout and add the timeline. Because the timeline doesn't have much to do with D3, we won't explain the code, but you can find it in listing D.14.4 of appendix D and in the `14.5.4` folder of this chapter's code files. You can also take it as a challenge to build it on your own! The completed static layout with the timeline is shown in figure 14.17.

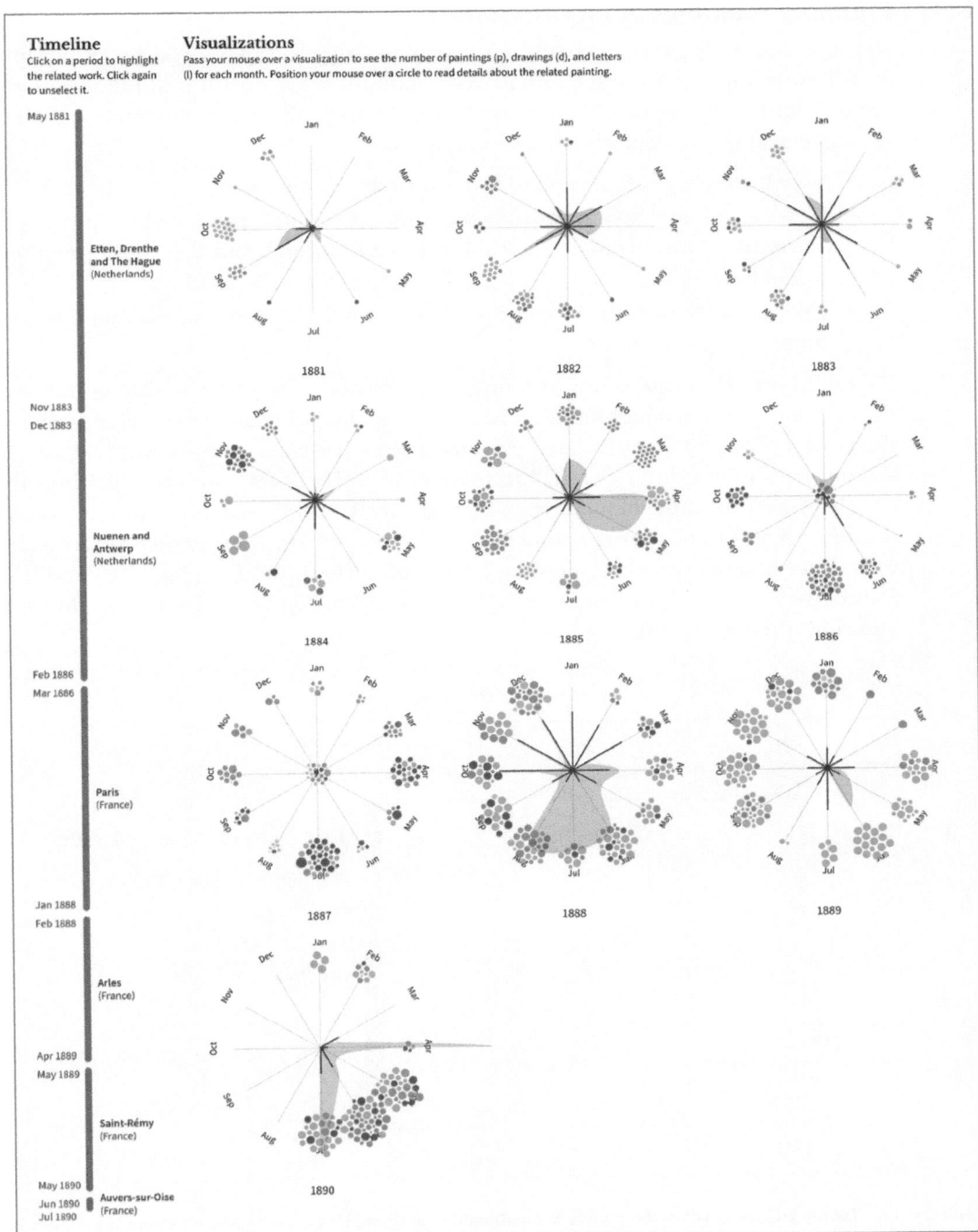

Figure 14.17   The completed static layout includes a timeline of where Van Gogh lived between 1881 and 1890, as well as his artistic production visualized for each year.

14.6   *Planning meaningful interactions*

Now that our static project is ready, it's essential to take a step back and consider how future users might want to explore it. What additional information will they be looking for? Which questions will they ask? Can we answer those with interactions? Here are three examples of questions a user might ask:

- Which painting is represented by each circle? Can I see it?
- How can I know how many drawings and letters were produced in June 1885? Currently, I can estimate the values with the legend, but seeing the numbers would be better.
- How can I connect the cities where Van Gogh lived, shown in the timeline, and his artistic production?

We can answer those questions with simple interactions: the first two with tooltips and the last one with cross-highlighting. Because this chapter is already getting long and such interactions aren't D3 related (in a framework, we tend to avoid using D3's event listener because we don't want D3 to interact with the DOM), we won't get into the details of how to implement them. The main focus of this section is to give you an example of how to plan interactions that are meaningful to your project. You can play with those interactions on the online hosted project (http://mng.bz/z8rg) and find the code in the 14.6 folder of this chapter's code files. Figures 14.18, 14.19, and 14.20 also show them in action.

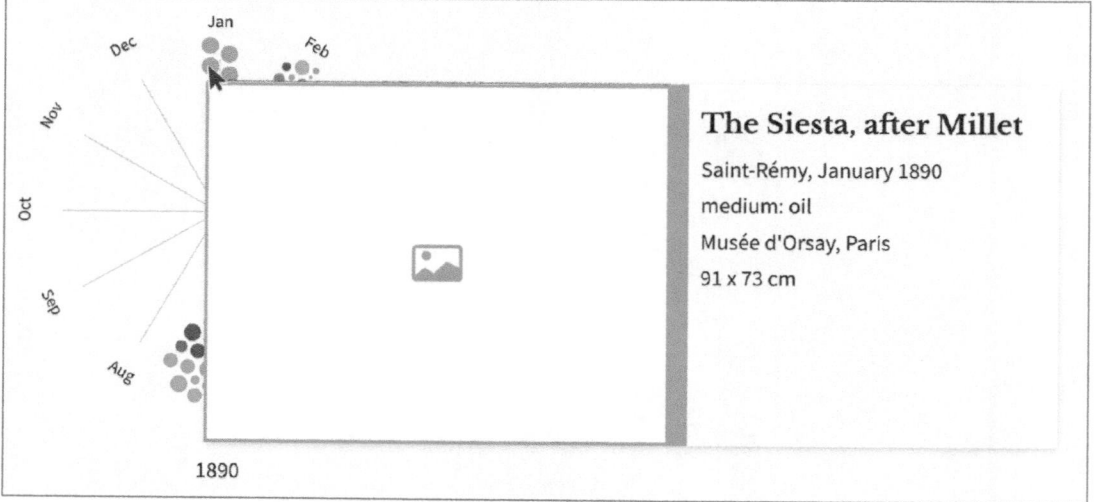

Figure 14.18   Tooltip triggered when the mouse is positioned over a painting's circle and revealing the details of this painting

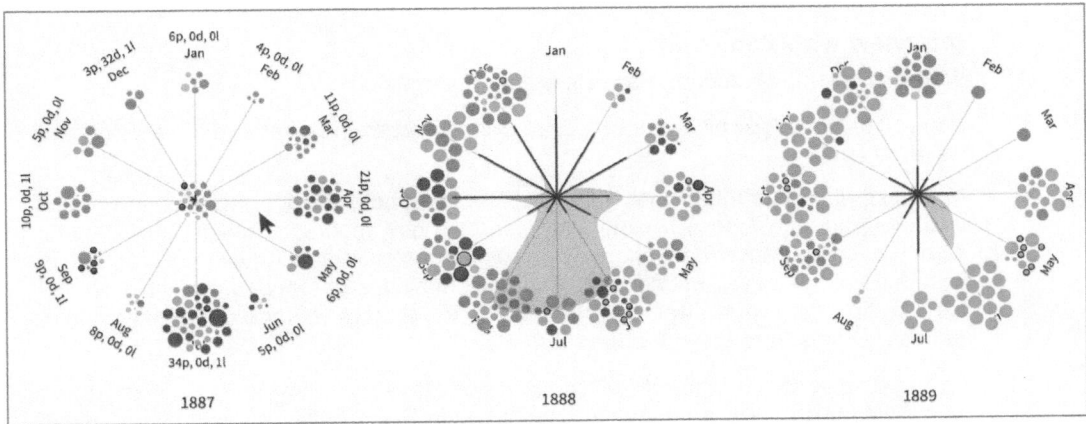

Figure 14.19 Tooltip triggered when the mouse is positioned over a visualization and revealing the number of paintings, drawings, and letters for each month

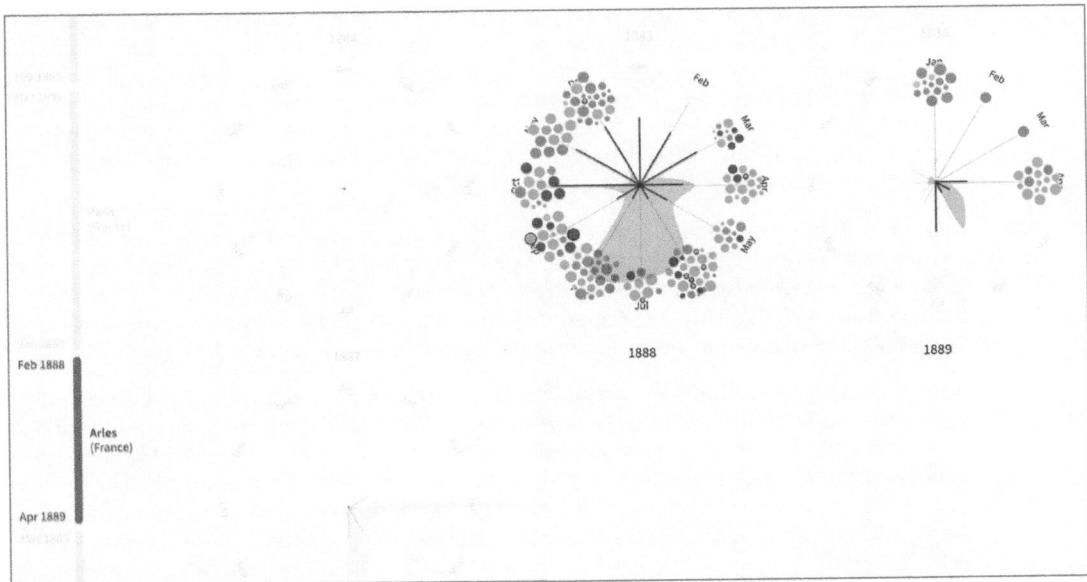

Figure 14.20 When a period is selected on the timeline, only the paintings created during that period are visible on the visualization.

And that wraps up our project! We hope it inspired you to get creative with your visualizations. If you want to dig deeper into combining D3 with Svelte for interactive data visualizations, we highly recommend the *Better Data Visualizations with Svelte* course by Connor Rothschild (http://mng.bz/jXVV).

Interview with Zane Wolf

Wolf is a scientist, teacher, data storyteller and rock climber.

Can you tell us a little bit about your background and how you entered the field of data visualization?

My background is a bit all over the place. I studied both biology and applied physics in undergrad with research experiences in copepod mating behavior, phylogenetic algorithm comparative function, and neutron star astrophysics, while my PhD projects were a Frankensteinian hodgepodge of biomechanics, soft robotics, and fluid dynamics. I wasn't sure what I wanted to research, so I took advantage of as many opportunities as I could to explore different fields.

During grad school, I realized that the parts of research I enjoyed most were when I was diving in to learn a new topic or tool, when I was building things, when I was exploring the data, and when I was spreading the gospel of science to others. So basically, all the bits of research without the actual research topic. On the one hand, pretty cool, points for insightful epiphanies; on the other, not good when facing a career in academia, where you have to pick a specific research topic.

During the summer of 2020, I was part of a virtual online teaching conference for teaching assistants a few days before the semester started. In one of the workshops, we all took a minute to describe the class we were going to teach. Another TA described their class, and I immediately wrote to them in the chat asking for the course information. It was CS 171: Intro to Data Visualization. I thought it sounded not only useful but fun—and it fulfilled my last course requirement for my degree—so I signed up to take it that day.

I found in data visualization everything I loved about science—constantly diving into new topics to understand the data, building visualizations from scratch, learning new tools and skills, and communicating discoveries with others. I felt at home in the field immediately. And I quickly developed massive work-crushes on Nadieh Brehmer and Shirley Wu, whose works were featured throughout the class.

After the class, I started working at the Learning Lab at the Derek Bok Center for Teaching and Learning at Harvard as a Media & Design Fellow. Here I learned more about website design and development. Online interactive data visualizations need to be placed in an online site of some sort, so it seemed like a worthwhile investment. I spent the year working with the engineering department to create visualizations of their faculty data, with a professor to make a website for their course, and with the learning lab hosting my own data visualization workshops, teaching basics from Gestalt principles to specific tools like Mapbox. Since then, I've mostly been working on personal projects where I'm interested in the topic or trying to learn a new skill or tool.

Do you use visualization tools other than D3? What's the place of D3 in your current data visualization workflow?

My current data visualization workflow mostly depends on the final product. If I'm making basic chart types for data exploration or for academic publication, or doing any sort of statistical modeling, I use R or Python. If I need to prototype a chart quickly or create a dashboard with basic chart types, Tableau. If I'm making a more complex or custom visualization or one that needs to be interactive online, I turn to D3. And finally, if I want to make a custom visualization that doesn't need to be interactive and has a non-updating data source, then I might use Affinity Designer.

Choosing the best tool for the job can alleviate a lot of headaches before they start. Even if you're choosing to specialize in a particular tool, such as D3, simply being aware of the alternatives, their pros and cons, can be quite the advantage.

Featured project: "Horror Novels" (www.zanewolf.com/projects/horror-novels)

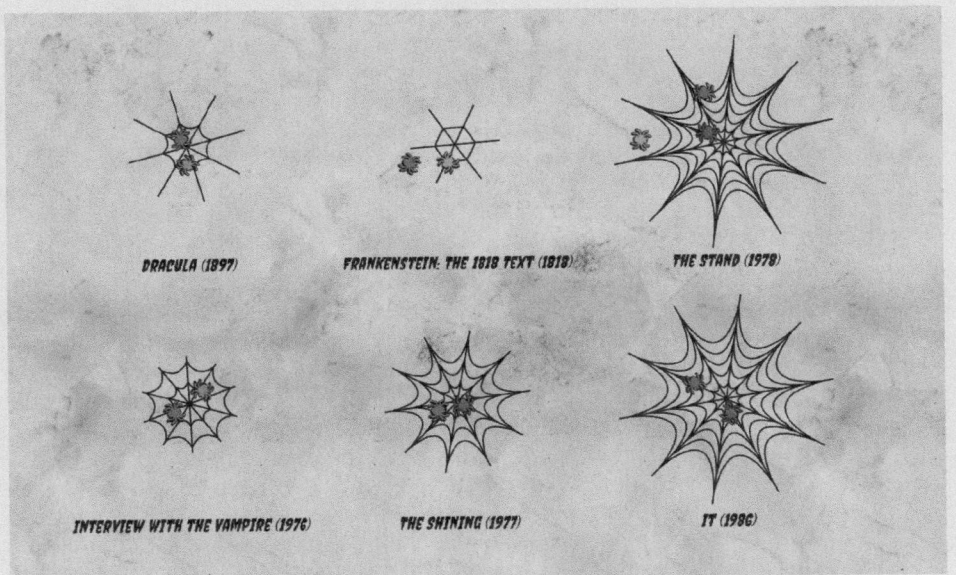

This project by Zane Wolf visualizes the top 20 horror novels, as listed by Goodreads.

Please describe your project, "Horror Novels."

"Horror Novels" is a data visualization tribute to my favorite holiday, Halloween, and one of my main inspirations in learning data visualization and D3, Shirley Wu and her "Film Flowers" visualization (https://shirleywu.studio/filmflowers/). I took the top 20 horror novels, as defined by Goodreads, and visualized each individual book as a spiderweb. The characteristics of the spiderweb, such as the size, the number of spindles and concentric rings, and even the number of spiders on the web, are all determined by the data from each book, like the number of pages, genres, age, and the general rating of the book out of 5.

Can you explain the process of creating this project?

I originally wanted to visualize the *New York Times* bestseller data, but unfortunately the datasets I found were either only looking at the past decade or so or didn't include

(continued)

the information I was hoping to find for each book, like genre, rating, page count, etc. More often than not, the perfect dataset doesn't exist, and you'll have to cobble together a dataset from multiple sources or collect the data yourself. I used Zenodo's Best Books Ever Dataset, which contained data from Goodread's most inclusive and gargantuan list, Best Books Ever—over 50,000 books. Then I found the Goodread's Definitive Horror Book List and used that to whittle down the dataset of 50,000 books to 20.

Now that I have the raw data, what do I make with it? I doodled and googled a variety of spiderweb designs to get an idea of the diversity of design. What aspects of a spiderweb could I map the data to, what could I vary design-wise and still have a spiderweb at the end of the day? I settled on size, of course, as well as the number of spindles, number of concentric rings, and the "sagginess" of the web (that is, are the concentric rings connecting the spindles strung tight, or floppy?). Lastly, I knew I wanted to map genre to color, but spiderwebs aren't known for their vibrancy. I kept a few options in mind, but it wasn't until I was finishing coding the webs that I settled on using colorful spiders. You don't need to have every piece of the puzzle figured out during the sketching phase. In R, I explored the data and figured out how I needed to transform the raw data into data I could use to make webs (such as converting publication date to age).

The next part of the process was coding the webs. I broke the spiderweb creation process into three distinct steps. First, I mapped the cleaned data (for example, age, genre, rating, page number) to plotting variables (for example, radius, number of spindles, angle between spindles, number of concentric rings) using a variety of D3 scales (linear, quantile, threshold). The specific scale used depended on the data's distribution of values. I opted for the ones that created the most visual diversity. If the ratings of the top 20 horror novels are only between 3.8 and 4.3 on the out-of-5 scale, how do I squeeze as much spiderweb diversity from a 0.5 spread as possible? And as I made the spiderwebs, I changed the mapping (which data elements were matched with which spiderweb aspect) to ensure the spiderwebs had the look I wanted. Don't be afraid to go back to the drawing board and revise the game plan!

Next, I needed to create the functions that created the SVG paths that, when fed to D3, would create spiderwebs. I used pseudocoding and basic trigonometry to figure out how to go from variables like radius and angle to actual spiderwebs. And yes, I had to google basic trigonometry. Using center coordinates generated from a function that figured out where each spiderweb needed to be placed on the page, radius, and angle between spindles, I could create the SVG paths for just the spindles, the straight lines of the web. Then, using radius, angle, center coordinates, number of concentric rings, and sagginess, I could calculate where the rings should go (how far from center) and how saggy they should be. And I used one more function to determine how the spiders' positions could be calculated to maximize diversity in placement while limiting overlap. I found a cute little SVG spider icon online instead of creating my own spiders. When making a car, don't be afraid to buy your tires at the tire factory instead of building them yourself.

Because the visualization wasn't interactive and didn't need to be able to accommodate potential new data, I felt the step of plotting the actual webs and spiders was rather simple compared to the previous step. A few path elements and I had the spiderwebs and spiders on the page. Creating legends with D3 can be simultaneously challenging and monotonous since you have to create the data for the legend, figure out where it goes, plot it, and rinse and repeat for every variable. But once the content was on the page, I started adding the design components like an old parchment-looking background and a font resembling those from old B-rated monster movie posters. This step took it from a collection of spiderwebs to something that I'd expect to see on a poster in a library.

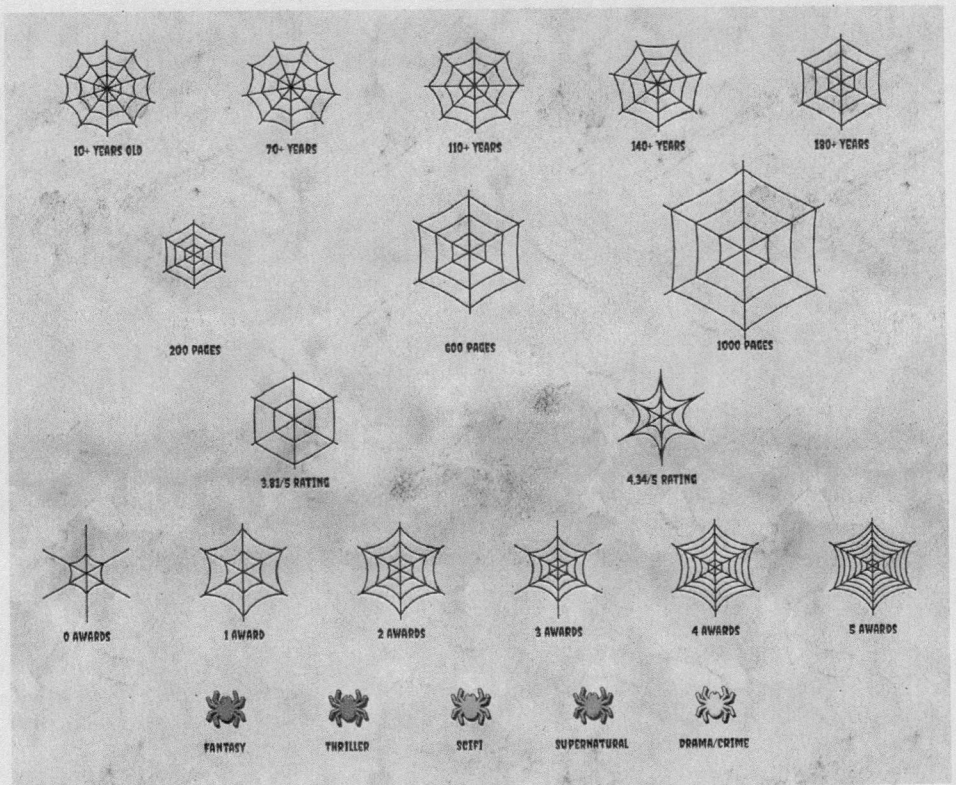

Figure 14.21 The novels' data is visualized with the size, number of spindles, number of concentric rings, and the "sagginess" of the spiderwebs, as well as the color of the associated spiders.

And don't forget to check any colors you add, from the spiders to the background colors, for color accessibility! You might not be able to create a 100% fully accessible color palette (I was limited by the number of colors that were Halloween-themed), but you can be strategic by assigning problematic colors to the variables that are less represented in the dataset.

(continued)

The last part of the process was a small one, but it brings me so much joy. I went back into the code and added as much randomness and easter eggs as I could. For example, I added random rotation to the spiderwebs and spiders so that each time the page is refreshed, the orientation of each web and each spider is different. These little touches make the visualization unique for every person who sees it, despite the visualization not being interactive or updating.

On your website, you explain how pseudocoding was helpful when planning how to draw the spiderweb shapes on the screen. Can you tell us more about this approach and the edge it gives you?

Pseudocoding is a way of describing code in a natural language. Every coding language has a different syntax, and you might not remember the exact way to write an if-statement or for-loop in R or Python or MATLAB, but you can write out the intent of the code: "for every item in the array, do this." By pseudocoding before writing code, you focus on the function of the code itself, what you want it to do, without having to worry about how exactly to write the code yet. This is especially helpful in situations where you don't know all the steps to get from input to desired output. For example, I needed a function that would, with just a few inputs like radius and angle, return the code for a spiderweb. That's not something I immediately know how to code off the top of my head, weirdly enough. After figuring out the math, pseudocoding is where I figured out how to rewrite the math into discrete, codable steps. These steps take me from my inputs, radius and theta, to my desired output, a spiderweb.

Pseudocoding can be as simple as commenting the individual steps in your editor of choice. If it's a straightforward or short function, this is always how I do it. Then, after commenting the steps, I go back in and write the code under the corresponding comment and voilà—beautifully commented code. If I need to figure out math or visualize something and draw it out, I pseudocode with pen and paper, or recently the E Ink version, before jumping into the editor.

The last part of the process, of course, is translating those pseudocoded steps into actual code with the appropriate syntax and punctuation. And if you're anything like me, I can never remember more than a few basic functions and syntaxes for any given language and have to google everything I want to code. But I've already figured out what I need the code to do in each step; those written steps are my ready-to-go search queries. The entire process feels very efficient.

It may seem obvious to say that you need to figure out what you're going to write in code before you write the code, but it is all too easy to sit down at the computer and then feel like an idiot who doesn't know how to code because you don't know all the steps in making a spiderweb. It feels ridiculous, but avoiding that negative headspace is one of those "an ounce of prevention is worth a pound of cure" situations, especially when you're still learning to code, and especially if you feel like coding is out of your comfort zone and incredibly challenging. It is all too easy to get frustrated and discouraged with coding, and pseudocoding is a secret weapon for avoiding all that negativity from the start. By pseudocoding, you are explicitly decoupling the problem of figuring out what the code needs to do from the problem of figuring out how to write the code. When you just start writing code from scratch without a game plan first, you force yourself to try to solve both problems at the same time. That is, for me, one of the key reasons coding can feel so hard. Pseudocoding is not a magic wand, but it eases the friction greatly.

Which one of the books you visualized is your favorite? Mine is without a doubt It, *by Stephen King!*

In a terrific moment of irony, I'm not a horror fan! The only one of these books I've read is *Frankenstein*, and it was so long ago I only remember the generic plot. I suppose it wins by default? Growing up, the extra anxiety was the last thing I wanted to experience when I had enough time to read for fun. And adult me feels the same. But I've been forced to watch some of the movies over the years, and *Silence of the Lambs* is probably top of the rewatch list.

What types of projects are you hoping to work on in the future?

I am actually not all that sure. I still feel very new to this field, and I'm still learning about the sheer diversity in data visualization projects and what they can do. I'm hoping to find a working environment that has more of a variety of projects going on so that I can explore my interests and find a more concrete answer to this question. In general, though, I'm obviously very passionate about sharing science, and I like the idea of building bridges between the isolated islands of academia and those that need to see or are in positions to use the science to effect change.

Summary

- One of the main selling points of D3 is how it empowers us to create innovative visualizations.
- When working on a visualization project, we tend to follow these steps: gathering data, cleaning and exploring the data, sketching the visualization layout, building the project skeleton, implementing the visualization elements, and adding interactions.
- We can use our JavaScript skills to extract data from a web page.
- When exploring data, it's helpful to list the quantitative and qualitative data attributes at our disposal because we use different channels to visualize them.
- To create innovative data visualizations, we need to break down our desired visual channels into building blocks. Knowing which D3 modules contain the methods necessary to implement those blocks is useful.
- When creating radial visualizations, we work in a polar coordinate system. We can use basic trigonometric functions to calculate the positions of the different visualization elements.
- To plan meaningful interactions, ask yourself which questions your user will want to answer while exploring your visualization.

Rendering visualizations with Canvas

This chapter covers

- Examining the pros and cons of using Canvas over SVG
- Rendering basic shapes with Canvas
- Applying mixed-mode rendering to a custom data visualization
- Exploring a strategy to handle Canvas interactions

Throughout this book, we've rendered our data visualizations with SVG elements. Because they provide such a crisp rendering on all screen sizes and resolutions and are easily made responsive, accessible, performant, and interactive, SVG elements are the default support for digital data visualizations. But in specific circumstances, such as when the SVG approach implies adding a very high number of SVG elements to the DOM (more than 1,000), the performance of SVG can plummet, making HTML Canvas a better choice.

In this chapter, we'll compare SVG with Canvas and discuss when we should use one over the other. Then we'll render basic shapes in a canvas element, revisiting the *Gallery of SVG Shapes* exercise from chapter 1. We'll also use a mixed-mode rendering technique to improve the performance of our Van Gogh project (from chapter 14) by rendering the painting circles with Canvas instead of SVG. Finally, we'll explore a strategy for handling interactions with a data visualization rendered with Canvas.

15.1 What is Canvas and when to use it

SVG and Canvas are two technologies used to draw in web browsers. While SVG is vectorial and uses a *declarative* approach (we tell the browser the result we want but not how to get there), Canvas generates raster graphics (with pixels) and uses a more *imperative* approach (we tell the browser how to draw with JavaScript commands).

SVG is usually the preferred way to render digital data visualizations because most charts don't imply adding a ton of elements to the DOM. But we might want to consider Canvas if we work with large datasets, have multiple data visualizations on the same page, or need complex animations and color gradients. As a rule of thumb, if you need to append more than a thousand elements to the DOM, then it might be time to use Canvas instead of SVG. But remember that this limit keeps being pushed as the browsers and our computers get more performant.

Table 15.1 enumerates the main factors to consider when comparing SVG to Canvas. The primary reasons we opt for SVG are for the crisp look of the images they generate and because every individual element is accessible in the DOM, making those graphics stylable with CSS, and easy to animate, make interactive, and debug. It's also easier to provide an accessible experience with SVG. On the other end, Canvas really shines when it comes to intricate graphics that may involve color gradients and numerous animations. In such cases, they can dramatically improve performance.

Table 15.1   Comparing SVG with Canvas

Feature	SVG	Canvas
Image quality	(+) Vectorial image: crisp looking on all screen sizes, resolutions, and zoom levels	(-) Raster image: the image tends to look a little blurry, especially when zooming in or on high-resolution screens. This is especially problematic when the visualization includes text labels.
Performance	(+) Not performant for large numbers of elements but very performant otherwise	(+) Very performant when rendering complex animated graphics. For smaller, less complex data visualizations, SVG graphics tend to have a better performance than raster images.
Can be styled with CSS	(+) Yes. SVG also supports CSS transitions and animations.	(-) No
Interactions	(+) Event listeners can be attached to SVG elements.	(-) Event listeners can be attached to the canvas element itself but not to the drawings inside of it. We must put additional strategies in place to add interactivity.
Animations	(+) SVG can be animated with CSS and JavaScript, but not suited for a high level of complexity like the one we find in games.	(+) Suited for handling lots of animations with intricate details and gradients

Table 15.1 Comparing SVG with Canvas *(continued)*

Feature	SVG	Canvas
Debugging	(+) Each SVG element is accessible in the DOM and can be manipulated and inspected.	(-) Only the canvas element is rendered into the DOM, and the image it generates can't be manipulated or inspected with the browser's inspector tool.
Accessibility	(+) SVG makes it easier to build an accessible experience because all the SVG elements are available in the DOM, and the text SVG elements are accessible to screen readers.	(-) The canvas element can be given an `aria-label` attribute but otherwise is treated like a regular raster image by screen readers.

Here are a few data visualization projects that use solely Canvas or a mixed SVG-Canvas approach. Use your browser's inspector tool to explore where those creators have used Canvas versus SVG:

- "An Interactive Visualization of Every Line in Hamilton," by Shirley Wu (https://pudding.cool/2017/03/hamilton/).
- "Mapping Diversity," by Sheldon Studio (https://mappingdiversity.eu/greece/athens/).
- "The Inside Scoop of Ben & Jerry's," by Hesham Eissa and Lindsey Poulter (https://benjerry.heshlindsdataviz.com/).

15.2 *Rendering basic shapes with Canvas*

Before jumping into complex graphics, let's learn how to draw basic shapes with Canvas. To do so, we'll reuse the *Gallery of SVG Shapes* exercise performed in chapter 1 and redo it with Canvas. You can find the completed project at http://mng.bz/WEqd. While explaining the concept of the Canvas context and introducing a few commands, we'll draw the line, rectangles, circle, ellipse, and SVG-path-inspired shapes displayed in figure 15.1.

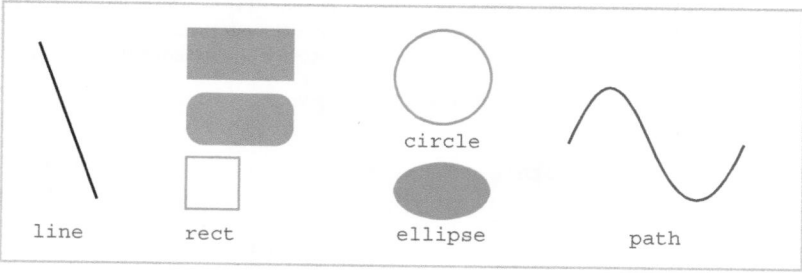

Figure 15.1   With basic commands, we can draw lines, rectangles, circles, and SVG-path-inspired shapes with Canvas.

To get started with this exercise, open the start folder from http://mng.bz/8wGW in Visual Studio Code (VS Code). Start your local development environment by clicking on the Go Live option in the status bar. If you don't see this option, it's probably because you haven't installed the Live Server extension yet. Refer to appendix A for detailed instructions.

15.2.1 *The <canvas> element*

The HTML canvas element is used in combination with JavaScript to draw on the screen, thanks to the Canvas API, which largely focuses on 2D graphics. Although we won't discuss it in this book, we can alternatively use the Web Graphics Library (WebGL) API to draw hardware-accelerated 2D and 3D graphics.

This exercise's code files include an HTML file (index.html) that contains the SVG markup of our *Gallery of SVG Shapes* built in chapter 1. At the bottom of that file, you'll also find a div with an ID of "canvas". This is where we'll inject our canvas element in a moment. In the /js folder, you'll find a file named main.js. This is where we'll write our code. Note that the D3 library and main.js are already loaded into index.html via a <script> tag.

Before we start drawing, we need to append a canvas element into the DOM. In the next listing, we use D3 to select the div with an ID of "canvas", append a canvas element into it, and give it a 1 px black border.

> **Listing 15.1 Appending a canvas element to the DOM (main.js)**

```
const canvas = d3.select("#canvas")
  .append("canvas")
    .style("border", "1px solid black");
```

If you look at your project in the browser and open the inspector tool, you'll see that the canvas element has a default size of about 300 × 150 px, as demonstrated by figure 15.2.

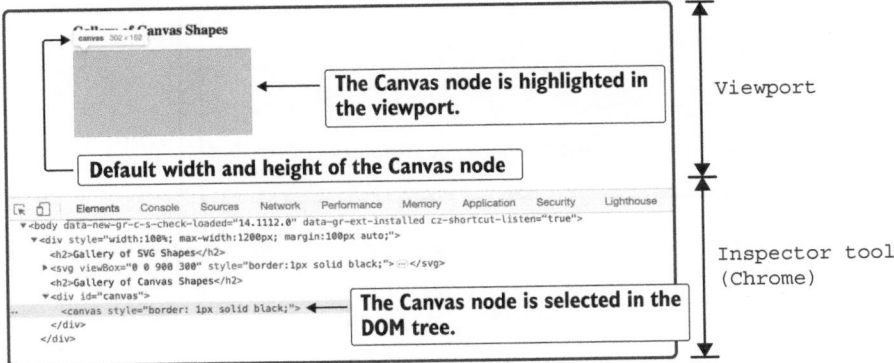

Figure 15.2 By default, the canvas element has a size of about 300 × 150 px.

We could use CSS to set the width and height of the canvas element, but because Canvas renders raster graphics, this might result in a blurry image. Instead, it's better to set the size of the canvas element via its `width` and `height` attributes.

Listing 15.2 expands on listing 15.1 by grabbing the `div` with an ID of `"canvas"` and saving it into a constant named `container`. Then we set the `width` and `height` attributes of the canvas element. The width is equal to the one of the `container`, while the height is one-third of that width.

> **Listing 15.2   Setting the `width` and `height` attributes (`main.js`)**

```
const canvas = d3.select("#canvas")
  .append("canvas")
    .style("border", "1px solid black");

const container = document.querySelector("#canvas");

const width = container.offsetWidth;
const height = 0.333 * width;

canvas
  .attr("width", width)
  .attr("height", height);
```

Grab the div with an ID of "canvas", and save it into a constant named container.

Set the width and height attributes of the canvas element. The width is the same as the one of the div parent, while the height equals one-third of that width.

If you go back to your browser and resize your screen, you'll see that the canvas element is now responsive and adapts to the size of its parent element, as shown in figure 15.3.

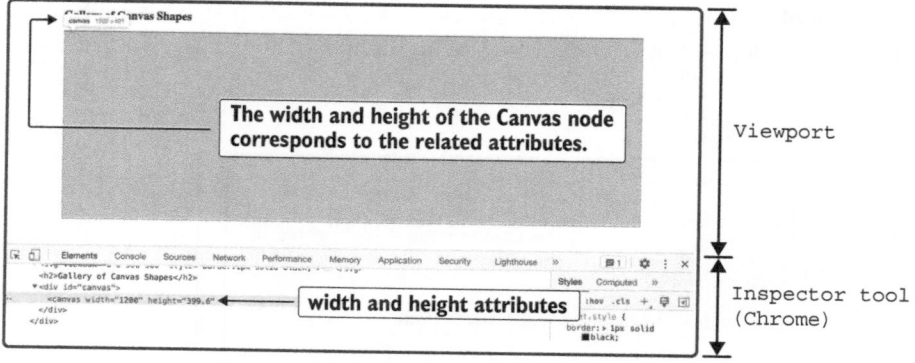

The width and height of the Canvas node corresponds to the related attributes.

Viewport

width and height attributes

Inspector tool (Chrome)

Figure 15.3   The `width` and `height` attributes are responsible for setting the dimensions of the canvas element.

One last thing we need to address is the pixel density of the canvas element. Some screens have a higher pixel density than others, which means that they pack more pixels per square centimeter. You probably know that raster images look blurry on such screens unless you double or triple their resolution. We need to adopt the same strategy for Canvas graphics.

Fortunately, the solution is simple! The `window` object has a `devicePixelRatio` property that provides the ratio of the resolution in *logical pixels* to the resolution in *physical pixels* of the current device. This property returns one on a traditional screen and two on a High Dots Per Inch (HiDPI) screen. In listing 15.3, we simply multiply the width and height by this value, and then cap the CSS `max-width` property of the canvas element to 100%. If we're working with a Retina screen, the `devicePixelRatio` is 2, so we double the width and height of the canvas element. But because this element can't be wider than its parent, the density of the logical pixels inside the canvas element will be twice as big, and the resolution of the graphics will be corrected.

Listing 15.3   Correcting the resolution (`main.js`)

```
const canvas = d3.select("#canvas")
  .append("canvas")
    .style("border", "1px solid black")
    .style("max-width", "100%");          ← Ensure the canvas element
                                            doesn't get wider than its parent.

const container = document.querySelector("#canvas");      Get the devicePixelRatio
const devicePixelRatio = window.devicePixelRatio;    ←    property of the window object,
                                                          and save it into a constant.

const setCanvasSize = () => {
  const width = container.offsetWidth;
  const height = 0.333 * width;

  canvas
    .attr("width", width * devicePixelRatio)
    .attr("height", height * devicePixelRatio);       Multiply the width and height
};                                                    attributes of the canvas element
                                                      by the device's pixel ratio.

setCanvasSize();
window.addEventListener("resize", setCanvasSize);
```

The last thing we need to do before starting to draw is initialize the `context` of the canvas element. This `context` is an object with properties and methods that we'll use to draw in a moment. In listing 15.4, we grab the node associated with the D3 selection and set its drawing `context` to `"2d"`. If we wanted to work with WebGL instead, the `context` would be `"webgl"`. We save this `context` into a constant named `context` so that we can call it easily.

Because we're correcting the number of logical pixels rendered by Canvas, we need to apply a scaling transformation to the Canvas units with the `scale()` method. By default, 1 Canvas unit corresponds to 1 px. If we apply a transformation of `scale(2, 2)`, every Canvas unit will correspond to 2 px, and shapes will be drawn at twice their normal size.

Listing 15.4 Setting the Canvas context (main.js)

```
const canvas = d3.select("#canvas")
  .append("canvas")
    .style("border", "1px solid black")
    .style("max-width", "100%");

...

const context = canvas.node().getContext("2d");
context.scale(devicePixelRatio, devicePixelRatio);
```

Get the node associated with the D3 selection, and set its drawing context to "2d".

Apply a horizontal and vertical scale transformation to the canvas units.

We're now ready to start drawing! In Canvas, we draw with the help of JavaScript commands applied to the `context` created in listing 15.4. Fortunately, those commands are often self-explanatory.

15.2.2 Line

In Canvas, a line is a path, so we call command `beginPath()` to start a new path. If we had drawn other paths earlier, this command would also reset the `context` from the previous path commands. In listing 15.5, we set the starting point of our line with command `moveTo()`, which takes the x and y coordinates as argument. It's like taking a pen, lifting it, and putting it down at the coordinate (66, 60). We then slide our pen onto the canvas to draw a line until the coordinate (186, 300) with command `lineTo()`. Finally, `context.stroke()` outlines the path onto the canvas. Note that the coordinates are the same as the ones used as the starting and ending point of the SVG line included in the HTML file. Figure 15.4 recapitulates the steps to draw a line with Canvas.

Listing 15.5 Drawing a line (main.js)

```
context.beginPath();
context.moveTo(66, 60);
context.lineTo(186, 300);
context.stroke();
```

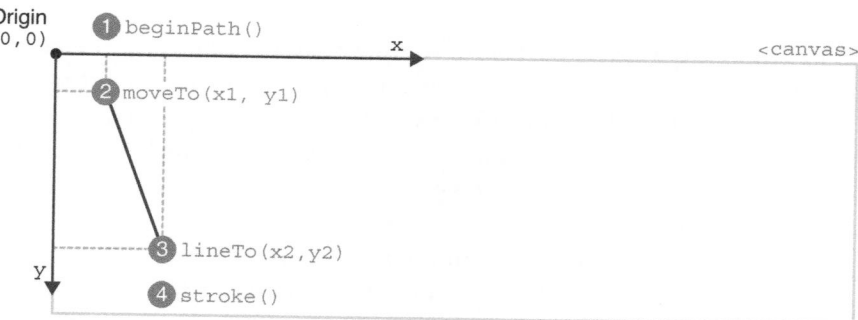

Figure 15.4 Drawing a line with Canvas requires four commands: `beginPath()` to start a new path, `moveTo()` to set the starting point, `lineTo()` to set the endpoint, and `stroke()` to draw the path's stroke.

15.2.3 Rectangle

Drawing a rectangle is even more straightforward. Its shape is defined with the single command `rect()`, which takes four arguments:

- `x`—The horizontal position of the rectangle's top-left corner
- `y`—The vertical position of the rectangle's top-left corner
- `width`—The width of the rectangle
- `height`—The height of the rectangle

The following snippet draws the first rectangle in our *Gallery of Canvas Shapes*. The top-left corner of this rectangle is positioned at (346, 33), its width is 160 px, and its height is 80 px. Note how we use the `fill()` command instead of `stroke()` to render the shape this time. As their names suggest, the `fill()` command fills a shape, while the `stroke()` command draws a shape's border:

```
context.rect(346, 33, 160, 80);
context.fill();
```

If you save your code and take a look in your browser, you'll see a black rectangle, as in figure 15.5. As with SVG, the default color in Canvas is black. It we want to use another color, we need to set the `context`'s `fillStyle` property before drawing the shape, as in the following snippet:

```
context.rect(346, 33, 160, 80);
context.fillStyle = "#6ba5d7";
context.fill();
```

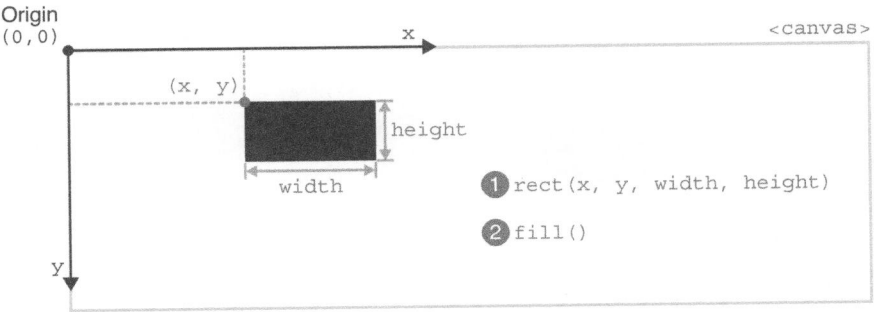

Figure 15.5 To draw a rectangle, we use `rect()` followed by `fill()`. We could also use `stroke()` to add a stroke to the shape.

To render a rectangle with rounded corners, we use the `roundRect()` command. This command takes the same arguments as `rect()` but needs an additional one: an array of the corners' radii. If only one value is passed into this array, all four corners will have the same radius.

Note how we're batching the drawing of the first two rectangles in listing 15.6. We first declare their dimensions, set the `fillStyle` property of the `context`, and draw them both at the same time with the `fill()` command. We then declare a third rectangle, for which we only want to draw the border. We do that by setting the `strokeStyle` property of the `context`, and then use the `stroke()` command to draw the border.

Note also how we used the `beginPath()` command to reset the current path. In Canvas, strokes are drawn as paths. Without this reset, the previous path (the line we drew in listing 15.5) will automatically take the same styles as the current `strokeStyle` of the `context`.

Listing 15.6 Drawing different rectangles (`main.js`)

```
context.rect(346, 33, 160, 80);                  Declare two rectangles—
context.roundRect(346, 133, 160, 80, [20]);      the second one with
                                                 rounded corners.
context.fillStyle = "#6ba5d7";      Set the fillStyle() property of the context to a
context.fill();                     blue color, and draw the first two rectangles.

context.beginPath();           ⟵   Reset the current path.
context.rect(346, 233, 106, 80);         Declare a new rectangle, set the strokeStyle()
context.strokeStyle = "#6ba5d7";         property of the context to a blue color, and
context.stroke();                        draw the border of that rectangle.
```

As you can see, we can group shapes with similar styles and draw them in batches. Every time we want to switch colors, we update the `fillStyle` and/or the `strokeStyle` properties of the `context`. At this point, your canvas should contain three rectangles, as in figure 15.6.

Figure 15.6 We've used a series of commands to draw a line and three rectangles.

15.2.4 Circle

There's no method in Canvas.to draw a circle, but rather one to draw arcs. The `arc()` method requires five arguments:

- x—The horizontal position of the arc's center
- y—The vertical position of the arc's center

- `radius`—The radius of the arc
- `startAngle`—The angle of the arc's starting point (in radians)
- `endAngle`—The angle of the arc's endpoint (in radians)

If the start angle meets the end angle, we have a circle! We draw an elliptical shape with a similar command: `ellipse(x, y, radiusX, radiusY, startAngle, endAngle)`, where `radiusX` and `radiusY` are the radii in the horizontal and vertical directions, as shown in figure 15.7.

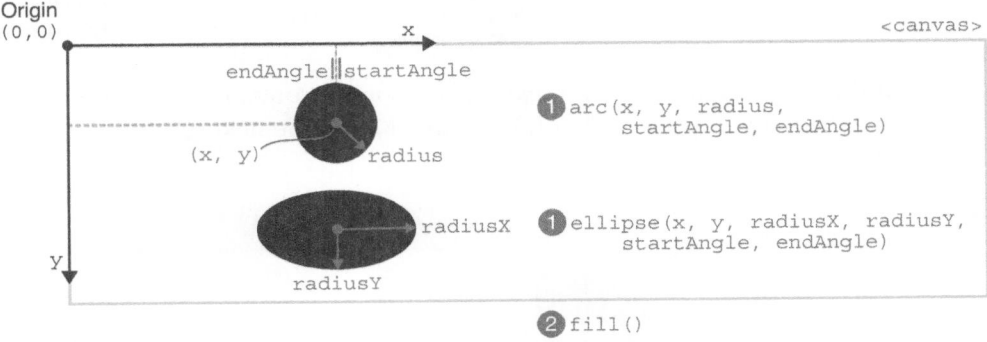

Figure 15.7   In Canvas, we draw circles with the `arc()` command and ellipses with `ellipse()`.

In listing 15.7, we draw the stroke of a circle and a filled ellipse. To obtain closed shapes, we set the `startAngle` to 0, and the `endAngle` to 2π radians, which is the equivalent of 360 degrees. We also introduce a new property, `lineWidth`, to set the `context`'s stroke width.

Note that we had to reset the current path with `beginPath()` before drawing both the circle and the ellipse. Try commenting out those lines to see what happens!

Listing 15.7   Drawing a circle and an ellipse (`main.js`)

```
context.beginPath();
context.arc(706, 106, 66, 0, 2 * Math.PI);     Reset the current path, and
context.strokeStyle = "#81c21c";               draw the stroke of a circle.
context.lineWidth = 3;
context.stroke();

context.beginPath();
context.ellipse(706, 273, 66, 40, 0, 0, 2 * Math.PI);   Reset the current path,
context.fillStyle = "#81c21c";                          and draw a filled ellipse.
context.fill();
```

15.2.5   Path

We often rely on D3's shape generator to draw complex SVG paths. In Canvas, we can directly use the `d` attribute returned by those generators to draw the same shapes. The

Canvas API exposes a constructor called `Path2D()` that accepts the `d` attribute of an SVG path as an argument. When passed to the `context`'s `stroke()` property, as shown in the next listing, this path object draws the same shape as we would get in SVG.

Listing 15.8 Drawing a path (`main.js`)

```
const path = new Path2D("M900 200 C 945 110, 965 110,
➥ 1010 200 S 1075 293, 1120 200");
context.strokeStyle = "#773b9a";
context.stroke(path);     ◁──┐ Draw the path by passing
                              the object to the context's
                              stroke() property.
```

Instantiate a new Path2D object, and pass the d attribute of the corresponding SVG path element as an argument.

At this point, your *Gallery of Canvas Shapes* should contain a line, rectangles, a circle, an ellipse, and a path, as shown in figure 15.8. In the next subsection, we'll add text labels.

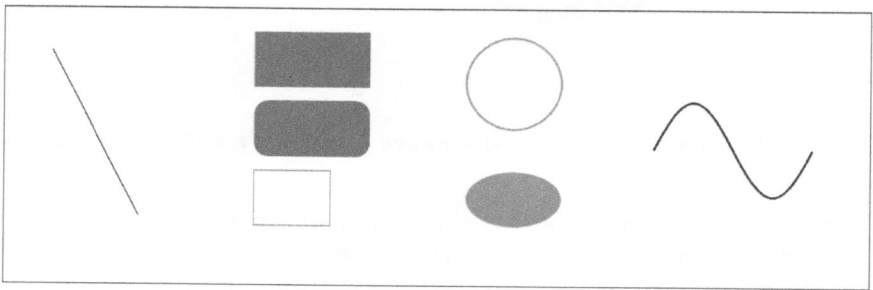

Figure 15.8   We've added all the shapes to our gallery.

15.2.6 *Text*

Displaying text with Canvas requires learning a few additional commands. The first one is `fillText()`, which takes as arguments both the text itself and its coordinates and draws the text onto the Canvas. In listing 15.9, we set the color of the text with the `context`'s `fillStyle`, and we set the font size and family with the `font` property.

The text is left-aligned by default. If we want to center it horizontally around its coordinates, we use the `context`'s `textAlign` property.

Listing 15.9   Adding text (`main.js`)

```
context.fillStyle = "#636466";
context.font = "16px monospace";
context.fillText("line", 80, 346);
context.fillText("rect", 346, 346);
context.fillText("path", 973, 346);
```

Set the text's color, font size, and font family.

With the fillText() command, we set the text and its position at the same time.

```
context.textAlign = "center";
context.fillText("circle", 706, 206);
context.fillText("ellipse", 706, 346);
```

Add two more labels that are horizontally centered around their coordinates.

That completes our *Gallery of Canvas Shapes*, shown in figure 15.9! As you can see, drawing Canvas graphics isn't necessarily complicated but is a little more verbose than SVG. In addition, we don't use D3 to append shapes directly into the DOM as we do when working in SVG, other than the canvas element itself. Instead, all the drawing commands rely on the Canvas API.

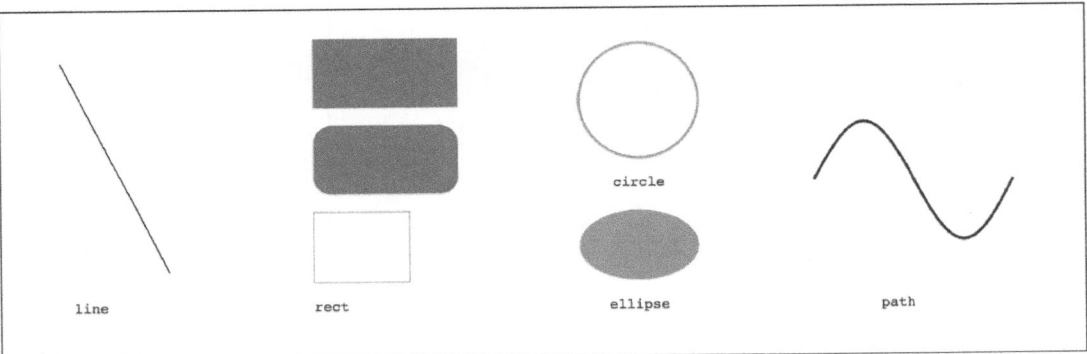

Figure 15.9   Completed *Gallery of Canvas Shapes*

Exercise: Create a Canvas graphic

Now it's your turn! Create the Canvas graphic shown in the following figure. You can work in the `start` folder inside `15.2-Exercise` of this chapter's code files (http://mng.bz/EZED). Here are a few guidelines:

1 Create a responsive canvas element with a maximum width and height of 400 px. If the screen is smaller than 400 px, the canvas element should take the entire width of the screen. The same width-to-height ratio should be maintained at all times.

2 You can give a gray border to the canvas element to see the space you're working in.

3 Draw a square shape with a width and a height of 200 px. Center it within the Canvas container, and give it a transparent fill and a 3 px black stroke.

4 Add a circle with a radius of 100 px to the center of the Canvas container. Set its `fill` attribute to the CSS color name `"plum"`.

5 Draw two diagonal black lines with a stroke of 3 px: one goes from the top-left corner of the square to its bottom-right corner, and the other one goes from the top-right corner of the square to its bottom-left corner.

6 Add the text `"Canvas is awesome!"` above the square, and center it within the Canvas container. Give the text the following style properties: a font size of 18 px and a font family of `"sans-serif"`.

(continued)

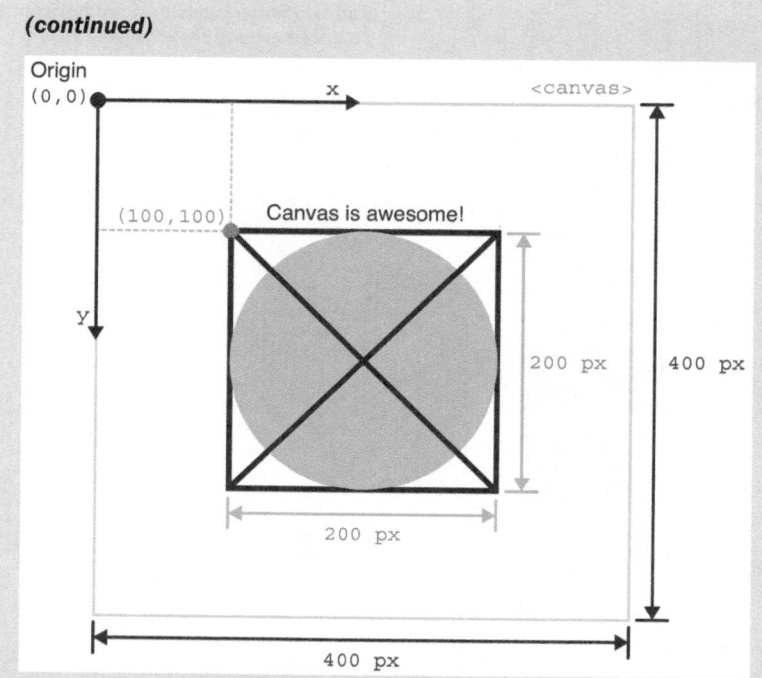

We encourage you to build this Canvas graphic to reinforce the
concepts discussed in this section.

You'll find the solution in listings D.15.1 and D.15.2 of appendix D and folder
`15.2-Exercise/end` of this chapter's code files. We encourage you to try to complete it on your own.

15.3   *Mixed-mode rendering*

So far, in this chapter, we've been comparing Canvas with SVG. Although you can totally choose to generate a project only with SVG or only with Canvas, another approach, called mixed-mode rendering, allows you to render a portion of a data visualization with SVG and another with Canvas, combining the best of both worlds. Let's take our Van Gogh project from chapter 14 as an example.

This project includes a series of small multiples visualizations, each one representing a year and visualizing the paintings, drawings, and letters produced by the artist during that period. A sample from this visualization is shown in figure 15.10. You can also find the completed project at http://mng.bz/z8rg. In each visualization, the number of drawings created each month is visualized with a radial area chart, and the number of letters with a radial bar chart. Each painting created by Van Gogh is depicted by a circle whose size is proportional to the dimensions of the actual painting, and the color represents its subject (portrait, landscape, still life, etc.).

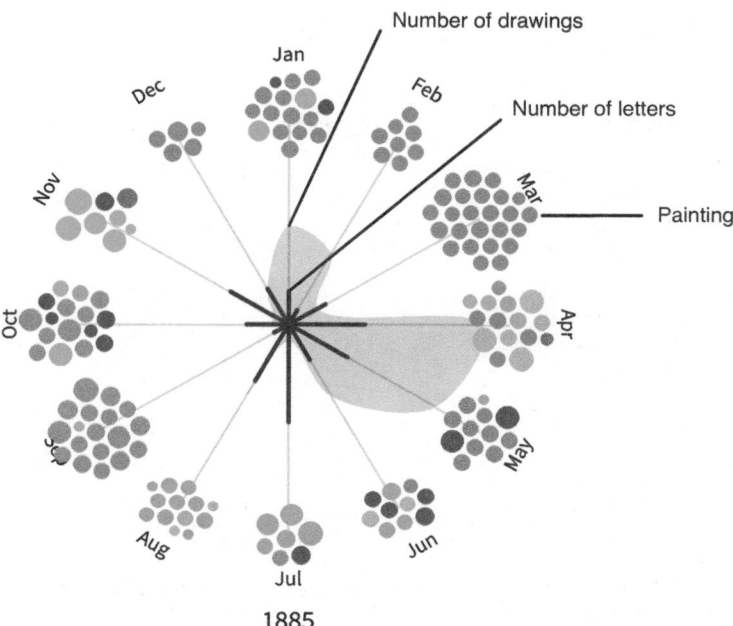

Figure 15.10   **The project consists of a series of small multiples visualizations, each representing a year in Van Gogh's artistic production. The number of drawings created each month is visualized with a radial area chart, and the number of letters with a radial bar chart. Each painting is depicted with a circle, whose size is proportional to the dimensions of the actual painting, and the color represents its subject.**

Because Van Gogh's artistic production spans more than 10 years, during which he created over 1,000 paintings, rendering each of them with an SVG circle element, as we did in chapter 14, can be challenging for the browser. It's not critical, but at the time of writing, Chrome was sometimes working hard to handle the force layout calculations behind the positioning of the circles, while Firefox tended to be okay (your experience might differ depending on the versions of your browsers and the computer you work with).

Those circles are a great example of a portion of a visualization that can be rendered with Canvas. In mixed-mode rendering, we plan our work as multiple layers displayed on top of each other, like the layers in a cake. Depending on the result we're after and the interactions we plan to add to our project, we decide in which order we want to add those layers to the page. This project requires only two layers: the first layer made of an SVG element and rendering the axes, drawings area chart, and paintings bar chart, and the second layer made of a canvas element and responsible for displaying the painting circles, as shown in figure 15.11. By positioning the canvas element on top of the SVG container, we ensure that the painting circles will appear on top of the other visual elements.

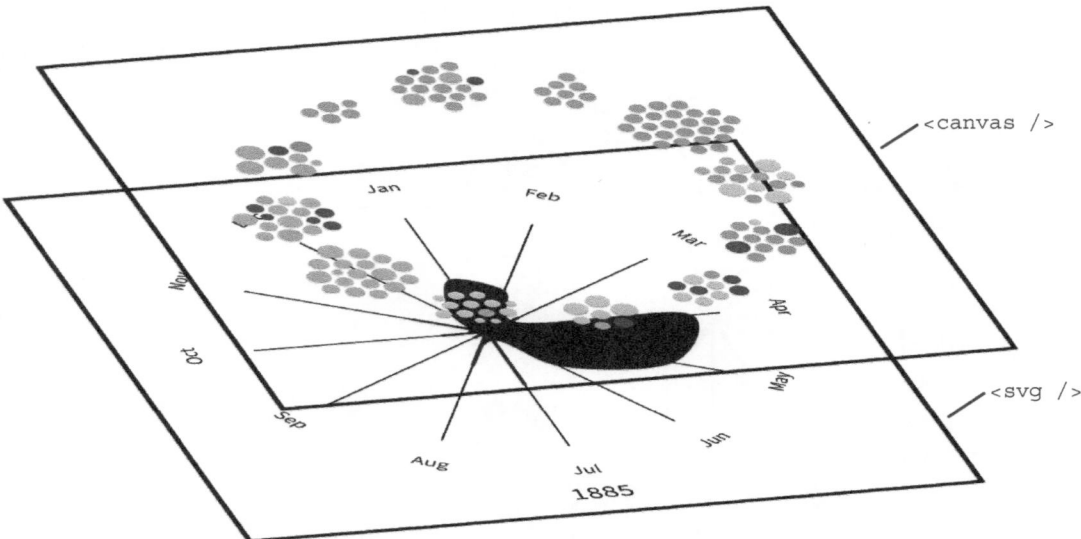

Figure 15.11   **Adopting the mixed-mode rendering approach, we use an SVG container to display the axes, drawings, and letters, and we add a canvas element on top that renders the painting circles.**

To follow along with the instructions in this section, open the start folder from http://mng.bz/NRnx in your code editor. This project is built with Svelte, and you'll find explanations about its architecture in chapter 14. To run the project locally, in a terminal window, run command npm install, followed by npm run dev. The localhost port number will be indicated in your terminal window (it's usually http://localhost :5173/).

Listing 15.10 contains the code included in the Paintings.svelte file, which you'll find in the chart_components folder. We've removed all the code that was dealing with SVG elements in chapter 14 and kept only the color scale and the force simulation. The color scale is responsible for returning the color associated with each painting circle, while the force simulation calculates their positions. We won't explain the ins and outs of D3's force simulation here because this isn't the focus of the chapter, but you can refer to chapters 11 and 14 for explanations. If you're not familiar with Svelte, you'll find a brief introduction in appendix E.

Listing 15.10   Starting point (Paintings.svelte)

```
<script>
 import { forceSimulation, forceX, forceY,
   forceCollide }
     from "d3-force";                                    Import dependencies.
 import { scaleOrdinal } from "d3-scale";
 import { subjects } from "../utils/subjects";
```

```
export let paintingAreaScale;
export let paintingDefaultRadius;
export let monthScale;
export let radius;
export let isTooltipVisible = false;
export let tooltipMeta = {};
```

Import props from the
parent component.

```
export let width;
export let height;
export let paintings;
export let yearsTranslations;
```

Initialize variables.

```
const colorScale = scaleOrdinal()
  .domain(subjects.map((d) => d.subject))
  .range(subjects.map((d) => d.color));
```

Declare an ordinal scale that returns the
color associated with the painting subjects.

```
let simulation = forceSimulation(paintings);
let nodes = [];
simulation.on("tick", () => {
  nodes = simulation.nodes();
});
```

Initialize the nodes array and
the force simulation. After each
simulation tick, call the
simulation's nodes() method.

```
$: {
  simulation
    .force(
      "x",
      forceX((d) => {
       const translation = yearsTranslations.find(
         (y) => y.year === d.year
       ).translationX;
       return d.month !== ""
         ? translation + radius * Math.sin(
             monthScale(d.month))
         : translation;
     }).strength(0.5)
    )
    .force(
      "y",
      forceY((d) => {
        const translation = yearsTranslations.find(
          (y) => y.year === d.year
        ).translationY;
        return d.month !== ""
          ? translation - radius * Math.cos(
              monthScale(d.month))
          : translation;
      }).strength(0.5)
    )
    .force(
      "collide",
      forceCollide()
        .radius((d) =>
          d.width_cm === null && d.height_cm === null
            ? paintingDefaultRadius + 1
            : Math.sqrt(paintingAreaScale(d.area_cm2)
```

Apply positioning
and collision forces.

```
                    / Math.PI) + 1
        )
        .strength(1)
    )
    .alpha(0.5)
    .alphaDecay(0.1);
  }
</script>
```

Apply positioning
and collision forces.

If you inspect the project's DOM, you'll find that the visualization is rendered in an SVG container. Per the strategy illustrated in figure 15.11, we'll add a canvas element on top of it. In listing 15.11, we add a canvas element to the component's markup and set its `width` and `height` attributes to the corresponding values received as props. Those are the same as the width and the height of the SVG container and are updated dynamically if we resize the screen. Therefore, the canvas element will always have the exact same size as the SVG container. We also correct those attributes with the window's `devicePixelRatio` to ensure a sufficient resolution, as discussed in section 15.2.1.

Finally, we use an absolute CSS position to move the canvas element on top of the SVG container. Note that the parent `<div>` of the SVG container and the canvas element already has its CSS position property set to `relative`, ensuring a proper alignment.

Listing 15.11 Adding a canvas element (`Paintings.svelte`)

```
<script>
  ...
</script>

<canvas
  width={width * window.devicePixelRatio}
  height={height * window.devicePixelRatio}
/>

<style>
  canvas {
    position: absolute;
    top: 0;
    left: 0;
    max-width: 100%;
  }
</style>
```

Add a canvas element to the DOM, and set its width and height attributes with the width and height props. Correct those with the window's devicePixelRatio property to ensure sufficient resolution.

Use an absolute CSS position to move the canvas element on top of the SVG container.

If you go back to your browser's inspector, you should see that the canvas element has been added as a sibling of the SVG container and is displayed on top of it, as illustrated by figure 15.12.

We now need to initialize the Canvas context. For that, we need a reference to the canvas node, which in Svelte is done with the `this` binding, as you can see in listing 15.12. This binding points to variable `canvasElement`, which is initialized higher in the `<script>` tags.

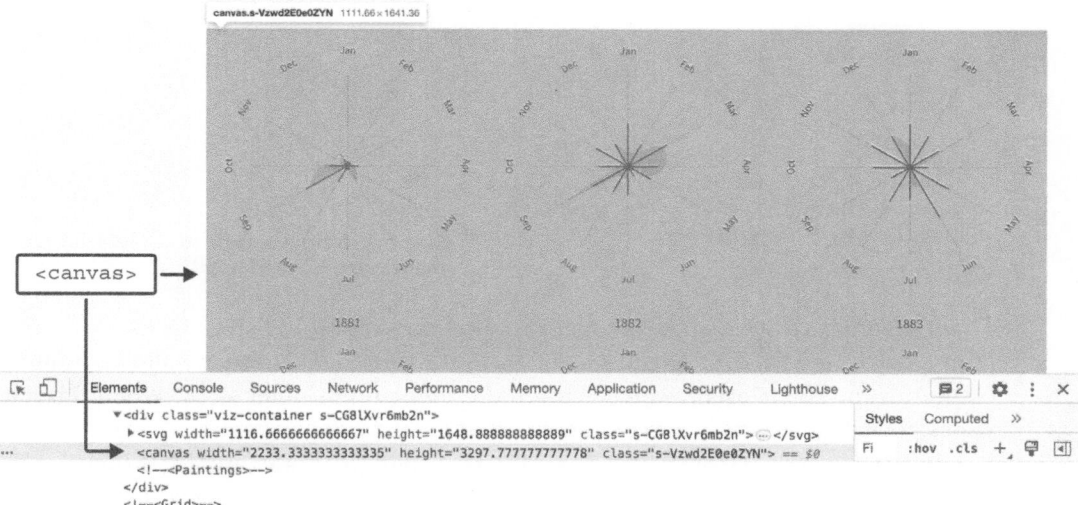

Figure 15.12 The canvas element is positioned on top of the SVG container.

We also initialize the Canvas `context` by calling Canvas API method `getContext` (`"2d"`) onto the canvas element. We need to do that inside the `onMount()` life cycle method to ensure that the `canvas` node has been added to the DOM before we initialize the `context`. Finally, we apply a horizontal and vertical scale transformation to the canvas units to take our previous resolution correction into account.

Note that we declared those variables before running the force simulation. This is because we'll call on those later from the simulation.

Listing 15.12 Initializing the Canvas `context` (`Paintings.svelte`)

```
<script>
  ...

  let simulation = forceSimulation(paintings);
  let nodes = [];
  simulation.on("tick", () => {
    nodes = simulation.nodes();
  });
  let canvasElement;
  let context;
  onMount(() => {
    context = canvasElement.getContext("2d");
    context.scale(window.devicePixelRatio,
      window.devicePixelRatio);
  });
```

Declare variable canvasElement, which will be bound to the <canvas> node.

Set the Canvas context inside the onMount() life cycle function to ensure that the <canvas> node already exists in the DOM.

Apply a scale transformation to take into account the resolution correction performed earlier.

```
$: {
  simulation
    .force ...
}
</script>

<canvas
  width={width * window.devicePixelRatio}
  height={height * window.devicePixelRatio}
  bind:this={canvasElement}
/>
```

Bind the <canvas> node to
the variable canvasElement.

With the Canvas all set up, we're ready to draw the circles! In listing 15.13, we create a
function named handleSimulationEnd(). In the force simulation, we add an event listener for the "end" event, which is when the simulation's timer stops. When this happens, we call handleSimulationEnd().

Inside handleSimulationEnd(), we loop through the nodes and draw them on the
Canvas one by one. Because each circle has a color corresponding to the painting's
subject and a border representing the medium, we set the context's fillStyle and
strokeStyle properties accordingly. We then use the commands discussed in section
15.2.4 to draw the circle:

1 Start a new path with beginPath().
2 Set the circle's position and dimensions with arc(x, y, radius, startAngle,
   endAngle).
3 Draw the circle's fill and stroke with methods fill() and stroke().

Listing 15.13 Drawing the circles (Paintings.svelte)

```
<script>
  ...

  let simulation = forceSimulation(paintings);
  let nodes = [];
  simulation.on("tick", () => {
    nodes = simulation.nodes();
  });

  let canvasElement;
  let context;
  onMount(() => {
    context = canvasElement.getContext("2d");
    context.scale(window.devicePixelRatio, window.devicePixelRatio);
  });

  const handleSimulationEnd = () => {
    nodes.forEach((node) => {
```

Loop through
the nodes.

```
      context.fillStyle = colorScale(node.subject);
      switch (node.medium) {
        case "oil":
          context.strokeStyle = "#FFFAFC";
          break;
        case "watercolor":
          context.strokeStyle = "#160E13";
          break;
        case "print":
          context.strokeStyle = "#BC5D9A";
          break;
      };
```

> Set the context's fillStyle and strokeStyle properties to the desired circle's color and border.

```
      context.beginPath();
      context.arc(
        node.x,
        node.y,
        node.area_cm2
          ? Math.sqrt(paintingAreaScale(node.area_cm2)
              / Math.PI)
          : paintingDefaultRadius,
        0,
        2 * Math.PI
      );
      context.fill();
      context.stroke();
    });
  };

  $: {
    simulation
      .force ...
      .alpha(0.5)
      .alphaDecay(0.1)
      .on("end", handleSimulationEnd);
  }
</script>

<canvas
  width={width * window.devicePixelRatio}
  height={height * window.devicePixelRatio}
  bind:this={canvasElement}
/>
```

> Draw the circle.

> When the force simulation ends, call function handleSimulationEnd() to draw the circles.

And voilà—the painting circles are back via the canvas element, as shown in figure 15.13.

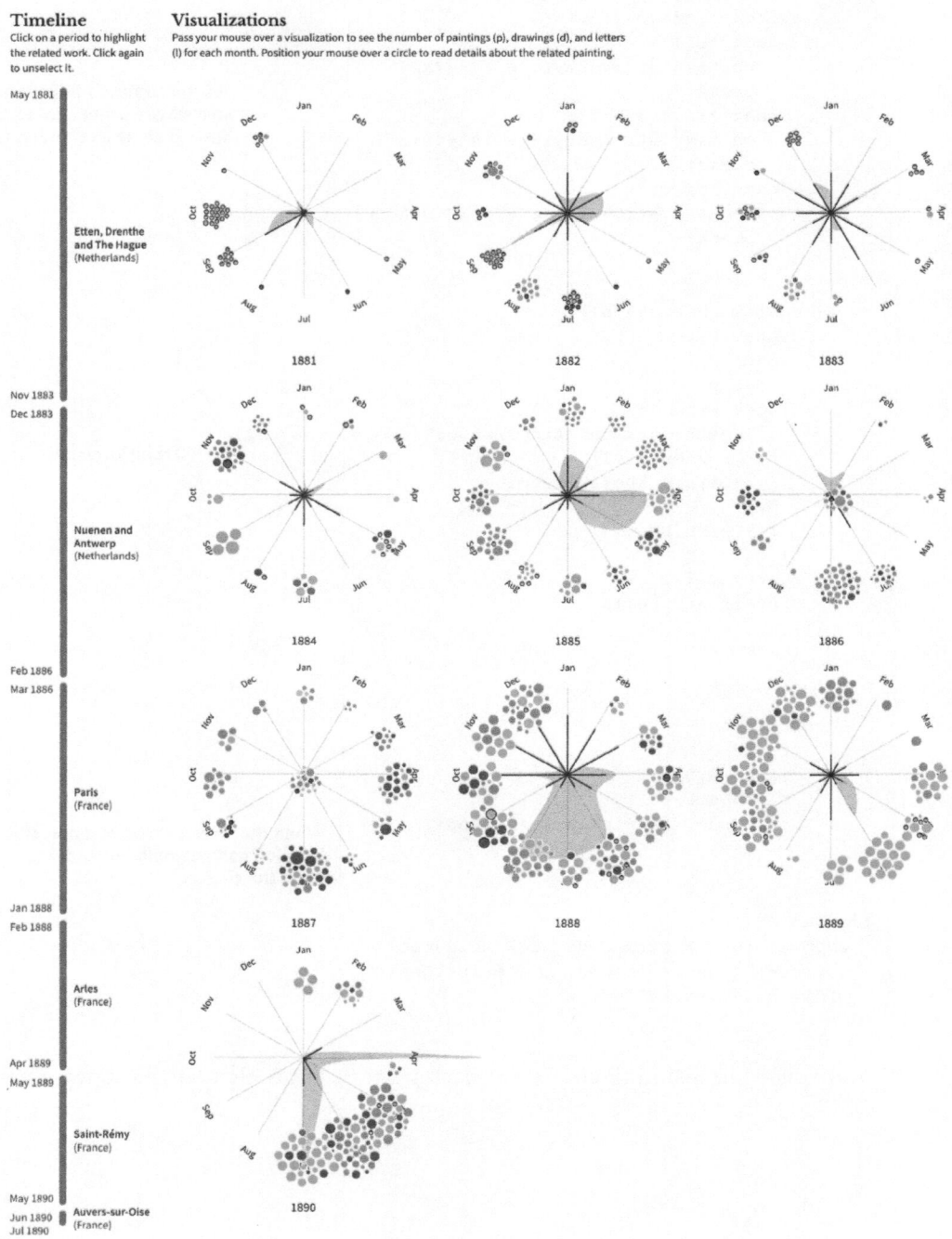

Figure 15.13   The paintings circles from chapter 14 are back, except this time we drew them with Canvas!

15.4 A strategy for Canvas interactions

We mentioned earlier that handling interactions with Canvas is trickier than with SVG. We can't rely on regular event listeners like we learned to do in the previous chapters because Canvas exists as a single DOM element, and what it renders can't be accessed. But there are a few strategies we can apply.

First, we can detect mouse events on the canvas element itself. This event returns a bunch of information, including the x and y positions of the mouse on the Canvas. If we render simple geometric shapes and know their position, we can determine if the mouse is positioned over one of those elements and react accordingly. The logic behind this approach is relatively simple, but putting it into practice can quickly become complex, especially when working with irregular shapes.

The second approach is unexpected, but clever and relatively easy to implement. Let's use our Van Gogh example again and add another canvas element on top of the one created in the previous section, as shown in figure 15.14. With this new canvas element, we display again the same painting circles, but this time, we give each circle a random and unique color. As we proceed, we store all the paintings' data and the random colors associated with them. Then we set the CSS `opacity` property of this canvas to `0`. From this point, we'll call it the "hidden" canvas.

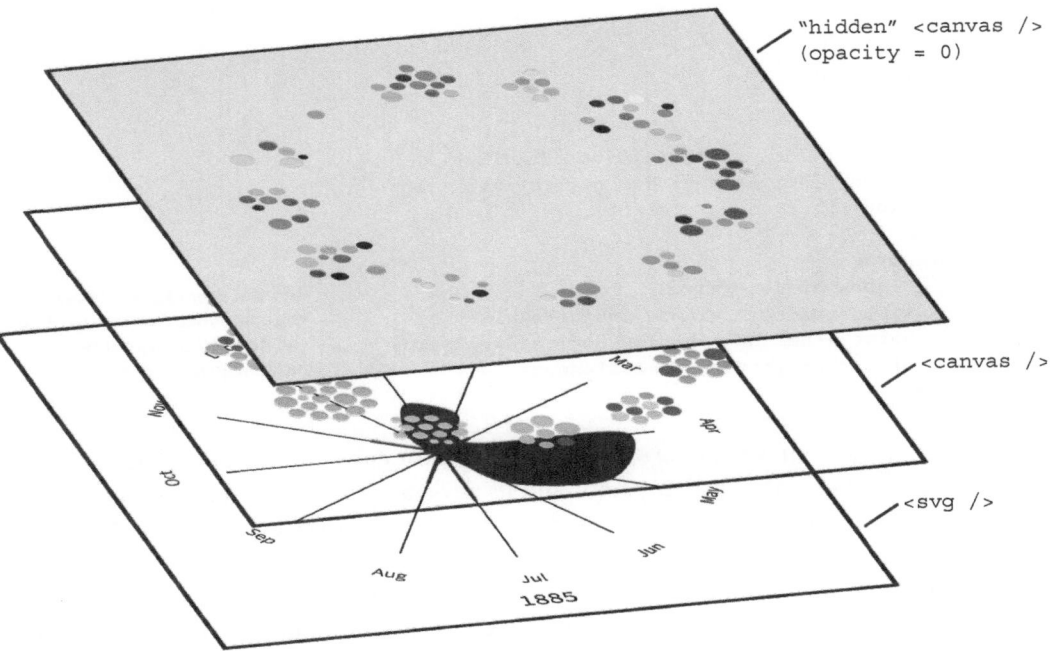

Figure 15.14 To detect when the mouse is positioned over one of the painting's circles, we add an additional Canvas layer, in which each circle is given a random and unique color. This layer is hidden from the user by setting its CSS `opacity` property to `0`.

Let's put those steps into action before explaining this technique further. In listing 15.14, we add a second canvas element to the component's markup and bind this node to a new variable named `hiddenCanvasElement`. We also set the `context` of the new canvas element and save it in a variable named `hiddenContext`. Because this `context` will be used to handle frequent interactions, we set its `willReadFrequently` property to `true`.

Listing 15.14 Adding a new canvas element (`Paintings.svelte`)

```
<script>
  ...

  let canvasElement;                         Declare variable hiddenCanvasElement,
  let context;                               which will be bound to the new
  let hiddenCanvasElement;                   <canvas> node and its context.
  let hiddenContext;
  onMount(() => {
    context = canvasElement.getContext("2d");
    context.scale(window.devicePixelRatio, window.devicePixelRatio);
    hiddenContext = hiddenCanvasElement.getContext(
      "2d", { willReadFrequently: true }        Initialize the new Canvas context.
    );
    hiddenContext.scale(window.devicePixelRatio, window.devicePixelRatio);
  });

  ...
</script>

<canvas
  width={width * window.devicePixelRatio}
  height={height * window.devicePixelRatio}
  bind:this={canvasElement}
/>
<canvas
  class="hidden-canvas"                      Add the new canvas element to
  width={width * window.devicePixelRatio}    the component's markup. Bind
  height={height * window.devicePixelRatio}  the node to the variable
  bind:this={hiddenCanvasElement}            hiddenCanvasElement.
/>
```

The next step is to generate a unique color for each circle that we'll draw on the new canvas. We'll also save this color and its associated node into a JavaScript `Map()` object so that we can easily retrieve nodes for their colors later. Listing 15.15 contains two new functions. The first one, `generateColor()`, returns an array of three numbers between 0 and 255. Then, in `addNodeColor()`, we assemble those numbers into an RGB color. If that color doesn't yet exist in the `nodesColor` map, we set a new key-value pair with the RGB color and its associated node. In `handleSimulationEnd()`, we call `addNodeColor()` to get a unique color for each node's circle and draw those circles onto the Canvas.

Listing 15.15 Giving a unique color to each node (`Paintings.svelte`)

```
<script>
  ...

  let canvasElement;
  let context;
  let hiddenCanvasElement;
  let hiddenContext;
  onMount(() => {
    ...
  });

  const nodesColors = new Map();
```

Declare a new
JavaScript Map class.

```
  const generateColor = () => {
    let colorArray = [];
    for (let i = 0; i < 3; i++) {
      const randomNumber = Math.floor(Math.random()
        * 255);
      colorArray.push(randomNumber);
    }
    return colorArray;
  };
```

Generate and return an
array of three numbers
between 0 and 255.

```
  const addNodeColor = (node) => {
    let isNewGeneratedColor = false;
    while (!isNewGeneratedColor) {
      const colorArray = generateColor();
      const colorRGB = `rgb(${colorArray.join(",")})`;
      if (!nodesColors.get(colorRGB)) {
        nodesColors.set(colorRGB, node);
        isNewGeneratedColor = true;
        return colorRGB;
      }
    }
  };
```

Get a new array of three
numbers, and assemble
it into an RGB color.

If the nodesColors map doesn't contain
a key corresponding to the RGB color,
set a new key-value pair with the color
and the node data. Return that color.

```
  const handleSimulationEnd = () => {
    nodes.forEach((node) => {
      ...

      const color = addNodeColor(node);
      hiddenContext.fillStyle = color;
      hiddenContext.strokeStyle = color;
```

Call addNodeColor() to get a new
RGB color. Set the context's fill and
stroke properties with that color.

```
      hiddenContext.beginPath();
      hiddenContext.arc(
        node.x,
        node.y,
        node.area_cm2
          ? Math.sqrt(paintingAreaScale(node.area_cm2)
              / Math.PI)
          : paintingDefaultRadius,
        0,
        2 * Math.PI
```

Draw the
new circle.

```
    );
    hiddenContext.fill();
    hiddenContext.stroke();
  });
};

  ...
</script>
```

⬆ **Draw the new circle.**

At this point, if you look at your project in the browser, you'll see that the circles of the new Canvas are positioned on top of the previous ones. They probably have very flashy colors as well! But don't worry—we can now hide them. In the following listing, we set the CSS `opacity` property of the new canvas to `0`.

Listing 15.16 Hiding the new Canvas (`Paintings.svelte`)

```
<script>

  ...

</script>

<canvas
  width={width * window.devicePixelRatio}
  height={height * window.devicePixelRatio}
  bind:this={canvasElement}
/>
<canvas
  class="hidden-canvas"
  width={width * window.devicePixelRatio}
  height={height * window.devicePixelRatio}
  bind:this={hiddenCanvasElement}
/>

<style>
  canvas {
    position: absolute;
    top: 0;
    left: 0;
    max-width: 100%;
  }
  .hidden-canvas {
    opacity: 0;
  }
</style>
```

We're ready to detect mouse events over the circles. Here's how we'll proceed: the Canvas 2D API exposes method `getImageData()`, to which we can pass a position on the canvas, and returns the corresponding pixel's color. When the `mousemove` event is detected over the canvas element, we'll use the mouse position provided by the Java-Script event and retrieve the corresponding color. The fun part is that it works even if the canvas element isn't visible. Then the `Map()` created when attributing a unique color to each node will allow us to retrieve the painting corresponding to the circle on which the mouse is positioned. So now we'll know when to show a tooltip and which information it should include!

In listing 15.17, we add an event listener to the hidden canvas to detect the mouse-move event. When this event is detected, we call function `handleMouseMove()`. Inside this function, we call method `getImageData()` on the hidden Canvas context. With this method, we can define a rectangle from which we'll extract image data. Because we want to detect the color at the exact position of the mouse, we'll say that this rectangle has a width and height of 1 px. So when calling `getImageData()`, we pass four arguments: the x and y coordinates of the mouse, and the width and height of 1 px. Note how we correct the x and y coordinates with the screen's resolution. This is necessary because we applied a scale transformation to the Canvas earlier.

The first three values of the image data's property named `data` are the three values of the corresponding RGB color, so it basically works like a color picker! All we have to do then is to reconstruct the RGB color, find the corresponding node in the nodes-Color `Map()`, and send that information to the tooltip component built in chapter 14.

Listing 15.17 Detecting hovered circles (`Paintings.svelte`)

```
<script>

  ...

  let currentColor = "";                          Get the coordinates
  const handleMouseMove = (event) => {            of the mouse relative
    const mouseX = event.layerX;                  to the Canvas.
    const mouseY = event.layerY;

    const imageData = hiddenContext.getImageData(
      mouseX * window.devicePixelRatio,
      mouseY * window.devicePixelRatio,
      1,
      1).data;                                    Extract the color at the
    const colorRGB = `rgb(                        location of the mouse.
      ${imageData[0]},
      ${imageData[1]},
      ${imageData[2]}
    )`;

    if (colorRGB !== currentColor) {
      if (colorRGB !== "rgb(0,0,0)") {
        currentColor = colorRGB;                  Find the node associated
        const nodeInfo = nodesColors.get(colorRGB);   with that color.
        if (nodeInfo) {
          isTooltipVisible = true;
          tooltipMeta = {
            x: mouseX,
            y: mouseY,                            Populate the
            screenY: event.clientY,              tooltip's data,
            url: nodeInfo.imageLink,             and set its
            title: nodeInfo.title,               visibility to true.
            createdIn: nodeInfo.created_in,
            date:
```

```
        nodeInfo.month !== ""
          ? `${nodeInfo.month} ${nodeInfo.year}`
          : nodeInfo.year,
      medium: nodeInfo.medium,
      currentLocation: nodeInfo.current_location,
      width: nodeInfo.width_cm,
      height: nodeInfo.height_cm,
      subject: nodeInfo.subject,
    };
  }
  } else {
    isTooltipVisible = false;
  }
  }
};

...

</script>

<canvas
  width={width * window.devicePixelRatio}
  height={height * window.devicePixelRatio}
  bind:this={canvasElement}
/>
<canvas
  class="hidden-canvas"
  width={width * window.devicePixelRatio}
  height={height * window.devicePixelRatio}
  bind:this={hiddenCanvasElement}
  on:mousemove={handleMouseMove}
/>
```

Populate the tooltip's data, and set its visibility to true.

Attach an event listener to the hidden canvas.

The tooltip, shown in figure 15.15, is now working again! As you can see, handling data visualization interactions is more complicated with Canvas than it is with SVG. Still, using the Canvas API `getImageData()` method allowed us to work around those limitations.

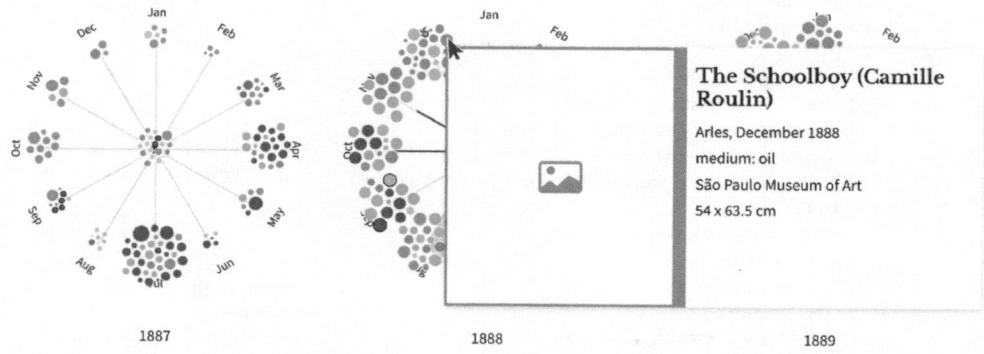

Figure 15.15   When working with Canvas, we must find different strategies to capture user interactions. In this project, we applied unique colors to the paintings' circles drawn on a hidden Canvas, retrieved those colors on mouse interaction with the Canvas API getImageData() method, and retrieved the associated painting.

Interview with Julian Fell

Fell is a journalist and developer.

Can you tell us a little bit about your background and how you entered the field of data visualization?

I worked in software development for about six years doing a broad mix of things, so I ended up with a rather unspecialized set of coding skills. While I was at the ABC (Australian Broadcasting Corporation) as an engineer, I got an opportunity to backfill on a team that specializes in data visualization. This story was actually my first one I did during that period—input from experienced members of the team had a lot to do with how well it turned out.

Which data visualization tools do you mainly use or have a preference for? What's the place of D3 in your current data visualization workflow?

I mainly use a combination of Svelte, D3, and vanilla CSS. The strengths of D3's data manipulation can be applied directly to declarative SVG markup in Svelte components. Svelte allows for lightweight componentization (some things like axes are often reusable, but most of them tend not to be). It also supplies animation utilities and state management. D3 provides all the tried-and-tested utilities that simplify data processing.

One tool I'm excited about (but didn't use on this project) is Layer Cake (https://layercake.graphics/), as it adds some helpful structure to building charts with these tools.

Featured project: "How the Seeds of the 2022 Election Result Were Sown Years Ago" (http://mng.bz/Ddzg)

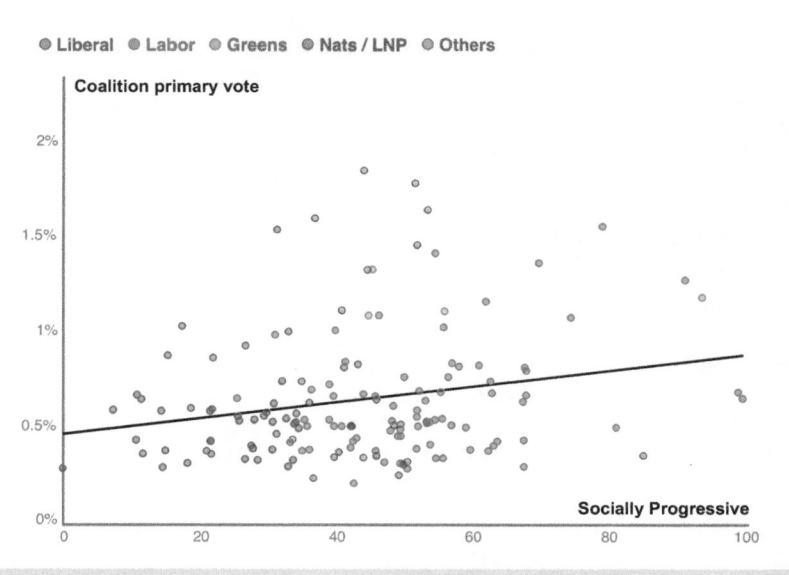

Scatterplot generated from Fell's builder, similar to the ones published in the article

(continued)

Please briefly describe your project.

Our team was already doing a series of stories explaining the mechanics of the 2022 federal election in Australia. For this piece, we wanted to explain the trends that might have driven the outcome. To do that, we used scatterplots to look for correlations between the vote in each of Australia's 151 electorates and the demographics of the people who lived in them.

We found several patterns—around climate, the economy, wealth, geography, ancestry—that had carried over from the previous election. These trends, and two outliers who swung ahead of the other seats in 2019, came together to pose a possible explanation for why so many traditionally "safe" seats fell at the election.

Can you explain the process of creating this project?

When time is on our side leading up to an event, we try to prepare as much of the code, design, and data ahead of time. For the data, I sourced as many datasets as I could that were broken down by electorate (most of these came from Australia's Bureau of Statistics). The design was done by my colleague Ben Spraggon.

The ABC's engineering team provided an API with the live results that we were able to integrate with ahead of time as well. For the code, I built a generic—and configurable—scatterplot component using Svelte and D3. This component was probably the simplest part of the project to build, but it's the only visible part—an indication that choosing the right data and building the flexibility into your visualization are key to telling a compelling story.

Finally, I built what we call a "builder" interface (http://mng.bz/v8xq) that let us configure the state of the chart, that is, which datasets to use, labels for the axes, toggles for the trendline, and coloring electorates by winning party, on the night without touching the code—these configurations can then be dropped into the story to configure the states of the chart.

I love how the scrollytelling format of this article makes it easy to follow and understand the story. The data visualizations fully support the reader's understanding. As a journalist, do you see a significant difference in your writing process for the stories with and without interactive data visualizations?

Definitely. I tend to keep the copy simple for the first draft, mainly focusing on the flow and ordering of the visuals. Then, once the charts are in the right order and the transitions between them are working well, I fill in the details. This means actually telling the story in the data. The last stage is fine-tuning the pacing and prose. When using a chart that's tricky to interpret for a general audience, it's so important to hold their hand through it. Quite a lot of this story is actually just an explanation of how to read a scatterplot, which was necessary to unlock all the fascinating patterns that turned up in the data.

How do you manage working for a news organization where things are by definition fast-paced, along with the creation of interactive stories, which can sometimes take time to produce?

Our team is lucky enough to be given the time to prepare for major events like elections, so most of the design, coding, and data collection are done ahead of the night. High-quality data visualization takes time, and it shows if you rush it. This is seen as a bit of a crime in some parts (I used to think this!), but I often copy and paste entire components from old projects to use as a base, then tweak from there. By the time you parametrize every aspect of a chart for packing up into a reusable component, you lose many of the benefits of coding it yourself.

What types of projects are you hoping to work on in the near future?

Lately, I've been looking for ways to blend data visualization and more feature-style stories. These two styles of communication are complementary, and I think there's real power in adding the weight of numbers and data to contextualize human stories.

Summary

- SVG and Canvas are two technologies used for drawing in web browsers. While SVG is vectorial, Canvas produces raster images from JavaScript commands.
- We mainly opt for Canvas for performance reasons when our visualizations contain more than a thousand elements, complex animations, and/or complex color gradients.
- The Canvas rendering context exposes multiple properties and methods for drawing on the surface of the canvas element.
- We're not bound to using solely SVG or Canvas. With the mixed-mode rendering approach, we superpose SVG and canvas elements to create the desired effect while enjoying the best of each option.
- While it's possible to attach events directly onto SVG elements, the drawings rendered by Canvas can't be accessed in the DOM.
- To allow the user to interact with data visualizations rendered in Canvas, we need to use different strategies. One of them consists of applying unique colors to a hidden canvas element and associating those colors with data. Then the `getImageData()` method from the Canvas API allows us to retrieve those colors and the data associated with them.

appendix A
Setting up a local development environment

A.1 *Visual Studio Code*

If you don't have Visual Studio Code (VS Code) already installed on your computer, follow these instructions:

1. Go to https://code.visualstudio.com/Download.
2. Select the version corresponding to your operating system (Windows, Linux, or Mac), and download the installer.

Windows

1. If you downloaded VS Code for Windows, run the installer, and follow the instructions.
2. Once the VS Code installation is complete, select the Launch Visual Studio Code option, and click the Finish button.

Mac OS

1. If you're working with the Mac version, locate and double-click the downloaded zip file to expand it.
2. Drag the expanded file, named `Visual Studio Code.app`, to your `Applications` folder.
3. Double-click on the application icon to open VS Code.

Linux

1. If you downloaded VS Code for Linux, your installation strategy will depend on your operating system. Go to https://code.visualstudio.com/docs/setup/linux to find detailed instructions.
2. Once you're done, open VS Code.

A.2   Installing and using the Live Server extension

VS Code offers a large number of extensions that you can browse and install directly from the code editor's window. One of these extensions, *Live Server*, allows you to launch a local web server with the click of a button. It also has an auto-reload feature, which is pretty neat. Follow these steps to install Live Server:

1   In VS Code, locate the Extensions icon on the left side of the screen, as shown in figure A.1.

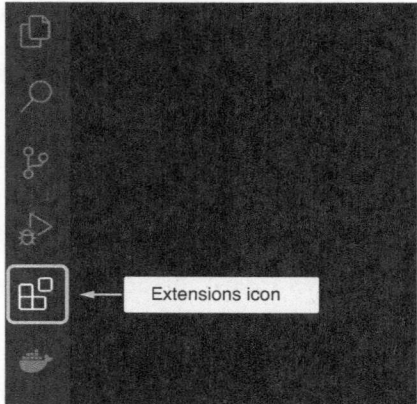

Figure A.1   Finding the Extensions icon in VS Code's interface

2   Click on the icon to open the Extensions search bar.
3   In the search bar, enter `live server`.
4   The Live Server extension will likely appear as the first result, as in figure A.2. Select it to open the extension's details page.

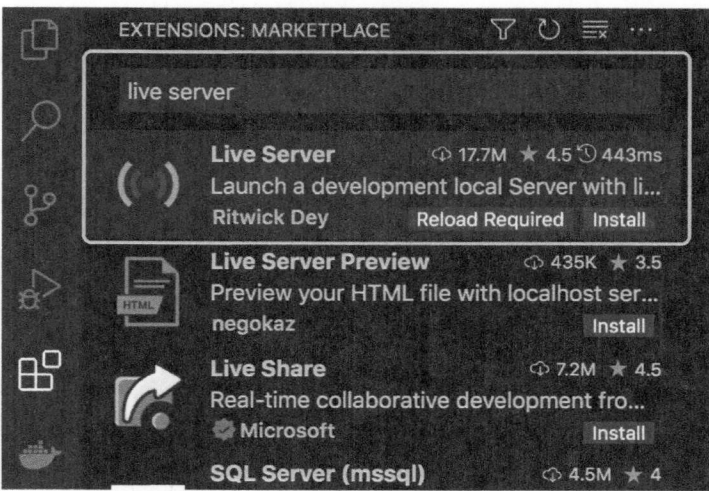

Figure A.2 Searching for the Live Server extension

5 On the details page, click the Install button shown in figure A.3.

Figure A.3   Installing the Live Server extension from its detail page

6 Reload VS Code. Quit the application, and relaunch it.
7 Open any web project in VS Code. Here we use the start folder of chapters 2's coding files (http://mng.bz/Xqjv):
  – To do so, open a VS Code window, go to File > Open in the menu bar, and browse to the start folder's location. If you're working on a Mac, you can also locate the folder with Finder and drag it onto the VS Code icon.
8 Whenever the Live Server extension detects that a web project is available, the Go Live option becomes available in the status bar at the bottom of the VS Code window, as in figure A.4. Click on it to start a local web server.

Figure A.4   Click on the Go Live button to start a local web server.

9 The project automatically opens as a new tab in your default browser. For now, it's a simple white page containing the title "You are about to start working with D3!", as in figure A.5. If a new browser tab doesn't open automatically, see step 10.

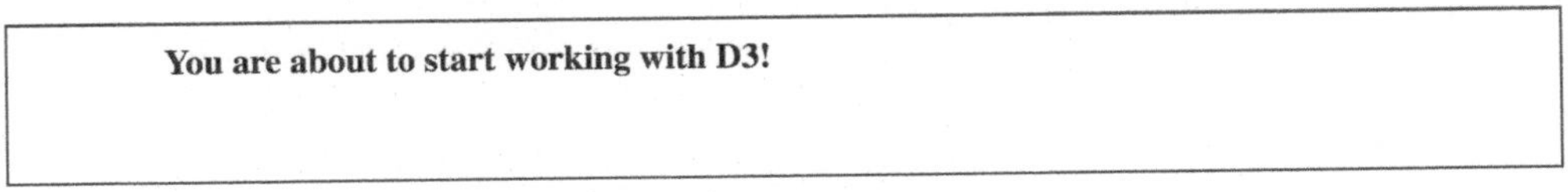

You are about to start working with D3!

Figure A.5   Your project will automatically open as a new tab in your default browser.

10 In the status bar, note that the Go Live button has been replaced by the port on which the project is running, like Port: 5500 in figure A.6. You can open the

project in the browser of your choice by entering `localhost:port_number` (e.g., `localhost:5500`) in the URL bar.

Figure A.6   The port on which the project is running is displayed in the status bar. Click on it to stop the web server.

11   To test the auto-reload feature, change the text of the `h1` title in the `index.html` file, and save the project. It will automatically reload the page and show your changes.

12   When you're done working on a project, you can stop the server by clicking on the Port number in the status bar.

appendix B
Selecting a scale

This appendix aims at helping you select the right D3 scales for your data visualization projects. For further information, refer to the documentation of the d3-scale module (https://d3js.org/d3-scale).

Scales are simply functions. The values they accept as an input are part of what we call the *domain* (the spectrum of possible input values from the data), while the values they return as an output are part of the *range* (the spectrum of possible output values). The domain and the range can be made of continuous or discrete values. *Continuous* values can exist anywhere within a predetermined spectrum, such as a floating-point number between 0 and 100 or a date between June 2020 and January 2021. On the other hand, *discrete* values have a predetermined set of values, for instance, a collection of t-shirts available in the sizes XS, S, M, L, and XL or a group of colors such as blue, green, yellow, and red.

There are four scale families, introduced in chapter 3. The difference between them is the type of values (continuous or discrete) they accept as input and output. To get started, pick a family from the following list, and go to the indicated section:

- Continuous input, continuous output: section B.1
- Continuous input, discrete output: section B.2
- Discrete input, continuous output: section B.3
- Discrete input, discrete output: section B.4

B.1 Continuous input, continuous output

The first family of scales can be subdivided into three categories: continuous, sequential, and diverging scales. The continuous category covers most of our scale needs, while the sequential and diverging scales are mostly used to map values over a continuous color spectrum.

The scales from this family provide four types of transformation: linear, power, logarithmic, and symlog. With *linear transformations,* the output is linearly proportional to the input, as shown in figure B.1.

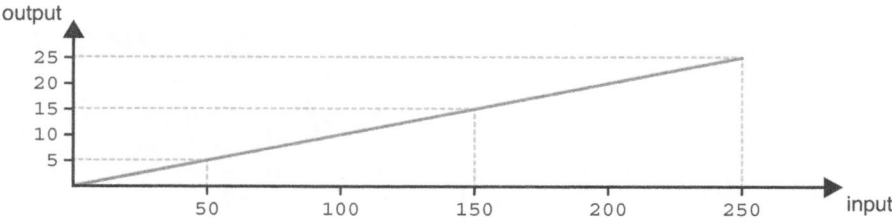

Figure B.1   With a linear transformation, the output is linearly proportional to the input.

With *power transformations,* an exponential transform is applied to the input to compute the output. As you can see in figure B.2, the greater the exponential, the steeper the slope.

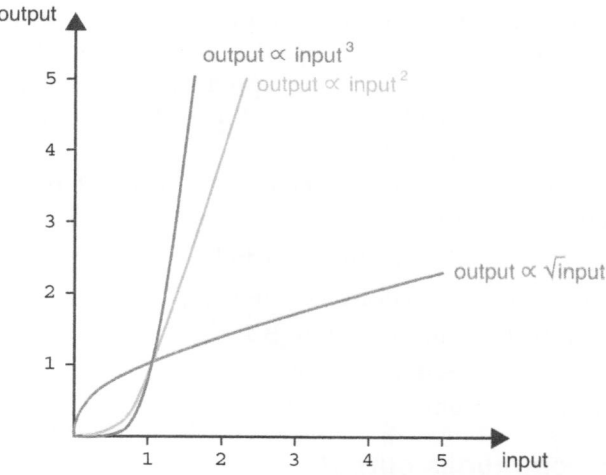

Figure B.2   With power scales, an exponential transform is applied to the input to compute the output.

The *logarithmic transformation* allows you to display several orders of magnitude in the same visualization. When working with such transformations, it's important to remember that the log of zero is undefined, so 0 cannot be included in the domain, as shown in figure B.3.

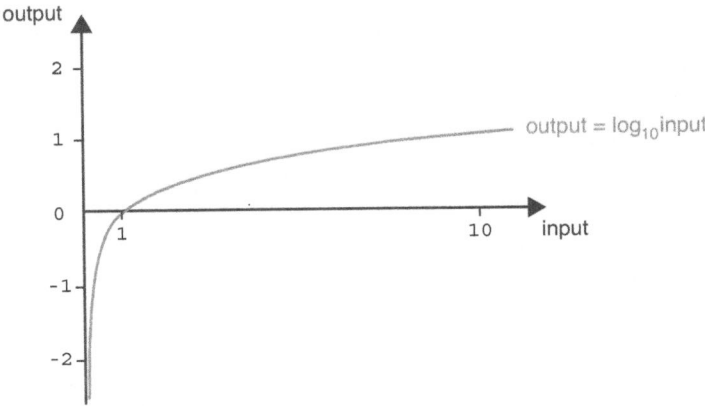

Figure B.3   Logarithmic transformation allows you to visualize several orders of magnitude together.

The symlog transformation is a by-symmetric logarithmic transformation that can include the value 0, as shown in figure B.4.

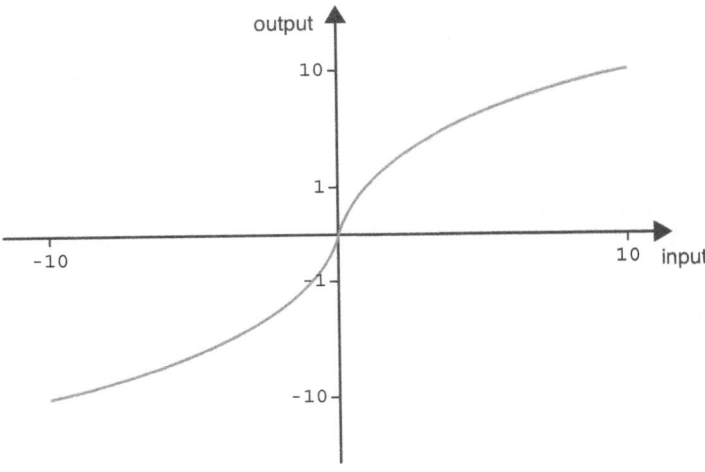

Figure B.4   Contrary to the logarithmic transformation, symlog functions are definite at 0.

B.1.1   Continuous scales

With continuous scales, both the domain and the range are expressed as an array of two values: the minimum and the maximum.

LINEAR SCALE

The value returned by a linear scale is linearly proportional to the input, as illustrated in figure B.5. If not clamped, linear scales can extrapolate values outside of the declared domain and range.

Method: `d3.scaleLinear()`
Transformation: Linear
Example of use: Students' grades

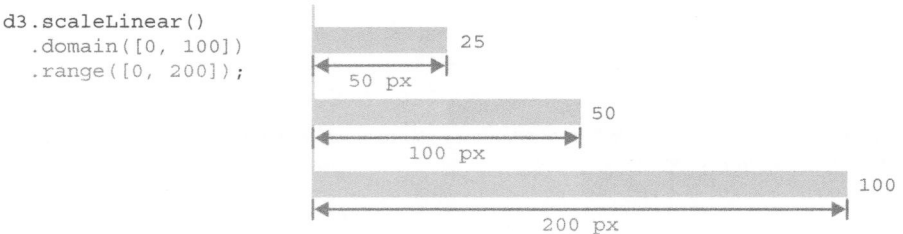

```
d3.scaleLinear()
  .domain([0, 100])
  .range([0, 200]);
```

Figure B.5   The linear scale is probably the most used of all D3 scales because it preserves proportional differences.

TIME SCALE

The domain of a time scale is expressed as an array of two JavaScript `Date()` objects (local time), as on the timeline in figure B.6, while the range is an array of two numbers. The value returned by a time scale is linearly proportional to the input.

Method: `d3.scaleTime()`
Transformation: Linear
Example of use: Timeline of events

```
d3.scaleTime()
  .domain([new Date(2023, 5, 1), new Date(2023, 8, 12)])
  .range([0, 200]);
```

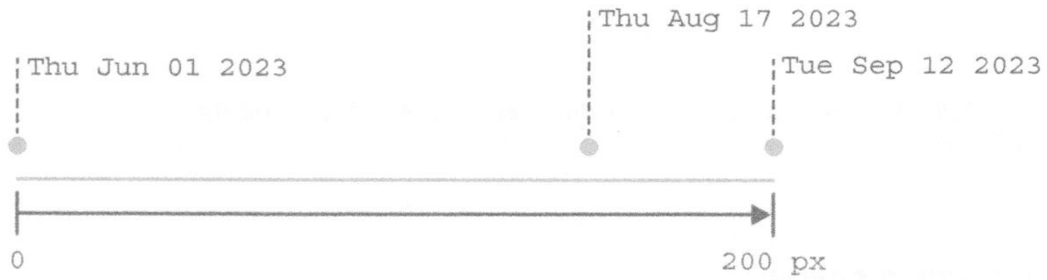

Figure B.6   The time scale accepts a `Date()` object as an input and returns the corresponding numerical value.

UTC SCALE

The UTC scale is like the time scale, except that the time is expressed in Coordinated Universal Time (UTC), the number of milliseconds since January 1, 1970, 00:00:00 UTC, rather than local time, as in the timeline in figure B.7. The UTC scale is used to avoid confusion about time zones or daylight savings time. We can use the JavaScript `Date.UTC()` method to handle UTC date values.

Method: `d3.scaleUtc()`

Transformation: Linear

Example of use: Weather forecast

```
const utcDate1 =  new Date(Date.UTC(2023, 5, 1, 11, 45, 5));
const utcDate2 =  new Date(Date.UTC(2023, 8, 12, 11, 45, 5));
d3.scaleUtc()
  .domain([utcDate1, utcDate2])
  .range([0, 200]);
```

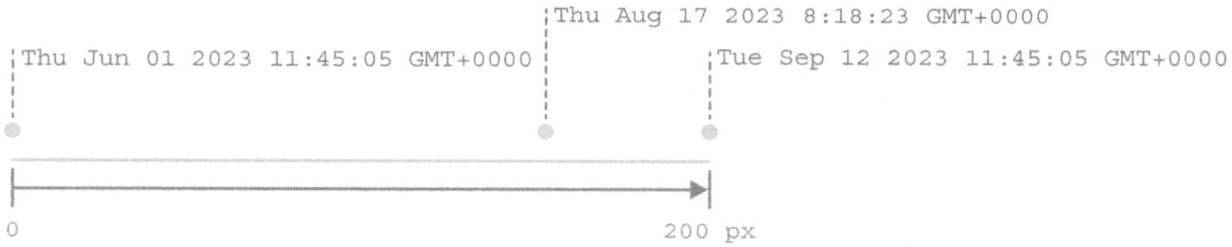

Figure B.7   The UTC scale accepts a `Date.UTC()` object as an input and returns the corresponding numerical value.

IDENTITY SCALE

An identity scale is a particular case of linear scale where the domain and the range are identical, as illustrated in figure B.8.

Method: `d3.scaleIdentity()`

Transformation: Linear

Example of use: Occasionally useful when working with pixel coordinates in combination with the `d3.zoom()` and `d3.brush` methods

```
d3.scaleIdentity()
  .domain([0, 1])
  .range([0, 1]);
```

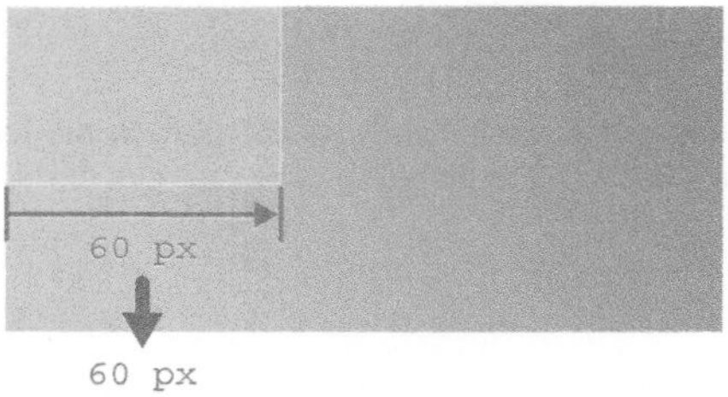

Figure B.8   The identity scale is based on the mathematical identity function, which always returns the same value that was used as its argument.

POWER SCALE

The power scale applies an exponent to the input before returning the output, as shown in figure B.9. If the exponent isn't specified, it defaults to 1, which is the equivalent of a linear scale.

Method: `d3.scalePow().exponent()`

Transformation: Power

Example of use: Spread of an infectious disease

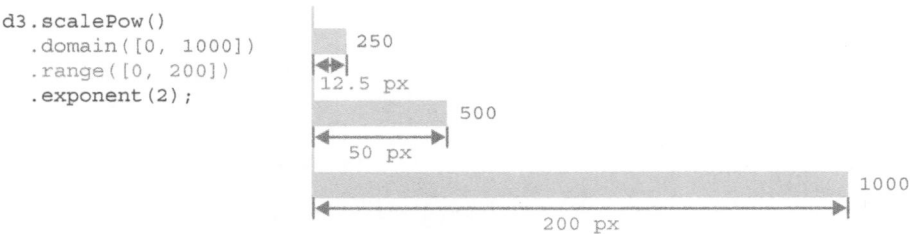

```
d3.scalePow()
    .domain([0, 1000])
    .range([0, 200])
    .exponent(2);
```

Figure B.9　The power scale calculates the output by applying an exponent to the input.

SQUARE ROOT SCALE

The square root scale is a special case of the power scale, where the exponent is always equal to 0.5. This scale is especially useful for visualizing data with the radius of a circle, as shown in figure B.10.

Method: `d3.scaleSqrt()`

Transformation: Power

Example of use: Radius of a circle

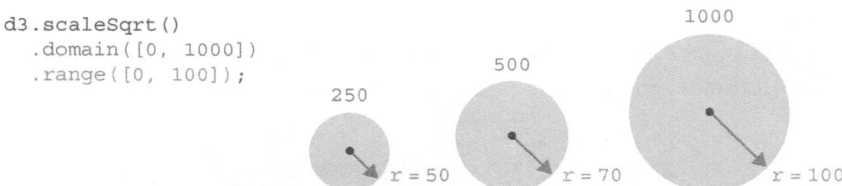

```
d3.scaleSqrt()
    .domain([0, 1000])
    .range([0, 100]);
```

Figure B.10　The square root scale is handy for calculating the radius of circles for which the area is proportional to the domain.

RADIAL SCALE

Contrarily to the power scale, the range is squared in a radial scale so that the input is proportional to the squared output. This scale is useful to calculate the inner and outer radii in radial charts, as illustrated in figure B.11.

Method: d3.scaleRadial()

Transformation: Power

Example of use: Inner and outer radius in radial charts

```
d3.scaleRadial()
  .domain([0, 1000])
  .range([100, 400]);
```

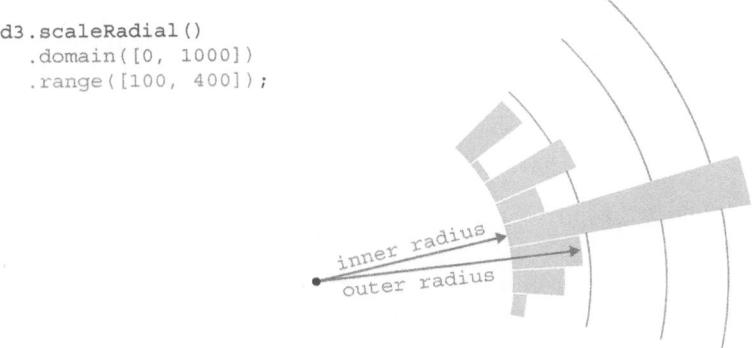

Figure B.11   **The radial scale is mainly used to calculate the inner and outer radii of radial charts.**

LOG SCALE

In a log scale, a logarithmic transform is applied to the input to compute the output. Such a scale allows visualizing several orders of magnitude within the same chart, as shown in figure B.12. The domain must be strictly positive or strictly negative because the log of zero doesn't exist ($\log(0) = -\infty$).

Method: d3.scaleLog()

Transformation: Logarithmic

Example of use: Display several orders of magnitude in the same visualization

```
d3.scaleLog()
  .domain([1, 10M])
  .range([0, 500]);
```

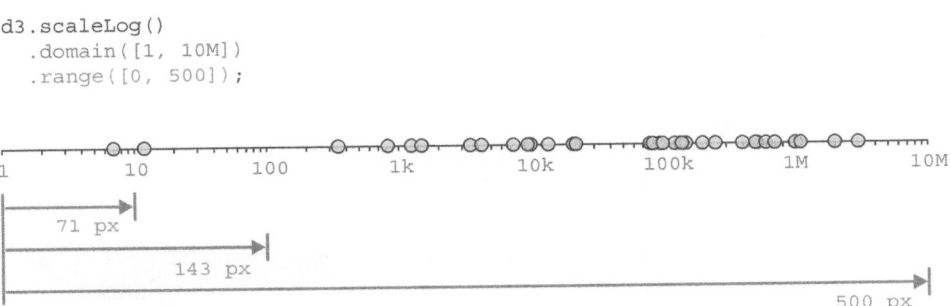

Figure B.12   **With the logarithmic scale, we can display several orders of magnitude in the same visualization.**

SYMLOG SCALE

The symlog scale offers a by-symmetric logarithmic transformation (with negative and positive values), as shown in figure B.13. The domain can include 0.

Method: `d3.scaleSymlog()`

Transformation: Symlog

Example of use: As suggested by the D3 documentation, can be applied to a representation of time where the days around now are much denser than the past and future

```
d3.scaleSymlog()
  .domain([-13.8B, 5B])
  .range([0, 500]);
```

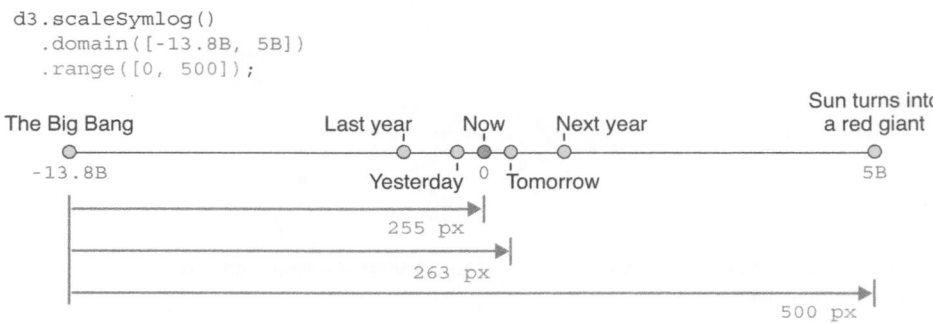

Figure B.13   The symlog scale creates a by-symmetric transformation where an input of 0 is allowed.

B.1.2   *Sequential scales*

The output of sequential scales is returned by an interpolator function. They are typically used to map a continuous input onto a continuous color range.

SEQUENTIAL SCALE

The output of a sequential scale is typically expressed by a sequential color scheme, where the color variation is linearly proportional to the input value, as shown in figure B.14.

Method: `d3.scaleSequential()`

Transformation: Linear

Example of use: Grades expressed as color

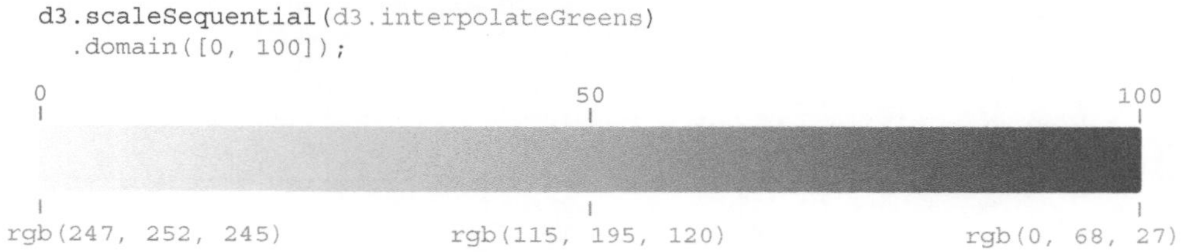

```
d3.scaleSequential(d3.interpolateGreens)
  .domain([0, 100]);
```

0   50   100

rgb(247, 252, 245)   rgb(115, 195, 120)   rgb(0, 68, 27)

Figure B.14   The sequential scale can map data over a linear color spectrum.

SEQUENTIAL POWER SCALE

A sequential power scale returns the value from an interpolator function while applying an exponential transform, analogous to the power scale. You can see the output in figure B.15.

Method: `d3.scaleSequentialPow().exponent()`

Transformation: Power

Example of use: Spread of an infectious disease expressed as color

```
d3.scaleSequentialPow(d3.interpolateGreens)
  .domain([0, 100])
  .exponent(2);
```

Figure B.15 The sequential power scale applies an exponential transformation to the input.

SEQUENTIAL SQUARE ROOT SCALE

The sequential square root scale is a special case of the sequential power scale where an exponent of 0.5 is applied as a transformation, analogous to a square root scale, as shown in figure B.16.

Method: `d3.scaleSequentialSqrt()`

Transformation: Power

Example of use: Expressing the percentage of return as a function of the risk in finance

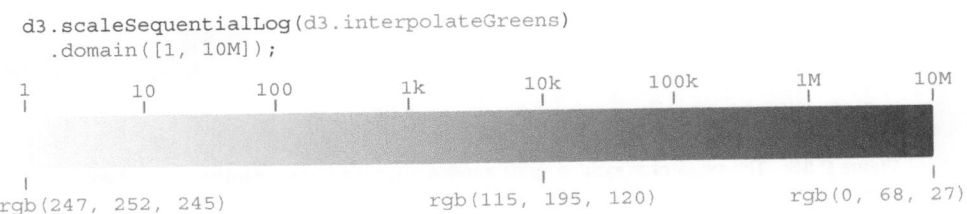

```
d3.scaleSequentialLog(d3.interpolateGreens)
  .domain([1, 10M]);
```

Figure B.16 The sequential square root scale is a special case of the sequential power scale with an exponent of 0.5.

SEQUENTIAL LOG SCALE

The sequential log scale applies a logarithmic transformation to the input and returns the corresponding value from an interpolator function, as shown in figure B.17. The domain must be strictly positive or strictly negative because the log of zero doesn't exist ($\log(0)$ = -∞).

Method: d3.scaleSequentialLog()

Transformation: Logarithmic

Example of use: Several orders of magnitude expressed as color

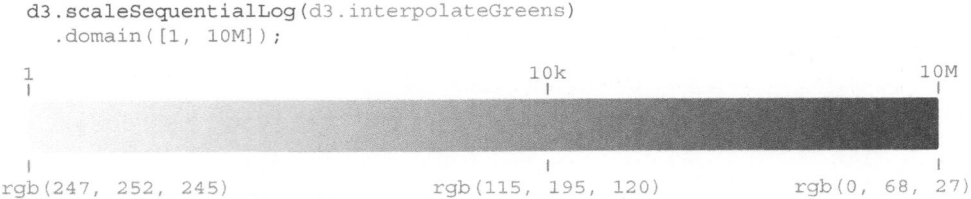

Figure B.17   **The sequential log scale applies a logarithmic transformation to the input.**

SEQUENTIAL SYMLOG SCALE

The sequential symlog scale offers a by-symmetric logarithmic transformation (with negative and positive values), as shown in figure B.18. The domain can include 0.

Method: d3.scaleSequentialSymlog()

Transformation: Symlog

Example of use: As suggested by the D3 documentation, can be applied to a representation of time where the days around now are much denser than the past and future

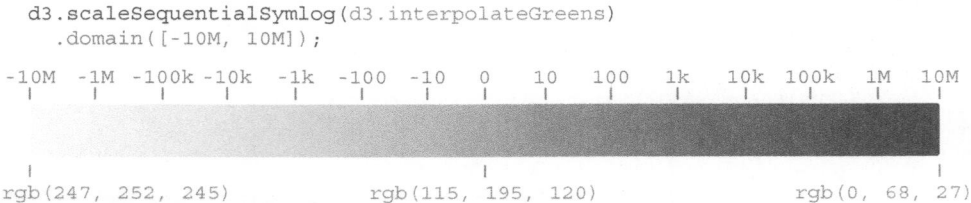

Figure B.18   **The sequential symlog scale applies a symlog transformation to the input, which gives more emphasis to the values in the center.**

B.1.3   *Diverging scales*

Like sequential scales, the output of diverging scales is returned by an interpolator function. The domain of diverging scales contains exactly three values (minimum, neutral, and maximum). Their output returns values going in opposite directions, often colors.

DIVERGING SCALE

The output of a diverging scale is typically expressed by a diverging color scheme, where the color changes linearly between three values, as shown in figure B.19.

    Method: `d3.scaleDiverging()`

    Transformation: Linear

    Example of use: Global temperature trends in Celsius

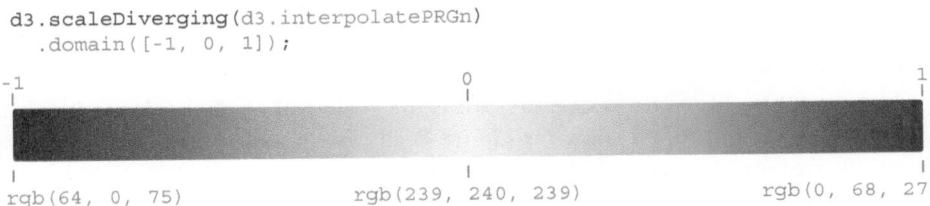

Figure B.19 **The diverging color scale returns a continuous color scheme going in two opposite directions.**

DIVERGING POWER SCALE

The diverging power scale is like the diverging scale but applies an exponent to the input, as shown in figure B.20.

    Method: `d3.scaleDivergingPow().exponent()`

    Transformation: Power

    Example of use: Spread of an infectious disease expressed as color

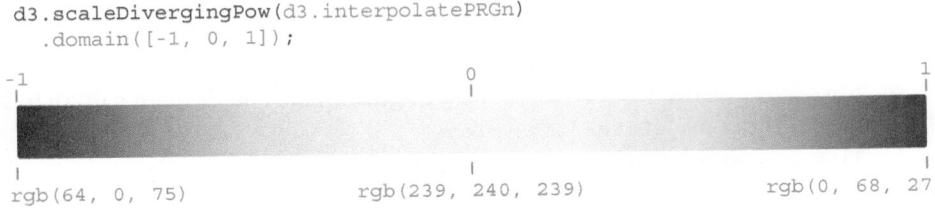

Figure B.20 **The diverging power scale applies an exponent to the input.**

DIVERGING SQUARE ROOT SCALE

The diverging square root scale is like the diverging scale but with an exponent of 0.5, as shown in figure B.21.

    Method: `d3.scaleDivergingSqrt()`

    Transformation: Power

    Example of use: Expressing the percentage of return as a function of the risk in finance

```
d3.scaleDivergingSqrt(d3.interpolatePRGn)
  .domain([-1, 0, 1]);
```

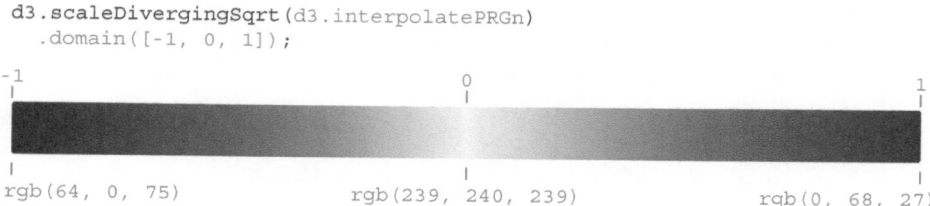

Figure B.21   **The diverging square root scale applies an exponent of 0.5 to the input.**

DIVERGING LOG SCALE

The diverging log scale is like the diverging scale but applies a logarithmic transformation to the input. As shown in figure B.22, the domain must be strictly positive or strictly negative because the log of zero doesn't exist ($\log(0) = -\infty$).

Method: d3.scaleDivergingLog()

Transformation: Logarithmic

Example of use: Several orders of magnitude expressed as color

```
d3.scaleDivergingLog(d3.interpolatePRGn)
  .domain([1, 100k, 10M]);
```

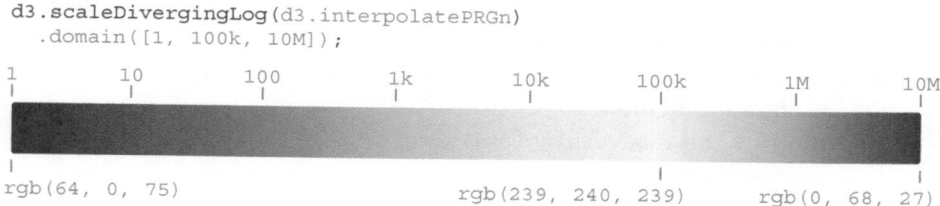

Figure B.22   **The diverging log scale applies a logarithmic transformation to the input.**

DIVERGING SYMLOG SCALE

The diverging symlog scale offers a by-symmetric logarithmic transformation (with negative and positive values), as shown in figure B.23. The domain can include 0.

Method: d3.scaleDivergingSymlog()

Transformation: Symlog

Example of use: As suggested by the D3 documentation, can be applied to a representation of time where the days around now are much denser than the past and future

```
d3.scaleDivergingSymlog(d3.interpolatePRGn)
  .domain([-10M, 0, 10M]);
```

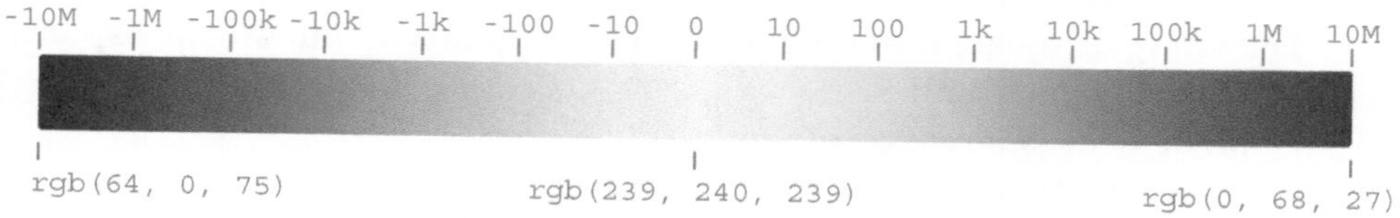

Figure B.23   **The diverging symlog scale applies a symlog transformation to the input, which gives more emphasis to the values in the center.**

B.2 Continuous input, discrete output

The second family of scales includes scales with a continuous domain and a discrete range.

QUANTIZE SCALE

The input domain of a quantize scale is divided into regular intervals corresponding to the number of discrete elements in the range, as shown in figure B.24.

Method: `d3.scaleQuantize()`

Example of use: Separate values into categories

```
d3.scaleQuantize()
  .domain([0, 100])
  .range(["yellow", "orange", "green", "purple"]);
```

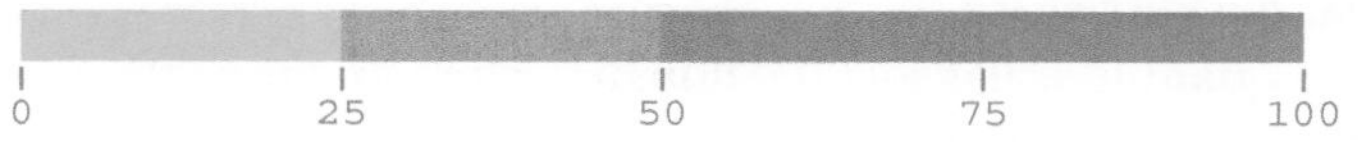

Figure B.24 The quantize scale separates continuous values into discrete categories.

THRESHOLD SCALE

The threshold scale is similar to the quantize scale except that we decide on which subset of the domain the range is mapped, as you can see in figure B.25. The domain is continuous but is specified as a sample of discrete values.

Method: `d3.scaleThreshold()`

Example of use: Choropleth map

```
d3.scaleThreshold()
  .domain([5, 7, 12])
  .range(["yellow", "orange", "green", "purple"]);
```

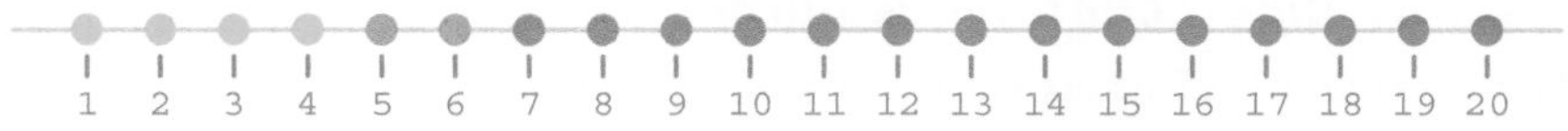

Figure B.25 The threshold scale lets us decide which subset from the domain is mapped onto which subset from the range.

QUANTILE SCALE

In the quantile scale, the range is mapped onto quantiles of the sampled input domain. Quantiles are groups containing a similar number of elements. If the range contains four colors, the domain is divided into four quantiles, and each color is attributed to a segment, as shown in figure B.26. The domain is continuous but is specified as a sample of discrete values.

Method: `d3.scaleQuantile()`

Example of use: Choropleth map

```
d3.scaleQuantile()
  .domain([1, 2, 5, 6, 8, 9, 10, 11, 12, 18, 19, 20])
  .range(["yellow", "orange", "green", "purple"]);
```

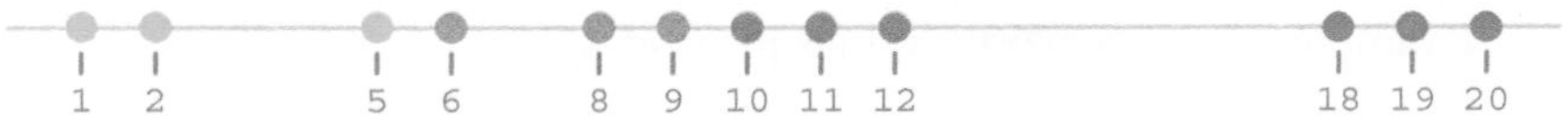

Figure B.26   The quantile scale divides a discrete sample domain into four groups containing a similar number of elements. It then accepts continuous values from that domain.

SEQUENTIAL QUANTILE SCALE

Sequential quantile scales sort the domain values and map them onto the output from an interpolation function to create specific step sizes, as shown in figure B.27.

Method: `d3.scaleSequentialQuantile()`

Example of use: Choropleth map

```
d3.scaleSequentialQuantile(d3.interpolatePRGn)
  .domain([0, 2, 5, 9]);
```

Figure B.27   The sequential quantile scale maps quantiles onto the output from an interpolation function.

B.3   *Discrete input, continuous output*

The third family of scales maps a discrete input onto a continuous output.

BAND SCALE

The band scale distributes discrete elements over a continuous range, giving each element a bandwidth based on the space available and the padding required. This scale is mostly used for bar charts, as shown in figure B.28.

Method: `d3.scaleBand()`

Example of use: Distributing the rectangles of a bar chart onto the length of an axis

```
d3.scaleBand()
  .domain(["apple", "apricot", "banana"])
  .range([0, 300])
  .padding(0.1);
```

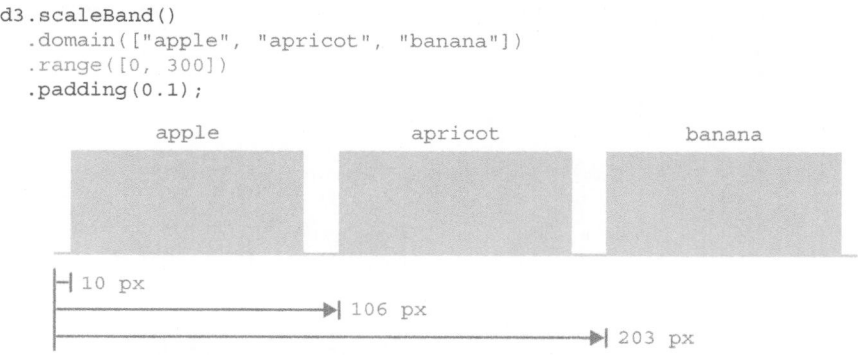

Figure B.28   The band scale is the tool of choice for distributing rectangles in a bar chart.

POINT SCALE

The point scale is similar to the band scale, but each element has a bandwidth of 0, as shown in figure B.29.

Method: `d3.scalePoint()`

Example of use: Scatterplots with a categorical dimension

```
d3.scalePoint()
  .domain(["apple", "apricot", "banana"])
  .range([0, 300]);
```

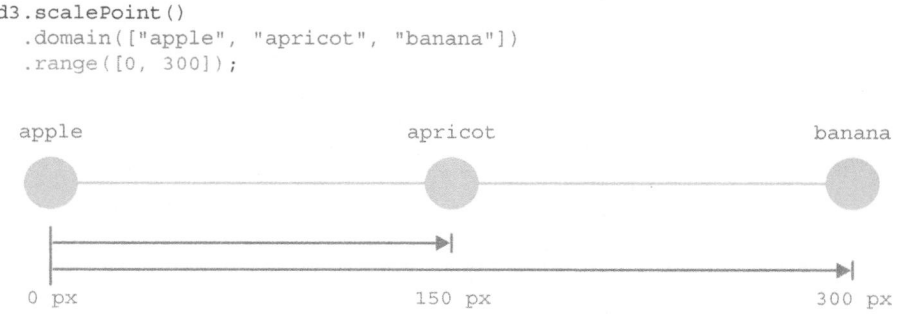

Figure B.29   The point scale behaves like the band scale, except that the bandwidth of each element is 0.

B.4   Discrete input, discrete output

The last family maps a discrete input onto a discrete output.

ORDINAL SCALE

The ordinal scale maps an array of elements from the domain onto another array from the range. As illustrated in figure B.30, the first value from the domain takes the first value from the range, the second value from the domain takes the second value from the range, and so on. If the range contains fewer values than the domain, D3 will cycle through the range values.

Method: `d3.scaleOrdinal()`

Example of use: Mapping categories onto a set of colors

```
d3.scaleOrdinal()
  .domain(["pop", "rock", "hip-hop",  "funk"])
  .range(["yellow", "orange", "green", "purple"]);
```

Figure B.30   The ordinal scale maps a discrete domain onto a discrete range.

appendix C
An overview of D3 modules

The D3 library is split into multiple modules. This appendix gives you an overview of those modules and explains when we use them. Generally, we avoid using them when combining D3 with a JavaScript framework such as React or Svelte because it can generate conflicts.

Table C.1 An overview of D3 modules

Preprocessing		Drawing a data visualization on the screen	Finishing touches	
Data preparation	Layout calculation		Interactions	Animations
d3-array	d3-chord	d3-axis*	d3-brush*	d3-ease
d3-color	d3-contour	d3-selection*	d3-dispatch*	d3-timer
d3-dsv	d3-delaunay		d3-drag*	d3-transition*
d3-fetch	d3-force		d3-zoom*	
d3-format	d3-geo			
d3-random	d3-hierarchy			
d3-time	d3-interpolate			
d3-time-format	d3-path			
	d3-polygon			
	d3-quadtree			
	d3-scale			
	d3-scale-chromatic			
	d3-shape			

* Contains methods that require access to the DOM. You might want to avoid this module if combining D3 with a JavaScript framework such as React or Svelte. Refer to chapter 8 for explanations and workarounds.

591

appendix D
Exercise solutions

D.1   Solutions chapter 1

D.1.1   Build an SVG graphic

Listing D.1   Building an SVG graphic (`index.html`)

```html
<!DOCTYPE html>
<html>
<head>
  <meta charset="UTF-8">
  <meta name="viewport" content="width=device-width, initial-scale=1.0">
  <title>SVG Exercise | D3.js in Action</title>
</head>
<body>
  <div style="width:100%; max-width:400px; margin:0 auto;">
    <svg viewBox="0 0 400 400" style="border:1px solid black;">

      <rect x="100" y="100" width="200" height="200" fill="transparent"
      ➥ stroke="black" stroke-width="5" />

      <circle cx="200" cy="200" r="100" fill="plum" />

      <line x1="100" y1="100" x2="300" y2="300" stroke="black"
      ➥ stroke-width="5" />
      <line x1="100" y1="300" x2="300" y2="100" stroke="black"
      ➥ stroke-width="5" />

      <text x="200" y="90" text-anchor="middle" style="font-size:18px;
      ➥ font-family:sans-serif">SVG is awesome!</text>

    </svg>
  </div>
</body>
</html>
```

D.2   Solutions chapter 6

D.2.1   Build a pyramid chart

Listing D.2   Building a pyramid chart (`pyramid.js`)

```
const dataWomen = data.filter(d =>
  d.gender === "Female");
const binsWomen = d3.bin()
  .value(d => d.salary)(dataWomen);

const dataMen = data.filter(d => d.gender === "Male");
const binsMen = d3.bin()
  .value(d => d.salary)(dataMen);
```

Create separate bins for women's and men's salaries.

```
const xScaleWomen = d3.scaleLinear()
  .domain([15, 0])
  .range([0, innerWidth/2]);
const xScaleMen = d3.scaleLinear()
  .domain([0, 15])
  .range([innerWidth/2, innerWidth]);
```

Initialize two linear scales for the horizontal axis: one for women extending along the first half of the x-axis and one for men along the second half.

```
const minSalary = binsWomen[0].x0;
const maxSalary = binsWomen[binsWomen.length - 1].x1;
const yScale = d3.scaleLinear()
  .domain([minSalary, maxSalary])
  .range([innerHeight, 0]);
```

Initialize a linear scale for the vertical axis, spreading from 0 to the maximum salary.

```
const pyramidContainer = innerChart
  .append("g")
    .attr("stroke", white)
    .attr("stroke-width", 2);
```

Append an SVG group to the inner chart. Save this selection in a constant named pyramidContainer, and set its stroke and stroke-width attributes. The children of this group will inherit those attributes.

```
pyramidContainer
  .selectAll(".bar-women")
  .data(binsWomen)
  .join("rect")
    .attr("class", "bar-women")
    .attr("x", d => xScaleWomen(d.length / data.length
      * 100))
    .attr("y", d => yScale(d.x1))
    .attr("width", d => innerWidth/2 -
      xScaleWomen(d.length / data.length * 100))
    .attr("height", d => yScale(d.x0) - yScale(d.x1))
    .attr("fill", womenColor);

pyramidContainer
  .selectAll("bar-men")
  .data(binsMen)
  .join("rect")
    .attr("class", "bar-men")
    .attr("x", innerWidth/2)
    .attr("y", d => yScale(d.x1))
    .attr("width", d => xScaleMen(d.length /
      data.length * 100) - innerWidth/2)
    .attr("height", d => yScale(d.x0) - yScale(d.x1))
    .attr("fill", menColor);
```

Using the data-binding pattern, append SVG rectangles for the women's and men's bars. Use the scales to calculate the bars' position and length, the latter being proportional to the percentage of data points found in the corresponding bin compared to the total number of data points.

```
const bottomAxisFemales = d3.axisBottom(xScaleWomen)
  .tickValues([15, 10, 5, 0])
  .tickSizeOuter(0);
innerChart
  .append("g")
    .attr("transform", `translate(0, ${innerHeight})`)
    .call(bottomAxisFemales);
const bottomAxisMales = d3.axisBottom(xScaleMen)
  .tickValues([5, 10, 15])
  .tickSizeOuter(0);
innerChart
  .append("g")
    .attr("transform", `translate(0, ${innerHeight})`)
    .call(bottomAxisMales);
svg
  .append("text")
    .text("Percent")
    .attr("text-anchor", "middle")
    .attr("x", margin.left + innerWidth/2)
    .attr("y", height - 3);
```

To draw the x-axis, declare separate bottom-axis generators for women and men, and pass the corresponding scales as a reference. You can define the ticks displayed on each axis with the accessor function tickValues(). Append a label to the x-axis with the text "Percent".

```
const leftAxis = d3.axisLeft(yScale);
innerChart
  .append("g")
    .call(leftAxis);
svg
  .append("text")
    .text("Yearly salary (USD)")
    .attr("x", 0)
    .attr("y", 20);
```

Declare a left-axis generator, and pass yScale as a reference. Append a label to the axis with the text "Yearly salary (USD)".

D.2.2   Append axes to the violin charts

Listing D.3   Appending the axes to the violin charts (`violins.js`)

```
const bottomAxis = d3.axisBottom(xScale)
  .tickSizeOuter(0);
innerChart
  .append("g")
    .attr("transform", `translate(0, ${innerHeight})`)
    .call(bottomAxis);
```

Declare a bottom-axis generator, and pass xScale as a reference. Append this axis to the inner chart.

```
const leftAxis = d3.axisLeft(yScale);
innerChart
  .append("g")
    .call(leftAxis);
svg
  .append("text")
    .text("Yearly salary (USD)")
    .attr("x", 0)
    .attr("y", 20);
```

Declare a left-axis generator, and pass yScale as a reference. Append this axis to the inner chart and a label with the text "Yearly salary (USD)".

D.2.3 Add the interquartile ranges and the mean values to the violin plots

Listing D.4 Interquartile ranges and mean values (`violins.js`)

```
roles.forEach(role => {

  ...

  const width = 8;
  roleContainer
    .append("rect")
      .attr("x", xScale(role.id) - width/2)
      .attr("y", yScale(role.quartiles[2]))
      .attr("width", width)
      .attr("height", yScale(role.quartiles[0]) -
      ➥ yScale(role.quartiles[2]))
      .attr("rx", 4)
      .attr("ry", 4)
      .attr("fill", gray);

  roleContainer
    .append("circle")
      .attr("cx", d => xScale(role.id))
      .attr("cy", d => yScale(role.mean))
      .attr("r", 3)
      .attr("fill", white);

};
```

Append a rectangle element for each role. The rectangle is centered with the role's centerline and extends vertically from the first to the third quartile. To round the rectangle's corners, we set the attributes rx and ry.

Append a circle element for each role. The circle is centered with the role's centerline and is aligned vertically with the position of the mean value.

D.3 Solutions chapter 7

D.3.1 Create the axis and append the circles to the scatterplot

Listing D.5 Drawing a scatterplot (`scatterplot.js`)

```
const bottomAxisGenerator = d3.axisBottom(xScale);
innerChart
  .append("g")
    .attr("class", "axis-x")
    .attr("transform", `translate(0, ${innerHeight})`)
    .call(bottomAxisGenerator);
const leftAxisGenerator = d3.axisLeft(yScale);
innerChart
  .append("g")
    .attr("class", "axis-y")
    .call(leftAxisGenerator);

svg
  .append("text")
    .text("Estimated population")
    .attr("text-anchor", "end")
    .attr("x", margin.left + innerWidth + 20)
    .attr("y", height - 3)
    .style("font-size", "18px");
```

Declare the bottom axis generator, and append the axis to the inner chart.

Declare the left axis generator, and append the axis to the inner chart.

Append a label for each axis.

```
svg
  .append("text")
    .text("Max size (m)")
    .attr("dominant-baseline", "hanging")
    .attr("y", 15)
    .style("font-size", "18px");
innerChart
  .selectAll(".cetacean")
  .data(data)
  .join("circle")
    .attr("class", "cetacean")
    .attr("cx", d => xScale(
      d.global_population_estimate))
    .attr("cy", d => yScale(d.max_size_m))
    .attr("r", d => rScale(d.max_weight_t))
    .attr("fill", d => colorScale(d.status))
    .attr('fill-opacity', 0.6)
    .attr("stroke", d => colorScale(d.status))
    .attr("stroke-width", 2);
```

Append a label for each axis.

Use the data-binding pattern to append one circle for each cetacean in the dataset.

Set the circles' cx, cy, r, and fill attributes using the logarithmic, linear, radial, and color scales declared earlier. Set the opacity of the fill attribute to 60%, and add a stroke of 2 px to the circles.

D.3.2 Create a tooltip

Listing D.6   Adding event listeners (scatterplot.js)

```
innerChart
  .selectAll(".cetacean")
  .data(data)
  .join("circle")
    .attr("class", "cetacean")
    ...
    .on("mouseenter", showTooltip)
    .on("mouseleave", hideTooltip);
```

Add an event listener for when the mouse enters a circle. When that happens, call the function showTooltip (this function is declared in listing D.7).

Add an event listener for when the mouse leaves a circle. When that happens, call the function showTooltip (this function is declared in listing D.7).

Listing D.7   Creating and handling the tooltip (interactions.js)

```
const appendTooltip = () => {
  const tooltip = innerChart
    .append("text")
      .attr("class", "tooltip")
      .attr("text-anchor", "middle")
      .attr("fill", "#192e4d")
      .style("opacity", 0);
};

const showTooltip = (e, d) => {
  const cx = e.target.getAttribute("cx");
  const cy = e.target.getAttribute("cy");
  const r = e.target.getAttribute("r");

  d3.select(".tooltip")
    .attr("x", cx)
    .attr("y", cy - r - 10)
    .text(d.common_name)
```

Append an SVG text element to the inner chart that will serve as a tooltip. Give it a class name of "tooltip" so that you can easily select it later. Set its opacity to 0.

When the mouse enters a circle, get the position and radius of the circle from its attributes. Set the tooltip's text based on the datum attached to the circle. Position the tooltip above the circle, and transition its opacity to 100%.

```
        .transition()
        .style("opacity", 1);
};
```

△ **When the mouse enters a circle, get the position and radius of the circle from its attributes. Set the tooltip's text based on the datum attached to the circle. Position the tooltip above the circle, and transition its opacity to 100%.**

```
const hideTooltip = (e, d) => {
  d3.select(".tooltip")
    .attr("y", -500)
    .style("opacity", 0);
};
```

When the mouse leaves the tooltip, translate it away from the chart, and set its opacity to 0.

Listing D.8 Handling the entering selection (`interactions.js`)

```
const handleClickOnFilter = (data) => {

  ...

  d3.selectAll(".filter")
    .on("click", (e, datum) => {
      if (!datum.isActive) {

        innerChart
          .selectAll("circle")
          .data(updatedData, d => d.uid)
          .join(
            enter => enter
              .append("circle")
              ...
              .on("mouseenter", showTooltip)  ⟵
              .on("mouseleave", hideTooltip)  ⟵
              ...,
            update => update,
            exit => exit
              ...
          )

      }
    });
};
```

Add an event listener for when the mouse enters a circle from the enter selection. When that happens, call the function showTooltip (this function is declared in listing D.7).

Add an event listener for when the mouse leaves a circle from the enter selection. When that happens, call the function showTooltip (this function is declared in listing D.7).

D.4   Solutions chapter 8

D.4.1   Bar chart

Listing D.9 Passing the data and color scale (`Chart.js`)

```
const Charts = props => {
  ...

  return (
    <h1>Front-end Frameworks</h1>
    <div className='row'>
      ...
      <div className='row'>
```

```
        ...
      <div className='col-12'>
        <BarChart
          data={props.data.experience}
          margin={margin}
          colorScale={colorScale}
        />
      </div>
    </div>
  </div>
  );
};
```

Listing D.10   Setting the rectangle's attributes (`Rectangle.js`)

```
const Rectangle = props => {
  return (
    <rect
      x={props.x}
      y={props.y}
      width={props.width}
      height={props.height}
      fill={props.fill}
    />
  )
};
```

Listing D.11   Preparing the axis of type band (`Axis.js`)

```
const AxisBandBottom = props => {
  return (
    <g className="axis" transform={`translate(0, ${props.innerHeight})`} >
      <line x1={0} y1={0} x2={props.innerWidth} y2={0} />
      {props.ticks.map(tick => (
        <text
          key={tick}
          textAnchor="end"
          alignmentBaseline="middle"
          transform={`translate(${props.scale(tick) + props.scale.bandwidth()
          ⮕ / 2}, 8) rotate(-90)`}
        >
          {tick}
        </text>
      ))}
    </g>
  );
};
```

Listing D.12   Drawing the bar chart (`BarChart.js`)

```
import * as d3 from "d3";
import Card from '../UI/Card';
import ChartContainer from '../ChartComponents/ChartContainer';
```

```
import Axis from "../ChartComponents/Axis";
import Rectangle from "../ChartComponents/Rectangle";

const BarChart = props => {
  const width = 300;
  const height = 245;
  const marginBottom = 85;
  const innerWidth = width - props.margin.left - props.margin.right;
  const innerHeight = height - props.margin.top - marginBottom;

  const awarenessData = [];
  props.data.forEach(d => {
    const awareness = {
      id: d.id,
      name: d.name,
      awareness_percentage: d.awareness[d.awareness.length- 1]
        .percentage_question
    };
    awarenessData.push(awareness);
  });
  awarenessData.sort((a, b) => b.awareness_percentage -
    a.awareness_percentage);

  const xScale = d3.scaleBand()
    .domain(awarenessData.map(d => d.name))
    .range([0, innerWidth])
    .padding(0.2);
  const yScale = d3.scaleLinear()
    .domain([0, 100])
    .range([innerHeight, 0]);

  return (
    <Card>
      <h2>Awareness</h2>
      <ChartContainer ... >
        <Axis
          type="band"
          scale={xScale}
          ticks={awarenessData.map(d => d.name)}
          innerWidth={innerWidth}
          innerHeight={innerHeight}
        />
        <Axis
          type="left"
          scale={yScale}
          innerWidth={innerWidth}
          innerHeight={innerHeight}
          label={"Awareness %"}
        />
        {awarenessData.map(framework => (
          <Rectangle
            key={`rectangle-${framework.id}`}
            x={xScale(framework.name)}
            y={yScale(framework.awareness_percentage)}
            width={xScale.bandwidth()}
```

Extract awareness data, and sort it in descending order.

Declare a band scale responsible for spreading the rectangles horizontally and a linear scale for calculating their height.

Append an axis of type "band". Pass the xScale and ticks as props.

Append an axis of type "left". Pass the yScale and a label of "Awareness %" as props.

Append a rectangle for each framework. Pass the x, y, width, height, and fill attributes as props.

```
            height={innerHeight - yScale(framework
              .awareness_percentage)}
            fill={props.colorScale(framework.id)}
        />
      ))}
    </ChartContainer>
  </Card>
 )
};
```

> △
> **Append a rectangle for each framework. Pass the x, y, width, height, and fill attributes as props.**

D.4.2   *Ranking badges*

Listing D.13   Creating the `Badge` component (`Badge.js`)

```
import Circle from "../ChartComponents/Circle";

const Badge = props => {
  return (
    <g style={{ transform: `translate(${props.
      translation[0]}px,${props.translation[1]}px)`}}>
      <Circle
        cx={0}
        cy={0}
        r={18}
        fill={"#fff"}
        stroke={props.strokeColor}
        strokeWidth={3}
      />
      <text
        textAnchor="middle"
        alignmentBaseline="middle"
        fill="#374f5e"
        style={{ fontSize: "12px", fontWeight: "bold" }}
      >
        {props.label}
      </text>
    </g>
  );
};

export default Badge;
```

> **Translate the group element using a prop that will be passed from the Rankings component.**

> **Call the Circle component and pass its attributes as props.**

> **Display a text element that receives its value as a prop.**

Listing D.14   Calling the `Badge` component (`Rankings.js`)

```
const Rankings = props => {
  ...

  return (
    <Card>
      <h2>Rankings</h2>
      <RankingFilters ... />
      <ChartContainer ... >
        ...
        {props.data.experience.map((framework, i) => (
```

```
                    <g key={`curve-${framework.id}`}>
                      <Curve ... />
                      ...
                      {framework[activeFilter].map((selection,i)
                        => (                                   <Fragment
                          key={`${framework.id}-selection-${i}`}>
                          {selection.rank &&
                            <Badge
                              translation={[xScale(selection
                              .year), yScale(selection.rank)]}
                              strokeColor={props.colorScale(framework.id)}
                              label={`${Math.round(selection.percentage_question)}%`}
                            />
                          }
                        </Fragment>
                      ))}
                    </g>
                  ))}
                </ChartContainer>
              </Card>
          )
        };
```

Append a Fragment wrapper for each item in the array corresponding to the active filter, for example, the satisfaction array.

If the rank property is not null, display a Badge component. Pass its translation, stroke color, and label as props.

D.5 Solutions chapter 9

D.5.1 Change the orientation of the bar chart on mobile

Listing D.15 Creating a horizontal bar chart (`BarChartMobile.js`)

```javascript
import * as d3 from "d3";
import Card from "../UI/Card";
import ChartContainer from "../ChartComponents/ChartContainer";
import Axis from "../ChartComponents/Axis";
import Rectangle from "../ChartComponents/Rectangle";

const BarChartMobile = props => {
  const width = 300;
  const height = 400;
  const marginRight = 38;
  const marginLeft = 95;
  const innerWidth = width - marginLeft - marginRight;
  const innerHeight = height - props.margin.top - props.margin.bottom;

  const awarenessData = [];
  props.data.forEach(d => {
    const awareness = {
      id: d.id,
      name: d.name,
      awareness_percentage: d.awareness[d.awareness.length -
      ➥ 1].percentage_question
    };
    awarenessData.push(awareness);
  });
```

```
awarenessData.sort((a, b) => b.awareness_percentage -
  a.awareness_percentage);

const xScale = d3.scaleLinear()
  .domain([0, 100])
  .range([0, innerWidth]);
const yScale = d3.scaleBand()
  .domain(awarenessData.map(d => d.name))
  .range([0, innerHeight])
  .padding(0.2);

return (
  <Card>
    <h2>Awareness</h2>
    <ChartContainer
      width={width}
      height={height}
      margin={{ top: props.margin.top, right: marginRight, bottom:
        props.margin.bottom, left: marginLeft }}
    >
      <Axis
        type="bandLeft"
        scale={yScale}
        ticks={awarenessData.map(d => d.name)}
        innerWidth={innerWidth}
        innerHeight={innerHeight}
      />
      {awarenessData.map(framework => (
        <g
          key={`rectangle-${framework.id}`}
          className="axis"
        >
          <Rectangle
            x={0}
            y={yScale(framework.name)}
            width={xScale(framework.awareness_percentage)}
            height={yScale.bandwidth()}
            fill={props.colorScale(framework.id)}
          />
          <text
            x={xScale(framework.awareness_percentage) + 5}
            y={yScale(framework.name) + yScale.bandwidth()/2}
            alignmentBaseline="middle"
            style={{ fontSize: "13px" }}
          >
            {`${Math.round(framework.awareness_percentage)}%`}
          </text>
        </g>
      ))}
    </ChartContainer>
  </Card>
);
};

export default BarChartMobile;
```

D.6   Solutions chapter 10

D.6.1   Create SVG patterns

Listing D.16   Creating a vertical bars pattern (`scatterplot.js`)

```
const verticalLinesPattern = defs
  .append("pattern")
    .attr("id", "pattern-vertical-lines")
    .attr("width", 4)
    .attr("height", 4)
    .attr("patternUnits", "userSpaceOnUse");
verticalLinesPattern
  .append("rect")
    .attr("x", 0)
    .attr("y", 0)
    .attr("width", "100%")
    .attr("height", "100%")
    .attr("fill", "#fff");
verticalLinesPattern
  .append("line")
    .attr("x1", 3)
    .attr("y1", 0)
    .attr("x2", 3)
    .attr("y2", 4)
    .attr("stroke", colorScale("VU"));
```

Append a new pattern to the defs element and set its ID to "pattern-vertical-lines". Give it a width and height of 4 px, and set its patternUnits attribute to userSpaceOnUse to ensure that its children dimensions correspond to the coordinate system of the SVG container.

Append a white rect element for the background of the tile.

Append a vertical line in the middle of the pattern container. Set its fill attribute with the color associated with the "Vulnerable" conservation status.

D.7   Solutions chapter 11

Listing D.17   Adding a section for the treemap (`index.html`)

```html
<!DOCTYPE html>
<html>
  ...
<body>
  <div class="container">

    ...

    <section>
      <h2>Treemap</h2>
      <div id="treemap"></div>
    </section>
  </div>

  <script type="module" src="./js/main.js"></script>
</body>
</html>
```

Add a section containing a div with an ID of "treemap".

Listing D.18   Drawing the treemap (`treemap.js`)

```javascript
import { treemap } from "d3-hierarchy";
import { select, selectAll } from "d3-selection";
import { colorScale } from "./scales";

export const drawTreemap = (root, leaves) => {
```

```
const width = 850;
const height = 600;

const treemapLayoutGenerator = treemap()
  .size(([width, height]))
  .paddingInner(1)
  .paddingOuter(1)
  .round(true);
treemapLayoutGenerator(root);
```

Create a treemap layout generator. Set the dimensions of the chart and the padding between the rectangles. Pass the hierarchical data (root) to the layout generator.

```
const svg = select("#treemap")
  .append("svg")
    .attr("viewBox", `0 0 ${width} ${height}`);
```

Append an SVG container to the div with an ID of "treemap".

```
const nodes = svg
  .selectAll(".node-container")
  .data(leaves)
  .join("g")
    .attr("class", "node-container")
    .attr("transform", d => `translate(${d.x0},
      ${d.y0})`);
```

Using the data-binding pattern, append an SVG group for each leaf node, and transition the group to the position indicated by the keys x0 and y0 in the data calculated by the layout generator. This step will make it easier to position the rectangles and labels together.

```
nodes
  .append("rect")
    .attr("class", "treemap-node")
    .attr("x", 0)
    .attr("y", 0)
    .attr("width", d => d.x1 - d.x0)
    .attr("height", d => d.y1 - d.y0)
    .attr("rx", 3)
    .attr("ry", 3)
    .attr("fill", d => colorScale(
      d.parent.data.parent));
```

Append a rectangle for each leaf node. Their width can be calculated by the difference between xl and x0, and their height calculated by the difference between yl and y0. Set their fill attribute with the color scale based on their language family.

```
nodes
  .append("text")
    .attr("class", d => `treemap-label day
      -${d.id.replaceAll(" ", "-")
      .replaceAll("'", "")}`)
    .attr("x", 5)
    .attr("y", 15)
    .attr("fill", "white")
    .style("font-size", "12px")
    .style("font-weight", 500)
    .text(d => d.id);
```

Append a text element for each leaf node. Set its position over the corresponding rectangle and text to the related language.

```
selectAll(".treemap-label")
  .style("opacity", d => {
    const textElement = document.querySelector(
      `.treemap-label-${d.id.replaceAll(" ", "-")
      .replaceAll("'", "")}`);
    const textWidth = textElement.getBBox().width;
    return ((d.y1 - d.y0) >= 25) && ((d.x1 - d.x0)
      >= textWidth + 10) ? 1 : 0;
  });
};
```

Optional: hide the text labels that are smaller than their corresponding rectangles.

Listing D.19 Calling `drawTreemap` (`main.js`)

```
...
import { drawTreemap } from "./treemap.js";


...

drawTreemap(root, leaves);
```

D.8 Solutions chapter 12

Listing D.20 Drawing an adjacency matrix (`matrix.js`)

```
import { select, selectAll } from "d3-selection";
import { max } from "d3-array";
import { scaleLinear } from "d3-scale";

export const drawMatrix = (nodes, edges) => {

  ...

  const innerWidth = nodes.length * (squareWidth +
    padding);
  const innerHeight = nodes.length * (squareWidth +
    padding);
  const margin = { top: 130, right: 0,
    bottom: 0, left: 130 };
  const width = innerWidth + margin.right +
    margin.left;
  const height = innerHeight + margin.top +
    margin.bottom;
```

Calculate the width and height of the matrix based on the number of nodes, their dimensions, and the padding between them.

```
  const svg = select("#matrix")
    .append("svg")
      .attr("viewBox", `0 0 ${width} ${height}`)
    .append("g")
      .attr("transform", `translate(${margin.left},
        ${margin.top})`);
```

Append an SVG container to the div with an ID of "matrix" and a group for the inner chart, per the strategy explained in chapter 4.

```
  const maxWeight = max(edges, d => d.weight);
  const opacityScale = scaleLinear()
    .domain([0, maxWeight])
    .range([0, 1]);

  svg
    .selectAll(".grid-quare")
    .data(matrix)
    .join("rect")
      .attr("class", "grid-quare")
      .attr("x", d => d.x)
      .attr("y", d => d.y)
      .attr("width", squareWidth)
      .attr("height", squareWidth)
      .attr("fill", "#364652")
      .attr("fill-opacity", d =>
        opacityScale(d.weight));
```

Append a rect element for each item in the matrix array. Set its position with the x and y keys and its fill attribute to "#364652". Calculate its fill-opacity based on the weight of the link. The maximum weight available gets an opacity of 100%.

```
const labelsContainer = svg
  .selectAll(".matrix-label")
  .data(nodes)
  .join("g")
    .attr("class", "matrix-label")
    .attr("dominant-baseline", "middle")
    .style("font-size", "13px");

labelsContainer
  .append("text")
    .attr("class", "label-top")
    .attr("x", -8)
    .attr("y", (d, i) => i * (squareWidth + padding)
      + squareWidth / 2)
    .attr("text-anchor", "end")
    .text(d => d.name);

labelsContainer
  .append("text")
    .attr("class", "label-left")
    .attr("transform", (d, i) => `translate(
    ${i*(squareWidth+padding) + squareWidth/2}, -8)
    rotate(-90)`)
    .text(d => d.name);

});
```

Append a label for each node on the left side of the grid.

Append a label for each node on the top of the grid. Rotate the text elements vertically.

D.9   Solutions chapter 13

Listing D.21   Nobel laureates' birth cities (`map-france.js`)

```
...
import { max } from "d3-array";
import { getCityRadius } from "./scales";

export const drawFranceMap = (laureates, france) => {

  ...

  const franceLaureates = laureates.filter(laureate =>
    laureate.birth_country === "France");

  const cities = [];
  franceLaureates.forEach(laureate => {
    if (cities.find(city => city.name ===
      laureate.birth_city)) {cities.find(city =>
      city.name === laureate.birth_city)
      .laureates.push(laureate);
    } else {
      cities.push({
        name: laureate.birth_city,
        latitude: laureate.birt_city_latitude,
        longitude: laureate.birt_city_longitude,
        laureates: [laureate]
      });
    }
  });
```

Filter the laureates' data to keep only the ones that were born in France.

Create an array that contains the cities where the French laureates were born. For each city, store its latitude, longitude, and an array of the corresponding laureates.

```
const maxLaureatesPerCity = max(cities, d => d.laureates.length);

svg
  .selectAll(".france-city-circle")
  .data(cities)
  .join("circle")
    .attr("class", "france-city-circle")
    .attr("cx", d => projection([d.longitude,
      d.latitude])[0])
    .attr("cy", d => projection([d.longitude,
      d.latitude])[1])
    .attr("r", d => getCityRadius(d.laureates.length,
      maxLaureatesPerCity))
    .attr("fill", "#35a7c2")
    .attr("fill-opacity", 0.5)
    .attr("stroke", "#35a7c2");

};
```

> **Use the data-binding pattern to append a circle for each city.**

> **Pass the city's longitude and latitude to the projection to obtain their position on the map.**

> **Call getCityRadius to obtain the radius of the circle.**

D.10 Solutions chapter 14

Listing D.22 Importing the letters dataset (`Grid.svelte`)

```
<script>
  import letters from "../data/letters.json";

  ...
</script>

<svelte:window bind:innerWidth={windowWidth} />

{#if svgWidth && svgHeight}
  <svg width={svgWidth} height={svgHeight}>
    {#each years as year, i}
      <g
        transform="translate(
          {(i % numColumns) * smWidth},
          {Math.floor(i / numColumns) * smHeight})"
      >
        <rect x={0} y={0} width={smWidth} height={smHeight} />
        <GridItem
          {smWidth}
          {smHeight}
          {year}
          {paintingAreaScale}
          {paintingDefaultRadius}
          paintings={paintings.filter((painting) =>
            painting.year === year)}
          {maxDrawings}
          drawings={yearlyDrawings.find((d) => d.year === year).months}
          letters={letters.filter((letter) =>
            letter.year === year)}
        />
      </g>
    {/each}
```

> **Pass the letters corresponding to the current year to the GridItem component.**

```
    </svg>
  {/if}
```

Listing D.23 Passing data to `Letters.svelte` (`GridItem.svelte`)

```
<script>
  import Letters from "../chart_components/Letters.svelte";

  export let letters;

  ...
</script>

<g transform="translate({smWidth / 2}, 0)">
  <g transform="translate(0, {padding + radius})">
    <circle ... />
    ...
    <Drawings {drawings} {monthScale} {radialScale} />
    <Letters {letters} {monthScale} {radialScale} />
  </g>
  <text ... >{year}</text>
</g>
```

Pass the required props to the Letters component.

Listing D.24 Drawing the radial bar chart (`Letters.svelte`)

```
<script>
  import { months } from "../utils/months";

  export let letters;
  export let monthScale;
  export let radialScale;
</script>

{#each months as month}
  <line
    x1={0}
    y1={0}
    x2={radialScale(letters.find(l => l.month===month)
      .number_of_letters)
      * Math.sin(monthScale(month))}
    y2={radialScale(letters.find(l => l.month===month)
      .number_of_letters)
      * Math.cos(monthScale(month))}
    stroke-width={2}
    stroke-linecap="round"
  />
{/each}

<style lang="scss">
  line {
    stroke: $secondary;
    pointer-events: none;
  }
</style>
```

Append a line element for each month.

Set the starting point of the line to the origin of the visualization.

Calculate the endpoint of the line by passing the number of letters to the radial scale and using a trigonometric function.

Listing D.25 Drawing the timeline (`Timeline.svelte`)

```
<script>
  import { scaleTime } from "d3-scale";
  import { timeFormat } from "d3-time-format";
  import timeline from "../data/timeline.json";

  let height;

  const startDate = new Date(
    timeline[0].start_year,
    timeline[0].start_month,
    1
  );
  const endDate = new Date(
    timeline[timeline.length - 1].end_year,
    timeline[timeline.length - 1].end_month,
    0
  );

  $: timeScale = scaleTime()
      .domain([startDate, endDate])
      .range([0, height]);
</script>

<div class="timeline-container"
  bind:clientHeight={height}>
  {#each timeline as period}
    <div
      class="period-container"
      style="top: {timeScale(new Date(
                    period.start_year,
                    period.start_month,
                    1))}px;
              height: {timeScale(new Date(
                    period.end_year,
                    period.end_month,
                    25)) -
                    timeScale(new Date(
                    period.start_year,
                    period.start_month,
                    0))}px;"
    >
      <div class="dates-container">
        <div class="start-date">
          {timeFormat("%b %Y")(new Date(
                               period.start_year,
                               period.start_month,
                               1))}
        </div>
        <div class="end-date">
          {timeFormat("%b %Y")(new Date(
                               period.end_year,
                               period.end_month,
                               1))}
        </div>
```

Set the starting date of the timeline by creating a new JavaScript Date object.

Proceed similarly for the end date, passing 0 as the day to target the last day of the month.

Declare a time scale that takes a date as an input and returns the corresponding vertical position on the timeline.

Bind the value of the height variable to the actual height of the timeline container.

Loop through each period in the timeline dataset.

Set the top and height style properties of each period by calling the time scale and passing the period's dates.

```
      </div>
      <div class="period" />
        <div class="location">
          <div class="city">{period.city}</div>
          <div class="country">({period.country})</div>
        </div>
      </div>
  {/each}
</div>

<style lang="scss">
  .timeline-container {
    height: 100%;
    font-size: 1.6rem;
    line-height: 1.2;
    color: $secondary;
  }
  .period-container {
    display: flex;
    align-items: stretch;
    position: absolute;
    left: 0;
    padding: 3px 0;
    cursor: pointer;
    transition: opacity 100ms ease;
  }
  .period {
    width: 10px;
    background-color: rgba($secondary, 0.7);
    border-radius: 8px;
  }
  .dates-container {
    display: flex;
    flex-direction: column;
    justify-content: space-between;
    width: 70px;
  }
  .location {
    display: flex;
    flex-direction: column;
    justify-content: center;
    width: 120px;
    padding-left: 10px;
  }
  .city {
    font-weight: 600;
  }
</style>
```

D.11 Solutions chapter 15

Listing D.26 Styling the canvas container (`index.html`)

```
<!DOCTYPE html>
<html>
```

```
<head>
  <meta charset="UTF-8">
  <meta name="viewport" content="width=device-width, initial-scale=1.0">
  <title>Gallery of Canvas Shapes | D3.js in Action</title>
</head>
<body>
  <div id="canvas" style="max-width: 400px;
    margin: 0 auto;"></div>
```

Ensure the div that will contain the canvas element is never larger than 400 px and is centered on the screen.

```
  <script src="https://d3js.org/d3.v7.min.js"></script>
  <script src="./js/main.js"></script>
</body>
</html>
```

Listing D.27 Appending the canvas and drawing shapes (`main.js`)

```
const canvas = d3.select("#canvas")
  .append("canvas")
    .style("border", "1px solid gray")
    .style("max-width", "100%");
```

Append a Canvas element to the DOM, give it a gray border, and ensure that it's never wider than its container.

```
const container = document.querySelector("#canvas");
const devicePixelRatio = window.devicePixelRatio;

const width = container.offsetWidth;
const height = width;

canvas
  .attr("width", width * devicePixelRatio)
  .attr("height", height * devicePixelRatio);
```

Set the width and height attributes of the Canvas element, and correct them based on the screen's pixel density.

```
const context = canvas.node().getContext("2d");
context.scale(devicePixelRatio, devicePixelRatio);
```

Initialize the Canvas's 2D context, and scale it based on the screen's pixel density.

```
context.rect(100, 100, 200, 200);
context.lineWidth = 3;
context.stroke();
```

Draw the 3 px black stroke of a square of 200 by 200 px, centered inside the Canvas element.

```
context.beginPath();
context.arc(200, 200, 100, 0, 2 * Math.PI);
context.fillStyle = "plum";
context.fill();
```

Draw a circle of 200 px radius with a fill color of "plum".

```
context.beginPath();
context.moveTo(100, 100);
context.lineTo(300, 300);
context.moveTo(300, 100);
context.lineTo(100, 300);
context.stroke();
```

Draw two diagonal black lines of 3 px width across the square.

```
context.font = "18px sans-serif";
context.fillStyle = "#000";
context.textAlign = "center";
context.fillText("Canvas is awesome!", 200, 90);
```

Add a label above the square, centered inside the Canvas element.

appendix E
A very brief
introduction to Svelte

This appendix covers

- Recognizing the structure of a Svelte file
- Sharing information between components
- Adding rendering logic
- Using reactive variables and functions

This appendix provides an overview of Svelte, a JavaScript library that is popularly used in combination with D3.js. If you aren't familiar with Svelte, this appendix will give you the knowledge you need to follow along with the projects from chapters 14 and 15.

E.1 The structure of a Svelte file

Svelte files can be recognized by their `.svelte` extension. By convention, their name starts with an uppercase letter. Svelte files are made of three sections: the script, the markup, and the styles. At the top of the file, the `<script>` tags contain any JavaScript code you need for the component. This is where you'll run your D3 code. Then we add our markup, such as the `<div>` tag in the following snippet. Note how we can dynamically use JavaScript variables within the markup by including them